656.62 [illegible]   P.
11/09

KU-524-863

WITHDRAWN
FROM
MIC-SPCT

St Patrick's College
Thurles
17765

FOR
REFERENCE ONLY

The Entrepreneurial Process

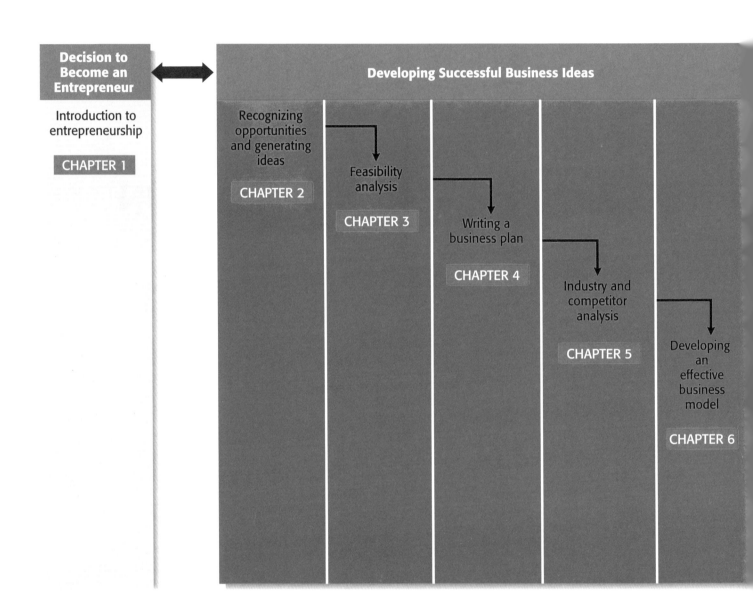

Decision to Become an Entrepreneur

Introduction to entrepreneurship

CHAPTER 1

Developing Successful Business Ideas

Recognizing opportunities and generating ideas

CHAPTER 2

Feasibility analysis

CHAPTER 3

Writing a business plan

CHAPTER 4

Industry and competitor analysis

CHAPTER 5

Developing an effective business model

CHAPTER 6

Passion plus

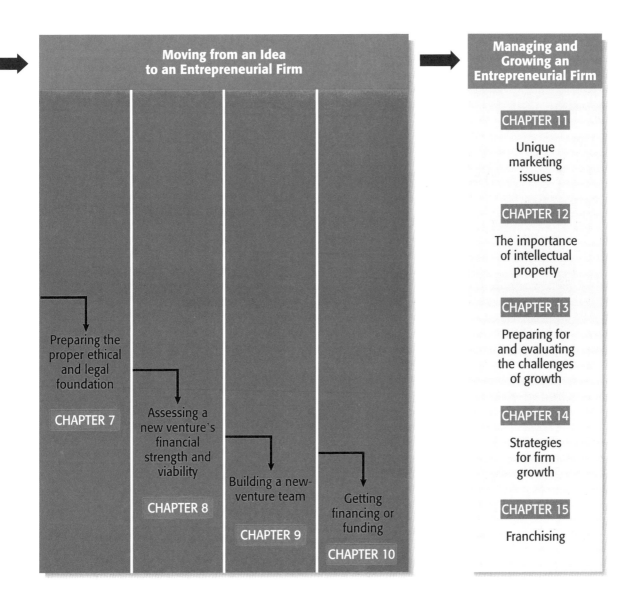

Moving from an Idea to an Entrepreneurial Firm

Preparing the proper ethical and legal foundation

CHAPTER 7

Assessing a new venture's financial strength and viability

CHAPTER 8

Building a new-venture team

CHAPTER 9

Getting financing or funding

CHAPTER 10

Managing and Growing an Entrepreneurial Firm

CHAPTER 11

Unique marketing issues

CHAPTER 12

The importance of intellectual property

CHAPTER 13

Preparing for and evaluating the challenges of growth

CHAPTER 14

Strategies for firm growth

CHAPTER 15

Franchising

Where a great idea meets a great process

Introducing the
Prentice Hall Entrepreneurship Series...

The Entrepreneurship Series by Prentice Hall is a compilation of brief, practical, and engaging titles that focus on the latest research findings, issues, and trends that guide successful entrepreneurs today. Written by experts of selected areas of entrepreneurship, each title is perfect for covering a special topic or to enhance your textbook material.

Series Editors

R. Duane Ireland, Mays Business School, Texas A&M University
Michael H. Morris, William S. Spears School of Business, Oklahoma State University

Current Series Titles

Kathleen Allen, *Entrepreneurship for Scientists and Engineers*, ISBN 0-13-235727-5
Bruce R. Barringer, *Preparing Effective Business Plans: An Entrepreneurial Approach*, ISBN 0-13-231832-6
Arthur C. Brooks, *Social Entrepreneurship: A Modern Approach to Social Value Creation*,
     ISBN 0-13-233076-8
Jeffrey Cornwall, *Bootstrapping*, ISBN 0-13-604425-5
Gerard George and Adam J. Bock, *Inventing Entrepreneurs: Technology Innovators and Their Entrepreneurial
     Journey*, ISBN 0-13-157470-1
Frank Hoy and Pramodita Sharma, *Entrepreneurial Family Firms*, ISBN 0-13-157711-5
Donald F. Kuratko and Jeffrey S. Hornsby, *New Venture Management: The Entrepreneur's Roadmap*,
     ISBN 0-13-613032-1
Minet Schindehutte, Michael H. Morris, and Leyland F. Pitt, *Rethinking Marketing: The Entrepreneurial
     Imperative*, ISBN 0-13-239389-1

Future Titles in the Series*

Jeffrey J. Reuer, Paul M. Olk, and Africa Ariño, *Entrepreneurial Alliances*, ISBN 0-13-615636-3
Thomas Dean, *Sustainable Venturing*, ISBN 0-13-604489-1
Daniel Davidson and Lynn Forsythe, *The Entrepreneur's Legal Companion*, ISBN 0-13-607723-4
James Davis, *Go to Market: What to do After the Business Plan is Written*, ISBN 0-13-606016-1
Ray Smilor and John Eggers, *Entrepreneurial Leadership*, ISBN 0-13-603237-0
Jeffrey A. Stamp, *Bold Thinking for Entrepreneurs: Creating and Managing Ideas That Matter*,
     ISBN 0-13-611969-7
Jeff Shay and Siri Terjesen, *International Entrepreneurship*, ISBN 0-13-611964-6
Donald F. Kuratko and Jeffrey S. Hornsby, *Innovation and Entrepreneurship*, ISBN 0-13-602148-4

*We will be publishing new titles every year.
Please visit www.pearsonhighered.com/entrepreneurship for an up-to-date list.

Interested?
For more information on these titles or to request an examination copy for
adoption consideration, please contact your local Prentice Hall sales representative.

Entrepreneurship

Successfully Launching New Ventures

Global Edition

Third Edition

Bruce R. Barringer
Oklahoma State University

R. Duane Ireland
Texas A&M University

Boston   Columbus   Indianapolis   New York   San Francisco   Upper Saddle River
Amsterdam   Cape Town   Dubai   London   Madrid   Milan   Munich   Paris   Montreal   Toronto
Delhi   Mexico City   Sao Paulo   Sydney   Hong Kong   Seoul   Singapore   Taipei   Tokyo

Coláiste Mhuire Gan Smál Luimneach	
Class	658.42
Suff	BAR
MI	

Editorial Director: Sally Yagan
Editor in Chief: Eric Svendsen
Acquisitions Editor: Kim Norbuta
Acquisitions Editor, Global Edition: Steven Jackson
Editorial Project Manager: Claudia Fernandes
Director of Marketing: Patrice Lumumba Jones
Director of International Marketing: Ann Oravetz
Marketing Manager: Nikki Jones
Senior Managing Editor: Judy Leale
Project Manager: Ann Pulido
Senior Operations Supervisor: Arnold Vila
Senior Art Director: Steve Frim
Text and Cover Designer: Judy Allan
Manager, Visual Research: Beth Brenzel
Manager, Rights and Permissions: Zina Arabia
Image Permission Coordinator: Kathy Gavilanes
Manager, Cover Visual Research & Permissions: Karen Sanatar
Lead Media Project Manager: Lisa Rinaldi
Full-Service Project Management: Sharon Anderson/BookMasters, Inc.
Composition: BookMasters, Inc.
Printer/Binder: Quebecor World Color/Versailles
Cover Printer: Lehigh-Phoenix Color/Hagerstown
Cover Image: © elemental imaging – Fotolia.com
Text Font: 10/12, Bookman old style

Credits and acknowledgments borrowed from other sources and reproduced, with permission, in this textbook appear on appropriate page within text.

Microsoft® and Windows® are registered trademarks of the Microsoft Corporation in the U.S.A. and other countries. Screen shots and icons reprinted with permission from the Microsoft Corporation. This book is not sponsored or endorsed by or affiliated with the Microsoft Corporation.

If you purchased this book within the United States or Canada you should be aware that it has been imported without the approval of the Publisher or the Author.

Copyright © 2010, 2008, 2006 Pearson Education, Inc., publishing as Prentice Hall, One Lake Street, Upper Saddle River, New Jersey. All rights reserved. Manufactured in the United States of America. This publication is protected by Copyright, and permission should be obtained from the publisher prior to any prohibited reproduction, storage in a retrieval system, or transmission in any form or by any means, electronic, mechanical, photocopying, recording, or likewise. To obtain permission(s) to use material from this work, please submit a written request to Pearson Education, Inc., Permissions Department, One Lake Street, Upper Saddle River, New Jersey 07458.

Many of the designations by manufacturers and seller to distinguish their products are claimed as trademarks. Where those designations appear in this book, and the publisher was aware of a trademark claim, the designations have been printed in initial caps or all caps.

10 9 8 7 6 5 4 3 2 1

ISBN 10:   0-13-815808-8
ISBN 13: 978-0-13-815808-8

Dedication

To my parents, Robert and Delores Barringer. Thanks for more than 50 years of encouragement and support. Also, thanks to my brother, Brian, and my sisters, Mary Anne and Barbara. Your encouragement, support, and friendship are also appreciated. Of course I owe a tremendous amount to my wife, Janet, and my children, John, Jennifer, and Emily. You are my inspiration and the joys of my life.

—Bruce R. Barringer

To my grandson, Jackson Blair Funkhouser:
With each day, you are working on your dreams. Keep dreaming as the foundation for forming and pursuing your goals, Jackson. For you, everything is possible. I love you.

—R. Duane Ireland

BRIEFCONTENTS

CONTENTS

PREFACE

INTRODUCTION

We are truly excited about the third edition of our book and the promise it brings to you. The main reason for our excitement is that there has never been a more invigorating time to study entrepreneurship. Across the world, even during what are challenging economic conditions on a global basis, entrepreneurial ventures are creating and bringing to market new products and services that make our lives easier, enhance our productivity at work, improve our health, and entertain us in new and fascinating ways. As you will see from reading this book, entrepreneurs are some of the most passionate and inspiring people you'll ever meet. This is why successful firms have been launched in a variety of unexpected places such as garages and an array of coffeehouses with wireless hot spots. Indeed, we never know the amount of success the person sitting next to us drinking coffee might achieve after launching an entrepreneurial venture!

As you might anticipate, the passion an entrepreneur has about a business idea, rather than fancy offices or other material things, is typically the number one predictor of a new venture's success. Conversely, a lack of passion often leads to entrepreneurial failure.

The purpose of our book is to introduce you, our readers and students of entrepreneurship, to the entrepreneurial process. We do this because evidence suggests that it is important for entrepreneurs to thoroughly understand the parts of the entrepreneurial process as well as how to effectively use those parts. The fact that in the United States alone roughly one-third of new firms fail within the first two years while another 20 percent fail within four years of their launching is the type of evidence we have in mind. These failure rates show that while many people are motivated to start new firms, motivation alone is not enough; indeed, motivation must be coupled with accurate and timely information, a solid business idea, an effective business plan, and sound execution to maximize chances for success. In this book, we discuss many examples of entrepreneurial ventures and the actions separating successful firms from unsuccessful ones.

This book provides a thoughtful, practical guide to the process of successfully launching and growing an entrepreneurial venture. To do this, we provide you with a thorough analysis of the entrepreneurial process. We model this process for you in the first chapter and then use the model's components to frame the book's remaining parts. Because of its importance, we place a special emphasis on the beginnings of the entrepreneurial process—particularly opportunity recognition and feasibility analysis. We do this because history shows that many entrepreneurial ventures struggle or fail not because the business owners weren't committed or didn't work hard, but because the idea they were pushing to bring to the marketplace wasn't the foundation for a vibrant, successful business.

NEW TO THIS EDITION

We are committed to presenting you with the most up-to-date and applicable treatment of the entrepreneurial process available in the marketplace. While serving your educational interests, we want to simultaneously increase the likelihood that you will become excited by entrepreneurship's promise as you read and study current experiences of entrepreneurs and their ventures as well as the findings springing from academic research.

To verify currency, thoroughness, and reader interest, we have made several important changes, as presented next, while preparing this third edition of our book:

Opening Profile.   Each chapter opens with a profile of an entrepreneurial venture that was started by one or more students while completing their university-level educational experience. Thirteen of the 15 Opening Profiles are new to this edition, and the remaining two have been updated. These descriptions of real-life entrepreneurs demonstrate that many of us have the ability to be entrepreneurs even while enrolled as a college student. Each profile is specific to a chapter's topic. We completed extensive interviews with each student entrepreneur(s) to obtain the required materials.

Student Entrepreneurs' Insights.   At the bottom of each Opening Profile, we present entrepreneurs' answers to a series of questions. In providing answers to these questions, the entrepreneurs who launched their venture while enrolled in school express their perspectives about various issues. An important benefit associated with thinking about these responses is that those reading this book today have opportunities to see that they, too, may indeed have the potential to launch an entrepreneurial venture quicker than originally thought.

Updated Features.   Over 75 percent of the "What Went Wrong?" "Savvy Entrepreneurial Firm," "Partnering for Success," and "You Be the VC" features are new to this edition. The features we did retain have been updated. The newness shown by these features benefits readers by allowing them to consider contemporary issues facing today's entrepreneurial ventures. The new and updated "You Be the VC" features allow readers to decide if the potential of a proposed entrepreneurial venture is sufficient to warrant funding.

New and Updated Cases.   Many of the pairs of end-of-chapter cases are new to this edition. Those retained have been updated. Comprehensive in nature, these cases were written with the purpose of presenting readers with opportunities to use chapter-specific concepts to identify problems and propose solutions to situations facing actual entrepreneurial ventures. Questions appearing at the end of each case can be used to stimulate classroom discussions.

Updated References.   The amount of academic research examining entrepreneurship topics continues to grow. To provide you, our readers, with the most recent insights from the academic literature, we draw from newly published articles. Similarly, we relied on the most current articles appearing in business publications such as the *Wall Street Journal*, *Entrepreneur*, and *Business 2.0*, among others, to present you with examples of the actions being taken by today's entrepreneurial ventures.

HOW IS THIS BOOK ORGANIZED?

To explain the entrepreneurial process and the way it typically unfolds, we divide our book into four parts and 15 chapters. The four parts of the entrepreneurial process model are:

Part 1: Decision to Become an Entrepreneur
Part 2: Developing Successful Business Ideas
Part 3: Moving from an Idea to an Entrepreneurial Firm
Part 4: Managing and Growing an Entrepreneurial Firm

We believe that this sequence will make your journey toward understanding the entrepreneurial process both enjoyable and productive. The model is shown here. The step in the model that corresponds to the chapter being introduced is highlighted to help you, our readers, form a picture of where each chapter fits in the entrepreneurial process.

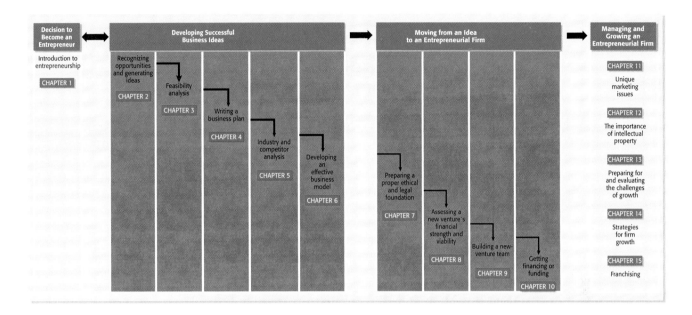

WHAT ARE THE BOOK'S BENEFICIAL FEATURES?

To provide as thorough and meaningful an introduction to the entrepreneurial process as possible, we include several features, as follows, in each chapter of the book:

FEATURE INCLUDED IN EACH CHAPTER	BENEFIT
Learning objectives	Help focus the reader's attention on the major topics in the chapter
Chapter opening profile	Introduces the chapter's topic by focusing on a company that was started while its founder or founders were still in college
Boldfaced key terms	Draw the reader's attention to key concepts
Examples and anecdotes	Liven up the text and provide descriptions of both successful and unsuccessful approaches to confronting the challenges discussed in each chapter
End-of-chapter summary	Integrates the key topics and concepts included in each chapter
20 review questions	Allow readers to test their recall of chapter material
15 application questions	Allow readers to apply what they learned from the chapter material

4 case discussion questions	Provide opportunities to use concepts examined following each case in each chapter to evaluate situations faced by entrepreneurs
2 case application questions	Provide opportunities to use a chapter's materials following each case for situations readers might face as entrepreneurs

WHAT ARE SOME OTHER UNIQUE FEATURES OF THIS BOOK?

While looking through your book, we think you'll find several unique features, as presented next, that will work to your benefit as a student of entrepreneurship and the entrepreneurial process.

UNIQUE FEATURE OF THE BOOK	EXPLANATION
Focus on opportunity recognition and feasibility analysis	The book begins with strong chapters on opportunity recognition and feasibility analysis. This is important, because opportunity recognition and feasibility analysis are key activities that must be completed early when investigating a new business idea.
What Went Wrong? boxed feature	Each chapter contains a boxed feature titled "What Went Wrong?" We use these features to explain the missteps of seemingly promising entrepreneurial firms. The purpose of these features, as you have no doubt already guessed, is to highlight the reality that things can go wrong when the fundamental concepts in the chapters aren't carefully followed.
Partnering for Success boxed feature	Each chapter contains a boxed feature titled "Partnering for Success." The ability to partner effectively with other firms is becoming an increasingly important attribute for successful entrepreneurial ventures.
Savvy Entrepreneurial Firm boxed feature	Each chapter contains a boxed feature titled "Savvy Entrepreneurial Firm." These features illustrate the types of business practices that facilitate the success of entrepreneurial ventures. As such, these are practices you should strongly consider putting into play when you are using the entrepreneurial process.
You Be the VC end-of-chapter features	Two features, titled "You Be the VC," are provided at the end of each chapter. These features present a "pitch" for funding from an emerging entrepreneurial venture. The features are designed to stimulate classroom discussion by sparking debate on whether a particular venture should or shouldn't receive funding. All the firms featured are real-life entrepreneurial start-ups. Thus, you'll be talking about real—not hypothetical or fictitious—entrepreneurial ventures.
A total of 30 original end-of-chapter cases	Two medium-length cases are featured at the end of each chapter. The cases are designed to stimulate classroom discussion and illustrate the issues discussed in the chapter.

A total of 5 comprehensive cases

Five comprehensive cases, authored by leading entrepreneurship writers and scholars, are included at the end of the book. Each case deals with topics from several chapters. These cases are suitable for individual assignments, group assignments, or exams. A notation is made at the end of each chapter alerting you and your professor to the comprehensive cases that complement that particular chapter.

STUDENT RESOURCES

- **Companion Website: www.pearsonglobaleditions.com/barringer**—contains free access to a student version of the PowerPoint package, chapter quizzes, and links to featured Web sites.
- **Business Feasibility Analysis Pro, ISBN: 0136132014**—This wizard-based software is a step-by-step guide and an easy-to-use tool for completing a feasibility analysis of a business idea. The program allows instructors the flexibility to assign each step in the feasibility analysis separately or to assign the entire feasibility analysis as a semester-long project. It can be packaged with the textbook at a nominal cost.

ACKNOWLEDGMENTS

We are pleased to express our sincere appreciation to four groups of people for helping bring both editions of our book to life.

Prentice Hall Professionals. A number of individuals at Prentice Hall have worked with us conscientiously and have fully supported our efforts to create a book that will work for those both studying and teaching the entrepreneurial process. From Prentice Hall, we want to extend our sincere appreciation to our editor, Kim Norbuta; our director of marketing, Patrice Jones; and our project manager, Claudia Fernandes. Each individual provided us invaluable guidance and support, and we are grateful for their contribution.

Student Entrepreneurs. We want to extend a heartfelt "thank you" to the student entrepreneurs who contributed to the opening features in our book. Our conversations with these individuals were both informative and inspiring. We enjoyed getting to know these bright young entrepreneurs, and wish them nothing but success as they continue to build their ventures.

Nate Alder, *Brigham Young University*

Eben Bayer, *Rensselaer Polytechnic Institute*

Joshua Boltuch, *Brown University*

David Brim, *University of Central Florida*

Misa Chien, *UCLA*

Matt Davidson, *University of California Berkeley*

Jordan Goldman, *Wesleyan University*

Jon Goodman, *St. John's University*

Merrill Guerra, *University of Michigan*

Joe Keeley, *St. Thomas University*

Kathryn Kerrigan, *Loyola University Chicago*

Craig Martyn, *University of California Riverside*

Sarah Schupp, *University of Colorado*

Amy Shukla, *Chapman University*

Andy Tabar, *Belmont University*

Academic Reviewers. We want to thank our colleagues who participated in reviewing individual chapters of the book while they were being written. We gained keen insight from these individuals (each of whom teaches courses in entrepreneurship) and incorporated many of the suggestions of our reviewers into the final version of the book.

Thank you to these professors who participated in reviews:

Dr. Richard Bartlett, *Columbus State Community College*

Greg Berezewski, *Robert Morris College*

Jeff Brice, Jr., *Texas Southern University*

Ralph Jagodka, *Mt. San Antonio College*

Christina Roeder, *James Madison University*

Aron S. Spencer, *New Jersey Institute of Technology*

Vincent Weaver, *Greenville Technical College*

Lisa Zidek, *Florida Gulf Coast University*

Academic Colleagues. We thank this large group of professors whose thoughts about entrepreneurial education have helped shape our book's contents and presentation structure:

David C. Adams, *Manhattanville College*

Sol Ahiarah, *SUNY—Buffalo State College*

Frederic Aiello, *University of Southern Maine*

James J. Alling Sr., *Augusta Technical College*

Jeffrey Alstete, *Iona College*

Jeffrey Alves, *Wilkes University*

Joe Aniello, *Francis Marion University*

Mary Avery, *Ripon College*

Jay Azriel, *Illinois State University*

Richard Barker, *Upper Iowa University*

Jim Bell, *Texas State University*

Robert J. Berger, *SUNY Potsdam*

Jenell Bramlage, *University of Northwestern Ohio*

Barb Brown, *Southwestern Community College*

James Burke, *Loyola University—Chicago*

Lowell Busenitz, *University of Oklahoma*

John Butler, *University of Texas—Austin*

Jane Byrd, *University of Mobile*

Art Camburn, *Buena Vista University*

Carol Carter, *Louisiana State University*

Gaylen Chandler, *Utah State University*

James Chrisman, *Mississippi State University*

Delena Clark, *Plattsburgh State University*

Dee Cole, *Middle Tennessee State University*

Roy Cook, *Fort Lewis College*

Andrew Corbett, *Rensselaer Polytechnic Institute*

Simone Cummings, *Washington University School of Medicine*

Suzanne D'Agnes, *Queensborough Community College*

Douglas Dayhoff, *Indiana University*

Frank Demmler, *Carnegie Mellon University*

David Desplaces, *University of Hartford/Barney*

Vern Disney, *University of South Carolina—Sumter*

Dale Eesley, *University of Toledo*

Alan Eisner, *Pace University*

Susan Everett, *Clark State Community College*

Henry Fernandez, *North Carolina Central University*

Charles Fishel, *San Jose State University*

Dana Fladhammer, *Phoenix College*

Brenda Flannery, *Minnesota State University*

John Friar, *Northeastern University*

Barbara Fuller, *Winthrop University*

Barry Gilmore, *University of Memphis*

Caroline Glackin, *Delaware State University*

Cheryl Gracie, *Washtenaw Community College*

Frederick Greene, *Manhattan College*

Lee Grubb, *East Carolina University*

Brad Handy, *Springfield Technical Community College*

Carnella Hardin, *Glendale College*

Ashley Harmon, *Southeastern Technical College*

Steve Harper, *University of North Carolina at Wilmington*

Alan Hauff, *University of Missouri—St. Louis*

Gordon Haym, *Lyndon State College*

Andrea Hershatter, *Emory University*

Richard Hilliard, *Nichols College*

Jo Hinton, *Copiah Lincoln Community College*

Dennis Hoagland, *LDS Business College*

Frank Hoy, *University of Texas at El Paso*

Jeffrey Jackson, *Manhattanville College*

Grant Jacobsen, *Northern Virginia Community College-Woodbridge*

Susan Jensen, *University of Nebraska—Kearney*

Alec Johnson, *University of St. Thomas*

James M. Jones, *University of the Incarnate Word, ERAU, Del Mar College*

Jane Jones, *Mountain Empire Community College*

Joy Jones, *Ohio Valley College*

Tom Kaplan, *Fairleigh Dickinson University—Madison*

Elizabeth Kisenwether, *Penn State University*

James Klingler, *Villanova University*

Edward Kuljian, *Saint Joseph's University*

James Lang, *Virginia Tech University*

Allon Lefever, *Eastern Mennonite University*

Anita Leffel, *University of Texas—San Antonio*

Gary Levanti, *Polytechnic University—LI Campus*

Benyamin Lichtenstein, *University of Massachusetts, Boston*

Bruce Lynskey, *Vanderbilt University*

Janice Mabry, *Mississippi Gulf Coast Community College*

Jeffrey Martin, *University of Texas—Austin*

Greg McCann, *Stetson University*

Elizabeth McCrea, *Pennsylvania State—Great Valley*

Brian McKenzie, *California State University—Hayward*

Chris McKinney, *Vanderbilt University*

Dale Meyer, *University of Colorado*

Steven C. Michael, *University of Illinois Urbana—Champaign*

Angela Mitchell, *Wilmington College*

Bryant Mitchell, *University of Maryland—Eastern Shore*

Rob Mitchell, *University of Oklahoma*

Charlie Nagelschmidt, *Champlain College*

William Naumes, *University of New Hampshire*

Connie Nichols, *Odessa College*

Gary Nothnagle, *Nazareth College*

Edward O'Brien, *Scottsdale Community College*

Haesun Park, *Louisiana State University*

Joseph Picken, *University of Texas at Dallas*

Emmeline de Pillis, *University of Hawaii—Hilo*

John Pfaff, *University of the Pacific*

Carol Reeves, *University of Arkansas*

John Richards, *Brigham Young University*

Christo Roberts, *University of Minnesota—Twin Cities*

George Roorbach, *Lyndon State College*

Janice Rustia, *University of Nebraska Medical Center*

James Saya, *The College of Santa Fe*

William Scheela, *Bemidji State University*

Gerry Scheffelmaier, *Middle Tennessee State University*

Gerald Segal, *Florida Gulf Coast University*

Cynthia Sheridan, *St. Edward's University*

Donald Shifter, *Fontbonne University*

C. L. J. Spencer, *Kapi'olani Community College*

Joseph Stasio, *Merrimack College*

Deborah Streeter, *Cornell University*

Dara Szyliowicz, *University of Denver*

Craig Tunwall, *Empire State College*

Clint B. Tankersley, *Syracuse University*

Barry Van Hook, *Arizona State University*

George Vozikis, *University of Tulsa*

David Wilemon, *Syracuse University*

Charlene Williams, *Brewton Parker College*

Doug Wilson, *University of Oregon*

Diana Wong, *Eastern Michigan University*

Finally, we want to express our appreciation to our home institutions (Oklahoma State University and Texas A&M University) for creating environments in which ideas are encouraged and supported.

We wish each of you—our readers—all the best in your study of the entrepreneurial process. And, of course, we hope that each of you will be highly successful entrepreneurs as you pursue the ideas you'll develop at different points in your careers.

Pearson wish to acknowledge and thank the following people for their work on the Global Edition:

Mansor Isa, *University of Malaysia,* Malaysia.

Eslyn Isaacs, School of Business and Finance, *University of the Western Cape.* South Africa.

Dr Stephen Ko, Department of Management and Marketing, *The Hong Kong Polytechnic University,* Hong Kong.

Teena Lyons

ABOUT THE AUTHORS

Bruce R. Barringer   Bruce R. Barringer holds the Johnny D. Pope Chair in Entrepreneurship in the Department of Entrepreneurship and Emerging Enterprises, Spears School of Business, Oklahoma State University. Previously, he served on the faculty of the University of Central Florida. He obtained his Ph.D. from the University of Missouri and his MBA from Iowa State University. His research interests include feasibility analysis, business planning, firm growth, and corporate entrepreneurship.

Bruce's research has been published in *Strategic Management Journal, Journal of Management, Journal of Business Venturing, Journal of Small Business Management, Journal of Developmental Entrepreneurship,* and in several other outlets. In addition to this book, Bruce is the co-author or author of three additional books, including *Preparing Effective Business Plans, The Truth About Starting a Business, and What's Stopping You? Shatter the 9 Most Common Myths Keeping You From Starting Your Own Business.*

Bruce's outside interests include running, trail biking, and swimming.

R. Duane Ireland   R. Duane Ireland is a Distinguished Professor of Management and holds the Foreman R. and Ruby S. Bennett Chair in Business in the Mays Business School, Texas A&M University. Previously, he served on the faculties at University of Richmond, Baylor University, and Oklahoma State University. His research interests include strategic entrepreneurship, corporate entrepreneurship, entrepreneurship in emerging economies, strategic alliances, and effectively managing organizational resources.

Duane's research has been published in journals such as *Academy of Management Journal, Academy of Management Review, Academy of Management Executive, Strategic Management Journal, Administrative Science Quarterly, Journal of Management, Journal of Business Venturing, Decision Sciences, Human Relations, Entrepreneurship Theory and Practice, Long Range Planning, Human Relations,* and *British Journal of Management,* among others. He is a co-author of both scholarly books and textbooks, including best-selling strategic management texts. Along with Mike Morris (Oklahoma State University), Duane serves as a co-editor for the Prentice Hall Entrepreneurship Series. Several books in the series have already been released (including *Business Plans for Entrepreneurs,* which is authored by Bruce Barringer) and others are soon to be released. Each book in the series offers an in-depth treatment of a specific entrepreneurship topic.

Duane has served or is serving on the editorial review boards for a number of journals, including *AMJ, AMR, AME, JOM, JBV, ETP, European Management Journal,* and *Journal of Business Strategy.* He is the current editor of the *Academy of Management Journal.* He has completed terms as an associate editor for *AMJ* and *AME* as a consulting editor for *ETP* and has served as a guest co-editor for special issues of *AMR, AME, SMJ, Journal of Engineering and Technology Management, JBV,* and *Organizational Research Methods.* He is a Fellow of the Academy of Management and has served as a member of the Board of Governors for the Academy. He is the recipient of multiple teaching and research awards.

Running, reading, listening to a variety of music, spending time with his family, and playing with his grandson are Duane's outside interests.

PART 1

Decision to Become an Entrepreneur

CHAPTERONE **Introduction to *Entrepreneurship***

NATE ALDER
Founder, Klymit
BS, Brigham Young University,
expected spring 2010

Getting Personal

with Nate Alder

CURRENTLY IN MY IPOD
MOTAB (Mormon Tabernacle Choir), Goldfinger, Cake, King Floyd

BEST ADVICE I'VE RECEIVED
"No other success in life can compensate for failure in the home." (David O. McKay)

MY BIGGEST WORRY AS AN ENTREPRENEUR
Rapid growth

BEST PART OF BEING A STUDENT
Expert professors as mentors, community support, learning

MY BIGGEST SURPRISE AS AN ENTREPRENEUR
The limelight of early success

MY ADVICE FOR NEW ENTREPRENEURS
Get mentors who have been there before; they will help you find the greatest steps to success

CHAPTERONE
Introduction to *Entrepreneurship*

OPENING PROFILE

In summer 2006, Nate Alder, a business student at Brigham Young University, was scuba diving off the coast of Brazil. Alder learned that divers using dry suits in Arctic conditions used noble gases to insulate their wet suits when they were in cold water. Back home in Utah, Alder was a snowboard instructor and knew all about being cold. He wondered why noble gases couldn't be used in ski jackets to keep skiers and snowboarders warm.

The idea stuck with Alder and when he returned home he enlisted the help of business student Nick Sorensen and engineering PhD candidate Brady Woolford to see if noble gases could be used to warm jackets. After studying noble gases and experimenting with how they could be used to warm apparel products, the three became more enthusiastic about the idea and started working on a business plan. The basic idea was to create a jacket with a series of connected, airtight chambers. A small cartridge, filled with pressurized argon gas, would be stored in a pocket, and would have a small dial on it. When the dial was turned to the right, gas would flow into the chambers and the skier would get warmer. Turn the dial to the left and gas would escape and the skier would cool down. The secret to how the system works is grounded in the properties of argon gas. Its large molecules block the cold and keep in the heat. It's also nonflammable, nontoxic, odorless, and 100 percent environmentally friendly. To make matters even better, using argon gas to warm a jacket instead of bulky fabrics results in a thinner, lighter, and more comfortable jacket that can always stay warm, even when totally wet.[1]

To further build on their idea, and get feedback from experienced businesspeople, Alder and his team entered a number of business plan competitions in spring 2007 and spring 2008. By this time the business had a name, Klymit, and Alder had expanded his founding team. The Klymit team took the business plan competitions very seriously, seeing them as a way to solicit feedback, raise funds, and hone their plan, which they eventually planned to present to investors. Incredibly, the team placed first or second place in 11 business plan or innovation competitions, raking in more than $175,000 in prize money. To convince the judges that Klymit was an attractive opportunity, Klymit's basic pitch was:

1. Existing insulation materials for ski jackets and other cold weather gear are inefficient.
2. High-volume, bulky fabrics force skiers and other outdoor enthusiasts to sacrifice mobility for warmth.
3. There is no way to regulate the overheating of bulky gear to accommodate for changing temperatures.

Learning Objectives

After studying this chapter you should be ready to:

1. Explain entrepreneurship and discuss its importance.

2. Describe corporate entrepreneurship and its use in established firms.

3. Discuss three main reasons people decide to become entrepreneurs.

4. Identify four main characteristics of successful entrepreneurs.

5. Explain the five common myths regarding entrepreneurship.

6. Explain how entrepreneurial firms differ from salary-substitute and lifestyle firms.

7. Discuss the changing demographics of entrepreneurs in nations around the world.

8. Discuss the impact of entrepreneurial firms on economies and societies.

9. Identify ways in which large firms benefit from the presence of smaller entrepreneurial firms.

10. Explain the entrepreneurial process.

Alder's passion for Klymit, and approach to participating in business plan competitions, is reflected in an answer he provided to an interviewer who asked about how the Klymit team prepared for competitions:

We just had so much fun with it that it makes up for all our other sacrifices. Before each event we always made sure we had gotten plenty of sleep, ate a healthy meal, always avoiding alcohol, tobacco, or any other substance that could impact our minds or bodies. All these things combined really helped us stay relaxed and focused to perform well and have a lot of fun doing so.[2]

If you go to YouTube and type in "Klymit," several of the team's pitches and promos for the company have been posted.

In terms of the business side of Klymit, the company plans to make money by licensing its technology to major outdoor gear and apparel companies like Atomic and The North Face and partnering with companies to refill the canisters that contain the argon gas. Klymit's second source of revenue, selling the refill gas canisters, is particularly attractive for creating a residual income. Similar to the printer industry that sells printers and then has a constant source of revenue from selling replacement cartridges, Klymit will have a steady stream of revenue from people who buy Klymit-equipped jackets and other products and periodically need new canisters of argon gas. Klymit has applied for patents that will protect its unique system of using gas to insulate gear and apparel products and for the technology needed to refill them.

Klymit now has a working prototype of its first product, a ski jacket. Its system has the potential to insulate almost any product that keeps people warm, including pants, boots, gloves, and sleeping bags. Like most start-ups, Klymit had a tough road raising funds, but has been able to secure sufficient investment capital to continue moving forward. Alder and his team have also bootstrapped Klymit's start-up expenses where they could. For example, the patent attorney and law firm that filed Klymit's patent applications agreed to delay compensation until after the company starts making money.

Klymit appears to have substantial upside potential. The company hopes to start generating revenue in 2009, and Klymit-equipped gear and clothing should hit stores in 2009–2010. Nate Alder's dream is that Klymit will revolutionize the outdoor industry the way the iPod has the portable music industry. "Like Velcro," he says, "it's a simple solution to a big problem."[3]

In this first chapter of your book about the successful launching of an entrepreneurial firm, we define entrepreneurship and discuss why some people decide to become entrepreneurs. We then look at successful entrepreneurs' characteristics, the common myths surrounding entrepreneurship, the different types of start-up firms, and the changing demographics of entrepreneurs in the United States and in nations throughout the world. We then examine entrepreneurship's importance, including the economic and social impact of new firms as well as the importance of entrepreneurial firms to larger businesses. To close this chapter, we introduce you to the entrepreneurial process. This process, which we believe is the foundation for successfully launching a start-up firm, is the framework we use to present the book's materials to you.

INTRODUCTION TO ENTREPRENEURSHIP

There is tremendous interest in entrepreneurship around the world. Although this statement may seem bold, there is evidence supporting it, some of which is provided by the Global Entrepreneurship Monitor (GEM). GEM, which is a joint research effort by Babson College and the London Business School, tracks entrepreneurship in 42 countries. Of particular interest to GEM is early-state entrepreneurial activity, which consists of businesses that are just being set up and businesses that have been in existence for less than $3\frac{1}{2}$ years. A sample of the rate of early-stage entrepreneurial activity in countries included in the GEM study is shown in Table 1.1. While the highest rates of entrepreneurial start-up activities occur in low-income countries, where good jobs are not plentiful, the rates are also impressive in high-income countries like Ireland (8.2 percent), Spain (7.6 percent), and the United States (9.6 percent).[4]

The GEM study also identifies whether its respondents are starting a new business to take advantage of an attractive opportunity, they desire independence, or they want to increase their income, rather than a lack of career prospects. The majority of people in high-income countries are drawn to entrepreneurship for the former rather than the latter reasons. The reverse is true of people in low-income countries, who tend to be drawn to entrepreneurship primarily because of the lack of traditional career opportunities.[5]

One criticism of entrepreneurship, which is often repeated in the press, is that the majority of new businesses fail. It simply isn't true. The often used statistic that 9 out of 10 businesses fail in their first few years is an exaggeration. According to Brian Headd, an economist for the U.S. Small Business Administration, after four years 50 percent of new businesses are still open,

Table 1.1 RATES OF EARLY-STATE ENTREPRENEURIAL ACTIVITY (AGES 18–64)

Country	Percent of Population Staring a New Business
Brazil	12.7%
China	16.4%
Hong Kong	10.0%
Iceland	12.5%
Peru	25.9%
Russia	2.7%
Spain	7.6%
Thailand	26.9%
United Kingdom	5.5%
United States	9.6%

Source: N. Bosma, K. Jones, E. Autio, and J. Levie, *Global Entrepreneurship Monitor 2007 Executive Report* (Babson College and London Business School, 2007). Permission to reproduce a section of the GEM 2007 Global Report, which appears here, has been kindly granted by the copyright holders. The GEM is an international consortium and this report has been produced from data collected in, and received from, 43 countries in 2007. Our thanks go to the authors, national teams, researchers, funding bodies and other contributors who have made this possible.

33 percent have failed, and 17 percent are closed but were considered to be successful by their owners.[6] While overall these figures are heartening, the 33 percent of start-ups that fail show that a motivation to start and run a business isn't enough; it must be coupled with a solid business idea, good financial management, and effective execution to maximize chances for success. In this book, we will discuss many examples of entrepreneurial firms and the factors separating successful new ventures from unsuccessful ones.

Many people see entrepreneurship as an attractive career path. Think about your friends and others you know. In all probability, you are acquainted with at least one or two people who want to become an entrepreneur—either now or at some point in the future. The number of books dealing with starting one's own business is another indication entrepreneurship is growing in popularity. Amazon.com, for example, currently lists over 45,000 books dealing with entrepreneurship and over 118,000 books focusing on small business. On college campuses an emphasis on entrepreneurship education is growing at an impressive in that country rate. In 1985, there were about 250 entrepreneurship courses offered across all college campuses in the United States. Today, more than 5,000 entrepreneurship courses are now offered in two-year and four-year institutions in that country.[7] The fact is that universities and colleges around the world are offering a growing number of courses in entrepreneurship.[8]

What Is Entrepreneurship?

The word *entrepreneur* derives from the French words *entre*, meaning "between," and *prendre*, meaning "to take." The word was originally used to describe people who "take on the risk" between buyers and sellers or who "undertake" a task such as starting a new venture.[9] Inventors and entrepreneurs differ from each other. An inventor creates something new. An entrepreneur assembles and then integrates all the resources needed—the money, the people, the business model, the strategy, and the risk-bearing ability—to transform the invention into a viable business.[10]

H. H. Stevenson and J. C. Jarillo, two highly regarded academics, define **entrepreneurship** as the process by which individuals pursue opportunities without regard to resources they currently control.[11] Others, such as venture capitalist Fred Wilson, define it more simply, and see entrepreneurship as the art of turning an idea into a business. The essence of entrepreneurial behavior is identifying opportunities and putting useful ideas into practice.[12] The tasks called for by this behavior can be accomplished by either an individual or a group and typically require creativity, drive, and a willingness to take risks. Nate Alder, the cofounder of Klymit, exemplifies all these qualities. Alder saw an *opportunity* to use argon gas to warm ski jackets and other apparel products, he *risked* his career by passing up alternatives to work on Klymit full-time, and he's now *working hard* to put Klymit in a position to deliver a *creative* and *useful* product to its customers.

In this book, we focus on entrepreneurship in the context of an entrepreneur or team of entrepreneurs launching a new business. However, ongoing firms can also behave entrepreneurially. Typically, established firms with an entrepreneurial emphasis are proactive, innovative, and risk-taking. For example, Apple Inc. is widely recognized as a firm in which entrepreneurial behaviors are clearly evident. Steve Jobs is at the heart of Apple's entrepreneurial culture. With his ability to persuade and motivate others' imaginations, Jobs continues to inspire Apple's employees as they develop innovative product after innovative product. To consider the penetration Apple has with some of its innovations, think of how many of your friends own an iPod or an iPhone![13] Similarly, studying Cisco Systems' ability to grow and succeed reveals a history of entrepreneurial behavior at multiple levels within the firm.[14] In addition, many of the firms traded

Learning Objective

1. Explain entrepreneurship and discuss its importance.

on the NASDAQ, such as Yahoo!, Intuit, Amazon.com, and Google, are commonly thought of as entrepreneurial firms. The NASDAQ is the largest U.S. electronic stock market, with over 3,200 companies listed on the exchange.

We want to note here that established firms with an orientation to acting entrepreneurially practice **corporate entrepreneurship**.[15] All firms fall along a conceptual continuum that ranges from highly conservative to highly entrepreneurial. The position of a firm on this continuum is referred to as its **entrepreneurial intensity**.[16] As we mentioned previously, entrepreneurial firms are typically proactive innovators and are not averse to taking calculated risks. In contrast, conservative firms take a more "wait and see" posture, are less innovative, and are risk averse.

One of the most persuasive indications of entrepreneurship's importance to an individual or to a firm is the degree of effort undertaken to behave in an entrepreneurial manner. Firms with higher entrepreneurial intensity regularly look for ways to cut bureaucracy. For example, Virgin Group, the large British conglomerate, works hard to keep its units small and instill in them an entrepreneurial spirit. Virgin is the third most recognized brand in Britain and is involved in businesses as diverse as airlines and music. In the following quote, Sir Richard Branson, the founder and CEO of Virgin, describes how his company operates in an entrepreneurial manner:

> Convention . . . dictates that "big is beautiful," but every time one of our ventures gets too big we divide it up into smaller units. I go to the deputy managing director, the deputy sales director, and the deputy marketing director and say, "Congratulations. You're now MD [managing director], sales director and marketing director—of a new company." Each time we've done this, the people involved haven't had much more work to do, but necessarily they have a greater incentive to perform and a greater zeal for their work. The results for us have been terrific. By the time we sold Virgin Music, we had as many as 50 subsidiary record companies, and not one of them had more than 60 employees.[17]

Why Become an Entrepreneur?

The three primary reasons that people become entrepreneurs and start their own firms are to be their own boss, pursue their own ideas, and realize financial rewards.

Learning Objective

2. Describe corporate entrepreneurship and its use in established firms.

Learning Objective

3. Discuss three main reasons people decide to become entrepreneurs.

Paul Sakuma/AP Wide World Photos

Steve Jobs is perhaps America's best-known entrepreneur. He cofounded Apple Computer in 1976, and has since built the company into a premier entrepreneurial firm. Apple's latest innovations include the widely popular Apple iTunes Music Store and the Apple iPod.

Be Their Own Boss The first of these reasons—being one's own boss—is given most commonly. This doesn't mean, however, that entrepreneurs are difficult to work with or that they have trouble accepting authority. Instead, many entrepreneurs want to be their own boss because either they have had a long-time ambition to own their own firm or because they have become frustrated working in traditional jobs. The type of frustration that some entrepreneurs feel working in conventional jobs is exemplified by Wendy DeFeudis, the founder of VeryWendy, a company that makes customized social invitations. Commenting on how her experiences working for herself have been more satisfying than working for a large firm, DeFeudis remarked:

> I always wanted to be my own boss. I felt confined by the corporate structure. I found it frustrating and a complete waste of time—a waste to have to sell my ideas to multiple people and attend all kinds of internal meetings before moving forward with a concept.[18]

Sometimes the desire to be their own boss results from a realization that the only way they'll achieve an important personal or professional goal is to start their own business. Christopher Jones, David LaBat, and Mary McGrath started a business for this reason. The three, who are educational psychologists, had secure jobs at a public school in the Santa Clarita Valley, north of Los Angeles. Over time, they felt inhibited by the limited range of services they were able to provide students in a school setting, so they left their jobs to start Dynamic Interventions, a more full-service educational psychology and counseling center. Recalling why it was necessary for him and his colleagues to leave their jobs to become their own bosses Jones said:

> The idea came from some general frustrations with not being able to practice the breadth of service that [we wanted to]. And instead of going to work and being angry about it for the next 30 years, we decided to do something about it. With Dynamics Interventions, our service doesn't stop at the end of the school day. We can go more in-depth and be more beneficial to the whole family."[19]

Pursue Their Own Ideas The second reason people start their own firms is to pursue their own ideas.[20] Some people are naturally alert, and when they recognize ideas for new products or services, they have a desire to see those ideas realized. Corporate entrepreneurs who innovate within the context of an existing firm typically have a mechanism for their ideas to become known. Established firms, however, often resist innovation. When this happens, employees are left with good ideas that go unfulfilled.[21] Because of their passion and commitment, some employees choose to leave the firm employing them in order to start their own business as the means to develop their own ideas.

This chain of events can take place in noncorporate settings, too. For example, some people, through a hobby, leisure activity, or just everyday life, recognize the need for a product or service that is not available in the marketplace. If the idea is viable enough to support a business, they commit tremendous time and energy to convert the idea into a part-time or full-time firm. In Chapters 2 and 3, we focus on how entrepreneurs spot ideas and determine if their ideas represent viable business opportunities.

An example of a person who left a job to pursue an idea is Daryn Kagan, a former reporter for CNN. Kagan became discouraged with her career trajectory and decided to leave the cable network to do something she had thought about for a long time, create a Web cast (a streaming video on a Web site) that features good news. Reflecting on the circumstances that caused her to quit her job to start her own business Kagan recalls:

> After 12 years at CNN, it became clear that I wasn't going to have the kind of opportunities that I wanted. I see that as the nudge I needed to move on. I had

been thinking of stories I have been drawn to—the kind that make your heart go zing. It was one of those moments in your life where you have the chance to sit back and think, "If I could do anything in my life, what would it be?[22]

If you'd like to see the fruits of Kagan's efforts, you can go to www.darynkagan.com and view her daily "good news" Web cast. The stories she posts are both heartfelt and inspiring.

Pursue Financial Rewards   Finally, people start their own firms to pursue financial rewards. This motivation, however, is typically secondary to the first two and often fails to live up to its hype. The average entrepreneur does not make more money than someone with a similar amount of responsibility in a traditional job. The financial lure of entrepreneurship is its upside potential. People such as Michael Dell of Dell Inc., Jerry Yang of Yahoo!, and Larry Page and Sergey Brin of Google made hundreds of millions of dollars building their firms. But these people insist that money wasn't their primary motivation. Marc Andreessen, founder of Netscape, said, "[Money] is not the motivator or even the measure of my success."[23] Some entrepreneurs even report that the financial rewards associated with entrepreneurship can be bittersweet if they are accompanied by losing control of their firm. For example, Sir Richard Branson, after selling Virgin Records, wrote, "I remember walking down the street [after the sale was completed]. I was crying. Tears . . . [were] streaming down my face. And there I was holding a check for a billion dollars. . . . If you'd have seen me, you would have thought I was loony. A billion dollars."[24] For Branson, it wasn't just the money—it was the thrill of building the business and of seeing the success of his initial idea.

Characteristics of Successful Entrepreneurs

Learning Objective

4. Identify four main characteristics of successful entrepreneurs.

Although many behaviors have been ascribed to entrepreneurs, several are common to those who are successful. Those in new ventures and those who are already part of an entrepreneurial firm share these qualities, which are shown in Figure 1.1 and described in the following section.

Passion for the Business   The number one characteristic shared by successful entrepreneurs is a **passion for their business**, whether it is in the context of a new firm or an existing business. This passion typically stems from the entrepreneur's belief that the business will positively influence people's lives.

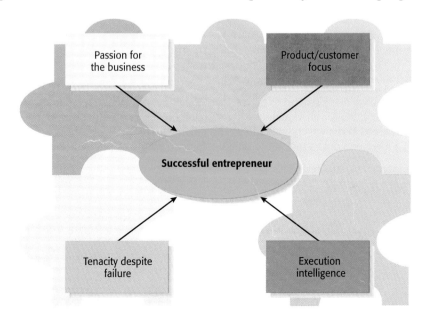

FIGURE 1.1

Four Primary Characteristics of Successful Entrepreneurs

Consider John Plaza, the founder of Seattle Biodiesel, a company that makes biodiesel, an environmentally friendly substitute for regular diesel fuel. Plaza, a former airline pilot, quit his job flying commercial airplanes to pursue an interest in alternative fuels. A single flight sparked his passion for environmental stewardship and caused him to decide to make a career change.

> I was flying from Anchorage to Tokyo, and I started thinking about how much fuel that flight used. I figured out that in a 6 hour flight, we used enough fuel to power my personal vehicle for 42 years. I had to make a change.[25]

This passion explains why people leave secure jobs to start their own firms and why billionaires such as Bill Gates of Microsoft, Michael Dell of Dell Inc., and Larry Page and Sergey Brin of Google continue working after they are financially secure. They strongly believe that the product or service they are selling makes a difference in people's lives and makes the world a better place to live in. It also explains why many start-ups do so well in spite of stiff competition. If a business owner is willing to work long hours and commit him- or herself passionately to see a business succeed, that's a combination that's hard to replicate in a regular firm.

Passion is particularly important for entrepreneurs because, although rewarding, the process of starting and building a new firm is demanding. Entrepreneurship isn't for the person who is only partially committed. Investors watch like hawks to try to determine an entrepreneur's passion for his or her business idea. Michael Rovner, a partner in AV Labs, a venture capital firm in Austin, Texas, expresses this sentiment:

> Everyone has a different concept of what starting a business is like. We look for people who are highly motivated—people who are passionate about providing their solution to customers, people who really want to make a new company fly.[26]

Additional examples of how entrepreneurs view passion are shown in Table 1.2. In each instance, the presence of passion is depicted as an essential characteristic of successful entrepreneurs.

Table 1.2 THE IMPORTANCE OF "PASSION" IN LAUNCHING A SUCCESSFUL NEW VENTURE

Entrepreneur and Company Founded	View on the Importance of Passion
Matthew Dunn Music IP Monrovia, CA	If you don't have a fundamental "can't walk away from it" **passion** for what you're going to do, you're probably going to have a hard time making it unless you're lucky and even if you do, you'll be tired. I'm never tired of this; I wish there were more hours in the day so that we could do this better and do it faster and do more of it.
Paul Freed Startup Academy Seattle, WA	I always had the urge and **passion** to do my own company, but I just did not know what that was going to be. After enough experience in recruiting I had some lucky breaks with some clients that believed in me which gave me the confidence to go on my own since the barriers to entry were so low and I only saw the recruiting industry getting hotter so the time was right!
Oleg Tscheltzoff Fotolia New York, NY	The most important thing [about starting a business] is to be **passionate** about what you do. I think it is very difficult to enter a business that you don't understand or have passion for.
Peter Flint Trulia.com San Francisco, CA	The key is to have **passion** and to never give up. This is imperative because it creates a drive to solve business problems.

Source: nPost homepage, www.npost.com (accessed October 28, 2008). Used with permission of nPost.com.

What Went WRONG?

How a Lack of Passion Can Kill a Business

Launched in 2006, ProtectMyPhotos was an online photo backup service with quite a few bells and whistles. It was fully automated, meaning that once you downloaded the software and set your preferences (on what you wanted to back up), it would automatically back up your pictures without any intervention on your part. Most photo sharing sites, like Flickr and Zooomr, require the user to manually upload photos. ProtectMyPhotos was also very user-friendly in the way it allowed users to browse, display, and manipulate photos. Over time, the site offered backup services for data files as well as photos. Its customer satisfaction ratings were high and CNET called it the "best photo backup ever." It cost $40 per year for very generous storage space. Yet, at the end of 2007, instead of acquiring new customers its founders were closing its doors. What went wrong?

Technically, ProtectMyPhotos was strong. Although the photo storage market was crowded, the firm had strong product features and satisfied customers. The reasons it failed, according to Chris Shaw, the company's cofounder, were threefold. First, Protect MyPhotos aggressively courted Best Buy, hoping to either license its service to Best Buy or bundle its service with Best Buy products. Although ProtectMyPhotos received plenty of positive feedback from Best Buy and its executives, the company just couldn't make a decision. Second, ProtectMyPhotos didn't grow as fast as anticipated. Although market research showed that 97 percent of people would be distraught if they lost their photos, Shaw and his team quickly learned that just because people say they're concerned about something doesn't mean they'll spend money to do something about it. Finally, in a very heartfelt and blunt blog post about why ProtectMyPhotos failed, Shaw admitted that he and his management team grew bored with running an online storage company. Shaw wrote:

> In the end, we realized that our creativity was being crushed by an idea that put us to sleep. My business partner and I came to the realization that what fires us up to come to work everyday is the feeling that we can build really cool things that people care about. Sorry but no one is "passionate" about their backup storage.

Although there were other issues that played a role in ProtectMyPhotos' failure, Shaw harkened back to this later point to end his blog post. "The biggest lesson we (Shaw and his cofounder) learned of all: Do what you're passionate about. In the startup world, if you're bored, you might as well be dead."

Questions for Critical Thinking

1. Why do you think Chris Shaw didn't better anticipate that his passion for ProtectMyPhotos might quickly wane? Describe what you believe are the keys to ensuring that a person is truly passionate about a business idea before moving forward with the idea.
2. Do you think it would have been difficult for anyone to have remained passionate about ProtectMyPhotos and the service it was offering?
3. In what ways did Chris Shaw and ProtectMyPhotos reflect the classic definition of an entrepreneurial firm?
4. How could ProtectMyPhotos have been saved?

Sources: C. Shaw, "Cliff Shaw on Lessons Learned and Moving Forward," www.coloradostartups.com (accessed September 13, 2008); M. Kirkpatrick, "ProtectMyPhotos," www.techcrunch.com, (accessed September 13, 2008).

A note of caution is in order here: While entrepreneurs should have passion, they should not wear rose-colored glasses. It would be a mistake to believe that all one needs is passion and anything is possible. It is important to be enthusiastic about a business idea, but it is also important to understand its potential flaws and risks. In addition, entrepreneurs should understand that the most effective business ideas take hold when their passion is consistent with their skills and is in an area that represents a legitimate business opportunity.

To illustrate the importance of passion, as well as other factors that are critical in determining a firm's success or failure, we include a boxed feature titled "What Went Wrong?" in each chapter. The feature for this chapter shows how ProtectMyPhotos, an online photo backup service, got off to a good start but ultimately failed because its founders were not able to remain passionate about their business idea.

Product/Customer Focus   A second defining characteristic of successful entrepreneurs is a **product/customer focus**. This quality is exemplified by Steven Jobs, the cofounder of Apple Inc., who wrote, "The computer is the most remarkable tool we've ever built . . . but the most important thing is to get them in the hands of as many people as possible."[27] This sentiment underscores an understanding of the two most important elements in any business—products and customers. While it's important to think about management, marketing, finance, and the like, none of those functions makes any difference if a firm does not have good products with the capability to satisfy customers.

Developing products that enhance people's lives is an aspect of the entrepreneurial process that many business owners find very rewarding. This sentiment is expressed by Joy Pierson, the founder of Candle Café and Candle 79, two restaurants in New York City. Her restaurants serve organic and vegan food, which provide options to people who not only prefer a certain diet but have strict dietary restrictions because of allergies or other health concerns. Person said her greatest success is:

> the opportunity to touch people's lives in a profound way through feeding them. We offer menus for people with Celiac disease, who cannot tolerate wheat. One day a child with Celiac disease dined in our restaurant. She was about nine years old and had never been to a restaurant before . . . she couldn't risk the possibility of cross-contamination from wheat products. She and her family were thrilled that they were able to experience being in a restaurant together to celebrate a special occasion.[28]

Watching entrepreneurs create products that meet unfilled needs is fascinating. The idea for the Apple Macintosh, for example, originated in the early 1980s when Steven Jobs and several other Apple employees took a tour of a Xerox research facility. They were astounded to see computers that displayed graphical icons and pull-down menus. The computers also allowed users to navigate desktops using a small, wheeled device called a mouse. Jobs decided to use these innovations to create the Macintosh, the first user-friendly computer. Throughout the $2\frac{1}{2}$ years the Macintosh team developed this new product, it maintained an intense product/customer focus, creating a high-quality computer that is easy to learn, is fun to use, and meets the needs of a wide audience of potential users.[29]

Tenacity Despite Failure   Because entrepreneurs are typically trying something new, the failure rate associated with their efforts is naturally high. In addition, the process of developing a new business is somewhat similar to what a scientist experiences in the laboratory. A chemist, for example, typically has to try multiple combinations of chemicals before finding an optimal combination that can accomplish a certain objective. In a similar fashion, developing a new business idea may require a certain degree of experimentation before a success is attained. Setbacks and failures inevitably occur during this process. The litmus test for entrepreneurs is their ability to persevere through setbacks and failures.

In some instances, tenacity is important because it shows a potential customer the degree of commitment that an entrepreneur has to a new product or service. For example, when his company was just getting started, J. Darius Bikoff, the founder of Glacéau, the company that makes vitaminwater, pounded the streets of New York City trying to drum up interest in his product. When he made a sale he would deliver the product himself, thinking that a personal touch would gain him the loyalty of shopkeepers. Joe Doria, a grocer in Bikoff's New York City neighborhood, vividly recalls the amount of tenacity that Bikoff displayed:

> I'll never forget it. Darius comes in and says, "Hey Joe, will you sell this for me?" He was just a customer of the store, but it impressed me that he was delivering the product himself and pushing it. You've got to respect that.

Today, Doria's grocery store devotes 12 linear feet of cooler space to vitaminwater, as well as fruitwater and smartwater, two other Glacéau brands. Doria says he won't sell any other brand of enhanced health water—even Pepsi's Propel, the top seller in the United States. "Darius was the first, and I have an allegiance to him." Bikoff's tenacity didn't wane as his company grew, and he continues to make personal deliveries of Glacéau products in select areas. Today, Glacéau bottled water is available in 50,000 outlets, including Albertson's, Safeway, Publix, and a large number of independent stores.[30]

An extremely compelling example of tenacity is provided in the boxed feature titled "Savvy Entrepreneurial Firm." In each chapter, this feature will provide an illustration of the exemplary behavior of one or more entrepreneurial firms or will provide an example of a tool or technique that well-managed entrepreneurial firms use to improve their performance.

Execution Intelligence   The ability to fashion a solid idea into a viable business is a key characteristic of successful entrepreneurs. Rob Adams, a senior partner in AV Labs, calls this ability **execution intelligence**.[31] In many cases, execution intelligence is the factor that determines whether a start-up is successful or fails. An ancient Chinese saying warns, "To open a business is very easy; to keep it open is very difficult."

The ability to effectively execute a business idea means developing a business model, putting together a new venture team, raising money, establishing partnerships, managing finances, leading and motivating employees, and so on. It also demands the ability to translate thought, creativity, and imagination into action and measurable results. As Jeff Bezos, the founder of Amazon.com, once said, "Ideas are easy. It's execution that's hard."[32] For many entrepreneurs, the hardest time is shortly after they launch their firm. This reality was expressed by Jodi Gallaer, the founder of a lingerie company, who said, "The most challenging part of my job is doing everything for the first time."[33]

To illustrate solid execution, let's look at Starbucks. Although Starbucks is not growing as fast and profitably as it once did and even though the firm's growth plans were adjusted downward in late 2008, it is still a remarkable success story. The business idea of Howard Schultz, the entrepreneur who purchased Starbucks in 1987, was his recognition of the fact that most Americans didn't have a place to enjoy coffee in a comfortable, quiet setting. Seeing a great opportunity to satisfy customers' needs, Schultz attacked the marketplace aggressively to make Starbucks the industry leader and to establish a national brand. First, he hired a seasoned management team, constructed a world-class roasting facility to supply his outlets with premium coffee beans, and focused on building an effective organizational infrastructure. Then Schultz recruited a management information systems expert from McDonald's to design a point-of-sale system capable of tracking consumer purchases across 300 outlets. This decision was crucial to the firm's ability to sustain rapid growth over the next several years. Starbucks succeeded because Howard Schultz knew how to execute a business idea.[34] He built a seasoned management team, implemented an effective strategy, and used information technology wisely to make his business thrive.[35] These fundamental aspects of execution excellence should serve Schultz and Starbucks when it comes to

Savvy Entrepreneurial FIRM

Guitar Hero and iRobot: Why Tenacity Is One of the Most Important Entrepreneurial Characteristics

www.guitarhero.com
www.irobot.com

Most everyone is familiar with Guitar Hero, the enormously popular series of music video games. To play Guitar Hero, a person holds a plastic guitar-shaped controller to simulate playing the guitar, represented on-screen by colored notes that correspond to fret buttons on the controller. The games support individual play as well as cooperative and competitive modes for two players. The games in the series use a range of both licensed and independent rock music tracks from the 1960s. The series has sold over 21 million copies for over $1 billion.

Impressive, isn't it? But here's the rest of the story. Even though Guitar Hero is published by RedOctane in partnership with Activision (both large video game companies), it was developed by Harmonix Music Systems, a much smaller company. Harmonix was founded in 1995. The founders met at the MIT Media Lab and created Harmonix to find ways to help non-musicians experience the joy of making music. Their efforts often sputtered. During the early years, they joked that the only thing they could sell was company stock. The company produced eight video games prior to Guitar Hero, with only modest results. Guitar Hero was Harmonix's ninth game and came 10 years after the company was founded. Harmonix was recently acquired by MTV Networks for $175 million.

iRobot, the maker of the popular Roomba robotic vacuum cleaner, has a similar story. The company was launched in 1990 with the idea of creating robots to improve people's everyday lives. The first idea was a wireless massager that could climb up a person's back and, with thermal sensors, detect and rub sensitive areas. That idea was scrapped as being too expensive. Over the next 10 years, the company worked on a number of consumer robotic products, with limited success. It was able to stay afloat by getting contracts to build specialized robots for the military, such as roving search robots used in Afghanistan. In the late 1990s, it pushed harder to crack the consumer marketplace. In 2000, it created a doll called My Real Baby, which giggled when its feet were tickled and displayed other human characteristics. The Roomba, the robotic vacuum cleaner for which the company is now known, didn't come along until 2001, 11 years after iRobot was founded. Even then, the Roomba took a tremendous amount of work and perseverance to develop. It went through nearly

20 iterations before it was ready for market. iRobot is now a successful company listed on the NASDAQ. In 2007 it reported 249.1 million in sales and a $9.1 million profit.

Both stories cause one to stop and ponder: What would have happened to Harmonix Music Systems and iRobot if their founders had thrown in the towel three years, five years, or even nine years into their existence? Neither company had an impressive product at that point or had produced much profit. What they both did have, however, were founders with steadfast visions and the tenacity to hang in there until their visions were realized. Both Guitar Hero and the Roomba vacuum cleaner are a little lucky that they exist. Had the founders of their respective companies not had the tenacity that makes many entrepreneurs successful, neither product would be in existence today.

Questions for Critical Thinking

1. Contrast Guitar Hero and iRobot with ProtectMy Photos, the company featured in the "What Went Wrong" boxed feature. Why have Guitar Hero and iRobot survived and thrived while ProtectMyPhotos failed?
2. Do you think you'd be able to "hang in there" as long as the founders of Guitar Hero and iRobot did before they produced a breakthrough product? What do you believe are the keys to remaining "tenacious" when things take longer than planned?
3. Why do you think Guitar Hero has been so successful?
4. Although the case doesn't provide specific information to help you answer these questions, give them a stab anyway. Why do you think the founders of Guitar Hero and iRobot stuck with their firms as long as they did? Wouldn't it have made perfect sense for the founders of Guitar Hero and iRobot to have thrown in the towel years before they produced their breakthrough products?

Sources: D. Dodge, "Guitar Hero a 10 Year Overnight Success," http://dondodge.typepad.com/the_next_big_thing/2008/05/guitar-hero-a-1.html (accessed September 17, 2008); J. Saranow, "Robot Vacuum Nips at Uprights," *Wall Street Journal*, August 27, 2003.

Stephen Simpson/Getty Images, Inc.–Taxi

You might describe an entrepreneur as an independent thinker, an innovator, or perhaps a risk taker. These entrepreneurial employees are passionate enough to work out of their garages if that's what it takes to get the company up and running. Consider Bill Gates, who was so enthusiastic about computers that he dropped out of Harvard University to pursue his vision.

dealing with the competitive challenges facing the firm in 2008 and at least through 2009. In contrast to what Schultz has accomplished at Starbucks, the cost of ignoring execution is high, as explained by Bob Young, the founder of several entrepreneurial firms. When asked "What was your hardest lesson or biggest mistake?" Young replied, "In my first two businesses, my interest was always in 'the new thing,' so I wasn't paying attention to details. As a result of my lack of interest in getting the repetitive stuff right, we never achieved the profitability we should have."[36]

Common Myths About Entrepreneurs

There are many misconceptions about who entrepreneurs are and what motivates them to launch firms to develop their ideas. Some misconceptions are due to the media covering atypical entrepreneurs, such as a couple of college students who obtain venture capital to fund a small business that they grow into a multimillion-dollar company. Such articles rarely state that these entrepreneurs are the exception rather than the norm and that their success is a result of carefully executing an appropriate plan to commercialize what inherently is a solid business idea. Indeed, the success of many of the entrepreneurs we study in each chapter's Opening Profile is a result of carefully executing the different aspects of the entrepreneurial process. Let's look at the most common myths and the realities about entrepreneurs

Myth 1: Entrepreneurs are born, not made. This myth is based on the mistaken belief that some people are genetically predisposed to be entrepreneurs. The consensus of many hundreds of studies on the psychological and sociological makeup of entrepreneurs is that entrepreneurs are not genetically different from other people. This evidence can be interpreted as meaning that no one is "born" to be an entrepreneur and that everyone has the potential to become one. Whether someone does or doesn't is a function of environment, life experiences, and personal choices.[37] However, there are personality traits and characteristics

Learning Objective

5. Explain the five common myths regarding entrepreneurship.

Table 1.3 COMMON TRAITS AND CHARACTERISTICS
OF ENTREPRENEURS

Achievement motivated	Optimistic disposition
Alert to opportunities	Persuasive
Creative	Promoter
Decisive	Resource assembler/leverager
Energetic	Self-confident
Has a strong work ethic	Self-starter
Is a moderate risk taker	Tenacious
Is a networker	Tolerant of ambiguity
Lengthy attention span	Visionary

commonly associated with entrepreneurs; these are listed in Table 1.3. These traits are developed over time and evolve from an individual's social context. For example, studies show that people with parents who were self-employed are more likely to become entrepreneurs.[38] After witnessing a father's or mother's independence in the workplace, an individual is more likely to find independence appealing.[39] Similarly, people who personally know an entrepreneur are more than twice as likely to be involved in starting a new firm as those with no entrepreneur acquaintances or role models.[40] The positive impact of knowing an entrepreneur is explained by the fact that direct observation of other entrepreneurs reduces the ambiguity and uncertainty associated with the entrepreneurial process.

Myth 2: Entrepreneurs are gamblers.   A second myth about entrepreneurs is that they are gamblers and take big risks. The truth is, entrepreneurs are usually **moderate risk takers**, as are most people.[41] The idea that entrepreneurs are gamblers originates from two sources. First, entrepreneurs typically have jobs that are less structured, and so they face a more uncertain set of possibilities than managers or rank-and-file employees.[42] For example, an entrepreneur who starts an e-business consulting service has a less stable job than one working for a governmental agency. Second, many entrepreneurs have a strong need to achieve and often set challenging goals, a behavior that is sometimes equated with risk taking.

Myth 3: Entrepreneurs are motivated primarily by money.   It is naïve to think that entrepreneurs don't seek financial rewards. As discussed previously, however, money is rarely the primary reason entrepreneurs start new firms. Considering what motivated him to start Siebel Systems, a successful Silicon Valley firm, Tom Siebel wrote

> [It] was never about making money. It was never about going public; it was never about the creation of wealth. This was about an attempt to build an incredibly high-quality company. I suppose if I was a great musician that maybe I would play the guitar, if I was a great golfer maybe I would go out on tour, but I can't play the guitar and my golf game is pretty horrible. So what I think, frequently under those circumstances, what you do is do what you do best. And I think that maybe what I do best is start and operate information technology companies.[43]

Some entrepreneurs warn that the pursuit of money can be distracting. Media mogul Ted Turner said, "If you think money is a real big deal . . .

you'll be too scared of losing it to get it."[44] Similarly, Sam Walton, commenting on all the media attention that surrounded him after he was named the richest man in America by *Forbes* magazine in 1985, said:

> Here's the thing: money never has meant that much to me, not even in the sense of keeping score. . . . We're not ashamed of having money, but I just don't believe a big showy lifestyle is appropriate for anywhere, least of all here in Bentonville where folks work hard for their money. We all know that everyone puts on their trousers one leg at a time. . . . I still can't believe it was news that I get my hair cut at the barbershop. Where else would I get it cut? Why do I drive a pickup truck? What am I supposed to haul my dogs around in, a Rolls-Royce?[45]

Myth 4: Entrepreneurs should be young and energetic. The most active age range for business ownership is 35 to 45 years old.[46] Later in this chapter, we'll discuss the reality that today, an increasing number of both younger and older individuals are being attracted to the entrepreneurial process.

Although it is important to be energetic, investors often cite the strength of the entrepreneur (or team of entrepreneurs) as their most important criterion in the decision to fund new ventures.[47] In fact, a sentiment that venture capitalists often express is that they would rather fund a strong entrepreneur with a mediocre business idea than fund a strong business idea and a mediocre entrepreneur. What makes an entrepreneur "strong" in the eyes of an investor is experience in the area of the proposed business, skills and abilities that will help the business, a solid reputation, a track record of success, and passion about the business idea. The first four of these five qualities favor older rather than younger entrepreneurs.

Myth 5: Entrepreneurs love the spotlight. Indeed, some entrepreneurs are flamboyant; however, the vast majority of them do not attract public attention. In fact, many entrepreneurs, because they are working on proprietary products or services, avoid public notice. Consider that entrepreneurs are the source of the launch of many of the 3,200 companies listed on the NASDAQ, and many of these entrepreneurs are still actively involved with their firms. But how many of these entrepreneurs can you name? Maybe a half dozen? Most of us could come up with Bill Gates of Microsoft, Jeff Bezos of Amazon.com, Michael Dell of Dell Inc., and maybe Larry Page and Sergey Brin of Google. Whether or not they sought attention, these are the entrepreneurs who are often in the news. But few of us could name the founders of Electronic Arts, Intel, or GAP even though we frequently use these firms' products and services. These entrepreneurs, like most, have either avoided attention or been passed over by the popular press. They defy the myth that entrepreneurs, more so than other groups in our society, love the spotlight.

Types of Start-Up Firms

As shown in Figure 1.2, there are three types of start-up firms: salary-substitute firms, lifestyle firms, and entrepreneurial firms.

Salary-substitute firms are small firms that yield a level of income for their owner or owners that is similar to what they would earn when working for an employer. Dry cleaners, convenience stores, restaurants, accounting firms, retail stores, and hairstyling salons are examples of salary-substitute firms. The vast majority of small businesses fit into this category. Salary-substitute

Learning Objective

6. Explain how entrepreneurial firms differ from salary-substitute and lifestyle firms.

FIGURE 1.2

Types of Start-Up Firms

Salary-Substitute Firms	Lifestyle Firms	Entrepreneurial Firms
Firms that basically provide their owner or owners a similar level of income to what they would be able to earn in a conventional job	Firms that provide their owner or owners the opportunity to pursue a particular lifestyle, and make a living at it	Firms that bring new products and services to the market by creating and seizing opportunities regardless of the resources they currently control

firms offer common, easily available products or services to customers that are not particularly innovative.

Lifestyle firms provide their owner or owners the opportunity to pursue a particular lifestyle and earn a living while doing so. Lifestyle firms include ski instructors, golf pros, and tour guides. These firms are not innovative, nor do they grow quickly. Commonly, lifestyle companies promote a particular sport, hobby, or pastime and may employ only the owner or just a handful of people. Tahoe Trips & Trails, owned by Hanna Sullivan, is an example of a lifestyle firm. The company leads multiday outdoor adventure trips for private groups and corporate clients to Lake Tahoe, Yosemite, Death Valley, Jackson Hole, and similar locations. Sullivan left a prestigious job with Freemont Ventures, a private investment company, to start Tahoe Trips & Trails because it better accommodates her preferred lifestyle.

Entrepreneurial firms bring new products and services to market. As we noted earlier in this chapter, the essence of entrepreneurship is creating value and then disseminating that value to customers. In this context, "**value**" refers to worth, importance, or utility. Entrepreneurial firms bring new products and services to market by creating and then seizing opportunities. Google, eBay, and Apple are well-known, highly successful examples of entrepreneurial firms. Having recognized an opportunity, companies of this type create products and services that have worth, that are important to their customers, and that provide a measure of usefulness to their customers that they wouldn't have otherwise.

Next, we describe the newly emerging characteristics of today's entrepreneurs. You may be surprised to learn about the types of individuals who are choosing to become entrepreneurs! While reading these characteristics, think about people you know who are accurately described by these characteristics. Do you think any of these people will choose to become entrepreneurs?

CHANGING DEMOGRAPHICS OF ENTREPRENEURS

Learning Objective

7. Discuss the changing demographics of entrepreneurs in the United States.

Over the past 10 years, the demographic makeup of entrepreneurial firms has changed in the United States and around the world. Of the 26 million businesses in the United States, for example, a growing number are owned by women, minorities, seniors, and young people. Although there are no solid numbers on how many of the 26 million businesses are entrepreneurial firms rather than salary-substitute or lifestyle firms, there is growing anecdotal evidence that an increasing number of women, minorities, seniors, and young people are becoming actively involved in the entrepreneurial process. This is an exciting development for entrepreneurship.

Women Entrepreneurs   In the United States, there were 6.5 million women-owned businesses in 2002, the most recent year the U.S. Census Bureau

Bruce Ayres/Getty Images Inc.–Stone Allstock

The demographic makeup of entrepreneurs continues to change, as more women, minorities, and seniors launch entrepreneurial firms. These four women own and operate a clothing design studio.

collected business ownership data. That number is up 20 percent from 1997. In addition to the 6.5 million women-owned businesses, there are 2.7 million firms that are equally male/female owned. Although historically women-owned firms have primarily been in health care and professional services, that emphasis is changing. Between 1997 and 2002, the fastest-growing areas of women-owned firms were construction (30 percent increase), agricultural services (24 percent increase), transportation (20 percent increase), communications (20 percent increase), and public utilities (20 percent increase). In addition, there were 117,069 women-owned firms in 2002 with total sales of $1 million or more. Recent studies show that women-owned firms are just as profitable as male-owned businesses.[48] Collectively, these statistics reflect the growing breadth and economic prowess of women-owned businesses in the United States.[49]

Minority Entrepreneurs Minorities owned approximately 18 percent of the 23 million U.S. businesses in 2002, up 10 percent from 1997. African American–owned firms had the highest growth rate between 1997 and 2002, up 45 percent. Hispanics and Latinos constituted the largest minority business community in 2002, owning 6.6 percent of all U.S. firms. The percentage of minority women owning businesses also rose between 1997 and 2002. For example, 29 percent of African American–owned businesses with paid employees and 47 percent of African American nonemployer firms were owned by women.

An important factor facilitating the increased prevalence of minority-owned businesses is the number of organizations that promote and provide assistance to minority entrepreneurs in the United States. Examples include the Asian Business Association, Hispanic Business Women's Alliance, National Black Chamber of Commerce, and the National Indian Business Association.

Senior Entrepreneurs Although the U.S. Census Bureau does not collect data on senior entrepreneurs (people 55 years old and older), there is strong evidence to suggest that the number of older people choosing entrepreneurial careers is increasing rapidly. A recent study from researchers affiliated with the U.S. Bureau of Labor Statistics and Boston College found that self-employment levels increase with age, and one-third of male workers between the ages of 51 and 61 are self-employed.[50] Similarly, unpublished government data obtained by Challenger, Gray & Christmas, an outplacement consulting firm, indicates that 2.1 million Americans 55 years of age and older owned their own businesses in 2005, an increase of 22 percent from 2000.[51] The dramatic increase in the number of senior entrepreneurs is attributed to a number of factors, including corporate downsizing, an increasing desire among older workers for more personal fulfillment in their lives, and growing worries among seniors that they need to earn additional income to pay for future health care services and other expenses.[52] A growing number of seniors may also see themselves as ideal candidates to start their own businesses. Many people in the 55 and older age range have substantial business experience, financial resources that they can draw upon, and excellent vigor and health.

Young Entrepreneurs Although the total number of young entrepreneurs is far less than women, minority, or senior entrepreneurs, interest among young people (ages 21 years and younger) in entrepreneurship is growing. At the high school level, a Gallup study revealed that 27 percent of high school students take an entrepreneurial business course, and 7 out of 10 high school students want to start their own companies. More specifically, 6 in 10 females, 7 in 10 Hispanics, and 8 in 10 African American high school students are interested in starting a business.[53] Interestingly, statistics also show that 90 percent of adult Americans would either approve or strongly approve of their son or daughter becoming an entrepreneur.[54]

An emphasis on entrepreneurship education is starting to appear in some areas as early as grade school. Harper Arrington Publishing is publishing a series of books titled *The Little Entrepreneur—Takes Flight*. The series is designed to teach kids how to turn their hobbies into businesses and is suitable for children as young as 8. The National Foundation for Teaching Entrepreneurship (NFTE) targets students in grades 7 through 12. It offers a number of different entrepreneurship-related programs in public schools and through nonprofits, like the YMCA and the Boys & Girls Clubs of America. The NFTE Comprehensive course is the most extensive. An abbreviated version of the course is taught as a Summer "Biz-Camp." The course requires students ages 13 to 18 to write a business plan for a real business, and the best plans receive "venture capital grants" that range from $50 to $500. Since its founding in 1987, the NFTE has reached over 186,000 young people and has more than 1,000 Certified Entrepreneurship Teachers.[55]

On college campuses, interest in entrepreneurship education is at an all-time high, as will be described throughout this book. According to Judith Cone, vice president of the Ewing Marion Kauffman Foundation, more than 2,000 colleges and universities in the United States, which is about two-thirds of the total, offer at least one course in entrepreneurship.[56] Although the bulk of entrepreneurship education takes place within business schools, many other colleges and departments are offering entrepreneurship courses as well—including engineering, agriculture, theater, dance, education, law, and nursing. The tide is also turning in regard to the attractiveness of an entrepreneurial career in almost every major. Commenting on this issue, Jerome Katz, a professor of management at St. Louis University who has studied this trend, said, "Twenty years ago students who dared to say they wanted to start their own companies would be sent for counseling. Today, entrepreneurship is the fastest-growing course of study on campuses nationwide."[57]

Entrepreneurship is a particularly attractive option for college students for a number of reasons, including their understanding of the attractiveness of the youth market, their ability to find low-cost labor in the form of other students, their access to resources that are available to them at their colleges or universities, and their intuitive recognition of the reality that if they fail they can pick up where they left off and pursue another venture or a conventional career. In addition, if a student's business was developed through an entrepreneurship program or was competitive in a business plan competition, the business may be seen as less risky than other start-ups.

ENTREPRENEURSHIP'S IMPORTANCE

Learning Objective

8. Discuss the impact of entrepreneurial firms on economics and societies.

Entrepreneurship's importance to an economy and the society in which it resides was first articulated in 1934 by Joseph Schumpeter, an Austrian economist who did the majority of his work at Harvard University. In his book *The Theory of Economic Development*, Schumpeter argued that entrepreneurs develop new products and technologies that over time make current products and technologies obsolete. Schumpeter called this process **creative destruction**. Because new products and technologies are typically better than those they replace and the availability of improved products and technologies increases consumer demand, creative destruction stimulates economic activity. The new products and technologies may also increase the productivity of all elements of a society.[58]

The creative destruction process is initiated most effectively by start-up ventures that improve on what is currently available. Small firms that practice this art are often called "innovators" or "agents of change." The process of creative destruction is not limited to new products and technologies; it can include new pricing strategies (e.g., discount airlines such as Southwest), new distribution channels (such as FedEx or Amazon.com), or new retail formats (such as IKEA in furniture and Whole Foods Market in groceries).

Now let's look more closely at entrepreneurship's importance.

Economic Impact of Entrepreneurial Firms

For two reasons, entrepreneurial behavior has a strong impact on an economy's strength and stability.

Innovation **Innovation** is the process of creating something new, which is central to the entrepreneurial process.[59] According to the National Federation for Independent Businesses, small firms (fewer than 500 employees) are twice as innovative per employee as larger firms. In addition, small innovative firms produce 13 times more patents per employee than large patenting firms, and their patents are twice as likely as large firm patents to be among the 1 percent most cited (which is an indication of their influence).[60]

Job Creation In the past two decades, economic activity has moved increasingly in the direction of smaller entrepreneurial firms, possibly because of their unique ability to innovate and focus on specialized tasks. Small businesses employ more than half of all private sector employees in the United States and create about two-thirds of new jobs. In addition, small businesses provide the first job for most new entrants to the labor force. Small businesses represent 99.7 percent of all employers, and small firms with fewer than 500 employees represent 99.9 percent of the 26 million businesses in the United States.[61]

Entrepreneurial Firms' Impact on Society

The innovations of entrepreneurial firms have a dramatic impact on a society. Think of all the new products and services that make our lives easier, enhance our productivity at work, improve our health, and entertain us. For example, Amgen, an entrepreneurial firm that helped launch the biotech industry, has produced a number of drugs that have dramatically improved people's lives. An example is NEUPOGEN, a drug that decreases the incidence of infection in cancer patients who are undergoing chemotherapy treatment. Sensipar is another of Amgen's important products. Patients with chronic kidney disease and who are on dialysis take this drug as a secondary treatment of hyperparathyroidism.[62]

In addition to improved health care, consider cellular phones, personal computing, Internet shopping, overnight package delivery, digital photography, and microwave ovens. All these products are new to this generation, yet it's hard to imagine our world without them.

However, innovations do create moral and ethical issues with which societies are forced to grapple. For example, bar-code scanner technology and the Internet have made it easier for companies to track the purchasing behavior of their customers, but this raises privacy concerns. Similarly, bioengineering has made it easier to extend the shelf life of many food products, but some researchers and consumers question the long-term health implications of bioengineered foods.

A particularly interesting example of a company that makes a product that is intended for good but some people oppose is VeriChip. VeriChip makes tiny, implantable microchips that hold medical records that can be implanted just beneath a person's skin. Emergency room physicians can scan the chips and gain immediate access to a person's medical records in the event of an emergency. The chips are controversial because they are actually implanted under a person's skin and because they raise privacy concerns. There is a perception in some quarters that the chips could be used to track people, steal their identities, or violate a patient's privacy in other ways.[63] As an individual, how do you react to this product? Would you be willing to use it? Why or why not?

Entrepreneurial Firms' Impact on Larger Firms

Learning Objective

9. Identify ways in which large firms benefit from the presence of smaller entrepreneurial firms.

In addition to the impact that entrepreneurial firms have on the economy and society, they also have a positive impact on the effectiveness of larger firms. For example, some entrepreneurial firms are original equipment manufacturers, producing parts that go into products that larger firms manufacture and sell. Thus, many exciting new products, such as DVD players, digital cameras, and improved prescription drugs, are not solely the result of the efforts of larger companies with strong brand names, such as Sony, Kodak, and Johnson & Johnson. They were produced with the cutting-edge component parts or research and development efforts provided by entrepreneurial firms.

The evidence shows that many entrepreneurial firms have built their entire business models around producing products and services that help larger firms be more efficient or effective. For example, an increasing number of U.S. firms want to advertise on Spanish sites and purchase media exposure in Latin American companies. Latin Edge, a 2002 start-up, helps its larger clients achieve these objectives. Similarly, large food retailers are increasingly on the lookout for methods to ensure that the food products they sell are safe. TraceRegister Inc., a tiny Seattle start-up, has developed software that is helping Wal-Mart and other large retailers ensure that their seafood is safe. TraceRegister's software provides seafood buyers an Internet-based tool that traces every step that a specific order of farm-raised seafood has taken, from growing pen to the retail store.

In many instances, entrepreneurial firms partner with larger companies to reach mutually beneficial goals. Participation in business partnerships accelerates a firm's growth by giving it access to some of its partner's resources, managerial talent, and intellectual capacities. We examine the idea of partnering throughout this book. In each chapter, look for the boxed feature titled "Partnering for Success," which illustrates how entrepreneurial firms are using business partnerships to boost their chances for success. The feature in this chapter discusses how a large media company is helping small producers of children's DVDs band together to create boxed sets of videos to compete head-to-head with Disney and other large companies at big-box stores like Sam's Warehouse Club and Costco.

Partnering for SUCCESS

Topics Entertainment: Helping the Makers of Children's DVDs Band Together to Take on Larger Rivals

www.topics-ent.com

A problem that small producers of educational DVDs for children have is mustering enough clout to get into big-box stores like Costco, Wal-Mart, and Best Buy. These stores prefer to deal with Disney's Baby Einstein division and other large producers. Recognizing this problem, Greg James, the founder of Topics Entertainment, a large media company, had an idea. What if his company, a producer of language-learning software and similar software products, utilized its relationships with major retailers and created "boxed sets" of educational children's DVDs, featuring the best products from smaller producers. And what if a set of four DVDs could be priced at $9.99, as opposed to $19.99, which is the price of one Baby Einstein DVD?

James's pitch worked. Topics Entertainment is now partnering with several small producers of children's educational DVDs and has created boxed sets under the "Little Steps" and the "Wild Animal Baby" brands. Each contributor is paid a licensing fee. The Little Steps boxed sets, named Animal Baby, Little Scholars, and ABCs, feature colorful graphics, creative characters, and interactive fun. The Wild Animal Baby boxed sets, including Counting, Phonics, Colors, and several others, promote literacy, teach simple math concepts, and help children develop motor skills through imitating animals. Both series of boxed sets are appropriate for children ages 2 and up.

The small companies that are partnering with Topics Entertainment have high-quality DVDs to sell, but their limited product lines and lack of relationships with large retailers make it nearly impossible to get noticed beyond small specialty markets. By partnering with Topics Entertainment they crack bigger

markets, free themselves to focus on making DVDs rather than cold-calling retailers, and expose their work to a wide audience. They're also free to build their brand beyond the Topics Entertainment relationship. The downside is that they allow some of their best work to be bundled with the work of others and branded as Little Steps or Wild Animal Baby DVDs rather than DVDs under their brand. While the individual producers are credited on the back or inside flap of the boxes, it's the Little Steps or Wild Animal Baby name on the front.

Questions for Critical Thinking

1. What was Topics Entertainment able to do for the smaller producers of children's educational DVDs that they would have never had been able to do on their own?
2. For a small firm, what are the advantages and disadvantages of having its products sold through a large retailer like Sam's or Costco?
3. What risks do the small firms mentioned in the article take partnering with a larger company like Topics Entertainment, other than the risks mentioned in the article? Think about all aspects of entrepreneurship when formulating your answer.
4. If you were the founder/CEO of one of the small firms mentioned in the article would you have accepted Topic's partnership offer? If so, explain why.

Sources: C. Penttila, "All Together Now," *Entrepreneur*, August 2007, 92; R. Flandez, "Small Makers of Children's DVDs Unite to Take on Big Rivals," *Wall Street Journal*, February 6, 2007, B4.

THE ENTREPRENEURIAL PROCESS

The entrepreneurial process consists of four steps:

Step 1   Deciding to become an entrepreneur

Step 2   Developing successful business ideas

Step 3   Moving from an idea to an entrepreneurial firm

Step 4   Managing and growing the entrepreneurial firm

Figure 1.3 models the entrepreneurial process. This process is the guide or framework around which we develop this book's contents. The double-headed arrow between the decision to become an entrepreneur and the development

Learning Objective

10. Explain the entrepreneurial process.

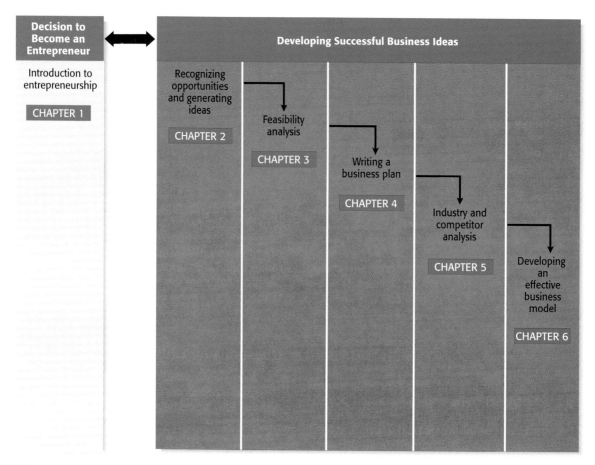

FIGURE 1.3

Basic Model of the Entrepreneurial Process

of successful business ideas indicates that sometimes the opportunity to develop an idea prompts a person to become an entrepreneur. Each section of Figure 1.3 is explained in the following sections.

Decision to Become an Entrepreneur (Chapter 1)

As discussed earlier, people become entrepreneurs to be their own bosses, to pursue their own ideas, and to realize financial rewards. Usually, a **triggering event** prompts an individual to become an entrepreneur.[64] For example, an individual may lose her job and decide that the time is right to start her own business. Or a person might receive an inheritance and for the first time in his life have the money to start his own company. Lifestyle issues may also trigger entrepreneurial careers. For example, a woman may wait until her youngest child is in school before she decides to launch her own entrepreneurial venture.

Developing Successful Business Ideas (Chapters 2–6)

Many new businesses fail not because the entrepreneur didn't work hard but because there was no real opportunity to begin with. Developing a successful business idea includes opportunity recognition, feasibility analysis, writing a business plan, industry analysis, and the development of an effective business model. Chapter 2 takes a scientific look at how entrepreneurs recognize opportunities and describes how the opportunity recognition process typically unfolds. Chapter 3 focuses on feasibility analysis: the way to determine whether

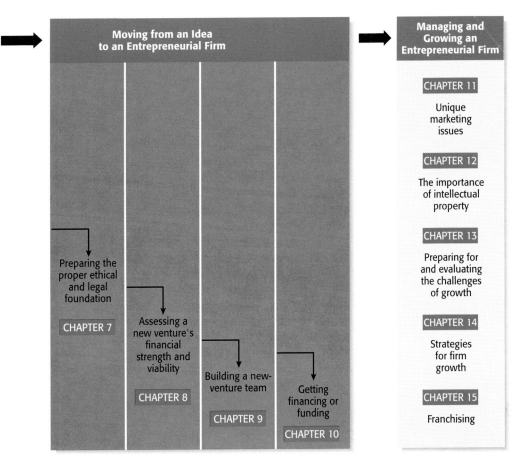

FIGURE 1.3

(Continued)

an idea represents a viable business opportunity. Chapter 4 describes how to write a business plan. A **business plan** is a written document that describes all the aspects of a business venture in a concise manner. It is usually necessary to have a written business plan to raise money and attract high-quality business partners. Some entrepreneurs are impatient and don't want to spend the time it takes to write a business plan.[65] This approach is usually a mistake. Writing a business plan forces an entrepreneur to think carefully through all the aspects of a business venture. It also helps a new venture establish a set of milestones that can be used to guide the early phases of the business rollout. Industry and competitor analysis is our concern in Chapter 5. Knowing the industry in which a firm will choose to compete is crucial to an entrepreneur's success. Chapter 6 focuses on the important topic of developing an effective business model. A firm's **business model** is its plan for how it competes, uses its resources, structures its relationships, interfaces with customers, and creates value to sustain itself on the basis of the profits it generates.

Moving from an Idea to an Entrepreneurial Firm (Chapters 7–10)

The first step in turning an idea into reality is to prepare a proper ethical and legal foundation for a firm, including selecting an appropriate form of business ownership. These issues are discussed in Chapter 7. Chapter 8 deals with the important topic of assessing a new venture's financial strength and viability. Important information is contained in this chapter about completing and analyzing both historical and pro forma financial statements. Chapter 9 focuses on building a new-venture team. Chapter 10 highlights the important task of getting financing or funding and identifies the options that a firm has for raising money.

Managing and Growing an Entrepreneurial Firm (Chapters 11–15)

Given today's competitive environment, all firms must be managed and grown properly to ensure their ongoing success. This is the final stage of the entrepreneurial process.

Chapter 11 focuses on the unique marketing issues facing entrepreneurial firms, including selecting an appropriate target market, building a brand, and the four Ps—product, price, promotion, and place (or distribution)—for new firms. Chapter 12 examines the important role of intellectual property in the growth of entrepreneurial firms. More and more, the value of "know-how" exceeds the value of a company's physical assets. In addition, we will talk about protecting business ideas through intellectual property statutes, such as patents, trademarks, copyrights, and trade secrets.

Preparing for and evaluating the challenges of growth is the topic of Chapter 13. We'll look at the characteristics and behaviors of successful growth firms. In Chapter 14, we'll study strategies for growth, ranging from new product development to mergers and acquisitions. We conclude with Chapter 15, which focuses on franchising. Not all franchise organizations are entrepreneurial firms, but franchising is a growing component of the entrepreneurial landscape. When you finish studying these 15 chapters, you will have been exposed to all components of the entrepreneurial process—a process that is vital to entrepreneurial success.

Chapter Summary

1. Entrepreneurship is the process by which individuals pursue opportunities without regard to resources they currently control.
2. Corporate entrepreneurship is the conceptualization of entrepreneurship at the organizational level. Entrepreneurial firms are proactive, innovative, and risk taking. In contrast, conservative firms take a more "wait and see" posture, are less innovative, and are risk averse.
3. The three primary reasons that people decide to become entrepreneurs and start their own firms are as follows: to be their own boss, to pursue their own ideas, and to realize financial rewards.
4. Passion for the business, product/customer focus, tenacity despite failure, and execution intelligence are the four primary characteristics of successful entrepreneurs.
5. The five most common myths regarding entrepreneurship are that entrepreneurs are born, not made; that entrepreneurs are gamblers; that entrepreneurs are motivated primarily by money; that entrepreneurs should be young and energetic; and that entrepreneurs love the spotlight.
6. Entrepreneurial firms are the firms that bring new products and services to market by recognizing and seizing opportunities regardless of the resources they currently control. Entrepreneurial firms stress innovation, which is not the case for salary-substitute and lifestyle firms.
7. The demographic makeup of those launching entrepreneurial firms is changing in the United States and around the world. There is growing evidence that an increasing number of women, minorities, seniors, and young people are becoming actively involved in the entrepreneurial process.
8. There is strong evidence that entrepreneurial behavior has a significant impact on economic stability and strength. The areas in which entrepreneurial firms contribute the most are innovation and job creation. Entrepreneurial behavior also has a dramatic impact on society. It's easy to think of new

products and services that have helped make our lives easier, that have made us more productive at work, that have improved our health, and that have entertained us in new ways.

9. In addition to the impact that entrepreneurial firms have on an economy and society, entrepreneurial firms have a positive impact on the effectiveness of larger firms. There are many entrepreneurial firms that have built their entire business models around producing products and services that help larger firms increase their efficiency and effectiveness.

10. The four distinct elements of the entrepreneurial process, pictured in Figure 1.3, are deciding to become an entrepreneur, developing successful business ideas, moving from an idea to establishing an entrepreneurial firm, and managing and growing an entrepreneurial firm.

Key Terms

Business model, **49**

Business plan, **49**

Corporate entrepreneurship, **31**

Creative destruction, **45**

Entrepreneurial firms, **42**

Entrepreneurial intensity, **31**

Entrepreneurship, **30**

Execution intelligence, **37**

Innovation, **45**

Lifestyle firms, **42**

Moderate risk takers, **40**

Passion for their business, **33**

Product/customer focus, **36**

Salary-substitute firms, **41**

Triggering event, **48**

Value, **42**

Review Questions

1. Increasingly, entrepreneurship is being practiced in countries throughout the world. Why do you think this is the case? Do you expect entrepreneurship to continue to spread throughout the world, or do you think its appeal will subside over time?

2. What key insights does the GEMS study provide us about entrepreneurship?

3. What evidence is available suggesting that the often reported statistic that 9 out of 10 new businesses fail is an exaggeration? What is a more realistic failure rate for new firms?

4. What is entrepreneurship? How can one differentiate an entrepreneurial firm from any other type of firm? In what ways is an entrepreneur who just launched a restaurant different from someone who just took a job as the general manager of a restaurant owned by a major restaurant chain?

5. What are the three main attributes of firms that pursue high levels of corporate entrepreneurship? Would these firms score high or low on an entrepreneurial intensity scale?

6. What are the three primary reasons people become entrepreneurs? Which reason is given most commonly? Which reason best describes why you may choose to become an entrepreneur?

7. Some people start their own firms to pursue financial rewards. However, these rewards are often far fewer than imagined. Why is this so?

8. What are the four primary traits and characteristics of successful entrepreneurs?

9. Why is passion such an important characteristic of successful entrepreneurs? What is it about passion that makes it particularly compatible with the entrepreneurial process?

10. Why is a product/customer focus an important characteristic of successful entrepreneurs?

11. What is it about "tenacity" that makes it such an important characteristic for entrepreneurs?

12. What are the five common myths of entrepreneurship?

13. What evidence do we have that debunks the myth that entrepreneurs are born, not made?

14. What are the major differences among salary-substitute firms, lifestyle firms, and entrepreneurial firms?

15. How would you characterize the risk-taking propensity of most entrepreneurs?

16. What factors favor older entrepreneurs as opposed to younger entrepreneurs?

17. What did Joseph Schumpeter mean by the term *creative destruction*?

18. In general, what effects does entrepreneurship have on economies around the world?

19. How is the demographic makeup of entrepreneurs changing? What do you believe is accounting for these changes?

20. Describe several examples of the impact that entrepreneurial firms have on a society.

Application Questions

1. Reread the opening case, and then list all the smart or effective moves Nate Alder made in the early days of building Klymit. Which three moves were most instrumental in Klymit's early success? Be prepared to justify your selections.

2. Imagine that you're the dean of your college and you've suggested that more entrepreneurship courses be taught throughout your college's curriculum. You're getting resistance from some professors who think that entrepreneurship is a fad. Make the argument that entrepreneurship isn't a fad and is an extremely important topic.

3. Suppose you were talking to a friend who told you that her father was thinking about quitting his job to start a business in an area that he's passionate about, but has decided to pass on the opportunity because he just read that 9 out of 10 new businesses fail. What would you advise your friend to tell her dad?

4. Karen Jenkins has a good job working for the city of Rapid City, South Dakota, but is weary of 2 percent per year pay raises. Because she has read magazine articles about young entrepreneurs becoming extremely wealthy, she decides to start her own firm. Do you think Karen is starting a firm for the right reason? Do you think the money she likely will earn will disappoint her? Do you think Karen's reason for starting a firm will contribute in a positive manner or a negative manner to the tenacity that is required to successfully launch and run an entrepreneurial venture?

5. Mark, a friend of yours, has always had a nagging desire to be his own boss. He has a good job with AT&T but has several ideas for new products that he can't get AT&T interested in. Mark has done a good job saving money over the years and has over $100,000 in the bank. He asks you, "Am I crazy for wanting to leave AT&T to start my own businesses? How do I know that I have what it takes to be a successful entrepreneur"? What would you tell him?

6. Describe someone you know who is a good candidate to be an entrepreneur and someone who is a poor candidate.

7. People are sometimes puzzled by the fact that entrepreneurs who have made millions of dollars still put in 60- to 80-hour weeks helping their companies innovate and grow. After reading the chapter, why do you think millionaire and multimillionaire entrepreneurs still get up and go to work every day? If you were one of these entrepreneurs, do you think you would feel the same way? Why or why not?

8. The "Savvy Entrepreneurial Firm" boxed feature focuses on Guitar Hero and iRobot. Is iRobot a salary-substitute, a lifestyle, or an entrepreneurial firm? In what ways has iRobot demonstrated a product/customer focus? (You may want to look at the company's Web site along with the information in the "Savvy Entrepreneurial Firm" boxed feature.) On a scale of 1 to 5 (5 is high), how instrumental has iRobot's product/market focus been to its success?

9. You just made a trip home and are visiting with your dad. He is 56 years old and has spent the past nine years working in various management positions for Home Depot. Prior to that, he served 24 years in the U.S. Army. Your father has always loved to fish and has several ideas for new fishing tackle and gear. He's made several prototypes of his ideas and has received positive feedback from other fishermen. He wonders if he is too old to start a firm and if his management experience and his military background will be helpful in a new-venture context. If your dad asked you for your advice, what would you tell him?

10. Shelia Patterson is 26 years old and is thinking about starting a digital media firm. She knows that an increasing number of women are starting their own firms, but she doesn't know where to go to learn about the start-up process. She would also like to network with other women, who are approximately her own age, who have started their own firms. Do some Internet research to provide Shelia suggestions about where to go to accomplish her objectives.

11. Jacob Lacy is an MBA student at a Big 12 school in the Midwest. He has an idea to start an Internet-based firm that will help high school students prepare for the SAT exam in an innovative manner. Jacob just talked to a trusted family friend, who told him that college is a poor time and place to launch a firm. The family friend told Jacob, "Try to distance yourself from the college atmosphere before you start your firm." Do you think Jacob is getting good advice? Why or why not?

12. "You Be the VC 1.1" feature focuses on Pie Face, which plans to make the humble pie an inviting alternative to fast food with a range of distinctive gourmet pies. Do some research on Pie Face and write a short summary of where the firm is today in regard to its early success (or failure) and how effectively it has executed its business plan.

13. A friend of yours just bought a Sony digital camera. While showing it to you, he said, "You think entrepreneurial firms are so smart, look at what Sony has done. It has produced a sophisticated digital camera that allows me to take pictures, download them to my PC, and e-mail them to family members. Sony's a big company, not a small entrepreneurial firm. What do you have to say to that?" If you were to defend the role of entrepreneurial firms in developing new technologies, how would you respond?

14. Read Case 1.2, which focuses on Aquaflow Bionomic Corporation. What similarities, if any, do you see between Aquaflow Bionomic Corporation's start-up story and the start-up stories of Harmonix Music Systems (the company behind Guitar Hero) and iRobot, the two firms featured in the "Savvy Entrepreneurial Firm" feature in the chapter?

15. Go to the Web site of Spark Craft Studios, a company that was started by two student entrepreneurs at Boston University. Spend some time looking at the Web site and reading about Spark Craft Studio's history and current offerings. Do you consider Spark Craft Studio to be a salary-substitute, lifestyle, or entrepreneurial firm? What unique value does Spark Craft Studios offer to its customers? In what ways, if any, does Spark Craft Studios contribute to the economy, to society, and to the success of larger firms?

You Be the VC 1.1

Company: Pie Face

www.pieface.com.au

Business Idea: Most people have a favorite pie shop, but entrepreneurs in Australia have ambitions to open a national chain of Pie Face gourmet pie restaurants, making the process of buying a humble pie an inviting alternative to fast food.

Pitch: Fast-food restaurants often have such similar formats that they have lost their appeal as fun and appealing destinations to some consumers.

Australian fashion entrepreneurs Betty Fong and Wayne Homschek came up with the idea to breathe new life into the fast-food industry after serving up pies at the end of one of their catwalk shows. The pies met with an enthusiastic response by the stylish crowd, and the pair decided to explore the idea further. After a lengthy brainstorming session, Fong and Homschek decided to give the humble pie an up-to-the-minute makeover by putting wacky faces on each crust that, as well as giving each pie a personality, also denotes the filling inside. So, for example, a smiley face indicates a chicken pie, while a wiggly mouth in the shape of an M is the code for beef mince and a V is for vegetable.

The Pie Face franchise operation, launched in Sydney, makes the premium pies in nine flavors, including unusual gourmet variations such as Thai chicken curry or Mexican vegetable. They come in an assortment of sizes such as mini, lunch, couples, and family and are all made in a central kitchen, with faces all piped on by hand before daily deliveries to franchisees. Each store, which is as bright and different in personality as the pies themselves, then bakes the goods freshly in front of customers, as well as producing a selection of cookies, muffins, croissants, wraps, and good coffee.

The unique pies come with gourmet "smash" and gravy. The term for when the three are put together is a "Stack," which is a Pie Face specialty.

The brand appeals to all ages, but younger buyers have particularly responded to the irreverence of the Pie Face name, which can be interpreted locally in two ways, as either a pie with a face, or a slang term for having drunk a little too much. Stores are open 24 hours, which appeals to late-night partygoers, as much as office lunch buyers and founders have carried on the jokey branding with the choice of tags for cold take-aways, "Take me home!!!" and hot eat-in pies, "Have me now!!!"

Fifty percent of customers are women, possibly due to the fact that many of the recipes are low or reduced in fat and the pastry is kept deliberately thin for the health conscious.

Pie Face currently has 10 franchises, which are each required to invest upward of $150,000, but the growth strategy includes plans to expand to more than 50 stores nationally.

Q&A: Based on the material covered in this chapter, what questions would you ask the firm's founders before making your funding decision? What answers would satisfy you?

Decision: If you had to make your decision on just the information provided in the pitch and on the company's Web site, would you fund this firm? Why or why not?

You Be the VC 1.2

Company: Jott

www.jott.com

Business Idea: Create a service that allows a user to call a specific phone number and leave a voice message (for a specific person, a group of people, or for him- or herself), and have the message converted to text and delivered to the recipient(s) as an e-mail or text message.

Pitch: Have you ever had a thought while driving your car and wished there was a convenient way to leave a message for yourself before you forgot the idea? Or have you ever been away from your office and wanted to send a message to a colleague but didn't have access to e-mail? How about this one: Say you have four adult children and want to remind them that their mother's birthday is in three days, but at the time you think of it you're away from your computer and don't have time to make four phone calls?

Jott is the solution to these and similar problems. It's a voice-to-text transcription service that allows its users to call a toll-free number and leave up to a 30-second message. The message is then translated into text (using a combination of software and human transcribers), and is delivered to the intended recipient(s) via e-mail, text message, or both. You can send the message to yourself or anyone on the list that you've established with Jott. The recipient or recipients can choose between reading the message or listening to the original voice recording. Because Jott uses software for most of its translations, the text messages often aren't perfect, but they're pretty close. There are other ways that you can use Jott. For example, events can be added to your Google calendar and updates can be sent to Twitter simply by calling Jott and initiating these actions with your voice. You can also set up a to-do list, which Jott calls Remember the Milk, and remind yourself of things. Imagine you're on your way to work and you just remembered that you need to pick up a loaf of bread on the way home. You can call Jott, ask to

"Jott" (or access) your Remember the Milk list, and say "Remember to pick up a loaf of bread on the way home tonight." On your way home, you can check your Remember the Milk list and your earlier voice message will be played back to you.

Jott offered its service for free during its beta phase, racking up 420,000 users. The service is now out of beta and is being monetized through a tiered service and payment plan. Jott Basic is free but is ad supported. Jott (regular version) costs $3.95 per month and Jott Pro costs $12.95 per month. Both are free from ads and offer increasingly desirable features.

Q&A: Based on the material covered in this chapter, what questions would you ask the firm's founders before making your funding decision? What answers would satisfy you?

Decision: If you had to make your decision on just the information provided in the pitch and on the company's Web site, would you fund this company? Why or why not?

CASE1.1

eHarmony: Passion and a Product/Customer Focus Has Helped Facilitate over 50,000 Marriages
www.eharmony.com

Bruce R. Barringer
Oklahoma State University
R. Duane Ireland
Texas A & M University

Every day in the United States over 225 people get married who met on eHarmony. Founded in 2000, eHarmony matches men and women looking for mates on 29 key dimensions of compatibility. The company has experienced remarkable success. It now has over 10 million registered users in 200 countries. About 15,000 people a day fill out its matchmaking questionnaire. Incredibly, over 100,000 babies have been born to people who met on eHarmony. Top that for an entrepreneurial success story! There are over 100,000 children alive today who may have never been born if a single entrepreneur hadn't started eHarmony.

Founding Story

eHarmony was founded on August 22, 2000, by Dr. Neil Clark Warren, a 65-year-old clinical psychologist. Dr. Warren spent the majority of his career counseling married couples and speaking out on how men and women develop healthy marriage relationships. He came to the conclusion that the single biggest factor that determines a marriage's success is picking the right partner. He also felt he had a keen sense of the dimensions of compatibility that led to a good match. Determined to do something about it, Dr. Warren launched eHarmony to leverage the power of the Internet to

(continued)

share his strategies with singles looking for marriage partners.

The early going wasn't easy. Dr. Warren crisscrossed central Texas, eHarmony's initial home, talking to groups as small as three to four people, sharing his vision for eHarmony. In a stroke a good luck, Dr. Warren pitched his idea to Greg Waldorf, an investor and entrepreneur. Waldorf was so taken with Dr. Warren's passion and vision that he invested and signed on as eHarmony's CEO. The company struggled until Dr. Warren appeared on a national radio program hosted by Dr. James Dobson, founder of Focus on the Family, an evangelical Christian ministry. The appearance resulted in 100,000 new subscribers to eHarmony's Web site, and the company was off and running.

How It Works

eHarmony users fill out a 436-question questionnaire that produces a personality profile. Some of the questions, like "I work much better if people follow my lead," are answered on a 1 to 5 scale; and others, like "Other than your parents, who has been the most influential person in your life, and why?" are fill in the blank. The site then gives you a set of potential matches—usually five at a time. Unlike other matchmaking sites you can't browse through profiles and pick who you'd like to contact. You only get access to the potential matches that eHarmony provides you. It costs $59 a month

or $251 a year to subscribe to the service. eHarmony doesn't directly supervise how you contact your potential matches, but it provides advice and guidance for how to proceed sensibly and safely.

Passion and Product/Customer Focus

In managing and tweaking eHarmony since 2000, Dr. Warren and his team have had tough calls to make, which have tested their passion and commitment to their customers versus increased financial rewards. For example, to maintain their commitment to facilitating healthy marriages, the company has turned down over 1.5 million potential customers. There are an initial set of rules. For example, you can't participate if you're already married, have been married and divorced more than three times, or are severely depressed. In addition, if you don't answer the questionnaire truthfully (based on sophisticated methods that eHarmony has for testing this) you'll be excluded. All told, eHarmony figures it has passed up more than $100 million in revenue by turning people away that it felt weren't good candidates for healthy marriage relationships. Another example is that early on eHarmony didn't allow photos. Dr. Warren wanted people to select one another strictly on the basis of compatibility rather than physical attractiveness. That didn't work—people wanted photos. After some serious soul searching, the company decided to allow photos based on the notion that the matches that a

The number of people in this stadium is approximately the same number of babies who have been born to couples who met on eHarmony.com.

person gets are all compatible matches. More importantly, a person is eight times more likely to get contacted by a potential mate if a photo is included in their profile. Financial considerations aside, Dr. Warren didn't want people to leave eHarmony and go to an alternative site just over the photo issue. The company also invests heavily in continually improving its questionnaire. It has five PhD-trained psychologists on staff who spend their time tweaking and improving the questionnaire.

The passion that eHarmony's employees have for facilitating healthy marriage relationships is genuine. Dr. Warren (who stars in eHarmony's television commercials) started the company at the age of 65, after he had had a successful career. Greg Waldorf, eHarmony's CEO, was a professional investor and reentered the workforce to lead the company. Particularly telling is a comment that Waldorf made in a speech given at Stanford University in its Entrepreneurial Thought Leaders Series on February 14, 2007 (Valentine's Day). Waldorf remarked that there is an old cliché that says that at the end of their career nobody ever says that they wished they'd spent more time at the office. While he admitted that he likes getting away, he said that there is a very tangible feeling among the people at eHarmony that the company is helping people accomplish something that they're extremely excited about. That, according to Waldorf, is something worth spending time at the office helping accomplish.

Opportunities and Challenges Ahead

eHarmony plans to continue to grow its matchmaking service and slowly expand into related areas. In addition to its staple service, it operates eHarmony Labs, a relationship research facility, and publishes eHarmony Advice, a relationship advice service for married couples. The company has expanded to Canada and Australia. The "eHarmony" name provides it the ability to expand into other relationship service areas. It is currently exploring the possibility of offering a service that helps children strengthen their relationship with their parents and a service centered on successful parenting.

Although the company has experienced impressive success, it has only scratched the surface regarding the number of potential users of its site. There are between 80 million and 90 million singles in the United States over the age of 18. Of these people, 15 million to 30 million visit a dating or marriage matchmaking site every year, but only

3 to 4 million sign up. While these numbers suggest eHarmony and its competitors have tremendous upside potential, they also illustrate the resistance than many singles have to participating in an online dating or matchmaking service.

While many industry observers see social networking sites like MySpace and Facebook as potential rivals for eHarmony, Waldorf didn't seem worried during his remarks in his speech at Stanford. Instead, he indicated that his biggest worry was the ingenuity of individual entrepreneurs. Since a large percentage of the singles population in the United States isn't currently using eHarmony or its competitors' sites, there is always a possibility that an entrepreneur will find a new and fresh way to motivate singles to engage in an online matchmaking start-up.

Discussion Questions

1. Describe the ways in which eHarmony practices "execution intelligence." How important of a part of eHarmony's success do you think these practices represent?
2. To what degree does eHarmony's founding story debunk one or more of the common myths of entrepreneurship?
3. In what ways has eHarmony sacrificed short-term financial gains to build as healthy a business as possible for the long run?
4. What do you think? Do you think eHarmony will be able to grow beyond a matchmaking Web site, or do you think the company will have a difficult time expanding its menu of services?

Application Questions

1. Why do you think eHarmony is able to persuade people to fill out a 436-question questionnaire and accept the fact that they'll only be provided potential matches that the "company" deems appropriate?
2. What is it about eHarmony, and the people behind it, that make it special? Would it be easy or difficult for another firm to imitate what eHarmony is doing?

Sources: G. Waldorf, Stanford Technology Ventures Entrepreneurial Through Leaders Podcast, February 14, 2007; D. Kirkpatrick, "eHarmony Does What Tech Ought to Do," http://cnnmoney.com (accessed September 30, 2008, posted on September 14, 2007).

CASE 1.2

Aquaflow Bionomic Corporation:
Passion Has Helped Turn Green Slime into Black Gold—Its Success Now Hinges on Execution Intelligence
www.aquaflowgroup.com

Introduction

Ask most gardeners, fish keepers, or pool owners about algae and it is doubtful there will be a positive response. However, you will get an altogether different reaction from a group of antipodean entrepreneurs, who believe that far from being smelly, slimy, and revolting, algae is actually beautiful stuff. Their innovation, which transforms algae grown on sewage into a substitute for crude oil, is now being hailed as the answer to finding a fuel supply that doesn't exacerbate global warming.

Nick Gerritsen's Passion for Clean Technology

New Zealand–born entrepreneur Nick Gerritsen has two main passions: protecting the environment and making the seemingly impossible happen. His attention was drawn to the lack of communication between innovators and investors while he worked as an intellectual property consultant following his graduation. It was a gap in the market that he could see was preventing some vital environmental technologies from getting off the ground. Setting himself up as "an enabler," his goal was to specialize in discovering start-up technology companies and developing them by bringing in other people, often financiers, to help them grow. He told New Zealand's *Listener* magazine that he often reduces hardworking scientists to tears by asking them about their real dreams and ambitions. It seems that no one ever bothered to ask them about what it is they really want to achieve, and their talents get ignored.

Developments in "clean technology" particularly interested Gerritsen, and that led him to a group that was attempting to convert wood into biofuel. Although this technology was unsuccessful, Gerritsen was hooked. He then read a U.S. Energy Office report naming algae as the best land-based solution for sustainable resources for biofuel. The

reasons are threefold: Algae grow continuously and don't require extensive land cropping or intensive chemical input, algae don't compete with other agricultural or horticultural uses of land, and the process produces a sustainable net energy gain by capturing free solar energy from the sun.

From that report, the idea for a company that brings algae-based biofuel to the world was born. In October 2008, three years after the company was set up, Aquaflow Bionomic Corporation announced it had produced the world's first sample of green-crude oil from wild algae using a proprietary process. Just three months later, Gerritsen announced another major breakthrough and predicted that the world's first test flight using wild-algae-based jet fuel was possibly just months away. The company had produced the world's first sample of synthetic paraffinic kerosene (SPK) converted from compounds derived from wild algae. The SPK meets Jet A-1 industry specifications for commercial aircraft fuel, which include density, flash point, and freeze point and are vital in persuading a highly safety-conscious industry that this is a viable product for the $48 billion world airline fuel market.

Balanced Expertise

Aquaflow's entry into the biofuel market coincided with the heightened international debate over the future of the technology. Questions are being increasingly raised about the carbon footprint of the first generation of biofuel production from crops like corn, maize, and rapeseed, while serious food shortages and price hikes have been blamed on rising demand for food crops for fuel.

Faith in algae to provide energy is growing. In January 2008, fuel-giant Shell announced a joint venture with HR Biopetroleum to construct a demonstration plant to harvest algae. Meanwhile, the Commercial Aviation Alternative Fuels Initiative, an alliance of aircraft manufacturers, industry organizations, and entrepreneurs, is seeking a biojet fuel that could come from algae; and a recent San Francisco "algae summit" drew more than 300 delegates.

To make the Aquaflow business model work, and take its place in the market for biofuel, it was important to combine strong skills across the board with strengths in scientific, business, political, and entrepreneurial disciplines.

Cofounders Vicki Buck, the former mayor of Christchurch, and Barrie Leay, the former executive director of New Zealand's Electricity Supply Association, had both worked with Gerritsen before and were inspired to join him in pursuing algae's role as an intelligent alternative in the contentious biofuel debate. Leay, a British-educated geologist, began investigating biofuels 20 years earlier. He says the difference between refining oil from algae and that pumped from beneath the earth's surface is that Aquaflow is just taking a few million years out of the process. Harvesting algae is creating energy from "new sunlight," whereas oil and gas taken from the ground is the product of "old sunlight." For Buck, who as well as her corporate and mayoral experience has served on the Government's Science and Innovation Advisory Council, the attraction of the venture was taking something that's a waste product and turning it into something useful. To complete the team, technical advisers including organic chemist Dr. Ian Miller and fuel expert Dr. Chris Bumby were brought in, along with a number of biochemists and aquaculturists.

Initial trials began at the Blenheim sewage treatment plant on New Zealand's South Island, and the resultant 5 percent algae-based component, extracted from the algae's natural oils, produces 90 percent less emissions than regular diesel. The process also produces millions of gallons of clean water along the way, which can be released back into the community for irrigation, industrial washing or cooling. It has an impressive oil yield of 16,500 pounds per acre, which compares with palm oil's 5,500 and soybean's 1,000 pounds. In 2006, just one year after launching the company, Aquaflow staged the world's first wild algae biodiesel test drive in Wellington.

Aquaflow's Three-Part Plan

Gerritsen, Buck, and Leay's goal is that algae from waste will address the worldwide problem of the increasing volatility in crude oil supplies and pricing, increasing demand and stresses on water supplies, and instability of the global markets due to fears over climate change and the nonsustainability of fossil fuels. It is backed by the

knowledge that if something as ubiquitous as sewage can be used to make a valuable transport fuel and if the process of removing the algae makes water reusable at the same time, it is an exciting proposition with global implications. The trio's plan to make algae-based biofuels a competitive player in the world market is summarized in the following table.

First, following the successful trials, Aquaflow must show that algae harvesting and conversion can work on a commercial scale in a world that urgently needs renewable fuel and clean water. This will entail working on the conversion process to give a better energy balance and developing lower-cost algae harvesting technologies. Put simply, the technology has to be cheap enough to be adopted anywhere. To fund these aims, the company embarked on an investment round to raise $20 million in funding in late 2008.

Second, in order to encourage increased production of algae-based biofuel and get the product to market as fast as possible, the company plans to license the technology to various parties worldwide and link into established companies that have the capacity to establish, service, and maintain the technology in their own territories. The company has already joined forces with a division of U.S. conglomerate Honeywell, UOP. Processes developed by UOP will be used to convert algae into fuel products that meet international standards. UOP, which is already involved with aviation biofuel research with Airbus and Boeing, will be involved in the secondary processing stage, refining the crude oil into products ready for industrial use.

Finally, Aquaflow is committed to encouraging more governmental urgency on climate-change issues, increased commitment to carbon neutrality, and any legislative moves that will encourage the switch to sustainable biofuels.

Aquaflow's Three-Part Plan to Drive Down the Cost of Biodiesel

Step 1 Increase the commercial scale of Aquaflow and implement process efficiencies.
Step 2 Increase the production of algae-based biofuels by licensing the technology worldwide.
Step 3 Support any legislative moves to encourage the switch to sustainable biofuels.

The Ultimate Importance of Execution Intelligence

The future of Aquaflow hinges on the ability of Gerritsen, Buck, and Leay to execute this carefully conceived plan. While passion is important, the entrepreneurs know that a process

(continued)

featuring sharp planning and execution must be in place and used to help a venture grow. There is still a great deal of ongoing research and development to do in the field, but at stake is a massive worldwide market in a number of different disciplines. Aquaflow has already been approached from interested parties involved in wastewater treatment, biopharmaceutical development, and jet fuel production.

Discussion Questions

1. What degree of confidence do you have that Gerritsen, Buck, and Leay will be able to execute their three-point plan? What factors have to come together for the plan to work? What advantages does Aquaflow have in its efforts to execute the plan and continue to grow?
2. To what extent did passion play a role in the founding of Aquaflow and its early success? Do you think that someone without passion for alternative fuels could have successfully founded the firm? Why or why not?
3. Which of the myths of entrepreneurs are dispelled by Nick Gerritsen's involvement in Aquaflow?

4. To what extent does Aquaflow have the potential to (1) make an economic impact on New Zealand, (2) make an impact on society, and (3) make an impact on larger firms?

Application Questions

1. To what extent is Aquaflow creating a network of stakeholders that have a vested interest in seeing the company succeed? Make a list of these people or groups. Comment on how each group's success is linked to Aquaflow's ultimate success.
2. Make a list of 10 people you know who might help you if you decided to start a firm. Briefly comment on the ways that each individual could offer you assistance. In each case, make a note of what you are doing, or should be doing, to solidify and nurture these relationships.

Source: www.aquaflowgroup.com; *Listener*, May 24, 2008; "Black Gold," *IBM Business Insight* (accessed November 17, 2008); *Good: New Zealand's Guide to Sustainable Living;* "Boeing Planes Successfully Fly with Biofuels," *Biodiesel Magazine*, February 2009.

Endnotes

1. E. Maltby, "Ultimate Ski Jackets," www.CNNMoney.com (accessed April 10, 2008).
2. Business in General Blog, "A Conversation with Klymit Technology," http://blog.bplans.com/index.php/2008/05/09/a-conversation-with-klymit-technology (accessed December 3, 2008).
3. S. Johnson, "Klymit Turns Up the Heat," *BYU Magazine*, Fall 2008.
4. N. Bosma, K. Jones, E. Autio, and J. Levie, *Global Entrepreneurship Monitor 2007 Executive Report* (Babson College and London Business School, 2007).
5. N. Bosma, K. Jones, E. Autio, and J. Levie, *Global Entrepreneurship Monitor 2007 Executive Report* (Babson College and London Business School, 2007).
6. B. Headd, "Redefining Business Success: Distinguishing Between Closure and Failure," *Small Business Economics* 21 (2003): 51–61.
7. "Entrepreneurship in American Higher Education," A Report from the Kauffman Panel on Entrepreneurship Curriculum in Higher Education (Kansas City, MO: Ewing Marion Kauffman Foundation, 2006).
8. AAC&U News, Building a Better Entrepreneurial Education, www.aacu.org (accessed November 9, 2008).
9. B. Bolton and J. Thompson, *Entrepreneurs* (Oxford: Butterworth-Heinemann, 2002).
10. P. Sharma and J. J. Chrisman, "Toward a Reconciliation of the Definitional Issues in the Field of Corporate Entrepreneurship," *Entrepreneurship Theory and Practice* 23, no. 3 (1999): 11–27.
11. H. H. Stevenson and J. C. Jarillo, "A Paradigm for Entrepreneurship: Entrepreneurial Management," *Strategic Management Journal* 11 (1990): 17–27.
12. R. D. Ireland and J. W. Webb, "A Cross-Disciplinary Exploration of Entrepreneurship Research," *Journal of Management* 33 (2007): 891–927.
13. M. G. Siegler. "45 Million iPhones Sold by 2009," *VentureBeat*, www.venturebeat.com (accessed November 10, 2008); C. Kirby and M. Yi. "Apple Turns 30," *San Francisco Chronicle OnLine*, www.sfgate.com (accessed May 22, 2006).

14. "Cisco to Build R215m Innovation Centre," *SouthAfrica.info*, www.southafrica.info (accessed November 10, 2008); M. V. Copeland and O. Malik, "How to Ride the Fifth Wave," *Business 2.0*, July 2005; D. Bunnell, *Making the Cisco Connection* (New York: John Wiley & Sons, 2000).

15. R. D. Ireland, J. G. Covin, and D. F. Kuratko, "Conceptualizing Corporate Entrepreneurship Strategy," *Entrepreneurship Theory and Practice* (2009): in press; J. G. Covin and D. P. Slevin, "A Conceptual Model of Entrepreneurship as Firm Behavior," *Entrepreneurship Theory and Practice* 16 (1991): 7–25.

16. B. R. Barringer and A. C. Bluedorn, "The Relationship Between Corporate Entrepreneurship and Strategic Management," *Strategic Management Journal* 20 (1999): 421–44; M. H. Morris, *Entrepreneurial Intensity Sustainable Advantages for Individuals, Organizations, and Societies* (Westport, CT: Quorum Books, 1998).

17. R. Branson, *Losing My Virginity* (New York: Time Warner, 1999).

18. Ladies Who Launch homepage, www.ladieswholaunch.com (accessed April 12, 2006).

19. A. Clark, "A Risk Worth Taking," *The Signal*, October 26, 2006.

20. L. Smolin, "Mixed Reactions to No New Einstein," *www.physicstoday.org*, January 2006; S. Shane, L. Kolvereid, and P. Westhead, "An Exploratory Examination of the Reasons Leading to New Firm Formation Across Country and Gender," *Journal of Business Venturing* 6 (1991): 431–46.

21. R. D. Ireland and J. W. Webb, "Strategic Entrepreneurship: Creating Competitive Advantage Through Streams of Innovation," *Business Horizons*, 50 (2007): 49–59; C. M. Christensen, *The Innovator's Dilemma* (Boston: Harvard Business School Press, 1997).

22. Ladies Who Launch homepage, www.ladieswholaunch.com (accessed February 5, 2007).

23. S. Hamm, "The Education of Marc Andreessen," *BusinessWeek,* Industrial/Technology edition, April 13, 1998: 92.

24. D. Carnoy, "Richard Branson," *Success,* April 1998, 62–63.

25. "Seattle Biodiesel Closes $2 Million Financing: New CEO with Package," Green Car Congress, July 18, 2005, www.greencarcongress.com/2005/07/seattle_biodiesel.html (accessed November 4, 2008).

26. R. Adams, *A Good Hard Kick in the Ass* (New York: Crown Business, 2002).

27. K. Farrell and L.C. Farrell, *Entrepreneurial Age* (New York, Allworth Press, 2001).

28. Ladies Who Launch homepage, www.ladieswholaunch.com (accessed November 1, 2008).

29. R. D. Jager and R. Ortiz, *In the Company of Giants* (New York, McGraw-Hill, 2007).

30. G. Bounds, "Move Over, Coke," *Wall Street Journal*, January 30, 2006, R1.

31. Adams, *A Good Hard Kick in the Ass.*

32. L. Hazleton, "Profile: Jeff Bezos," *Success,* July 1998: 60.

33. Ladies Who Launch homepage, www.ladieswholaunch.com (accessed April 16, 2006).

34. N. Koehn, *Brand New: How Entrepreneurs Earned Consumers' Trust from Wedgwood to Dell* (Boston: Harvard Business School Press, 2001).

35. Koehn, *Brand New.*

36. S. Baillie, "High Tech Heroes," *Profit,* December 2000/January 2001.

37. J. Cope, "Toward a Dynamic Learning Perspective of Entrepreneurship," *Entrepreneurship Theory and Practice* 29 (2005): 373–97; Morris, *Entrepreneurial Intensity.*

38. P. Davidsson and B. Honig, "The Role of Social and Human Capital Among Nascent Entrepreneurs," *Journal of Business Venturing* 18 (2003): 301–31.

39. F. W. Kellermanns, "Family Firm Resource Management: Commentary and Extensions," *Entrepreneurship Theory and Practice* 29 (2005): 313–19; E. B. Roberts, *Entrepreneurs in High Technology* (New York: Oxford University Press, 1991).

40. P. D. Reynolds, W. D. Bygrave, E. Autio, L. Cox, and M. Hay, *Global Entrepreneurship Monitor 2002 Executive Report* (Kansas City, MO: Kauffman Foundation Center for Entrepreneurship Leadership, 2002).

41. Morris, *Entrepreneurial Intensity.*

42. P. J. Bearse, "A Study of Entrepreneurship by Region and SMSA Size," in *Frontiers of Entrepreneurship Research* (Wellesley, MA: Babson College, 1982), 78–112.

43. T. Siebel, "Betting It All," in *The Entrepreneurs of Technology* ed. M. S. Malone (New York: John Wiley & Sons, 2002), 84.

44. C. Williams, *Lead, Follow, or Get Out of the Way* (New York: Times Books, 1981), 111.

45. S. Walton, *Made in America: My Story* (New York: Doubleday, 1992).

46. J. Ballou, T. Barton, D. DesRoches, F. Potter, E. J. Reedy, A. Robb, S. Shane, and Z. Zhao, *The Kauffman Firm Survey* (Kansas City, MO: Ewing Marion Kauffman Foundation, March 2008), 15.
47. J. M. Hite, "Evolutionary Processes and Paths of Relationally Embedded Network Ties in Emerging Entrepreneurial Firms," *Entrepreneurship Theory and Practice* 29 (2005): 113–44; R. Quindlen, *Confessions of a Venture Capitalist* (New York: Warner Books, 2000).
48. E. Kepler and S. Shane, "Are Male and Female Entrepreneurs Really That Different?" *Small Business Research Summary* (Washington, DC: SBA Office of Advocacy: 2007).
49. U.S. Census Bureau 2006 Report, U.S. Census Bureau homepage, www.census.gov (accessed May 18, 2006).
50. M. Giandria, K. Cahill, and Joseph F. Quinn, "Self-Employment Transitions Among Older Workers with Career Jobs," *Boston College Department of Economics Working Papers* (Boston, MA: Boston College, 2008).
51. J. A. Challenger, "As Entrepreneurs, Seniors Lead U.S. Start-Ups," *Franchising World*, August 2005.
52. P. Weber and M. Schaper, "Understand the Grey Entrepreneur," *Journal of Enterprising Culture* 12 (2004), 147–64.
53. SCORE homepage, www.score.org (accessed May 18, 2006).
54. The National Foundation for Teaching Entrepreneurship homepage, www.nfte.com (accessed November 4, 2008).
55. The National Foundation for Teaching Entrepreneurship homepage, www.nfte.com (accessed November 4, 2008).
56. J. Cone, "Teaching Entrepreneurship in Colleges and Universities: How (and Why) a New Academic Field Is Being Built" (Kansas City, MO: Ewing Marion Kauffman Foundation, 2008).
57. P. B. Gray, "Can Entrepreneurship Be Taught?" *Fortune Small Business*, March 10, 2006.
58. J. A. Schumpeter, *The Theory of Economic Development* (Cambridge, MA: Harvard University Press, 1994).
59. R. D. Ireland, D. F. Kuratko, and M. H. Morris, "Is Your Firm Ready for Corporate Entrepreneurship?" *Journal of Business Strategy* 27, no. 1 (2006): 10–17; M. Hammer, "Deep Change: How Operational Innovation Can Transform Your Company," *Harvard Business Review* 82, no. 4 (2004): 84–93.
60. National Federation of Independent Businesses homepage, www.nfib.com (accessed November 4, 2008).
61. National Federation of Independent Businesses homepage, www.nfib.com (accessed November 4, 2008).
62. "Amgen," *Standard & Poor's Stock Report*, www.standardandpoors.com (accessed April 3, 2004).
63. E. Welsch, "VeriChip IPO Bets an Implant Is in Your Future," *Wall Street Journal*, January 11, 2006, A12A.
64. S. Downing, "The Social Construction of Entrepreneurship: Narrative and Dramatic Processes in the Coproduction of Organizations and Identities," *Entrepreneurship Theory and Practice* 29 (2005): 185–204.
65. B. Barringer, *Preparing Effective Business Plans* (Upper Saddle River, NJ: Prentice Hall), 2009.

PART 2

Developing Successful Business Ideas

Getting
Personal

with Kathryn Kerrigan

CURRENTLY IN MY IPOD
Adele, Britney Spears, and
Jack Johnson

BEST ADVICE I'VE RECEIVED
1—Be very cautious of
people who want to help you
for FREE; 2—Ask for help
from people you trust

**FIRST ENTREPRENEURIAL
EXPERIENCE**
Sitting in front of a banker
and pitching my ideas

**WHAT I DO WHEN I'M NOT
WORKING**
Work out, travel with my
fiancé, and be inspired by my
super creative and talented
gal pals

**HARDEST PART OF GETTING
FUNDING**
Getting others to believe in
you. The secret: Believe in
yourself 1,000 percent
FIRST and everything falls
into place.

**WHAT I'D LIKE TO BE DOING
IN 10 YEARS**
Raising a family and being
a venture capitalist

KATHRYN KERRIGAN

Founder and President,
Kathryn Kerrigan
MBA, Loyola University Chicago, 2005

CHAPTERTWO

Recognizing *Opportunities* and Generating Ideas

OPENING PROFILE

KATHRYN KERRIGAN
Filling a Gap in the $24 Billion Women's Shoe Industry
www.kathrynkerrigan.com

Kathryn Kerrigan, who is six feet tall, has always had trouble finding shoes. She began wearing boys' athletic shoes after a growth spurt in elementary school, and as a teenager, she had trouble finding shoes for special events. Her dad remembers those days well, "When she was in high school, I had to drive her all over looking for prom shoes. Within 20 miles, there are six regional malls. We hit them all!"[1]

Kerrigan's difficulties finding shoes continued through high school and college. At Lake Forest College, where she played basketball, she didn't mind wearing athletic shoes and flip-flops, but the lack of fashionable shoes was a problem when she graduated. She saw herself and her teammates (all tall women) as future businesswomen, trendsetters, and mothers, who wanted fashionable and elegant shoes in sizes 11, 12, and 13. All they could find were bland shoes that didn't seem to go well with anything.

In 2003, Kerrigan entered the MBA program at Loyola University Chicago. During her last semester, she took a course, taught by clinical instructor Eve Geroulis, where she was required to come up with a business idea and write a business plan. She decided to write a plan to start a company to design and sell fashionable shoes for women with large shoe sizes. She never thought the plan would turn into a company—it was simply an assignment to complete the class.

As Kerrigan started researching her business idea, she became intrigued. She didn't realize how many tall women there were and how big the gap in the marketplace was. In the course of writing the plan, she talked to 200 tall women and 175 of them had the same complaint—no fashionable size 11, 12, or 13 shoes. She tried to find hard data, from the Shoe Retailers Association and elsewhere, that explained why fashionable shoes weren't available in large sizes, but she had no luck. In the back of her head, Kerrigan had the sneaking suspicion that the shoe companies just weren't supplying these sizes, and that a large untapped market for fashionable size 11, 12, and 13 women's shoes existed. Through her research, she found that women's shoe sizes are increasing. She figured that the reason for this was increased participation in women's sports: Women who play sports from the time they are young will invariably have larger feet and require bigger shoes when they become adults. This was another reason to expect a continued increase in demand for larger-sized women's shoes.

After Kerrigan received her MBA, she took her business plan to a bank to see if she could get a loan and actually start a business. The banker was impressed, not so much with the plan, but with the fact that Kerrigan prepared it, and that she knew the shoe industry and could talk the industry's language. She got a $35,000 loan, which allowed her to travel to trade shows and start the business. She named her business Kathryn

Learning Objectives

After studying this chapter you should be ready to:

1. Explain why it's important to start a new firm when its "window of opportunity" is open.

2. Explain the difference between an opportunity and an idea.

3. Describe the three general approaches entrepreneurs use to identify opportunities.

4. Identify the four environmental trends that are most instrumental in creating business opportunities.

5. List the personal characteristics that make some people better at recognizing business opportunities than others.

6. Identify the five steps in the creative process.

7. Describe the purpose of brainstorming and its use as an idea generator.

8. Describe how to use library and Internet research to generate new business ideas.

9. Explain the purpose of maintaining an idea bank.

10. Describe three steps for protecting ideas from being lost or stolen.

Kerrigan to build a personal brand. The first obstacle that Kerrigan had to overcome, as silly as it sounds, was that she didn't know much about designing and selling shoes. Luckily, she got good advice from her parents and their extended network, and traveled to trade shows talking to suppliers and industry insiders. Another big obstacle was finding a contract manufacturer to make the shoes she had in mind. Because she was proposing something new—fashionable women's shoes in big sizes—manufacturers didn't want to take a chance on an unproven idea. She finally found a factory in Alicante, Spain, a Mediterranean region known for high-quality shoe making, that was willing to work with her. She spent seven months apprenticing in the factory—learning the shoe business inside out. Back home, she studied import laws, tariffs, and the like, becoming an expert in how to import shoes into the United States. She also designed her initial order of large-sized fashionable shoes and boots, aided by craftsmen she had met in Northern Italy, to be made by the factory in Spain.[2]

Kerrigan sold her first shoes in fall 2006. In her first six weeks of operations, her company had $26,950 in sales, depleting most of her stock. Kerrigan's business has grown steadily, and she's outgrown the single manufacturing facility in Spain. While producing fashionable women's shoes in large sizes remains her primary focus, she has expanded her product line. In July 2007, she opened her own flagship store in Libertyville, Illinois, and in August 2007, she added a clothing line for tall women. Her products are now sold online, in catalogs, and through women's fashion boutiques across the United States and in Europe.

In 2007, Kerrigan was named the top female entrepreneur under the age of 30 in America by *Inc.* Along with continuing to build her company, Kerrigan is now an adjunct professor of entrepreneurship at her alma mater, Loyola University of Chicago.

IDENTIFYING AND RECOGNIZING OPPORTUNITIES

Essentially, entrepreneurs recognize an opportunity and turn it into a successful business.[3] An **opportunity** is a favorable set of circumstances that creates a need for a new product, service, or business. Most entrepreneurial ventures are started in one of two ways. Some ventures are externally stimulated. In this instance, an entrepreneur decides to launch a firm, searches for and recognizes an opportunity, and then starts a business, as Jeff Bezos did when he created Amazon.com. In 1994, Bezos quit his lucrative job at a New York City investment firm and headed for Seattle with a plan to find an attractive opportunity and launch an e-commerce company.[4] Other firms are internally stimulated. An entrepreneur recognizes a problem or an **opportunity gap** and creates a business to fill it.

Regardless of which of these two ways an entrepreneur starts a new business, opportunities are tough to spot. Identifying a product, service, or business opportunity that isn't merely a different version of something already available is difficult. A common mistake entrepreneurs make in the opportunity recognition process is picking a

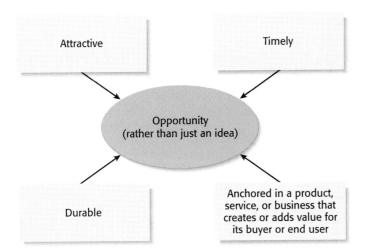

FIGURE 2.1

Four Essential Qualities of an Opportunity

currently available product or service that they like or are passionate about and then trying to build a business around a slightly better version of it. Although this approach seems sensible, such is usually not the case. The key to opportunity recognition is to identify a product or service that people need and are willing to buy, not one that an entrepreneur wants to make and sell.[5]

As shown in Figure 2.1, an opportunity has four essential qualities: It is (1) attractive, (2) durable, (3) timely, and (4) anchored in a product, service, or business that creates or adds value for its buyer or end user.[6] For an entrepreneur to capitalize on an opportunity, its **window of opportunity** must be open.[7] The term *window of opportunity* is a metaphor describing the time period in which a firm can realistically enter a new market. Once the market for a new product is established, its window of opportunity opens. As the market grows, firms enter and try to establish a profitable position. At some point, the market matures, and the window of opportunity closes. This is the case with Internet search engines. Yahoo!, the first search engine, appeared in 1995, and the market grew quickly, with the addition of Lycos, Excite, Hotbot, AltaVista, and others. Google entered the market in 1998, sporting advanced search technology. Since then, the search engine market has matured, and the window of opportunity has essentially closed. Today, it would be very difficult for a new start-up search engine firm to be successful unless it offered compelling advantages over already established competitors or targeted a niche market in an exemplary manner.

It is important to understand that there is a difference between an opportunity and an idea. An **idea** is a thought, an impression, or a notion.[8] An idea may or may not meet the criteria of an opportunity. This is a critical point because many entrepreneurial ventures fail not because the entrepreneurs that launched them didn't work hard, but rather because there was no real opportunity to begin with. Before getting excited about a business idea, it is crucial to understand whether the idea fills a need and meets the criteria for an opportunity.

Now let's look at the three approaches to use to identify an opportunity, as depicted in Figure 2.2. Once you understand the importance of each approach, you'll be much more likely to look for opportunities and ideas that fit each profile.

Learning Objective

1. Explain why it's important to start a new firm when its "window of opportunity" is open.

Learning Objective

2. Explain the difference between an opportunity and an idea.

Learning Objective

3. Describe the three general approaches entrepreneurs use to identify opportunities.

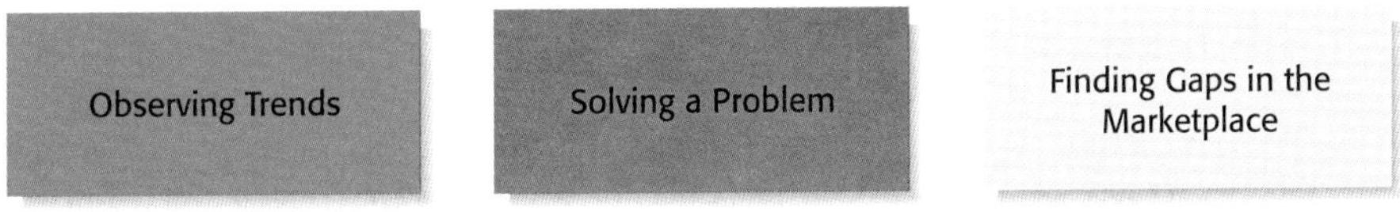

Observing Trends   Solving a Problem   Finding Gaps in the Marketplace

FIGURE 2.2

Three Ways to Identify an Opportunity

Observing Trends

The first approach to identifying opportunities is to observe trends and study how they create opportunities for entrepreneurs to pursue. The most important trends to follow are economic trends, social trends, technological advances, and political action and regulatory changes. As an entrepreneur or potential entrepreneur, it's important to remain aware of changes in these areas. This sentiment is affirmed by Michael Yang, the founder of Become.com, a comparison shopping site, who believes that keen observation skills and a willingness to stay on top of changing environmental trends are key attributes of successful entrepreneurs:

> One of the most important attributes of a good entrepreneur is having a keen observation ability. Basically seeing what's needed in people's everyday lives and coming up with innovative new ideas and services that meet those needs . . . I always believe the entrepreneurs that anticipate trends and maintain observations of what's needed . . . to solve those needs will have a higher chance of succeeding in the marketplace.[9]

When looking at environmental trends to discern new business ideas, there are two caveats to keep in mind. First, it's important to distinguish between trends and fads. New businesses typically do not have the resources to ramp up fast enough to take advantage of a fad. Second, even though we discuss each trend individually, they are interconnected and should be considered simultaneously when brainstorming new business ideas. For example, one reason the Apple iPod is so popular is because it benefits from several trends converging at the same time, including teenagers with increased disposable income (economic trend), an increasingly mobile population (social trend), and the continual miniaturization of electronics (technological trend). If any of these trends weren't present, the iPod wouldn't be as successful as it is.

Figure 2.3 provides a summary of the relationship between the environmental factors just mentioned and identifying opportunity gaps. Next, let's look at how each of these factors helps entrepreneurs spot business, product, and service opportunity gaps.

Learning Objective

4. Identify the four environmental trends that are most instrumental in creating business opportunities.

FIGURE 2.3

Environmental Trends Suggesting Business or Product Opportunity Gaps

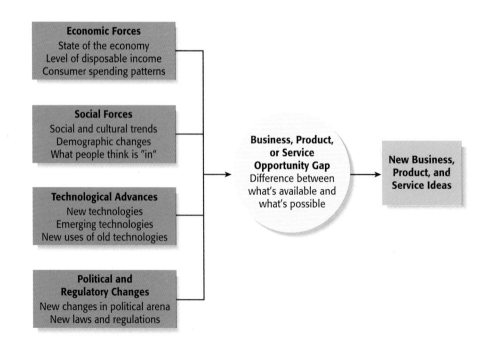

Stephen Derr/Getty Images Inc.-Image Bank

As baby boomers age, opportunities will grow for firms that provide unique products and services to this age group. Look for the resulting expansion of entrepreneurial opportunities in health care, organic food, insurance, travel, and entertainment.

Economic Forces An understanding of economic trends is helpful in determining areas that are ripe for new business ideas as well as areas to avoid.[10] When the economy is strong, people have more money to spend and are willing to buy discretionary products and services that enhance their lives. In contrast, when the economy is weak, not only do people have less money to spend, but they are typically more reluctant to spend the money they have, fearing the economy may become even worse—and that in turn, they might lose their jobs because of a weakening economy. Paradoxically, a weak economy provides business opportunities for start-ups that help consumers save money. Examples include GasBuddy and GasPriceWatch.com, two companies started to help consumers save money on gasoline.

When studying how economic forces affect opportunities, it is important to evaluate who has money to spend and what they spend it on. For example, an increase in the number of women in the workforce and the subsequent increase in their disposable income is largely responsible for the number of boutique clothing stores targeting professional women that have opened in the past several years. Some of the boutiques, like Ellen Tracy and Tory Burch, compete on a national scale, while others, like Olivine, in Seattle, are single-store boutiques that individual entrepreneurs have opened. Similarly, as more teens enter the workforce, demand increases for products they buy, such as designer clothing, MP3 players, and concert tickets. High-end clothing stores like Abercrombie & Fitch, for example, have expanded so quickly in part because teenagers have increasing levels of cash to spend.

Another trend that is affected by economic factors is pressure on firms to cut costs to compensate for increased prices in other areas such as those related to the purchase of raw materials required to build or make their products.[11] For example, 2008 was a tough year to be in the pizza business. Compared to just 18 months earlier, cheese prices were up 50 percent, flour prices were up 64 percent, and gas prices (for delivery vehicles) were setting all-time highs. Facing consumer resistance to higher prices, the companies are responding by trying to squeeze more costs out of their supply chains. This strategy suggests there may be opportunities for start-ups that help pizza chains and similar businesses optimize their supply chains through more efficient inventory control, better routing of delivery vehicles, more cost-effective procurement of supplies, and so forth. AMR Research forecasts that spending on supply-chain software will rise from $2.7 billion in 2007 to $3.9 billion by 2011.[12]

An understanding of economic trends can also help identify areas to avoid. For example, this is not a good time to start a company that relies on fossil fuels, such as airlines or trucking, because of high fuel prices. There are also certain product categories that suffer as result of economic circumstances. This is not a good time to open a store or franchise that sells premium-priced food products like cookies or ice cream. Mrs. Fields Cookies, for example, recently filed bankruptcy, and a number of its franchises are closing largely as the result of a decline in demand for its products.[13]

Social Forces   An understanding of the impact of social forces on trends and how they affect new product, service, and business ideas is a fundamental piece of the opportunity recognition puzzle. Often, the reason that a product or service exists has more to do with satisfying a social need than the more transparent need the product fills. The proliferation of fast-food restaurants, for example, isn't primarily because of people's love of fast food but rather because of the fact that people are busy and often don't have time to cook their own meals. Similarly, social networking sites like Facebook and MySpace aren't popular because they can be used to post music and pictures on a Web site. They're popular because they allow people to connect and communicate with each other, which is a natural human tendency.

Changes in social trends alter how people and businesses behave and how they set their priorities. These changes affect how products and services are built and sold. Here is a sample of the social trends that are currently affecting how individuals behave and set their priorities:

- Retirement of baby boomers
- The increasing diversity of the workforce
- Increasing interest in healthy foods and "green" products
- New forms of music and other types of entertainment
- The increasing focus on health care, fitness, and wellness
- Emphasis on alternative forms of energy
- Increased globalization of business
- Increased availability of inexpensive yet relatively powerful personal computers

Each of these trends is providing the impetus for new business ideas. For example, the increasing emphasis on alternative forms of energy is spawning business ideas ranging from solar power to alternative types of biofuels. One new company, Mariah Power (the subject of the "You Be the VC 2.2" feature at the end of the chapter), is now selling efficient, quiet, and sleek wind power turbines that can be used by both businesses and home owners to harness the power of the wind to produce electricity. The turbines are priced at just under $5,000, and produce enough electricity to supply roughly 25 to 30 percent of the power needed for an average home.[14] The increasing emphasis on green products throughout the world is another social trend that is spawning interesting new business ideas. An example of a recent start-up in this arena is South West Trading Co., a business that specializes in earth-friendly, alternative fibers and textiles such as yarns made from bamboo, corn, and even recycled crab shells.

Technological Advances   Advances in technology frequently dovetail with economic and social changes to create opportunities.[15] In most cases, the technology isn't the key to recognizing business opportunities. Instead, the key is to recognize how technologies can be used and harnessed to help satisfy basic or changing human needs. For example, the creation of the cell phone is a technological achievement, but it was motivated by an increasingly mobile population that finds many advantages to having the ability to communicate with its coworkers, customers, friends, and families from anywhere and everywhere. Similarly, many e-commerce sites are technological marvels, allowing a customer to order products, pay for them, and choose how quickly they're shipped. But again, it isn't so much the technology that makes e-commerce attractive. The ultimate reason most people buy online is because they are busy and prefer to shop when they have free time rather than being restricted to traditional store hours and store locations.

Technological advances also provide opportunities to help people perform everyday tasks in better or more convenient ways. For example, OpenTable.com is a Web site that allows users to make restaurant reservations online and now covers most of the United States. If you're planning a trip to Chicago, for example, you can access OpenTable.com, select the area of the city you'll be visiting, and view descriptions, reviews, customer ratings, and in most cases the menus of the restaurants in the area. You can then make a reservation at the restaurant and print a map and the directions to it. The basic tasks that OpenTable.com helps people perform have always been done—looking for a restaurant, comparing prices and menus, soliciting advice from people who are familiar with competing restaurants, and getting directions. What OpenTable.com does is help people perform these tasks in a more convenient and expedient manner.

Another aspect of technological advances is that once a technology is created, products often emerge to advance it. For example, the creation of the Apple iPod and the Apple iPhone has in turned spawned entire industries that produce iPod and iPhone accessories. An example is H2OAudio, a company that was started by four former San Diego State University students, which makes waterproof housings for the iPod and the iPod nano. The waterproof housings permit iPod users to listen to their iPods while swimming, surfing, snowboarding, or engaging in any activity where the iPod is likely to get wet. There is a wide variety of other accessories available for the iPod, from designer cases to car rechargers. It is now estimated that for every $3 spent on an iPod, at least $1 is spent on an accessory.[16]

Political Action and Regulatory Changes   Political and regulatory changes also provide the basis for opportunities.[17] For example, new laws create opportunities for entrepreneurs to start firms to help companies, individuals, and governmental agencies comply with these laws. For example, in the United States the No Child Left Behind Act of 2002, which is based on the notion of outcome-based education, requires states to develop criterion-based assessments in basic skills to be periodically given to all students in certain grades. Shortly after the act was passed, Kim and Jay Kleeman, two high school teachers, started Shakespeare Squared, a company that produces materials to help schools comply with the act.

On some occasions, changes in government regulations motivate business owners to start firms that differentiate themselves by "exceeding" the regulations. For example, several years ago, the U.S. Federal Trade Commission changed the regulation about how far apart the wood or metal bars in an infant crib can be. If the bars are too far apart, a baby can get an arm or leg caught between the bars, causing an injury. An obvious business idea that might be spawned by this type of change is to produce a crib that is advertised and positioned as "exceeding" the new standard for width between bars and is "extra safe" for babies and young children. The change in regulation brings attention to the issue and provides ideal timing for a new company to reassure parents by providing a product that not only meets but exceeds the new regulation.

Some businesses and industries are so dependent on favorable government regulations that their literal survival is threatened if a regulation changes. An example of a business that fits this profile is Almost Family, a company that provides home health nursing services. Almost Family receives the majority of its income via fixed payments from Medicare based on the level of care that it provides its clients. As a result, the company's profitability is highly sensitive to any changes in Medicare reimbursement policies.[18]

Political change also engenders new business and product opportunities. For example, global political instability and the threat of terrorism have resulted in many firms becoming more security conscious. These companies need new products and services to protect their physical assets and intellectual property as well as to protect their customers and employees. The backup data storage industry, for example, is expanding because of this new trend in the tendency to feel the need for data to be more protected than in the past. An example of a recent start-up in this area is Box.net, which was funded by Mark Cuban, the owner of the Dallas Mavericks. Box.net provides customers with a "better solution than FTP."[19] Box.net believes its data security services are superior because customers use their web browser to access the firm's services. Moreover, there are no start-up costs, no software to download, and no equipment for customers to manage when using Box.net.

Table 2.1 offers additional examples of changes in environmental trends that provided fertile soil for opportunities and subsequent concepts to take advantage of them.

Table 2.1 EXAMPLES OF HOW CHANGES IN ENVIRONMENTAL TRENDS PROVIDE OPENINGS FOR NEW BUSINESS AND PRODUCT OPPORTUNITIES

Changing Environmental Trend	Resulting New Business, Product, and Service Opportunities	Companies That Resulted
Economic Trends		
Search for alternatives to traditional fossil fuels like gasoline	Ethanol, biodiesel, solar power, wind-generated power	Mariah Power, Solix Biofuels, Seattle Biodiesel
Teenagers with more cash and disposable income	Designer clothes, MP3 players, game consoles, electronic games	Hot Topic, Karma Loop, SanDisk, Alienware
Social Trends		
Increased interest in different, tastier, and healthier food	Healthy-fare restaurants, organic foods, healthy-focused grocery stores	Chipotle, Great Wraps, White Wave, Whole Foods
Increased interest in fitness as the result of new medical information warning of the hazards of being overweight	Fitness centers, in-house exercise equipment, weight-loss centers, health food stores	Curves International, Expresso Fitness, Fitbit, Snap Fitness
Technological Advances		
Development of the Internet	E-commerce, improved supply chain management, social networking	Google, Amazon.com, MySpace, Facebook
Miniaturization of electronics	Laptop computers, MP3 players, PDAs	Digital Lifestyle Outfitters, Research in Motion, Palm
Political and Regulatory Changes		
Increased EPA and OSHA standards	Consulting companies, software to monitor compliance	ESS, PrimaTech, Compliance Consulting Services, Inc.
Sarbanes-Oxley Act of 2002	Software vendors, consulting companies	CEBOS, OiWare

Solving a Problem

The second approach to identifying opportunities is to recognize problems and find ways to solve them.[20] These problems can be recognized by observing the challenges that people encounter in their daily lives and through more simple means, such as intuition, serendipity, or chance. There are many problems that have yet to be solved. Commenting on this issue and how noticing problems can lead to the recognition of business ideas, Philip Kotler, a marketing expert, said:

> Look for problems. People complain about it being hard to sleep through the night, get rid of clutter in their homes, find an affordable vacation, trace their family origins, get rid of garden weeds, and so on. As the late John Gardner, founder of Common Cause, observed: "Every problem is a brilliantly disguised opportunity."[21]

Consistent with this observation, many companies have been started by people who have experienced a problem in their own lives, and then realized that the solution to the problem represented a business opportunity. For example, in 1991, Jay Sorensen dropped a cup of coffee in his lap because the paper cup was too hot. This experience led Sorensen to invent an insulating cup sleeve and to start a company to sell it. Since launching his venture, the company, Java Jacket, has sold over 1 billion cup sleeves. Additional examples of companies that were started by people solving problems in their everyday lives are provided in the "Savvy Entrepreneurial Firm" boxed feature.

Advances in technology often result in problems for people who can't use the technology in the way it is sold to the masses. For example, some older people find traditional cell phones hard to use—the buttons are small, the text is hard to read, and it's often difficult to hear someone on a cell phone in a noisy room. To solve these problems, GreatCall Inc., a recent start-up, is producing a cell phone called the Jitterbug, which is designed specifically for older users. The Jitterbug features large buttons, easy-to-read text, and a cushion that cups around the ear to improve sound quality. Another company, Firefly

One of the most pressing problems facing countries is finding alternatives for fossil fuels. A large number of entrepreneurial firms are being launched to take on this challenge. Among the potential solutions is wind-generated power.

Dave King © Dorling Kindersley

Savvy Entrepreneurial FIRM

iHearSafe, ZUCA, and J.J. Creations: Companies Started by Ordinary People Solving Problems in Their Everyday Lives

www.ihearsafe.com
www.zuca.com
www.jjmatis.com

Although it's easy to imagine that most business ideas are formulated by product development specialists working in laboratories, just the opposite is the case. Most business ideas are conceived by ordinary people who solve problems in their own lives, and realize that the solution might be helpful to others and represent a viable business opportunity.

In 2006, Christine Ingemi, a mother of four children under 11, became concerned by how loud her children were playing their MP3 players. She said she could hear music coming through her children's MP3 players' earphones when she was driving her van with the music on. To prevent her children from playing their MP3 players too loud, she and her husband Rick did some research, interviewed several audiologists, and invented a set of earbuds that limit the volume entering the user's ears. After her kids started using the earbuds, Ingemi began getting inquiries from other parents asking where they could get a similar device. To make the device available to others, Ingemi started a business called Ingemi Corporation to sell her iHearSafe earbuds.

Similarly, Laura Udall, another mother, invented an alternative to traditional backpacks when her fourth-grade daughter complained daily that her back hurt from carrying her backpack. After conducting research, obtaining feedback from student focus groups, and building several prototypes, Udall invented the ZUCA, a backpack on rollers that strikes the ideal balance between functionality and "cool" for kids. It also includes a fold-out seat and is strong enough that a child can sit on the backpack while waiting for the school bus. ZUCA is now a successful company, and its rolling backpacks can be purchased online or through a number of retailers.

Finally, in 1999, J.J. Matis was looking for something that she could use to carry her water bottle, peanuts, binoculars, and radio when going to a Los Angeles Dodgers game. When she couldn't find anything out of the ordinary, she created a bag (she had

been sewing since she was a teenager) that looked like a baseball. At the game, she was inundated by people asking her where she got her bag, which made her think that she might have a business idea. She took her idea to Mike Nygren, the merchandising manager for the Dodgers. Nygren encouraged her to make some additional samples and incorporate the project into her MBA program at California Lutheran University. After receiving her MBA, Matis started her business. The business now sells bags for a variety of sports teams, politicians, and rock groups. Her "flag-bags" are even featured in the Senate Gift Shop on Capitol Hill in Washington, DC.

Questions for Critical Thinking

1. Do you think that Christine Ingemi, Laura Udall, and J.J. Matis are extraordinary people (in terms of their observational abilities and business skills) or ordinary people, like most of the people who own this book? What does this feature tell you about your own ability to come up with a promising business idea?
2. Evaluate each of the ideas mentioned on all four dimensions of an opportunity. Rank each idea on a scale of 1 to 5 (5 is high) regarding how strongly it satisfies the four dimensions.
3. Was each idea a result of observing trends, solving a problem, filling a gap in the marketplace, a combination of two of these things, or all three?
4. Pick one of the three companies mentioned in this feature and provide an update on how the company is doing.

Sources: K. Spiller, "Low-Decibel Earbuds Keep Noise at a Reasonable Level," *Nashua Telegraph*, August 13, 2006; "Laura Udall" (Mom Inventor's Inc), www.mominventors.com (accessed September 16, 2008); "J.J. Matis," Ladies Who Launch, http://applications.ladieswholaunch.com/featuredlady.cfm/featureid/41 (accessed September 16, 2008).

Mobile, has created a cell phone designed specifically for tweens, ages 8 to 12. The phone only weighs 2 ounces and is designed to fit in a kid's hand. The phone includes appropriate limitations for a young child and speed-dial keys for Mom and Dad.

Some problems are solved by entrepreneurs who frame a problem differently than it's been thought of before, and then propose an appropriate solution. The solution is often easier and less expensive than traditional fixes. An example of a problem that was solved in this manner is illustrated through a story told by Matt Linderman, an employee of 36signals, on the company's blog. The story's about a multistory building in New York City where tenants were complaining about long elevator wait times. Several of the tenants threatened to break their leases and move out of the building unless something was done. A study found that because of the age of the building, nothing could be done to speed up the elevators. The tenants would just have to live with the problem. The desperate manager of the building called a meeting of his staff, which included a young, recently hired graduate in personnel psychology. Instead of focusing on the speed of the elevators, the young new-hire wondered why people complained about waiting for only a few minutes. He concluded that the complaints were a consequence of boredom, rather than the few minutes that people waited, and the solution was to give people something to do while waiting for an elevator. He suggested installing mirrors in elevator boarding areas so that those waiting could look at each other or themselves (without appearing to do so) while waiting for an elevator. The manager accepted his suggestion. Mirrors were installed quickly and relatively inexpensively. Remarkably, the complaints about waiting stopped. Today, mirrors in elevator lobbies and even on elevators are commonplace.[22]

Some business ideas are gleaned from the recognition of problems in emerging trends. For example, Symantec Corporation created Norton antivirus software to rid computers of viruses, and computer firewall firms such as McAfee developed software to secure computer systems and guard them against attack from hackers or unauthorized users. These companies took advantage of the problems that surface when new technology is introduced. Other companies are founded to deal with annoyances or inefficiencies that technology causes, which are commonplace but no one has proposed a solution to an obvious problem. Think of how many times you've printed a document from the Internet and the page you want is followed by several pages that you immediately throw away, because they only include the site's URL, contain ads, or contain legal jargon. Greenprint, a recent start-up, eliminates wasteful pages by analyzing each page of every document sent to a printer for typical waste characteristics.[23]

Additional examples of people who launched businesses to solve problems are included in Table 2.2.

Table 2.2 BUSINESSES CREATED TO SOLVE A PROBLEM

Entrepreneur(s)	Year	Problem	Solution	Name of Business That Resulted
Arlene Harris	2006	Many cell phones are too complicated and the buttons are too small for older people	Design cell phones that are easy to use and have large buttons	GreatCall
Scott Kliger	2006	411 (directory assistance) calls are expensive	Create a free, nationwide advertiser-supported directory assistance service	Jingle Networks
David Bateman	2002	No way for apartment renters to pay their monthly rent online	Create a software product that allows apartment complexes to enable their tenants to pay online	Property Solutions
Lisa Druxman	2002	No fitness routine available to help new mothers stay fit and be with their newborns at the same time	Create a franchise organization that promotes a workout routine that mothers and their babies can do together	Stroller Strides
Richard Cole	1999	No service available to help people with computer problems at home	Create an organization that makes "house calls" and helps people solve computer problems at home	Geeks on Call

FINDING GAPS IN THE MARKETPLACE

The third source of business ideas is gaps in the marketplace. There are many examples of products that consumers need or want that aren't available in a particular location or aren't available at all. Part of the problem is created by large retailers, like Wal-Mart and Costco, which compete primarily on price and offer the most popular items targeted toward mainstream consumers. While this approach allows the large retailers to achieve economies of scale, it leaves gaps in the marketplace. This is the reason that clothing boutiques and specialty shops exist. These businesses are willing to carry merchandise that doesn't sell in large enough quantities for Wal-Mart and Costco to carry.

Product gaps in the marketplace represent potentially viable business opportunities. For example, in 2000, Tish Cirovolo realized that there were no guitars on the market made specifically for women. To fill this gap, she started Daisy Rock guitars, a company that makes guitars just for women. Daisy Rock guitars are stylish, have feminine names (e.g., Candy Apple Pink, Rainbow Sparkle, and Red Pearl), and incorporate design features that accommodate a woman's smaller hand and build. A more common example of a company that is filling a gap in the marketplace is Shade Clothing, which is a relatively new online store that designs and sells clothing for women who want apparel that is stylish yet not too revealing.[24] Recall that Kathryn Kerrigan (who is featured in this chapter's Opening Profile) started a business to fill a gap for larger-sized women's shoes. Additional examples of companies started to fill gaps in the marketplace are provided in Table 2.3.

A common way that gaps in the marketplace are recognized is when people become frustrated because they can't find a product or service that they need and recognize that other people feel the same way. This scenario played out for Lorna Ketler and Barb Wilkins, who became frustrated when they couldn't find stylish "plus-sized" clothing that fit. In response to their frustration, they started Bodacious, a store that sells fun and stylish "plus size" clothing that fits. Ketler and Wilkins's experience illustrates how compelling a business

Table 2.3   Businesses Created to Fill a Gap in the Marketplace

Gap in the Marketplace	Resulting New Business Opportunity	Name of Businesses That Resulted
No fitness centers designed specifically for women	Fitness centers that are just for women, featuring workouts and exercises designed specifically for women, and fits the time and budgetary constraints of its female clientele	Curves International Lady of America, Slim & Tone
Lack of toy stores that focus on a child's intellectual development	Toy stores, toy manufacturers, and Web sites that sell educational toys	Discovery Toys, Sprig Toys, Kazoo & Company
Restaurants that are both fast and serve good food	Fast-casual restaurants that combine the advantages of fast-food (fast service) and casual dining (good food)	Panera Bread, Chipotle, Cosi, Bruegger's
Shortage of clothing stores that sell fashionable clothing for hard-to-fit people	Boutiques and retail chains that sell fashionable clothing for hard-to-fit people, including plus size clothing and clothing for tall or short people	Casual Male, Ashley Stewart, iGigi, RealKidz

Adapted from I. S. Servi, *New Product Development and Marketing* (New York: Praeger, 1990). Copyright © 1990. Reproduced with permission of Greenwood Publishing Group, Inc., Westport, CT.

idea can be when it strikes just the right chord by filling a gap that deeply resonates with a specific clientele. Reflecting on the success of Bodacious, Wilkins said:

> It's so rewarding when you take a risk and it pays off for you and people are telling you every single day, "I am so glad you are here." We've had people cry in our store. It happens a lot. They're crying because they're so happy (that they're finding clothes that fit). One woman put on a pair of jeans that fit her, and she called me an hour later and said, "They still look good, even at home!" Sometimes people have a body change that happens, whether they have been ill or had a baby, and there's lots of emotion involved in it. If you can go and buy clothes that fit, that helps people feel good about themselves.[25]

A related technique for generating new business ideas is to take an existing product or service and create a new category by targeting a completely different target market. This approach essentially involves creating a gap and filling it. An example is PopCap games, a company that was started to create a new category in the electronic games industry called "casual games." The games are casual and relaxing rather than flashy and action-packed and are made for people who want to wind down after a busy day. Currently, 90 percent of the company's customers are women 25 years old or older, which is a completely different demographic than the young males that the mainstream game manufacturers target.[26]

One thing a new firm has to be careful about is that if it says it's capitalizing on an environmental trend, solving a problem, or filling a gap in the marketplace, it has to deliver on its promises. If start-ups' initial customers find out it's more hype than substance, they will quickly abandon it. This unfortunate scenario played out for Clearly Canadian when it first started, as illustrated in the "What Went Wrong?" boxed feature.

Personal Characteristics of the Entrepreneur

How did Michael Dell come up with the idea of a "build it yourself" computer company? How did Dave Roberts, the founder of PopCap Games, figure out that there is a large and growing market for "casual" electronic games?

Researchers have identified several characteristics that tend to make some people better at recognizing opportunities than others. Before we talk about them, there is an important yet subtle difference between two key terms pertaining to this topic. We've already defined an opportunity as a favorable set of circumstances that create the need for a new product, service, or business. But, the term **opportunity recognition** refers to the process of *perceiving* the possibility of a profitable new business or a new product or service. That is, an opportunity cannot be taken until it's *recognized*.[27] Now let's look at some specific characteristics shared by those who excel at recognizing an opportunity.

Prior Experience   Several studies show that prior experience in an industry helps entrepreneurs recognize business opportunities.[28] For example, a report about the *Inc.* 500 founders revealed that 43 percent of those studied got the idea for their new businesses while working for companies in the same industries.[29] This finding is consistent with research conducted by the National Federation of Independent Businesses.[30] There are several explanations for these findings. By working in an industry, an individual may spot a market niche that is underserved. It is also possible that while working in a particular area, an individual builds a network of social contacts in that industry that may provide insights that lead to opportunities.[31]

Learning Objective

5. List the personal characteristics that make some people better at recognizing business opportunities than others.

What Went WRONG?

Clearly Canadian: What Happens When You Don't Deliver on Your Promises

www.clearly.ca

If a new product or service seems like the perfect option to solve a problem or capitalize on an environmental trend, but its customers find out it can't deliver on its promises, they will quickly jump ship. This is what happened to Clearly Canadian, one of the first bottled drinks to position itself in the new-age or wellness category.

Clearly Canadian introduced a line of fruit-flavored bottled water in the early 1990s. Its efforts were clearly an attempt to jump on an environmental trend—an increased interest in wellness. It positioned its drinks as a healthy alternative to soft drinks such as Coke, Pepsi, and Mountain Dew. Its bottles, labels, and packaging all supported the notion that the drinks were pure and fresh. Canadian fruits, which have a fresh and robust flavor, were the basis for the six flavors in the initial Clearly Canadian line. Its Canadian origins invoked images of clean lakes, pristine mountain ranges, rushing streams, and grassy plains. It was easy for someone to assume that they were doing their body a favor by buying and drinking a Clearly Canadian beverage.

But as Clearly Canadian's drinks spread, consumers started reading the fine print on the labels. It turned out that Clearly Canadian drinks weren't any healthier than soft drinks at the time. Its bottled water had about 160 calories, the same as a regular Pepsi. How could that be—it was water! It turned out that to sweeten and color its water, Clearly Canadian was using essentially the same artificial flavors, sweeteners, and preservatives that the soft drink companies were using. Customers quickly bailed and found more legitimate alternatives, like Snapple, which came out

at about the same time. The company has since reformulated its ingredients and is a healthier alternative to soft drinks than it once was, but it's never gained much traction in the flavored bottled water wellness category.

The message from this firm's experience is simple yet powerful—it takes more than talk and savvy marketing to capitalize on an environmental trend, solve a problem, or fill a gap in the marketplace. A company has to actually deliver on one of those promises to be successful.

Questions for Critical Thinking

1. Evaluate Clearly Canadian's initial fruit-flavored bottled water on all four dimensions of an opportunity.
2. When you pick up a drink that's clearly marketed as a healthy alternative to soda and sugared drinks, do you read the label to see if the drink is truly healthier than the alternatives? If it isn't, do you feel deceived by the marketing?
3. How can a start-up that has good intentions make sure that its product is truly meeting the need that it was designed to meet?
4. Evaluate Clearly Canadian's marketing of its products and the ingredients in its products today. Is the marketing and the products themselves in better sync than the products were when the drink was introduced in the early 1990s?

Source: C. L. Hodock, *Why Smart Companies Do Dumb Things* (Amherst, NY: Prometheus Books, 2007).

Once an entrepreneur starts a firm, new venture opportunities become apparent. This is called the **corridor principle**, which states that once an entrepreneur starts a firm, he or she begins a journey down a path where "corridors" leading to new venture opportunities become apparent.[32] The insight provided by this principle is simply that once someone starts a firm and becomes immersed in an industry, it's much easier for that person to see new opportunities in the industry than it is for someone looking in from the outside.

Cognitive Factors Opportunity recognition may be an innate skill or a cognitive process.[33] There are some who think that entrepreneurs have a "sixth sense" that allows them to see opportunities that others miss. This sixth sense is called **entrepreneurial alertness**, which is formally defined as the ability to notice things without engaging in deliberate search.[34] Most entrepreneurs see themselves in this light, believing they are more "alert" than others.[35] Alertness is largely a learned skill, and people who have more knowledge of an area tend to be more alert to opportunities in that area than others. A computer engineer, for example, would be more alert to needs and opportunities within the computer industry than a lawyer would be.

The research findings on entrepreneurial alertness are mixed. Some researchers conclude that alertness goes beyond noticing things and involves a more purposeful effort.[36] For example, one scholar believes that the crucial difference between opportunity finders (i.e., entrepreneurs) and nonfinders is their relative assessments of the marketplace.[37] In other words, entrepreneurs may be better than others at sizing up the marketplace and inferring the likely implications.

Social Networks   The extent and depth of an individual's social network affects opportunity recognition.[38] People who build a substantial network of social and professional contacts will be exposed to more opportunities and ideas than people with sparse networks.[39] This exposure can lead to new business starts.[40] In a survey of 65 start-ups, half the founders reported that they got their business ideas through social contacts.[41] A similar study examined the differences between **solo entrepreneurs** (those who identified their business ideas on their own) and **network entrepreneurs** (those who identified their ideas through social contacts). The researchers found that network entrepreneurs identified significantly more opportunities than solo entrepreneurs but were less likely to describe themselves as being particularly alert or creative.[42]

An important concept that sheds light on the importance of social networks to opportunity recognition is the differential impact of strong-tie versus weak-tie relationships. Relationships with other people are called "ties." We all have ties. **Strong-tie relationships** are characterized by frequent interaction and ties between coworkers, friends, and spouses. **Weak-tie relationships** are characterized by infrequent interaction and ties between casual acquaintances. According to research in this area, it is more likely that an entrepreneur will get a new business idea through a weak-tie than a strong-tie relationship[43] because strong-tie relationships, which typically form between like-minded individuals, tend to reinforce insights and ideas the individuals already have. Weak-tie relationships, on the other hand, which form between casual acquaintances, are not as apt to be between like-minded individuals, so one person may say something to another that sparks a completely new idea.[44] An example might be an electrician explaining to a restaurant owner how he solved a business problem. After hearing the solution, the restaurant owner might say, "I would never have heard that solution from someone in my company or industry. That insight is completely new to me and just might help me solve my problem."

One way that entrepreneurs network with one another is through membership in industry trade associations, as illustrated in the "Partnering for Success" boxed feature.

Creativity   **Creativity** is the process of generating a novel or useful idea. Opportunity recognition may be, at least in part, a creative process.[45] On an anecdotal basis, it is easy to see the creativity involved in forming many products, services, and businesses. Increasingly, teams of entrepreneurs working within a company are sources of creativity for their firm.[46]

For an individual, the creative process can be broken into five stages, as shown in Figure 2.4.[47] Let's examine how these stages relate to the opportunity recognition process.[48] In the figure, the horizontal arrows that point from box to box suggest that the creative process progresses through five stages. The vertical arrows suggest that if at any stage an individual (such as an entrepreneur) gets "stuck" or doesn't have enough information or insight to continue, the best choice is to return to the preparation stage—to obtain more knowledge or experience before continuing to move forward.

Learning Objective

6. Identify the five steps in the creative process.

Partnering for SUCCESS
Networking: The Importance of Joining Industry Trade Associations

Trade associations are typically nonprofit organizations formed by firms in the same industry to collect and disseminate information, offer legal and technical advice, furnish industry-related training and marketing materials, and provide a forum for the people in the industry to network.

To accomplish these goals, many trade organizations organize annual meetings and trade shows. For example, the Internet Society (ISOC) is a professional trade association with more than 80 organizations and 28,000 individual members. Members of the association meet in local chapters and come together once a year for an annual conference to discuss issues related to the Internet. The Game Manufacturers Association is another example. The association, which services the tabletop game industry, sponsors an annual trade show, which is attended by more than 15,000 people every year.

For many people, the biggest advantage of belonging to a trade association is the opportunity to network with industry peers. This is one reason busy CEOs and entrepreneurs are willing to donate their time to serve on the board of directors of their respective associations. Serving on the board or on an association committee gives them the opportunity to exchange ideas with their peers.

Recognizing the benefits of networking, some associations have even created online forums. For example, the American Booksellers Association (which restricts its membership to independent bookstores, thus eliminating the potential divergent interests of bookstore chains like Borders and Barnes & Noble) hosts a number of password-protected online forums, where its members can ask each other questions and collectively brainstorm the best ways to compete against big-box competitors. Another example is the Craft & Hobby Association. Along with providing its members traditional trade association benefits, it offers business-building seminars, workshops, and social events for its members.

Questions for Critical Thinking

1. What is an industry "trade show?" How do entrepreneurs benefit by attending trade shows?
2. What are the risks associated with networking? For example, are their risks involved with sharing information with other trade association members about how your firm competes?
3. Does participating in a trade association allow an entrepreneur to establish strong-tie relationships, weak-tie relationships, or both? How can an entrepreneur deliberately try to establish more weak-tie relationships through trade association membership?
4. Spend some time looking at the Web site of the Craft & Hobby Association. Make a list of networking opportunities made available via membership in this organization.

Sources: B. Barringer and J. Harrison, "Walking a Tightrope: Creating Value Through Interorganizational Relationships," *Journal of Management* 26, no. 3 (2000): 367–403. Internet Society homepage www.isoc.org (accessed November 5, 2008; Game Manufacturers Association homepage www.gama.org (accessed November 5, 2008); American Booksellers Association homepage www.bookweb.org (accessed November 5, 2008); Craft & Hobby Association homepage www.hobby.org (accessed November 5, 2008).

Preparation. Preparation is the background, experience, and knowledge that an entrepreneur brings to the opportunity recognition process. Just as an athlete must practice to excel, an entrepreneur needs experience to spot opportunities. Studies show that 50 to 90 percent of start-up ideas emerge from a person's prior work experience.[49]

Incubation. Incubation is the stage during which a person considers an idea or thinks about a problem; it is the "mulling things over" phase.

FIGURE 2.4

Five Steps to Generating Creative Ideas

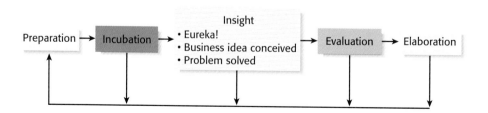

Sometimes incubation is a conscious activity, and sometimes it is unconscious and occurs while a person is engaged in another activity. One writer characterized this phenomenon by saying that "ideas churn around below the threshold of consciousness."[50]

Insight. Insight is the flash of recognition—when the solution to a problem is seen or an idea is born. It is sometimes called the "eureka" experience. In a business context, this is the moment an entrepreneur recognizes an opportunity. Sometimes this experience pushes the process forward, and sometimes it prompts an individual to return to the preparation stage. For example, an entrepreneur may recognize the potential for an opportunity but may feel that more knowledge and thought is required before pursuing it.

Evaluation. Evaluation is the stage of the creative process during which an idea is subjected to scrutiny and analyzed for its viability. Many entrepreneurs mistakenly skip this step and try to implement an idea before they've made sure it is viable. Evaluation is a particularly challenging stage of the creative process because it requires an entrepreneur to take a candid look at the viability of an idea.[51] The process of evaluating the feasibility of new business ideas is discussed in Chapter 3.

Elaboration. Elaboration is the stage during which the creative idea is put into a final form: The details are worked out and the idea is transformed into something of value, such as a new product, service, or business concept. In the case of a new business, this is the point at which a business plan is written.

Figure 2.5 illustrates the opportunity recognition process. As shown in the figure, there is a connection between an awareness of emerging trends and the personal characteristics of the entrepreneur because the two facets of opportunity recognition are interdependent. For example, an entrepreneur with a well-established social network may be in a better position to recognize emerging technological trends than an entrepreneur with a poorly established social network. Or the awareness of an emerging technology trend, such as digitization, may prompt an entrepreneur to attend conferences or workshops to learn more about the topic, expanding the social network.

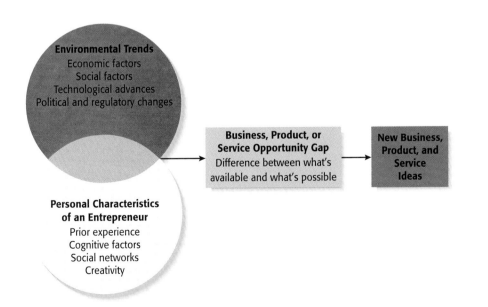

FIGURE 2.5

The Opportunity Recognition Process

TECHNIQUES FOR GENERATING IDEAS

In general, entrepreneurs identify more ideas than opportunities[52] because many ideas are typically generated to find the best way to capitalize on an opportunity. Several techniques can be used to stimulate and facilitate the generation of new ideas for products, services, and businesses. Let's take a look at some of them.

Brainstorming

Learning Objective

7. *Describe the purpose of brainstorming and its use as an idea generator.*

A common way to generate new business ideas is through **brainstorming**. In general, brainstorming is simply the process of generating several ideas about a specific topic. The approaches range from a person sitting down with a yellow legal pad and jotting down interesting business ideas to formal "brainstorming sessions" led by moderators that involve a group of people.

In a formal brainstorming session, the leader of the group asks the participants to share their ideas. One person shares an idea, another person reacts to it, another person reacts to the reaction, and so on. A flip chart or an electronic whiteboard is typically used to record all the ideas. A productive session is free-wheeling and lively. The session is not used for analysis or decision making—the ideas generated during a brainstorming session need to be filtered and analyzed, but this is done later. There are four strict rules for conducting a formal brainstorming session, which are shown in Table 2.4. As shown, the number one rule for a brainstorming session is that no criticism is allowed, including chuckles, raised eyebrows, or facial expressions that express skepticism or doubt. Criticism stymies creativity and inhibits the free flow of ideas.

Brainstorming sessions dedicated to generating new business ideas are often less formal. For example, as described in more detail in Case 11.2, during the creation of Proactiv, a popular acne treatment product, Dr. Katie Rodan, one of the company's founders, hosted dinner parties at her house and conducted brainstorming sessions with guests. The guests included business executives, market researchers, marketing consultants, an FDA regulatory attorney, and others. Rodan credits this group with helping her and her cofounder brainstorm a number of ideas that helped shape Proactiv and move the process of starting the company forward.[53] Similarly, Sharelle Klause, the founder of Dry Soda, a

An increasing number of firms are using whiteboards to record ideas and conduct ongoing brainstorming sessions. Here, a young entrepreneur is brainstorming alternative designs for a retail store.

Ryan McVay/Getty Images, Inc.-Photodisc.

Table 2.4   RULES FOR A FORMAL BRAINSTORMING SESSION

Rule	Explanation
1	No criticism is allowed, including chuckles, raised eyebrows, or facial expressions that express skepticism or doubt. Criticism stymies creativity and inhibits the free flow of ideas.
2	Freewheeling, which is the carefree expression of ideas free from rules or restraints, is encouraged; the more ideas, the better. Even crazy or outlandish ideas may lead to a good idea or a solution to a problem.
3	The session moves quickly, and nothing is permitted to slow down its pace. For example, it is more important to capture the essence of an idea than to take the time to write it down neatly.
4	Leapfrogging is encouraged. This means using one idea as a means of jumping forward quickly to other ideas.

company that makes an all-natural soda that's paired with food the way wine is in upscale restaurants, tested her idea by first talking to her husband's colleagues, who were in the food industry, and then tapped into the professional network of a friend who owned a bottled water company. Through the process, she met a chemist, who was instrumental in helping her develop the initial recipes for her beverage. Klause also went directly to restaurant owners and chefs to ask them to sample early versions of her product.[54] While this approach only loosely fits the definition of brainstorming, the spirit is the same. Klause was bouncing ideas and early prototypes of her product off others to get their reactions and generate additional ideas.

Approaches to brainstorming are only limited by a person's imagination. For example, to teach her students an approach to utilizing brainstorming to generate business ideas, Marcene Sonneborn, an adjunct professor at the Whitman School of Management at Syracuse University, uses a tool she developed called the *"bug report"* to help students brainstorm business ideas. She instructs her students to list 75 things that "bug" them in their everyday lives. The number 75 was chosen because it forces students to go beyond thinking about obvious things that bug them (campus parking, roommates, scraping snow off their windshields in the winter), and think more deeply. On occasions, students actually hold focus groups with their friends to brainstorm ideas and fill out their lists.

While most brainstorming sessions involve a group of people planning a start-up or the employees of an existing organization, Kodak hosts pizza video parties where groups of customers meet with the company's technical people to discuss problems and needs and to brainstorm potential solutions. Similarly, some companies make brief brainstorming sessions a routine part of facility tours.[55]

Focus Groups

A **focus group** is a gathering of 5 to 10 people who are selected because of their relationship to the issue being discussed. Although focus groups are used for a variety of purposes, they can be used to help generate new business ideas.

Focus groups typically involve a group of people who are familiar with a topic, are brought together to respond to questions, and shed light on an issue through the give-and-take nature of a group discussion. Focus groups usually work best as a follow-up to brainstorming, when the general idea for a business has been formulated, such as casual electronic games for adults, but further refinement of the idea is needed. Usually, focus groups are conducted by trained moderators. The moderator's primary goals are to keep the group "focused" and to generate lively discussion. Much of the effectiveness of a focus group session depends on the moderator's ability to ask questions and keep the discussion on track. For example, a retail establishment in which coffee is sold, such as Starbucks, might conduct a focus group consisting of 7 to 10 frequent customers and ask the group, "What is it that you *don't* like about our coffee shop?" A customer may say, "You sell 1-pound bags of your specialty ground coffees for people to brew at home. That's okay, but I often run out of the coffee in just a few days. Sometimes it's a week before I get back to the shop to buy another bag. If you sold 3-pound or 5-pound bags, I'd actually use more coffee because I wouldn't run out so often. I guess I could buy two or three 1-pound bags at the same time, but that gets a little pricey. I'd buy a 3- or 5-pound bag, however, if you'd discount your price a little for larger quantities." The moderator may then ask the group, "How many people here would buy 3-pound or 5-pound bags of our coffee if they were available?" If five hands shoot up, the coffee shop may have just uncovered an idea for a new product line.

Some companies utilize hybrid focus group methodologies to achieve specific insights and goals. An example is "college drop-ins." This approach involves paying college students to host a party at their campus and providing them a budget to buy food and snacks. During the party, the hosts interview and videotape other students about specific market issues. Everything is up-front—the partygoers are told that the information is being collected for a market research firm (on behalf of a client).[56]

Library and Internet Research

Learning Objective

8. Describe how to use library and Internet research to generate new business ideas.

A third approach to generate new business ideas is to conduct library and Internet research. A natural tendency is to think that an idea should be chosen, and the process of researching the idea should then begin. This approach is too linear. Often, the best ideas emerge when the general notion of an idea, like creating casual electronic games for adults, is merged with extensive library and Internet research, which might provide insights into the best type of casual games to create.

Libraries are often an underutilized source of information for generating business ideas. The best approach to utilizing a library is to discuss your general area of interest with a reference librarian, who can point out useful resources, such as industry-specific magazines, trade journals, and industry reports. Simply browsing through several issues of a trade journal on a topic can spark new ideas. Very powerful search engines and databases are also available through university and large public libraries, which would cost hundreds or thousands of dollars to access on your own. An example is IBIS World (www.ibisworld.com), a company that publishes market research on all major industries and subcategories within industries. IBIS World published a 48-page report on the electronic game industry, for example, on July 23, 2008, that includes key statistics (about industry growth and profitability), a complete industry analysis, and an outlook for the future. Spending time reading through this report could spark new ideas for electronic games or help affirm an existing idea.

Internet research is also important. If you are starting from scratch, simply typing "new business ideas" into Google or Yahoo! will produce links to newspaper and magazine articles about the "hottest" and "latest" new business ideas. Although these types of articles are general in nature, they represent a starting point if you're trying to generate new business ideas from scratch. If you have a specific idea in mind, a useful technique is to set up a Google or Yahoo! "e-mail alert" using keywords that pertain to your topic of interest. Google and Yahoo! alerts are e-mail updates of the latest Google or Yahoo! results including press releases, news articles, and blog posts based on your topic. This technique, which is available for free, will feed you a daily stream of news articles and blog postings about specific topics.

Other Techniques

Firms use a variety of other techniques to generate ideas. Some companies set up **customer advisory boards** that meet regularly to discuss needs, wants, and problems that may lead to new ideas. Other companies conduct varying forms of anthropological research, such as **day-in-the-life research**. A company that practices a variation of this technique is Intuit, the focus of Case 3.2. The company routinely sends teams of testers to the homes and businesses of its users to see how its products are working and to seek insights for new product ideas.

ENCOURAGING AND PROTECTING NEW IDEAS

In many firms, idea generation is a haphazard process. However, entrepreneurial ventures can take certain concrete steps to build an organization that encourages and protects new ideas. Let's see what these steps are.

Establishing a Focal Point for Ideas

Some firms meet the challenge of encouraging, collecting, and evaluating ideas by designating a specific person to screen and track them—for if it's everybody's job, it may be no one's responsibility.[57] Another approach is to establish an **idea bank** (or vault), which is a physical or digital repository for storing ideas. An example of an idea bank would be a password-protected location on a firm's **intranet** that is available only to qualified employees. It may have a file for ideas that are being actively contemplated and a file for inactive ideas. Other firms do not have idea banks but instead encourage employees to keep journals of their ideas.

Learning Objective

9. Explain the purpose of maintaining an idea bank.

Encouraging Creativity at the Firm Level

There is an important distinction between creativity and innovation. Innovation, as mentioned in Chapter 1, refers to the successful introduction of new outcomes by a firm. In contrast, creativity is the process of generating a novel or useful idea but does not require implementation. In other words, creativity is the raw material that goes into innovation. A team of employees may come up with a hundred legitimate creative ideas for a new product or service, but only one may eventually be implemented. Of course, it may take a hundred creative ideas to discover the one that ideally satisfies an opportunity.

An employee may exhibit creativity in a number of ways, including solving a problem or taking an opportunity and using it to develop a new product or service idea. Although creativity is typically thought of as an individual attribute, it can be encouraged or discouraged at the firm level.[58] The extent to which an organization encourages and rewards creativity affects the creative output of its employees.[59] Table 2.5 provides a list of actions and behaviors that encourage and discourage creativity at both the organizational level and the individual supervisor level.

Table 2.5   ACTIONS AND BEHAVIORS THAT ENCOURAGE AND DISCOURAGE CREATIVITY

Creativity Enhancers

Organizational Level	Individual Supervisory Level
• Elevating creativity's importance throughout the organization • Offering tangible rewards to those generating new ideas • Investing in resources that help employees sharpen their creative skills • Hiring people different from those currently working in the company	• Listening attentively in order to acknowledge and provide early support to ideas • Dealing with employees as equals to show that status isn't very important • Speculating, being open, and building on others' ideas • Protecting people who make honest mistakes and are willing to learn from them

Creativity Detractors

Organizational Level	Individual Supervisory Level
• Not attempting to hire creative people • Maintaining a "stiff" organizational culture with no room for different behaviors • Pigeonholing employees; keeping them in the same job for years • Promoting a mentality suggesting that the best solutions to all problems have already been found	• Being pessimistic, judgmental, and critical • Punishing mistakes or failed ideas • Being cynical or negative and insisting on early precision • Being inattentive, acting distant, and remaining silent when employees want to discuss new ideas

Source: Adapted from I. S. Servi, *New Product Development and Marketing* (New York: Praeger, 1990).

Protecting Ideas from Being Lost or Stolen

Learning Objective

10. *Describe three steps for protecting ideas from being lost or stolen.*

Intellectual property is any product of human intellect that is intangible but has value in the marketplace. It can be protected through tools such as patents, trademarks, copyrights, and trade secrets, which we'll discuss in depth in Chapter 12. As a rule, a mere idea or concept does not qualify for intellectual property protection; that protection comes later when the idea is translated into a more concrete form. At the opportunity recognition stage, however, there are three steps that should be taken when a potentially valuable idea is generated:

Step 1   The idea should be put into a tangible form—either entered into a physical idea logbook or saved on a computer disk—and dated. When using a physical logbook, be sure that it is bound so that it cannot be alleged that a page was added. Make all entries in ink and have them witnessed. If an idea has significant potential, the signature of the person who entered the idea into the logbook and the witness should be notarized.

Putting the idea into tangible form is important for two reasons. First, if the idea is in concrete form, is original and useful, and is kept secret or is disclosed only in a situation where compensation for its use is contemplated, the idea may qualify as a "property right" or "trade secret" and be legally protected under a variety of statutes.

Second, in the case of an invention, if two inventors independently come up with essentially the same invention, the right to apply for the patent belongs to the first person who invented the product. A properly maintained idea log provides evidence of the date that the idea for the invention was first contemplated.

Once an invention demonstrates feasibility, a form called a "Disclosure Document," which describes an invention, can be filed with the U.S. Patent and Trademark Office. The purpose of the form is to provide evidence of the date of an invention's conception.[60]

Step 2 The idea, whether it is recorded in a physical idea logbook or saved in a computer file, should be secured. This may seem like an obvious step, but it is one that is often overlooked. The extent to which an idea should be secured depends on the circumstances. On the one hand, a firm wants new ideas to be discussed, so a certain amount of openness in the early stages of refining a business idea may be appropriate. On the other hand, if an idea has considerable potential and may be eligible for patent protection, access to the idea should be restricted. In the case of ideas stored on a computer network, access to the ideas should be at a minimum password protected.

Step 3 Avoid making an inadvertent or voluntary disclosure of an idea in a way that forfeits your claim to its exclusive rights. In general, the intellectual property laws seek to protect and reward the originators of ideas as long as they are prudent and try to protect the ideas. For example, if two coworkers are chatting about an idea in an elevator in a public building and a competitor overhears the conversation, the exclusive rights to the idea are probably lost.

In summary, opportunity recognition is a key part of the entrepreneurial process. As mentioned, many firms fail not because the entrepreneurs didn't work hard, but because there was no real opportunity to begin with.

Chapter Summary

1. Once an opportunity is recognized, a window opens, and the market to fill the opportunity grows. At some point, the market matures and becomes saturated with competitors, and the window of opportunity closes.
2. An idea is a thought, an impression, or a notion. An opportunity is an idea that has the qualities of being attractive, durable, and timely and is anchored in a product or service that creates value for its buyers or end users. Not all ideas are opportunities.
3. Observing trends, solving a problem, and finding gaps in the marketplace are the three general approaches entrepreneurs use to identify an opportunity.
4. Economic forces, social forces, technological advances, and political action and regulatory changes are the four environmental trends that are most instrumental in creating opportunities.
5. Prior experience, cognitive factors, social networks, and creativity are the personal characteristics researchers have identified that tend to make some people better at recognizing business opportunities than others.
6. For an individual, the five steps in the creative process are preparation, incubation, insight, evaluation, and elaboration.
7. Brainstorming is a technique used to quickly generate a large number of ideas and solutions to problems. One reason to conduct a brainstorming session is to generate ideas that might represent product, service, or business opportunities.
8. A focus group is a gathering of 5 to 10 people who have been selected on the basis of their common characteristics relative to the issue being discussed. One reason to conduct a focus group is to generate ideas that might represent product or business opportunities.

9. An idea bank is a physical or digital repository for storing ideas.
10. The three main steps that can be taken to protect ideas from being lost or stolen are putting the idea into tangible form by such means as entering it in a logbook or saving it in a computer file, securing the idea, and avoiding making an inadvertent or voluntary disclosure of an idea in a manner that forfeits the right to claim exclusive rights to it if it falls into someone else's hands.

Key Terms

Brainstorming, **82**
Corridor principle, **78**
Creativity, **79**
Customer advisory boards, **85**
Day-in-the-life research, **85**
Entrepreneurial alertness, **78**
Focus group, **83**

Idea, **67**
Idea bank, **85**
Intellectual property, **86**
Intranet, **85**
Network entrepreneurs, **79**
Opportunity, **66**
Opportunity gap, **66**

Opportunity recognition, **77**
Solo entrepreneurs, **79**
Strong-tie relationships, **79**
Weak-tie relationships, **79**
Window of opportunity, **67**

Review Questions

1. What is a product opportunity gap? How can an entrepreneur tell if a product opportunity gap exists?
2. What is an opportunity? What are the qualities of an opportunity, and why is each quality important?
3. What four environmental trends are most instrumental in creating business opportunities? Provide an example of each environmental trend and the type of business opportunity that it might help create.
4. Explain how "solving a problem" can create a business opportunity. Provide an example that was not mentioned in the chapter of a business opportunity that was created in this way.
5. Explain how finding a gap in the marketplace can create a business opportunity.
6. What is meant by opportunity recognition?
7. In what ways does prior industry experience provide an entrepreneur an advantage in recognizing business opportunities?
8. What is the corridor principle? How does this corridor principle explain why the majority of business ideas are conceived at work?
9. What is entrepreneurial alertness?
10. In what ways does an extensive social network provide an entrepreneur an advantage in recognizing business opportunities?
11. Describe the difference between strong-tie relationships and weak-tie relationships. Is an entrepreneur more likely to get new business ideas through strong-tie or weak-tie relationships? Why?
12. Define creativity. How does creativity contribute to the opportunity recognition process?
13. Briefly describe the five stages of the creative process.
14. Explain the difference between an opportunity and an idea.
15. Describe the brainstorming process. Why is "no criticism" the number one rule for brainstorming?
16. Describe how a focus group is set up and how it is used to generate new business ideas.
17. Describe how library and Internet research can be used to generate new business ideas.
18. What is the purpose of day-in-the-life research?

19. What is the purpose of an idea bank? Describe how an idea bank can be set up in a firm.

20. What are the three main steps to protect ideas from being lost or stolen?

Application Questions

1. Tammy, a product development specialist at Procter & Gamble, plans to write an e-mail message to her father asking for a loan. The purpose of the loan will be to start a company to sell an environmentally friendly line of home cleaning supplies that Tammy has spent the past two years developing in her spare time. Tammy wants to convince her father that the idea represents an attractive business opportunity. In your opinion, what should Tammy include in the e-mail message?

2. Jason is very perceptive and believes he has identified an opportunity for a new business in the beverage industry. He wants to make sure, however, that he isn't just following a hunch—that the opportunity is sound. What criteria can Jason use to determine whether he has identified an attractive opportunity?

3. Go to DEMO's Web site at www.demo.com. Watch several "Alumni Videos," which are short videos of start-ups pitching their product ideas to investors and other DEMO participants. Identify a start-up that is pitching a business idea that "solves a problem." Write a short description of the idea and your assessment of its potential.

4. The "You Be the VC 2.1" feature focuses on Freedirectoryenquiries, a company that has launched the first free national directory enquiry service. Does freedirectoryenquiries meet the tests of an opportunity (as opposed to an idea)? Justify your answer.

5. Identify three start-ups, other than those discussed in the chapter or listed in Table 2.1, which were started to satisfy a changing environmental trend.

6. Marshall Hanson, the founder of Santa Fe Hitching Rail, a chain of nine steak restaurants in New Mexico, is considering expanding his menu, which is currently restricted to steak, hamburger, potatoes, and fries. He has just read a book about entrepreneurship and learned that entrepreneurs should study social trends to help identify new product opportunities. List the social trends that might help Marshall choose items to add to his menu. Given the trends you list, what items do you suggest Marshall add?

7. Make a list of the three to five most compelling "social changes" that have occurred in your country since you entered college. Think of at least two new product ideas that have emerged from each of these changes. To what extent do you believe each of these changes will continue spawning new product ideas?

8. Recognizing a problem and proposing a solution to it is one way entrepreneurs identify opportunities. Think about your current activities as well as others in which you have an interest. Identify a problem with the activity you are considering and recommend a business to solve the problem.

9. Go to Vator.tv's Web site at www.vator.tv. Watch several of the "Tech Startups" pitches. Describe the most compelling pitch that you watched and identify whether the business idea satisfies a changing environmental trend, solves a problem, or fills a gap in the marketplace.

10. Megan Jones owns a small chain of fitness centers in Kansas City. In general, her centers are successful, but she feels they are getting "stale" and could benefit from new ideas. Suggest to Megan some ways she could generate new ideas for her centers.

11. As mentioned in the chapter, "prior experience" in an industry helps entrepreneurs recognize business opportunities. This concept extends to prior experience in any aspect of life—whether it is in sports, music, or a volunteer activity. In what area or areas do you have a good amount of "prior experience"? How could this position you to start a business drawing on your experiences?

12. Make a list of your strong-tie and weak-tie relationships. (Include at least five names on each list.) Select two names from your list of weak-tie relationships and speculate on the types of new business ideas that you think these individuals would be uniquely qualified to assist you with.

13. How could FLAVORx and CarePages, the two companies featured in Case 2.2, use brainstorming to generate new ideas for their companies?

14. How could the founders of Pie Face, the subject of the "You Be the VC 1.1" feature at the end of Chapter 1, have utilized library and Internet research to flesh out their business idea? What information would have been most helpful to them?

15. Freedom Electronics is a start-up with about 20 sales representatives. The company has a solid product line but knows that to remain competitive it must continue recognizing opportunities for new products and services. The firm has not developed a systematic way for its sales staff to report new ideas. Suggest some ways that Freedom can record and protect the ideas of its sales representatives.

You Be the VC 2.1

Company: Freedirectoryenquiries

www.freedirectoryenquiries.com

Business Idea: Launch the first free national directory enquiry service.

Pitch: Since the U.K. directory enquiry market was deregulated in 2003, call numbers have fallen by more than half. In surveys, consumers say they are put off by the wide diversity of 118 (directory enquiry) suppliers and high charges. Most companies charge a fixed price per call, plus the caller searching for the number is charged per second throughout the call. So, for example, Yellow Pages charges a fixed charge of $1.20 per call and then 21 cents per minute, while the most frequently used service, The Number, costs $1.05 to call, plus 29 cents per minute.

Freedirectoryenquiries launched in February 2008 aims to get a slice of the 76 million calls made to 118 numbers each year. Callers pay nothing for the service, but must listen to an advertisement for 20 seconds before their requested number is read out. Advertisers already signed up with the 0800 100 100 service include EDF Energy, NatWest, Simply Switch, ASDA, and Eurostar.

The advertisement being played often relates to the number being requested (i.e., a query about a restaurant might prompt an ad for a pizza delivery firm). The caller is able to connect with the advertiser for free at the end of the call.

Freedirectoryenquiries was founded by business partners Isabel Megan-Campbell and Murray McPherson, who were previously involved with the launch of a paid directory enquiry service. Their research into callers' reactions to advertisements being played has had a positive response. Consumers felt that 20 seconds was not an intrusion given that they were getting the number for free. The business model is expected to appeal to the corporate market too. Of the $450 million spent a year on directory enquiry calls, an estimated 20 percent are made from workplace phones.

Regular users of directory enquiry services are typically young and affluent and want to get the number of a taxi or restaurant, so it is little wonder that advertisers are keen to get involved with this new way of targeting them. The number is also free for mobile phone callers who will then receive a text message with the requested number, along with an offer from one of the advertising companies.

Q&A: Based on the material covered in this chapter, what questions would you ask the firm's founders before making your funding decision? What answers would satisfy you?

Decision: If you had to make your decision on just the information provided in the pitch and on the company's Web site, would you fund this firm? Why or why not?

You Be the VC 2.2

Company: Mariah Power

http://mariahpower.com

Business Idea: Manufacture an efficient, quiet, and sleek wind power turbine that both businesses and home owners can use to harness the power of the wind to produce electricity.

Pitch: Although wind power is clean and increasingly cost-competitive, it is largely confined to large wind farms in rural areas. The primary obstacle to building windmills in more densely populated areas is the "not-in-my-backyard" sentiment. This sentiment arises from the large scale of most wind-powered devices, the noise and shadows that are created, and the height of traditional windmills, which normally exceed local zoning regulations.

Mariah Power's mission is to make wind power available to businesses and home owners by avoiding these complications. The company has invented and is selling a low-cost, attractive, plug-n-produce wind power appliance that can fit within the aesthetic schemes of many business and residential environments. The appliance, called the Windspire, doesn't look like a traditional windmill or wind generator. It is 30 feet tall and 2 feet wide, ultra quiet, and is distinguished by its sleek propeller-free design. The device is priced at just under $5,000. In many areas, the cost can be partially defrayed by rebates from the local power company and the government.

To make the Windspire more palatable for business and residential environments, it is manufactured with a corrosion-resistant soft silver paint that can be re-painted in any color. At 30 feet (which is equivalent to a three-story building), it is below typical residential and urban zoning requirements its uniquely slender vertical axis design allows it to operate with a low speed ratio, which makes it quiet and more visible to birds. In a business setting, several Windspires clustered together can be visually appealing and can display a company's commitment to environmental stewardship. Like other sources of wind power, a Windspire generates clean, renewable energy that doesn't require the burning of fossil fuels.

Windspire is sold in a "kit" form and includes everything that is needed except the concrete foundation. It can be installed by a professional installer in a matter of hours. Maintenance is limited to oiling the bearings, which are 9 feet off the ground, once a year. The 1.2 kilowatt (or 1,200 watts) Windspire will produce approximately 2,000 kilowatt hours per year in 12 mile per hour average wind. This amount of electricity is sufficient to supply roughly 25 to 30 percent of the power needed for an average house. A household that spends $3,600 a year on electricity could recoup its investment in a Windspire in just over five years.

Q&A: Based on the material covered in this chapter, what questions would you ask the firm's founders before making your funding decision? What answers would satisfy you?

Decision: If you had to make your decision on just the information provided in the pitch and on the company's Web site, would you fund this company? Why or why not?

CASE2.1

23andMe: Is This an Opportunity or Just an Interesting Idea?

www.23andMe.com

Bruce R. Barringer
Oklahoma State University
R. Duane Ireland
Texas A&M University

Introduction

Many people are intensely interested in how they can prevent the onset of health-related problems, from the common cold to a debilitating disease. To translate their concerns into action people exercise, watch their diets, take vitamins, and undergo routine physicals. Now there is a new way for people to understand the health-related issues to which they

(continued)

are susceptible. 23andMe is a Silicon Valley start-up that can provide you access to your genetic information. By providing the company a sample of your DNA, you can receive a comprehensive profile of your risks for heart attacks, multiple sclerosis, lung cancer, depression, and 90 other conditions.

23andMe has attracted quite a bit of media buzz, not only because of its cutting-edge technology, but because one of its cofounders, Anne Wojcicki, is married to Google cofounder Sergey Brin. Google has invested $3.9 million in the company. In September 2008, Brin disclosed, in a heartfelt post on his blog, that his DNA had been examined by 23andMe, and the results show that his genetic makeup includes a mutation of a gene known as LRRK2, which several studies have linked to Parkinson's disease. While he acknowledged that the implications of the discovery were "not entirely clear," he added, "It is clear that I have a markedly higher chance of developing Parkinson's in my lifetime than the average person."

Since Brin's revelation, 23andMe has receive both positive and negative attention. Supporters of genetic testing argue that DNA tests provide crucial information. The hope is that by alerting people to their risk factors they will take steps to deal with them. But people from doctors to government regulators are lining up against 23andMe and genetic testing in general. They argue that the tests are inconclusive and may cause psychological problems if people begin to worry about a disease they "might" get years in the future.

So is 23andMe a legitimate business opportunity or just an idea? Read the following information and then you decide.

How It Works

You access the company's Web site, sign a consent form, and pay $399. In a few days you receive a Spit Kit in the mail. The kit includes everything you need to provide 23andMe a saliva-based DNA sample. You send the sample to a certified lab where more than a half-million points in your DNA are analyzed and converted into digital data. Your data is then loaded onto 23andMe's encrypted Web site, and a genetic profile is created. You're notified by e-mail that your profile is ready, and you can log onto your account and view your results.

The profile provides you with two sets of information. The first set deals with your ancestry. By comparing your genetic information to that of people around the globe, via a technique called "genotyping," 23andMe provides you with maps of the world that show where both your mother's and your father's ancestors came from. 23andMe also describes for you the role your mother's and father's ancestors played in human history. If multiple members of your family have their DNA

analyzed by 23andMe, you can construct a family tree and see how specific genes have been passed down within your own family. The ancestry data is particularly useful for people who are adopted, immigrants, Native Americans, or anyone whose ancestors left few historical records. Besides being informative it can also be fun. If all four of a child's grandparents, for example, are alive and participate in 23andMe's service, the child can pinpoint characteristics that were inherited from a specific grandparent.

The second set of information deals with health and traits. There are four categories of information.

1. Disease Risks. This section tells you whether you have an elevated risk for more than 90 diseases such as cystic fibrosis, Parkinson's disease, rheumatoid arthritis, and type 2 diabetes.
2. Traits. This section tells you what your genes indicate with regard to physical attributes, from earwax consistency to eye color to lactose intolerance.
3. Carrier Status. This section tells you if you are a carrier for inherited diseases such as cystic fibrosis and sickle-cell anemia. It also tells you whether you pass positive resistances to diseases through your genes, like malaria resistance.
4. New and Recently Updated. This section, which changes as new information becomes available, keeps you updated on health and trait information.

Once you view your 23andMe profile, you'll be asked to participate in the company's research arm, which is called 23andWe. This involves (on a volunteer basis) participating in studies of conditions and traits that are applicable to you. Part of the lure for participating in 23andWe-sponsored studies is access to social networks of people who care about the same things you do. For example, 23andWe is currently building a social network of women who have survived breast cancer and/or are participating in 23andWe breast cancer research studies.

23andMe's Web site illustrates the breadth of information and services that the company offers to its participants.

Points of Contention

There are two points of contention regarding 23andMe's service and genetic testing in general. The first is whether genetic tests truly provide useful information. The main concern is that many gene-disease relationships are statistically very small, making it a stretch to make predictions. Also, in many cases, it's still unclear whether

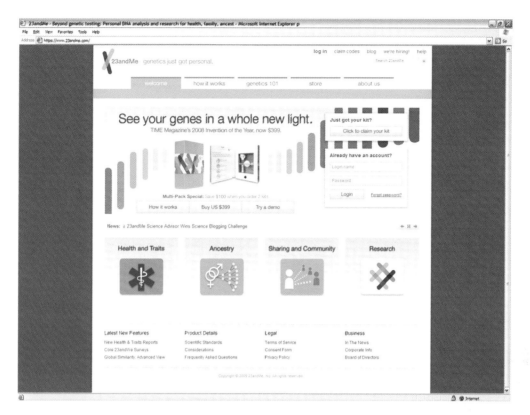

a relationship between a particular genetic marker and a disease, like lung cancer, plays a role in the onset of the disease or whether the gene is just along for the ride. In addition, even if the tests can tell someone they are predisposed to a specific disease, there is often no cure. And for many diseases, like heart disease and diabetes, doctors already have reliable and inexpensive ways of telling people whether they are at risk. Affirming these concerns, in January 2008, the *New England Journal of Medicine* published an article criticizing the popularity of genetic testing by companies like 23andMe. The authors of the article coined the phrase "recreational gemonics" for this type of testing. The article argued that the science of genetic testing is still too premature to be put into a commercial setting.

The second point of contention is that people often don't take affirmative steps even if they're told that they have an elevated risk for a disease. Surprisingly, the research on this topic is sparse. There is a study underway, by San Diego's Scripps Translational Science Institute, which will assess whether people undergoing genetic testing change their behaviors as a result of the tests. No similar study has been completed.

Collectively, these concerns suggest that people will spend $399 to receive a report that may alarm and worry them, and in many cases leave them with little they can do to respond. Parkinson's disease is a case in point. Since there is no known way to prevent Parkinson's, 23andMe critics argue

that the main value of the report is to cause people to worry.

Reaction from Supporters of 23andMe and Genetic Testing in General

In reaction to these criticisms, supporters of 23andMe argue that people who have an interest in their genetic information have a right to have it. In fact, 23andMe's mantra is to "democratize personal genetics" by making it possible for the average person to have access to his or her genetic information. They also point out that science is never done evolving so there's a risk in saying that a technology is too "premature" to share with the public. Based on that notion, it may never be shared. In addition, despite what the skeptics think, proponents of genetic testing argue that simple common sense says that raising an individual's awareness of their risk of contracting a specific disease is a good thing. Even if it causes some worry, it may prompt some people to exercise more, watch their diets, or take specific steps that delay or prevent the onset of a serious disease.

What Do You Think?

So what do you think? Is 23andMe a legitimate business opportunity or just an idea? Will the company still be in business three years or five years from today?

(continued)

Discussion Questions

1. What environmental trends are working in 23andMe's favor? If 23andMe has uncovered a promising business opportunity, what environmental trends have made 23andMe's system possible and potentially attractive to consumers?
2. Of the two separate sets of information 23andMe provides its clients (ancestry and health risks), which set do you think will prove to be of the most interest to the people who use the service?
3. Which of the "points of contention" is the biggest threat to 23andMe's business idea? How can 23andMe overcome this threat?
4. So what do you think? Is 23andMe a legitimate business opportunity or just an idea?

Application Questions

1. Do you think 23andMe will be able to establish credibility with the medical community (i.e., doctors, hospital administrators, health insurance providers) or do you think it's going to be an uphill battle for the company? What steps can 23andMe take to assure the medical community and the general public that it's providing a valuable service?
2. Think about the challenges in your own life that might represent a business opportunity. If you don't think of something right away, don't give up. All of us encounter problems and challenges in our everyday lives that might represent the basis of a promising business opportunity. Be prepared to describe to others one of the challenges or problems you encounter and how it represents a potential business opportunity.

Source: www.23andMe.com (accessed October 15, 2008).
© 23andMe, Inc. 2009. All rights reserved; distributed pursuant to a Limited License from 23andMe.

CASE2.2

FLAVORx and CarePages:
How Solving a Personal Problem Can Trigger the Recognition of a Promising Business Opportunity
www.FLAVORx.com
www.carepages.com

Bruce R. Barringer
Oklahoma State University
R. Duane Ireland
Texas A&M University

Introduction

Many business opportunities are recognized by people who are trying to solve a personal problem. The problem can arise in a person's job because of financial issues, while participating in recreational and/or volunteer activities, or because of a family issue. As many of us would agree, when a problem arises in a person's family for which there isn't an obvious solution, the need to find a solution can become urgent. In these instances, if a creative solution is found, it often represents a solution that other families, facing the same problem, might find useful. In some instances, the solution is compelling enough that it represents the basis for launching a new entrepreneurial venture.

This case provides examples of two businesses that were started in this manner. In each case, the recognition of the business opportunity was triggered by a set of parents grappling with an urgent family-related issue.

FLAVORx

In 1992, Kenny Kramm's second daughter, Hadley, was born premature. As an infant, she developed a medical disorder that required her to take medicine four times a day. The medicine tasted awful, and it was difficult for Kramm and his wife to help Hadley keep it down. The Kramms grew increasingly concerned about this situation. Every time Hadley had a hard time keeping the medicine down, her condition worsened. "We were ending up in the emergency room on a weekly basis," Kramm recalls. There was literally nothing that Hadley's doctors or nurses could do other than to urge the Kramms to help Hadley keep her medicine down—in any way they could.

Kenny Kramm worked in his parent's pharmacy. To help Hadley, Kenny and his father (a pharmacist for 40 years) started experimenting with concentrated flavors that could be mixed with Hadley's medicine to mask its bitter taste. Eventually, they produced a banana flavor concentrate that they were able to safely mix with the medicine; they were elated when Hadley started accepting the flavored medicine in its entirety. Almost immediately her condition stabilized, both medically and emotionally.

Over the next three years, Kramm and his father continued to experiment with adding flavors to Hadley's various medicines. There were other medicine flavoring products available at the time, but none of them worked well enough to cover the bitter taste of most children's medications. Gradually,

Kramm started seeing his pursuit as a business idea. Surely many other parents faced the same challenges that he and his wife had faced with Hadley, he thought. In 1995, he decided to incorporate and named the business FLAVORx. To move the business forward, he partnered with one of the largest flavoring companies in the world to help develop custom flavors that would be safely mixed with medicines. After months of testing, FLAVORx's first flavor additives were formally approved.

FLAVORx's additives are now available in most pharmacies in the United States and are frequently used to improve the taste of both child and adult medicines. Medicines mixed with FLAVORx's formulas not only taste better; they improve medicinal compliance and make it possible for some people to take their entire prescribed dosage. Not all FLAVORx-treated medicines taste like candy, but they all make medicines taste better. And Kenny Kramm's instincts were right on target. FLAVORx has been a lifesaver for thousands of parents who faced the same challenge that he and his wife did with Hadley. The following is a sample of customer testimonials posted on FLAVORx's Web site. You can sense the relief in lives of the parents, doctors, and children who wrote the testimonials.

Customer Testimonials from FLAVORx's Web Site
December 2008

Lauren Noto, 10 years old
Evans, Georgia

I love this stuff because it works. I used the Strawberry FLAVORx flavor when I was younger and it helped so much when I took liquid medications. But I take swallowers (pills) now.

Dr. Bart Schmitt,
Denver Children's Hospital

I love the idea of making medicine easier for sick children to take. We need all the help we can get . . .

Nancy Lantz
Glen Ellyn, Illinois

My child has a seizure disorder and was supposed to take Zarontin liquid. It was horrible tasting: I tasted it. We could not get her to keep it down. This medication was crucial to her survival. We knew if she did not keep it down she would end up in the hospital. We then heard about FLAVORx and tried it. It was a miracle! Now she takes her medicine just as the doctor directed.

FLAVORx remains an independent company, and Kenny Kramm is still at the helm. It has 42 FDA-approved flavorings for both over-the-counter and prescription medications, and is in over 35,000 pharmacies worldwide. It recently added a veterinary division and now makes flavor additives for pet medications. As for Hadley, her father's solution was just what she needed. From the time she took her first dose of banana-flavored

medicine, she has never had another medicine-related hospital visit.

CarePages

About six years after Kenny Kramm and his wife were struggling to help Hadley keep her medicine down, another couple, Eric and Sharon Langshur, were facing an equally difficult situation. Their son

(continued)

Matthew, who was born with a heart defect, needed a series of surgeries. Along with dealing with doctors, nurses, and caring for Matthew, the Langshurs had to find a way to keep their family and friends up-to-date on Matthew's progress. Sharon's brother came up with an idea. He created a Web site, which resembled a modern day blog, which allowed Eric and Sharon to post updates about Matthew. The site also allowed people to write back and offer words of support. By the time Matthew had his last surgery (at 18 months old), the site was receiving several thousand unique hits a day, from family, friends, and people who heard about Matthew and were following his progress.

The Langshurs were overwhelmed by the support they received through the Web site as well as the positive feedback from people using it. Eric saw it as a business idea, and in 2000 CarePages was born. Rather than market CarePages directly to individuals, Eric decided to market it to hospitals, which could make it available to patients and family members who were leading their care. The hospitals could promote the service and attach their brand, and benefit through improved patient satisfaction and patients and families who were more at ease because of the support they were receiving through their CarePages community.

A CarePage page includes sections that allow for updates and replies, a photo gallery (of the patient), and a section labeled "About Patient," which provides a history of the patient and his or her medical condition. The page is very easy to set up. A running tally is displayed that shows how many times a site has been accessed and how many messages have been left. It's not uncommon for the messages to run into the thousands. A CarePage page includes a link labeled "Invite Others" that allows a user to invite other people to start visiting a page. Because of this, many people who have a relative or friend in the hospital will invite coworkers, neighbors, people they go to church with, and others who don't directly know the patient to start visiting the page and offering support. Many CarePage pages are very touching as parents share updates about a child who is facing surgery or treatment for a serious medical condition, and family, friends, and people the patient doesn't even know post words of encouragement and support. A CarePage page also includes a link labeled CareCompliment. The link allows patients, family members, and others to leave compliments for nurses, doctors, and hospital staff. This aspect of CarePages is very popular with hospital personnel.

Today, over 700 health care facilities are CarePage clients and offer the service to their patients. There is no advertising on a CarePage page. The health care facilities pay CarePage for the service and offer it to their patients for free. The health care facilities benefit through improved customer satisfaction (30 percent, on average, from people who use the CarePage service), positive PR that leads to referrals, and the benefit they receive from patients and families who are more emotionally healthy during their hospital stay because of the support they receive through their CarePages network.

In early 2007, CarePages was acquired by RevolutionHealth, a multifaceted customer-centric health care company. CarePages' mission and strategy are not expected to change. In its new release, RevolutionHealth indicated that Care-Pages, which was founded in 2000, is now generating more than 30 million page views per month.

Discussion Questions

1. In this chapter, an opportunity is defined as being (1) attractive, (2) durable, (3) timely, and (4) anchored in a product or service that creates value for its buyer or end user. To what extent do FLAVORx and CarePages meet each of these tests of an opportunity?
2. Why do you think the idea for FLAVORx wasn't developed by a large pharmaceutical company long before Kenny Kramm came along, and the idea for CarePages wasn't developed by a hospital long before Eric Langshur came up with the idea?
3. Why do you think CarePages markets its product to hospitals rather than directly to consumers, like MySpace and Facebook do?
4. What similarities do you see between FLAVORx and CarePages? What does each company teach you about the opportunity recognition process?

Application Questions

1. How could FLAVORx and CarePages effectively use focus groups to strengthen their existing products and solicit suggestions for related product ideas?
2. Think about the service that CarePages offers. Brainstorm other situations that people are in where it might make sense to set up a Web site or blog that allows a person to provide frequent updates and receive notes of encouragement and support from friends. Pick your best idea. Could a business be set up to facilitate the process for others?

Sources: Flavorx homepage, www.flavorx.com (accessed December 12, 2008); Storm Pilot Tribune, "BVRMC, CarePages Helps Keep Young Cancer Patient in Touch," January 5, 2009; Bernoff, L. *Groundswell*, New York: Forrester Research, Inc., 2008.

Endnotes

1. K. Milkus, "If the Shoe Fits . . . Entrepreneur's Larger Size Give Many Women a Reason to Smile," *Daily Herald* (Arlington Heights, IL), February 3, 2006.
2. D. Cohen, "If the Shoe Doesn't Fit, Start a Company," *Reuters*, July 14, 2008. http://features.us.reuters.com/entrepreneur/news/B63568A8-51DC-11DD-B959-334B5BFC.html (accessed December 2, 2008).
3. C. Hsieh, J. A. Nickerson, and T. R. Zenger, "Opportunity Discovery, Problem Solving and a Theory of the Entrepreneurial Firm," *Journal of Management Studies* 44, no. 7 (2008): 1253–77.
4. Amazon.Com Company Report, *Standard and Poor's Stock Report*, May 27, 2006; *Time*, "Amazing Person.com," December 27, 1999.
5. A. Ulwich, *What Customers Want* (New York: McGraw-Hill, 2005).
6. J. E. Cliff, P. D. Jennings, and R. Greenwood, "New to the Game and Questioning the Rules: The Experiences and Beliefs of Founders Who Start Imitative Versus Innovative Firms," *Journal of Business Venturing* 21 (2006): 633–63; J. A. Timmons, "Opportunity Recognition," in *The Portable MBA in Entrepreneurship*, ed. W. D. Bygrave (New York: John Wiley & Sons, 1997), 27.
7. D. N. Sull, "The Three Windows of Opportunity," *Harvard Business School Working Knowledge*, June 6, 2005.
8. D. B. Audretsch and E. Lehmann, "Entrepreneurial Access and Absorption of Knowledge Spillovers: Strategic Board and Managerial Composition for Competitive Advantage," *Journal of Small Business Management* 44, no. 2 (2006): 155–66; *New Webster's Dictionary* (New York: Delair Publishing, 1981).
9. M. Yang, nPost homepage, www.npost.com (accessed November 6, 2008. Originally posted on April 24, 2006).
10. H. S. Alhorr, C. B. Moore, and G. T. Payne, "The Impact of Economic Integration on Cross-Border Venture Capital Investments: Evidence from the European Union," *Entrepreneurship Theory and Practice*, 32, no. 5 (2008): 897–917.
11. B. Steverman, "Cutting Costs to Increase Profits," *Business Week Online*, www.businessweek.com (accessed November 25, 2008).
12. B. Worthen, "Weak Links in the Food (Supply) Chain," *Wall Street Journal*, June 24, 2008.
13. E. Chasan, "Cookie Chain Mrs. Fields to File for Bankruptcy," *Reuters*, August 15, 2008.
14. Miriah Power homepage, http://mariahpower.com (accessed November 6, 2008).
15. J. L. Woolley and R. M. Rottner, "Innovation Policy and Nanotechnology Entrepreneurship," *Entrepreneurship Theory and Practice*, 32, no. 5 (2008): 791–811.
16. D. Darlin, "The iPod Ecosystem," *New York Times*, February 3, 2006.
17. M. Minniti, "The Role of Government Policy on Entrepreneurial Activity: Productive, Unproductive, or Destructive?" *Entrepreneurship Theory and Practice*, 32, no. 5 (2008): 779–90.
18. Almost Family Inc. 10-K Annual Report filed with the Securities and Exchange Commission, March 12, 2008.
19. Box.net homepage, www.box.net.com (accessed November 27, 2008).
20. D. Smagalla, "The Truth About Software Startups," *MIT Sloan Management Review* (Winter 2004): 7.
21. P. Kotler, *Marketing Insights from A to Z* (New York: John Wiley & Sons, 2003), 128.
22. M. Linderman, Signals Vs. Noise Blog, www.37signals.com/svn/posts/1244-definiing-the-problem-of-elevator-waiting-times (accessed September 17, 2008).
23. Greenprint homepage, www.printgreener.com (accessed November 6, 2008).
24. Shade Clothing homepage, www.shadeclothing.com (accessed November 6, 2008).
25. Ladies Who Launch homepage, www.ladieswholaunch.com (accessed October 4, 2007).
26. nPost homepage, www.npost.com (accessed November 6, 2008. Originally posted April 6, 2007).
27. V. Mahnke, M. Venzin, and S. A. Zahra, "Governing Entrepreneurial Opportunity Recognition in MNEs: Aligning Interest and Cognition Under Uncertainty," *Journal of Management Studies*, 44, no. 7 (2007): 1278–98.
28. J. Wiklund and D. A. Shepherd, "Portfolio Entrepreneurship: Habitual and Novice Founders, New Entry, and Mode of Organizing," *Entrepreneurship Theory and Practice*, 32, no. 4 (2008): 701–25; G. D. Markham and R. A. Baron,

"Person–Entrepreneurship Fit—Why Some People Are More Successful as Entrepreneurs Than Others," *Human Resource Management Review* 13, no. 2 (2003): 281–301.

29. J. Case, "The Origins of Entrepreneurship," *Inc.*, June 1989.

30. A. C. Cooper, W. Dunkelberg, C. Woo, and W. Dennis, *New Business in America: The Firms and Their Owners* (Washington, DC: National Federation of Independent Business, 1990).

31. R. L. Sorenson, C. A. Folker, and K. H. Brigham, "The Collaborative Network Orientation: Achieving Business Success Through Collaborative Relationships," *Entrepreneurship Theory and Practice* 32, no. 4 (2008): 615–34.

32. E. Stam, D. Audretsch, and J. Meijaard, "Renscent Entrepreneurship," *Journal of Evolutionary Economics*, 18, no. 3 (2008): 493–507; R. Ronstadt, "The Corridor Principle," *Journal of Business Venturing*, 3, no. 1 (1988): 31–40.

33. G. T. Lumpkin and B. B. Lichtenstein, "The Role of Organizational Learning in the Opportunity-Recognition Process," *Entrepreneurship Theory and Practice* 29, no. 4 (2005): 451–72.

34. I. M. Kirzner, *Perception, Opportunity, and Profit: Studies in the Theory of Entrepreneurship* (Chicago: University of Chicago Press, 1979).

35. S. A. Alvarez and J. B. Barney, "Entrepreneurial Alertness," in *The Blackwell Encyclopedia of Management—Entrepreneurship,* eds. M. A. Hitt and R. D. Ireland, (Malden, MA: Blackwell Publishing, 2005), 63–64.

36. C. M. Gaglio and J. A. Katz, "The Psychological Basis of Opportunity Identification: Entrepreneurial Alertness," *Small Business Economics* 16, no. 2 (2001): 95–111.

37. I. M. Kirzner, "The Primacy of Entrepreneurial Discovery," in *The Prime Mover of Progress*, ed. A. Seldon (London: Institute of Economic Affairs, 1980), 5–30.

38. S. C. Parker, "The Economics of Formal Business Networks," *Journal of Business Venturing* 23, no. 6 (2008): 627–40; G. Kingsley and E. J. Malecki, "Networking for Competitiveness," *Small Business Economics* 23, no. 1 (2004): 71–84.

39. A. C. Cooper and X. Yin, "Entrepreneurial Networks," in *The Blackwell Encyclopedia of Management—Entrepreneurship*, eds. M. A. Hitt and R. D. Ireland (Malden, MA: Blackwell Publishing, 2005), 98–100.

40. D. B. Audretsch, W. Bonte, and M. Keilbach, "Entrepreneurship Capital and Its Impact on Knowledge Diffusion and Economic Performance," *Journal of Business Venturing* 23, no. 6 (2008): 687–98; P. Davidsson and B. Honig, "The Role of Social and Human Capital Among Nascent Entrepreneurs," *Journal of Business Venturing* 18, no. 3 (2003): 301–31.

41. R. H. Koller, "On the Source of Entrepreneurial Ideas," in *Frontiers of Entrepreneurship Research* (Wellesley, MA: Babson College, 1988), 194–207.

42. G. E. Hills, R. C. Shrader, and G. T. Lumpkin, "Opportunity Recognition as a Creative Process," in *Frontiers of Entrepreneurship Research* (Wellesley, MA: Babson College, 1999), 216–27.

43. R. Braun, "In the Eye of the Beholder: How Construing Situations Affects Opportunity Recognition," *Social Science Research Network*, 2008, http://papers.ssrn.com; R. P. Singh, G. E. Hills, R. C. Hybels, and G. T. Lumpkin, "Opportunity Recognition Through Social Network Characteristics of Entrepreneurs," in *Frontiers of Entrepreneurship Research* (Wellesley, MA: Babson College, 1999), 228–38.

44. C. J. Medlin, "Self and Collective Interests in Business Relationships," *Journal of Business Research* 59, no. 7 (2006): 858–65; M. Granovetter, "The Strength of Weak Ties," *American Journal of Sociology* 78, no. 6 (1973): 1360–80.

45. A. Ardichvili, R. Cardozo, and S. Ray, "A Theory of Entrepreneurial Opportunity Identification and Development," *Journal of Business Venturing* 18, no. 1 (2003): 105–23.

46. D. A. Harper, "Towards a Theory of Entrepreneurial Teams," *Journal of Business Venturing* 23, no. 6 (2008): 613–26.

47. J. J. Kao, *Entrepreneurship, Creativity, and Organization* (Upper Saddle River, NJ: Prentice Hall, 1989).

48. Hills et al., "Opportunity Recognition," 168–72.

49. W. Bygrave, "The Entrepreneurial Process," in *The Portable MBA in Entrepreneurship,* ed. William B. Bygrave (New York: John Wiley & Sons, 1997), 1–26.

50. M. Csikszentmihalyi, *Creativity* (New York: HarperCollins, 1996).

51. E. Edmonds and L. Candy, "Creativity, Art Practice, and Knowledge," *Communications of the ACM* 4, no. 10 (2002): 91–95.

52. J. S. Park, "Opportunity Recognition and Product Innovation in Entrepreneurial High-Tech Start-Ups: A New Perspective and Supporting Case Study," *Technovation* 2, no. 7 (2005): 739–52; R. P. Singh, *Entrepreneurial Opportunity Recognition* (New York: Garland Publishing, 2000).

53. K. Rodan, Entrepreneurial Thought Leaders Podcast, Stanford Technology Ventures Program, http://stvp.stanford.edu (accessed April 2006).

54. G. Galant and S. Klause, Venture Voice Podcast, Show 35, www.venturevoice.com (accessed March 2006).

55. R. G. Cooper and S. J. Edgett, *Product Development for the Service Sector* (Cambridge, MA: Perseus Books, 1999).

56. College Drop-Ins homepage, http://collegedropins.com (accessed November 4, 2008).

57. A. Majchrzak, D. Logan, R. McCurdy, and M. Kirchmer, "Four Keys to Managing Emergence," *MIT Sloan Management Review* 47, no. 2 (2006): 14–18.

58. J. A. Goncalo and B. M. Staw, "Individualism-Collectivism and Group Creativity," *Organizational Behavior and Human Decision Processes* 100 (May 2006): 96–109.

59. S. H. Thomke, "Capturing the Real Value of Innovation Tools," *MIT Sloan Management Review* 47, no. 2 (2006): 24–32; A. Cummings and G. R. Oldham, "Enhancing Creativity: Managing Work Contexts for the High Potential Employee," *California Management Review* 40, no.1 (1997): 22–38.

60. United States Patent and Trademark Office, "Disclosure Document Program," www.uspto.gov/web/offices/pac/disdo.html (accessed June 4, 2002).

MATT DAVIDSON

Founder, Think Gum LLC
BS, University of California,
Berkley, 2006

Getting Personal

with Matt Davidson

CURRENTLY IN MY IPOD
Weezer

BEST ADVICE I'VE RECEIVED
You can't score if you don't
take a shot

**WHAT I'D LIKE TO BE DOING
IN 10 YEARS**
Making the lives of people
more enjoyable

**MY BIGGEST SURPRISE
AS AN ENTREPRENEUR**
How willing people are to help
if they believe in your idea

**HARDEST PART OF GETTING
FUNDING**
Finding someone who can
contribute more than just
money

**MY ADVICE TO NEW
ENTREPRENEURS**
Don't get discouraged when
you hear "No" because you
will hear it all the time

CHAPTERTHREE
Feasibility *Analysis*

OPENING PROFILE

THINK GUM
The Value of Validating a Business Idea
www.thinkgum.com

As an undergraduate student at the University of California, Berkeley, Matt Davidson picked a tough major—molecular and cellular biology. One course he took, MCB 62, was particularly interesting. The course was titled "Drugs and the Brain" and focused on the effects of drugs on mental processes such as attention, motivation, learning, and memory. Davidson learned that certain scents, like rosemary and peppermint, can be used to improve concentration and reduce careless errors. He even put some of what he learned to work by picking rosemary from bushes on campus and putting it on gum before classes. He figured that combining rosemary with peppermint gum would improve his concentration and memory.

The idea of combining herbs with gum to sharpen mental functions stuck with Davidson, and he started reading every scientific article that he could find about the effects of herbs on concentration and memory. He slowly developed the idea of producing a gum that would help students do better on exams and presentations.

After graduation in spring 2006, Davidson spent a year working at a research lab in New York City to prepare for graduate school. He also worked on his business idea. Rather than producing something quickly, he decided to take it slow and test the feasibility of his idea before he sank a lot of money into it. After getting some advice from industry experts, he bought small quantities of every supplement and herb known to have brain-boosting power. He established two criteria to determine whether an ingredient would become part of his gum: (1) is there scientific evidence to support the claim that it has brain-boosting power and (2) does it taste good. Some supplements, for example, are extremely potent but taste terrible. Davidson eventually settled on four ingredients: ginkgo biloba, bacopa, guarana, and vinpocetine. Over the next six months, five test batches of gum were produced, and Davidson distributed the gum to anyone who would provide valuable feedback. Each new batch improved on the previous one. Although Davidson was diligent in selecting wholesome ingredients to place in his gum, he was aided by fairly lax regulatory statutes regarding supplements. As long as the herbs and supplements he used were already approved as dietary supplements, he didn't need any further approvals to test or eventually sell his gum.

In fall 2007, Davidson simultaneously entered a PhD program at Stanford University and launched his company, which he named Think Gum LLC. The gum included six ingredients: peppermint (for awareness), rosemary (to energize and improve memory), vinpocetine (to improve short-term memory), bacopa (to speed cognitive processing), gingko biloba (to enhance memory), and guarana (which contains natural caffeine for an energy boost). These ingredients converge to produce the effects that Davidson was after. Not only is Think Gum a good concentration and memory booster,

Learning Objectives

After studying this chapter you should be ready to:

1. Explain what a feasibility analysis is and why it's important.

2. Discuss the proper time to complete a feasibility analysis when developing an entrepreneurial venture.

3. Describe the purpose of a product/service feasibility analysis and the two primary issues that a proposed business should consider in this area.

4. Explain a concept statement and its contents.

5. Describe the purpose of a buying intentions survey and how it's administered.

6. Explain the importance of library, Internet, and gumshoe research.

7. Describe the purpose of industry/market feasibility analysis and the two primary issues to consider in this area.

8. Discuss the characteristics of an attractive industry.

9. Describe the purpose of organizational feasibility analysis and list the two primary issues to consider in this area.

10. Explain the importance of financial feasibility analysis and list the most critical issues to consider in this area.

but it facilitates an action referred to as "context-dependent memory." The idea behind context-dependent memory is that if you learn something in the presence of a certain stimuli (like chewing Think Gum), then when you're in the presence of the same stimuli again (like chewing Think Gum during a test) your memory will be improved. It's akin to what happens to people when they're exposed to the aroma of pumpkin pie. Most people respond favorably to the aroma of pumpkin pie and become visibly more content and relaxed because the smell triggers pleasant memories of happy Thanksgiving family gatherings.

Along with creating Think Gum, Davidson also educated himself on how gum is produced. It turns out that gum manufacturers are risk averse and aren't excited about taking a chance on a new type of gum. As a result, Davidson had to do some convincing to find a manufacturer to work with. After finding a manufacturer and learning the costs involved, he ran the numbers to make sure that his venture was financially feasible. To make his forecasts as accurate as possible, he got quotes on everything—from the cost of the gum to the cost of getting trademarks to the cost of packaging. Satisfied, he finally was ready to go and in spring 2007 ordered an initial batch of 100,000 pieces of Think Gum.

Davidson's patient approach has been rewarded. His initial batch of gum sold out in about two months. He placed successively larger orders, and as of winter 2008, had sold over 1,000,000 pieces of Think Gum in 12-piece packages. The gum is for sale on Davidson's Web site and in several retail locations in California. It's also for sale in Canada and Great Britain. Davidson's next goal is to expand distribution and get his product in more retail outlets.[1]

In this chapter, we'll discuss the importance of feasibility analysis. Failure to conduct a feasibility analysis can result in disappointing outcomes, as illustrated in this chapter's "What Went Wrong?" boxed feature (which deals with the failure of many eBay drop-off stores).

FEASIBILITY ANALYSIS

Feasibility analysis is the process of determining if a business idea is viable. As shown in Figure 3.1, the most effective businesses emerge from a process that includes (1) recognizing a business idea, (2) testing the feasibility of the idea, (3) writing a business plan, and (4) launching the business. If a business idea falls short on one or more of the four components of feasibility analysis, it should be dropped or rethought, as shown in the figure. Many entrepreneurs make the mistake of identifying a business idea and then jumping directly to writing a business plan to describe and gain support for the idea. This sequence often omits or provides little time for the important step of testing the feasibility of a business idea before the business plan is written.

A mental transition needs to be made when completing a feasibility analysis from thinking of a business idea as just an idea to thinking of it as a business. A feasibility analysis is an assessment

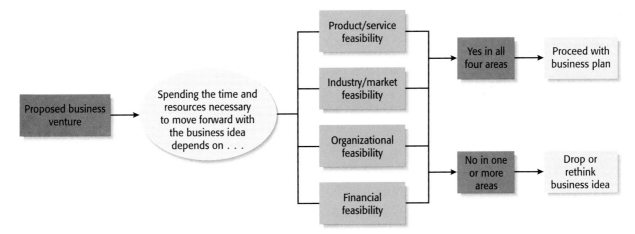

FIGURE 3.1

Role of Feasibility Analysis in Developing Successful Business Ideas

Learning Objective

1. Explain what a feasibility analysis is and why it's important.

Learning Objective

2. Discuss the proper time to complete a feasibility analysis when developing an entrepreneurial venture.

of a potential business rather than strictly a product or service idea. The sequential nature of the steps shown in Figure 3.1 cleanly separates the investigative portion of thinking through the merits of a business idea from the planning and selling portion of the process. Feasibility analysis is investigative in nature and is designed to critique the merits of a proposed business. A business plan is more focused on planning and selling. The reason it's important to complete the entire process, according to John W. Mullins, the author of the highly regarded book *The New Business Road Test*, is to avoid falling into the "everything about my opportunity is wonder" mode. In Mullins's view, failure to properly investigate the merits of a business idea before the business plan is written runs the risk of blinding an entrepreneur to inherent risks associated with the potential business and results in too positive of a plan.[2] This scenario may explain the large number of eBay drop-off stores that were opened in the mid-2000s only to quickly fail as described in the "What Went Wrong?" boxed feature.

This chapter provides a methodology for conducting a feasibility analysis by describing its four key areas: product/service feasibility, industry/market feasibility, organizational feasibility, and financial feasibility. We introduce supplemental material in two appendixes to the chapter. Appendix 3.1 contains a tool called First Screen, which is a template for completing a feasibility analysis. Appendix 3.2 contains an Internet Resource Table that provides information on Internet resources that are helpful in completing First Screen.

An outline for the approach to feasibility analysis depicted in this chapter is provided in Table 3.1. Completing a feasibility analysis requires both primary and secondary research. **Primary research** is research that is collected by the person or persons completing the analysis. It normally includes talking to industry experts, obtaining feedback from prospective customers, conducting focus groups, and administering surveys. **Secondary research** probes data that is already collected. The data generally includes industry studies, census bureau data, analyst forecasts, and other pertinent information gleaned through library and Internet research. The Internet Resource Table in Appendix 3.2 is useful for conducting secondary research.

Jim Clark, the founder of Silicon Graphics and cofounder of Netscape, affirms the importance of feasibility analysis. Clark is very blunt in the value he places on feasibility analysis—particularly the importance of getting out and talking to potential customers about the merits of a business idea:

> The reason so few companies are a success is that most people don't have a lot of common sense about what will sell and what won't. You need to be very pragmatic about whether people will pay for a product based on your great idea. "This should be great and I am sure the world will beat a path to my door." Once you

What Went WRONG?

eBay Drop-Off Stores: How Feasible Were They?

Sounds like a good idea. You're replacing your laptop computer with a new one, but your current laptop still works and should be worth something. You'd like to sell it on eBay but don't want to hassle with setting up an eBay account, listing the laptop, and following the auction. The alternative is to take the laptop to an eBay drop-off store, which will sell your laptop for you on eBay. You'll then get a check less a commission taken by the store.

In the mid-2000s a number of eBay drop-off stores started to do just this. Nonexistent in 2003, by 2005 there were thousands of independent and franchise eBay Drop-Off Stores across America; today, only a handful remain. What went wrong?

The eBay drop-off store idea was initiated primarily by two franchise organizations—iSoldit and QuickDrop. Although the idea made sense to many—there were 7,000 drop-off stores by mid-2005—skeptics questioned their feasibility from the beginning. The lure of the drop-off store idea is that nearly everybody has something in their closet or garage they'd like to sell on eBay. So the market's almost unlimited. But the skeptics wondered how much "quality" merchandise would actually come in. It's one thing to manage an auction for a $600 laptop and another to manage one for a $20 baseball card. With commissions in the 40 percent range (that's what the stores were getting), what was most likely to come in? It was easy to envision someone, the skeptics maintained, thinking to themselves, "I'm not going to give up 40 percent of my $600 laptop computer ($240). I'll manage the auction myself," while the same person might gladly give up 40 percent of a $20 baseball card because the total amount of money involved isn't that much. If this type of thinking was pervasive, the drop-off stores would be stuck selling a large amount of low-ticket items rather than high-ticket products. Another thing the skeptics questioned was the diversity of the items the stores were willing to sell. Could the same store owners be experts managing auctions for diamond rings, baseball cards, boats, cameras, computers, decorative plates, rare photos, and countless other things? One of the pitches the drop-off stores made was that they would help their clients know what a fair price was for the items they hoped to sell.

Regrettably, many of the skeptics' worries came true. Literally hundreds of eBay drop-off stores have closed. The main complaint, by the store owners who have called it quits, is that their profit margins were either nonexistent or too low. They simply dealt with too many one-time sellers and one-of-a-kind items to develop a cadence of repeat business and efficient processing. They also found that the cost of processing an item was the same whether it was a $30 decorative plate or a $15,000 boat. Processing each item included talking to a customer, researching a price, taking a photo, writing a description, posting the item on eBay, following the auction, shipping the product to the buyer, getting paid by the buyer, and paying the customer. Not much money would be left over from a 40 percent commission on a $30 decorative plate after all of that.

There are now many disgruntled former eBay drop-off store owners. The initial capital outlay and working capital for a franchise like iSoldit was between $100,000 and $150,000. One former owner of an iSoldit franchise, Karen McGinn, is so mad that she and her partner maintain a Web site, Am I the Only One? (www.amitheonlyone.org), to provide updates about eBay drop-off store problems. While it's difficult to verify the information on the site, it does illustrate how high emotions are running regarding the eBay drop-off store concept. QuickDrop, one of the pioneers of the eBay drop-off store industry, closed shop in early 2008 and stopped selling franchises and supporting existing franchisees.

Not all is lost. There are still eBay drop-off stores in existence, as illustrated by the iSoldit Web site. Yet the numbers are small compared to original projections. At one time, iSoldit had ambitions to open 3,000 stores in the United States and more overseas. At the time this feature was written, the company had 96 domestic stores listed on its Web site.

Questions for Critical Thinking

1. How many owners of eBay drop-off stores do you think conducted a feasibility analysis before they opened their stores? If you think the number is low, what's the explanation?
2. Describe the difference between eBay drop-off stores as an "idea" and as an actual business. Is it possible for something to be an enticing business idea but a poor business?
3. Why do you think people bought into eBay drop-off stores toward the end of the downward spiral of the category?
4. What can a start-up learn from the experience of the eBay drop-off store industry about the importance of feasibility analysis?

Sources: S. Pooler, "If You Own a QuickDrop eBay Drop Store Franchise What Will You Do Now?" http://ezinearticles.com/?If-You-Own-A-Quickdrop-Ebay-Drop-Store-Franchise-What-Will-You-Do-Now?&id=930650 (accessed September 27, 2008, posted on January 15, 2008); F. Fortunato, "The State of eBay Drop-Off Stores," www.ecommerce-guide.com/news/news/article.pap/3631266 (accessed September 27, 2008, posted September 11, 2006).

Table 3.1   FEASIBILITY ANALYSIS

Part 1: Product/Service Feasibility

    A. Product/service desirability

    B. Product/service demand

Part 2: Industry/Target Market Feasibility

    A. Industry attractiveness

    B. Target market attractiveness

Part 3: Organizational Feasibility

    A. Management prowess

    B. Resource sufficiency

Part 4: Financial Feasibility

    A. Total start-up cash needed

    B. Financial performance of similar businesses

    C. Overall financial attractiveness of the proposed venture

Overall Assessment

have an idea for a product or service, you need to test the market. Talk to potential customers about what they want. And don't try to make the product do everything for everyone. Engineers often make mistakes. It's the Swiss Amy knife mentality. They want to put everything in. Don't. Go out and talk to customers as quickly as you can and put a copy of the product in front of them to get their feedback. When we went out to sell our first product at Silicon Graphics people came back and said, "We don't want this." We (after making adjustments) sold them what they wanted.[3]

Clark's sentiments reflect exactly what Matt Davidson did with Think Gum and what other entrepreneurs who believe in the importance of feasibility analysis do.

It should be emphasized that while a feasibility analysis tests the merits of a specific idea, it allows ample opportunity for the idea to be revised, altered, and changed as a result of the feedback that is obtained and the analysis that is conducted. The whole idea behind feasibility analysis is to put an idea to the test—by talking to industry experts, surveying prospective customers, studying industry trends, thinking through the financials, and scrutinizing it in other ways. These types of activities not only help determine whether an idea is feasible but also help shape and mold the idea.

Now let's turn our attention to the four areas of feasibility analysis. The first area we'll discuss is product/service feasibility.

Product/Service Feasibility Analysis

Product/service feasibility analysis is an assessment of the overall appeal of the product or service being proposed. Although there are many important things to consider when launching a new venture, nothing else matters if the product or service itself doesn't sell. There are two components to product/service feasibility analysis: product/service desirability and product/service demand.

Learning Objective

3. Describe the purpose of a product/service feasibility analysis and the two primary issues that a proposed business should consider in this area.

Often, the most effective thing an entrepreneur can do while completing a product/service feasibility analysis is hit the streets and talk to potential customers. Here, a senior entrepreneur collects feedback from a prospective customer about a new product idea.

Spencer Grant/Photo Researchers, Inc.

Product/Service Desirability   The first component of product/service feasibility is to affirm that the proposed product or service is desirable and serves a need in the marketplace. You should ask the following questions to determine the basic appeal of the product or service:

- Does it make sense? Is it reasonable? Is it something consumers will get excited about?
- Does it take advantage of an environmental trend, solve a problem, or fill a gap in the marketplace?
- Is this a good time to introduce the product or service to the market?
- Are there any fatal flaws in the product or service's basic design or concept?

The proper mind-set at the feasibility analysis stage is to get a general sense of the answers to these and similar questions, rather than to try to reach final conclusions. One way to achieve this objective is to administer a concept test.

Learning Objective

4. Explain a concept statement and its contents.

Concept Test   A concept test involves showing a preliminary description of a product or service idea, called a **concept statement**, to industry experts and prospective customers to solicit their feedback. It is a one-page document that normally includes the following:

- A description of the product or service. This section details the features of the product or service; many include a sketch of it as well.
- The intended target market. This section lists the consumers or businesses who are expected to buy the product or service.
- The benefits of the product or service. This section describes the benefits of the product or service and includes an account of how the product or service adds value and/or solves a problem.
- A description of how the product or service will be positioned relative to competitors. A company's position describes how its product or service is situated relative to its rivals.
- A brief description of the company's management team

FIGURE 3.2

New Venture Fitness
Drinks' Concept
Statement

New Business Concept
New Venture Fitness Drinks Inc.

Product

New Venture Fitness Drinks will sell delicious, nutrition-filled, all-natural fitness drinks to thirsty sports enthusiasts. The drinks will be sold through small storefronts (600 sq. ft.) that will be the same size as popular smoothie restaurants. The drinks were formulated by Dr. William Peters, a world-renowned nutritionist, and Dr. Michelle Smith, a sports medicine specialist, on behalf of New Venture Fitness Drinks and its customers.

Target Market

In the first three years of operation, New Venture Fitness Drinks plans to open three or four restaurants. They will all be located near large sports complexes that contain football and cricket playing fields. The target market is sports enthusiasts.

Why New Venture Fitness Drinks?

The industry for sports drinks continues to grow. New Venture Fitness Drinks will introduce exciting new sports drinks that will be priced between $1.50 and $2.50 per 16-ounce serving. Energy bars and other over-the-counter sports snacks will also be sold. Each restaurant will contain comfortable tables and chairs (both inside and outside) where sports enthusiasts can congregate after a game. The atmosphere will be fun, cheerful, and uplifting.

Special Feature—No Other Restaurant Does This

As a special feature, New Venture Fitness Drinks will videotape select sporting events that take place in the sports complexes nearest its restaurants and will replay highlights of the games on video monitors in their restaurants. The "highlight" film will be a 30-minute film that will play continuously from the previous day's sporting events. This special feature will allow sports enthusiasts, from kids playing football to adults in cricket leagues, to drop in and see themselves and their teammates on television.

Management Team

New Venture Fitness Drink is led by its cofounders, Jack Petty and Peggy Wills. Jack has 16 years of experience with a national restaurant chain, and Peggy is a certified public accountant with seven years of experience at a Big 4 accounting firm.

After the concept statement is developed, it should be shown to at least 10 people who are familiar with the industry that the firm plans to enter and who can provide informed feedback. The temptation to show it to family members and friends should be avoided because these people are predisposed to give positive feedback. Instead, it should be distributed to people who will provide candid and informed feedback and advice. A short survey should be attached to the statement. The items that should be placed in the survey are shown in Table 3.2. The information gleaned from the survey should be tabulated and carefully read. If time permits, the statement can be used in an iterative manner to strengthen the product or service idea. For example, you might show the statement to a group of prospective customers, get feedback, tweak the idea, show it to a second group of prospective customers, tweak the idea some more, and so on.

The concept statement for a fictitious company named New Venture Fitness Drinks is provided in Figure 3.2. New Venture Fitness Drinks sells a line of

Table 3.2 SHORT SURVEY TO ATTACH TO THE CONCEPT STATEMENT

1. List three things you like about the product or service idea described in this statement.

2. Provide three suggestions for making the idea better.

3. Do you think the idea is feasible (i.e., is a realistic or viable business idea)?

4. Provide any additional comments or suggestions you think might be helpful (including red flags).

nutritious fitness drinks and targets sports enthusiasts. Its strategy is to place small restaurants, similar to smoothie restaurants, near large sports complexes. It is important to keep a concept statement relatively short (no more than one page) to increase the likelihood that it will be read.

Rather than developing a formal concept statement, some entrepreneurs conduct their initial product/service feasibility analysis by simply talking through their ideas with people or conducting focus groups to solicit feedback. Jeremy Jaech, the founder of Trumba.com, an online calendar service, talked through his idea with a number of people before he finalized his product design. In describing how his company conducted its initial product/service feasibility analysis, Jaech recalls:

> The first thing we (did) was to go out and talk to a lot of different people. We talked to about 25 couples about their calendaring, and what they did to manage all the different aspects of their lives. The first hurdle was determining if our idea held water with this broader group of people, what they were using today, and how difficult we thought it would be to switch them over to our solution.[4]

While not a complete approach, there is merit to the give-and-take that entrepreneurs like Jaech experience by talking with prospective customers rather than just handing them a concept statement and asking them to complete a questionnaire. The ideal combination is to do both—distribute a concept statement to 10 or more people who can provide informed feedback and engage in verbal give-and-take with as many industry experts and prospective customers as possible. Some entrepreneurs go to extraordinary lengths to talk about their product or service idea with others before deciding to move forward. Scott Dunlap, the founder of NearbyNow, which is the focus of Case 3.1, talked to over 2,000 people about his product idea before he incorporated his firm. NearbyNow enables shoppers to determine if stores in a mall have a specific item in their inventory.

Product/Service Demand   The second component of product/service feasibility analysis is to determine if there is demand for the product or service. There are two techniques for making this determination: administering a buying intentions survey and conducting library, Internet, and gumshoe research.

Learning Objective

5. Describe the purpose of a buying intentions survey and how it's administered.

Buying Intentions Survey   A **buying intentions survey** is an instrument that is used to gauge customer interest in a product or service. It consists of a concept statement or a similar description of a product or service with a short survey attached. The statement and survey should be distributed to 20 to 30 potential customers (people who completed the concept statement test should not be asked to complete this survey). Each participant should be asked to read the statement and complete the survey. The format for the survey is shown in Table 3.3.

To gauge customer interest, the number of people who indicate they definitely would buy is typically combined with the number of people who indicate they probably would buy. It's getting increasingly easy to administer buying intentions surveys. Internet sites like SurveyMonkey.com allow you to set up a small-scale (less than 100 respondents) survey for free or administer a larger survey for a small fee.[5]

One caveat is that people who say that they intend to purchase a product or service don't always follow through; as a result, the numbers resulting from this activity are almost always optimistic. The survey also doesn't normally tap a scientifically random sample. Still, the results give a potential entrepreneur a general sense of the degree of customer interest in the product or service idea. If the optional questions shown in Table 3.3 are included in the survey, additional insights can be obtained regarding pricing and sales and distribution.

Table 3.3 BUYING INTENTIONS SURVEY

*Distributed to a different group of people than those who completed
the initial concept statement test*

How likely would you be to buy the product or service described above, if we make it?

_____ Definitely would buy

_____ Probably would buy

_____ Might or might not buy

_____ Probably would not buy

_____ Definitely would not buy

Additional questions that are sometimes included in the survey:

How much would you be willing to pay for the product or service?

Where would you expect to find this product or service for sale?

One approach to finding qualified people to talk to about a product or service idea or to react to a concept statement is to contact trade associations and/or attend industry trade shows. If your product idea is in the digital media space, for example, you may be able to call the Digital Media Association (which is a national trade association devoted primarily to the online audio and video industries) and get a list of members who live in your area. Attending trade shows in the industry you're interested in will place you in direct contact with numerous people who might be of assistance. A Web site that provides a directory of trade associations is included in the Internet Resource Table in Appendix 3.2.

Library, Internet, and Gumshoe Research The second way to assess demand for a product or service idea is by conducting library, Internet, and gumshoe research. While administrating a buying intentions survey is important, more data is needed. Think of yourself as a lawyer preparing to defend a client in court. You can't just tell the jury that you "think" your client is innocent or that 25 out of 30 people you surveyed think that acquitting him is a good idea. The jury will want more evidence. So you have to dig it up. In a feasibility analysis context, you have a similar task. You have to accumulate evidence that there will be healthy demand for your product or service. Three important ways to do this are via library, Internet, and gumshoe research.

As mentioned in Chapter 2, reference librarians can often point you toward resources to help investigate a business idea, such as industry-specific magazines, trade journals, and industry reports. For example, the "You Be the VC 3.2" feature focuses on CADI Scientific, a Singapore-based start-up that is making SmartSense, a wireless patient monitoring system, which enhances patient care by continuously measuring vital medical data and transmitting the information to health practitioners. Sounds like a good idea. But "sounds like a good idea" isn't enough—we need facts to discern whether there is a demand for SmartSense units. What's the trajectory of the medical monitoring industry? What do industry experts say are the most important factors that health practitioners consider when they buy their medical equipment? Has this idea been tried before? If so, what were the results? Are there alternative solutions to tackle this problem of unobtrusive monitoring of patients in the hospital and in the home? If so, is this segment growing or shrinking? Is there a trade association for the makers of medical monitoring equipment that already has scads of statistics about market demand for such devices?

Learning Objective

6. Explain the importance of library, Internet, and gumshoe research.

A well-documented feasibility analysis usually requires library research to discern industry trends and collect other valuable information. Here, two college-aged entrepreneurs are utilizing the reference section of their university's library to document the demand for a product idea.

The overarching point is that for your particular product or service idea you need to accumulate evidence about likely demand. Your university or college library is a good place to start, and the Internet is a marvelous resource. By simply typing "market demand for patient monitoring systems" into the Google search box, we quickly found an article describing research in the U.S. market that bodes well for SmartSense. One survey from the United States, for example, found demand will grow by 5.9 percent every year through to 2012 and that growth in this sector was based on the ability of remote monitors to transmit data either online or over the telephone. This, and other surveys, tells us a lot about likely demand for SmartSense units, and it's just a start. Another report says the patient monitoring market in Europe is poised for robust growth in the years ahead. There is a wealth of information from around the globe.[6]

Simple gumshoe research is also important for gaining a sense of the likely demand for a product or service idea. A gumshoe is a detective or an investigator that scrounges around for information or clues wherever they can be found. Don't be bashful. Ask people what they think about your product or service idea. If your idea is to sell educational toys, spend a week volunteering at a day care center and watch how children interact with toys. Take the owner of a toy store to lunch and discuss your ideas. Spend some time browsing through toy stores and observe the types of toys that get the most attention. If you actually launch a business, there is simply too much at stake to rely on gut instincts and cursory information to assure you that your product or service will sell. Collect as much information as you can within reasonable time constraints.

Industry/Target Market Feasibility Analysis

Learning Objective

7. Describe the purpose of industry/market feasibility analysis and the two primary issues to consider in this area.

Industry/target market feasibility is an assessment of the overall appeal of the industry and the target market for the product or service being proposed. There is a distinct difference between a firm's industry and its target market, which should be clearly understood. An **industry** is a group of firms producing a similar product or service, such as computers, children's toys, airplanes, or tires. A firm's target market is the limited portion of the industry that it goes after or to which it wants to appeal. Most firms do not try to service their entire industry. Instead, they select or carve out a specific target market and try to service that market very well. SmartSense is not trying to target the entire medical equipment industry. Its target market is medical authorities that are looking for a more modern and patient-friendly care system.

There are two components to industry/target market feasibility analysis: industry attractiveness and target market attractiveness.

Industry Attractiveness   Industries vary in terms of their overall attractiveness.[7] In general, the most attractive industries have the characteristics depicted in Table 3.4. The top three factors are particularly important. Industries that are young rather than old, are early rather than late in their life cycle, and are fragmented rather than concentrated are more receptive to new entrants than industries with the opposite characteristics. You also want to pick an industry that is structurally attractive—meaning start-ups can enter the industry (in various target markets) and compete. Some industries are characterized by such high barriers to entry or the presence of one or two dominant players that potential new entrants are essentially shut out.

Learning Objective

8. Discuss the characteristics of an attractive industry.

Other factors are also important. For example, the degree to which environmental and business trends are moving in favor rather than against the industry are important for the industry's long-term health and its capacity to spawn new target or niche markets. Are changing economic and societal trends helping or hurting industry incumbents? Are profit margins increasing or falling? Is innovation accelerating or waning? Are input costs going up or down? Are new markets for the industry's staple products opening up or are current markets being shut down by competing industries? You can't cover every facet of an industry; but you should gain a sense of whether the industry you're entering is a good one or a poor one for start-ups.

Information that addresses each of these issues is available via industry reports published by IBISWorld, Mintel, Standard & Poor's NetAdvantage, and similar fee-based databases that are typically free if assessed through a university or large public library's Web site. These resources are listed in the Internet Resource Table in Appendix 3.2. The First Screen, which is the feasibility analysis template included in Appendix 3.1, includes a section that draws attention to the most important issues to focus on regarding industry attractiveness during the feasibility analysis stage of investigating a business idea.

Target Market Attractiveness   As mentioned, a target market is a place within a larger market segment that represents a narrower group of customers with similar needs. Most start-ups simply don't have the resources needed to participate in a broad market, at least initially. Instead, by focusing on a

Table 3.4   CHARACTERISTICS OF ATTRACTIVE INDUSTRIES

- Are young rather than old
- Are early rather than late in their life cycle
- Are fragmented rather than concentrated
- Are growing rather than shrinking
- Sell products or services that customers "must have" rather than "want to have"
- Are not crowded
- Have high rather than low operating margins
- Are not highly dependent on the historically low price of a key raw material, like gasoline or flour, to remain profitable

smaller target market, a firm can usually avoid head-to-head competition with industry leaders and can focus on serving a specialized market very well. It's also not realistic, in most cases, for a start-up to introduce a completely original product idea into a completely new market. In most instances, it's just too expensive to be a pioneer in each area. Most successful start-ups either introduce a new product into an existing market (like SmartSense introducing monitoring equipment into the existing medical market) or introduce a new market to an existing product.

The challenge in identifying an attractive target market is to find a market that's large enough for the proposed business but is yet small enough to avoid attracting larger competitors at least until the entrepreneurial venture can get off to a successful start. An example of a company that has targeted a market that meets these criteria is Dogster, a social networking site for dog owners and the subject of Case 10.1. The site allows its users to create profiles for their dogs, participate in dog-related forums, post photos and video clips of their dogs, and perform a number of other activities. The site, which was started in 2004 with its sister site Catster, now has more than 500,000 profiles of dogs and cats. In October 2008, it exceeded 1 million page views for a single month. It makes money by placing ads on its sites and has attracted blue-chip advertisers like Netflix, Disney, and Target.[8] Although Dogster operates in the $38 billion pet industry, it has carved out a specialized target or niche market for itself and is profitable. It has gotten off to a good start largely because it has remained laser-focused on a clearly defined target market (social networking for dog and cat owners) within a larger industry.

While it's generally easy to find good information to assess the attractiveness of an entire industry, discerning the attractiveness of a small target market within an industry is tougher, particularly if the start-up is pioneering the target market. Often, under these circumstances, information from more than one industry and/or market must be collected and synthesized to make an informed judgment. For example, H2OAudio, first introduced in Chapter 2, makes waterproof housings for the iPod and the iPod nano. The waterproof housings permit iPod users to listen to their iPods while swimming, surfing, skiing, or engaging in any activity where the iPod might get wet. The question for a product like this is what market to assess? There are no SIC (Standard Industrial Classification) or NAICS (North American Industry Classification System) codes for the "waterproof iPod housing" industry or market. Obviously, a combination of markets must be studied, including the MP3 or iPod market, the iPod accessory market, and the market for water and snow sports. It would be important to not only know how well iPod accessories are selling but also what the current trends in water and snow sports are. If iPod accessories are selling like hotcakes but water and snow sports are on a sharp decline, the target market that H2OAudio is pioneering would be much less attractive than if iPods were selling well and interest in water sports and snow sports were rapidly increasing.

The sources of information to mine and tap are also not as transparent when investigating target market attractiveness opposed to industry attractiveness. Say you wanted to piggyback on H2OAudio's idea and create super-durable airtight housings (which are near indestructible and don't allow any dirt or dust in) for iPhones for people who participate in extreme sports (i.e., mountain biking, hang-gliding, skateboarding, motocross, etc.). How to best assess the attractiveness of this target market is not entirely clear. Table 3.5 includes a list of suggestions, which illustrates the type of creativity that's required to find information on a narrowly defined target market. Ultimately, it will require a synthesis of data and facts collected from various sources to get a sense of whether creating super-durable airtight housings for iPhones for extreme sports participants is an attractive target market. You'll need to construct a similar list of potential sources of information to

Table 3.5 POTENTIAL SOURCES OF INFORMATION TO ASSESS TARGET MARKET ATTRACTIVENESS FOR SUPER-DURABLE AIRTIGHT iPHONE HOUSINGS FOR EXTREME SPORTS PARTICIPANTS

- Type "iPhone accessories industry" into the Google or Yahoo! search bar to gain general information about the trajectory of iPhone accessory sales.
- Go to a site that reviews or sells iPhone accessories, such as iPhoneGold.org, and see if a similar product is already for sale. If it is, go to the company's' Web site to see what evidence it reports about market attractiveness. This company may have already done much of your work for you.
- Try to determine if there is a trade association or an annual trade show for iPhone accessories manufacturers and the manufacturers of extreme sports clothing and gear. Contact the relevant organizations to ask if they have data that might be helpful.
- Search for newspaper and magazine articles on iPhone accessories using public search engines such as Find Articles (www.findarticles.com) and MagPortal (www.magportal.com), and more powerful search engines such as ProQuest and LexisNexis Academic, which are usually available through a university or large public library Web site.
- Search newspaper and magazine articles on extreme sports, looking specifically for how extreme sport enthusiasts protect the products they carry while participating in their sport. Search engines are also getting extremely smart. Try entering into Google, Yahoo!, or ProQuest "iPhone accessories + extreme sports" and see what happens.
- Contact a company that focuses on extreme sports to ask for leads in finding industry-wide sales data and to ask if super-durable airtight housings for iPhones currently exist. If they don't, ask if it would carry the product if it were available (you might even get your first customer this way). Don't be shy. Adrenalina, which is a retail chain that specializes in extreme sports clothing and gear (and is also the focus of "You Be the VC 14.1"), lists the phone numbers and e-mail addresses of each of its retail stores and its corporate office right on its Web site.

assess the attractiveness of the target market your product or service will attempt to appeal to.

Organizational Feasibility Analysis

Organizational feasibility analysis is conducted to determine whether a proposed business has sufficient management expertise, organizational competence, and resources to successfully launch its business.[9] There are two primary issues to consider in this area: management prowess and resource sufficiency.

Learning Objective

9. Describe the purpose of organizational feasibility analysis and list the two primary issues to consider in this area.

An important part of organizational feasibility analysis is assessing the degree of passion that a sole entrepreneur or team of entrepreneurs has for a business idea. A good indication of passion is the willingness of a young team to do what it takes to complete a sound feasibility analysis for a business idea.

Triangle Images/Getty Images-Digital Vision

Management Prowess   A proposed business should evaluate the prowess, or ability, of its initial management team, whether it is a sole entrepreneur or a larger group.[10] This task requires the individuals starting the firm to be honest and candid in their self-assessments. Two of the most important factors in this area are the passion that the solo entrepreneur or the management team has for the business idea and the extent to which the management team or solo entrepreneur understands the markets in which the firm will participate.[11] There are no practical substitutes for strengths in these areas.[12]

A collection of additional factors help define management prowess. Managers with extensive professional and social networks have an advantage in that they are able to reach out to colleagues and friends to help them plug experience or knowledge gaps. In addition, a potential new venture should have an idea of the type of new-venture team that it can assemble. A **new-venture team** is the group of founders, key employees, and advisers that either manage or help manage a new business in its start-up years. If the founder or founders of a new venture have identified several individuals they believe will join the firm after it is launched and these individuals are highly capable, that knowledge lends credibility to the organizational feasibility of the potential venture. The same rationale applies for highly capable people who a new venture believes would be willing to join its board of directors or board of advisers.

One thing that many potential business founders find while assessing management prowess is that they may benefit from finding one or more partners to help them launch their business. Tips for finding an appropriate business partner are provided in the "Partnering for Success" boxed feature.

Resource Sufficiency   The second area of organizational feasibility analysis is to determine whether the proposed venture has or is capable of obtaining sufficient resources to move forward. The focus in organizational feasibility analysis is on nonfinancial resources. The objective is to identify the most important nonfinancial resources and assess whether they are available. An example is a start-up that will require employees with specialized skills. If a firm launches in a community that does not have a labor pool that includes people with the skill sets the firm needs, a serious resources sufficiency problem exists.

Another key resource sufficiency issue is the ability to obtain intellectual property protection on key aspects of the business. This issue doesn't apply to all start-ups but is critical to companies that have invented a new product or are introducing a new business process that adds value to the way a product is manufactured or a service is delivered. For example, Laura Udall, introduced in the "Savvy Entrepreneurial Firm" boxed feature in Chapter 2, invented ZUCA, a new type of backpack for kids that is on rollers and is sturdy enough that a child can sit on it (on a built-in seat) while waiting for the school bus. ZUCA Inc. has two utility patents and two design patents on its backpacks. If there was nothing unique or distinct enough about Udall's backpacks to make patent protection possible, then creating ZUCA would have been riskier because a larger competitor could create exact duplicates of ZUCA backpacks if they were a hit.

A resource sufficiency issue that varies in importance depending on the type of business that is being contemplated is the availability of an appropriate and affordable location to operate from. This issue is expounded on in the Savvy Entrepreneurial boxed feature.

To test resource sufficiency, a firm should list the 6 to 12 most critical nonfinancial resources that it will need to move its business idea forward and determine if those resources are available.

Partnering for SUCCESS
Finding the Right Business Partner

One thing that becomes clear to many potential business founders, while conducting organizational feasibility analysis, is that they need one or more partners to help launch their business. You might be a Web developer who has a great idea for a Web 2.0 cooking site, for example, but have no experience in marketing or sales. In this instance, you may need to find a partner with marketing and sales experience to successfully launch and run the firm. There are five key criteria to look for in a business partner. You want to get this right because picking the wrong partner or partners can lead to a lot of heartaches and business challenges.

1. Know the skills and experiences you need. Make an honest assessment of the skills and experience you bring to the business and the gaps that remain. Pick someone who fills the gaps. For example, if you're an experienced Web designer you probably don't want to partner with another experienced Web designer. Pick someone who brings other competencies that you need to the venture, like marketing or finance.
2. Make sure your personalities and work habits are compatible. While you don't need someone who is just like yourself, you do need to be comfortable with the person you'll be in business with. For example, if you'd rather work 16 hours a day if that is what it takes to finish a project on time, and your partner would rather quit after 8 hours a day and try to renegotiate the due date for the project, that difference in work styles will invariably cause conflict. Similarly, if you like to wear a coat and tie when meeting with clients and your partner thinks wearing blue jeans is fine, obvious disagreements could arise.
3. Make sure you and your partner have common goals and aspirations. Be sure that you and your partner are shooting for the same target. For example, if your goal is to build a billion-dollar company but your partner would be perfectly satisfied growing the company to $10 million in sales and then selling out, obvious problems could ensue.

4. Look in the right places. If you don't have someone already in mind, it's important to know where to look for a potential partner. Generic networking events, like Chamber of Commerce mixers, are usually ineffective for finding a business partner. Instead, if you're looking for an engineer, contact engineering trade associations for leads or attend engineering trade fairs. Social networking sites for professionals, like LinkedIn, can be an effective way to make contacts. There are also Web sites, like PartnerUp (www.partnerup.com), that help people identify business partners.
5. Hire a lawyer. When you have identified a potential partner and you're confident that the criteria shown previously have been satisfied, you should hire a lawyer to sit down with the two (or more) of you to help hammer out the details. You should decide what each partner will contribute to the business, how the equity in the business will be split, what form of business ownership to select, what each partner's role in the company will be, and so forth. It's important to hire someone who's not loyal to any specific partner (even if it's you). Hire someone who is impartial and everyone feels good about.

Questions for Critical Thinking

1. Think about your personality and work habits. What type of person (in terms of personality and work habits) do you think you'd work well with and what type of person do you think you'd be in constant conflict with?
2. Do you think it's a good idea or a bad idea to form a business partnership with a close friend? How could you go about discerning if a good friend would make for a good business partner?
3. Provide some suggestions, other than those mentioned in the feature, for places (online or offline) for finding a business partner.
4. Spend some time looking at PartnerUp. To what extent would you be comfortable using this service to try to locate a business partner?

Financial Feasibility Analysis

Financial feasibility analysis is the final component of a comprehensive feasibility analysis. For feasibility analysis, a preliminary financial assessment is usually sufficient. More rigor at this point is typically not required because the specifics of the business will inevitably evolve, making it impractical to spend a lot of time early on preparing detailed financial forecasts.

Learning Objective

10. Explain the importance of financial feasibility analysis and list the most critical issues to consider in this area.

Savvy Entrepreneurial FIRM

A Business's Location: A Resource that Varies in Importance Depending on the Type of Business

A factor that's important to some businesses in the feasibility analysis stage is whether an appropriate location is available at an affordable cost. For some businesses location is key while for others it's not. For example, many service businesses, such as plumbers, electricians, and mail-order companies, don't maintain a storefront so their physical location isn't a major issue. In fact, these businesses often seek out nondescript locations to economize on costs. In contrast, location is an extremely crucial issue for retail stores, certain service businesses and professional practices (like doctor's offices) that deal directly with the public.

If Location Is Important, What Type of Location Will Work the Best?

If location is important, the first step is to determine what type of location is suitable for the business you're considering. Start by asking yourself the following questions:

- Will my customers come on foot, or will they drive and need a place to park?
- Will more customers come if the business is located near other similar businesses?
- Will more customers come if the business is located near complementary businesses?
- Do the demographics of the trade area the business will be located in make a difference?

Answering these four questions can go a long way in helping you determine if an appropriate location is available. For example, if you're opening an urban bagel shop or a similar type of business, you'll want to locate in an area that has a high amount of foot traffic. In contrast, if you're opening an auto parts store or a convenience store, you'll want to be on a busy street where the store can be seen by drivers who can pull into your parking lot. In terms of being near similar businesses, clothing stores and jewelry stores, for example, often benefit by being near similar businesses, since people like to comparison shop. A hair salon or barber shop, where comparison shopping isn't as much of an issue, may do better by itself. Some businesses benefit by locating near a big box store like Wal-Mart or Home Depot, because their customer bases are similar and they benefit from the increased traffic. An example is Sally's Beauty Supply, which appears in 26 percent of U.S. Wal-Mart-anchored shopping centers.

Another important issue is whether the demographic makeup of a trade area is suitable for a particular business. A high-end clothing boutique, for example, needs to be in an affluent area. Stores that sell children's clothing do better in areas with a high percentage of young families than in areas with a high percentage of retirement-age people. You can obtain the demographic breakdown of most communities census bureau Web sites.

How Much Will It Cost?

The second thing to find out is how much the appropriate location will cost. This is a tough issue, because the best locations are typically the most expensive. Most businesses that aren't home-based businesses rent or lease property rather than build or buy, which reduces the cost some. The best way to determine the rental or lease rates for a particular area is to talk to a real estate broker or agent. At the feasibility analysis stage, you may not be able to make a final call regarding whether the lease rates you're hearing are affordable. But it's another piece of information that will help you gain a sense of whether a particular business opportunity is feasible. Knowing the cost of a good location also helps a prospective business establish priorities. In some cases, a business, like an urban bagel shop, may opt to dedicate resources to a prime location, and cut back in other areas, like on computer equipment and the restaurant's décor.

Questions for Critical Thinking

1. Think of a business that you believe has an exceptionally good location and a business that has a poor location. Briefly explain how the good location benefits the business you're thinking about and how the poor location hurts the other business.
2. Use either American FactFinder or City-Data.com to study the demographic makeup of the community in which your college of university is located. If your college or university is located in a city, analyze the area of the city that surrounds your college or university. Report the key findings from your search.
3. Other than Sally's Beauty Shop, name several businesses that may benefit from being located near a big-box store, like Wal-Mart, Target, or

Costco. Name several businesses that would be at a disadvantage in similar circumstances.

4. If you were thinking about opening an urban bagel shop and found a location you felt was appropriate and affordable, what factors would you consider to determine whether the building itself was feasible for your business? For example, buildings that contain

restaurants often have to be vented in a particular way or have special plumbing or electrical work in place.

Sources: Adapted from B. Barringer, *The Truth About Starting a Business* (Upper Saddle River, NJ: Financial Times, 2009); S. McLinden, "Who's Afraid of the Giant," Shopping Centers Today, June 2006, http://www.icsc.org/srch/sct/sct0606/cozy_walmart.php.

The most important issues to consider at this stage are total start-up cash needed, financial performance of similar businesses, and the overall financial attractiveness of the proposed venture.

If a proposed new venture moves beyond the feasibility analysis stage, it will need to complete pro forma (or projected) financial statements that demonstrate the firm's financial viability for the first one to three years of its existence. In Chapter 8, we'll provide you with specific instructions for preparing these statements.

Total Start-Up Cash Needed   This first issue refers to the total cash needed to prepare the business to make its first sale. An actual budget should be prepared that lists all the anticipated capital purchases and operating expenses needed to get the business up and running. After determining a total figure, an explanation of where the money will come from should be provided. Avoid cursory explanations such as "I plan to bring investors on board" or "I'll borrow the money." Although you may ultimately involve investors or lenders in your business, a more thoughtful account is required of how you'll provide for your initial cash needs. We'll cover funding and financing in Chapter 10.

If the money will come from friends and family or is raised through other means, such as credit cards or a home equity line of credit, a reasonable plan should be stipulated to repay the money. Showing how a new venture's start-up costs will be covered and repaid is an important issue. Many new ventures look promising as ongoing concerns but have no way of raising the money to get started or are never able to recover from the initial costs involved. When projecting start-up expenses, it is better to overestimate rather than underestimate the costs involved. Murphy's Law is prevalent in the start-up world—things will go wrong. It is a rare start-up that doesn't experience some unexpected expenses during the start-up phase.

There are worksheets posted online that help entrepreneurs determine the start-up costs to launch their respective businesses. Start-up cost worksheets are available via SCORE (www.score.org) and the Small Business Administration (www.sba.gov).

Financial Performance of Similar Businesses   The second component of financial feasibility analysis is estimating a proposed start-up's potential financial performance by comparing it to similar, already established businesses. Obviously, this effort will result in approximate rather than exact numbers. There are several ways of doing this, all of which involve a little gumshoe labor.

First, substantial archival data is available online, which offers detailed financial reports on thousands of individual firms. The easiest data to obtain is on publicly traded firms through Hoovers or a similar source. These firms are typically too large, however, for meaningful comparisons to proposed new ventures. The trick is to find the financial performance of small, more comparable firms. Samples of Web sites that are helpful in this regard are provided in the Internet Resource table in Appendix 3.2. Both IBISWorld and Mintel provide data on the average sales and profitability for the firms in the industries they track. For example, IBISWorld reports that the average music store makes a pre-tax profit of 6 percent of revenues. Guitar Center makes 8 percent.[13] This means if you were thinking about opening a music store and projected $300,000 in first-year revenues, you could expect profits of around $18,000 unless you exceeded the industry average. Reference USA provides revenue estimates for many private firms, but fewer libraries subscribe to its service. (This resource is more commonly available at large city libraries.) On the expense side, a very useful Web site is BizStats.com, where an entrepreneur can type in the projected revenue of his or her firm, by industry classification, and receive a mock income statement in return that shows the average profitability and expense percentages of U.S. businesses in the same category. IBISWorld also normally provides a chart of the average expenses (as a percentage of sales) for major items like wages, rent, office and administrative expenses, and utilities for firms in the industries they follow. Another source to help estimate a firm's sales and net profit is BizMiner (www.bizminer.com). BizMiner provides a printout of the average sales and profitability for firms in the industries they follow and provides more detail than similar reports. BizMiner is a fee-based site, and the reports cost between $69 and $99.[14]

There are additional ways to obtain financial data on smaller firms. If a start-up entrepreneur identifies a business that is similar to the one he or she wants to start, and the business isn't likely to be a direct competitor, it's not inappropriate to ask the owner or manager of the business to share sales and income data. Even if the owner or manager is only willing to talk in general terms (i.e., our annual sales are in the $3 million range, and we're netting around 9 percent of sales), that information is certainly better than nothing. Simply Internet, ProQuest, and LexisNexis Academic searches are also helpful. If you're interested in the sports apparel industry, simply typing "sports apparel industry sales" and "sports apparel industry profitability" will invariably result in links to stories about sports apparel companies that will mention their sales and profitability.

A final way to obtain sales data for similar businesses is through simple observation and legwork. This approach is suitable in some cases and in others it isn't. For example, if you were proposing to open a new smoothie shop, you could gauge the type of sales to expect by estimating the number of people, along with the average purchase per visit, who patronize similar smoothie shops in your area. A very basic way to do this is to frequent these stores and count the number of customers who come in and out of the stores during various times of the day.

Overall Financial Attractiveness of the Proposed Venture   A number of other factors are associated with evaluating the financial attractiveness of a proposed venture. These evaluations are based primarily on a new venture's projected sales and rate of return (or profitability), as just discussed. At the feasibility analysis stage, the projected return is a judgment call. A more precise estimation can be computed by preparing pro forma (or projected) financial statements, including one- to three-year pro forma statements of cash flow, income statements, and balance sheets (along with accompanying financial ratios). This work can be done if time and circumstances allow, but is typically done at the business plan stage rather than the feasibility analysis stage of a new venture's development.

To gain perspective, a start-up's projected rate of return should be weighed against the following factors to assess whether the venture is financially feasible.

■ The amount of capital invested

■ The risks assumed in launching the business

■ The existing alternatives for the money being invested

■ The existing alternatives for the entrepreneur's time and efforts

Table 3.6 FINANCIAL FEASIBILITY

- Steady and rapid growth in sales during the first five to seven years in a clearly defined market niche
- High percentage of recurring revenue—meaning that once a firm wins a client, the client will provide recurring sources of revenue
- Ability to forecast income and expenses with a reasonable degree of certainty
- Internally generated funds to finance and sustain growth
- Availability of an exit opportunity (such as an acquisition or an initial public offering) for investors to convert equity into cash

As promising as they seem on the surface, some opportunities simply may not be worth it financially. For example, it makes no economic sense for a group of entrepreneurs to invest $10 million in a capital-intense risky start-up that offers a 5 percent rate of return. Five percent interest can be earned through a money market fund with essentially no risk. The adequacy of returns also depends on the alternatives the individuals involved have. For example, an individual who is thinking about leaving a $150,000-per-year job to start a new firm requires a higher rate of return than the person thinking about leaving a $50,000-per-year job.[15]

Other factors used to weigh the overall financial attractiveness of a new business are listed in Table 3.6.

First Screen

First Screen, shown in Appendix 3.1, is a template for completing a feasibility analysis. It is called First Screen because a feasibility analysis is an entrepreneur's (or a group of entrepreneurs') initial pass at determining the feasibility of a business idea. If a business idea cuts muster at this stage, the next step is to complete a business plan.

The mechanics for filling out the First Screen worksheet are straightforward. It maps the four areas of feasibility analysis described in the chapter, accentuating the most important points in each area. The final section of the worksheet, "Overall Potential," includes a section that allows for suggested revisions to a business idea to improve its potential or feasibility. For example, a business might start out planning to manufacture its own product, but through the process of completing First Screen, learn that the capital needed to set up a manufacturing facility is prohibitive in terms of both the money that would need to be raised and the extended time to break even for the business. As a result, two of five items in Part 5, "Initial Capital Investment" and "Time to Break Even," might be rated "low potential." This doesn't need to be the end of the story, however. In the column labeled "Suggestions for Improving the Potential," the founders of the business might write, "Consider contract manufacturing or outsourcing as an alternative to manufacturing the product ourselves." The value of the First Screen worksheet is that it draws attention to issues like this one and forces the founders to think about alternatives. If this particular suggestion is realistic and is determined to be a better way to proceed, a revised version of First Screen might rate the two factors referred to previously, "Initial Capital Requirements" and "Time to Break Even," as "high potential" rather than "low potential" because of the change in the business concept that was made. Business ideas, at the feasibility analysis stage, should always be seen as fluid and subject to change. Little is lost if several versions of First Screen are completed for the same business idea, however, there is much more to be lost if a start-up gets half way through writing a business plan and concludes that the business isn't feasible, or actually launches a business without having all the kinks worked out.

Although completing First Screen does take some research and analysis, it is not meant to be a lengthy process. It is also not meant to be a shot in the dark. The best ideas are ones that emerge from analysis that is based on facts and good information, rather than speculation and guesses, as emphasized throughout the chapter. Appendix 3.2 contains the Internet Resource Table that may be particularly helpful in completing a First Screen analysis. It is well worth your time to learn how to use these resources—they are rich in terms of their content and analysis.

It's important to be completely candid when completing First Screen for your business idea. No business scores "high potential" on every item. There is also no definitive way of discerning, after the worksheet is completed, if an idea is feasible. First Screen, like the feasibility analysis itself, is meant to convey an overall impression or sense of the feasibility of a business idea.*

Chapter Summary

1. Feasibility analysis is the process of determining whether a business idea is viable. It is a preliminary evaluation of a business idea, conducted for the purpose of determining whether the idea is worth pursuing.

2. The proper time to conduct a feasibility analysis is early in thinking through the prospects for a new business idea. It follows opportunity recognition but comes before the development of a business plan.

3. Product/service feasibility analysis is an assessment of the overall appeal of the product or service being proposed. The two components of product/service feasibility analysis are product desirability and product demand.

4. A concept statement is a preliminary description of a product idea.

5. Two techniques for determining the likely demand for a product or service are administering a buying intentions survey and conducting library, Internet, and gumshoe research.

6. Industry/market feasibility analysis is an assessment of the overall appeal of the market for the product or service being proposed. For feasibility analysis, there are two primary issues that a business should consider in this area: industry attractiveness and target market attractiveness.

7. A target market is a place within a larger market segment that represents a narrower group of customers with similar needs. Most start-ups simply don't have the resources needed to participate in a broad market, at least initially. Instead, by focusing on a smaller target market a firm can usually avoid head-to-head competition with industry leaders and can focus on serving a specialized market very well.

8. Organizational feasibility analysis is conducted to determine whether a proposed business has sufficient management expertise, organizational competence, and resources to successfully launch its business. There are two primary issues to consider in this area: management prowess and resource sufficiency.

9. Financial feasibility analysis is a preliminary financial analysis of whether a business idea is worth pursuing. The most important areas to consider are the total start-up cash needed, financial performance of similar businesses, and the overall financial attractiveness of the proposed business.

*Copies of the First Screen worksheet, in both MS Word and PDF format, are available at www.pearsonglobaleditions.com/barringer.

10. First Screen is a template for completing a feasibility analysis. It is called First Screen because a feasibility analysis is an entrepreneur's (or group of entrepreneurs') initial pass at determining the feasibility of a business idea.

Key Terms

buying intentions survey, **108**
concept statement, **106**
concept test, **106**
feasibility analysis, **102**
financial feasibility analysis, **115**
follow-me-home testing, **128**

industry, **110**
industry/market feasibility analysis, **113**
new-venture team, **114**
organizational feasibility analysis, **113**

primary research, **103**
product/service feasibility analysis, **105**
secondary research, **103**

Review Questions

1. What is a feasibility analysis? What is it designed to accomplish?
2. Briefly describe each of the four areas that a properly executed feasibility analysis explores.
3. What is a product/service feasibility analysis?
4. Describe the difference between primary research and secondary research.
5. What is a concept statement?
6. What is a buying intentions survey, and what does it accomplish?
7. What are the two ways that entrepreneurs assess the likely product demand for the proposed product or service they are analyzing?
8. What is gumshoe research in the context of product/service feasibility analysis?
9. What is industry/target market feasibility analysis?
10. Describe the attributes of an attractive industry for a new venture.
11. What is a target market? Why do most start-ups focus on relatively small target markets to begin with rather than larger markets with more substantial demand?
12. What are some of the ways to determine the attractiveness of a small target market within a larger industry?
13. What is organizational feasibility analysis?
14. Briefly describe each of the two primary issues to consider when conducting an organizational feasibility analysis.
15. What is a new venture team?
16. What is financial feasibility analysis?
17. Identify and briefly describe the three separate components of financial feasibility analysis.
18. What are some of the techniques a start-up can use to estimate its potential financial performance by comparing it to similar, already established businesses?
19. What are some factors that make a potential start-up attractive from an overall financial perspective?
20. What is the purpose of a First Screen analysis?

Application Questions

1. Ann Myers, a friend of yours, just told you an interesting story. She was at her parents' house over the weekend and her father saw this book lying next to her backpack. He pickup it up and read Chapter 3. He told Ann, "When you were growing up, I started and sold three successful businesses

and never completed a feasibility analysis once. I wonder what the authors of your entrepreneurship book would say about that." If you could advise Ann about how to respond to her father, what would you tell her to say?

2. Jason Willis just applied for a bank loan to finance a sporting goods store that he plans to open. The banker asked Jason if he conducted any primary research to assess the feasibility of the store, and Jason replied that he spent countless evenings and weekends in the library and on the Internet collecting data on the feasibility of sporting good stores, and he is confident that his store will be successful. He said that he even did careful research to make sure that sporting goods stores do well in demographic areas that are similar to the area where he plans to open his store. If you were the banker, how would you react to Jason's statement?

3. Assume that you were one of the recipients of New Venture Fitness Drink's concept statement. What type of feedback would you have given the company about the viability of its product idea?

4. Shelly Mills, who has considerable experience in the home security industry, is planning to launch a firm that will sell a new line of home security alarms that she believes will be superior to anything currently on the market. Shelly knows how to develop a concept statement and administer a buying intentions survey but is less clear about the type of library and Internet research that might be helpful in assessing the likely demand for her product. If Shelly turned to you for help, what would you tell her?

5. Assess the industry attractiveness for the industry that Freedirectory-enquiries, the subject of the "You Be the VC 2.1" feature at the end of Chapter 2, will be participating in.

6. Skip ahead to Chapter 4 and look at the "You Be the VC 4.2" feature, which focuses on Icon Aircraft. How would you access the likely demand for Icon's initial aircraft?

7. Carrie Wells is planning to open a store to sell DVDs in Nashville. As part of her feasibility study, she hands out a questionnaire to 500 people in her trade area, asking them to indicate whether they would shop at her store. Carrie is pleased to find that 75 percent of the people surveyed said they would either "definitely" or "probably" shop in her store at least once a month. Should Carrie plan her business based on the 75 percent figure? Why or why not?

8. Recently, you were telling a friend about Intuit, in particular about the company's "follow-me-home" usability testing methodology. This methodology is discussed in Case 3.2 in this chapter. To help you prepare your answer to this question, skip ahead to read about this methodology in Case 3.2. Your friend, who plans to launch a business to sell and make modifications on all-terrain vehicles (ATVs), was intrigued by the story. Describe how your friend could use the follow-me-home methodology to improve the quality of usability testing for his business.

9. Steve Ambrose, who is a physical therapist, is thinking about starting a firm in the medical instruments industry. He would like to know more about the industry, however, before proceeding. Provide Steve with suggestions for conducting primary and secondary research on the industry.

10. Pete Campbell, a classmate of yours, is completing the "management prowess" portion of a feasibility analysis he is conducting for an Internet business he plans to start. Pete is an excellent Web designer and programmer, but doesn't have any experience in marketing or finance. Pete is wondering about his options for plugging these competency gaps. What would you tell him?

11. What do you think were the 8 to 10 most important nonfinancial resources that the founders of DanceJam, the subject of the "You Be the VC 3.1" feature, needed to have in place before they launched their new venture?

12. Some neighbors of yours are hoping to open a Thai restaurant near an industrial area of the city you live in. They have a limited budget so it is

very important to them to have as good of an idea as possible of what their total start-up costs will be. How would you recommend that they estimate the total start-up costs of opening the restaurant?

13. Look at the Web site of Rufus Shirts, a company that was launched by first-time entrepreneur April Singer and makes high-end shirts for men. During the financial feasibility analysis stage of the process of investigating the merits of her new venture, how could Singer have gone about estimating the financial performance of Rufus Shirts by comparing it to similar, existing businesses?

14. What are some of the red flags that would suggest that the overall financial attractiveness of a proposed new venture is poor?

15. A friend of yours just completed a First Screen analysis for an e-commerce site that she hoped to launch to sell horse riding supplies, including saddles, tack, lead ropes, and feed buckets. She's disappointed because she rated 10 of the 25 items on First Screen as either low or moderate potential. She says to you, "Well that's that. Good thing I completed a feasibility analysis. I sure don't want to start that business." Is your friend right?

You Be the VC 3.1

Company: DanceJam

http://dancejam.com

Business Idea: To create a social media destination for people interested in being entertained by dance, having fun with dance, competing in dance, and wanting to learn how to dance.

Pitch: DanceJam is all things dance. It's a social media Internet destination, created by rap star M.C. Hammer, which allows people to enjoy and participate in all facets of dance. On the site, dancers can upload videos of themselves dancing, watch other people dance, slow down videos to learn new dance moves, and compete in dance contests. Visitors can also search by type of dance or search geographically to find videos of specific dances or dancers they're interested in. To create excitement and attract new users, DanceJam plans to sponsor dance tournaments on a continual basis. For example, at the time of this writing, DanceJam was promoting a tournament where users could enter and vote on tournament brackets for things like "Best Choreography." The winners earn cash prizes. Similar contests, tournaments, and special events are in the works.

DanceJam is also forging partnerships within the entertainment industry to create additional buzz for its site. For example, it formed a partnership with Janet Jackson to host auditions for one of her reality shows. Contestants were instructed to submit their audition videos on DanceJam's Web site. For the user interested in the day-to-day features of DanceJam's site,

there is plenty available. Users can upload videos of themselves, allow viewers to rate them, and index videos of others. In addition, the site provides demonstrations and information on a wide variety of dances. All genres of dance are included—from break dancing, to rap, to hip hop, to line dancing, to ballet. Forums are provided for people to post information and talk about the genre of dance they're interested in. DanceJam also hopes to use other social networks' success to fuel its growth. DanceJam users will be able to embed videos of themselves dancing on Facebook, MySpace, and similar sites.

DanceJam plans to make money via online advertising. Dance is considered to be on the rise in the United States. For example, the YouTube video "Evolution of Dance" has been viewed more times than any video on the site (watch this video if you haven't already done so—it's really entertaining). The television show *Dancing with the Stars* is also contributing to a resurgence of interest in dance.

Q&A: Based on the material covered in this chapter, what questions would you ask the firm's founders before making your funding decision? What answers would satisfy you?

Decision: If you had to make your decision on just the information provided in the pitch and on the company's Web site, would you fund this company? Why or why not?

You Be the VC 3.2
Company: CADI Scientific—SmartSense
www.cadi.com.sg

Business Idea: Produce and sell the first wireless patient monitoring system, enhancing patient care by continuously measuring vital medical data and transmitting the information to health practitioners.

Pitch: Monitoring a sick patient can be a delicate balancing act. Although the patient needs uninterrupted sleep to aid with recovery, medical staff must also regularly check vital signs such as temperature and blood pressure. The two needs are not always fine bedfellows.

Four entrepreneurial scientists have come up with a solution: a wireless gadget called SmartSense, which is now being used in hospitals in Singapore, Bangkok, Taipei, and the Middle East. The 1.2-inch wide SmartSense is taped to a patient's body to continuously measure vital signs. Radio frequency technology then transfers the data wirelessly via ceiling-mounted transmitters to computers in the nurses' station.

The inspiration for the idea came out of a coffee break conversation between CADI Scientific founder Zenton Goh and a colleague. The colleague had a sick child and said he and his wife were waking the infant every two hours through the night to take her temperature. Goh thought of the idea of an automated wireless sensing system to monitor a baby's body temperature,

so that both parents and children could enjoy uninterrupted sleep. The idea evolved into SmartSense.

Nurses can now dispense with the task of manually checking temperatures and blood pressure every few hours, and patients get an uninterrupted rest. SmartSense also cuts down on any possibility of human error in the checks and reduces nurses' workloads. Doctors also can check on the data on-the-go via WiFi-enabled digital assistants, or on PCs anywhere in the hospital.

Another bonus to introducing this system into crowded wards is it is now very easy to quickly spot clusters of patients developing a fever at the same time. At a time of growing incidences of hospital-acquired infections, this is an important early warning signal. Plans are also underway to introduce a consumer version of SmartSense, which can monitor temperature and blood pressure at home.

Q&A: Based on the material covered in this chapter, what questions would you ask the firm's founders before making your funding decision? What answers would satisfy you?

Decision: If you had to make your decision on just the information provided in the pitch and on the company's Web site, would you fund this company? Why or why not?

CASE3.1

NearbyNow: Hands-On Product Feasibility Analysis
www.nearbynow.com

Bruce R. Barringer
Oklahoma State University
R. Duane Ireland
Texas A & M University

Introduction

In mid-2006 Scott Dunlap accompanied his wife on a trip to the mall. Dunlap's wife saw a pair of UGG boots she liked in a magazine, and was taking the magazine from store to store to see if they had the boots. Dunlap wanted out of there—he wasn't a shopper. He wondered, "Why isn't there a search engine for malls where shoppers can go online to see if a product is available and where it's the cheapest?"

Dunlap, who had worked for several Silicon Valley start-ups, wrote the idea in his "idea" logbook. He kept a list of business ideas that occurred to him.

Redpoint Ventures

At the time of the trip to the mall, Dunlap was an entrepreneur in residence at Redpoint Ventures. Redpoint is a venture capital firm that specializes in first-round investments in Internet and broadband start-ups. Dunlap had just come off three successful jobs at Netscape, E.piphany, and Loudcloud. He was taking a break and was sitting in on pitches that Redpoint's partners were listening to. He was also thinking about launching his own start-up. He kept his idea logbook handy and frequently shared ideas with Redpoint partners. He narrowed his list of 100 ideas to two or three, and finally settled on creating a way for shoppers to search the inventories of local malls. He named the venture NearbyNow.

Unlike some start-up stories, Dunlap's selection of a business idea wasn't a bolt out of the blue. He had been talking to shoppers, retailers, and mall managers for some time about how to use the Internet to enhance the retail experience. His conversations with mall managers were particularly revealing. They were more technologically savvy than Dunlap would have guessed. They were fascinated by search engines, like Google, but realized that Google searches largely directed people to places where they could buy things online rather than in stores. This frustration peaked Dunlap's interest in finding a way to help people search for products online but buy them at a local store. Some Internet sites allowed shoppers to enter their postal codes and find the location of the nearest store that carried a product. But no site told a shopper if a specific store had a particular product in inventory or where the cheapest place to buy the product was. NearbyNow's vision was to be the solution to these shortcomings.

Product Feasibility Analysis

Before moving aggressively forward, Dunlap settled into a "product feasibility analysis" mode. He decided that NearbyNow's first target would be malls. The primary reason was a little-known fact: Approximately 90 percent of all malls in the United States are controlled by six companies. If Dunlap could convince even one of those companies to give NearbyNow a chance, he'd instantly be in a large number of malls.

The thing Dunlap wanted to learn the most, at this point, was whether people really needed the service. He figures he talked to about 2,000 people, some in focus groups and some one-to-one. One technique he used was to sit on a stool, at a local mall, next to the mall directory. As people walked up to try to figure out which store they were going to, he'd say, "Can I help you find something, and by the way, on the way out if you tell me if you found it I'll put your name in a hat for a $500 gift certificate." Collectively, these methods convinced Dunlap that there was a need and an enthusiastic thirst for the solutions that NearbyNow planned to offer.

From the industry feasibility analysis side, one thing that was heartening to Dunlap was signs that although people like to search and do price comparisons online, they prefer to shop offline so they can touch and feel a product—especially for higher-priced items. This sentiment was later affirmed by a 2007 study by the National Retail Federation and Forrester Research, which found that while online sales are climbing, shoppers still like to be able to feel and touch their products, especially clothes and shoes, before they buy.

NearbyNow

Dunlap didn't incorporate NearbyNow until after the product feasibility analysis was completed. Subsequently Dunlap built a team, raised funding, and built the service. The following table shows how NearbyNow works. The company is presently restricted to searching malls. An

---

How NearbyNow Works

Step 1 A shopper goes to a mall's Web site and under "Find a Product" types in the name of a product such as iPod. The results will list the stores in the mall that carry iPods or iPod accessories. Try it. Go to the Westfield Montgomery Mall in Bethesda, Maryland, at www.westfield.com/montgomery. You can access your local mall via NearbyNow's Web site.

Step 2 You page through the listings to find the item you want and determine where it's the cheapest. In some cases, the listings will show whether the item is in stock and will ask if you'd like the store to place it on hold for you.

Step 3 Next, you're asked how you'd like to be notified to make sure the product is in stock. You can choose either e-mail or text message. You'll usually hear back in 10 minutes or so.

Step 4 If the item is available, you go to the store to buy the item. If the item isn't available at the store, you may be given the option to buy it online.

Other • You can search a mall by brand name, like "iPod," or by a generic product category, like "men's jeans."
   • The search results are based on what previous searchers entered and clicked on. So if you type in "iPod" you may get three stores that sell iPods (along with their prices), plus stores that sell iPod cases, iPod earbuds, etc.
   • If you're already at the mall, an alternative is to send a text message to "nearby" (632729) to go through the same process.

(continued)

ambition Dunlap has is to grow the service beyond malls in 2010.

As shown in the table, NearbyNow's service is straightforward. A limitation of the system is that there's still quite a bit of variability among stores regarding how accurately they track their inventory. As a result, not all stores can quickly tell a shopper whether an item is in stock. Another limitation is participation. Some high-end retailers don't like their products seen side by side with less expensive alternatives. Once NearbyNow becomes well-known in a specific mall, however, most retailers eventually come on board, not wanting to be left out of the search results.

NearbyNow makes money via ads and revenue-sharing arrangements with the retailers to whom they send customers. It wasn't an easy service to build and isn't an easy one to run. Dunlap had to do a lot of missionary work up front to get the first few retailers to share their inventory data with NearbyNow. Dunlap recruited former coworkers from E.piphany to build the service. As the service grows, the number of employees in NearbyNow's call center will grow in a similar manner. Once a request to reserve an item is made, a NearbyNow employee calls the store to verify the item is in stock and then contacts the shopper. If an item is placed on hold, a personalized claim check is generated that tells the shopper exactly who to ask for when they pick up the item.

Learning the Unexpected

One thing that happens to companies during their initial beta or test phase of a product or service is that things are learned that were totally unexpected. This is why it's important to have a beta or test phase. In NearbyNow's case, it found that one of the most valuable aspects of its service was that when shoppers saw that a store didn't have an item, they didn't call the store to ask about it. For example, when the Nintendo Wii was hot, stores, which ran out of Wiis, would answer calls all day from shoppers looking for the product. By logging onto NearbyNow's service, shoppers could see which stores were sold out of Wiis, and they wouldn't call them. This is a concept referred to as "local call buffering," something Dunlap had never even heard of before. As an added bonus, NearbyNow would keep a list of customers and their e-mail addresses that were looking for a Wii at a particular store, and would send out an e-mail message to the shopper when the Wii was available again.

Poised for Future Growth

NearbyNow is presently in about 200 malls, with 50 percent of U.S. consumers within 30 miles of a NearbyNow-enabled mall. The company hopes to be in the vast majority of malls by 2009. It will then take its service beyond malls, in a still to be determined fashion. The company has captured the attention of several strong advocates. In April 2008, it raised a fresh round of $11.75 million in funding, which raised its total to $19.25 million since 2006. How big NearbyNow is able to grow is open to question. "NearbyNow is one of those that is still up in the air," says venture capitalist Howard Hartenbaum, a NearbyNow investor. "It could be really big. For other companies, people might be happy if we make two times our money or if it's big, then 10 times. NearbyNow, if everything works, could be a billion dollar business."

Discussion Questions

1. Write a concept statement for NearbyNow. If NearbyNow was still in the start-up stage and Scott Dunlap asked you who he should distribute the concept statement to, what would you have told him?
2. What types of gumshoe research did Dunlap benefit from, and what additional gumshoe research could he have conducted while he was investigating the feasibility of NearbyNow?
3. Did you know that the majority of malls in the United States are owned by six companies? If not, how might you have discovered this information if you were conducting a feasibility analysis for a product or service that would be placed in malls?
4. Complete a First Screen analysis for NearbyNow. What do you learn from the analysis?

Application Questions

1. What types of insights do you think Dunlap picked up, about the feasibility of NearbyNow, by sitting on a stool next to the directories in malls?
2. Read the "You Be the VC 3.1" feature in this chapter. If you had started DanceJam, how would you have set up its product/service feasibility analysis?

Sources: S. Dunlap and N. Eyal, Innovate Podcast, February 17, 2008; "NearbyNow CEO in It for the Long Run," *Silicon Valley Business Journal*, January 25, 2008; J. Haberkorn, "The *Washington Times* Retail and Hospitality Column," *Knight Ridder Tribune Business News*, July 2, 2007.

CASE3.2

Intuit: The Value of Validating Business Ideas
www.intuit.com

Bruce R. Barringer
Oklahoma State University
R. Duane Ireland
Texas A & M University

Introduction

Intuit is the leading provider of financial management software and related services. Its flagship products—Quicken, QuickBooks, and TurboTax—simplify personal finance, small-business management, payroll processing, and tax preparation. The company prides itself first on its customer focus and second on its technological prowess. Its customer focus is directly tied to its culture of ongoing product/service feasibility analysis and usability testing.

Intuit's Founding

Intuit's founding is an excellent example of how a strong business idea, coupled with properly executed feasibility analysis, leads to business success. Scott Cook, a business consultant, started the company in 1983. After watching his wife painstakingly pay bills by hand, Cook wondered whether a software product could be developed to help people manage their personal finances. He drew up a preliminary business plan and partnered with Tom Proulx, a computer science student at Stanford University, to found Intuit and develop a product that was to be named Quicken.

Cook's background in consumer marketing was a true advantage during the product's development. Cook spent several years as a brand manager with Procter & Gamble earlier in his career and had a thorough understanding of feasibility analysis and marketing research as a result. Cook insisted that he and Proulx first determine exactly what consumers wanted in a personal finance program before any initial prototypes were developed. When asked how he approached this task, Cook answered,

> The only way to find that information was to talk to households. So I'd make calls and I got my sister-in-law to call households. We asked upper-income consumers—they were the only people buying computers—about their financial lives. We did this to build a real gut knowledge about how real people did

their finances: their behaviors, their likes, and their dislikes. We looked at behavioral data as well. It became very clear to us that people wanted a way to take the hassle out of doing their finances. Who likes to pay bills and write in checkbooks?

An important component of Cook's approach was a keen understanding that because personal financial management software was a product that consumers hadn't seen before, it wouldn't work to simply ask them what they would like in this type of product. So, in addition to the phone interviews, Cook and Proulx actually watched people managing their finances. Quicken was developed only after they were confident that they knew what consumers needed to make personal financial management easier. Cook said this about understanding a customer's needs:

> The key to business success is knowing your customer cold. We had spent time understanding the customer. We clearly understood customer behavior and had data showing that our solution was vastly better according to customers' decision-making criteria.

Since it's founding, Intuit has developed or employed a number of techniques to determine customers' needs and ensure that its products are easy to use and meet customer expectations. Its most useful techniques, which serve as models for all firms to consider, are as follows.

In-House Usability Testing

Intuit didn't invent the notion of usability testing, but was the first company to apply usability testing to software products. The goal of usability testing is to design products in a way that best meets customer needs. To meet this goal, one thing Intuit does is invite both users and nonusers of its products to visit its usability-testing lab at its California headquarters. At the lab, participants are seated in front of PCs and are asked to work with

(continued)

software products that are being developed. A soundproof room is attached to the lab, where Intuit programmers and designers observe the participants. A "logger" is typically assigned to record usability problems or any comments participants make during the test, and the sessions are taped for further review. The participants are usually given copies of Intuit products in appreciation for their time and efforts. The objective of the testing is to uncover and work out problems relating to Intuit products "before" rather than after they reach the marketplace.

Follow-Me-Home Test

A hybrid form of usability testing that Scott Cook invented is referred to as follow-me-home testing. In the early days of Intuit, Cook's committed focus on understanding customers' needs found him going into stores where Intuit's software was being sold and waiting for someone to buy one of his products. He would then ask if he could follow the customer home and watch while the customer installed the software and tried to use it.

Over the years, this form of testing at Intuit has become more formalized but retains the original spirit of Cook's early efforts. The company routinely sends teams of testers to the homes and businesses of its users to see how its products are working. A team typically consists of three Intuit employees, including someone from the User Experience Group, someone from Quality Assurance, and someone from Engineering or Technical Documentation. Technically, the program is a form of ethnography, which is research based on firsthand observation of how people behave in a certain situation. According to Cook, who has participated in many follow-me-home tests, "You watch their eyebrows, where they hesitate, where they have a quizzical look. Every glitch, every momentary hesitation is our fault." The testing helps the company uncover areas needing improvement that potentially couldn't be uncovered in any other way.

A side benefit of the follow-me-home program is that it demonstrates to users the extent to which Intuit is serious about meeting their needs and is genuinely open to their comments and suggestions. This sentiment was affirmed by Wendy Padmos, a Quicken user, who volunteered to participate in the follow-me-home program in 2004. Commenting on her experience, Padmos said,

> When the Quicken team came to my house, I thought they just wanted to find out how they could better advertise to me and people like me, but it wasn't that at all. It was much more customer-focused. They wanted to know how I use the product, what was important to me, and what was not important to me. I told them I would like the ability to see my current spending against my average spending over the last 12 months, and now it's in the product!

Other Techniques

Intuit utilizes a variety of other techniques to better understand its customers and test its products. The company routinely runs surveys to see how its products are doing. Similarly, the company has a beta tester program that it recruits for on an ongoing basis. The program allows customers to test prerelease software products and then provide Intuit software engineers real-world quality and usability feedback. It is a hands-on program that facilitates a dialogue between Intuit and its users during rather than after the development of a software product. Users aren't paid for their participation—instead they are provided the opportunity to help shape the design of Intuit products and in some cases are able to buy Intuit products at a discount.

Intuit Today

Today, Intuit is one of the largest software companies in the world with over $3 billion in annual sales. Between 2007 and 2008, the company grew by 14.9 percent and is consistently ranked by *Fortune* magazine as one of the "Top 100 Companies to Work For" in America. All of the programs described here are active and are part of Intuit's ongoing efforts to better understand its customers and their needs.

Discussion Questions

1. What kinds of things to you think Scott Cook and Tom Proulx learned by actually watching people manage their finances that they could never have learned via secondary research?
2. What are three examples of tips or techniques that you picked up from this case that you would consider using if you conducted a feasibility analysis for a consumer product?
3. To what extent do you think Intuit's industry is attractive? If Intuit conducted an industry/market feasibility analysis on the main industries in which it participates, what do you believe would be the outcome?
4. Why do you think Intuit puts so much effort into collecting primary research about its users and their experiences? Would it be cheaper for Intuit to hire a marketing research firm to collect data on user preferences? What would Intuit lose if it pursued this approach?

Application Questions

1. The "You Be the VC 3.2" feature at the end of the chapter focuses on SmartSense. Which of the forms of Intuit's feasibility analysis and usability testing do you think would work for SmartSense? Describe how you would adapt Intuit's practices to help SmartSense better understand its users and test its products.

2. Would you enjoy participating in Intuit's beta tester program? Locate information about the program on Intuit's Web site and read more about it. What aspects of the program, if any, would motivate you to participate?

Sources: Intuit homepage, www.intuit.com (accessed November 8, 2008); "Show Me the Money: Quicken 2006 Provides Instant Insights into Spending Habits; Personal Finance Software Boasts 121 New Features and Improvements Including Ability to Attach Electronic Documents and Statements," *TMCnet*, August 1, 2005; R. D. Jager and R. Ortiz, *In the Company of Giants* (New York: McGraw-Hill, 1997).

Endnotes

1. Think Gum Press Kit, www.thinkgum.com (accessed December 3, 2008).
2. J. Mullins, *The New Business Road Test* (London: Prentice Hall, 2003).
3. "The World According to Clark," *Business 2.0*, May 2005.
4. N. C. Kaiser, "Jeremy Jaech, CEO of Trumba.com," nPost.com, www.npost.com (accessed August 8, 2005).
5. SurveyMonkey homepage, www.surveymonkey.com (accessed November 9, 2008).
6. "Patient Monitoring Systems," www.freedoniagroup.com (accessed March 19, 2009). "Remote Patient Monitoring Technologies Get Patients Wired for Health and Wellness," www.forst.com (accessed March 19, 2009).
7. P. Avida and I. Vertinsky, "Firm Exits as a Determinant of New Entry: Is There Evidence of Local Creative Destruction?" *Journal of Business Venturing* 23, no. 3 (2008): 257–79.
8. Dogster homepage, www.dogster.com (accessed November 8, 2008).
9. C. G. Brush, T. S. Manolova, and L. F. Edelman, "Properties of Emerging Organizations: An Empirical Test," *Journal of Business Venturing*, 23 no. 5 (2008): 547–66.
10. L. He, "Do Founders Matter? A Study of Executive Compensation, Governance Structure and Firm Performance," *Journal of Business Venturing* 23, no. 3 (2008): 257–79.
11. M. S. Cardon, C. Zietsma, P. Saparito, B. P. Matherne, and C. Davis, "A Tale of Passion: New Insights into Entrepreneurship from a Parenthood Metaphor, *Journal of Business Venturing* 20 (2005): 23–45.
12. M. Vivarelli, "Are All the Potential Entrepreneurs So Good?" *Small Business Economics* 23, no. 1 (2004): 41–49.
13. IBISWorld, *U.S. Musical Instrument & Supply Stores Industry Market Research Report,* www.ibisworld.com (accessed November 8, 2008).
14. BizMiner homepage, www.bizminer.com (assessed November 8, 2008).
15. J. R. Van Slyke, H. H. Stevenson, and M. J. Roberts, "How to Write a Winning Business Plan," in *The Entrepreneurial Venture*, ed. W.A. Sahlman and H. H. Stevenson (Boston: Harvard Business School Press, 1992), 127–37.

Appendix 3.1   FIRST SCREEN

Part 1: Strength of Business Idea

For each item, circle the most appropriate answer and make note of the (−1), (0), or (+1) score.

	Low Potential (−1)	Moderate Potential (0)	High Potential (+1)
1. Extent to which the idea: • Takes advantage of an environmental trend • Solves a problem • Addresses an unfilled gap in the marketplace	Weak	Moderate	Strong
2. Timeliness of entry to market	Not timely	Moderately timely	Very timely
3. Extent to which the idea "adds value" for its buyer or end user	Low	Medium	High
4. Extent to which the customer is satisfied by competing products that are already available	Very satisfied	Moderately satisfied	Not very satisfied or ambivalent
5. Degree to which the idea requires customers to change their basic practices or behaviors	Substantial changes required	Moderate changes required	Small to no changes required

Part 2: Industry-Related Issues

	Low Potential (−1)	Moderate Potential (0)	High Potential (+1)
1. Number of competitors	Many	Few	None
2. Stage of industry life cycle	Maturity phase or decline phase	Growth phase	Emergence phase
3. Growth rate of industry	Little or no growth	Moderate growth	Strong growth
4. Importance of industry's products and/or services to customers	"Ambivalent"	"Would like to have"	"Must have"
5. Industry operating margins	Low	Moderate	High

Part 3: Target Market and Customer-Related Issues

	Low Potential (−1)	Moderate Potential (0)	High Potential (+1)
1. Identification of target market for the proposed new venture	Difficult to identify	May be able to identify	Identified
2. Ability to create "barriers to entry" for potential competitors	Unable to create	May or may not be able to create	Can create
3. Purchasing power of customers	Low	Moderate	High
4. Ease of making customers aware of the new product or service	Low	Moderate	High
5. Growth potential of target market	Low	Moderate	High

Part 4: Founder- (or Founders-) Related Issues

	Low Potential (−1)	Moderate Potential (0)	High Potential (+1)
1. Founder's or founders' experience in the industry	No experience	Moderate experience	Experienced
2. Founder's or founders' skills as they relate to the proposed new venture's product or service	No skills	Moderate skills	Skilled
3. Extent of the founder's or founders' professional and social networks in the relevant industry	None	Moderate	Extensive
4. Extent to which the proposed new venture meets the founder's or founders' personal goals and aspirations	Weak	Moderate	Strong
5. Likelihood that a team can be put together to launch and grow the new venture	Unlikely	Moderately likely	Very likely

Part 5: Financial Issues

	Low Potential (−1)	Moderate Potential (0)	High Potential (+1)
1. Initial capital investment	High	Moderate	Low
2. Number of revenue drivers (ways in which the company makes money)	One	Two to three	More than three
3. Time to break even	More than two years	One to two years	Less than one year
4. Financial performance of similar businesses	Weak	Modest	Strong
5. Ability to fund initial product (or service) development and/or initial start-up expenses from personal funds or via bootstrapping	Low	Moderate	High

Overall Potential

Each part has five items. Scores will range from −5 to +5 for each part. The score is a guide—there is no established rule of thumb for the numerical score that equates to high potential, moderate potential, or low potential for each part. The ranking is a judgment call.

Score (−5 to +1)	Overall Potential of the Business Idea Based on Each Part		Suggestions for Improving the Potential
Part 1: Strength of Business Idea	High potential	☐	
	Moderate potential	☐	
	Low potential	☐	
Part 2: Industry-Related Issues	High potential	☐	
	Moderate potential	☐	
	Low potential	☐	
Part 3: Target Market and Customer-Related Issues	High potential	☐	
	Moderate potential	☐	
	Low potential	☐	

(continued)

Score (−5 to +1)	Overall Potential of the Business Idea Based on Each Part		Suggestions for Improving the Potential
Part 4: Founder- (or Founders-) Related Issues	High potential	☐	
	Moderate potential	☐	
	Low potential	☐	
Part 5: Financial Issues	High potential	☐	
	Moderate potential	☐	
	Low potential	☐	
Overall Assessment	High potential	☐	
	Moderate potential	☐	
	Low potential	☐	

Summary

Briefly summarize your justification for your overall assessment:

Appendix 3.2   INTERNET RESOURCE TABLE

Resources to Help Complete the First Screen Worksheet in Appendix 3.1

Source	Description	Applicable Parts of First Screen	Cost/ Availability
American Factfinder (www.factfinder.census.gov)	An easy-to-use portal for obtaining census data. One quick way to retrieve data is to get a "Fact Sheet" on a geographic area (by city, county, or postal code), which provides population, medium household income, demographic breakdown (age, gender, race), and other information.	Part 3	Free
BizStats (www.bizstats.com)	Has a variety of detailed financial data on various retail categories. On the site, a user can type in the projected income of a firm, by industry, and receive a mock income statement in return.	Parts 2 and 5	Free
Business & Company Resource Center (www.gale.com/ BusinessRC)	Access to information on the organization and structure of industries, current industry trends, and other information.	Parts 1 and 2	Fee based; typically free if accessed through a university library
City-Data.com (www.city-data.com)	Contains detailed information on cities, including median resident age, median household income, ethnic mix of residents, and aerial photos.	Part 3	Free
County Business Patterns (www.census.gov/epcd/cbp/ view/cbpview.html)	Good resources for looking at business activity, including the number of competitors, at a city, county, or state level. For example, you can find the number of dry cleaners (or any other business) in a specific postal code or city.	Parts 2 and 3	Free
Hoovers Online (www. hoovers.com)	Brief histories and financial information on companies, industries, people, and products. Premium service provides access to detailed finan-cial information and 10-K reports for publicly traded firms.	Parts 2, 3, and 5	Free; premium version available on a fee basis or typically for free if accessed through a university library

Source	Description	Applicable Parts of First Screen	Cost/ Availability
IBISWorld (www.ibisworld.com)	Detailed reports available on hundreds of industries, including industry statistics, trends, buyer behavior, and expected returns.	Parts 1, 2, 3, and 5	Fee based; typically free if accessed through a university library
LexisNexis Academic (www.lexisnexis.com)	Provides access to sales data for public and private firms, which can be searched in a number of useful ways. Helps start-ups estimate the financial performance of similar businesses. Go to "Business" and then "Company Financial."	Part 5	Fee-based; typically free if accessed through a university library
MagPortal.com (www.magportal.com)	Search engine and directory for finding online magazine articles. Helps start-ups by providing access to magazine articles about their product/service and industry of interest. This information may be helpful in all areas of feasibility analysis.	Parts 1, 2, 3, 4, and 5	Free
Mergent Online (www.mergentonline.com)	Provides near instant access to financial data, including income statements, balance sheets, and cash flows, on more than 10,000 U.S. public corporations.	Parts 2 and 5	Fee based; typically free if accessed through a university library
Mintel (www.mintel.com)	Detailed reports available on hundreds of industries, including industry statistics, trends, buyer behavior, and expected returns.	Parts 1, 2, 3, and 5	Fee based; typically free if accessed through a university library
ProQuest (no public Web site available)	Very robust search engine for searching publications such as the *Wall Street Journal* and the *New York Times*. Useful for all areas of feasibility analysis.	Parts 1, 2, 3, 4, and 5	Fee based; typically free if accessed through a university library
Quickfacts (http://quickfacts.census.gov)	A very quick way to access census bureau data, including population, median household income, census breakdowns by age and other demographic characteristics, and so on.	Parts 2 and 3	Free
ReferenceUSA (www.referenceusa.com)	Provides contact information, estimated annual sales, credit rating score, year established, news, and other information on both public and private companies. Contains more information on private firms than many similar sites. Helps start-ups estimate the financial performance of similar businesses.	Part 5	Free
Standard & Poor's NetAdvantage (www.netadvantage. standardpoor.com)	Detailed reports available on hundreds of industries, including industry statistics, trends, buyer behavior, and expected returns.	Parts 1, 2, 3, and 5	Fee based; typically free if accessed through a university library
Trade (and Professional) Association Directories (http://idii.com/resource/ associations.htm) (www. weddles.com/associations/ index.cfm) (www.ipl.org/div/aon)	Directories provide access to the Web site addresses of trade associations in all fields. The trade associations can be contacted to obtain information on all areas of feasibility.	Parts 1, 2, 3, 4, and 5	Free
Yahoo! Industry Center (http://biz.yahoo.com/ic)	Provides a directory of industries, along with a list of the companies in each industry, the latest industry-related news, and performance data on the top companies in an industry.	Parts 2, 3, and 5	Free

Getting Personal

with David Brim

CURRENTLY IN MY IPOD
Anything from classical to Jay Z to John Mayer

MY BIGGEST WORRY AS AN ENTREPRENEUR
Not having the resources to make my venture reach its full potential

MY ADVICE FOR NEW ENTREPRENEURS
Take the ready-aim-fire approach and don't get discouraged

MY BIGGEST SURPRISE AS AN ENTREPRENEUR
All the doors that open up once you get things rolling

BEST PART OF BEING A STUDENT
Learning and being able to tap into the resources accessible to you

WHAT I DO WHEN I'M NOT WORKING
Fishing, reading, learning, and spending time with friends

DAVID BRIM
Cofounder, Group Table
BS, College of Business, University of Central Florida, 2008

SCOTT WALL
Cofounder, Group Table
BS, College of Business, University of Central Florida, 2007

CARL HENDERSON
Cofounder, Group Table
BS, College of Business, University of Central Florida, expected 2009

CHAPTERFOUR

Writing a *Business* Plan

OPENING PROFILE

GROUP TABLE
Proceeding on the Strength of a Winning Business Plan

www.grouptable.com

On March 29, 2008, David Brim was someplace he never imagined he'd ever be. He was in a limousine circling the Indianapolis 500 Motor Speedway pitching his business idea to a group of judges. Brim and the other two cofounders of GroupTable were selected as finalists in the 2008 Nascent 500 Business Challenge, sponsored by Ball State University's Entrepreneurship Center. An unusual twist of the competition is that the finalists get the time it takes to circle the Indianapolis Motor Speedway once to pitch their idea to a group of judges.

Brim is one of the cofounders of GroupTable, a Web-based platform that helps students work more effectively in groups. The idea for GroupTable occurred to Brim and his partners, fellow University of Central Florida students Scott Wall and Carl Henderson, over a period of time. All three had participated in groups in various classes, and had firsthand knowledge of the advantages and disadvantages of working in groups. One of the biggest disadvantages is that students have conflicting schedules, which always makes it difficult to find a time for groups to meet. Another downside is that it's often hard for all of the members of a group to focus at the same time. To avoid these complications, students often use e-mail to exchange the work they're doing on a group project. This process is often clumsy as the members of a group try to route the portion of a project they're working on to others.

Brim and his partners are very tech-savvy, and the first version of GroupTable was created just for themselves—to help them better manage the groups they were a part of. As they worked on the project and got feedback from others, they started seeing GroupTable as a business idea. One thing that Brim, Wall, and Henderson noticed was that the group collaboration platforms already available on the Web were built with businesses in mind. Their goal was to do something different—to build a group collaboration platform with students in mind. In the summer and fall of 2007, they hosted focus groups to discern the functionality to build into GroupTable to make it particularly suitable for student groups. They also shaped GroupTable to resemble a social network, thinking that anyone familiar with Facebook or MySpace would catch on to how to use GroupTable quickly.

To test the merits of their ideas, in November 2007, the three entered GroupTable into the Sunshine State Venture Challenge, the U.S. state of Florida's collegiate business plan competition. Bolstered by positive feedback, in the spring of 2008 they entered the Nascent 500 Business Challenge referred to earlier and Joust, a business plan competition sponsored by the Center for Entrepreneurship and Innovation at the University of Central Florida. Brim and Wall had won Joust the previous year for a different business idea. They won again, this time with GroupTable. The first-place

Learning Objectives

After studying this chapter you should be ready to:

1. Explain the purpose of a business plan.

2. Describe the two primary reasons for writing a business plan.

3. Describe who reads a business plan and what they're looking for.

4. Explain the difference between a summary business plan, a full business plan, and an operational business plan.

5. Explain why the executive summary may be the most important section of a business plan.

6. Describe a milestone and how milestones are used in business plans.

7. Explain why it's important to include separate sections on a firm's industry and its target market in a business plan.

8. Explain why the "Management Team and Company Structure" section of a business plan is particularly important.

9. Describe the purposes of a "sources and uses of funds" statement and an "assumptions sheet."

10. Detail the parts of an oral presentation of a business plan.

finish included a $12,000 cash prize and a free year in the UCF Technology Incubator.

The $12,000 prize money was enough to launch GroupTable as a functioning firm. Brim, Wall, and Henderson have complementary skills—Brim in marketing, Wall in finance, and Henderson in MIS—which served the three well as the business started to take shape. GroupTable was opened to a larger group of beta users in the spring and early summer of 2008, and Brim, Wall, and Henderson continued to obtain feedback as student groups started to use it. For example, third-year law students on a mock trial team at Barry University Law School used GroupTable to share documents, discuss their cases, and organize for a competition, with positive results.[1]

GroupTable is now fully functional, and over 1,300 students have used the service. It's currently free while Brim, Wall, and Henderson accumulate a critical mass of users and settle on a business model. The number of users will be boosted considerably in 2009, as GroupTable has contracted with a university to preload subscriptions to its service to all of the university's students. The university anticipates using GroupTable in the majority of its classes to help its students work more effectively in groups.

Brim, Wall, and Henderson credit their participation in business plan competitions, and the business plan they've written for GroupTable, as important vehicles for structuring their thoughts about GroupTable, building in the correct functionality, and helping the company come together. The prize money they've won has also been instrumental in getting GroupTable off the ground. GroupTable is gaining momentum, and Brim and his partners plan to continue working on the business plan and entering business plan competitions.[2]

This chapter discusses the importance of writing a business plan. Although some new ventures simply "wing it" and start doing business without the benefit of formal planning, it is hard to find an expert who doesn't recommend preparing a business plan. A **business plan** is a written narrative, typically 25 to 35 pages long, that describes what a new business intends to accomplish and how it intends to accomplish it. For most new ventures, the business plan is a dual-purpose document used both inside and outside the firm. Inside the firm, the plan helps the company develop a "road map" to follow to execute its strategies and plans. Outside the firm, it introduces potential investors and other stakeholders to the business opportunity the firm is pursuing and how it plans to pursue it.[3]

To begin this chapter, we discuss issues with which entrepreneurs often grapple when facing the challenge of writing a business plan. Topics included in the first section of the chapter are reasons for writing a business plan, a description of who reads the business plan and what they're looking for, and guidelines to follow when preparing a written business plan. In the chapter's second section, we present an outline of a business plan with a description of the material in each section of the plan. The third section of the chapter deals with strategies for how to present the business plan to potential investors and others.

THE BUSINESS PLAN

As illustrated in the basic model of the entrepreneurial process shown in Chapter 1, the time to write a business plan is midway through the step of the entrepreneurial process titled "Developing Successful Business Ideas." It is a mistake to write a business plan too early. The business plan must be substantive enough and have sufficient details about the merits of the new venture to convince the reader that the new business is exciting and should receive support. Much of this detail is accumulated in the feasibility analysis stage of investigating the merits of a potential new venture.

A large percentage of entrepreneurs do not write business plans for their new ventures. In fact, only 31 percent of the 600 entrepreneurs who participated in a recent Wells Fargo/Gallup Small Business Study indicated that they had started their venture with a business plan.[4] This statistic should not deter an entrepreneur from writing a business plan, however. Consider that we do not know how many of the entrepreneurs participating in the Wells Fargo/Gallup Small Business study who did not write a business plan wish they had done so. We're also not sure how many aspiring entrepreneurs never got their businesses off the ground because they didn't have a business plan. One academic study found that potential entrepreneurs who completed a business plan were six times more likely to start a business than individuals who did not complete a business plan.[5]

Reasons for Writing a Business Plan

We show the two primary reasons to write a business plan in Figure 4.1. First, writing a business plan forces a firm's founders to systematically think through each aspect of their new venture.[6] This is not a trivial effort—it usually takes several days or weeks to complete a well-developed business plan—and the founders will usually meet regularly to work on the plan during this period. An example of how much work is sometimes involved, and how a well-planned new business unfolds, is provided by Gwen Whiting and Lindsey Wieber, the cofounders of The Laundress, a company that sells specially formulated laundry detergents and other fabric care products. Whiting and Wieber met at Cornell University while studying fabrics, and after graduating the pair decided to start a business together. The following vignette comes from an interview they gave to Ladies Who Launch, a Web site that highlights the accomplishments of female entrepreneurs:

> *Gwen*: Lindsey and I went to college and studied textiles at Cornell together and always wanted to be in business together. We knew it was going to happen. We always talked about ideas. We were talking about this concept, and it was the right time for us. The first thing we did was the business plan and then a cash flow analysis. We wanted to do as much research as possible before developing the products.

> *Lindsey*: We spent Memorial Day weekend (2003) doing our business plan. We spent the Fourth of July weekend doing our cash flow. After we had our ideas on

Learning Objective

1. Explain the purpose of a business plan.

Learning Objective

2. Discuss the two primary reasons for writing a business plan.

Internal Reason	External Reason
Forces the founding team to systematically think through every aspect of their new venture	Communicates the merits of a new venture to outsiders, such as investors and bankers

FIGURE 4.1

Two Primary Reasons for Writing a Business Plan

paper, we went back to Cornell, met with a professor there, and had a crash course in chemistry. She worked with us on the formulation of the products.

Gwen: I found a manufacturer on Columbus Day. Every piece of free time we had, we dedicated to the business. We weren't at the beach with our friends anymore.[7]

The payoff for this level of dedication and hard work, which involved the preparation of a formal business plan, is that Whiting and Wieber now have a successful business. Their products are sold through their Web site and in many stores.

The second reason to write a business plan is to create a selling document for a company. It provides a mechanism for a young company to present itself to potential investors, suppliers, business partners, key job candidates, and others.[8] Imagine that you have enough money to invest in one new business. You chat informally with several entrepreneurs at a conference for start-ups and decide that there are two new ventures that you would like to know more about. You contact the first entrepreneur and ask for a copy of his business plan. The entrepreneur hesitates a bit and says that he hasn't prepared a formal business plan but would love to get together with you to discuss his ideas. You contact the second entrepreneur and make the same request. This time, the entrepreneur says that she would be glad to forward you a copy of a 30-page business plan, along with a 10-slide PowerPoint presentation that provides an overview of the plan. Ten minutes later, the PowerPoint presentation is in your e-mail in-box with a note that the business plan will arrive the next morning. You look through the slides, which are crisp and to the point and do an excellent job of outlining the strengths of the business opportunity. The next day, the business plan arrives just as promised and is equally impressive.

Which entrepreneur has convinced you to invest in his or her business? All other things being equal, the answer is obvious—the second entrepreneur. The fact that the second entrepreneur has a business plan not only provides you with detailed information about the venture but also suggests that the entrepreneur has thought through each element of the business and is committed enough to the new venture to invest the time and energy necessary to prepare the plan. Having a business plan also gives an investor something to react to. Very few, if any, investors will free up time to "listen" to your idea for a new business, at least initially. Investors prefer to vet or evaluate business ideas by

These three young entrepreneurs plan to open a women's fashion boutique. They have completed a feasibility analysis and are working on their business plan. A garment they plan to feature in their store is draped over the table they're working at.

Dana Edmunds/Getty Images, Inc.-Taxi

looking through business plans (or the executive summaries of business plans) initially before they are willing to invest more of their time and effort.[9]

Who Reads the Business Plan—And What Are They Looking For?

There are two primary audiences for a firm's business plan. Let's look at each of them.

Learning Objective

3. *Describe who reads a business plan and what they're looking for.*

A Firm's Employees   A clearly written business plan, which articulates the vision and future plans of a firm, is important for both the management team and the rank-and-file employees. Some experts argue that it's a waste of time to write a business plan because the marketplace changes so rapidly that any plan will become quickly outdated. Although it's true that marketplaces can and often do change rapidly, the process of writing the plan may be as valuable as the plan itself. Writing the plan forces the management team to think through every aspect of its business and agree on its most important priorities and goals.[10] Just imagine the managers of a new firm sitting at a conference table hammering out the content of their business plan. In most instances, many heated discussions are likely to take place as the founders reach agreement on the most important aspects of their firm's operations.

A clearly written business plan also helps a firm's rank-and-file employees operate in sync and move forward in a consistent and purposeful manner. The existence of a business plan is particularly useful for the functional department heads of a young firm. For example, imagine that you are the newly hired vice president for management information systems for a rapidly growing start-up. The availability of a formal business plan that talks about all aspects of the business and the business's future strategies and goals can help you make sure that what you're doing is consistent with the overall plans and direction of the firm.

Investors and Other External Stakeholders   External stakeholders who are being recruited to join a firm such as investors, potential business partners, and key employees are the second audience for a business plan. To appeal to this group, the business plan must be realistic and not reflective of overconfidence on the firm's part.[11] Overly optimistic statements or projections undermine a business plan's credibility, so it is foolish to include them. At the same time, the plan must clearly demonstrate that the business idea is viable and offers potential investors financial returns greater than lower-risk investment alternatives. The same is true for potential business partners, customers, and key recruits. Unless the new business can show that it has impressive potential, investors have little reason to become involved with it.

A firm must validate the feasibility of its business idea and have a good understanding of its competitive environment prior to presenting its business plan to others. Sophisticated investors, potential business partners, and key recruits will base their assessment of the future prospects of a business on facts, not guesswork or platitudes, as emphasized in Chapter 3. The most compelling facts a company can provide in its business plan are the results of its own feasibility analysis and the articulation of a distinctive and competitive business model. A business plan rings hollow if it is based strictly on an entrepreneur's predictions of a business's future prospects.

In addition to the previously mentioned attributes, a business plan should disclose all resource limitations that the business must meet before it is ready to start earning revenues. For example, a firm may need to hire service people before it can honor the warranties for the products it sells. It is foolhardy for a new venture to try to downplay or hide its resource needs. One of the main reasons new ventures seek out investors is to obtain the capital needed to hire key personnel, further develop their products or services, lease office space, or fill some other gap in their operations. Investors understand this, and experienced investors are typically willing to help the firms they fund plug resource or competency gaps.

Guidelines for Writing a Business Plan

There are several important guidelines that should influence the writing of a business plan. It is important to remember that a firm's business plan is typically the first aspect of a proposed venture that an investor will see. If the plan is incomplete or looks sloppy, it is easy for an investor to infer that the venture itself is incomplete and sloppy.[12] It is important to be sensitive to the structure, content, and style of a business plan before sending it to an investor or anyone else who may be involved with the new firm. Table 4.1 lists some of the "red flags" that are raised when certain aspects of a business plan are insufficient or miss the mark.

Structure of the Business Plan   To make the best impression, a business plan should follow a conventional structure, such as the outline shown in the next section. Although some entrepreneurs want to demonstrate creativity in everything they do, departing from the basic structure of the conventional business plan format is usually a mistake. Typically, investors are very busy people and want a plan where they can easily find critical information. If an investor has to hunt for something because it is in an unusual place or just isn't there, he or she might simply give up and move on to the next plan.[13]

Many software packages are available that employ an interactive, menu-driven approach to assist in the writing of a business plan. Some of these programs are very helpful.[14] However, entrepreneurs should avoid a boilerplate plan that looks as though it came from a "canned" source. The software package may be helpful in providing structure and saving time, but the information in the plan should still be tailored to the individual business. Some businesses hire consultants or outside advisers to write their business plans. Although there is nothing wrong with getting advice or making sure that a plan looks as professional as possible, a consultant or outside adviser shouldn't be the primary author of the plan. Along with facts and figures, a business plan needs to project

Table 4.1   RED FLAGS IN BUSINESS PLANS

Red Flag	Explanation
Founders with none of their own money at risk	If the founders aren't willing to put their own money at risk, why should anyone else?
A poorly cited plan	A plan should be built on hard evidence and sound research, not guesswork or what an entrepreneur "thinks" will happen. The sources for all primary and secondary research should be cited.
Defining the market size too broadly	Defining the market for a new venture too broadly shows that the true target market is not well defined. For example, saying that a new venture will target the $550-billion-per-year pharmaceutical industry isn't helpful. The market opportunity needs to be better defined. Obviously, the new venture will target a segment or a specific market within the industry.
Overly aggressive financials	Many investors skip directly to this portion of the plan. Projections that are poorly reasoned or unrealistically optimistic lose credibility. In contrast, sober, well-reasoned statements backed by sound research and judgment gain credibility quickly.
Sloppiness in any area	It is never a good idea to make a reader wade through typos, balance sheets that don't balance, or sloppiness in any area. These types of mistakes are seen as inattention to detail, and hurt the credibility of the entrepreneur.

a sense of anticipation and excitement about the possibilities that surround a new venture—a task best accomplished by the creators of the business themselves.[15]

Content of the Business Plan   The business plan should give clear and concise information on all the important aspects of the proposed new venture. It must be long enough to provide sufficient information, yet short enough to maintain reader interest. For most plans, 25 to 35 pages are sufficient. Supporting information, such as the résumés of the founding entrepreneurs, can appear in an appendix.

After a business plan is completed, it should be reviewed for spelling, grammar, and to make sure that no critical information has been omitted. There are numerous stories about business plans sent to investors that left out important information, such as significant industry trends, how much money the company needed, or what the money was going to be used for. One investor even told the authors of this book that he once received a business plan that didn't include any contact information for the entrepreneur. Apparently, the entrepreneur was so focused on the content of the plan that he or she simply forgot to provide contact information on the business plan itself. This was a shame, because the investor was interested in learning more about the business idea.[16]

Style or Format of the Business Plan   The plan's appearance must be carefully thought out. It should look sharp but not give the impression that a lot of money was spent to produce it. Those who read business plans know that entrepreneurs have limited resources and expect them to act accordingly. A plastic spiral binder including a transparent cover sheet and a back sheet to support the plan is a good choice. When writing the plan, avoid getting carried away with the design elements included in word-processing programs, such as boldfaced type, italics, different font sizes and colors, clip art, and so forth. Overuse of these tools makes a business plan look amateurish rather than professional.[17]

One of the most common questions that the writers of business plans ask is, "How long and detailed should it be?" The answer to this question depends on the type of business plan that is being written. There are three types of business plans, each of which has a different rule of thumb regarding length and level of detail. Presented in Figure 4.2, the three types of business plans are as follows:

- **Summary plan:** A **summary business plan** is 10 to 15 pages and works best for companies that are very early in their development and are not prepared to write a full plan. The authors may be asking for funding to conduct the analysis needed to write a full plan. Ironically, summary business plans are also used by very experienced entrepreneurs who may be thinking about a new venture but don't want to take the time to write a full business plan. For example, if someone such as Mark Zuckerberg, the founder and CEO of Facebook, was thinking about starting a new business, he might write a summary business plan and send it out to selected investors to get feedback on his idea. Most investors know about Zuckerberg's success with Facebook and don't need detailed information.

Learning Objective

4. Explain the difference between a summary business plan, a full business plan, and an operational business plan.

Summary Business Plan	Full Business Plan	Operational Business Plan
10–15 pages	25–35 pages	40–100 pages
Works best for new ventures in the early stages of development that want to "test the waters" to see if investors are interested in their idea	Works best for new ventures that are at the point where they need funding or financing; serves as a "blueprint" for the company's operations	Is meant primarily for an internal audience; works best as a tool for creating a blueprint for a new venture's operations and providing guidance to operational managers

FIGURE 4.2

Types of Business Plans

■ **Full business plan:** A **full business plan**, which is the focus of this chapter, is typically 25 to 35 pages long. This type of plan spells out a company's operations and plans in much more detail than a summary business plan, and it is the format that is usually used to prepare a business plan for an investor.

■ **Operational business plan:** Some established businesses will write an **operational business plan**, which is intended primarily for an internal audience. An operational business plan is a blueprint for a company's operations. Commonly running between 40 and 100 pages in length, these plans can obviously feature a great amount of detail. An effectively developed operational business plan can help a young company provide guidance to operational managers.

It's not uncommon for an investor to initially ask for a copy of the executive summary or a set of PowerPoint slides featuring an overview of the proposed business rather than a full business plan. This is normal so don't be alarmed if it happens to you. If the investor's interest is peaked, he or she will ask for more information. Don't misinterpret the signals that investors are sending by not asking for a full business plan. It's still important to write one. This sentiment is affirmed by Brad Feld, a venture capitalist based in Boulder, Colorado, who wrote:

> Writing a good business plan is hard. At one point it was an entry point for discussion with most funding sources (angels and VCs). Today, while a formal business plan is less critical to get in the door, the exercise of writing a business plan is incredibly useful. As an entrepreneur, I was involved in writing numerous business plans. It's almost always tedious, time consuming, and difficult but resulted in me having a much better understanding of the business I was trying to create.[18]

A cover letter should accompany a business plan sent to an investor or other stakeholders through the mail. The cover letter should briefly introduce the entrepreneur and clearly state why the business plan is being sent to the individual receiving it. As discussed in Chapter 10, if a new venture is looking for funding, it is a poor strategy to obtain a list of investors and blindly send the plan to everyone on the list. Instead, each person who receives a copy of the plan should be carefully selected on the basis of being a viable investor candidate.

Recognizing the Elements of the Plan May Change   A final guideline for writing a business plan is to recognize that the plan will usually change as it is being written. New insights invariably emerge when an entrepreneur or a team of entrepreneurs immerse themselves in writing the plan and start getting feedback from others. This process continues throughout the life of a company, and it behooves entrepreneurs to remain alert and open to new insights and ideas. As a result of this phenomenon, entrepreneurs who have written business plans and have launched successful businesses stress that a business plan is a living, breathing document, rather than something that is set in stone. This sentiment is affirmed by Calvin Tang, the founder of Newsvine, an online social news platform that was recently acquired by MSNBC. In regard to business plans being living, breathing documents, Tang said:

> My advice to other entrepreneurs would be to stay true to your business plan and your vision. But at the same time, be nimble enough to be able to read the environment and weigh options against each other and try to make the best decision.[19]

The spirit of Tang's comment is reflected in the "Savvy Entrepreneurial Firm" feature. The feature focuses on the challenge of determining how closely to stick to your business plan once your business is launched.

Savvy Entrepreneurial FIRM
Know When to Hold Them, Know When to Fold Them

www.exorogame.com
www.mydestinationinfo.com
www.catchacorp.com

One of the challenges that business owners have is determining how closely to stick to their business plans once the business is launched and they start getting consumer feedback. In almost all cases, some changes will need to be made. But the degree to which business plans pan out as their founders' envisioned varies. In some cases, a business plan is spot-on and the worst thing a founder could do is vary from the plan. In other cases, a plan needs to be significantly tweaked, and in still other cases it needs to be thrown out the window, and the business needs to start over. The following are brief descriptions of businesses that have experienced these various outcomes.

No Changes Needed

ExoroGame is the brainchild of five undergraduates from the National University of Singapore (NUS) who wanted to spark students' interest in running a business. Their aim was to create a social enterprise to promote youth entrepreneurship more widely, rather than a commercial venture for pure profit.

In 2005, the team launched ExoroGame (*exoro* is Latin for "success through persuasion"), an interactive business simulation game dubbed "Entrepreneurship for Dummies." Players increase "their" company's valuation through strategic decisions on buying goods, marketing, sales development, and logistics management.

Students were initially reluctant to take up the challenge, but several months of further trials and enhancements saw the game's popularity soar among undergraduates. ExoroGame has gained a following in educational establishments across Singapore and China. Take-up has been enhanced by a series of ExoroGame Youth Challenge competitions. Although ExoroGame has an appeal among consumers as the "new board game in town," the team has stuck to its original plan to promote youth entrepreneurs. Online portals for universities and schools and even a computer game version are being developed.

Minor Changes Needed

Like so many students, U.K.-based business administration student Neil Waller could not help but get distracted by the thought of a beach holiday getaway, and the Spanish resort of Marbella particularly caught his eye. Unfortunately, when he turned to the Internet for information on hotels, restaurants, and local events, Waller was disappointed at what he found.

Waller was inspired to set up a Web site to help tourists, and Marbellainfo.com was born. While he quickly generated sponsorship from dozens of local companies that were understandably keen to get involved, when Waller studied the traffic on the rapidly growing site, he got a surprise. As well as attracting a strong tourist following, Marbellainfo.com had rapidly evolved into a community site used by local residents to find local services, exchange information, and even get real estate prices. So, his business plan shifted. Recognizing that there was an opportunity for combined tourist and community sites, he has rolled out the business as a worldwide franchise operation. The franchise, now named Mydestinationinfo.com, has coverage from Cape Town to Sydney. It is run by local operators who have access to vital information about their destinations and who are well placed to understand and respond to the community around them.

Major Changes Needed

Catcha.com was the local icon in Malaysia for the 1990s dot-com craze, with its business formed out of the merger and rebranding of three local Web sites: Searchsingapore.com, Malaysiasearch.com, and Searchindonesia.com. The original strategy from the four entrepreneurs who began Catcha.com in 1999 was to rapidly build up a network of regional Web portals that included local content, community news, and listings, all supported by aggressive marketing of the Catcha.com brand.

Expansion was rapid into 2000, with sites for the Philippines, Thailand, and Australia added in as many months, but costs were high too. At the same time, U.S. search directories such as Yahoo! Inc. and Microsoft Corp's MSN all began to target the Asian market and were complementing their local sites with global Internet content. Lycos Inc. teamed up with Singapore Telecommunications in a $50 million venture to set up sites in 10 Asian markets.

The writing was on the wall for Catcha.com. Portals and search engines make money from advertising and e-commerce, and they need as much traffic as possible. Only a handful of search engines can succeed in each market. By late 2000, Catcha.com did not have enough funds to maintain the business thanks to a combination of overexpansion, competition from established and well-financed companies, and the bursting of the dot-com bubble that spooked the markets and shelved Catcha.com's planned stock market flotation.

Catcha.com's founders were forced to completely rethink their business model, and using their local knowledge switched to media, publishing, and event management. Catcha Media Group has gone on to become one of the largest English-language publishing groups in Southeast Asia. It has also ventured back into the Internet arena with iProperty.com, which is now listed on the Australian Securities Exchange (ASX).

Questions for Critical Thinking

1. Does ExoroGame's evaluation of its current status and its decision to stick with its business plan make sense? Why or why not?
2. What do you think would have happened to Marbellainfo.com if it hadn't changed its business plan? What do you think would have happened to Catcha.com?
3. Why do you think some start-ups find it difficult to change their business plan, even when presented

with evidence that their current business plan isn't working?
4. Look at the "You Be the VC" features at the end of Chapter 3, which focus on Dance Jam and SmartSense, and the "You Be the VC" features at the end of this chapter, which focus on WIN Detergent and Icon Aircraft. For the information in the features and on each of the company's Web sites, which company do you think will have the easiest time sticking to its original business plan? Which company do you think will have the hardest time? Explain your selections.

Sources: "Exoro-lating–The New Board Game in Town," *The Sun U!* April 15, 2008; "Interview with the Exoro Team," *SG Entrepreneurs,* October 11, 2006; "Catcha.com to Focus on Technology for Its Content Distribution," *ZDNet Asia,* May 15, 2000; "Once Bitten," *The Business Times,* February 19, 2009.

OUTLINE OF THE BUSINESS PLAN

A suggested outline of the full business plan appears in Table 4.2. Specific plans may vary, depending on the nature of the business and the personalities of the founding entrepreneurs. Most business plans do not include all the elements introduced in Table 4.2; we include them here for the purpose of completeness. Each entrepreneur must decide which specific elements to include in his or her business plan.

Exploring Each Section of the Plan

Cover Page and Table of Contents   The cover page should include the company's name, address, phone number, the date, the contact information for the lead entrepreneur, and the company's Web site address if it has one. The contact information should include a land-based phone number, an e-mail address, and a cell phone number. This information should be centered at the top of the page. Because the cover letter and the business plan could get separated, it is wise to include contact information in both places. The bottom of the cover page should include information alerting the reader to the confidential nature of the plan. If the company already has a distinctive trademark, it should be placed somewhere near the center of the page. A table of contents should follow the cover letter. It should list the sections and page numbers of the business plan and the appendices.

Learning Objective

5. Explain why the executive summary may be the most important section of a business plan.

Executive Summary   The **executive summary** is a short overview of the entire business plan; it provides a busy reader with everything she needs to known about the new venture's distinctive nature.[20] As mentioned earlier, in many instances an investor will first ask for a copy of a firm's executive summary and will request a copy of the full business plan only if the executive summary is sufficiently convincing. The executive summary, then, is arguably the most important section of the business plan.[21] After reading the executive summary, investors should have a relatively good understanding of what will be presented in greater detail throughout the plan. The most important point to remember when writing an executive summary is that it is not an introduction or preface to the business plan. Instead, it is meant to be a summary of the plan itself.[22]

Table 4.2 BUSINESS PLAN OUTLINE

Cover Page

Table of Contents

I. Executive Summary

II. Company Description
Company History
Mission Statement
Products and Services
Current Status
Legal Status and Ownership
Key Partnerships (if any)

III. Industry Analysis
Industry Size, Growth Rate, and Sales Projections
Industry Structure
Nature of Participants
Key Success Factors
Industry Trends
Long-Term Prospects

IV. Market Analysis
Market Segmentation and Target Market Selection
Buyer Behavior
Competitor Analysis

V. Marketing Plan
Overall Marketing Strategy
Product, Price, Promotions, and Distribution

VI. Management Team and Company Structure
Management Team
Board of Directors
Board of Advisers
Company Structure

VII. Operations Plan
General Approach to Operations
Business Location
Facilities and Equipment

VIII. Product (or Service) Design and Development Plan
Development Status and Tasks
Challenges and Risks
Intellectual Property

IX. Financial Projections
Sources and Uses of Funds Statement
Assumptions Sheet
Pro Forma Income Statements
Pro Forma Balance Sheets
Pro Forma Cash Flows
Ratio Analysis

Appendices

An executive summary shouldn't exceed two single-spaced pages. The cleanest format for an executive summary is to provide an overview of the business plan on a section-by-section basis. The topics should be presented in the same order as they are presented in the business plan. Two identical versions of the executive summary should be prepared—one that's part of the business plan and one that's a stand-alone document. The stand-alone document should be used to accommodate people who ask to see the executive summary before they decide whether they want to see the full plan.

Even though the executive summary appears at the beginning of the business plan, it should be written last. The plan itself will evolve as it's written, so not everything is known at the outset. In addition, if you write the executive summary first, you run the risk of trying to write a plan that fits the executive summary rather than thinking through each piece of the plan independently.[23]

Company Description   The main body of the business plan begins with a general description of the company. Although at first glance this section may seem less critical than others, it is extremely important. It demonstrates to your reader that you know how to translate an idea into a business.

The company history section should be brief, but should explain where the idea for the company came from and the driving force behind its inception. If it is a start-up, simply mention that the company is in its start-up stage. If the story of where the idea for the company came from is heartfelt, tell it. For example, in Case 2.2, we introduced Eric and Sharon Langshur, the couple whose infant son, Matthew, was in the hospital facing multiple surgeries. You'll recall that the Langshurs struggled with not only caring for Matthew but with keeping their family and friends up-to-date on Matthew's progress. To help, Sharon's brother created a Web site, which not only allowed Eric and Sharon to post updates about Matthew but allowed people to write back and offer words of support. The Web site evolved into CarePages, a business that the Langshurs launched to help other caregivers in a similar situation. The Langshurs' story is interesting and is one that anyone can relate to. It might even cause the person reading the plan to pause and think, "I remember when my dad was in the hospital and was so sick—everyone wanted to know how he was doing. I wish we'd had access to a product like CarePages back then."

A **mission statement** defines why a company exists and what it aspires to become. We further define a mission statement in Chapter 6. If carefully written and used properly, a mission statement can define the path a company takes and act as its financial and moral compass. For a business plan, a well-written mission statement demonstrates that your business is focused and you can articulate its purpose clearly and distinctly. The products and services section should include an explanation of your product or service, beyond what is written in the executive summary. Include a description of how your product or service is unique and how you plan to position it in the marketplace. A product or service's **position** is how it is situated relative to its rivals. If you plan to open a new type of smoothie shop, for example, you should explain how your smoothie shop differs from others and how it will be positioned in the market in terms of the products it offers and the clientele it attracts. The product/service section is the ideal place for you to start reporting the results of your feasibility analysis. If the concept test, buying intentions survey, and library, Internet, and gumshoe research produced meaningful results, they should be reported here.

The current status section should reveal how far along your company is in its development. A good way to frame this discussion is to think in terms of milestones. A **milestone** is a noteworthy or significant event. If you have selected and registered your company's name, completed a feasibility analysis, written a business plan, and established a legal entity, you have already cleared several important milestones. The legal status and ownership section should indicate who owns the business and how the ownership is split up. You should also indicate what your current form of business ownership (i.e., LLC, Subchapter S Corp., etc.) is if that issue has been decided. We provide a full discussion of the different forms of business ownership in Chapter 7.

A final item a business should cover in this opening section is whether it has any key partnerships that are integral to the business. Many business plans rely on the establishment of partnerships to make them work. Examples of the types of partnerships that are common in business plans are shown in the "Partnering for Success" feature.

Learning Objective

6. Describe a milestone and how milestones are used in business plans.

Partnering for SUCCESS
Types of Partnerships That Are Common in Business Plans

Because new businesses are resource constrained they often make partnering an essential part of their business plans. As illustrated throughout this book, effective partnering can help a start-up in many ways. The following are examples of the types of partnering scenarios that are common in business plans.

Smaller Companies Partnering with Larger Companies to Bring Their Products to Market

Because the cost of bringing a new drug to market is so high, biotech companies normally partner with large pharmaceutical companies to bring their products to market. Biotech companies specialize in discovering and developing new drugs—it's what they're good at. In most cases, however, they have neither the money nor the experience to bring the products to market. In contrast, the large drug companies, like Merck and Pfizer, specialize in marketing and selling drugs and in providing information to doctors about them. It's what they're good at. As a result, most biotech firms' business plans plainly state that their mission is to discover, develop, and patent new drugs and that they'll partner with larger pharmaceutical companies to bring the products to market.

Smaller Companies Partnering with Larger Companies to Produce, Fulfill, and/or Ship Their Products

Many new firms, from the get-go, structure their business plans on the notion that partners will produce, fulfill, and ship their products. As a result, a start-up that develops a new type of board game may have the game made by a contract manufacturer in China, have it shipped from China to a warehouse and fulfillment company in the United States, and when an order is placed (by a retailer like Barnes & Noble or Target) the warehouse and fulfillment company ships the product to the buyer. While there are costs involved at every step in the process, this arrangement frees the board game company to focus on designing and marketing products and reduces its initial capital requirements. A variation of this approach, for catalog and Web-based companies that sell other manufacturers' products, is a method called drop shipping. Drop shippers like eBags, which is an online retailer that sells luggage, backpacks, and similar items, doesn't warehouse anything it sells. Instead, when it receives an order it passes the order onto the original manufacturer (or distributor), which fulfills the order, often in an

eBags box with an eBags invoice so it looks like it came directly from eBags. This arrangement costs eBags money, but it is integral to eBags' business plan of offering a wide selection of products to customers at affordable prices and not getting caught with outdated merchandise.

Smaller Companies Outsourcing Human Resources Management Tasks

An increasingly common feature in business plans is outsourcing human resource management tasks that are labor intensive and take specialized expertise. Some start-ups outsource only administrative tasks, such as payroll processing and benefits administration. These firms partner with a payroll accounting firms such as Paychex or Ceridian. Other start-ups outsource a broader range of their human resource management functions and partner with a company such as ADP or Administaff. These companies are called professional employer organizations (PEOs) and act like an off-site human resource department for a start-up or other firm. Along with doing everything that Paychex and Ceridian does, PEOs can help a start-up with hiring, firing, training, regulatory compliance, and other more in-depth human resource–related issues. Outsourcing these tasks can minimize a firm's investment in human resources management personnel and support (such as software products) and frees a company to focus on other core activities.

Questions for Critical Thinking

1. What factors in the business environment encourage firms to partner to compete?
2. What risks do small firms face when partnering with large, successful companies? What risks do large companies take when they partner with small start-ups?
3. What are three ways (that are not illustrated in the feature) that small firms can partner with larger firms to lessen their capital requirements?
4. The "You Be the VC 4.1" feature focuses on WIN Detergent, a company that is producing laundry detergent for athletes and people who exercise frequently, which completely removes odors from both cotton and synthetic fabrics. What types of partnerships could WIN Detergent form to lower its capital requirements and allow its top management team to focus on its distinctive competencies?

Learning Objective

7. Explain why it's important to include separate sections on a firm's industry and its target market in a business plan.

Industry Analysis   This section should begin by describing the industry the business will enter in terms of its size, growth rate, and sales projections. It is important to focus strictly on the business's industry and not its industry and target market simultaneously. Before a business selects a target market, it should have a good grasp of its industry—including where its industry's promising areas are and where its points of vulnerability are located. For example, as mentioned in Chapter 3, the toy industry in general is flat but the market for educational toys is promising.

Industry structure refers to how concentrated or fragmented an industry is. Fragmented industries are more receptive to new entrants than industries that are dominated by a handful of large firms. You should also provide your reader a feel for the nature of the participants in your industry. Issues such as whether the major participants in the industry are innovative or conservative and are quick or slow to react to environment change are the types of characteristics to convey. You want your reader to visualize how your firm will fit in or see the gap that your firm will fill. The key success factors in an industry are also important to know and convey. Most industries have 6 to 10 key factors that all participants must be competent in to compete. Most participants try to then differentiate themselves by excelling in two or three areas.

Industry trends should be discussed, which include both environmental and business trends. This is arguably the most important section of an industry analysis because if often lays the foundation for a new business idea in an industry. The most important environmental trends are economic trends, social trends, technological advances, and political and regulatory changes. Business trends include issues such as whether profit margins in the industry are increasing or falling and whether input costs are going up or down. The industry analysis should conclude with a brief statement of your beliefs regarding the long-term prospects for the industry.

Market Analysis   The industry analysis section of a business plan is normally followed by the market analysis. Whereas the industry analysis focuses on the industry that a firm will participate in (i.e., toy industry, beverage industry, women's clothing industry), the **market analysis** breaks the industry into segments and zeroes in on the specific segment (or target market) to which the firm will try to appeal. As mentioned in Chapter 3, most start-ups do not try to

If you plan to start a company in the fitness industry, it's important to document the health and future growth potential of the industry. A careful analysis of a firm's industry lays out what is realistically possible and what isn't realistically possible for a startup to achieve.

David Sacks/Getty Images, Inc.

service their entire industry. Instead, they focus on servicing a specific target market within the industry.

The first task that's generally tackled in a market analysis is to segment the industry the business will be entering and then identify the specific target market on which it will focus. This is done through **market segmentation**, which is the process of dividing the market into distinct segments. Markets can be segmented in many ways, such as by geography (city, state, country), demographic variables (age, gender, income), psychographic variables (personality, lifestyle, values), and so forth. Sometimes a firm segments its market on more than one dimension to drill down to a specific segment that the firm thinks it is uniquely capable of serving. For example, in its market analysis, GreatCall, the cell phone service provided for older people, probably segmented the cell phone market by age and by benefits sought. Some start-ups create value by finding a new way to segment an industry. For example, before Tish Ciravolo started Daisy Rock Guitar, a company that makes guitars just for women, the guitar industry had not been segmented by gender. Daisy Rock Guitar's competitive advantage is that it makes guitars that accommodate a woman's smaller hands and build.

It's important to include a section in the market analysis that deals directly with the behavior of the consumers in a firm's target market. The more a start-up knows about the consumers in its target market, the more it can gear products or services to accommodate their needs. Many start-ups find it hard to sell products to public schools, for example, because purchase decisions are often made by committees (which draws out the decision-making process), and the funding often has to go through several levels of administrators to get approved. A **competitor analysis**, which is a detailed analysis of a firm's competitors, should be included. Including a competitor analysis helps a firm understand the positions of its major competitors and communicates to the readers of your business plan that you have a complete understanding of your firm's competitive environment. A complete explanation of how to complete a competitor analysis is provided in Chapter 5.

Marketing Plan   The marketing plan focuses on how the business will market and sell its product or service. It deals with the nuts and bolts of marketing in terms of price, promotion, distribution, and sales. For example, GreatCall, the firm that makes cell phones for older users, may have a great product, a well-defined target market, and a good understanding of its customers and competitors, but it still has to find customers and persuade them to buy its product. The marketing section communicates your specific plans for meeting these objectives.

The best way to describe a company's marketing plan is to start by articulating its marketing strategy, positioning, and points of differentiation, and then talk about how these overall aspects of the plan will be supported by price, promotional mix and sales process, and distribution strategy. Obviously, it's not possible to include a full-blown marketing plan in the four to five pages permitted in a business plan for the marketing section, but you should hit the high points as best as possible.

A firm's **marketing strategy** refers to its overall approach for marketing its products and services. A firm's overall approach typically boils down to how it positions itself in its market and how it differentiates itself from its competitors. Sprig Toys, the educational toy company introduced in Chapter 3, is positioning itself as a toy company selling premium products to parents with the ability to pay and differentiates itself through the educational and developmental value of its toys and their environmentally friendly and safe properties. This overall strategy sets the tone and provides guidance for how the company should reach its target market via its product, pricing, promotional, and distribution tactics. For example, it will invariably promote and advertise its products in places that people in its target market are most likely to see. Similarly, it will most likely sell its products through specialty toy stores (like

Kazoo & Company, the subject of Case 4.1) and its own Web site rather than through mass merchandisers like Wal-Mart and Costco.

The next section should deal with your company's approach to product, price, promotion, and distribution. If your product has been adequately explained already, you can move directly to price. Price, promotion, and distribution should all be in sync with your positioning and points of differentiation, as described previously. Price is a particularly important issue because it determines how much money a company can make. It also sends an important message to your target market. If Sprig Toys advertised its toys as high-quality toys that are both educationally sound and environmentally friendly but also charged a low price, people in its target market would be confused. They would think, "This doesn't make sense. Are Sprig Toys high quality or aren't they?" In addition, the lower price wouldn't generate the profits that Sprig Toys needs to further develop its toys. You should also briefly discuss your plans regarding promotions and distribution.

Learning Objective

8. Explain why the "Management Team and Company Structure" section of a business plan is particularly important.

Management Team and Company Structure   This is a critical section of a business plan. Many investors and others who read business plans look first at the executive summary and then go directly to the management team section to assess the strength of the people starting the firm. Investors read more business plans with interesting ideas and exciting markets than they are able to finance. As a result, it's often not the idea or market that wins funding among competing plans, but the perception that one management team is better prepared to execute their idea than the others.

The management team of a new firm typically consists of the founder or founders and a handful of key management personnel. A brief profile of each member of the management team should be provided, starting with the founder or founders of the firm. Each profile should include the following information:

■ Title of the position
■ Duties and responsibilities of the position
■ Previous industry and related experience
■ Previous successes
■ Educational background

Although they should be kept brief, the profiles should illustrate why each individual is qualified and will uniquely contribute to the success of the firm. Certain attributes of a management team should be highlighted if they apply in your case. For example, investors and others tend to prefer team members who've worked together before. The thinking here is that if people have worked together before and have decided to partner to start a new firm, it usually means that they get along personally and trust one another.[24] You should also identify the gaps that exist in the management team and your plans and timetable for filling them. The complete résumés of key management team personnel can be placed in an appendix to the business plan.

If a start-up has a board of directors and/or a board of advisers, their qualifications and the roles they play should be explained and they should be included as part of your management team. A **board of directors** is a panel of individuals elected by a corporation's shareholders to oversee the management of the firm, as explained in more detail in Chapter 9. A **board of advisers** is a panel of experts asked by a firm's management to provide counsel and advice on an ongoing basis. Unlike a board of directors, a board of advisers possess no legal responsibility for the firm and gives nonbinding advice.[25] Many start-ups ask people who have specific skills or expertise to serve on their board of advisers to help plug competency gaps until the firm can afford to hire additional personnel. For example, if a firm is started by two Web designers and doesn't have anyone on staff with marketing expertise, the firm might place one or two people on its board of advisers with marketing expertise to provide guidance and advice.

The final portion of this section of your business plan focuses on how your company will be structured. Even if you are a start-up, you should outline how the company is currently structured and how it will be structured as it grows. It's important that the internal structure of a company makes sense and that the lines of communication and accountability are clear. Including a description of your company's structure also reassures the people who read the plan that you know how to translate your business idea into a functioning firm.

The most effective way to illustrate how a company will be structured and the lines of authority and accountability that will be in place is to include an organizational chart in the plan. An **organizational chart** is a graphic representation of how authority and responsibility are distributed within the company. The organizational chart should be presented in graphical format if possible.

Operations Plan   The operations plan section of the business plan outlines how your business will be run and how your product or service will be produced. You have to strike a careful balance between adequately describing this topic and providing too much detail. Your readers will want an overall sense of how the business will be run, but they generally will not be looking for detailed explanations. As a result, it is best to keep this section short and crisp.

A useful way to illustrate how your business will be run is to first articulate your general approach to operations in terms of what's most important and what the make-or-break issues are. You can then frame the discussion in terms of "back stage," or behind the scenes activities, and "front stage," or what the customer sees and experiences. For example, if you're opening a new fitness center, the back stage and the front stage issues might be broken down as follows:

Back Stage (Behind the Scenes Activities)	Front Stage (What the Members See)
• Staff selection	• Member tours
• Operations manual	• Operating hours
• Relationships with suppliers	• Staff assistance
• Relationships with city government	• Fitness classes and programs
• Development of marketing materials	• Fitness machines
• Employee orientation and training	• Workshops
• Emergency plans	• Monthly newsletter

Obviously you can't comment on each issue in the three to four pages you have for your operations plan, but you can lay out the key back stage and front stage activities and address the most critical ones.

The next section of the operations plan should describe the geographic location of your business. In some instances, location is an extremely important issue and in other instances it isn't. For example, one of the reasons that Jeff Bezos located Amazon.com in Seattle is that Seattle is a major distribution hub for several large book publishers. By locating near these distribution facilities, Amazon.com has enjoyed a cost advantage that it wouldn't have had otherwise. On a more fine-grained level, for restaurants and retail businesses, the specific location within a mall or shopping center, or a certain side of a busy street, may make a dramatic difference.

This section should also describe a firm's facilities and equipment. You should list your most important facilities and equipment and briefly describe how they will be (or have been) acquired, in terms of whether they will be purchased, leased, or acquired through some other means. If you will be producing a product and will contract or outsource your production, you should comment on how that will be accomplished. If your facilities are nondescript, such as a generic workspace for computer programmers, a lot of explanation is not needed.

Product (or Service) Design and Development Plan If you're developing a completely new product or service, you need to include a section in your business plan that focuses on the status of your development efforts. Many seemingly promising start-ups never get off the ground because their product development efforts stall or the actual development of the product or service turns out to be more difficult than expected. In addition, in many cases, building a working prototype of a product is not enough. A start-up must also have a credible plan for ramping up the production of a product to satisfy the sales estimates in its financial projections.

The first issue to address is to describe the present stage of the development of your product or service. Most products follow a logical path of development that includes product conception, prototyping, initial production, and full production. You should describe specifically the point that your product or service is at and provide a timeline that describes the remaining steps. If you are in the very early stages of your business and only have an idea, you should carefully explain how a **prototype**, which is the first physical depiction of a new product, will be produced. For a new product, a prototype is needed to test the merits of the product and get substantive feedback. In some instances, a virtual prototype, which is less expensive than a physical prototype, is sufficient. A **virtual prototype** is a computer-generated 3-D image of an idea. It displays an invention as a 3-D model that can be viewed from all sides and rotated 360 degrees.

A section labeled "Challenges and Risks" should be included and disclose any major anticipated design and development challenges and risks that will be involved in bringing your product or service to market. While you want to remain upbeat, the last thing you want to do is paint an overly rosy picture of how quickly and effortlessly your design and development process will unfold. Experienced readers know that product and service development is an inherently bumpy and challenging process and will want insights into the challenges and risks you anticipate with your particular offering.

A final section should describe any patents, trademarks, copyrights, or trade secrets that you have secured or plan to secure relative to the products or services you are developing. If your start-up is still in the early stages and you have not taken action on intellectual property issues yet, you should get legal advice so you can, at a minimum, discuss your plans in these areas. Intellectual property is discussed in Chapter 12.

Financial Projections The final section of a business plan presents a firm's pro forma (or projected) financial projections. Having completed the previous sections of the plan, it's easy to see why the financial projections come last. They take the plans you've developed and express them in financial terms.

The first thing to include is a **sources and uses of funds statement**, which is a document that lays out specifically how much money a firm needs (if the intention of the business plan is to raise money), where the money will come from, and what the money will be used for. The next item to include is an **assumptions sheet**, which is an explanation of the most critical assumptions that your financial statements are based on. Some assumptions will be based on general information, and no specific sources will be cited to substantiate the assumption. For example, if you believe that the U.S. economy will gain strength over the next three to five years, and that's an underlying assumption driving your sales projections, then you should state that assumption. In this instance, you wouldn't cite a specific source—you're reflecting a consensus view. (It's then up to your reader to agree or disagree.) Other assumptions will be based on very specific information, and you should cite the source for your assumptions. For example, if Sprig Toys has credible data that shows the educational segment of the children's toy industry is expected to grow at a rate of 10 to 12 percent per year for the foreseeable future, and this figure plays a large role in its belief that it can increase its

Learning Objective

9. Describe the purpose of a "sources and uses of funds" statement and an "assumptions sheet."

What Went WRONG?

What the Enthusiast Group Learned About Assumptions, the Hard Way

The idea behind the Enthusiast Group was to launch a series of community/social networking sites around various adventure sports such as rock climbing, mountain biking, running, and horseback riding. Its sites included YourMTB.com, YourClimbing.com, and YourHorseSports.com. The business plan relied on users to create content for each site by sharing stories, pictures, videos, and advice, and to make money via online advertising. The company was based in Boulder, Colorado, a seemingly perfect place to build a portfolio of outdoor adventure Web sites. One strength of the Enthusiast Group's business plan was that by relying on user-generated content it could keep costs down by not employing writers or paying freelancers for articles to populate the sites. What went wrong?

It didn't work. Although interest in mountain biking, climbing, and the other sports that the Enthusiast Group built Web sites for was increasing, the company was never able to attract enough traffic to its sites to make a go of it. It turns out that several of the assumptions that were key aspects of the Enthusiast Group's business plan simply didn't pan out. First, although relying on user-generated content sounds good, it's tough to rely primarily on users. Users will submit interesting photos, anecdotes, and videos, but people who visit the site will eventually miss the feature articles and well-researched material that professional writers create for magazines, newspaper, and premier Web sites. Second, while many Web sites are able to support themselves via ad revenue, it doesn't always work out. The founders of the Enthusiast Group discovered that the outdoor industry isn't progressive when it comes to online advertising, so it was difficult to convince them to go beyond banner and pay view ads. Finally, in formulating the company's business plan, the notion of creating niche Web sites for individual sports won out over the idea of a creating a mega-site that included individual sections for each sport. An advantage of the mega-site would have been to aggregate the traffic on one Web site, and hopefully become more attractive to advertisers. Whether going with a mega-site over the individual sites would have been a better option, we'll never know.

The Enthusiast Group's failure is a reminder that all business plans are based on key assumptions that should be carefully and thoroughly vetted as the plan takes shape. The best way to approach this task is to conduct a feasibility analysis prior to writing the business plan, and discuss the business plan and its key assumptions with as many people as possible. Even then, realize that all business plans entail risk. Reflecting on the failure of the Enthusiast Group, cofounder Derek Scruggs remarked, "We got lots of positive response to our business plan, but that didn't translate into success."

Questions for Critical Thinking

1. What assumptions, other than those mentioned in the feature, do you think were integral to the Enthusiast Group's business plan?
2. Review the "Savvy Entrepreneurial Firm" feature in this chapter. Were there changes that Catcha.com could have made that would have allowed the company to continue as a regional Web portal? If so, suggest changes that could have been made.
3. What, if anything, could the Enthusiast Group have done during its feasibility analysis stage to better anticipate the problems that eventually led to the firm's failure?
4. The "You Be the VC 4.2" feature focuses on Icon Aircraft, a company that plans to produce a sleek, affordable propeller-powered plane for recreational enthusiasts. What are some of the main assumptions that Icon Aircraft's business plan is based on?

Sources: R. Niles, "Lessons from Steve Outing's Enthusiast Group," www.ojr.org (accessed September 16, 2008); D. Scruggs, "Enthusiast Group Enters Deadpool Reflectively," www.coloradostartups.com (accessed September 16, 2008).

---

sales every year, then it should cite the sources of its information. The importance of identifying the most critical assumptions that a business is based on and thoroughly vetting the assumptions is illustrated in the "What Went Wrong?" feature. The Enthusiast Group, the company that's the focus of the feature, failed largely because several of its key assumptions proved to be incorrect.

The **pro forma (or projected) financial statements** are the heart of the financial section of a business plan. Although at first glance preparing financial statements appears to be a tedious exercise, it's a fairly straightforward process if the preceding sections of your plan are thorough. The financial statements also represent the finale of the entire plan. As a result, it's interesting to see how they turn out.

Table 4.3   THE 10 MOST IMPORTANT QUESTIONS A BUSINESS PLAN SHOULD ANSWER

1. Is the business just an idea, or is it an opportunity with real potential?
2. Is the product or service viable? Does it add significant value to the customer? Has a feasibility analysis been completed? If so, what are the results?
3. Is the business entering an exciting, growing industry, and has the firm identified an attractive position within the industry?
4. Does the business have a well-defined target market?
5. Does the business have points of differentiation that truly separate itself from its competitors? Are these points of differentiation sustainable?
6. Does the business have a sound marketing plan?
7. Is the management team experienced, skilled, and up to the task of launching the new firm?
8. Is the business's operations plan appropriate and sound?
9. Are the assumptions that the firm is basing its financial projections on realistic?
10. Are the financial projections completed correctly, and do they project a bright future for the firm?

A firm's pro forma financial statements are similar to the historical statements an established firm would normally prepare, except they look forward rather than track the past. Pro forma financial statements include the pro forma income statement, the pro forma balance sheet, and the pro forma cash flow statement. The statements are usually prepared in this order because information flows logically from one to the next. Most experts recommend three to five years of pro forma statements. If the company you're writing your plan for already exists, you should also include three years of historical financial statements. Most business plan writers interpret or make sense of a firm's historical or pro forma financial statements through **ratio analysis**. Ratios, such as return on assets and return on sales, are computed by taking numbers out of financial statements and forming ratios with them. Each ratio has a particular meaning in regard to the potential of the business.

We present a complete explanation of how to complete pro forma financial statements and ratio analysis in Chapter 8.

Appendix   Any material that does not easily fit into the body of a business plan should appear in an appendix—résumés of the top management team, photos or diagrams of product or product prototypes, certain financial data, and market research projections. The appendix should not be bulky and add significant length to the business plan. It should include only the additional information vital to the plan but not appropriate for the body of the plan itself.

Putting It All Together   In evaluating and reviewing the completed business plan, the writers should put themselves in the reader's shoes to determine if the most important questions about the viability of their business venture have been answered. Table 4.3 lists the 10 most important questions a business plan should answer. It's a good checklist for any business plan writer.

PRESENTING THE BUSINESS PLAN TO INVESTORS

If the business plan successfully elicits the interest of a potential investor, the next step is to meet with the investor and present the plan in person. The investor will typically want to meet with the firm's founders. Because investors ultimately fund only a few ventures, the founders of a new firm should make as positive an impression on the investor as possible.

The first meeting with an investor is generally very short, about one hour.[26] The investor will typically ask the firm to make a 20- to 30-minute presentation using PowerPoint slides and use the rest of the time to ask questions. If the investor is impressed and wants to learn more about the venture, the presenters will be asked back for a second meeting to meet with the investor and his or her partners. This meeting will typically last longer and will require a more thorough presentation.

The Oral Presentation of a Business Plan

When asked to meet with an investor, the founders of a new venture should prepare a set of PowerPoint slides that will fill the time slot allowed for the presentation portion of the meeting. The same format applies to most business plan competitions. The first rule in making an oral presentation is to follow instructions. If an investor tells an entrepreneur that he or she has one hour and that the hour will consist of a 30-minute presentation and a 30-minute question-and-answer period, the presentation shouldn't last more than 30 minutes. The presentation should be smooth and well rehearsed. The slides should be sharp and not cluttered with material.

The entrepreneur should arrive at the appointment on time and be well prepared. If any audiovisual equipment is needed, the entrepreneur should be prepared to supply the equipment if the investor doesn't have it. These arrangements should be made before the meeting. The presentation should consist of plain talk and should avoid technical jargon. Start-up entrepreneurs may mistakenly spend too much time talking about the technology that will go into a new product or service and not enough time talking about the business itself. The most important issues to cover in the presentation and how to present them are shown in Table 4.4. This presentation format calls for the use of 12 slides. A common mistake entrepreneurs make is to prepare too many slides and then try to rush through them during a 30-minute presentation.

Questions and Feedback to Expect from Investors

Whether in the initial meeting or on subsequent occasions, an entrepreneur will be asked a host of questions by potential investors. The smart entrepreneur has a good idea of what to expect and is prepared for these queries. Because investors often come across as being very critical,[27] it is easy for an entrepreneur to get discouraged, particularly if the investor seems to be poking holes in every aspect of the business plan. The same dynamic typifies the question-and-answer sessions that follow presentations in business plan competitions. It helps if the entrepreneur can develop a thick skin and remember that generally speaking, investors are simply doing their job. In fact, an investor who is able to identify weaknesses in a business plan or presentation does a favor for the entrepreneur. This is because the entrepreneur can take the investor's feedback to heart and use it to improve the business plan and/or the presentation.

In the first meeting, investors typically focus on whether a real opportunity exists and whether the management team has the experience and skills to pull off the venture. The investor will also try to sense whether the managers are highly confident in their own venture. The question-and-answer period is extremely important. Here investors are typically looking for how well entrepreneurs think on their feet and how knowledgeable they are

Learning Objective

10. Detail the parts of an oral presentation of a business plan.

Table 4.4 TWELVE POWERPOINT SLIDES TO INCLUDE IN AN INVESTOR PRESENTATION

Topic	Explanation
1. Title slide	Introduce the presentation with your company's name, the names of the founders, and the company logo if available.
2. Problem	Briefly state the problem to be solved or the need to be filled.
3. Solution	Explain how your firm will solve the problem or how it will satisfy the need to be filled.
4. Opportunity and target market	Articulate your specific target market. Talk about business and environmental trends that are providing your target market momentum.
5. Technology	This slide is optional but is normally included. Talk about your technology or any unusual aspects of your product or service. Don't talk in an overly technical manner. Make your descriptions easy to understand.
6. Competition	Explain specifically the firm's competitive advantage in the marketplace and how it will compete against more established competitors.
7. Marketing and sales	Describe your overall marketing strategy. Talk about your sales process. If you've administered a buying intentions survey or conducted other primary research regarding how people feel about your product, report the results here.
8. Management team	Describe your existing management team. Explain how the team came together and how their backgrounds and expertise are keys to the success of your firm. If you have a board of advisers or board of directors, briefly mention the key individuals involved. If you have gaps in your team, explain how and when they will be filled.
9. Financial projections	Briefly discuss the financials. Stress when the firm will achieve profitability, how much capital it will take to get there, and when its cash flow will break even. Use additional slides if needed to properly display your information, but don't go overboard.
10. Current status	Describe the current status of your firm in the context of the milestones you've achieved to date. Don't diminish the value of your accomplishments.
11. Financing sought	Lay out specifically how much financing you're seeking and how you'll use the money.
12. Summary	Bring the presentation to a close. Summarize the strongest points of your venture and your team. Solicit feedback from your audience.

B. Barringer, *Preparing Effective Business Plans: An Entrepreneurial Approach,* 1st Edition, © 2009, pp. 242–253. Adapted by permission of Pearson Education, Inc. Upper Saddle River, NJ.

about the business venture. Michael Rovner, a partner of Rob Adam's at AV Labs, put it this way: "We ask a lot of peripheral questions. We might not want answers—we just want to evaluate the entrepreneur's thought process."[28]

Chapter Summary

1. A business plan is a written narrative that describes what a new business intends to accomplish and how it plans to achieve its goals.

2. For most ventures, the business plan is a dual-purpose document used both inside and outside the firm. Inside the firm, it helps the company develop a road map to follow in executing its strategies. Outside the firm, it acquaints potential investors and other stakeholders with the business opportunity the firm is pursuing and describes how the business will pursue that opportunity.

3. There are two primary audiences for a firm's business plan: a firm's employees and investors and other external stakeholders.

4. The business plan should give clear and concise information on all the important aspects of the proposed venture. It must be long enough to provide sufficient information yet short enough to maintain reader interest.

5. A summary business plan is 10 to 15 pages and works best for companies in the early stages of development. These companies don't have the information needed for a full business plan but may put together a summary business plan to see if potential investors are interested in their idea. A full business plan, typically 25 to 35 pages, spells out a company's operations and plans in much more detail than a summary business plan and is the usual format for a business plan prepared for an investor. An operational business plan is usually prepared for an internal audience. It is 40 to 100 pages long and provides a blueprint for a company's operations.

6. Business plans usually change as they're written. As an entrepreneur or team of entrepreneurs immerse themselves in writing the plan and start getting feedback from others, new insights will invariably emerge that weren't initially apparent. This process continues throughout the life of a company, and it behooves entrepreneurs to remain alert and open to new insights and ideas.

7. The executive summary is a quick overview of the entire business plan and provides busy readers with everything they need to know about the distinctive nature of the new venture. In many instances, an investor will ask for a copy of a firm's executive summary and will request a copy of the full business plan only when the executive summary is sufficiently convincing.

8. An industry analysis describes the industry a business will enter. The market analysis, which is a separate section, breaks the industry into segments and zeroes in on the specific segment (or target market) to which the firm will seek to appeal.

9. The best way to describe a company's marketing plan is to start by articulating its marketing strategy, positioning, and points of differentiation, and then talk about how these overall aspects of the plan will be supported by product, price, promotions, and distribution.

10. The management team and company structure section of a business plan is critical. Many investors and others who read business plans look first at the executive summary and then go directly to the management team section to assess the strength of the people starting the firm.

11. The pro forma (or projected) financial statements are the heart of the financial section of a business plan. These include pro forma income statements, balance sheets, and cash flows.

Key Terms

assumptions sheet, **152**
board of advisers, **150**
board of directors, **150**
business plan, **136**
competitor analysis, **149**
executive summary, **144**
full business plan, **142**
market analysis, **148**
market segmentation, **149**

marketing strategy, **149**
milestone, **146**
mission statement, **146**
operational business plan, **142**
organizational chart, **151**
position, **146**
pro forma (or projected)
    financial statements, **153**

prototype, **152**
ratio analysis, **154**
sources and uses of funds
    statement, **152**
summary business plan, **141**
virtual prototype, **152**

Review Questions

1. What is a business plan? What are the advantages of preparing a business plan for a new venture? Explain your answer.
2. When is the appropriate time to write a business plan?
3. What are the two primary reasons for writing a business plan?
4. A business plan is often called a selling document for a new company. In what ways does a business plan provide a mechanism for a young company to present itself to potential investors, suppliers, business partners, and key job candidates?
5. It is often argued that the process of writing a business plan is as important as the plan itself, particularly for the top management team of a young firm. How is this so?
6. Who reads the business plan and what are they looking for?
7. Why is it necessary for a business plan to be realistic? How will investors typically react if they think a business plan is based on estimates and predictions rather than on careful thinking and facts? Where can entrepreneurs obtain facts to substantiate their business plans?
8. Why is it important for a business plan to follow a conventional structure rather than be highly innovative and creative?
9. What are the differences among a summary business plan, a full business plan, and an operational business plan?
10. Why should the executive summary, which is one of the first things that appears in a business plan, be written last?
11. What is a product or service's "position," and why is this concept important?
12. What is the difference between the industry analysis and the market analysis sections of a business plan?
13. What is the purpose of the "Marketing Plan" section of a business plan?
14. Why is the "Management Team and Company Structure" section of a business plan often touted as one of the most important sections of the plan?
15. What is the purpose of the "Operations Plan" section of a business plan?
16. If you're developing a completely new product or service, what type of information should you include in your business plan regarding the status of the development efforts?
17. What is the purpose of a sources and uses of funds statement?
18. What is the purpose of an assumptions sheet? Why is it important to include an assumptions sheet in a business plan's financial section?
19. What are the differences between historical financial statements and pro forma financial statements?
20. What is the number one rule in making an investor presentation?

Application Questions

1. Karen Jones is the chief financial officer of an electronic games start-up venture located in Minneapolis. Her firm has decided to apply for venture capital funding and needs a business plan. Karen told Phil Bridge, the firm's CEO, that she could have the plan done in two weeks. Phil looked at Karen with surprise and said, "Wouldn't it be better if the entire management team of our firm worked on the plan together?" Karen replied, "The only reason we're writing the plan is to get funding. Getting a lot of people involved would just slow things down and be a waste of their time." Do you agree with Karen? Why or why not?
2. Christina Smith, who lives near Seattle, just left her job with Microsoft to start a business that will sell a new type of fax machine. She knows she'll

need a feasibility analysis, a well-articulated business model, and a business plan to get funding, but she can't decide which project to tackle first. If Christina asked you for your advice, what would you tell her and what rationale for your decision would you provide to Christina?

3. A good friend or yours, Patsy Ford, has decided to leave her teaching job to launch a private tutoring company for grade school and middle school children. She is putting together her business plan and asks you, "I have lots of books and articles that tell me how to write a business plan, but I'm wondering if there is anything in particular I should be careful to avoid in putting my plan together." How would you respond to Patsy's question?

4. Spend some time looking at DanceJam, the focus of the "You Be the VC 3.1" feature. Name five things that DanceJam could have done in its feasibility analysis that would have been particularly helpful in supporting its business plan.

5. Suppose you have been asked by your local chamber of commerce to teach a two-hour workshop on how to write an effective business plan. The workshop will be attended by people who are thinking about starting their own business but don't currently have a business plan. Write a one-page outline detailing what you'd cover in the two-hour session.

6. John Brunner is a biochemist at a major university. He is thinking about starting a business to commercialize some animal vaccines on which he has been working. John just registered for a biotech investment conference in San Francisco. A number of venture capitalists are on the program, and John hopes to talk to them about his ideas. John hasn't written a business plan and doesn't see the need to write one. When asked about this issue, he told a colleague, "I can sell my ideas without the hassle of writing a business plan. Besides, I'll have plenty of time to talk to investors at the conference. If they need additional information, I can always write something up when I get home." Explain to John why his approach to the development of a business plan is unwise.

7. Imagine you just received an e-mail message from a friend. The message reads, "Just wanted to tell you that I just finished writing my business plan. I'm very proud of it. It's very comprehensive and is just over 100 pages. The executive summary alone is 9 pages. I plan to start sending it out to potential investors next week. Do you have any words of advice for me before I start sending it out? Be honest—I really want to get funding." How would you respond to your friend's request for feedback?

8. Joan Barnes, who is a family friend, heard you are taking an entrepreneurship course and invited you for coffee to talk to you about a business plan she is just starting. She was very proud when she met you because she completed her executive summary and told you that she plans to use the executive summary as a guide for writing the remaining sections of the plan. Is Joan pursuing a wise approach? Why or why not?

9. Write a mission statement for WIN Detergent, the subject of the "You Be the VC 4.1" feature. What is the rationale for the statement you wrote?

10. Segment the airplane industry in a way that shows where Icon Aircraft, the subject of the "You Be the VC 4.2" feature, is located in the industry. How does Icon's awareness of the segment it is in help it develop its marketing strategy?

11. Jackie Hunter and Katherine Jones are launching a personal finance software company. They're both very proficient programmers and are confident they have a strong product idea, but they have no finance and marketing expertise. Is it premature for Jackie and Katherine to write a business plan for their venture? If they do decide to write the plan, how can they handle their lack of finance and marketing expertise?

12. Bill Sharp, a friend of yours, has an idea for a new type of kitchen utensil, which will make it easier for busy people to scramble eggs in the morning. He showed his business plan to a local SCORE counselor who told Bill that the business plan was strong, but he needed to produce an actual prototype of his product before anyone would take his idea seriously. Bill can't understand why he needs to produce a prototype—it's easy to see on paper what the device will look like and how it will work. What would you tell Bill?

13. Laura Vaughn is thinking about opening a high-end fashion boutique in an affluent suburb of Kansas City, Missouri. Laura knows that she will need to complete an "assumptions sheet" as part of the financial section of her business plan. Explain to Laura the importance of an assumptions sheet, and give her three to five suggestions for assumptions to include based on the nature of her business.

14. Jeremy Collins just got off the phone with an angel investor and is ecstatic because the investor asked him and his cofounder to present their business plan next Monday at 1:00 P.M. The investor said the meeting would last one hour and that 30 minutes would be devoted to the presentation of the business plan and that the remaining 30 minutes would be devoted to a question-and-answer session. Jeremy wants to make the best of this opportunity and has turned to you for advice. How would you advise Jeremy to prepare for this meeting?

15. Suppose you are asked to serve as a judge for a local business plan competition. In preparing for the competition, the organizer has asked you to write a very brief article titled "What the Judges of Business Plan Competitions Look For" that she plans to pass along to the entrepreneurs who enter the competition. Write a 500- to 600-word article to accommodate this request.

You Be the VC 4.1

Company: WIN Detergent

www.windetergent.com

Business Idea: Produce a laundry detergent for athletes and people who exercise frequently, which completely removes odors from both cotton and synthetic fabric.

Pitch: For athletes and people who work out frequently, one of the most exciting innovations in recent years is the development of synthetic fabrics. Synthetic fabrics such as Nike Dri-FIT and Under Armour Coolmax, which are used to make popular tennis, running, cycling, and general fitness apparel, are designed to transfer moisture from your skin to the outside of the fabric where it can quickly evaporate. This process, known as "wicking," helps keep you cool and dry while you're exercising.

A problem with these fabrics is that they are harder to clean. By wicking moisture away from your skin, they embed perspiration residue deep in the fabric. Ordinary laundry detergent was designed to wash primarily cotton fabrics, and does an incomplete job of removing odors from synthetic fabrics. After a few workouts, even the best synthetic clothing typically develops a musty odor. This is where WIN Detergent comes in. WIN High Performance Sports Detergent is designed specifically to clean clothing made from synthetic fabrics. Its scientifically designed super-oxygenated ingredients directly target odors and stains. The same ingredients react with soil and organic materials causing them to either decolorize or disintegrate. The result—odor-free clothing. Two independent laboratory tests show that WIN Detergent outperforms the leading detergents and specialty products on removing sweat and odors from all fabrics. It's formulated to be safe and gentle for all colors and fabrics and works in washing machines or hand washing.

WIN Detergent's target market is sports enthusiasts. More than 5 million Americans exercise over 100 days a year, and an increasing number are wearing synthetic fabrics. WIN Detergent obtained a large boost in 2008 when it was named the official detergent of the U.S. Olympic Team. Although WIN paid to obtain this endorsement, it was a perfect fit. Many Olympians wear synthetic fabrics, and WIN Detergent is now able to place the Olympic Rings on the bottles of its detergent. It also enhances the company's story—that serious athletes rely on WIN Detergent. WIN Detergent is currently sold in sporting good stores and on the company's Web site.

Q&A: Based on the material covered in this chapter, what questions would you ask the firm's founders before making your funding decision? What answers would satisfy you?

Decision: If you had to make your decision on just the information provided in the pitch and on the company's Web site, would you fund this company? Why or why not?

You Be the VC 4.2
Company: Icon Aircraft
www.iconaircraft.com

Business Idea: Produce a sleek, affordable propeller-powered plane for recreational enthusiasts, which is small enough to be towed by a small truck or SUV and stored in a garage.

Pitch: Icon will enter the fast-growing light sport aircraft industry, with an innovative plane that will allow affluent thrill seekers and sports enthusiasts to swoop down for a hike near an isolated lake or enjoy aerial views with a friend on a lazy afternoon. The plane, which is the brainchild of Kirk Hawkins, a former Air Force pilot and aviation adventurer, weighs in at just over 1,400 pounds and can operate on land as well as water. The initial model, called the Icon A5, includes foldable wings so it can fit on a trailer like a boat and roll easily into a garage. The two-seater Icon A5 will be able to fly as slowly as 50 miles per hour or as fast as 120. A stripped-down version of the plan will cost about $140,000. Prototypes of the A5 exist and it has been successfully flown. Full-scale production will begin in 2010.

The market for the plane is recreational and sports enthusiasts, who already spend billions of dollars a year on activities such as boating, motorbiking, hang gliding, parasailing, and similar activities. The A5's amenities include a retractable landing gear, a single 100-horsepower engine that runs on regular gasoline, a sleek design, and an optional parachute for the plane. The passenger cabin is roomy, and the side cockpit windows pop out to provide a wind-in-the-hair feel. Icon is positioning the A5 as a product that encourages and facilitates outdoor fun and camaraderie among recreational enthusiasts. It is also promoting the A5 as a plane that can bring back the "romance and excitement to flying" that was evident in the early years of aviation. One flying enthusiast likened flying a small plane, like the Icon A5, to having your own IMAX theater when flying in the open air and immersed in the experience.

The existence of the Icon A5 is possible in part because of new U.S. Federal Aviation Administration (FAA) regulations. In 2004, the FAA created a new category of aircraft, called Light Sport Aircraft, and a new category of pilot, called Sport Pilot, which makes it less time consuming and cumbersome to obtain a license to fly the Icon A5. By restricting sport pilots to flying in daytime, in good weather, and in uncongested airspace, many of the complexities to learning to fly have been removed. Although Icon considers safety to be a paramount concern, a sports pilot license can be obtained in a matter of weeks as opposed to the months it normally takes to obtain a conventional pilot's license. Icon plans to market the Icon A5 through sales channels that are much broader than those used by traditional recreational aircraft manufacturers.

Q&A: Based on the material covered in this chapter, what questions would you ask the firm's founders before making your funding decision? What answers would satisfy you?

Decision: If you had to make your decision on just the information provided in the pitch and on the company's Web site, would you fund this company? Why or why not?

CASE4.1

Kazoo & Company: You Can Compete Against the Big Guys—If You Have the Right Plan

www.kazootoys.com

Bruce R. Barringer
Oklahoma State University
R. Duane Ireland
Texas A & M University

Introduction

There is no denying it. It's tough for an independent toy store to compete against Wal-Mart, Target, Toys "R" Us, and other large retailers selling products that entertain children and adults alike.

So how is it that Kazoo Toys, an independent toy store in Denver, Colorado, is thriving? It's thriving because of two things—the firm has a doggedly determined entrepreneur at the helm and it has a good business plan. After you read about Kazoo Toys, you'll nod your head and think to yourself, yup—that's a good plan!

Diana Nelson

In the early 1990s, Diana Nelson left the corporate world with the intention of spending more time with her two young sons. In 1998, she decided to reenter the workforce, but this time as an entrepreneur. Rather than starting a company from scratch, she set out looking for a business to buy. After ruling out fast food and flower shops, she came across a toy store named Kazoo & Company. She saw untapped potential in the store and decided to buy it. It wasn't easy to get the money together to close the deal. To finance the purchase, she cashed out her retirement accounts, put $25,000 on credit cards, borrowed money from her father, and set up a $500,000 SBA-guaranteed bank loan. "I gambled everything to buy a toy store," she says. The actions Nelson took to finance her venture demonstrate the courage that characterizes virtually all entrepreneurs.

From the outset, Nelson had no illusions that owning a toy store would be easy. When she bought Kazoo, independent toy stores were being tattered to pieces by Wal-Mart, Toys "R" Us, and other large retailers. So, she knew that the only way to beat them was to outthink them. In this regard, Nelson saw her challenge as that of designing and then implementing a business plan that would make a small toy store competitive. Here's how she did it.

Kazoo's Business Plan

The essence of Kazoo's business plan was to not try to be like Wal-Mart or Toys "R" Us. Instead, Nelson set out to build a business that would offer unique products and services to its clientele. The mistake that many small businesses make, in Nelson's thinking, is that they set themselves up to compete against the chains (e.g., Toys "R" Us) or a supercenter (Wal-Mart) by trying to duplicate what they do. In these instances, the best an entrepreneurial venture can expect to do is to come close to being as effective at what the "big boys" are skilled at doing. Instead of falling into that trap, Nelson took Kazoo in a different direction. "We changed our whole merchandise mix to not carry the same product (as the nationwide chains did)," she recalls, "so price competition isn't an issue." As a result of this strategy, Kazoo doesn't carry Mattel, Crayola, or Fisher-Price. Instead, the store sells unique items like Gotz Dolls from Germany and a wide range of educational toys. The key to making this strategy work, Nelson found, is to build strong relationships with vendors. To help do this, Nelson invites many of Kazoo's vendors to demo and test new products in her store. Doing this gives Kazoo first crack at many of the new products that its vendors make. While they are in her store, the vendors also tip their hand from time to time regarding what the big retailers are buying. This gives Nelson and Kazoo a heads-up about what not to buy.

In 1999, Nelson opened a Yahoo! store online. The site sold the same type of toys being sold in the store. Over time, Nelson increased her Internet prowess and now her Kazoo & Company's Web site sells many of the same products that are sold in the store, along with additional products that are drop shipped by vendors. At one point in the early 2000s, Nelson considered franchising Kazoo but decided to pass on the idea. Instead, she felt it was better to preserve Kazoo's "destination" image and build the e-commerce site. Now, with 10 years of experience as Kazoo's owner under her belt,

Nelson has decided to pursue franchising, and Kazoo & Company will begin franchising in 2009.

Points of Differentiation

Through all of this, Kazoo has established strong points of differentiation between itself and its much larger competitors, which has been the heart of Kazoo's business plan from the beginning. Along with carrying different products than its competitors, Kazoo is different from Wal-Mart, Toys "R" Us, and other large toy retailers in the following ways.

1. The company welcomes professionals, like speech therapists, to bring their patients into the store, to play with them and identify specific toys that might help them progress in their treatments. Observing professionals work with their patients (i.e., young children that have some type of disability) also helps Kazoo's staff know what to recommend when a parent comes in looking for a similar solution.
2. Kazoo's store design is unique. While the store itself is still fairly small, it is further broken down into smaller, more intimate departments. "When a particular consumer goes into a Toys "R" Us it has departments, but it's like a big warehouse," Nelson explains. "Here, it's very small. It's intimate, but it's also departmentalized, so you actually have a Playmobil department, and you have a Thomas the Tank Engine department."
3. The company focuses intently on customer service, from free gift wrapping to free parking. So whether it's a baby crying or a customer who can't find an item in the store, the company works hard to accommodate its customers in every way possible.
4. The company's specialty is selling educational, nonviolent toys, for birth to 12-year-old children. In fact, Kazoo's focus on selling toys that meet this criterion has won it a loyal clientele.
5. The inventory in the store is freshened up frequently, so regular customers see different toys each time they come into the store. "If you think about your regular customer, they don't want to see the same stuff on the shelf all the time, so we're always changing our inventory and our mix of what we do," Nelson said.

Kazoo's business plan and its sharp execution have paid off. Business is growing, and the company was selected as one of the Top 5 Specialty Retail Toy Stores in North America by the Toy Industry Association in 2003, 2004, 2005, and 2006. Its Internet site was voted the number one toy Internet site in 2006 and 2007 by *Playthings* magazine.

Challenges Ahead

Although Kazoo & Company has done well, there are many challenges that lie ahead. For one, a lot of the manufacturers of specialty toys, which have been Kazoo's bread-and-butter since Nelson bought the firm in 1998, are now selling into broader channels. Thus, the toys that at one time only Kazoo and other specialty toy stores could get their hands on will be popping up in other types of stores. Economic pressures also tend to hit specialty retailers particularly hard. Tough economic times drive more people to Wal-Mart and Target, as opposed to specialty stores.

As far as Diana Nelson is concerned, she is very content with her decision to become an entrepreneur and the lifestyle that accompanies that decision as the owner of Kazoo & Company. Commenting on how her young sons fared over the years with her decision to buy a toy store, she said, "Their friends think—how cool are they that their mom has a toy store and a toy business." How cool indeed!

Discussion Questions

1. To what extent do you sense that Diana Nelson got up to speed quickly on the dynamics of the toy industry when she took over Kazoo & Company in 1998? What impact would it have had on the ultimate success of Kazoo if Nelson had spent more time initially focused on the specifics of her business (i.e., store layout, hiring personnel, placing ads in local newspapers, writing press releases, setting up the accounting system, and so on) rather than gaining a complete understanding of the toy industry as part of her work to carefully develop a business plan?
2. When she first bought the store, do you think that Nelson could have convinced an investor that Kazoo & Company could successfully compete against the likes of giants such as Wal-Mart, Target, and Toys "R" Us? If not, who needed to believe that the business plan would work? How does an entrepreneur's level of belief in his or her own business plan affect how successful the business is, particularly in the early years?
3. Based on the information contained in the case, write the one-page executive summary of Kazoo's original business plan.
4. What is drop shipping? What are the advantages and the risks for a company like Kazoo & Company to engage in drop-shipping arrangements with its vendors?

Application Questions

1. If you had taken over Kazoo & Company in 1998 instead of Diana Nelson, would you have thought

(continued)

of all the things that Nelson did? Would you have been able to write Kazoo's original business plan? If your answer is *no* to these questions, what steps can you take now to better prepare yourself for the day that you might become an entrepreneur? Make your answer as specific as possible.

2. If you decided to buy a specialty store that competes against Wal-Mart, Target, or another big-box retailer, what type of store would you like to own? How would you differentiate your store from your larger competitors?

Sources: Kazoo & Company homepage, www.kazootoys.com (accessed November 15, 2008); B. Ruggiero, "Kazoo & Company Reaches Top 5 . . . Again," *TD Monthly*, June 2005; J. M. Webb, "When the Tools of the Trade Are Toys," *TD Monthly*, March 2006.

CASE4.2

Yelp!: How a Willingness to Let Its Business Plan Quickly Evolve Helped a Start-Up Get Its Offering Right
www.yelp.com

Bruce R. Barringer
Oklahoma State University
R. Duane Ireland
Texas A & M University

Introduction

Yelp is a Web site where anyone can post reviews of restaurants, coffee shops, doctors, dentists, or any business with which they are familiar. It differentiates itself from similar sites by giving reviewers an identity. Each reviewer has a profile that features their picture, lists their friends, and provides a history of their past reviews. As a result, you can be assured that a review on Yelp is authentic. Most local review sites allow anonymous reviews. A problem with this approach is how do you know if a positive review about a restaurant wasn't written by the restaurant's owner?

Yelp was launched in October 2004. Today, over 10.6 million people access Yelp's Web site each month, making it one of the top 100 most visited Web sites in the United States. The interesting thing is that Yelp's initial business plan bombed. Only by letting its business plan quickly evolve did Yelp's founders place it on the right track.

Initial Business Plan

Yelp was founded by Jeremy Stoppelman and Russell Simmons, two Silicon Valley tech entrepreneurs. Both were intrigued by the notion that when people are looking for a new restaurant, barber shop, or plumber they normally ask their friends for a recommendation, but no one had created a Web site to help people do this. Yelp was launched to give people the ability to e-mail a list of their friends to ask for a recommendation for a restaurant, doctor, barber, or any service provider in a specific geographic area. The message included a link that allowed the friend to easily provide a recommendation. The recommendation would go back to the person who asked for it and also be added to a directory of businesses that had been recommended in an area. As a result, if you lived in the Mission District of San Francisco and none of the people you e-mailed via Yelp could recommend a good eye doctor, you could look at Yelp's directory of eye doctors who had been recommended by other Yelp users in your area.

It didn't work. People started complaining that they were getting too many e-mail messages from friends and often didn't have a recommendation. In turn, people trying to get a recommendation often came up empty. Surprisingly, the one aspect of the site that worked was the ability to write your own review—a functionality that had been included by Yelp's founders almost as an afterthought. Rather than waiting until a friend asked for a recommendation about a restaurant or a doctor, people seemed to enjoy sharing information about their favorite restaurants or their doctor without being asked. Yelp's founders quickly concluded that their site was onto something, but their users were pointing them in a different direction than their original business plan.

Revised Business Plan

In February 2005, just four months after Yelp was launched, Stoppelman and Simmons revised their firm's business plan. The new plan dropped the e-mail your friends idea and focused on providing a platform for people to proactively write reviews of local businesses. The Web site itself was also redesigned. Yelp's initial site required people to sign up prior to using the service so Stoppelman and Simmons had a good idea of who its users were. Surprising to them, its users were mostly women. So they redesigned the site, changing the color scheme from a masculine gray and blue to softer more feminine colors. They also tweaked their name. Stoppelman worried that "Yelp" sounded like an angry dog, which may put off women. While they didn't drop "Yelp" they softened it by adding a burst at the end of the word that looks like a flower or ribbon bow.

The redesigned site and emphasis on local reviews immediately resonated with users. Traffic to the site grew, and the founders started hearing users say things like, "Oh, this is so much fun" and "it's addictive." These types of sentiments hadn't been expressed about the first version of the site. Stoppelman and Simmons knew that their concept was now right. They also saw the beginnings of a Yelp community emerge. The challenge now was how to flesh out their revised plan and implement it in a sensible manner.

Key Decisions to Flesh Out Yelp's Revised Business Plan

Several key decisions were made to flesh out Yelp's revised business plan. First, the founders decided not to pay for reviews. Some local search Web sites, to build a directory of reviews, paid people to write reviews. Others, like CitySearch, maintained a staff to write descriptions of business and editorial reviews. Yelp's founders wanted their site to be built by people who simply wanted to share their experiences. The only exception would be when Yelp expanded to a new city and needed to build an initial critical mass of local reviews. Second, rather than trying to go nationwide all at once, Stoppelman and Simmons decided to follow the Craigslist model and build Yelp city by city. Craigslist did not go nationwide initially. Instead, it established itself in San Francisco first and then expanded methodically from city to city until its service blanketed the nation. Yelp determined to follow the same approach. It would firmly establish itself in San Francisco before

expanding. Third, to add credibility to their site the founders came up with the idea of requiring reviewers to build profiles of themselves including photos, a friends list, and a listing of their past reviews. This initiative provided Yelp a social networking flavor. Yelp profiles are as lively and content rich as most Facebook and MySpace pages. As a result, many Yelp users have favorite reviewers and follow their recommendations for restaurants and other businesses.

Stoppelman and Simmons also decided to make Yelp fun. To connect with their users, and allow Yelp's users to meet each other face to face, they sponsored Yelp parties, a tradition that the company has kept up. They also sell Yelp apparel similar to what you'd find at a Planet Hollywood or Hard Rock Café.

One of Stoppelman and Simmons' toughest challenges was determining Yelp's revenue model. The company settled on selling what it calls sponsorships, which are somewhat controversial. By buying a "sponsorship" a business can bring favorable reviews to the top (of its listings), move negative reviews to the bottom, provide a photo slideshow, and post a message from the business's owner. The one thing Yelp won't do, which it feels is integral to its integrity as a local search site, is to completely remove negative reviews.

Challenges Ahead

Yelp's business plan is still evolving and it has challenges ahead. As of this writing (fall 2008) it has not reached profitability. Although it has an impressive critical mass of users in cities, it's unclear whether it will be able to replicate its success in small towns. Even though Yelp is a Web 2.0 Internet company, it sells it sponsorships largely through a traditional sales force, which must knock on doors like any other sales organization. As a result, Yelp will need to continue to expand the size of its sales force as it grows.

Discussion Questions

1. Go to Yelp's Web site and look up one of your favorite restaurants. What do you think? Do you think the company has an attractive enough offering that it will continue to increase its number of users? Will you use the service again? Why or why not?

2. What are the most important assumptions that Yelp's initial business plan is based on? How about its revised business plan? Compare and contrast the two.

3. What changes to Yelp did the company's founders make to effectively implement their revised business plan? Were the changes

(continued)

obvious or did it take careful observation on the founders' part to know what changes to make?

4. What do you think would have happened to Yelp, after it revised its business plan, if it had decided to go nationwide all at once?

Application Questions

1. Write a mission statement for Yelp. If Yelp already has one and you come across it in your research, write down the mission statement and comment on its appropriateness.

2. Think of a time in your life when you (1) committed yourself to achieve something substantial, (2) your first few attempts to achieve it failed, and (3) you eventually found a way to be successful. What made you persevere despite your early failures? Compare your experience to Jeremy Stoppelman and Russell Simmons's experience with Yelp.

Sources: G. Galant and J. Stoppelman, "VentureVoice Show #46—Jeremy Stoppelman of Yelp," Venture Voice Podcast, May 2008; Yelp homepage, www.yelp.com (accessed September 30, 2008).

Endnotes

1. "GroupTable.com Launches Beta Version of GroupTable Online Tool for Campus Study Groups," Press release, *UCF Technology Incubator*, February 21, 2008.
2. Personal Conversation with David Brim, December 8, 2008.
3. *Entrepreneur's Toolkit* (Boston: Harvard Business School Publishing, 2005).
4. Wells Fargo, "How Much Money Does It Take to Start a Small Business?" Wells Fargo/Gallup Small Business Index, August 15, 2006.
5. J. Liao and W. Gartner, "The Influence of Pre-Venture Planning on New Venture Creation," *Journal of Small Business Strategy* 18, no. 2 (Fall/Winter 2008): 21–30.
6. K. Shah, "SMEs Need to Beef Up Business Plans, Warns Lotus," *Financial Advisor*, FT Business, October 2, 2008.
7. "Meet Lindsey Wieber and Gwen Whiting," Ladies Who Launch, www.ladieswholaunch.com (accessed July 20, 2007, originally posted January 16, 2007).
8. P. Kennedy, "20 Reasons Why You Need a Business Plan," growthink, www.growthink.com, April 9, 2008 (accessed December 1, 2008); Adam Jolly, *From Idea to Profit* (Kogan Page: London, 2005).
9. K. Hindle and B. Mainprize, "A Systematic Approach to Writing and Rating Entrepreneurial Business Plans," *The Journal of Private Equity* 9, no. 3 (Summer 2006): 1–17; M. D. Foo, P. K. Wong, and A. Ong, "Do Others Think You Have a Viable Business Idea? Team Diversity and Judges' Evaluation of Ideas in a Business Plan Competition," *Journal of Business Venturing* 20, no. 3 (2005): 385–402.
10. B. Ford and J. Pruitt, *The Ernst & Young Business Plan Guide* (New York: Ernst & Young, 2007).
11. M. C. Mankins and R. Steele, "Turning Great Strategy into Great Performance," *Harvard Business Review* 85, no. 7 (2005): 78–89; D. Valentine, "Don Valentine: Sequoia Capital," in *Done Deals: Venture Capitalists Tell Their Stories*, ed. U. Gupta (Boston: Harvard Business School Press, 2000), 173.
12. Deloitte & Touche, *Writing an Effective Business Plan*, 4th edition, 2003.
13. G. Kawasaki, *The Art of the Start* (New York: Portfolio, 2004).
14. T. Needleman, "Business Plan Software Remains an Important App," *Accounting Today* 21, no. 3 (2007): 16.
15. J. L. Nesheim, *The Power of Unfair Advantage* (New York: Free Press, 2005).
16. Personal conversation with Michael Heller, January 20, 2002.
17. *Entrepreneur's Toolkit* (Boston: Harvard Business School Publishing, 2005).
18. B. Feld, "Should You Hire Someone to Write Your Business Plan?" *Ask the VC*, www.askthevc.com/blog/archives/2007/02/should-you-hire.php (accessed November 12, 2008).
19. C. Tang, Interview with Calvin Tang, nPost homepage, www.npost.com (accessed November 15, 2008).
20. U. Looser and B. Schlapfer, *The New Venture Adventure* (New York: Texere, 2001).

21. S. Rogers, *The Entrepreneur's Guide to Finance and Business* (New York: McGraw-Hill, 2003).
22. *Entrepreneur's Toolkit* (Boston: Harvard Business School Publishing, 2005).
23. B. Ford and J. Pruitt, *The Ernst & Young Business Plan Guide* (New York: Ernst & Young: 2007).
24. R. Rico, M. Sanchez-Manzanares, F. Gil, and C. Gibson, "Team Implicit Coordination Processes: A Team Knowledge-Based Approach," *Academy of Management Review* 33, no. 1 (2008): 163–84; K. Eisenhardt and C. Shoonhoven, "Organizational Growth: Linking Founding Team Strategy, Environment, and Growth Among U.S. Semiconductor Ventures, 1978–1988," *Administrative Science Quarterly* 35 (1990): 504–29.
25. A. Sherman, *Fast-Track Business Growth* (Washington, DC: Kiplinger Books, 2001).
26. J. L. Nesheim, *High-Tech Start Up* (New York, NY; The Free Press, 2000).
27. J. L. Nesheim, *High-Tech Start Up* (New York, NY; The Free Press, 2000).
28. R. Adams, *A Good Hard Kick in the Ass* (New York: Crown Books, 2002), 150.

Getting Personal

with Amy Shukla

CURRENTLY IN MY IPOD
Kanye West, T-plain,
Lil' Wayne

WHAT I DO WHEN I'M NOT WORKING
Watch movies with my business partner

MY ADVICE TO NEW ENTREPRENEURS
Don't let critics steer you away from your dream

BEST PART OF BEING A STUDENT
Knowing that my opportunities are endless

BEST ADVICE I'VE RECEIVED
My dad taught me "Under promise and over deliver" (P. K. Shukla)

FIRST ENTREPRENEURIAL EXPERIENCE
Selling bracelets with my sister and best friend in fifth grade

AMY SHUKLA
Cofounder, BusinessesAtoZ
BS, Computer Science, Chapman University, expected 2010

BHAVDIP BHAYANI
Cofounder, BusinessesAtoZ
BS, Engineering and Computer Science, Fullerton College, expected 2010

CHAPTERFIVE
Industry and Competitor *Analysis*

OPENING PROFILE
BUSINESSESATOZ
Occupying a Unique Position in a Difficult Industry—and Thriving
www.businessatoz.com

In high school, Amy Shukla and Bhavdip Bhayani earned extra income by developing Web sites for clients. They did "project" work, meaning that once a Web site was completed, they referred the client to a Web hosting company that charged a monthly fee to host its Web site. While the arrangement worked well, it was obvious to Shukla and Bhayani that they were leaving money on the table. If they could offer their own Web hosting service, they could keep the clients they built Web sites for and create a source of recurring income.

Shukla and Bhayani recall meeting at Denny's near their homes in Orange County, California, to hammer out how they could create a company to meet their objectives. Bhayani outlined the business on a napkin—a keepsake the two have to this day. What they designed is akin to what's referred to as a Web development firm. They would (1) design Web sites and (2) offer a Web hosting service. They picked a name for the company, but the Internet domain name was already taken. Shukla's dad owned the domain name www.businessesAtoZ.com, and agreed to let them use it. As a result, the business, which was launched in July 2007, was named BusinessesAtoZ.

By this time, Shukla was a math and computer science student at Chapman University and Bhayani was preparing to enter Fullerton College as an electrical engineering and computer science major. The two universities are only a few miles apart. Shukla and Bhayani made a good team, partly because they have complementary skills. Shukla's expertise is in graphic design and customer service, and Bhayani is an expert coder. The two knew that Web hosting is a tough industry, so they positioned BusinessesAtoZ carefully. The Web hosting industry is characterized by firms that represent two extremes. One extreme is small companies that own their own servers. While these companies offer customer service, the risk is if a server goes down a client's Web site could go dark. The other extreme is large companies like Yahoo! While a clients' Web site will never go down if it's hosted by Yahoo! (Yahoo! has ample redundancy in its operations), it's harder to get good customer service.

To capture the benefits of both extremes, Shukla and Bhayani positioned BusinessesAtoZ right in the middle. The company offers high levels of customer service. In fact, an innovation that Shukla and Bhayani came up with to bolster customer service is a "ticket" or work order system, where a client can "open a ticket" or submit a request for service and rate the urgency of the request on a scale of 1 to 10. That way Shukla and Bhayani can prioritize their work and deal with the most critical customer service issues first. In terms of the risks associated with small companies and servers going down, rather than owing their own equipment, Shukla and Bhayani lease servers from various companies. This gives them the same level of guaranteed uptime service as their larger competitors. As a result, BusinessesAtoZ captures the strengths of both extremes of the Web hosting industry—it offers high customer service (like the other little guys) and very little chance that a client's Web site will go down (like the big guys).

Learning Objectives

After studying this chapter you should be ready to:

1. Explain the purpose of an industry analysis.

2. Identify the five competitive forces that determine industry profitability.

3. Explain the role of "barriers to entry" in creating disincentives for firms to enter an industry.

4. Identify the nontraditional barriers to entry that are especially associated with entrepreneurial firms.

5. List the four industry-related questions to ask before pursuing the idea for a firm.

6. Identify the five primary industry types and the opportunities they offer.

7. Explain the purpose of a competitor analysis.

8. Identify the three groups of competitors a new firm will face.

9. Describe ways a firm can ethically obtain information about its competitors.

10. Describe the reasons for completing a competitive analysis grid.

The other benefit that Shukla and Bhayani offer, which is something that large firms have trouble matching, is hustle. They're passionate about their business, which is evident in the work they do, how quickly they respond to client requests, and in the extras they offer. For example, many Web hosting firms outsource much of what they offer their clients, like the shopping cart functionality that e-commerce sites have. BusinessesAtoZ builds every component from scratch, which saves money and avoids incompatibility issues. Similarly, through a job with a technology company, Bhayani has developed an expertise in backup solutions for Web sites. It's now possible for a company to have the data on its computers backed up in real time, so there is no possibility of data being lost. BusinessesAtoZ plans to offer this service to its Web hosting clients for free. If a competitor tries to match BusinessesAtoZ in this area, it will likely incur additional costs because it will have to outsource the service absent Bhayani's expertise.

Shukla and Bhayani plan to graduate from their respective universities in fall 2010. They credit academic mentors who have contributed to their success. Amy Shukla's father, Pradip Shukla, has been particularly helpful. He's an entrepreneurship professor at Chapman University. A challenge that Shukla and Bhayani will face moving forward is offering the same levels of customer service and amenities as their business grows.

BusinessesAtoZ is a success in part because of Amy Shukla and Bhavdip Bhayani's ability to analyze the Web hosting industry and precisely position BusinessesAtoZ within it. In this chapter, we'll look at industry analysis and competitor analysis. The first section of the chapter considers **industry analysis**, which is business research that focuses on the potential of an industry. An **industry** is a group of firms producing a similar product or service, such as music, fitness drinks, or electronic games. Once it is determined that a new venture is feasible in regard to the industry and the target market in which it will compete, a more in-depth analysis is needed to learn the ins and outs of the industry the firm plans to enter. This analysis helps a firm determine if the niche or target markets it identified during its feasibility analysis are accessible and which ones represent the best point of entry for the new firm.

We focus on competitor analysis in the second section of the chapter. A **competitor analysis** is a detailed evaluation of a firm's competitors. Once a firm decides to enter an industry and chooses a market in which to compete, it must gain an understanding of its competitive environment. We'll look at how a firm identifies its competition and the importance of completing a competitive analysis grid.

INDUSTRY ANALYSIS

Learning Objective

1. Explain the purpose of an industry analysis.

When studying an industry, an entrepreneur must answer three questions before pursuing the idea of starting a firm. First, is the industry accessible—in other words, is it a realistic place for a new venture to enter? Second, does the industry contain markets that are ripe for innovation or are underserved? Third, are there positions in the industry that will avoid some of the negative attributes of the industry as a whole? It is useful for a new venture to think about its **position** at both the company level and the product or service level. At the company level, a firm's position determines how the company is situated relative to its competitors, as discussed in Chapter 4. For example, Blue Maze Entertainment has positioned itself as a company that produces branded music products and manages branded music campaigns. This is a much different position than Warner Music or EMI, which are all-purpose music companies. Sometimes, through savvy positioning, a firm can enter an unattractive industry and do well. Because it found an attractive niche market and has nicely positioned itself in that market, Blue Maze is profitable even though it competes in a moderately unattractive industry.

The importance of knowing the competitive landscape, which is what an industry is, may have been first recognized in the fourth century B.C. by Sun-tzu, a Chinese philosopher. Reputedly he wrote *The Art of War* to help generals prepare for battle. However, the ideas in the book are still used today to help managers prepare their firms for the competitive wars of the marketplace. The following quote from Sun-tzu's work points out the importance of industry analysis:

> We are not fit to lead an army on the march unless we are familiar with the face of the country—its pitfalls and precipices, its marshes and swamps.[1]

These words serve as a reminder to entrepreneurs that regardless of how eager they are to start their businesses, they are not adequately prepared until they are "familiar with the face of the country"—that is, until they understand the industry or industries they plan to enter.

To illustrate the importance of the industry a firm chooses to enter, research evidence shows that both firm- and industry-specific factors contribute to a firm's profitability.[2] Firm-level factors include a firm's assets, products, culture, reputation, and other resources. Industry-specific factors include the threat of new entrants, rivalry among existing firms, the bargaining power of suppliers, and other factors discussed in this chapter. In various studies, researchers have found that from 8 to 30 percent of the variation in firm profitability is directly attributable to the industry in which a firm competes.[3] Two researchers (including Harvard University professor Michael Porter, the author of the five competitive forces model we discuss in this chapter) who are known for their studies of industry effects found that 19 percent of the variation in firm profitability is attributable to stable industry effects. Commenting on the 19 percent figure, Porter concluded, "This result provides strong support for the idea that industry membership has an important influence on [firm] profitability."[4]

Because both firm- and industry-level factors are important in determining a firm's profitability, there are firms that do well in unattractive or moderately attractive industries if they are well positioned and well managed. Still, the overall attractiveness of an industry should be part of the equation when an entrepreneur decides whether to pursue a particular opportunity. Two techniques that entrepreneurs have available for assessing industry attractiveness are studying industry trends and the five forces framework.

Studying Industry Trends

The first technique that an entrepreneur has available to discern the attractiveness of an industry is to study industry trends. The two trends that are the most important to focus on are environmental trends and business trends.

Environmental Trends   As discussed in Chapter 2, environmental trends are very important. The strength of an industry often surges or wanes not so much because of the management skills of the firms in the industry, but because environmental trends shift in favor or against the products or services sold by firms in the industry.

Economic trends, social trends, technological advances, and political and regulatory changes are the most important environmental trends for entrepreneurs to study. For example, any industry that sells products to seniors, such as the eyeglasses industry and the hearing aid industry, are benefiting from the aging of the population, a social trend. In contrast, industries that sell food products that are high in sugar, such as the candy industry and the sugared soft-drink industry, are suffering as the result of a renewed emphasis on health and fitness. Sometimes there are multiple environmental changes at work that set the stage for an industry's future. This point is illustrated in the following statement from Standard & Poor's NetAdvantage's assessment of the future of the motorcycle industry:

> Over time, we think factors that are likely to affect motorcycle sales are personal income and spending levels, consumer confidence, levels of unemployment, demographics, the amount of free time that people have available, and the extent to which brand recognition and appeal are created. We expect that an aging population, and the impact that this has on consumer demand, will limit opportunities for industry sales growth. In the U.S., we expect that efforts will increase to encourage the number of female motorcycle riders.[5]

This short statement illustrates the degree to which environmental change can affect one industry, and may cause an entrepreneur who was considering entering the motorcycle industry to pause. Similar forces are at work in all industries.

Some industries experience slow or no growth for years and then experience sudden upswings in growth and popularity as the result of savvy industry incumbents and/or entrepreneurs who realized that environmental change has turned in favor of the industry. A current example is the mattress industry. In *Business Week*'s 2007 list of "The Best (100) Small Companies to Watch," two of the companies, Select Comfort and Tempur-Pedic International, were mattress companies. Surprising, isn't it. Who would have thought that with all the high-tech and other interesting companies in the United States that two mattress companies would make the list? But a number of significant environmental trends are working in favor of the industry.[6]

■ Rising incomes have led to increased mattress sales at the high end of the market.

■ High shipping costs have limited imports (imports represent only 2.9 percent of U.S. mattress industry sales).

■ A recent upswing in hotel and motel construction has resulted in a spike in mattress demand from that sector.

■ There are approximately 2.7 million hospital and nursing home beds in the United States. These facilities typically purchase high-end mattresses with enhancements that allow them to be electronically adjusted. As the population ages, the health care market for mattresses will continue to expand.

■ An increased emphasis on wellness has created new markets for mattresses that will improve sleep quality and provide better neck and back support.

■ Technological improvements in spring design, foam usage, and overall construction of mattresses have stimulated additional demand for high-quality mattresses.

If you spend a few minutes browsing Select Comfort and Tempur-Pedic's Web sites, you'll see that they are tapping into these exact trends. An awareness of environmental trends can help start-ups better understand the industries they plan to enter and help them develop more successful businesses.

Business Trends   Other trends impact industries that aren't environmental trends per se but are important to mention. For example, the firms in some industries benefit from an increasing ability to outsource manufacturing or service functions to lower-cost foreign labor markets, while firms in other industries don't share this advantage. In a similar fashion, the firms in some industries are able to move customer procurement and service functions online, at considerable cost savings, while the firms in other industries aren't able to capture this advantage. Trends like these favor some industries over others.

One company that suffered as a result of not staying on top of social and business trends is Burberry, as illustrated in the "What Went Wrong?" feature. For decades Burberry was a heritage brand with a strong position in its industry. The company lost its way in the 1990s largely because it took its success for granted and lost sight of what made it a sought-after brand.

What Went WRONG?

Burberry: How a Traditional British Brand Lost Its Favorable Position in the Fashion Industry

Once a company establishes a favorable position in an industry, it must remain vigilant or its position can be lost. Burberry is a British fashion brand founded in 1856 and rich in history. The brand not only equipped polar explorer Sir Ernest Shackleton, but its waterproof coats were also worn in World War I by Army officers, which is the origin of the "trench coat" label. Women too flocked to the luxury brand and many a debutant "came out" wearing a floor-length Burberry dress in duchess satin.

Keeping an exclusive fashion brand relevant year after year is a delicate balancing act, yet Burberry managed it seamlessly for well over a century. On the one hand it was careful not to become too famous, because the minute a luxury brand becomes too accessible to the mass market it becomes devalued. On the other hand it steered clear of becoming too exclusive and alienating great swathes of well-off buyers.

By the 1970s, however, Burberry's popularity began to wane. Its association with the upper classes saw many contemporary fashion lovers begin to dismiss it as a bit stuffy, perhaps as rigid as its ubiquitous checks, which were introduced in the 1920s. In the early 1990s as a celebrity culture really began to take off, fueled by the Internet, a plethora of new television channels, and several magazine launches dedicated to what film and pop stars were wearing, Burberry made the fateful decision to pursue the burgeoning market for designer labels. The brand upped its advertising budget to target the mainstream audience and its trademark check, which was previously only used as a discreet lining, was prominently used on all its ranges. The check surfaced on everything from scarves to purses to handbags and skirts. When it rained, High Street was a sea of Burberry umbrellas. A flood of counterfeit Burberry stock appeared at market stalls up and down the country to satisfy the demand, and before long the brand gained a reputation as the hooligan's label of choice. The fall of the once-exclusive brand was declared complete when Danniella Westbrook, an actress from a down-market television soap opera, was pictured dressed head to toe in Burberry check with her baby and her pram dressed to match. The tabloid press had a field day, and the once-great Burberry brand was declared a national joke.

The change in status of the brand was so marked that major London department stores such as Harvey Nichols and Selfridges would no longer stock the ranges and Harrods would only carry the traditional raincoats. In 1997, Rose Marie Bravo was recruited from the New York department store Saks Fifth Avenue to become chief executive of Burberry. Her first step was to cut down on the reliance of what she termed "logoism." At the height of Burberry's fame, the check appeared on 20 percent of its outfits, it has now been pruned back to less than 5 percent. The group also discontinued many lines, such as the Burberry baseball cap, and undertook a strident clampdown on fakes.

Cutting-edge designer Christopher Bailey was brought in and pored over the brand archives looking for ways to tap into its rich history. He then redesigned the core range to feature "classics with a twist" by transforming the traditional trench into a bright fuchsia coat, for example. Under the younger Burberry Prorsum label, Bailey inspired a number of new trends, such as vertiginous shoes and expensive handbags fashioned from exotic skins.

(continued)

Rose Marie Bravo also recognized that Burberry's uniquely British reputation still had real appeal to fashion watchers around the world, despite its tattered reputation at home. Famed fashion photographer Mario Testino was hired to shoot a sophisticated black-and-white advertising campaign, which traded on the brand's heritage by using models that appeared to be members of the British aristocracy.

The reinvention of Burberry has not been an overnight phenomenon. It has been a long haul over several years. Sales are steadily rising, and Burberry has made considerable progress in turning itself into one of the top global luxury goods brands. However, although the brand is now firmly back in Britain's top department stores, just 15 percent of Burberry's sales come from the country itself. The rest mainly come from Asia and North America.

Questions for Critical Thinking

1. What steps, if any, could Burberry have taken to prevent the loss of its favorable position in the fashion industry in the early 1900s? How had it managed to avoid this problem previously?

2. Look at Burberry's Web site. How would you describe the positioning of the firm today? Look at other luxury goods and fashion brands such as Prada, Gucci, and LVMH. Which firm do you think has the most distinct positioning strategy? What industry trends do you think Burberry is relying on to continue its positive momentum?

3. Do you think it would be possible for a new or existing brand to successfully imitate what Burberry has done in positioning its brand?

4. Use Table 5.2 to complete an industry analysis on the fashion and luxury goods industry today. Is it an attractive industry? Would it be a good or poor industry for a start-up firm to enter?

Sources: "The Two Faces of Burberry," *The Guardian*, April 15, 2004; "The Luxury Brand with a Chequered Past, Burberry's Shaken Off Its Chav Image to Become the Fashionistas' Favourite Once More," *Daily Mail*, June 2, 2008.

The Five Competitive Forces Model

Learning Objective

2. Identify the five competitive forces that determine industry profitability.

The five competitive forces model is a framework for understanding the structure of an industry and was developed by Harvard professor Michael Porter. Shown in Figure 5.1, the framework is comprised of the forces that determine industry profitability.[7] These forces—the threat of substitutes, the entry of new competitors, rivalry among existing firms, the bargaining power of suppliers, and the bargaining power of buyers—determine the average rate of return for the firms in an industry.

Each of Porter's five forces impacts the average rate of return for the firms in an industry by applying pressure on industry profitability. Well-managed companies try to position their firms in a way that avoids or diminishes these forces—in an attempt to beat the average rate of return for the industry. For example, the rivalry among existing firms in the music industry is high. Blue Maze diminished the impact of this threat to its profitability by avoiding head-to-head competition with the major record labels.

FIGURE 5.1

Forces That Determine Industry Profitability

Source: Reprinted with permission of The Free Press, a Division of Simon & Schuster Adult Publishing Group, from *Competitive Strategy: Techniques for Analyzing Industries and Competitors* by Michael E. Porter. Copyright © 1980, 1998 by The Free Press. All rights reserved.

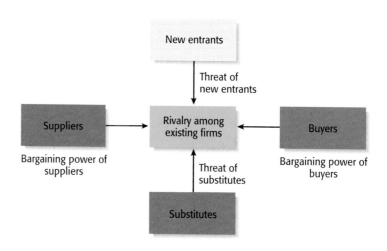

In his book *Competitive Advantage*, Porter points out that industry profitability is not a function of *only* a product's features. Although it was written in 1985 and the dynamics of the industries mentioned have changed, Porter's essential point continues to offer important insights for entrepreneurs:

> Industry profitability is not a function of what the product looks like or whether it embodies high or low technology but of industry structure. Some very mundane industries such as postage meters and grain trading are extremely profitable, while some more glamorous, high-technology industries such as personal computers and cable television are not profitable for many participants.[8]

The five competitive forces that determine industry profitability are described next. As mentioned in previous chapters, industry reports, produced by companies like Mintel, IBISWorld, and Standard & Poor's NetAdvantage, provide substantive information for analyzing the impact of the five forces on specific industries. All three of these resources are available free through many university library Web sites and are highlighted in the Internet Resources Table in Appendix 3.2.

Threat of Substitutes   In general, industries are more attractive when the threat of substitutes is low. This means that products or services from other industries can't easily serve as substitutes for the products or services being made and sold in the focal firm's industry. For example, there are few if any substitutes for prescription medicines, which is one of the reasons the pharmaceutical industry is so profitable. When people are sick, they typically don't quibble with the pharmacist about the price of a medicine. In contrast, when close substitutes for a product do exist, industry profitability is suppressed because consumers will opt not to buy when the price is too high. Consider the price of airplane tickets. If the price gets too high, businesspeople will increasingly utilize videoconferencing as a substitute for travel. This problem is particularly acute if the substitutes are free or nearly free. For example, if the price of express mail gets too high, people will increasingly attach documents to e-mail messages rather than sending them via UPS or FedEx. Actions such as these were becoming more common in late 2008, a time when there was a worldwide recession taking place.

The extent to which substitutes suppress the profitability of an industry depends on the propensity for buyers to substitute alternatives. This is why the firms in an industry often offer their customers amenities to reduce the likelihood of their switching to a substitute product, even in light of a price increase. Let's look at the coffee restaurant industry as an example of this. The coffee sold at Starbucks is relatively expensive. A consumer could easily find a less expensive cup of coffee at a convenience store or brew coffee at home rather than pay more at Starbucks. To decrease the likelihood that customers will choose either of these alternatives, Starbucks offers high-quality fresh coffee, a pleasant atmosphere, and good service. Starbucks doesn't do this just so its customers don't go to a different coffee restaurant. It offers the service so its customers won't switch to substitute products as well. Although this strategy is still working for Starbucks, it isn't as effective as it once was, given Starbucks' slowdown in growth in 2008 and 2009. Because of this slowdown, Starbucks was experimenting with offering less expensive coffees while maintaining its commitment to quality and providing customers with a unique experience.

Threat of New Entrants   In general, industries are more attractive when the threat of entry is low. This means that competitors cannot easily enter the industry to copy what the industry incumbents are doing. There are a number of ways that firms in an industry can keep the number of new entrants low. These techniques are referred to as barriers to entry. A **barrier to entry** is a

Learning Objective

3. Explain the role of "barriers to entry" in creating disincentives for firms to enter an industry.

Starbucks doesn't just sell coffee. It also offers its patrons a convenient and pleasant place to meet, socialize, and study. Starbucks offers these amenities in part to decrease the likelihood that its customers will "substitute" their Starbucks coffee for a less expensive alternative.

Carolyn A. McKeone/Photo Researchers, Inc.

condition that creates a disincentive way for a new firm to enter an industry.[9] Let's look at the six major sources of barriers to entry:

- **Economies of scale:** Industries that are characterized by large economies of scale are difficult for new firms to enter, unless they are willing to accept a cost disadvantage. **Economies of scale** occur when mass-producing a product results in lower average costs. For example, Intel has huge microchip factories that produce vast quantities of chips, thereby reducing the average cost of a chip. It would be difficult for a new entrant to match Intel's advantage in this area. There are instances in which the advantages of economics of scale can be overcome. For example, many microbreweries have successfully entered the beer industry by brewing their beer locally and relying on a local niche market clientele. This strategy counters the enormous economies of scale that national brewers like Anheuser-Busch and Miller have.

- **Product differentiation:** Industries such as the soft-drink industry that are characterized by firms with strong brands are difficult to break into without spending heavily on advertising. For example, imagine how costly it would be to compete head-to-head against Pepsi or Coca-Cola. Another way of achieving differentiation is through exclusive licensing agreements. For example, in 2004, Electronic Arts inked a five-year exclusive deal with the National Football League, making it the only company that can produce electronic games involving NFL players, teams, or stadiums.[10]

- **Capital requirements:** The need to invest large amounts of money to gain entrance to an industry is another barrier to entry. The airline industry is characterized by large capital requirements, although JetBlue, which launched in 1999, was able to overcome this barrier and raise substantial funds by winning the confidence of investors through the strength of its business model and its management team.

- **Cost advantages independent of size:** Entrenched competitors may have cost advantages not related to size that are not available to new entrants. Commonly, these advantages are grounded in the firm's history. For example, the existing competitors in an industry may have purchased land and equipment in the past when the cost was far less than new entrants would have to pay for the same assets at the time of their entry.

- **Access to distribution channels:** Distribution channels are often hard to crack. This is particularly true in crowded markets, such as the convenience store market. For a new sports drink to be placed on a convenience store shelf, it typically has to displace a product that is already there.
- **Government and legal barriers:** In knowledge-intensive industries, such as biotechnology and software, patents, trademarks, and copyrights form major barriers to entry. Other industries, such as banking and broadcasting, require the granting of a license by a public authority.

When a new firm tries to enter an industry with powerful barriers to entry, it must have a plan to overcome those barriers. Scott McNealy, the cofounder of Sun Microsystems, says that Sun was able to overcome the barriers to entry in many of its industries primarily through a program of partnering with other firms:

> Initially, Sun's business model was no different from that of its rivals. We wanted to beat our competitors, grow internally, build manufacturing plants, create new distribution channels, acquire promising new start-ups, and so on. What happened was that we realized we couldn't do it alone. The markets were vast, our competitors were huge, barriers to entry to some segments were overwhelming, we didn't have enough cash, and the pace of change in the industry was too fast. What we did was purely instinctive. We reached out to other companies that could help us. We leveraged their expertise and specialty products by forming strategic alliances.[11]

When start-ups create their own industries or create new niche markets within existing industries, they must create barriers to entry of their own to reduce the threat of new entrants. It is difficult for start-ups to create barriers to entry that are expensive, such as economies of scale, because money is usually tight. The biggest threat to a new firm's viability, particularly if it is creating a new market, is that larger, better-funded firms will step in and copy what it is doing. The ideal barrier to entry is a patent, trademark, or copyright, which prevents another firm from duplicating what the start-up is doing. Apart from these options, however, start-ups have to rely on nontraditional barriers to entry to discourage new entrants, such as assembling a world-class management team that would be difficult for another company to replicate. A list of nontraditional barriers to entry, which are particularly suited to start-up firms, is provided in Table 5.1.

Rivalry Among Existing Firms In most industries, the major determinant of industry profitability is the level of competition among the firms already competing in the industry. Some industries are fiercely competitive to the point where prices are pushed below the level of costs. When this happens, industry-wide losses occur. In other industries, competition is much less intense and price competition is subdued. For example, the personal computer industry is so competitive that profit margins are extremely thin. ASUSTeK Computer, for example, was selling its Eee PC laptop for $300 toward the end of 2008.[12] In contrast, the market for specialized medical equipment is less competitive, and profit margins are higher.

There are four primary factors that determine the nature and intensity of the rivalry among existing firms in an industry:

- **Number and balance of competitors:** The more competitors there are, the more likely it is that one or more will try to gain customers by cutting prices. Price-cutting causes problems throughout the industry and occurs more often when all the competitors in an industry are about the same size and when there is no clear market leader.
- **Degree of difference between products:** The degree to which products differ from one producer to another affects industry rivalry. For example,

Table 5.1 NONTRADITIONAL BARRIERS TO ENTRY

Barrier to Entry	Explanation	Example
Strength of management team	If a start-up puts together a world-class management team, it may give potential rivals pause in taking on the start-up in its chosen industry.	JetBlue
First-mover advantage	If a start-up pioneers an industry or a new concept within an existing industry, the name recognition the start-up establishes may create a formidable barrier to entry.	Facebook
Passion of management team and employees	If the key employees of a start-up are highly motivated by its unique culture, are willing to work long hours because of their belief in what they are doing, and anticipate large financial gains through stock options, this is a combination that cannot be replicated by a larger firm. Think of the employees of a biotech firm trying to find a cure for a disease.	Amgen
Unique business model	If a start-up is able to construct a unique business model and establish a network of relationships that make the business model work, this set of advantages creates a barrier to entry.	Dell
Internet domain name	Some Internet domain names are so "spot-on" in regard to a specific product or service that they give a start-up a meaningful leg up in terms of e-commerce opportunities. Think of www.1800flowers.com, www.1800gotjunk.com, and www.bodybuilding.com.	www.1800contacts.com
Inventing a new approach to an industry and executing the idea in an exemplary fashion	If a start-up invents a new approach to an industry and executes it in an exemplary fashion, these factors create a barrier to entry for potential imitators.	Wikipedia

Learning Objective

4. Identify the nontraditional barriers to entry that are especially associated with entrepreneurial firms.

commodity industries such as paper products producers tend to compete on price because there is no meaningful difference between one manufacturer's products and another's.

■ **Growth rate of an industry:** The competition among firms in a slow-growth industry is stronger than among those in fast-growth industries. Slow-growth industry firms, such as insurance, must fight for market share, which may tempt them to lower prices or increase quality to get customers. In fast-growth industries, such as pharmaceutical products, there are enough customers to go around to fill the capacity of most firms, making price-cutting less likely.

■ **Level of fixed costs:** Firms that have high fixed costs must sell a higher volume of their product to reach the break-even point than firms with low fixed costs. Once the break-even point is met, each additional unit sold contributes directly to a firm's bottom line. Firms with high fixed costs are anxious to fill their capacity, and this anxiety may lead to price-cutting.

Bargaining Power of Suppliers   In general, industries are more attractive when the bargaining power of suppliers is low. In some cases, suppliers can suppress the profitability of the industries to which they sell by raising prices or reducing the quality of the components they provide. If a supplier reduces the quality of the components it supplies, the quality of the finished product will suffer, and the manufacturer will eventually have to lower its price. If the suppliers are powerful relative to the firms in the industry to which they sell, industry profitability can suffer.[13] For example, Intel, with its Pentium chip, is a powerful supplier to the PC industry. Because most PCs feature Pentium chips, Intel can command a premium price from the PC manufacturers, thus directly affecting the overall profitability of the PC industry. Several factors have an impact on the ability of suppliers to exert pressure on buyers and suppress the profitability of the industries they serve. These include the following:

■ **Supplier concentration:** When there are only a few suppliers to provide a critical product to a large number of buyers, the supplier has an advantage. This is the case in the pharmaceutical industry, where relatively few drug manufacturers are selling to thousands of doctors and their patients.

■ **Switching costs:** Switching costs are the fixed costs that buyers encounter when switching or changing from one supplier to another. If switching costs are high, a buyer will be less likely to switch suppliers. For example, suppliers often provide their largest buyers with specialized software that makes it easy to buy their products. After the buyer spends time and effort learning the supplier's ordering and inventory management systems, it will be less likely to want to spend time and effort learning another supplier's system.

■ **Attractiveness of substitutes:** Supplier power is enhanced if there are no attractive substitutes for the products or services the supplier offers. For example, there is little the computer industry can do when Microsoft and Intel raise their prices, as there are relatively few if any practical substitutes for these firms' products.

■ **Threat of forward integration:** The power of a supplier is enhanced if there is a credible possibility that the supplier might enter the buyer's industry. For example, Microsoft's power as a supplier of computer operating systems is enhanced by the threat that it might enter the PC industry if PC makers balk too much at the cost of its software or threaten to use an operating system from a different software provider.

Bargaining Power of Buyers   In general, industries are more attractive when the bargaining power of buyers (a start-up's customers) is low. Buyers can suppress the profitability of the industries from which they purchase by demanding price concessions or increases in quality. For example, even in light of the problems it encountered in 2008 and 2009, the automobile industry remains dominated by a handful of large automakers that buy products from thousands of suppliers in different industries. This enables the automakers to suppress the profitability of the industries from which they buy by demanding price reductions. Similarly, if the automakers insisted that their suppliers provide better-quality parts for the same price, the profitability of the suppliers would suffer. Several factors affect buyers' ability to exert pressure on suppliers and suppress the profitability of the industries from which they buy. These include the following:

■ **Buyer group concentration:** If the buyers are concentrated, meaning that there are only a few large buyers, and they buy from a large number of suppliers, they can pressure the suppliers to lower costs and thus affect the profitability of the industries from which they buy.

■ **Buyer's costs:** The greater the importance of an item is to a buyer, the more sensitive the buyer will be to the price it pays. For example, if the component sold by the supplier represents 50 percent of the cost of the buyer's product, the buyer will bargain hard to get the best price for that component.

■ **Degree of standardization of supplier's products:** The degree to which a supplier's product differs from its competitors' affects the buyer's bargaining power. For example, a buyer who is purchasing a standard or undifferentiated product from a supplier, such as the corn syrup that goes into a soft drink, can play one supplier against another until it gets the best combination of features such as price and service.

■ **Threat of backward integration:** The power of a buyer is enhanced if there is a credible threat that the buyer might enter the supplier's industry. For example, the PC industry can keep the price of computer monitors down by threatening to make its own monitors if the price gets too high.

The bargaining power of buyers is such a pervasive threat that some new ventures opt out of particular industries when the extent of the bargaining power of buyers becomes clear. This scenario changed the course of history for the Sony Corporation, as explained in the boxed feature titled "Savvy Entrepreneurial Firm."

Savvy Entrepreneurial FIRM

How the Bargaining Power of Buyers Changed the Fate of Sony in Its Start-Up Years

www.sony.com

There are many variables that shape a company in its start-up years, but perhaps none are as powerful as Porter's five forces. Many companies, for example, establish strong brands or differentiate themselves in creative ways, primarily to establish barriers to entry and stem the tide of new entrants. Other companies, such as Starbucks and Barnes & Noble, offer amenities in their places of business to discourage customers from switching to less expensive substitute products. The story of Sony, however, tops them all. When Sony was a start-up, it changed its entire approach to doing business as the result of the bargaining power of buyers. In fact, if Sony hadn't responded to this threat in the way it did, it wouldn't be a household name today.

Sony was established in 1946 by Masaru Ibuka and Akio Morita, two Japanese businessmen, to make communication equipment for the reconstruction of Japan after World War II. One thing Ibuka and Morita learned quickly was that to make a sale, they had to win the confidence of the purchasing officers in the government agencies with whom they were dealing. This task often proved difficult, but their hard work typically paid off in orders from these purchasing officers. One day, however, early in the life of Sony, a purchasing agent who Morita had worked particularly hard to win over was transferred to a new position. This was frustrating to Morita because he had to start from square one to win the confidence of the purchasing officer's replacement.

After this scenario repeated itself several times, Morita considered the problem. While he liked the fact that large orders could be granted by the purchasing agents of government agencies and large firms, he was leery of the fact that Sony's sales hinged on the decisions of such a small number of people. After discussing this concern with Ibuka, Morita decided to take Sony in a different direction. Instead of placing the future of Sony in the hands of a few purchasing agents, Morita

decided that Sony would go after the consumer market. "In other words, we decided to do business with unspecified millions of individuals instead of with a specific few. On this basis we started to produce the first tape recorders and tapes in Japan," Morita later recalled.

This remarkable story illustrates the compelling nature of the real bargaining power of buyers. This clout is most formidable when there are only a few buyers and many sellers. Morita redirected Sony's entire future to avoid this threat. Today, as it has throughout the majority of its history, Sony's future lies in the hands of the millions of people who buy its products rather than in the hands of just a few powerful buyers.

Questions for Critical Thinking

1. Analyze the electronics industry using Porter's five forces model. What do you think are the biggest threats to the electronics industry today? What is Sony doing to try to deter these threats?
2. Think of examples of at least two other companies that are in industries that are subject to the strong bargaining power of buyers. Do you think the profitability of these firms is being suppressed by the strong bargaining power of their buyers? What, if anything, can these firms do to neutralize this threat?
3. How would you describe Sony's positioning strategy in the electronics industry?
4. What single industry do you think suffers the most from the bargaining power of buyers? How about the bargaining power of suppliers? Are entrepreneurial start-ups able to enter these industries? If so, how?

Source: A. Morita, "Moving Up in Marketing by Getting Down to Basics," in *The Book of Entrepreneurs' Wisdom*, ed. Peter Krass (New York: John Wiley & Sons, 1999), 315–23. Reproduced with the permission of John Wiley & Sons, Inc.

The Value of the Five Forces Model

Along with helping a firm understand the dynamics of the industry it plans to enter, the five forces model can be used in two ways: (1) to help a firm determine whether it should enter a particular industry and (2) whether it can carve out an attractive position in that industry. Let's examine these two positive outcomes.

First, the five forces model can be used to assess the attractiveness of an industry or a specific position within an industry by determining the level of threat to industry profitability for each of the forces, as shown in Table 5.2. This analysis of industry attractiveness should be more in-depth than the less rigorous analysis conducted during feasibility analysis. For example, if a firm filled out the form shown in Table 5.2 and several of the threats to industry profitability were high, the firm may want to reconsider entering the industry or think carefully about the position it will occupy in the industry. In the restaurant industry, for example, the threat of substitute products, the threat of new entrants, and the rivalry among existing firms are high. For certain restaurants, such as fresh-seafood restaurants, the bargaining power of suppliers may also be high (the number of seafood suppliers is relatively small compared to the number of beef and chicken suppliers). Thus, a firm that enters the restaurant industry has several forces working against it simply because of the nature of the industry. To help sidestep or diminish these threats, it must establish a favorable position. One firm that has accomplished this is Panera Bread, as discussed in Case 5.1 in this chapter. By studying the restaurant industry, Panera found that some consumers have tired of fast food but don't always have the time to patronize a sit-down restaurant. To fill the gap, Panera helped to pioneer a new category called "fast casual," which combines relatively fast service with high-quality food. Panera has been very successful in occupying this unique position in the restaurant industry. You'll learn more about Panera Bread's success while reading Case 5.1.

The second way a new firm can apply the five forces model to help determine whether it should enter an industry is by using the model

Table 5.2 DETERMINING THE ATTRACTIVENESS OF AN INDUSTRY USING THE FIVE FORCES MODEL

Competitive Force	Threat to Industry Profitability		
	Low	Medium	High
Threat of substitutes			
Threat of new entrants			
Rivalry among existing firms			
Bargaining power of suppliers			
Bargaining power of buyers			

Instructions:

Step 1   Select an industry.
Step 2   Determine the level of threat to industry profitability for each of the forces (low, medium, or high).
Step 3   Use the table to get an overall feel for the attractiveness of the industry.
Step 4   Use the table to identify the threats that are most often relevant to industry profitability.

Panera Bread offers a variety of alternatives to the typical burger and fries offered at many fast-food restaurants. In addition to a selection of fresh baked bread, Panera is also known for bagels, pastries, soups, sandwiches, salads, and coffee.

AP Wide World Photos

Learning Objective

5. List the four industry-related questions to ask before pursuing the idea for a firm.

FIGURE 5.2

Using the Five Forces Model to Pose Questions to Determine the Potential Success of a New Venture

pictured in Figure 5.2 to answer several key questions. By doing so, a new venture can assess the thresholds it may have to meet to be successful in a particular industry:

Question 1: Is the industry a realistic place for our new venture to enter? This question can be answered by looking at the overall attractiveness of an industry, as depicted in Table 5.2, and by assessing whether the window of opportunity is open. It is up to the entrepreneur to determine if the window of opportunity for the industry is open or closed.

Question 2: If we do enter the industry, can our firm do a better job than the industry as a whole in avoiding or diminishing the impact of the forces that suppress industry profitability? A new venture can enter an industry with a fresh brand, innovative ideas, and a world-class management team and perform better than the industry incumbents. This was the

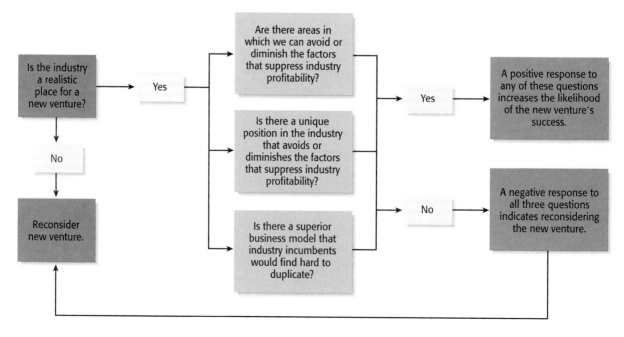

case when Google entered the Internet search engine industry and displaced Yahoo! as the market leader. Outperformance of industry incumbents can also be achieved if a new venture brings an attractive new product to market that is patented, preventing others from duplicating it for a period of time.

Question 3: Is there a unique position in the industry that avoids or diminishes the forces that suppress industry profitability?   As we've described, this is the advantage that both BusinessesAtoZ and Panera Bread have captured.

Question 4: Is there a superior business model that can be put in place that would be hard for industry incumbents to duplicate?   Keep in mind that the five forces model provides a picture of an industry "as is," which isn't necessarily the way a new venture has to approach it. Sometimes the largest firms in an industry are trapped by their own strategies and contractual obligations, providing an opening for a start-up to try something new. For example, when Dell started selling computers directly to consumers, its largest rivals—Hewlett-Packard, Compaq, and IBM—were not able to respond. They were locked into a strategy of selling through retailers. If they had tried to mimic Dell and sell directly to end users or customers, they would have alienated their most valuable partners—retailers such as Sears, and Best Buy. However, with the passage of time, Dell's competitors have learned how to effectively and efficiently sell directly to consumers, largely erasing Dell's historic advantage in the process of doing so.

The steps involved in answering these questions are pictured in Figure 5.2. If the founders of a new firm believe that a particular industry is a realistic place for their new venture, a positive response to one or more of the questions posed in Figure 5.2 increases the likelihood that the new venture will be successful.

Industry Types and the Opportunities They Offer

Along with studying the factors discussed previously, it is helpful for a new venture to study industry types to determine the opportunities they offer.[14] The five most prevalent industry types, depicted in Table 5.3, are emerging industries, fragmented industries, mature industries, declining industries, and global industries.[15] There are unique opportunities offered by each type of industry.

Learning Objective

6. Identify the five primary industry types and the opportunities they offer.

Emerging Industries   An **emerging industry** is a new industry in which standard operating procedures have yet to be developed. The firm that pioneers or takes the leadership of an emerging industry often captures a first-mover advantage. A **first-mover advantage** is a sometimes insurmountable advantage gained by the first significant company to move into a new market.

Because a high level of uncertainty characterizes emerging industries, any opportunity that is captured may be short-lived. Still, many new ventures enter emerging industries because barriers to entry are usually low and there is no established pattern of rivalry.

Fragmented Industries   A **fragmented industry** is one that is characterized by a large number of firms of approximately equal size. The primary opportunity for start-ups in fragmented industries is to consolidate the industry and establish industry leadership as a result of doing so. The most common way to do this is through a **geographic roll-up strategy**, in which one firm starts acquiring similar firms that are located in different geographic areas.[16] This is what Blockbuster did in the video rental industry. Prior to Blockbuster's arrival, thousands of small video stores were scattered throughout the United

Table 5.3 INDUSTRY STRUCTURE AND OPPORTUNITIES

Industry Type	Industry Characteristics	Opportunities	Examples of Entrepreneurial Firms Exploiting These Opportunities
Emerging industries	Recent changes in demand or technology; new industry standard operating procedures have yet to be developed	First-mover advantage	• Apple with its iTunes Music Store • Mariah Power in wind-generated power • MySpace.com with its online social networking Web site
Fragmented industries	Large number of firms of approximately equal size	Consolidation	• Starbucks in coffee restaurants • Clean Air Lawn Care in lawn service • Geeks on Call in home computer repairs
Mature industries	Slow increases in demand, numerous repeat customers, and limited product innovation	Process and after-sale service innovation	• Tesla Motors in automobiles • Sprig Toys in toys • Daisy Rock Guitars in guitars
Declining industries	Consistent reduction in industry demand	Leaders, niche, harvest, and divest	• Nucor in steel • JetBlue in airlines • Cirque du Soleil in circuses
Global industries	Significant international sales	Multinational and global	• Nike in athletic shoes • Electronic Arts in electronic games

States. Through internal growth and acquisitions, Blockbuster grew quickly, consolidating a previously fragmented industry. Of course, Netflix's model of delivering products via mail to customers reduced the strength of the advantage Blockbuster gained initially by consolidating in a fragmented industry.

Mature Industries A **mature industry** is an industry that is experiencing slow or no increase in demand, has numerous repeat (rather than new) customers, and has limited product innovation. Occasionally, entrepreneurs introduce new product innovations to mature industries, surprising incumbents who thought nothing new was possible in their industries. An example is Steve Demos, the founder of White Wave, a company that makes vegetarian food products. In 1996, the company introduced Silk Soymilk, which has quickly become the best-selling soymilk in the United States. Soymilk isn't really milk at all—it's a soybean-based beverage that looks like milk and has a similar texture. Still, it has made its way into the dairy section of most supermarkets in the United States and has positioned itself as a healthy substitute for milk. Who would have thought that a major innovation was possible in the milk industry?

Declining Industries A **declining industry** is an industry that is experiencing a reduction in demand, such as the retail photo finishing industry. Typically, entrepreneurs shy away from declining industries because the firms in the industry do not meet the tests of an attractive opportunity, described in Chapter 2. There are occasions, however, when a start-up will do just the opposite of what conventional wisdom would suggest and, by doing so, stakes out a position in a declining industry that isn't being hotly contested. That is what Cirque du Soleil did in the circus industry.

Entrepreneurial firms employ three different strategies in declining industries. The first is to adopt a **leadership strategy**, in which the firm tries to become the dominant player in the industry. This is a rare strategy for a start-up in a declining industry. The second is to pursue a **niche strategy**, which focuses on a narrow segment of the industry that might be encouraged to grow through product or process innovation. The third is a **cost reduction strategy**, which is accomplished through achieving lower costs than industry incumbents through process improvements. Initially a small firm but now quite large as a result of its success, Nucor Steel revolutionized the steel industry through the introduction of the "minimill" concept, and is an example of an entrepreneurially minded firm that pursued this strategy. Most steel mills in the United States use large blast furnaces that produce a wide line of products and require enormous throughput in order to be profitable. Nucor's minimills are smaller and produce a narrower range of products. They are, however, energy efficient and make high-quality steel.[17]

Nucor proved its concept and quickly found growth markets within the largely declining U.S. steel industry.

Global Industries   A **global industry** is an industry that is experiencing significant international sales. Many start-ups enter global industries and from day one try to appeal to international rather than just domestic markets. The two most common strategies pursued by firms in global industries are the multidomestic strategy and the global strategy. Firms that pursue a **multidomestic strategy** compete for market share on a country-by-country basis and vary their product or service offerings to meet the demands of the local market. In contrast, firms pursuing a **global strategy** use the same basic approach in all foreign markets. The choice between these two strategies depends on how similar consumers' tastes are from market to market. For example, food companies typically are limited to a multidomestic strategy because food preferences vary significantly from country to country. Firms that sell more universal products, such as athletic shoes, have been successful with global strategies. A global strategy is preferred because it is more economical to sell the same product in multiple markets.[18]

COMPETITOR ANALYSIS

After a firm has gained an understanding of the industry and the target market in which it plans to compete, the next step is to complete a competitor analysis. A competitor analysis is a detailed analysis of a firm's competition. It helps a firm understand the positions of its major competitors and the opportunities that are available to obtain a competitive advantage in one or more areas. These are important issues, particularly for new ventures.[19] In the words of Sun-tzu, quoted earlier in this chapter, "Time spent in reconnaissance is seldom wasted."

First we'll discuss how a firm identifies its major competitors, and then we'll look at the process of completing a competitive analysis grid, which is a tool for organizing the information a firm collects about its primary competitors.

Learning Objective

7. Explain the purpose of a competitor analysis.

Identifying Competitors

The first step in a competitive analysis is to determine who the competition is. This is more difficult than one might think. For example, take a company such as 1-800-FLOWERS. Primarily, the company sells flowers. But 1-800-FLOWERS is not only in the flower business. Because flowers are often given for gifts, the company is also in the gift business. If the company sees itself in the gift business rather than just the flower business, it has a broader set of competitors and opportunities to consider. In addition, some firms sell products or services that straddle more than one industry. For example, a company that makes computer software for doctors' offices operates in both the computer software industry and the health care industry. Again, a company like this has more potential competitors but also more opportunities to consider.

The different types of competitors a business will face are shown in Figure 5.3. The challenges associated with each of these groups of competitors are described here:

Learning Objective

8. Identify the three groups of competitors a new firm will face.

- **Direct competitors:** These are businesses that offer products identical or similar to the products of the firm completing the analysis. These competitors are the most important because they are going after the same customers as the new firm. A new firm faces winning over the loyal followers of its major competitors, which is difficult to do, even when the new firm has a better product.

- **Indirect competitors:** These competitors offer close substitutes to the product the firm completing the analysis sells. These firms' products are also important in that they target the same basic need that is being met by the new firm's product. For example, when people told Roberto Goizueta, the late CEO of Coca-Cola, that Coke's market share was at a maximum, he countered by saying that Coke accounted for less than 2 percent of the 64 ounces of fluid that the average person drinks each day. "The enemy is coffee, milk, tea [and] water," he once said.[20]

- **Future competitors:** These are companies that are not yet direct or indirect competitors but could move into one of these roles at any time. Firms are always concerned about strong competitors moving into their markets. For example, think of how the world has changed for Barnes & Noble since Amazon.com was founded. And, think of how cellular phone technology continues changing the nature of competition for a variety of firms including those selling entertainment services, telephone services, and the like.

It is impossible for a firm to identify all its direct and indirect competitors, let alone its future competitors. However, identifying its top 5 to 10 direct competitors and its top 5 to 10 indirect and future competitors makes it easier for the firm to complete its competitive analysis grid.

If a firm does not have a direct competitor, it shouldn't forget that the status quo can be the toughest competitor of all. In general, people are resistant to change and can always keep their money rather than spend it.[21] A product or service's utility must rise above its cost, not only in monetary terms but also in terms of the hassles associated with switching or learning something new, to motivate someone to buy a new product or service.[22]

One thing small firms in an industry often do is find a way to cooperate in an effort to remain competitive given the presence of larger rivals. This chapter's "Partnering for Success" feature offers an example of this scenario. It provides an example of a unique format that the owners of small coffee shops are utilizing to remain competitive in an industry that includes Starbucks and other much larger rivals.

FIGURE 5.3

Types of Competitors
New Ventures Face

Direct Competitors

Businesses offering identical or similar products

Indirect Competitors

Businesses offering close substitute products

Future Competitors

Businesses that are not yet direct or indirect competitors but could be at any time

Partnering for SUCCESS

Barista Exchange: Online Social Network Aiding Independent Coffeehouse Owners

www.baristaexchange.com

Many industries include a mix of small and large firms. Small firm owners often feel like they're at a disadvantage because they don't have the resources and national brand that their larger counterparts do. This issue is particularly apparent in the coffeehouse industry, where small independently owned coffee shops must compete against Starbucks and powerful regional brands.

Matt Milletto, the director of training for the American Barista & Coffee School in Portland, Oregon, had an idea to boost the chances of independent coffeehouse owners. Using Ning.com, a site that allows anyone to create a social network, he founded Barista Exchange, an online network for the specialty coffee industry. The idea was that if all the independent coffeehouse owners banded together to share information, support each other, and build a platform that allowed each independently owned store to better connect with its customers, the independents could become as strong as the national chains.

Since its launch in December 2007, the Barista Exchange has signed up about 3,000 members and is growing. The exchange allows its members to build profiles about themselves (or their business), post discussion topics, share information in chat rooms, and post photos, videos, and other material of interest to independent coffeehouse owners. Discussion topics range from the best espresso machines to buy to how to arrange trips to coffee growing countries. There's also a lot of talk about recent Starbucks store closings, and how independent coffeehouses can benefit and fill the gap. There is evidence that social exchanges like Barista Exchange are particularly effective for the owners of small businesses. Unlike their larger rivals, small firms can quickly respond to suggestions for buying equipment, adjusting their strategies, or for any other matter without a corporate bureaucracy to slow them down.

One smart thing that Milletto did when launching Barista Exchange was to aggressively promote the site by sending out e-mail messages to independent coffeehouse owners and by talking the site up on other coffee-related blogs. He also populated Barista Exchange with blog posts and discussion topics to get conversations going. A common mistake that the originators of social networks make is to set up a network and then stand by thinking that people will show up and start posting on the site. Social networking sites typically must be promoted by their originators and populated with good quality content before others will join in. Even after a site starts growing, the originators periodically have to add content to keep the site fresh and relevant for its members.

A particularly attractive aspect of Barista Exchange is that it allows its members to create their own social networks to interact with their customers and others. For example, through the Barista Exchange, Troy Reynard, owner of Cosmic Cup Coffee in Eaton, Pennsylvania, met a coffee shop owner on the site who is about 20 miles away. Now the two coffee shop owners refer customers to each other's shops.

Philip Kotler, a marketing expert and highly respected business professor, has made the statement that for a firm to be an effective competitor, it must also be "an effective cooperator." The small coffeehouse owners that participate in the Barista Exchange adhere to the spirit of Kotler's observation.

Questions for Critical Thinking

1. How can small coffee shop owners keep better abreast of changing industry trends by participating in the Barista Exchange?
2. Spend some time looking at the Barista Exchange's Web site. In what ways, other than to study industry trends, can a coffee shop owner utilize the Barista Exchange to be more competitive in the coffee shop industry?
3. What do you think Kotler means when he says that "firms must be effective cooperators to be effective competitors?" Given what you've read in this book and learned in your other courses, do you agree with Kotler's statement? Why or why not?
4. What are some appropriate and inappropriate ways that an owner of a small coffee shop could use the Barista Exchange to collect competitive intelligence?

Source: Wall Street Journal (Eastern Edition) by K. Sports. Copyright 2008 by Dow Jones & Company, Inc.

Sources of Competitive Intelligence

To complete a meaningful competitive analysis grid, a firm must first understand the strategies and behaviors of its competitors. The information that is gathered by a firm to learn about its competitors is referred to as

Learning Objective

9. Describe ways a firm can ethically obtain information about its competitors.

competitive intelligence. Obtaining sound competitive intelligence is not always a simple task. If a competitor is a publicly traded firm, a description of the firm's business and its financial information is available through annual reports filed with the Securities and Exchange Commission (SEC). These reports are public records and are available at the SEC's Web site (www.sec.gov). If one or more of the competitors is a private company, the task is more difficult. Private companies are not required to divulge information to the public. There are a number of ways that a firm can ethically obtain information about its competitors. A sample of the most common techniques is shown in Table 5.4.

Completing a Competitive Analysis Grid

Learning Objective

10. Describe the reasons for completing a competitive analysis grid.

As we mentioned previously, a **competitive analysis grid** is a tool for organizing the information a firm collects about its competitors. It can help a firm see how it stacks up against its competitors, provide ideas for markets to pursue, and, perhaps most importantly, identify its primary sources of competitive advantage. To be a viable company, a new venture must have at least one clear competitive advantage over its major competitors.

An example of a competitive analysis grid is provided in Table 5.5. This grid is for Expresso Fitness, a company that makes a high-end exercise bike and is the focus of the "You Be the VC 5.1" feature. The main competitive factors in the fitness equipment industry are product features, user engagement, durability, user feedback, health benefits, price, and customer service. These factors are placed on the vertical axis of Expresso Fitness's competitive analysis grid. The horizontal axis contains Expresso Fitness and its five main competitors. In each box, Expresso Fitness rates itself against its main competitors. The purpose of this exercise is for a company to see how it stacks up against its competitors and to illustrate the areas in which it has an advantage (and has a disadvantage). For example, Expresso Fitness rates itself as superior to its competitors in terms of

Table 5.4 SOURCES OF COMPETITIVE INTELLIGENCE

Source	Description/Benefit
Attend conferences and trade shows	Participants talk about the latest trends in the industry and display their most current products.
Purchase competitors' products	Purchasing and using a competitor's products can provide insight into their benefits and shortcomings. The purchase process itself can provide data about how a competitor treats its customers.
Study competitors' Web sites	Many companies put a lot of information on their Web sites, including product information and the latest news about the company.
Set up Google and Yahoo! e-mail alerts	E-mail alerts are updates of the latest Google or Yahoo! results, including press releases, news articles, and blog posts, on any keywords of interest. You can set up e-mail alerts using your company's name or the name of a competitor.
Read industry-related books, magazines, and Web sites	Many of these sources contain articles or features that contain information about competitors.
Talk to customers about what motivated them to buy your product as opposed to your competitor's product	Customers can provide a wealth of information about the advantages and disadvantages of competing products.

Courtesy of the Consumer Electronics Association

Many companies attend trade shows to display their products and see what their competitors are up to. This is a photo of the 2008 Consumer Electronics Trade Show, held in Las Vegas, which is America's largest annual tradeshow of any kind.

Table 5.5 COMPETITIVE ANALYSIS GRID FOR EXPRESSO FITNESS

Name	Expresso Fitness	Cybex	Star Trec	Nautilus	Life Fitness
Product features	Advantage	Advantage	Even	Even	Disadvantage
User engagement	Advantage	Even	Even	Disadvantage	Disadvantage
Durability	Even	Even	Even	Disadvantage	Disadvantage
User feedback	Advantage	Advantage	Even	Even	Even
Health benefits	Even	Even	Advantage	Even	Advantage
Price	Disadvantage	Disadvantage	Even	Advantage	Advantage
Customer service	Even	Even	Even	Advantage	Even

product features, user engagement, and user feedback. It will likely use this information in its advertising and promotions. An additional benefit of completing a competitive analysis grid is that it helps a company fine-tune its offering. For example, if Expresso Fitness rated itself at a disadvantage to its competitors on customer service, it might want to improve that component of its offering to remain competitive.

Chapter Summary

1. Industry analysis is business research that focuses on an industry's potential. The knowledge gleaned from an industry analysis helps a firm decide whether to enter an industry and if it can carve out a position in the industry that will provide it a competitive advantage. The two main components of "industry trends" are environmental trends and business trends. Environmental trends include economic trends, social trends, technological advances, and political and regulatory changes. Business trends include

other business-related trends that aren't environmental trends but are important to recognize.

2. Porter's five forces model includes threat of substitutes, threat of new entrants, rivalry among existing firms, bargaining power of suppliers, and bargaining power of buyers.

3. The threat of new entrants is one of the five forces that determine industry profitability. Firms try to keep other firms from entering their industries by erecting barriers to entry. A barrier to entry is a condition that creates a disincentive for a new firm to enter an industry. Economies of scale, product differentiation, capital requirements, cost advantages independent of size, access to distribution channels, and government and legal barriers are examples of barriers to entry.

4. The nontraditional barriers to entry that are particularly well suited to entrepreneurial firms include strength of the management team, first-mover advantage, passion of the management team and employees, unique business model, special internet domain name, and inventing a new approach to an industry and executing the approach in an exemplary manner.

5. The four industry-related questions that a firm should ask before entering an industry are the following: Is the industry a realistic place for a new venture? If we do enter the industry, can our firm do a better job than the industry as a whole in avoiding or diminishing the threats that suppress industry profitability? Is there a unique position in the industry that avoids or diminishes the forces that suppress industry profitability? Is there a superior business model that can be put in place that would be hard for industry incumbents to duplicate?

6. The five primary industry types and the opportunities they offer are as follows: emerging industry/first-mover advantage; fragmented industry/ consolidation; mature industry/emphasis on service and process innovation; declining industry/leadership, niche, harvest, and divest; and global industry/multidomestic strategy or global strategy.

7. A competitor analysis is a detailed analysis of a firm's competition. It helps a firm understand the positions of its major competitors and the opportunities that are available to obtain a competitive advantage in one or more areas.

8. The three groups of competitors a new firm will face are direct competitors, indirect competitors, and future competitors.

9. There are a number of ways a firm can ethically obtain information about its competitors, including attending conferences and trade shows; purchasing competitors' products; studying competitors' Web sites; setting up Google and Yahoo! e-mail alerts; reading industry-related books, magazines, and Web sites; and talking to customers about what motivated them to buy your product as opposed to your competitor's product.

10. A competitive analysis grid is a tool for organizing the information a firm collects about its competitors. This grid can help a firm see how it stacks up against its competitors, provide ideas for markets to pursue, and, perhaps most importantly, identify its primary sources of competitive advantage.

Key Terms

barrier to entry, **175**
competitive analysis grid, **188**
competitive intelligence, **188**
competitor analysis, **170**
cost reduction strategy, **185**
declining industry, **184**
economies of scale, **176**

emerging industry, **183**
first-mover advantage, **183**
fragmented industry, **183**
geographic roll-up
    strategy, **183**
global industry, **185**
global strategy, **185**

industry, **170**
industry analysis, **170**
leadership strategy, **184**
mature industry, **184**
multidomestic strategy, **185**
niche strategy, **184**
position, **170**

Review Questions

1. What is an industry? Provide an example of an industry and several firms in it.
2. What is the purpose of industry analysis?
3. What are the four primary categories of environmental trends? Provide an example of how a trend in each category could affect the toy industry.
4. Identify the five competitive forces that determine industry profitability.
5. Describe how the threat of substitute products has the potential to suppress an industry's profitability.
6. How does the threat of new entrants have the potential to suppress an industry's profitability?
7. What is meant by the term *barrier to entry*? Describe the six major sources of barriers to entry that firms use to restrict entry into their markets.
8. How does rivalry among existing firms have the potential to suppress an industry's profitability?
9. Describe the four primary factors that play a role in determining the nature and intensity of the bargaining power of suppliers. How does the bargaining power of suppliers have the potential to suppress an industry's profitability?
10. Describe the four primary factors that play a role in determining the nature and intensity of the bargaining power of buyers. How does the bargaining power of buyers have the potential to suppress an industry's profitability?
11. Identify the nontraditional barriers to entry that are particularly suitable for entrepreneurial firms.
12. How can a start-up avoid or sidestep the pressure applied by one of the five forces on industry profitability by establishing a unique "position" in an industry?
13. Describe the characteristics of a fragmented industry. What is the primary opportunity for new firms in fragmented industries?
14. Describe the characteristics of a mature industry. What is the primary opportunity for new firms in a mature industry?
15. What is a global industry? Describe the two most common strategies pursued by firms in global industries.
16. Describe the purpose of a competitor analysis. Make your answer as complete as possible.
17. Describe the differences between direct competitors, indirect competitors, and future competitors.
18. What is meant by the term *competitive intelligence*? Why is it important for firms to collect intelligence about their competitors?
19. Identify three sources of competitive intelligence.
20. What is the purpose of completing a competitive analysis grid?

Application Questions

1. Jason Murphy is thinking about starting a firm in the fitness drinks industry. When asked by a potential investor if he had studied the industry, Jason replied, "The fitness drink industry is so full of potential, it doesn't need formal analysis." Will Jason's answer satisfy the investor? In what ways will Jason limit his potential if his current attitude about the importance of industry analysis doesn't change?
2. The "You Be the VC 5.1" feature focuses on Expresso Fitness, a maker of high-end exercise bikes. Spend some time studying Expresso Fitness's Web site and other information about the company. How would you describe Expresso Fitness's positioning strategy? How will the strategy help Expresso Fitness avoid some of the downward pressure on the fitness equipment industry imposed by Porter's five forces?

3. Karen Sharp lives in a town of approximately 10,000 in Western Kentucky. There isn't a furniture store in the town and Karen is thinking about starting one. She has good business and marketing skills and is confident she can run the store, but she's not sure whether the furniture store industry is a good industry to enter. Karen's turned to you for help. What would you tell her?

4. The "You Be the VC 5.2" feature focuses on SRS Aviation, a company in the South African airline industry. Spend some time studying the airline industry and Sibongile Sambo's unique approach to the industry. Which environmental and business trends favor SRS Aviation's offering, and which environmental and business trends are likely to work against it?

5. Expresso Fitness operates at the high-end of the fitness equipment industry. What barriers to entry has Expresso Fitness erected (or can it erect) to deter other companies from entering the unique position that it has established?

6. Your friend Lisa Ryan is opening a smoothie shop that will sell a variety of smoothie drinks in the $4 to $5 price range. When you ask her if she is worried that the steep price of smoothies might prompt potential customers to buy a soda or a sports drink instead of a smoothie, Lisa answers, "You're right. Someone could substitute a soda or a sports drink for a smoothie and save a lot of money. Is there anything I can do to discourage that?" What do you tell her?

7. Starbucks has been very successfully selling high-priced coffee despite the fact that consumers could easily substitute Starbucks coffee for less expensive coffee or substitute its coffee for less expensive drinks like soda, bottled water, or fitness drinks. Why do you think Starbucks has historically been so successful avoiding substitutes? Do you think its advantage is eroding in this area? If so why? If its advantage is eroding, what could the firm do to change this situation?

8. Kendall Jones is in the process of opening a new pet store. The store will sell pet food, pet supplies, and a select variety of pets (excluding dogs and cats). It will also offer grooming services and dog obedience classes. In a recent *Fortune* magazine article, Kendall read that in industries where the bargaining power of suppliers is high, industry profitability suffers. Help Kendall determine if the bargaining power of suppliers is high in the pet store industry.

9. Look at Table 5.1 in the chapter and read Case 5.2, which focuses on Cirque du Soleil and Curves International. Which of the nontraditional barriers to entry have been the most helpful to Cirque du Soleil and Curves in terms of deterring new entrants into their industries?

10. Think of at least three entrepreneurial firms, not listed in Table 5.1, that benefit greatly from their Internet domain names. In each case, to what extent do you think the strength of their Internet domain names is instrumental to their ability to limit the number of new entrants in their industries?

11. As mentioned in this chapter, White Wave Inc. produces Silk Soymilk, a product that has done surprisingly well in the mature milk industry. Based on the material we've covered so far, why do you think Silk Soymilk has been so successful?

12. Make a list of Expresso Fitness's direct competitors, indirect competitors, and future competitors. On a scale of 1 to 5 (5 is high), how concerned should Expresso Fitness be about each category of competitors?

13. Sibongile Sambo, the founder of SRS Aviation, wants to do as good a job as possible collecting competitive intelligence in an ethical manner to stay on top of industry trends and the strategies and tactics of her major competitors. Suggest some specific trade shows, industry-related magazines and periodicals, and Web sites the company should pay attention to as part of its competitive intelligence efforts.

14. Dana Smith will soon be opening a fitness club in Tucson, Arizona. Having identified his competitors, he wants to display the information he has

collected in a way that will help him determine how he'll stack up against his competitors and pinpoint his sources of competitive advantage. Describe to Dana a technique that he could use to help achieve his objectives.

15. Complete a competitive analysis grid for Panera Bread.

You Be the VC 5.1

Company: Expresso Fitness

www.expressofitness.com

Business Idea: Produce an exercise bike that keeps its users engaged and motivated by turning the bike into a video game.

Pitch: More than 66.5 percent of Americans who are 20 years or older are overweight or obese. To lose weight and improve their fitness, many people join gyms and start working out on exercise machines, like stationary bikes, treadmills, and Stairmasters. However, for many people there's one big drawback to this approach. It's boring. The main complaint of people who use exercise bikes or walk on treadmills is that it's hard to stay motivated because the daily grind of using these types of machines is just too dull.

To combat this problem, Expresso Fitness has designed a stationary bike called the Spark. The new twist that the bike brings to the market is that it helps its riders stay motivated by turning the bike into a video game. The Spark has a built-in computer and flat-panel monitor that allows a user to race against virtual opponents through a variety of simulated outdoor courses, including one that simulates portions of the latest Tour de France course. Unlike the typical exercise bike, the Spark has movable handlebars to steer you through trails on the screen and a gearshift for tracking hills. And, just like a real bike, when you climb a hill on the screen, you have to downshift the bike to keep the pedaling from getting harder. If you're having a particularly good ride and are coming close to a personal record (the bike keeps a record of all of

your rides), a cyclist in a yellow jersey will appear and set the pace to help you meet the goal.

The Spark also has a built-in television and built-in music channels, but its main feature is its competitive riding courses. The machine is attached to the Internet so its owners can troubleshoot directly with the company in case of problems. It also allows the company to download new courses to its machines periodically and to keep track of which courses are the most popular. Exercisers can set goals and record and track their progress on Expresso Fitness's Web site. The bike sells in the $6,500 range, plus shipping and installation. Although the bike is designed primarily for gyms, fitness clubs, and corporate fitness centers, Espresso Fitness expects the Spark to appeal to highly motivated exercise enthusiasts as well.

A particularly appealing aspect of Expresso Fitness's offering is its revenue-sharing opportunities with fitness club owners. The company generates after-sale revenue from users through subscription services, contests, and special events.

Q&A: Based on the material covered in this chapter, what questions would you ask the firm's founders before making your funding decision? What answers would satisfy you?

Decision: If you had to make your decision on just the information provided in the pitch and on the company's Web site, would you fund this company? Why or why not?

You Be the VC 5.2

SRS Aviation

www.srsaviation.co.za

Business Idea: Build a network of professional private jet services across Africa that will offer personalized flight options to destinations around the world.

Pitch: Sibongile Sambo was meant to fly. The South African entrepreneur grew up close to an Air Force base and always had a love of planes. After a successful seven-year career in human resources, Sambo seized

(continued)

the opportunity presented by South Africa's Black Economic Empowerment Act of 2003 to realize her lifetime dream of setting up her own aviation company. The Act promotes affirmative action for previously disadvantaged groups, although Sambo conceded that her main obstacle to setting up and running an airline was being "young and female" in the male-dominated aviation industry.

In 2004, Sambo founded SRS Aviation, the first black female–owned aviation company in South Africa. From her previous work at diamond giant De Beers, Sambo could see that there was a significant demand for high-quality private jets in the increasingly prosperous business community. Although initially access to funding was difficult, the Black Economic Empowerment Act made all the difference in convincing the government to award Sambo her first contract; after all, the legislation was designed to promote economic transformation by enabling "meaningful participation of black people in the economy." The contract encouraged many companies who had previously refused support and partnership to open their doors to SRS Aviation. The government also provided business training and a consultant to help her with her business plan.

In 2005, SRS Aviation's first full year of trading, the firm generated revenues of $5 million, with three-quarters of the business coming from the government. With growing competition, the company keeps overhead low by employing a skeleton staff of nine employees, yet it is still committed to empowering socially disadvantaged groups, such as South African women, by training them to become pilots, cabin crew, technicians, and engineers. SRS also keeps costs down by only commissioning planes immediately before the flight, once the revenue has been received.

From its early beginnings as simply a broker of flights, the company now holds government licenses in helicopter operations and air transport for large and small aircraft. It undertakes VIP, cargo, and tourist charters, as well as emergency work such as medical evacuations and firefighting with the mission to offer flexibility, security, and "unparalleled service." Sambo won the international Black Woman in Business Award in 2007 and was selected for the prestigious Fortune mentoring program for women in the United States.

With South Africa as the transport hub for many goods coming into Africa, or being exported to Asia or the United States, Sambo now has plans to expand the business throughout the continent. SRS Aviation is also targeting international contracts for supplying food and other products to emergency areas across southern Africa. Sambo's ambition is to have a full network in place by the 2010 Football World Cup tournament, which will be held in South Africa.

Q&A: Based on the material covered in this chapter, what questions would you ask the firm's founders before making your funding decision? What answers would satisfy you?

Decision: If you had to make your decision on just the information provided in the pitch and on the company's Web site, would you fund this firm? Why or why not?

CASE5.1

Panera Bread: Occupying a Favorable Position in a Highly Competitive Industry
www.panerabread.com

Bruce R. Barringer
Oklahoma State University
R. Duane Ireland
Texas A & M University

Introduction

If you analyzed the restaurant industry using Porter's five forces model, you wouldn't be favorably impressed. Three of the threats to profitability—the threat of substitutes, the threat of new entrants, and rivalry among existing firms—are high. Despite these threats to industry profitability, one restaurant chain is moving forward in a very positive direction.

St. Louis–based Panera Bread, a chain of specialty bakery-cafés, has grown from 602 company-owned and franchised units in 2003 to 1,270 today. In 2008 alone, its sales increased by over 23 percent. So what's Panera's secret? How is it that this company flourishes while its industry as a whole is experiencing difficulty? As we'll see, Panera Bread's success can be explained in two words: positioning and execution.

Changing Consumer Tastes

Panera's roots go back to 1981, when it was founded under the name of Au Bon Pain Co. and consisted of three Au Bon Pain bakery-cafés and one cookie store. The company grew slowly until the mid-1990s, when it acquired Saint Louis Bread Company, a chain of 20 bakery-cafés located in the St. Louis area. About that time, the owners of the newly combined companies observed that people were increasingly looking for products that were "special"—that were a departure from run-of-the-mill restaurant food. Second, they noted that although consumers were tiring of standard fast-food fare, they didn't want to give up the convenience of quick service. This trend led the company to conclude that consumers wanted the convenience of fast food combined with a higher-quality experience. In slightly different words, they wanted good food served quickly in an enjoyable environment.

The Emergence of Fast Casual

As the result of these changing consumer tastes, a new category in the restaurant industry, called "fast casual," emerged. This category provided consumers the alternative they wanted by capturing the advantage of both the fast-food category (speed) and the casual dining category (good food), with no significant disadvantages. The owners of Au Bon Pain and Saint Louis Bread Company felt that they could help pioneer this new category, so they repositioned their restaurants and named them Panera Bread. The position that Panera moved into is depicted in the graphic titled "Positioning Strategy of Various Restaurant Chains." A market positioning grid provides a visual representation of the positions of various companies in an industry. About Panera's category, industry expert T. J. Callahan said, "I don't think fast casual is a fad; I think it's a structural change starting to happen in the restaurant industry."

Panera's Version of Fast Casual

To establish itself as the leader in the fast-casual category and to distinguish itself from its rivals, Panera (which is Latin for "time for bread") added a bonus to the mix—specialty food. The company has become known as a bread expert and offers a variety of artisan and other specialty breads, along with bagels, pastries, and baked goods. Panera Bread's restaurants are open for breakfast, lunch, and dinner and also offer hand-tossed salads, signature sandwiches, and hearty soups served in edible sourdough bread bowls, along with hot and cold coffee drinks. The company also provides catering services through its Via Panera catering business. Its restaurants provide an inviting neighborly atmosphere, adding to their appeal. Panera even suggests a new time of day to eat specialty foods, calling the time between lunch and dinner "chill-out" time.

With high hopes for future expansion, Panera Bread is now the acknowledged leader in the fast-casual category. Systemwide sales were $941 million in 2008. Its unique blend of fast-casual service and specialty foods also continues to gain momentum. This sentiment is captured in the following quote from Mark von Waaden, an investor and restaurateur who recently signed an agreement to open 20 Panera Bread restaurants in the Houston, Texas, area. Commenting on why he was attracted to Panera Bread as opposed to other restaurant chains, Mr. von Waaden said,

> My wife, Monica, and I fell in love with the fresh-baked breads and the beautiful bakery-cafés. We think the Panera Bread concept of outstanding bread coupled with a warm, inviting environment is a natural fit with the sophistication that the Houston market represents.

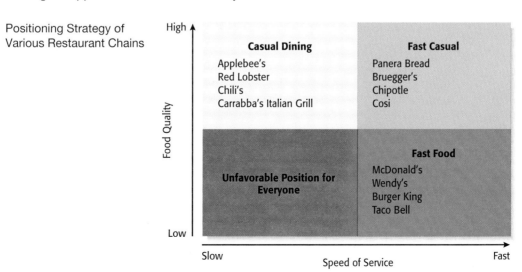

Positioning Strategy of Various Restaurant Chains

(continued)

The spirit of von Waaden's statement captures the essence of Panera's advantage. It isn't just another restaurant. By observing trends and listening to customers, its leaders helped the firm carve out a unique and favorable position in a difficult industry.

Present Status and Goal for the Future

Panera's leadership in the fast-casual category and its financial performance has drawn considerable attention to the company. The company's goal remains to make Panera a leading national brand. The company is counting on its unique positioning strategy, its signature foods, and savvy execution to make this goal a reality.

Discussion Questions

1. How has Panera Bread established a unique position in the restaurant industry? How has this unique position contributed to its success? Do you think Panera Bread will reach its goal of becoming a leading national brand in the restaurant industry? Why or why not?
2. Analyze the restaurant industry using Porter's five forces model. In what ways has Panera Bread successfully positioned itself against the forces that are suppressing the profitability of the restaurant industry as a whole?
3. What barriers to entry has Panera Bread created for potential competitors? How significant are these barriers?
4. What are Panera Bread's primary sources of competitive advantage? In your judgment, are these sources of advantage sustainable? Why or why not?

Application Questions

1. What are the ways that Panera Bread can conduct ethical and proper forms of competitive analysis to learn about potential competitors entering the fast-casual category?
2. Think of at least two other businesses that have established unique positions in their industries. How have their unique positions contributed to their success?

Sources: Panera Bread homepage, www.panerabread.com, (accessed November 18, 2008); Panera Bread Annual Report (2008); "Industry by Industry: A Look at the Start, Their Stocks—and Their Latest Picks, *Wall Street Journal*, May 12, 2003, R8.

CASE5.2

Cirque du Soleil and Curves International: Succeeding in Unattractive Industries via Blue Ocean Strategies
www.cirquedusoleil.com
www.curves.com

Bruce R. Barringer
Oklahoma State University
R. Duane Ireland
Texas A & M University

Introduction

At first glance, Cirque du Soleil and Curves International have little in common. One is a high-end entertainment company with only five permanent locations. The other is a fitness center for women, with close to 10,500 locations worldwide. But when it comes to this chapter's topic, industry and competitor analysis, the two have similar start-up stories as well as current performance-related outcomes. Indeed, although both companies were launched in what would be called unattractive industries, both are thriving today, primarily by attracting new customers to their industries and by changing the rules of competition in their respective industries.

Examining these firms shows that both Cirque du Soleil and Curves have started companies in what W. Chan Kim and Renee Mauborgne call "blue oceans." In their book *Blue Ocean Strategy*, Kim and Mauborgne ask their readers to imagine a market universe composed of two types of oceans: blue oceans and red oceans. In the red oceans, industry boundaries are well defined and the rules of the game are known. Companies slug it out for market share, and as the market gets increasingly crowded, prospects for growth and profits diminish, and cutthroat competition turns the oceans red. In contrast, blue oceans are defined by untapped market space and the opportunity for highly profitable growth. Most blue oceans are actually created within red oceans by expanding existing industry boundaries. When this happens, the industries experience a flood of new customers that rarely, if ever, participated before.

Although not all industries are ripe for blue ocean strategies, Cirque du Soleil and Curves are extraordinary examples of firms that rejuvenated unattractive industries by changing the rules of the game. They have succeeded *not* by taking customers away from their rivals, but by unlocking huge untapped markets in previously unattractive industries. Read on to see how they did it.

Cirque du Soleil

Cirque du Soleil (French for "circus of the sun") was started in Montreal, Canada, in 1984 by Guy Lailberté, a 23-year-old Montreal fire breather, and Daniel Gauthier, a 24-year-old hotel manager. At the time the circus industry was in decline. There was a growing sentiment against the use of animals in circuses and alternative forms of entertainment were increasing. The existing circus companies were focused on maximizing their share of the existing demand by tweaking their acts. This meant hiring more famous clowns and more spectacular circus acts, which resulted in higher costs with little or no corresponding increase in revenue and, subsequently, income.

Rather than trying to create a circus with better fun and more thrilling acts, Cirque du Soleil decided to redefine the boundaries of the circus by offering people at the same time (1) the thrill of the circus and (2) the artistic richness and the intellectual sophistication of the theater. By adopting this approach, Cirque du Soleil was able to eliminate many of the negatives associated with traditional circuses and add the positives associated with more upscale theater productions. In the process, it did away with animal shows, hiring star performers, aisle concession sales, and the "three rings" of the three-ring circus. Animals are expensive to maintain and are controversial in a circus setting. The so-called "circus stars" paled in popularity to movie stars and professional athletics. And the "three rings" of the three-ring circus not only created angst among spectators, who rapidly switched their attention from one ring to another, but drove costs up as well.

To the founders of Cirque du Soleil, the lasting allure of the circus came down to three essential elements: the tent, the clowns, and the acrobatic acts. So they retained these elements and dressed them up. To expand the richness and the boundaries of the circus, they added new elements, such as a story line, a refined environment, artistic music and dance, and permanent venues. In addition, a key decision made early in the life of the company set its direction in terms of quality. As word spread about Cirque du Soleil's early success, offers flooded in from agents and production companies wanting to finance numerous touring renditions of the show. But the founders refused. The supply of world-class circus performers was just too limited, they reasoned, to put dozens of Cirque du Soleil–branded shows on the road. Instead, they decided to strictly limit the number of shows they produced to avoid diluting their talent.

To visually see how Cirque du Soleil redefined the circus industry, refer to the figure titled "How Cirque du Soleil and Curves International Redefined the Industries in Which They Compete." This figure shows the factors that Cirque du Soleil eliminated from the traditional circus and the factors that it added. Among Cirque du Soleil's 18 current productions are *O*, an aquatic show in Las Vegas at MGM Mirage's Bellagio Hotel; *Love*, a Las Vegas show featuring music of the Beatles; and touring shows *Alegria* and *Quidam*. All of Cirque du Soleil's shows are unique and distinct. By offering the best of both the circus and the theater, the company has drawn people to its performances that would never have considered attending a traditional circus. Its prices, which range from $40 to $125 per ticket, are comparable to Broadway shows.

Cirque de Soleil's unique approach has created a blue ocean and a new form of live entertainment—which is neither circus nor theater. In just under 25 years, the company has brought in as much revenue as it took Barnum & Bailey and Ringling Brothers a combined 100 years to obtain.

Curves International

In the early 1990s, most fitness centers in the United States targeted people between the ages of 20 and 30. They focused on fitness and sports and typically offered exercise equipment and classes such as aerobics. Amenities ranged from towel service and showers to massages, swimming pools, and child care. Most centers sold annual or monthly memberships. Some of these memberships were expensive, running as high as $1,800 per year.

Like the founders of Cirque du Soleil, Gary and Diane Heavin, who founded Curves in 1992, had a different idea. They wanted to open a fitness center targeted at an underserved part of the market: overweight women who had never worked out

(continued)

How Cirque du Soleil and Curves Redefined the Industries in Which They Compete

Cirque du Soleil

Eliminated from Traditional Circuses	Unique Additions to the Circus Concept
• Star performers • Animal shows • Aisle concession sales • Multiple show arenas	• Theme • Refined environment • Artistic music and dance • Multiple productions

Curves International

Eliminated from Traditional Fitness Centers	Unique Additions to the Fitness Center Concept
• Full range of aerobic and strength machines • Locker room and showers • Aerobic classes • Juice bars	• Just for women • A tightly structured 30-minute workout • Affordable prices • Advocacy for women

before. The Heavins believed that many women 30 and older cared deeply about their health and appearance but didn't want to join a fitness center full of people who were already fit. They also figured that if they made the center convenient and affordable, and restricted it to females, it would inspire middle-aged women to give fitness a try.

To implement their idea, the Heavins stripped the fitness center concept down to what they felt would appeal to the emotional and physical needs of women and would fit into their budgets and busy lives. They started by eliminating many of the factors that drive up the cost of a fitness club membership and provide little value to many women: multiple aerobic and strength machines, locker rooms and showers, aerobic classes and juice bars. In their place, they implemented a tightly structured 30-minute workout on 8 to 12 exercise machines. The machines are located in a circle, and a recorded voice tells a member when to move from one machine to another. A member walks in, works out, and walks out, all in just over half an hour. This approach gives busy women the ability to participate without sacrificing a large portion of their day. It also allows them to shower and dress in the privacy of their homes.

What Curves has eliminated, and has uniquely added to the fitness center concept, is shown in the figure referred to earlier. As shown in the figure, the additions go beyond the workout itself. By creating a fitness center designed specifically for women, the company explicitly and implicitly told this group, "We know how you feel. We know it is not easy to go to a fitness center if you're a little embarrassed about how you look. You're important enough that we've created a company just for you. We care." By positioning itself in this way, Curves became an advocate for women 30 and older and expanded

the boundaries of the fitness industry. "What Curves has done is broken through the perception that you have to be fit, coordinated and thin to go to a gym," says Bill Howland, director of research for the International Health, Racquet and Sports Association. "They've carved out a niche within the population that had never been served." In different words, Curves has created a blue ocean out of an existing red ocean.

There are now close to 10,500 Curves locations worldwide with sales exceeding the $1 billion mark. Through its unique approach, Curves has attracted a large number of women to the fitness industry who would never have joined a fitness center before. Its unique approach has also made the opening of a Curves franchise affordable for a wider range of potential franchisees. A curves franchise can be opened for between $35,000 and $50,000. By comparison, a full-service fitness center can cost up to $1 million to build and fully equip.

Discussion Questions

1. What are the primary lessons learned from the Cirque du Soleil and the Curves cases? How do these lessons help the founders of a start-up better appreciate and understand the dynamics of the industry that they are about to enter?

2. What barriers to entry have both Cirque du Soleil and Curves established to deter competitors? Has capturing a first-mover advantage helped these firms deter new entrants from expanding their respective industries in the same ways that Cirque du Soleil and Curves did? Which company has established stronger barriers to entry— Cirque du Soleil or Curves?

3. Which of the nontraditional barriers to entry, shown in Table 5.1, were utilized by Cirque du

Soleil and which were utilized by Curves? To what extent have these nontraditional barriers to entry contributed to each company's success?

4. Develop a competitive analysis grid for Curves. Replicate the grid shown in Table 5.5, replacing the information provided for Expresso Fitness with similar information for Curves.

Application Questions

1. Provide an example of a company, other than Cirque du Soleil or Curves, that has expanded the market boundaries (that is, has created a blue

ocean) out of an unattractive industry (that is, from a red ocean). Briefly tell this company's story.

2. Do you think a fitness center designed specifically for men could be as successful in drawing new people into the fitness center industry as Curves has been with its fitness centers designed specifically for women? Explain your answer.

Sources: W. C. Kim and R. Mauborge, *Blue Ocean Strategy* (Boston: Harvard Business School Press, 2005); Cirque du Soleil homepage, www.cirquedusoleil.com (accessed November 15, 2008); Curves International homepage, www.curves.com (accessed November 15, 2008); H. W. Tesoriero, "A Slim Gym's Fat Success," *Time*, June 2003.

Endnotes

1. Sun-tzu, *The Art of War* (Mineola, NY: Dover Publications, 2002), chap. 7.
2. P. J. Derfus, P. G. Maggitti, C. M. Grimm, and K. G. Smith, "The Red Queen Effect: Competitive Actions and Firm Performance," *Academy of Management Journal* 51, no. 1 (2008): 61–80; R. P. Rumelt, "How Much Does Industry Matter?" *Strategic Management Journal* 12, no. 3 (1991): 167–85.
3. Y. E. Spanos, G. Zaralis, and S. Lioukas, "Strategy and Industry Effects on Profitability: Evidence from Greece," *Strategic Management Journal* 25 (2004), 139–65.
4. A. M. McGahan and M. Porter, "How Much Does Industry Matter, Really?" *Strategic Management Journal* 18, special issue (1997): 15–30.
5. "Motorcycle Manufacturers," Standard & Poor's NetAdvantage, www.netadvantage. standardpoor.com/NASApp/NetAdvantage/loadIndustriesPage.do?task=loadIndus triesPage (accessed November 16, 2008).
6. "Mattress Manufacturers in the U.S.: 33791," *IBISWorld Industry Report*, www. ibisworld.com.au (accessed October 8, 2008).
7. M. Porter, *Competitive Strategy: Techniques for Analyzing Industries and Competitors* (New York: Free Press, 1980).
8. Porter, *Competitive Strategy.*
9. Porter, *Competitive Strategy.*
10. T. Surette and C. Feldman, "Big Deal: EA and NFL Ink Exclusive Licensing Agreement," *Gamespot News*, www.gamespot.com (accessed December 13, 2004).
11. S. McNealy, "A Winning Business Model," in *The Book of Entrepreneurs' Wisdom*, ed. Peter Krass (New York: John Wiley & Sons, 1999), 171–89.
12. T. Tsai, "ASUSTeK Adds Online Storage to Low-Cost Eee PC," *Wall Street Journal*, September 5, 2008, B3.
13. M. Porter, "How Competitive Forces Shape Strategy," *Harvard Business Review* 57, no. 2 (1979): 137–45.
14. Geoffrey A. Moore, *Dealing with Darwin* (New York: Portfolio, 2005).
15. J. A. Barney and W. Hesterly, "Organizational Economics: Understanding the Relationship Between Organizations and Economic Analysis," in *Handbook of Organization Studies*, eds. Steward R. Clegg, Cynthia Hardy, and Walter R. Nord (London: Sage, 1996), 115–47.
16. M. Carpenter and W. Sanders, *Strategic Management,* 2nd ed. (Upper Saddle River, NJ: Prentice Hall, 2008).
17. J. Rodengen, *The Legend of Nucor Corporation* (Ft. Lauderdale, FL: Write Stuff Enterprises, 1997).
18. T. Levitt, *The Marketing Imagination* (New York: Free Press, 1986).
19. M-J. Chen, K-H. Su, and W. Tsai, "Competitive Tension: The Awareness-Motivation-Capability Perspective," *Academy of Management Journal* 50, no. 1 (2007): 101–18; M-J. Chen, "Competitor Analysis and Inter-Firm Rivalry: Toward a Theoretical Integration," *Academy of Management Review* 21, no. 1 (1996): 100–34.
20. P. Kotler, *Marketing Insights from A to Z* (Hoboken, NJ: Wiley, 2003), 23.
21. P. Coburn, *The Change Function* (New York: Portfolio, 2006).
22. J. L. Nesheim, *The Power of Unfair Advantage* (New York: Free Press, 2005).

Getting Personal

with Joshua Boltuch

BEST ADVICE I'VE RECEIVED
"Put yourself in their shoes. Then make the deal."

MY ADVICE FOR NEW ENTREPRENEURS
You can't do it alone, so bring in people you trust and who can do something better than you can

MY BIGGEST SURPRISE AS AN ENTREPRENEUR
There's always something to worry about

WHAT I DO WHEN I'M NOT WORKING
Concerts, see friends, watch baseball—big Oakland A's fan, gym, bowling, read, write

BEST PART OF BEING A STUDENT
Having next to zero responsibilities and a lot of free time (it never happens again)

WHAT I'D LIKE TO BE DOING IN 10 YEARS
Traveling all over the world

JOSHUA BOLTUCH
Cofounder, Amie Street
BA, College of Arts & Sciences, Brown University, 2006

ELLIOTT BREECE
Cofounder, Amie Street
BA, College of Arts & Sciences, Brown University, 2006

ELIAS ROMAN
Cofounder, Amie Street
BA, College of Arts & Sciences, Brown University, 2006

CHAPTERSIX
Developing an *Effective* Business Model

OPENING PROFILE

If you're a music fan and haven't heard about Amie Street, you're in for a treat. Amie Street is a music download service that was started by Joshua Boltuch, Elliott Breece, and Elias Roman, three Brown University students in 2006. The name "Amie Street" came from the street the three shared a house on in Providence, Rhode Island where Brown is located. The three are an eclectic trio. Boltuch was an English literature major, Breece was majoring in modern cultures and media, and Roman was an economics student. Breece is on the left, Boltuch is in the middle, and Roman is to the right in the picture.

In spring 2006, the three were preparing for graduation and thinking about business ideas. One thing that struck them about the music industry was that the majority of people who downloaded music from the Internet fell into one of two groups. The first group found ways to get music free—either legally or illegally. The second group paid 99 cents per song on iTunes, which was just getting off the ground at the time. What if they found a way to bridge the gap—and help people download music legally for free or for less than 99 cents? That type of approach would bring people who were downloading music illegally into an organized, proper system and motivate people to "try" new types of music because it was free or could be obtained at a nominal cost.

As Boltuch, Breece, and Roman kicked around different ideas, a unique business model emerged, which remains in place today. Amie Street is an online music store and social network that appeals primarily to independent musicians and their fans. A musician can upload a song to Amie Street, and the song is initially available for free. As people start downloading the song, it rises in price to a maximum of 98 cents. Along the way, it might be 10 cents, 20 cents, or 50 cents, depending on its popularity. Musicians keep 70 percent of the revenue, as long as they have made at least $5. Additionally, musicians are not required to sell their music exclusively through Amie Street and can remove a song anytime they like.

On the customer side, people who buy songs on Amie Street have a profile page, similar to a Facebook or MySpace page, except most of your profile automatically gets filled with your music tastes as you browse and purchase music on the site. One of the most unique benefits to Amie Street is its recommendation system. On Amie Street, when you REC (recommend) a song you get money added to your account! Every time you REC a song, and it continues to increase in price, you earn free downloads for having recommended it to other Amie Street members. Amie Street wants to encourage you to talk about the music you like because it helps everyone discover more music and artists reach more people. So they made it worth your while, and how much money you get depends on how popular that song gets—you can get up to 98 cents per REC!

Amie Street's core competencies are twofold: First, it's a fast and easy service that helps people discover new music they'll love; second, it generates revenue for artists and record labels. Along with its unique pricing strategy, key elements of Amie Street's business model include its partnership network and customer interface. To populate its

Learning Objectives

After studying this chapter you should be ready to:

1. Describe a business model.

2. Explain business model innovation.

3. Discuss the importance of having a clearly articulated business model.

4. Discuss the concept of the value chain.

5. Identify a business model's two potential fatal flaws.

6. Identify a business model's four major components.

7. Explain the meaning of the term *business concept blind spot.*

8. Define core competency and describe its importance.

9. Explain the concept of supply chain management.

10. Explain the concept of fulfillment and support.

site with a large critical mass of songs, Amie Street procures music in three ways. First, through independent musicians who upload songs to its site. Second, through distributors who aggregate songs and partner with Amie Street to list to them on its site. And third, through partnerships with record labels that partner with Amie Street to place additional songs on its Web site. Amie Street has a variety of additional partnerships, most of which help drive traffic to its site. In terms of customer interface, Amie Street has invested heavily in the user experience. The site, which underwent a complete makeover in late 2008, is easy to navigate, and a user can sort by genre, browse new releases, look at the top 25 albums and the top 25 songs, get personalized recommendations based on past purchases, and more. There are also extensive recommendations of songs by the Amie Street community. The company also maintains a blog and a very popular weekly newsletter that helps members discover music they never would have found otherwise.

Amie Street's business model has expanded beyond its music download service, but only in narrow ways. AmieTV is a weekly post on the company's blog that highlights eight popular music videos on YouTube from Amie Street artists. The company has also become involved in promoting some of its artists in live concerts, but in a limited fashion.

How is Amie Street's business model performing? While the company does not release financial results, Amazon.com invested in the site in spring 2007, it has 21 employees, 1.5 million songs on its Web site, and has exceeded the expectations of its founders, which is quite a step up from Boltuch, Breece, and Roman's initial idea—in their rented house on Amie Street in Providence their senior year in college.[1]

This chapter introduces the business model and explains why it's important for a new venture to develop a business model early in its life. In everyday language, a model is a plan that's used to make or describe something. More formally, a **business model** is a firm's plan or diagram for how it competes, uses its resources, structures its relationships, interfaces with customers, and creates value to sustain itself on the basis of the profits it earns.[2] As you'll see later in this chapter, a successful business model has four components.

The term *business model* first came into use with the advent of the personal computer (PC) and the spreadsheet. The spreadsheet made sensitivity analysis possible, giving managers the ability to ask "what-if" questions. A manager could sit at a computer, manipulate an item such as sales, and see how a shortfall or an upswing in sales would affect every other aspect of the business. In other words, a manager could "model" the behavior of the business.[3] Today, "business model" is used in a much broader context to include all the activities that define how a firm competes in the marketplace.[4]

It's important to understand that a firm's business model takes it beyond its own boundaries. Almost all firms partner with others to make their business models work. In Amie Street's case, the venture requires cooperation from record label companies who partner with Amie Street to provide additional songs the firm places on its site. Additionally, Amie Street works hard to create user-friendly interfaces with its customers so they can easily find and then enjoy music that interests them. Very similarly, the firm seeks to interact positively with the musicians who provide their creative works to Amie Street as a means of successfully distributing their music to a variety of listeners. Amie Street's business model would suffer without all of these collaborative relationships.

As our discussion to this point suggests, a company's business model involves its network of partners along with its products. It encompasses the capabilities of multiple individuals and entities, all of which must be willing and motivated to play along. Some early e-commerce firms that had plausible business models on paper failed because they couldn't get key partners to participate. An example is online beauty retailer Eve.com. The company struggled largely because many of the high-profile suppliers of women's beauty products wouldn't sell their products on its Web site. The suppliers were concerned that if they sold through Eve.com, they would offend their traditional channel partners, such as Nordstrom and Saks. Eve.com's business model never coalesced, and the firm eventually went out of business. Similarly, some business models fail because they become stale and are replaced by more attractive alternatives. Many people believe that the daily newspaper business model is headed in this direction. One newspaper, *The Christian Science Monitor*, recently dropped its daily print edition and has replaced it with a daily Web edition, a print weekend edition, and a daily e-mail service. In announcing the change, Jonathan Wells, the newspaper's publisher, described the newspaper industry as being in a "nexus of change" with readers increasingly migrating to the Web for information.[5]

In this chapter, we'll first discuss business models and their importance. Then we'll look at how business models emerge and examine some of their potential "fatal flaws." Finally, we'll examine the components of effective business models.

BUSINESS MODELS

There is no standard business model, no hard-and-fast rules that dictate how a firm in a particular industry should compete. In fact, it's dangerous for the entrepreneur launching a new venture to assume that the venture can be successful by simply copying the business model of another firm—even if that other firm is the industry leader. This is true for two reasons. First, it is difficult to precisely understand all of the components of another firm's business model. Second, a firm's business model is inherently dependent on the collection of resources it controls and the capabilities it possesses. For example, if FedEx employs the best group of supply chain managers possible and has established long-term trusting relationships with key suppliers, it may be the only company in the world that can effectively implement its business model. No other firm would have this unique set of capabilities, at least initially.

To achieve long-term success though, all business models need to be modified across time. The reason for this is that competitors can eventually learn how to duplicate the benefits a particular firm is able to create through its business model. In the late 2000s, for example, financial returns have suggested that competitors such as Hewlett-Packard are successfully duplicating some of the benefits of Dell's business model. When Dell's business model was first introduced, it was a **business model innovation**, which refers to a business model that revolutionizes how a product is produced, sold, or supported after the sale.[6] Figure 6.1 depicts Dell's approach to selling computers versus traditional manufacturers. As we've noted, Dell's competitors seem to be able today to duplicate the benefits of Dell's business model. Nonetheless, at the time of its introduction, Dell's business model was definitely revolutionary.

Firms are continually introducing business model innovations to find ways to add value in unique ways and revolutionize how products and services are

Learning Objective
1. Describe a business model.

Learning Objective
2. Explain business model innovation.

FIGURE 6.1

Dell's Approach to Selling PCs Versus Traditional Manufacturers'

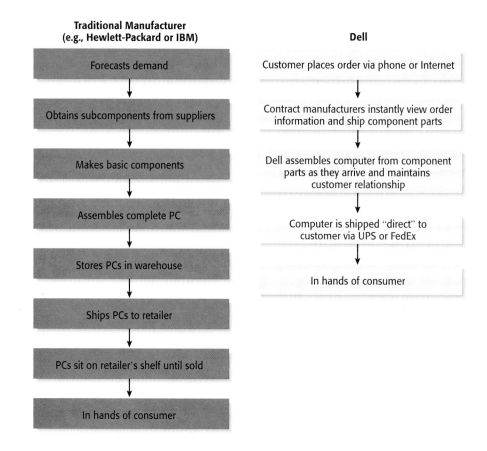

Traditional Manufacturer (e.g., Hewlett-Packard or IBM)

Forecasts demand

↓

Obtains subcomponents from suppliers

↓

Makes basic components

↓

Assembles complete PC

↓

Stores PCs in warehouse

↓

Ships PCs to retailer

↓

PCs sit on retailer's shelf until sold

↓

In hands of consumer

Dell

Customer places order via phone or Internet

↓

Contract manufacturers instantly view order information and ship component parts

↓

Dell assembles computer from component parts as they arrive and maintains customer relationship

↓

Computer is shipped "direct" to customer via UPS or FedEx

↓

In hands of consumer

sold in their industries. The "Savvy Entrepreneurial Firm" feature provides examples of business model innovations in solar power, software, and medical services.

A firm's business model is developed after the feasibility analysis stage of launching a new venture. If a firm has conducted a successful feasibility analysis and knows that it has a product or service with potential, the business model stage addresses how to surround it with a core strategy, a partnership model, a customer interface, distinctive resources, and an approach to creating value that represents a viable business.

An example of a business model innovation is Netflix, which was started by Reed Hastings in 1997. Netflix introduced a completely new way of renting DVDs. For a flat monthly fee, a subscriber gets up to three DVDs at a time, which may be kept as long as desired or exchanged for other DVDs. The DVDs are delivered by mail, saving Netflix subscribers a trip to a video rental store.

©Kimberly White/CORBIS, all rights reserved.

Savvy Entrepreneurial FIRM
Three Industries, Three Business Model Innovators

Business model innovation is an important part of the entrepreneurial process. Not only do entrepreneurs bring new products and services to market, but new business models often revolutionize how products and services are sold and bring considerable value to businesses and consumers. The following are examples of business model innovations in three industries.

SunEdison

Solar Energy seems like an ideal alternative to fossil fuels. However, the reality is that purchasing and installing a solar energy system is simply too expensive given the potential cost savings in most instances. Installing a solar energy system also requires a consumer or business to make a substantial capital outlay for future cost savings. Although there are obvious environmental benefits to consider, how would you like to pay your next five years of electric bills in advance? There's also the issue of maintenance. Once you buy a solar energy system you own it and are responsible for upkeep and repairs.

So how can solar energy be an affordable alternative to gaining access to an energy source? One innovative business model, pioneered by SunEdison, is to make solar energy a service rather than a product. The company, which was started by Jigar Shah, a former British Petroleum executive, purchases, installs, and maintains the solar panels placed on its customers' roofs in exchange for service contracts that provide SunEdison a steady stream of revenue to fund its operators. SunEdison's "solar as a service" business model is new and is now being copied by other firms.

Red Hat

In 1991, a student at the University of Helsinki named Linus Torvalds posted his Linux operating system on the Internet to compete with the Microsoft Windows operating system. Torvalds, a believer in free or "open" software, invited other programmers to try to improve it—for free. The only caveat is that if an individual or company downloads the source code and improves upon it, they must then make the upgraded version freely available to everyone else.

Linux quickly developed a global following among programmers and businesses. There are now many different forms of software that emulate the Linux "open source" or free model. Many companies, like Google and Amazon.com, use the Linux operating system rather than a system from Microsoft or a similar vendor to cut their technology costs.

The only problem with Linux is that even though it's free, it takes some expertise to download and properly

implement into a business's computer systems and products. Early on rogue programmers and hobbyists like Linus Torvalds showed people how to use it, but this type of approach has obvious limits. To solve this problem, in the late 1990s, Red Hat, a Raleigh, North Carolina, start-up, introduced an innovative business model to complement Linux software. Red Hat didn't sell Linux—that's not allowed. But it started supporting and customizing Linux for clients and developed applications to make Linux run smoother. There are now many companies like Red Hat that make money by supporting open-source software.

Charter Internal Medicine

This one's a little more controversial. In late 2008, Charter Internal Medicine, a clinic located in Columbia, Maryland, posted the following notice on its Web site:

> Beginning on January 1, 2009, Charter Internal Medicine, LLC will no longer participate in any health insurance plans or Medicare. Our goal is to provide you with personal health care and therefore we will no longer have 3 parties involved; your health care will be between you and your personal physician. Payment will be by retainer.

According to an article published in the *Baltimore Sun*, Charter's new business model works like this. In exchange for a $4,500 yearly fee, a family guarantees itself 24-hour access to doctors, unhurried appointments, home visits, and start-of-the-art annual physicals. The concept is referred to as "boutique" or "concierge" medical care. Charter Internal Medicine didn't pioneer the concept but is part of a pioneering effort to try to make the business model work. Doctors say that the model allows them to trim their patient loads and give patients quality care without the hassles of relying on insurance. Critics argue that the business model exacerbates the shortage of primary care doctors available to patients and creates an "elite" approach to health care for those who can afford it.

Questions for Critical Thinking

1. Which of the business models described here strikes you as the most revolutionary? Which business model do you think will have the largest long-term impact on its industry?
2. Write a mission statement for SunEdison (mission statements are described later in the chapter).
3. Do you think SunEdison stands to capture a first-mover advantage in the solar energy industry if its business model innovation catches on?

(continued)

4. Name two additional business model innovations not mentioned in the chapter. How is each business model innovation "adding value" in its industry?

Sources: J. Makower, *Strategies for the Green Economy* (New York: McGraw Hill: 2009); T. Dixon and K. Brewington, "For

a Little More, the Doctor Will See You Now," *Baltimore Sun*, www.baltimoresun.com/news/local/bal-te.md.doctors26 oct26,0,3508066.story (accessed October 26, 2008); Charter Internal Medicine homepage, www.charterinternalmedicine.com (accessed November 16, 2008).

The Importance and Diversity of Business Models

Having a well-thought-out business model is important for several reasons. Although some models are better than others, it is dangerous to link the performance of a firm solely to the configuration of its business model. In most cases, performance is a function of both the *choice* of a business model and how effectively it's implemented. For example, eBay's business model is straightforward. In exchange for providing a virtual meeting place for people to buy and sell things, it earns a fee. It isn't a complicated model. The trick is executing the model in a way that satisfies customers and makes a profit for eBay. If the customers aren't satisfied, the business model fails. If eBay can't make a profit, the business model fails.[7] The challenge for all companies is to *create* a sensible business model and to *implement* it effectively.

Learning Objective

3. Discuss the importance of having a clearly articulated business model.

Importance of Business Models   Having a clearly articulated business model is important because it does the following:

- Serves as an ongoing extension of feasibility analysis (a business model continually asks the question, Does the business make sense?)
- Focuses attention on how all the elements of a business fit together and how they constitute a working whole
- Describes why the network of participants needed to make a business idea viable is willing to work together
- Articulates a company's core logic to all stakeholders, including the firm's employees

A good way to illustrate the importance of these points is to describe a business model that *didn't* work. WebHouse Club was launched by Priceline.com founder Jay Walker in fall 1999 and failed just a year later after eating up nearly $350 million of its investors' money. Priceline.com allows customers to "bid" for airline tickets, hotel rooms, and home mortgages. WebHouse was set up to mimic Priceline.com's business model and extend it to grocery store items. WebHouse worked like this: A shopper obtained a plastic card with a unique number and a magnetic strip from a local grocery store or a newspaper insert. The card was used to activate an account on the WebHouse Internet site. Once an account was established, the shopper could then make a bid for a supermarket item, say $3.75 for a box of toasted corn flakes cereal. The shopper could specify the price but not the brand. In seconds, the shopper would learn whether a maker of toasted corn flakes cereal was willing to accept the price. If so, the shopper would pay WebHouse for the cereal with a credit card and would then pick up the cereal at a participating store using the WebHouse card. The cereal could be Kellogg's, General Mills, or any other brand.

Behind the scenes, WebHouse followed the same formula that Priceline.com had invented to sell airline tickets and hotel rooms. By aggregating shopper demand for products such as cereal, tuna, or diapers, WebHouse could go to producers such as Kellogg's and General Mills and negotiate discounts. The company could then pass along the discounts to consumers and take a small fee for bringing buyers and sellers together.[8]

Why didn't this business model work for WebHouse? Actually, several reasons describe the business model's failure in grocery stores. First, it assumed that companies such as Kellogg's would be willing to participate—not a wise assumption when you consider that Kellogg's has spent millions of dollars convincing consumers that Kellogg's Corn Flakes is better than competing brands. The WebHouse model teaches consumers to select products strictly on the basis of price rather than brand identity. So why would Kellogg's or any other producer want to help WebHouse do that? Second, the WebHouse model assumed that millions of shoppers would take the time to sit down at their computers and bid on grocery store items. It's easy to see why a consumer might take the time to get a better deal on an airline ticket or a stay in a four-star hotel room. But how many people have the time to sit down, log on to their computer, and interact with a Web site to save 50 cents on a box of cereal without even being able to choose the brand? As it turned out, not many people were willing to do so.

Ultimately, WebHouse failed because its business model was flawed. The company just couldn't motivate its suppliers or customers to participate at a sufficient scale to support the overhead of the business. WebHouse was asking suppliers to act against their self-interest and was asking shoppers to take too much time to save too little money. As busy as people are today, shoppers want to make the very best use of their limited time, meaning that they'll likely reject a time-consuming process that doesn't create obvious value for them.

Diversity of Business Models   As mentioned, there is no standard business model for an industry or for a target market within an industry. Firms approach their markets in different ways and devise different ways to make money. For example, there are five distinct ways that online companies make money. These approaches, shown in Table 6.1, are the core piece of their respective company's business models. The table illustrates one of the beauties of the Internet—you don't have to have a product or service to sell to make money online. If you know a great deal about a particular topic, such as cooking or home repair, you can launch a Web site; populate it with articles, tips, and other useful information; and make money online by essentially selling access to the people you attract to your Web site. This is possible by becoming an affiliate of another company, allowing pay-per-click ads to be placed on your Web site, or by selling direct ads that are placed on your Web site, as described in Table 6.1. All of these approaches were developed and pioneered by business model innovators. The result is that the Internet is essentially an ecosystem of varying business models that allow both online and offline companies to make money. A Web site that promotes BMX biking, for example, makes money by selling ads to companies that make BMX bikes and related equipment. The advertisers, in turn, make money when people respond to the ads and buy their products. Other companies, like Google and Yahoo!, make money by bringing Web sites and advertisers together.

Over time, the most successful business model (or models) in an industry predominate and the weaker models fall by the wayside. There are always opportunities for business model innovation. This fact is illustrated in the "Savvy Entrepreneurial Firm" feature earlier in the chapter. Think of Netflix in movie rentals, Wikipedia in encyclopedias, and Curves International in fitness clubs. These firms flourished by introducing new business models into their respective industries.

Table 6.1 FIVE DISTINCT WAYS OF MAKING MONEY ONLINE (THE WAY AN ONLINE COMPANY MAKES MONEY LARGELY DEFINES ITS BUSINESS MODEL)

Method for Making Money	Description
Affiliate programs	An affiliate program is a way for online merchants, like 1-800-FLOWERS, to get more exposure by offering a commission to Web sites and blogs that are willing to feature ads for its products or services. The merchant *pays* the affiliate a small commission every time someone clicks on the ads and buys one of its products.
Pay-per-click programs	A Web site or blog allows an advertiser's link to be placed on its site and gets *paid* a small commission every time someone clicks the ad. Examples include Google AdSense and Yahoo? Search Marketing. You've seen many Google AdSense ads. They are easy to spot because they have an emblem underneath that says "Ads by Google."
Direct ads	These are banner ads, skyscraper ads (all ads that run along the side of a Web page), or ads with pictures embedded in the content of a Web site. Web sites, blogs, and other online companies get *paid* for allowing these ads to be placed on their Web sites.
E-commerce	Direct sale of products online (i.e., Amazon.com, Dell.com). Online companies get *paid* directly by the individuals and businesses that buy their products.
Subscription services	These online companies provide services that have sufficient value that people in their niche market are willing to *pay* for on a yearly on monthly basis. For example, eHarmony charges an annual fee for access to its matchmaking service.

Source: Bruce R. Barringer and R. Duane Ireland, *What's Stopping You?: Shatter the 9 Most Common Myths Keeping You from Starting* Your *Own Business,* 1st Edition, ©2008, pp.162–170. Adapted by permission of Pearson Education, Inc., Upper Saddle River, NJ.

How Business Models Emerge

Learning Objective

4. *Discuss the concept of the value chain.*

The value chain is a model developed by an academic researcher[9] that many businesspeople as well as entrepreneurs use to identify opportunities to enhance their competitive strategies. The value chain also explains how business models emerge and develop. The **value chain** is the string of activities that moves a product from the raw material stage, through manufacturing and distribution, and ultimately to the end user. Depicted in Figure 6.2, the value chain consists of primary activities and support activities. The primary activities have to do with the physical creation, sale, and service of a product or a service, while the support activities provide reinforcement for the primary activities. Individual parts of the chain either add or do not add value as a product moves through the different stages of the value chain. The final product or service is an aggregate of the individual contributions of value made at the different stages of the chain.

By studying a product's or service's value chain, an organization can identify ways to create additional value and assess whether it has the means to do so. For example, Dell learned that it has customers who want technical support available on a 24-hour-per-day basis, 7 days a week (24/7), and that these customers are willing to pay extra to get it. Dell realized that it could "add value" to the value chain for selling computers by beefing up the "service" segment to include 24/7 technical support. This would work, however, only if Dell had enough trained personnel to offer the 24/7 support and could make money doing so. Additionally, if Dell could offer the 24/7 support and its competitors couldn't, the 24/7 service would become a point of profit-generating differentiation between Dell and its competitors. Dell spent 2007 and 2008 allocating additional resources to its support services in order to create more value for its customers. This example illustrates why

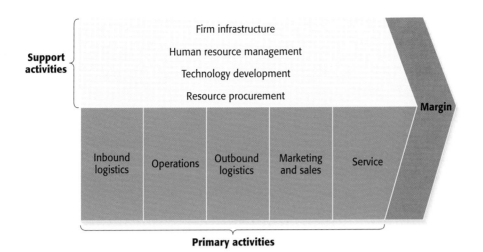

FIGURE 6.2

The Value Chain

Source: Reprinted with permission of The Free Press, a Division of Simon & Schuster Adult Publishing Group, from *Competitive Advantage: Creating and Sustaining Superior Performance* by Michael E. Porter. Copyright © 1985, 1998 by Michael E. Porter. All rights reserved.

Definitions of Terms

Inbound logistics: Involves a firm's relationship with its suppliers and involves all the activities of receiving, storing, and shipping component parts to the place where they will be added to the final product

Operations: Involves all the activities required to manufacture a product

Outbound logistics: Involves all the activities required to warehouse and ship a finished product

the value chain has been widely adopted as a tool for developing firm strategy and analyzing firm competitiveness.

Entrepreneurs look at the value chain of a product or a service to pinpoint where the value chain can be made more effective or to spot where additional "value" can be added in some meaningful way. This type of analysis may focus on (1) a single primary activity of the value chain (such as marketing and sales), (2) the interface between one stage of the value chain and another (such as the interface between operations, which are the activities required to manufacture a product, and outbound logistics, which are the activities required to warehouse and ship it), or (3) one of the support activities (such as human resource management). If a product's value chain can be strengthened in any one of these areas, it may represent an opportunity for the formation of a new firm to perform that activity. Table 6.2 provides examples of entrepreneurial firms that have enhanced the value chain of an existing product or service by focusing on one of the three previously mentioned areas.

A firm can be formed to strengthen the value chain for a product, but only if a viable business model can be created to support it. For example, Michael Dell's idea of selling computers directly to end users wouldn't have been possible if it weren't for low-cost shippers, such as UPS and FedEx, and manufacturers of computer components who were willing to sell their products to him.

Finally, some start-ups are launched with the defined purpose of providing the missing link in a potentially lucrative value chain that currently isn't plausible because of technical or economic limitations. For example, many consumers are interested in reducing their energy costs via solar power, but the investment required to buy solar panels and have the panels installed compared to the cost savings makes solar power impractical, as indicated in the "Savvy Entrepreneurial Firm" feature. ReadySolar, a recent start-up (and the focus of the "You Be the VC 6.1" feature), claims that it can significantly reduce the cost of installing solar panels via an IKEA-like "solar-in-a box" solution, where the system comes prepackaged and installs more easily and

Table 6.2   FIRMS FOUNDED TO ENHANCE THE VALUE CHAIN OF AN EXISTING PRODUCT
OR SERVICE

New Venture's Current Name	Value Chain Activity	Reason New Venture Was Started
Primary Activities		
Maersk, Viking Logistics	Inbound logistics	To provide efficient material management, warehousing, and inventory control
Celestica, Flextronics	Operations	To provide efficient contract manufacturing services for companies such as IBM, Microsoft, and Ericsson
FedEx, UPS	Outbound logistics	To provide new ways to warehouse and move goods effectively to the end user
Costco, Staples, Wal-Mart	Marketing and sales	To provide new ways to market and sell products
Contact America, Infosys	Service	To provide efficient call center, e-mail, and Web-based customer contact services
Support Activities		
Accenture, Headstrong	Firm infrastructure	To provide management support
ADP, Paychex	Human resource management	To provide payroll, tax, benefits administration, and other human resource services
Booz Allen, Unisys	Technology development	To help firms integrate emerging technologies into existing business systems
BASF, Grainger	Resource procurement	To help firms procure the raw materials and supplies needed for their production processes
The Interface Between One Stage of the Value Chain and Another		
Ariba, ChemConnect	Inbound logistics/operations	To help firms with the interface between inbound logistics and operations
Con-way Inc., UPS	Operations/outbound logistics	To help firms with the interface between operations and outbound logistics
Interstate Cold Storage	Outbound logistics/marketing and sales	To help firms with the interface between outbound logistics and marketing and sales
vCustomer, Eclipsys	Marketing and sales/service	To help firms with the interface between marketing and sales/service

inexpensively than competing systems. If ReadySolar is able to deliver on its promises, it will have solved, at least in part, one of the major problems currently confronting the value chain for solar power: the high cost of installation.

Potential Fatal Flaws of Business Models

Learning Objective

5. Identify a business model's two potential fatal flaws.

Two fatal flaws can render a business model untenable from the beginning: a complete misread of the customer and utterly unsound economics. Business models that fall victim to one of these two flaws have lost the race before leaving the starting gate.

In plain terms, a product must have customers to be successful. In the previously mentioned WebHouse example, the savings that were possible by

Getty Images, Inc.–Stone Allstock

Pets.com was known for its "spokespuppet," which appeared in Super Bowl ads and even in the Macy's Thanksgiving Day parade in New York City. The company's ads were larger than life, but when it came down to basic customer satisfaction Pets.com missed the mark, revealing fatal flaws in the company's business model. Pets.com closed its doors in early 2001.

bidding on grocery store items just weren't large enough to make it worthwhile for enough people to participate. The product had no customers. A similar misread of the customer sank Pets.com, a high-profile e-commerce flameout. Although it was convenient for consumers to have pet food and supplies delivered directly to their homes, the orders took several days to arrive—too long for customers who have access to the same products at the grocery store and at pet superstores such as PetSmart. Pets.com didn't realize that fast delivery was essential to its customers.

The second fatal flaw is pursuing unsound economics, as shown by the failure of many e-Bay drop-off stores, as illustrated in Chapter 3. The idea behind eBay drop-off stores (like iSoldit and QuickDrop) was that nearly everyone has something they'd like to sell on eBay, but many people don't want the hassles associated with setting up an eBay account, listing an item, following the auction, shipping the item to the buyer, and so forth.[10] While there are still some eBay drop-off stores still open and presumably making money, most store owners couldn't make the business model work. Their profit margins were just too small to justify their time and investment.[11]

COMPONENTS OF AN EFFECTIVE BUSINESS MODEL

Although not everyone agrees precisely about the components of a business model, many agree that a successful business model has a common set of attributes. For example, one team of academics thinks of a business model as a coordinated plan to design strategy along three vectors: customer interaction, asset configuration, and knowledge leverage.[12] Similarly, a noted business professor and writer, Gary Hamel, believes that a business model consists of four components: core strategy, strategic resources, customer interface, and value network.[13] We'll adopt a similar view and talk about a business model consisting of the following components:

- Core strategy (how a firm competes)
- Strategic resources (how a firm acquires and uses its resources)

Learning Objective

6. Identify a business model's four major components.

FIGURE 6.3

Components of
a Business
Model

Core Strategy	Strategic Resources	Partnership Network	Customer Interface
• Business mission • Product/market scope • Basis for differentiation	• Core competencies • Strategic assets	• Suppliers • Partners • Other key relationships	• Target customer • Fulfillment and support • Pricing structure

■ Partnership network (how a firm structures and nurtures its partnerships)

■ Customer interface (how a firm interfaces with its customers)

Each of these components has several subcomponents that we'll explore. We provide a summary of each component and its respective subcomponents in Figure 6.3.

If one of the four components of a start-up's business model doesn't take shape, the entire business model can fail. This is what happened to iContact, a company that was started to build a mobile social network. While its core strategy, strategic resources, and customer interface were strong, the firm couldn't motivate its key partners to cooperate, causing it to fail, as illustrated in the "What Went Wrong?" feature.

What Went WRONG?

What Happens When One of the Four Components of a Start-Up's Business Model Doesn't Take Shape?

In the early 2000s, David Cohen, a serial entrepreneur, set out to build a mobile social network named iContact. Social networks, like MySpace, were well known, but others like Facebook hadn't been started yet. There were no social networks built from the ground up to work on GPS-enabled mobile phones. Cohen and his cofounders felt that building a social network for mobile phone users would be profitable and fun.

The team raised about $600,000, half from themselves, and proceeded to develop the technology they needed. The social network they built wasn't much different than other social networks, except that it was very phone-centric. It included a number of nifty features, including the ability to stream your buddies' (people that had joined your network) favorite music and information on the events they were attending soon on your cell phone. Within a year, iContact had about 2,000 beta users. Unfortunately, it also had zero distribution by the cell phone companies.

The iContact team quickly realized that without the cell phone companies on board, they were dead in the water. After all, they had built a social network for cell phones. What they needed was for Verizon, T-Mobile, AT&T, and the other cell phone providers to provide a platform for their service in exchange for a cut of the revenue that was generated. This is what the cell phone companies did with their other partners.

Although they tried, the founders of iContact never struck a deal with a cell phone company or a company that had partnerships with a cell phone company. Once they were convinced that no deal was in the offing, they

shut the company down and returned 78 percent of their investor's money. The only financial plus that resulted from the venture is that the founders sold the iContact domain name for a tidy sum.

The moral of iContact's story is that if you don't have a way to distribute your product you don't have a viable business model. All four components of a start-up's business model (distribution is part of "Partnership Network") must be in place for a firm to function and have a chance to be successful.

Questions for Critical Thinking

1. Is there a way that iContact could have better foreseen the reluctance of cell phone companies to support its business model?
2. Do you think iContact would have a better chance to make its business model work today than it did in the early 2000s when the company was founded? Why or why not?
3. Is there a product on the market today that is similar to what iContact was trying to sell? If so, describe it.
4. Read the "You Be the VC 6.1" feature, which focuses on ReadySolar. What type of partnership arrangement will ReadySolar need to make its business model work?

Source: D. Cohen, "Life in the Deadpool," www.coloradostartups.com (accessed September 15, 2008). Used with permission of David Cohen.

Core Strategy

The first component of a business model is the **core strategy**, which describes how a firm competes relative to its competitors.[14] The firm's mission statement, the product/market scope, and the basis for differentiation are the primary elements of a core strategy.

Mission Statement   A firm's mission, or **mission statement**, describes why it exists and what its business model is supposed to accomplish.[15] Table 6.3 provides examples of the mission statements of five firms from very different industries. To varying degrees, the statements articulate the overarching priorities of the firms and set criteria to measure performance.

It is important that a firm's mission not be defined too narrowly. If it is, the business model that evolves may become too singularly focused and resistant to change. Take Xerox, for example. The firm styled itself as "The Document Company" with an implicit mission that focused on copiers and copying. This mission created what some call a **business concept blind spot**, which prevents a firm from seeing an opportunity that might fit its business model. Xerox viewed itself as a company that *reproduced* documents that already existed, causing the firm to be a late entrant into the market for computer printers, which print original documents stored electronically. This narrow focus allowed Hewlett-Packard to gain control of the printer market.[16]

Learning Objective

7. Explain the meaning of the term *business concept blind spot.*

Product/Market Scope   A company's **product/market scope** defines the products and markets on which it will concentrate. First, the choice of product has an important impact on a firm's business model. For example, Amazon.com started out as an online bookseller but has evolved to sell many other product lines, including CDs, DVDs, jewelry, apparel, and even groceries. Its business model has expanded to now include the challenge of managing relationships with a number of vendors and partners beyond those connected with books. Similarly, Yahoo! started as a company offering free Internet search services in an attempt to generate enough traffic to sell advertising space on its Web site. This business model worked until the e-commerce bubble burst in early 2000 and advertising revenues declined. Yahoo! is continually revising its business

Table 6.3   EXAMPLES OF MISSION STATEMENTS

Google

Organize the world's information and make it universally accessible and useful.

Pizza Fusion

Our mission is to uphold the highest level of integrity in all we do, from the quality and origin of our food to our care for the health of our customers and the environment.

Sprig Toys

Active, inspirational, fun toys made safely and sustainably.

Amgen

Amgen strives to serve patients by transforming the promise of science and biotechnology into therapies that have the power to restore health or even save lives. In everything we do, we aim to fulfill our mission to serve patients. And every step of the way, we are guided by the values that define us.

Southwest Airlines

The mission of Southwest Airlines is dedication to the highest quality of customer service delivered with a sense of warmth, friendliness, individual pride, and company spirit.

model to include additional subscription services to generate a more consistent income stream. Recent performance challenges found Microsoft making a bid for Yahoo!'s search business in late 2008. The outcome of this bid could obviously change Yahoo!'s business model quite substantially.[17]

The markets on which a company focuses are also an important element of its core strategy. For example, Dell targets business customers and government agencies, while Hewlett-Packard targets individuals, small businesses, and first-time computer buyers. For both firms, their choices have had a significant impact on the shaping of their business models.

New ventures should be particularly careful not to expand their product/market offerings beyond their capabilities. Even Dell had to resist this temptation, as illustrated by Michael Dell in his book *Direct from Dell*:

> Growing a company much faster than the industry is growing is great, but when your company grows by as much as 127 percent in one year, you can quickly outstrip your ability to manage it effectively. Our problem was not that Dell was in serious decline or that our customers didn't want to buy our products. Quite the opposite, we learned that it was possible to grow too quickly. The problem was that we had been over enthusiastically pursuing every opportunity that presented itself. We needed to learn that not only did we not have to jump at each and every one, as we once did—but that we couldn't or shouldn't, for our overall well-being.[18]

Basis for Differentiation   It is important that a new venture differentiate itself from its competitors in some way that is important to its customers and is not easy to copy.[19] If a new firm's products or services aren't different from those of its competitors, why should anyone try them?[20]

From a broad perspective, firms typically choose one of two generic strategies (cost leadership and differentiation) to establish a defensible position in the marketplace. Firms that have a **cost leadership strategy** strive to have the lowest costs in the industry, relative to competitors' costs, and typically attract customers by offering them a low, if not the lowest, price for the products they sell. ASSUSTeK Computer, the company that sells the $300 Eee PC laptop computer, clearly has a cost-leadership strategy. In contrast, firms using a **differentiation strategy** compete on the basis of providing unique or different products, typically on the basis of quality, service, timeliness, or some other dimension that is important to customers.[21] Historically, it has been difficult for a new venture to use a cost leadership strategy because cost leadership typically requires economies of scale that require time to develop.

Firms within the same industry often use different generic strategies. In the retail clothing industry, for example, Ross follows a cost leadership strategy by offering slightly out-of-date merchandise at a deep discount. In contrast, Abercrombie & Fitch uses a differentiation strategy. It rarely cuts prices and instead competes on the basis that its products are different and stylish enough that they should command a premium price.

The strategy a firm chooses greatly affects its business model.[22] A cost leadership strategy requires a business model that is focused on efficiency, cost minimization, and large volume. As a result, a cost leader's facilities typically aren't fancy, as the emphasis is on keeping costs low rather than on comfort. Conversely, a differentiation strategy requires a business model focused on developing products and services that are unique in ways that are important to targeted customers and that command a premium price.

Strategic Resources

A firm is not able to implement a strategy without adequate resources. This reality means that a firm's resources substantially affect how its business model is used. For a new venture, its strategic resources may initially be limited to the competencies of its founders, the opportunity they have identified, and the unique way they plan to service their market. The two most important resources are a firm's core competencies and its strategic assets.

Core Competencies   A **core competency** is a resource or capability that serves as a source of a firm's competitive advantage over its rivals. It is a unique skill or capability that transcends products or markets, makes a significant contribution to the customer's perceived benefit, and is difficult to imitate.[23] Examples of core competencies include Sony's competence in miniaturization and Dell's competence in supply chain management. A firm's core competencies determine where it creates the most value. In distinguishing its core competencies, a firm should identify the skills it has that are (1) unique, (2) valuable to customers, (3) difficult to imitate, and (4) transferable to new opportunities.[24]

Learning Objective

8. Define the term *core competency* and describe its importance.

A firm's core competencies are important in both the short and the long term. In the short term, it is a company's core competencies that allow it to differentiate itself from its competitors and create unique value. For example, Dell's core competencies historically have included supply chain management, efficient assembly, and serving corporate customers, so its business model of providing corporate customers computers that are price competitive, are technologically up-to-date, and have access to after-sale support makes sense. If Dell suddenly started assembling and selling musical instruments, analysts would be skeptical of the new strategy and justifiably ask, "Why is Dell pursuing a strategy that is outside its core competency?"

In the long term, it is important to have core competencies to grow and establish strong positions in complementary markets. For example, Dell has taken its core competencies in the assembly and sale of PCs and has moved them into the market for computer servers and other electronic devices. This process of adapting a company's core competencies to exploit new opportunities is referred to as **resource leverage**.

Strategic Assets   **Strategic assets** are anything rare and valuable that a firm owns. They include plant and equipment, location, brands, patents, customer data, a highly qualified staff, and distinctive partnerships. A particularly valuable strategic asset is a company's brand, which is discussed in detail in Chapter 11. Starbucks, for example, has worked hard to build the image of its brand, and it would take an enormous effort for another coffee retailer to achieve this same level of brand recognition. Companies ultimately try to combine their core competencies and strategic assets to create a **sustainable competitive advantage**. This factor is one to which investors pay close attention when evaluating a business.[25] A sustainable competitive advantage is achieved by implementing a value-creating strategy that is unique and not easy to imitate.[26] This type of advantage is achievable when a firm has strategic resources and the ability to use them in unique ways that create value for a group of targeted customers.[27]

Partnership Network

A firm's network of partnerships is the third component of a business model. New ventures, in particular, typically do not have the resources to perform all the tasks required to make their businesses work, so they rely on partners to perform key roles.[28] In most cases, a business does not want to do everything itself because the majority of tasks needed to build a product or deliver a service are not core to a company's competitive advantage.[29] For example, Dell historically sought to differentiate itself from competitors through its expertise in assembling computers but buys chips from others, primarily Intel. Dell could manufacture its own chips, but it didn't have a core competency in this area. Similarly, Dell relies on UPS and FedEx to deliver its products because it would be silly for Dell to build a nationwide system to deliver its computers. Firms also rely on partners to supply intellectual capital needed to produce complex products and services, as illustrated in the following observation from two authorities on business partnerships:

> Neither Boeing nor Airbus has one-tenth of the intellectual capital or coordination capacity to cost-effectively mine metals, create alloys, make fasteners, cast and machine parts, design avionics, produce control systems, make engines, and so on. The complex systems we call airplanes come together through the voluntary agreements and collaborations of thousands of companies operating in the global marketplace.[30]

One thing that firms must often work hard at, particularly when they are in their start-up stage, is convincing other firms to partner with them. Partnering with a start-up is risky, particularly if its business model is new and is untested in the marketplace. One thing that helps is if a start-up has a business model that elevates its partners and not just itself. Two start-ups that have been able to form successful partnerships for this reason are Getwine and WaveSecure, as illustrated in the "Partnering for Success" feature.

A firm's partnership network includes suppliers and other partners. Let's look at each of them.

Suppliers   A **supplier** (or vendor) is a company that provides parts or services to another company. Intel is Dell's primary supplier for computer chips, for example. A **supply chain** is the network of all the companies that participate in the production of a product, from the acquisition of raw materials to the final sale. Almost all firms have suppliers who play vital roles in the functioning of their business models.

Traditionally, firms maintained an arm's-length relationship with their suppliers and viewed them almost as adversaries. Producers needing a component part would negotiate with several suppliers to find the best price. Today, however, firms want to move away from contentious relationships with their suppliers and seek to partner with them to achieve mutually beneficial goals.[31] This shift resulted from competitive pressures that motivated managers to look up and down their value chains to find opportunities for cost savings, quality improvement, and improved speed to market. More and more, managers are focusing on **supply chain management**, which is the coordination of the flow of all information, money, and material that moves through a product's supply chain. The more efficiently an organization can manage its supply chain, the more effectively its entire business model will perform.[32]

Learning Objective

9. Explain the concept of supply chain management.

Firms are developing more collaborative relationships with their suppliers, finding ways to motivate them to perform at a higher level. Many firms are reducing the number of their suppliers and working more closely with a smaller group. Dell, for example, maintains close relationships with its suppliers and uses sophisticated systems to enhance the performance of its supply chain. Dell has accomplished a level of rigor in its supply chain that supports its core strategy of offering technologically up-to-date computers at affordable prices. Thomas Friedman in his best-selling book *The World Is Flat* illustrates the quick pace and value of Dell's supply chain:

> "In an average day, we sell 140,000 to 150,000 computers," explained Dick Hunter, one of Dell's three global production managers. "These orders come in over Dell.com or over the telephone. As soon as these orders come in, our

Partnering for SUCCESS

Getwine, South Africa, and WaveSecure, Singapore: Forging Valuable Relationships by Elevating the Performance of Their Partners

Getwine: www.getwine.co.za
WaveSecure: www.wavesecure.com

All firms must partner with others to make their business models work. A challenge that new firms have is forging partnerships and obtaining the cooperation they need to move forward. It's easy for new firms to face resistance, particularly if it looks like their business models will only benefit themselves. A better approach is to build a business model that not only works for yourself but elevates your partners. Firms that meet this criterion find it easier to establish partnerships and build an upbeat, can-do culture.

Getwine

Getwine is a wine company based in Cape Town, South Africa. It doesn't own a single vineyard or processing facility, but buys unlabelled surplus wines from vineyards and distributors and sells them online to consumers at very affordable prices. While Getwine competes with other wines that are available to consumers, it actually helps the industry by buying its excess wine.

Although South African wines are competing well on the world stage, the strengthening of the rand has considerably pushed up the cost of a bottle abroad. The practice of selling unlabelled wines, or clearskins as they are also known, works well in periods of currency imbalance. Many top estates are unable to export all of their annual wine harvests and are keen to shift surplus stock while avoiding the negative consequences of heavily discounting their brands. Getwine sources the unlabelled excess wines and sells them at cut prices across South Africa via an efficient e-commerce operation. The business model is a win-win proposition for everyone involved, and the country's wine experts have feted the Getwine selection.

WaveSecure

Mobile phones today host a whole suite of functions, such as a phone book, a camera, calendar, and e-mail, and users are becoming increasingly dependent on them. Losing one is not just frustrating, it can make life very difficult indeed. Like so many good entrepreneurial ideas, the origin for WaveSecure was a simple problem. One of the cofounders kept losing his mobile phone, and the team of graduates from the National University of Singapore put their heads together to find a solution.

WaveSecure phone security software allows users to lock their phones remotely, track its usage, back up personal contacts through the Internet, and even remotely wipe private data off the phone once it is lost. The phone can even be programmed to emit a piercing scream when stolen, even if in silent mode, in a bid to embarrass the finder of the device.

The idea was an immediate hit with the authorities, gaining high-profile clients such as the Singapore Police and the Defense Ministry. The consumer version, which was launched in December 2007, saw 60,000 users sign up to the $2-a-month service within three months. Large phone corporations were a little reluctant to partner with the unknown start-up at first, but once they saw the response from consumers, they became convinced that WaveSecure is a product that mobile phone users needed.

WaveSecure has now been adopted by most of the major phone companies including Nokia, O2, Sony Ericsson, and Motorola, with some offering it as a bundle with the phone contract and others including it as a value-added service charge on subscribers' bills.

Questions for Critical Thinking

1. Describe a firm, other than Getwine or WaveSecure, that has created a win-win business model for itself and its partners.
2. One a scale of 1 to 5 (5 is high), how do you rate the strength of both Getwine's and WaveSecure's business models? Explain your ratings.
3. Describe Getwine's core strategy and its customer interface. Do the same for WaveSecure's.
4. Look at the "You Be the VC 6.2" feature, which focuses on Minted, a company that utilizes an innovative business model to produce stationery and invitations. In what ways, if any, does Minted's business model elevate the performance of its partners?

Sources: "GetWine!" *The Times,* May 15, 2008; "New Code to Track Your Lost Mobile," *Economic Times,* October 25, 2008; "*Asia* WaveSecure Software to Go Commercial Soon," *CNET,* October 6, 2008.

suppliers know about it. They get a signal based on every component in the machine you ordered, so the supplier knows just what he has to deliver. If you are supplying power cords for desktops, you can see minute by minute how many power cords you are going to have to deliver." Every two hours, the Dell factory in Penang (Malaysia) sends an e-mail to the various SLCs (supplier logistic centers) nearby, telling each one what parts and what quantities of those parts it wants delivered within the next thirty minutes—and not one minute later. Within ninety minutes, trucks from the various SLCs around Penang pull up to the Dell manufacturing plant and unload the parts needed for all those notebooks ordered in the last two hours. This goes on all day, every two hours. As soon as those parts arrive at the factory, it takes thirty minutes for Dell employees to unload the parts, register their bar codes, and put them in the bins for assembly. "We know where every part in every SLC is in the Dell system at all times," said Hunter.[33]

Other Key Relationships Along with its suppliers, firms partner with other companies to make their business models work. As described in Table 6.4, strategic alliances, joint ventures, networks, consortia, and trade associations are common forms of these partnerships. A survey by PricewaterhouseCoopers found that more than half of America's fastest-growing companies have formed multiple partnerships to support their business models. According to the research, these partnerships have "resulted in more innovative products, more profit opportunities, and significantly high growth rates" for the firms involved.[34]

There are also hybrid forms of business partnerships that allow companies to maximize their efficiencies. One relatively new approach, referred to as **insourcing**, takes place when a service provider comes inside a partner's facilities and helps the partner design and manage its supply chain. An example is a unique partnership between Papa John's and UPS. Since 1996, UPS has managed, routed, and scheduled the delivery of tomatoes, pizza sauce, cheese, and other ingredients from Papa John's food service centers across the United States to its more than 2,000 pizza delivery stores twice a week. The ingredients are delivered in UPS trailers marked with Papa John's insignias.[35]

Table 6.4 THE MOST COMMON TYPES OF BUSINESS PARTNERSHIPS

Partnership Form	Description
Joint venture	An entity created by two or more firms pooling a portion of their resources to create a separate, jointly owned organization
Network	A hub-and-wheel configuration with a local firm at the hub organizing the interdependencies of a complex array of firms
Consortia	A group of organizations with similar needs that band together to create a new entity to address those needs
Strategic alliance	An arrangement between two or more firms that establishes an exchange relationship but has no joint ownership involved
Trade associations	Organizations (typically nonprofit) that are formed by firms in the same industry to collect and disseminate trade information, offer legal and technical advice, furnish industry-related training, and provide a platform for collective lobbying

Source: B. Barringer and J. Harrison, "Walking a Tightrope: Creating Value Through Interorganizational Relationships," *Journal of Management* 26, no. 3 (2000): 367–403. Reprinted by permission of Sage Publications.

There *are* risks involved in partnerships, particularly if a single partnership is a key component of a firm's business model. Many partnerships fall short of meeting the expectations of the participants for a variety of reasons. Through studies they have conducted, the international accounting firms of PricewaterhouseCoopers[36] and KPMG[37] estimate that the failure rate for business alliances is 50 percent and 60 to 70 percent, respectively. Many of the failures result from poor planning or the difficulties involved with meshing the cultures of two or more organizations to achieve a common goal. There are also potential disadvantages to participating in alliances, including loss of proprietary information, management complexities, financial and organizational risks, risk of becoming dependent on a partner, and partial loss of decision autonomy.[38]

Still, for the majority of start-ups, the ability to establish and effectively manage partnerships is a major component of their business models' success. For some firms, the ability to manage partnerships is the essence of their competitive advantage and ultimate success.

Customer Interface

Customer interface—how a firm interacts with its customers—is the fourth component of a business model. The type of customer interaction depends on how a firm chooses to compete. For example, Amazon.com sells books solely over the Internet, while Barnes & Noble sells through both its traditional bookstores and online.

For a new venture, the customer interface that it chooses is central to how it plans to compete and where it is located in the value chain of the products and services it provides.[39] The three elements of a company's customer interface are target market, fulfillment and support, and pricing structure. Let's look at each of these elements closely.

Target Market   A firm's **target market** is the limited group of individuals or businesses that it goes after or tries to appeal to, as discussed earlier in this book. The target market a firm selects affects everything it does, from the strategic resources it acquires to the partnerships it forges to its promotional campaigns.

Many start-ups interface with their customers over the phone to process orders, answer questions, or provide after-sale service. Here, a customer service representative helps a customer troubleshoot a problem with a software installation in a pleasant and reassuring manner.

Bruce Ayres/Getty Images Inc.-Stone Allstock

For example, the clothing retailer Abercrombie & Fitch targets 18- to 22-year-old men and women who are willing to pay full price for trendy apparel. So the decisions it makes about strategic resources, partnerships, and advertising will be much different from the decisions made by Chico's, a clothing store that targets 30- to 60-year-old women.

Typically, a firm greatly benefits from having a clearly defined target market. Because of the specificity of its targeted customer, Abercrombie & Fitch can keep abreast of the clothing trends for its market, it can focus its marketing and promotional campaigns, and it can develop deep core competencies pertaining to its specific marketplace. A company such as Gap has a larger challenge because its stores appeal to a broader range of clientele. In fact, when a retailer such as Gap starts offering too many products, it typically begins breaking itself down into more narrowly focused markets so that it can regain the advantages that are enjoyed by a singularly focused retailer such as Abercrombie & Fitch. Gap has done this successfully and now has a diversified collection of brands including Gap, Old Navy, Banana Republic, and Piperlime. Gap, GapKids, babyGap, and gapbody form the Gap brand.

Learning Objective

10. Explain the concept of fulfillment and support.

Fulfillment and Support   **Fulfillment and support** describes the way a firm's product or service "goes to market," or how it reaches its customers. It also refers to the channels a company uses and what level of customer support it provides.[40] All these issues impact the shape and nature of a company's business model.

Firms differ considerably along these dimensions. Suppose that a new venture developed and patented an exciting new cell phone technology. In forming its business plan, the firm might have several options regarding how to take its technology to market. It could (1) license the technology to existing cell phone companies such as Nokia and LG, (2) manufacture the cell phone itself and establish its own sales channels, or (3) partner with a cell phone company such as LG and sell the phone through partnerships with the cell phone service providers such as AT&T and Verizon. The choice a firm makes about fulfillment and service has a dramatic impact on the type of company that evolves and the business model that develops. For example, if the company licenses its technology, it would probably build a business model that emphasized research and development to continue to have cutting-edge technologies to license to the cell phone manufacturers. In contrast, if it decides to manufacture its own cell phones, it needs to establish core competencies in the areas of manufacturing and design and needs to form partnerships with cell phone retailers such as AT&T, Sprint, and Verizon.

The level of customer support a firm is willing to offer also affects its business model. Some firms differentiate their products or services and provide extra value to their customers through high levels of service and support. Customer service can include delivery and installation, financing arrangements, customer training, warranties and guarantees, repairs, layaway plans, convenient hours of operation, convenient parking, and information through toll-free numbers and Web sites.[41] Dell, as mentioned earlier, has a broad menu of tiered services available to provide its corporate clients the exact level of support they need and for which they are willing to pay. Making this choice of services available is a key component of Dell's business model.

Pricing Structure   A third element of a company's customer interface is its pricing structure, a topic that we discuss in more detail in Chapter 11. Pricing structures vary, depending on a firm's target market and its pricing philosophy. For example, some consultants charge a flat fee for performing a service (e.g., helping an entrepreneurial venture write a business plan), while others charge an hourly rate. In some instances, a company must also choose whether to charge its customers directly or indirectly through a service provider.

Firms differentiate themselves on the basis of their pricing structure in both common and unusual ways. In general, it is difficult for new ventures to differentiate themselves on price, which is a common strategy for larger firms with more substantial economies of scale, as discussed earlier in the chapter. There are exceptions, such as Amazon.com in books, Domino's in pizza, and LogoWorks in business logos, which have been price leaders since their inception. In contrast, there are several examples of firms that have started primarily on the basis of featuring innovative pricing models. The most noteworthy is Priceline.com, which pioneered the practice of letting customers explicitly set prices they are willing to pay for products and services. Another example is CarMax, which features a "no-haggle" pricing policy and sells new and used cars through its showrooms and Web site. The company's slogan is "The Way Car Buying Should Be." CarMax offers its customers a low-stress environment by presenting them with what it believes to be a fair price, with no negotiations.

In summary, it is very useful for a new venture to look at itself in a holistic manner and understand that it must construct an effective "business model" to be successful. Everyone that does business with a new firm, from its customers to its partners, does so on a voluntary basis. As a result, a firm must motivate its customers and partners to play along. The primary elements of a firm's business model are its core strategy, strategic resources, partnership network, and customer interface. Close attention to each of these elements is essential for a new venture's success.

Chapter Summary

1. A firm's business model is its plan or diagram for how it intends to compete, use its resources, structure relationships, interface with customers, and create value to sustain itself on the basis of the profits it generates.
2. Business model innovation refers to initiatives such as those undertaken by Michael Dell that revolutionize how products are sold in an industry.
3. The main reasons that having a clearly articulated business model is important are as follows: It serves as an ongoing extension of feasibility analysis, it focuses attention on how all the elements of a business fit together, it describes why the network of participants who are needed to make a business idea viable would be willing to work together, and it articulates the core logic of a firm to all its stakeholders.
4. The value chain shows how a product moves from the raw-material stage to the final consumer. The value chain helps a firm identify opportunities to enhance its competitive strategies and to recognize new business opportunities.
5. A complete misread of the customer and utterly unsound economics are the two fatal flaws that can make a business model a failure from the outset.
6. Core strategy, strategic resources, partnership networks, and customer interface are the four major components of a firm's business model.
7. A business concept blind spot prevents a firm from seeing an opportunity that might fit its business model.
8. A core competency is something that a firm does particularly well. It is a resource or capability that serves as a source of a firm's competitive advantage over its rivals.
9. Supply chain management refers to the flow of all information, money, and material that moves through a product's supply chain. The more efficiently

an organization can manage its supply chain, the more effectively its entire business model will perform.

10. A firm's target market is the limited group of individuals or business that it goes after or tries to appeal to at a point in time.

Key Terms

business concept
   blind spot, **213**
business model, **202**
business model innovation, **203**
core competency, **215**
core strategy, **213**
cost leadership strategy, **214**
customer interface, **219**

differentiation strategy, **214**
fulfillment and support, **220**
insourcing, **218**
mission statement, **213**
product/market scope, **213**
resource leverage, **215**
strategic assets, **215**
supplier, **216**

supply chain, **216**
supply chain
   management, **216**
sustainable competitive
   advantage, **215**
target market, **219**
value chain, **208**

Review Questions

1. Define the term *business model*. How can entrepreneurial firms benefit by developing and using a business model? What are the downsides for entrepreneurial ventures when an effective business model isn't put in place?
2. Explain what business model innovation means. Provide an example of business model innovation other than the examples included in the chapter.
3. List at least three reasons that demonstrate why having a business model is important.
4. Why did WebHouse's business model fail?
5. How does an understanding of the value chain help explain how business models emerge?
6. What are the two fatal flaws that can render a business model untenable?
7. What are the four primary components of a firm's business model? Briefly describe the importance of each component.
8. Describe what is meant by the term *core strategy* and why it is important.
9. Describe the purpose of a mission statement.
10. What is meant by the term *business model blind spot*? Provide an original example of a firm that suffered as the result of having a business model blind spot.
11. What is a firm's product/market scope? Why is the concept of product/market scope important in regard to crafting a successful business model?
12. Why is it important for firms to differentiate themselves from competitors?
13. In what ways does a focus on a cost leadership strategy lead to a very different business model than a focus on a differentiation strategy?
14. Define the term *core competency* and describe why it's important for a firm to have one or more core competencies. How do a company's core competencies help shape its business model?
15. What is meant by the term *resource leverage*? How does an understanding of this term help a firm exploit new product or service opportunities?
16. What is meant by the term *strategic asset*? Provide examples of the strategic assets of three well-known firms.
17. Why do firms typically need partners to make their business models work?
18. What is meant by the term *supply chain management*?
19. What is meant by the term *customer interface*? Explain how Dell and Hewlett-Packard differ from each other on this core dimension.
20. Describe the impact of a firm's pricing structure on its business model.

Application Questions

1. Write a brief critique of Amie Street business model. What do you think are the strengths and weaknesses of the model? Do you think that Amie Street has a sustainable competitive advantage? Why or why not?

2. Write a brief description of Apple Inc.'s business model.

3. Spend some time thinking about Charter Internal Medicine, the Columbia, Maryland, medical practice (highlighted in the "Savvy Entrepreneurial Firm" feature) that is pioneering a new business model. Which of the four components of a business model does Charter's business model emphasize? To what extent does the success or failure of Charter's business model rest on how much value its patients see in this portion of its model?

4. Carol Schmidt plans to open a company that will make accessories for cell phones. She has read that having a clearly articulated business model will help "all the elements of her business fit together." Carol isn't quite sure what that statement means. If Carol asked you to explain it to her, what would you say?

5. Since its founding in 1984, Cirque du Soleil, the focus of Case 5.2, has experienced enormous success. Do you consider the founders of Cirque du Soleil to be business model innovators? If so, why do you think an established circus company didn't pioneer a Cirque du Soleil type of business model before Cirque du Soleil did?

6. Jane Rowan is an experienced business consultant. Through working with clients, she has noticed that many companies have "business concept blind spots." How can having a business concept blind spot affect the strength of a firm's business model?

7. Write a mission statement for WaveSecure, one of the companies highlighted in the "Partnering for Success" feature. How can this statement help clarify and direct the core strategy component of WaveSecure's business model?

8. Select one of the following companies: Facebook, Google, or eBay. For the company you selected, identify its core competency and explain how its core competency strengthens its business model and contributes to its competitive advantage.

9. Using the same firm you selected for question 8, make a list of the firm's strategic assets. How does each of its strategic assets strengthen its business model?

10. Twitter (http://twitter.com) is a free networking and micro-blogging service that allows its users to send and read other users' updates (otherwise known as "tweets"). Although Twitter has hundreds of thousands of users and is growing rapidly, it has been criticized for not having a business model. Spend some time researching Twitter. How does the company make money? Does it have a business model? If so, describe it.

11. What are some examples of instances in which location is an important part of a firm's business model?

12. Jill Hopkins just received an e-mail message from an investor who has agreed to listen to her pitch her business idea. The investor said, "Your timing is good—I just happen to be sitting on $500,000 that I'm anxious to invest. One thing I'll warn you about ahead of time, however, is that you must show me that your business has the potential to achieve a sustainable competitive advantage. If you can't show me that, I won't invest." Jill has read about sustainable competitive advantage but is still a little hazy about the concept. Explain the concept to Jill.

13. Spend some time studying SunEdison, the solar power company highlighted in the "Savvy Entrepreneurial Firm" feature. What is found in the "strategic

resources" component of SunEdison's business model? How do this firm's strategic resources strengthen its business model and contribute to its success?

14. The "You Be the VC 6.2" feature at the end of the chapter focuses on Minted, a company that has adopted a "crowdsourcing" business model. What is a crowdsourcing business model? Do you think a crowdsourcing business model will work for Minted? Why or why not?

15. Do you think that the business models of daily newspapers are viable in the long run? If you were the owner of a daily newspaper in a major American city, would you try to maintain the print edition of your paper, evolve to strictly an online presence, or do something else?

You Be the VC 6.1

Company: ReadySolar

www.readysolar.com

Business Idea: Significantly reduce the cost of installing residential solar panels via an IKEA-like "solar-in-a box" solution, where the system comes prepackaged and installs more easily and inexpensively than competing systems.

Pitch: Although many consumers are interested in reducing their energy costs via solar power, in most cases cost is a critical concern. The cost of buying a solar energy system, including installation, amortized over the life of the system, is still normally more expensive than buying power from a utility. In many areas it's also difficult to find someone to design and install a solar energy system for an individual home. Because the sizes and shapes of roofs vary by home, it often takes considerable design work by a contractor or solar installer to plan the idea system for a particular roof.

ReadySolar is pioneering a new approach to selling and installing solar energy systems, aimed at lowering the cost and minimizing the hassles associated with installation. It sells modular solar-in-a-box packages. Each package includes everything that a contractor or solar installer needs to install a solar energy system, from the solar panels to the roof jacks. The packages are also modular, meaning that they are a standard size. As a result, when looking at a roof, all a contractor has to do is decide whether to install one, two, or three modules (normally), eliminating expensive design work. The panels are built in blocks, making them particularly easy to fit around skylights and other obstructions to a smooth roof.

According to ReadySolar, the collective benefits of its solar-in-a-box approach save the average home owner 30 to 50 percent on the cost of installing a solar energy system. As an added benefit, the ReadySolar system is aesthetically appealing. ReadySolar commissioned an independent firm to assess the three most important things that consumers look for in buying a solar energy system. The three things are price, reliability, and aesthetics. Because of the modular, building block nature of the ReadySolar solar panels, they look very attractive on most roofs.

ReadySolar's solar-in-a-box system is sold through resellers, who are typically contractors, solar installers, and real estate developers. An increasing number of consumers are expressing interest in solar energy systems, as the price of traditional energy continues to fluctuate with the long-term trend in pricing almost certainly upward in direction. Currently, U.S. electric rates are increasing at a rate of about 3 percent per year. Increases are sharper in densely populated U.S. states like California, which is currently experiencing an average increase of 6 percent per year. Many consumers are also interested in the environmental benefits of solar power. Tax and utility company rebates, which are becoming increasingly generous, provide an additional incentive for home owners to invest in solar power.

Q&A: Based on the material covered in this chapter, what questions would you ask the firm's founders before making your funding decision? What answers would satisfy you?

Decision: If you had to make your decision on just the information provided in the pitch and on the company's Web site, would you fund this company? Why or why not?

You Be the VC 6.2

Company: Minted

www.minted.com

Business Idea: Launch an online stationery store that provides consumers access to fresh, modern stationery and invitations.

Pitch: Minted's goal is to help its customers celebrate their most personal occasions through the availability of fresh, innovative stationary and invitations, printed on fine paper stock. In addition, the company offers complementary services such as custom design, calligraphy, and hand-addressing of envelopes.

To gain access to a continual flow of fresh stationery and invitation design ideas, Minted is relying on professional designers to submit designs, which it will resell on its Web site. It will pick the designs that are sold by allowing customers to vote on the designs. This business model is referred to as "crowdsourcing." The idea is to rely on an independent network of potentially hundreds of designers, all stretching their talents to produce fresh, new designs, rather than rely on a handful of in-house graphic artists. Allowing the Minted community to pick the submissions that will be sold takes the model one step further. Minted's approach is similar to Zazzle.com, which sources graphic art from its "crowd" to produce physical goods such as T-shirts, cards, posters, and coffee mugs. The difference between Minted's approach and Zazzle's is that Minted will only solicit designs from professional-level designers. Minted will also offer stationery and invitations from a selection of handpicked independent stationery brands.

To encourage designers to submit stationery and invitation designs, Minted sponsors contests, offering cash awards to the designs that are picked. Once a designer has a design selected, either through a contest or through the normal submission process, he or she receives a 5 percent commission on the retail sales of the resulting product. While a 5 percent commission sounds modest, it is nearly twice the commission an independent artist gets from a company like Hallmark. To sweeten the deal for the designer, all the cards and invitations that Minted sells that come from independent designers will have the designer's name emblazoned on the rear of the product.

The print stationery and card market is a $10 billion-a-year market. While Minted is starting with stationery and cards, it will likely expand into other products in the future, leveraging its crowdsourcing business model. It may also find channels beyond its Web site to sell its most successful stationery, invitation, and card designs.

Q&A: Based on the material covered in this chapter, what questions would you ask the firm's founders before making your funding decision? What answers would satisfy you?

Decision: If you had to make your decision on just the information provided in the pitch and on the company's Web site, would you fund this company? Why or why not?

CASE6.1

Place Your Bets: Netflix Versus the Field in DVD Rentals

www.netflix.com

Bruce R. Barringer
Oklahoma State University
R. Duane Ireland
Texas A & M University

Introduction

Many industries include firms with competing business models for bringing a product or service to market. Over time, some business models prove to be more successful than others, because they are simpler and more customer friendly or because they allow one firm to operate at a lower cost than its competitors.

The DVD rental industry provides an interesting venue to see competing business models at work and to speculate on which model is the strongest.

Netflix

The DVD rental industry was rocked to its core when Netflix introduced an innovative and simple business model in 1997. Prior to Netflix, people were accustomed to driving to a Blockbuster or other video rental store to pick up a video and then returning the video to the same store. A sore spot with customers was late fees charged by the stores. Netflix introduced a completely new way of renting DVDs. A subscriber pays a monthly fee and creates an order list, called a rental queue, of DVDs to rent on Netflix's Web site. The DVDs are delivered via the U.S. Postal Service. The subscriber can keep the DVDs as long as desired, and then return them to Netflix for another batch of DVDs. There is a limit to how many DVDs a subscriber can have at one time (determined by subscription level), but there are no late fees and no pressure to return the DVDs, as long as the monthly subscription is kept current. As of fall 2008, Netflix's most popular plan cost $16.99 a month and allowed a subscriber to have three DVDs out at one time. Netflix has over 100,000 DVDs to choose from. Its Web site features an extensive personalized video-recommendations system based on ratings and reviews by its customers, similar to the system maintained by Amazon.com.

Netflix also has a "Watch Instantly" feature available to all eligible subscribers. The feature enables subscribers, at no additional cost, to stream select movies and television shows instantly, depending on the strength of their Internet connection. Building on this service, in May 2008 Netflix, in partnership with Roku Inc., introduced a new set-top box that allows subscribers to stream videos from the Netflix Web site to their television sets. The box cost $99.99. Netflix and LG Electronics have also announced plans to sell an LG-branded DVD player that will show movies downloaded through Netflix on TVs.

Netflix has been building market share since its inception, and pieces of its business model have been copied by most of its competitors. Its sub-scriber base has grown from 670,000 in 2002 to 5.6 million in 2006 to 8.2 million in 2008. Blockbuster started offering a Netflix-like monthly subscription service in 2004. Wal-Mart began an online rental service in 2002, but abandoned the effort and now has a cross-promotional arrangement with Netflix.

There are two significant and emerging threats to Netflix's business model. The first threat is for Netflix to remain the most convenient way for consumers to rent and watch DVDs; the second threat is to stay on top of technological trends that are making it easier for companies to offer DVD-quality movies and televi-sion shows instantly online. Netflix's competitors are well aware of these potential vulnerabilities and are revising their business models accordingly. There

are also new business models emerging in the DVD rental industry. So it's Netflix versus the field—may the best business model(s) win.

The Field

The figure on the facing page depicts Netflix's business model versus its major competitors. Next, we'll briefly describe each competitor's business model. Notice how each business model is fashioned in a way that it attacks one of the potential vulnerabilities of Netflix's business model and features advantages of its own.

Blockbuster Blockbuster has both a traditional brick-and-mortar and an online DVD rental strategy. A customer can rent strictly online, strictly from a Blockbuster store, or rent a movie online, receive it in the mail, and swap it out for another movie at a Blockbuster store, rather than returning it via mail. (There are caps on monthly in-store exchanges unless you pay for a premium plan.) Netfix can't do this because it doesn't have brick-and-mortar stores. Blockbuster rents old movies for $1 for five days. It also gives its online customers two coupons per month for free in-store movie or game rentals.

Redbox Redbox, which was launched in 2002, has placed kiosks in retail stores and McDonald's restaurants across the United States. The kiosks are self-service and contain over 600 DVDs with 70 to 200 titles, and are updated weekly. Most of the titles are current hit movies. Customers can reserve DVDs online. DVDs can be returned the next day to any of the company's kiosks. A one-day rental costs $1 plus tax and it costs an additional $1 a day (up to 25 days, at which point you own the DVD) to keep a DVD. Redbox allows someone to grab a movie on a whim for $1 a day, something that Netflix can't do. The downsides are that Redbox is not available in all areas and it offers a limited selection of movies.

Hulu Hulu is the new kid on the block—founded in 2007 by NBC Universal and News Corp. It offers movies and television episodes online for free, anytime in the United States. Its movie collection is limited (around 100 titles in fall 2008) but is expected to grow. Its full-length television shows include select episodes of *The Simpsons*, *Family Guy*, *The Office*, and *House*. Hulu makes money via advertising. Most of the ads occur prior to the start of the selected movie or television episode. Hulu offers instant gratification and free viewing, something Netflix can't and doesn't do.

iTunes Movie Rental iTunes rents movies in an entirely different manner. After selecting a movie (or television episode), the user downloads the movie to a Mac or PC and it is available for 24 hours after viewing begins. (You have up to 30 days to start viewing.) After 24 hours, the movie is erased.

Blockbuster
- Brick-and-mortar stores
- Online subscriptions
- Old movies—$1 for 5 days
- Free coupons for in-store movies or games for online customers

Redbox
- Kiosks
- New movies
- $1 per day
- Instant gratification
- Limited selection/not available in all locations

Netflix
- Monthly subscriptions
- No late fees
- Wide selection
- View online for free
- No instant gratification

Versus

Hulu
- Online
- Free
- Ad supported
- Limited selection
- Instant gratification

iTunes Movie Rental
- Download movies
- Pay per movie
- Movies play on multiple platforms
- Movies only available for 24 hours

Movies can also be downloaded to an iPod, iPhone, or TV. Movies cost $2.99 for library titles and $3.99 for new releases. iTunes offers instant gratification and multiple platforms upon which a movie can be watched, which gives it an edge over Netflix in those areas.

Discussion Questions

1. Do you think Netflix has the strongest business model in the DVD rental industry, or do you favor the business model of one of its competitors?
2. Which of Netflix's competitors do you believe has the most innovative business model? Which competitor do you think worries the top management team of Netflix the most?
3. In what ways has Netflix's business model evolved because of (1) changing technologies and (2) the business model innovations of its competitors?
4. Is the level of competition that Netflix is experiencing about what you'd expect, or is it higher or lower than you might have expected? Do you think Netflix's industry will be more or less competitive three years from now? Explain your answers.

Application Questions

1. What is Netflix's core competency? What are its strategic assets? Is there anything in Netflix's business model that makes what it is doing hard to replicate? Explain your answer to this final question.
2. If you were advising Netflix, what would you tell it to do, that it isn't already doing, to remain the leader in the DVD rental industry?

Sources: R. Setty, "DVD Rental Battle Zone—Netflix vs. Blockbuster+Redbox+Hulu+Cable Networks," Life Beyond Code Blog, http://blog.lifebeyondcode.com/2008/08/24/dvd-rental-battle-zone-netflix-vs-blockbusterredboxhulucable-networks (accessed October 28, 2008, originally posted August 24, 2008); "Netflix," Wikipedia, http://en.wikipedia.org/wiki/Wikipedia (accessed October 28, 2008); "Blockbuster," Wikipedia, http://en.wikipedia.org/wiki/Blockbuster (accessed October 28, 2008); "Redbox," Wikipedia, http://en.wikipedia.org/wiki/Redbox (accessed October 28, 2008); "Hulu," Wikipedia, http://en.wikipedia.org/wiki/Hulu (accessed October 28, 2008); Apple information page on iTunes Movie Rental, www.apple.com/itunes/whatson/moview.html (accessed October 28, 2008).

CASE6.2

IKEA and ProFlowers:
Reconfiguring Industry Value Chains to Create Competitive Business Models

www.ikea.com
www.proflowers.com

Bruce R. Barringer
Oklahoma State University
R. Duane Ireland
Texas A & M University

Introduction

Although there are no hard-and-fast rules that dictate how a firm in a particular industry should compete, many industries have a standard way of doing business that most participants follow. When the tendency to follow these standards is strong, there is an opportunity for new entrants or industry incumbents to create new business models that revolutionize how products are sold in an industry. This practice is defined in the chapter as "business model innovation."

Both IKEA and ProFlowers are business model innovators. By reconfiguring the value chains in their respective industries, both companies have revolutionized the selling of products. This case explains how they did it.

IKEA

IKEA is a Swedish furniture company that is known for its brightly colored furniture and its approach of requiring customers to assemble their furniture for themselves. As of fall 2008, IKEA had 270 stores that were located in three countries, including the United States. The firm is famous for its functional yet stylish products that are sold at a very competitive price.

IKEA was founded in Almhult, Sweden, in 1943 by Ingvar Kamprad, who was then 17. The company's name is a composite of the first letters in his name in addition to the first letters of the names of the property and the village in which he grew up: **I**ngvar **K**amprad **E**lmtaryd **A**gunnaryd. Initially, the firm sold pens, wallets, picture frames, watches, and similar items. Furniture was added to IKEA's product lines in the late 1940s.

When IKEA first considered selling furniture, it closely studied the furniture industry value chain. In Sweden, furniture was manufactured and sold in the late 1940s much the same way it is still manufactured and sold throughout the world today. As shown in the figure on the facing page, furniture typically flows through a value chain, with all, or most, of the steps completed by the same company. After a piece of furniture is designed, the parts are typically made by the same company, which then assembles the parts and ships the finished product to a warehouse. The completed furniture then sits in a warehouse until it is delivered to a retail store or is delivered directly to a consumer. The only significant deviation from this process is that furniture companies are increasingly outsourcing the production and assembly of the furniture they sell. Still, the furniture industry value chain depicted in the figure has prevailed largely intact throughout most of IKEA's history.

To create a competitive advantage, IKEA decided to reconfigure the furniture value chain. The bottom part of the figure shows how they did it. IKEA still owns furniture design but outsources the manufacture of parts to a contract manufacturer. The "parts" (the disassembled pieces of the furniture) are then shipped in boxes to IKEA retail stores, where they are stacked on shelves in a large warehouse environment. Customers make their selections by looking at display models and then buy the furniture, still in the box, to assemble later on their own. Customers are also responsible for transporting the furniture to their home.

This reconfiguration of the furniture value chain gives IKEA several distinct advantages. First, by outsourcing the manufacture of the parts, it does not have to incur the cost of maintaining manufacturing facilities. The company also

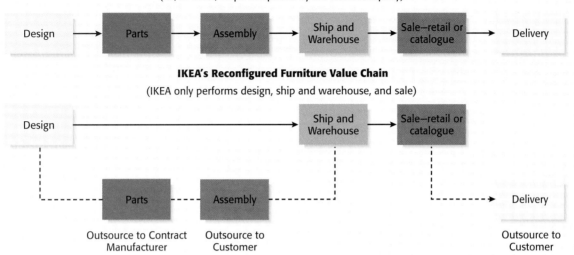

The Traditional Furniture Industry Value Chain

(All, or most, steps completed by the same company)

Design → Parts → Assembly → Ship and Warehouse → Sale—retail or catalogue → Delivery

IKEA's Reconfigured Furniture Value Chain

(IKEA only performs design, ship and warehouse, and sale)

Design → Ship and Warehouse → Sale—retail or catalogue

Parts — Assembly — Delivery

Outsource to Contract Manufacturer   Outsource to Customer   Outsource to Customer

basically "outsources" the assembly and delivery of furniture to the customer. This approach creates substantial cost savings for IKEA, which passes on a portion of the savings to customers. It also allows IKEA to target a segment of the market that is looking for a good value and doesn't mind assembling furniture. To make its offering even more unique, IKEA's stores feature playrooms for children and Swedish cuisine restaurants.

Analysts view IKEA's efforts as a resounding success. Because it is a private company, it doesn't release profitability figures. Although we don't know about the firm's profitability, we do know that according to Hoover's reports, the firm's sales increased 21.7 percent from 2007 to 2008. With effective control of its cost of goods sold, the increase in sales suggests that IKEA is earning profits.

ProFlowers

Launched in 1998, ProFlowers is an online retailer that sells and ships fresh flowers for all occasions. It is a subsidiary of Provide Commerce, which operates similar Web sites that sell and ship fresh fruit baskets, steak and seafood, and fresh desserts. Provide Commerce was started in 1997 by Jared Schutz Polis, the son of SPS Studios founders Stephen Schutz and Susan Polis Schutz. SPS Studios created Bluemountain.com, the first Web site to offer free online greeting cards in 1996.

Like IKEA, ProFlowers has created a competitive advantage by reconfiguring its industry's value chain.

The traditional value chain for flowers is depicted in the following figure. Flowers are raised by growers and then typically pass through the hands of an importer (or distributor), wholesaler, and retailer before they are sold to the customer. This process typically takes between 7 and 12 days. As a flower passes through the process, temperature and humidity often change, which degrades the flower's appearance and shortens its vase life. ProFlowers has sharply reduced the number of steps a flower must go through as it travels from the grower to the customer, as depicted in the figure. The advantage to the customer is fresher, higher-quality flowers that are normally delivered within three days and last longer once delivered. In addition, ProFlowers is able to offer a wider selection than most florists because it doesn't have to take physical possession of its flowers. The advantage to the grower (or supplier) is increased margins, broader customer reach, and better inventory management.

The way ProFlowers has made its approach work is by contracting with a global network of flower growers and suppliers. When an order is received via its Web site, ProFlowers routes the order to the appropriate grower. In turn, the grower fills the order and ships it via either FedEx or UPS utilizing proprietary technology provided by ProFlowers. This approach results in a considerable savings by eliminating steps in the traditional flower value chain. The savings ProFlowers captures are in part passed along to its customers through lower prices. It's difficult to quantify the value of the "freshness factor" made

(continued)

The Traditional Flower Industry Value Chain

(All, or most, steps completed by different companies)

Grower → Importer (distributor) → Wholesaler → Retailer → Customer

ProFlower's Reconfigured Flower Value Chain

(ProFlowers e-commerce platform enables the process)

Grower ────────────────────→ Customer

Flowers delivered to customer via
FedEx or UPS

possible by ProFlowers' approach. Flowers are often an emotional purchase, with the sender wanting the flowers to be delivered to the recipient in the best shape possible, because quality is intertwined with sincerity. To tout its freshness advantage, ProFlowers basically explains how it has reconfigured its industry's value chain in its advertising and promotions.

To date, ProFlowers has captured only a small portion of the total market for flowers and related products in the United States, although its sales are increasing. Provide Commerce was purchased by Liberty Interactive Group in December 2005 for $477 million. Liberty Interactive Group includes home shopping network QVC, along with an assortment of online and off-line properties.

Discussion Questions

1. At the beginning of this chapter, the statement is made that "in everyday language, a model is a plan that's used to make or describe something." Do you think IKEA and ProFlowers have plans that effectively describe what the firms offer to customers? How could these firms' models be changed so they would be more appealing?

2. What is IKEA's core competency? What are its strategic assets? Is there anything about IKEA's business model that makes what the company is doing hard to replicate? Explain your answer.

3. Suppose that you are the CEO of ProFlowers. You just received an e-mail from Carolyn Anderson, a highly reputable and sought-after rose grower, who is interested in learning more about your company. In her e-mail message to you, Anderson asks the following question:

"Describe to me your business model. Convince me that your organization has a good story and I should be part of it." How would you respond to this request?

4. How does ProFlowers' business model motivate its customers and partners (such as its contract growers) to participate in its business? On a scale of 1 to 10 (10 is high), rate how motivated you think each group is to do business with ProFlowers and help it succeed. How does ProFlowers' business model demonstrate that in some instances fewer business partners can be better than more business partners?

Application Questions

1. Which industries, other then furniture and flowers, are ripe for business model innovation? Provide an example of a product or a service with a value chain that could be reconfigured in a manner similar to the way that IKEA reconfigured the value chain of the furniture industry or ProFlowers reconfigured the value chain of the flower industry. Discuss how a start-up or an industry incumbent could benefit by reconfiguring its industry's value chain in this manner.

2. Why do you think IKEA hasn't grown more rapidly? Think about IKEA's business model in formulating your answer.

Sources: IKEA homepage, www.ikea.com (accessed November 16, 2008); ProFlowers homepage, www.proflowers.com (accessed November 16, 2008); Hoover's Online, www.hoovers.com (accessed November 16, 2008); N. Thornberry, *Lead Like an Entrepreneur* (New York: McGraw-Hill, 2006).

Endnotes

1. Personal interview with Joshua Boltuch, December 10, 2008.
2. H. Chesbrough and R. S. Rosenbloom, "The Role of the Business Model in Capturing Value from Innovation: Evidence from Xerox Corporation's Technology Spin-off Companies," *Industrial and Corporate Change* 11, no. 3 (2002): 529–55; A. J. Slywotzky, *Value Migration* (Boston: Harvard Business Review Press, 1996).
3. J. Magretta, "Why Business Models Matter," *Harvard Business Review* 80, no. 5 (2002): 86–94.
4. M. Morris, M. Schindehutte, and J. Allen, "The Entrepreneur's Business Model: Toward a Unified Perspective, *Journal of Business Research* 58 (2005): 726–35.
5. N. Herther, "The Christian Science Monitor Moves to a Web-Based Model—Is This the Future of News?" *Information Today Inc.,* http://newsbreaks.infotoday.com/nbReader.asp?ArticleID=51495 (accessed November 16, 2008).
6. G. Hamel, *Leading the Revolution* (New York: Plume, 2002).
7. C. Jordan, "Are Hidden Flaws in Your Business Preventing Your Success?" e-Firm Consultants, www.eventvibethevibe.com/Hidden_Flaws.asp (accessed November 16, 2008).
8. N. Wingfield, "New Battlefield for Priceline Is Diapers, Tuna," *Wall Street Journal,* September 20, 1999, B1.
9. M. Porter, *Competitive Advantage: Creating and Sustaining Superior Performance* (New York: Free Press, 1985).
10. H. Chu and S. Liao, "Defining and Categorizing Consumer Resale Behavior in Consumer-to-Consumer (C@C) E-Commerce," *International Journal of Business and Information* 2, no. 2 (2007): 159–84.
11. S. Pooler, "If You Own a QuickDrop eBay Drop Store Franchise What Will You Do Now?" http://ezinearticles.com/?If-You-Own-A-Quickdrop-Ebay-Drop-Store-Franchise-What-Will-You-Do-Now?&id=930650 (accessed September 27, 2008, posted January 15, 2008); F. Fortunato, "The State of eBay Drop-Off Stores," www.ecommerce-guide.com/news/news/article.pha/3631266 (accessed September 27, 2008, posted September 11, 2006).
12. N. Venkataraman and J. C. Henderson, "Real Strategies for Virtual Organizations," *Sloan Management Review* 40, no. 1 (1998): 33–48.
13. Hamel, *Leading the Revolution.*
14. R. D. Ireland, R. E. Hoskisson, and M. A. Hitt, *Understanding Business Strategy,* 2nd ed. (Mason, OH: South-Western Cengage Learning, 2009); M. E. Porter, *On Competition* (Boston: Harvard Business School Press, 1996).
15. "Mission Statement," About.com, www.sbinfocanada.about.com (accessed December 6, 2008).
16. Hamel, *Leading the Revolution.*
17. N. Wingfield, "Ballmer Wants Quick Yahoo Pact," *Wall Street Journal Online,* www.wsj.com (accessed December 6, 2008).
18. M. Dell, *Direct from Dell* (New York: HarperBusiness, 1999), 57.
19. R. J. Harrington and A. K. Tjan, "Transforming Strategy One Customer at a Time," *Harvard Business Review* 86, no. 3 (2008): 62–72.
20. Hamel, *Leading the Revolution.*
21. Porter, *Competitive Advantage.*
22. M. W. Johnson, C. M. Christensen, and H. Kagermann, "Reinventing Your Business Model," *Harvard Business Review* 86, no. 12 (2008): 50–59; J. Hedman and T. Kalling, "The Business Model Concept: Theoretical Underpinnings and Empirical Illustrations," *European Journal of Information Systems* 12 (2003): 49–59.
23. D. G. Sirmon, M. A. Hitt, and R. D. Ireland, "Managing Firm Resources in Dynamic Environments to Create Value: Looking Inside the Black Box," *Academy of Management Review* 32, no. 3 (2007): 273–92.
24. Hamel, *Leading the Revolution.*
25. R. Adner and P. Zemsky, "A Demand-Based Perspective on Sustainable Competitive Advantage," *Strategic Management Journal* 27 (2006): 215–39.
26. S. L. Newbert, "Value, Rareness, Competitive Advantage, and Performance: A Conceptual-Level Empirical Investigation of the Resource-Based View of the Firm," *Strategic Management Journal* 29, no 7 (2008): 745–68; J. Barney, "Firm Resources and Sustained Competitive Advantage," *Journal of Management* 17, no. 1 (1991): 99–120.

27. I. C. MacMillan and L. Selden, "The Incumbent's Advantage," *Harvard Business Review* 86, no. 10 (2008): 111–21; G. Hamel, "Management Innovation," *Harvard Business Review* 84, no. 2 (2006): 72–84.

28. R. L. Sorenson, C. A. Folker, and K. H. Brigham, "The Collaborative Network Orientation: Achieving Business Success Through Collaborative Relationships," *Entrepreneurship Theory and Practice* 32, no. 4 (2008): 615–34; F. T. Rothaermel and D. L. Deeds, "Alliance Type, Alliance Experience and Alliance Management Capability in High-Technology Ventures," *Journal of Business Venturing* 21 (2006): 429–60.

29. G. P. Pisano and R. Verganti, "Which Kind of Collaboration Is Right for You?" *Harvard Business Review* 86, no. 12 (2008): 78–86; G. Moore, *Living on the Fault Line* (New York: HarperBusiness, 2002).

30. E. Pinchot and G. Pinchot, "Leading Organizations into Partnerships," in *Partnering*, eds. L. Segil, M. Goldsmith, and J. Belasco (New York: AMACOM Books, 2002), 41–55.

31. B. Barringer, "The Effects of Relational Channel Exchange on the Small Firm: A Conceptual Framework," *Journal of Small Business Management* 35, no. 2 (1997): 65–79.

32. L. Xu and B. M. Beamon, "Supply Chain Coordination and Cooperation Mechanisms: An Attribute-Based Approach," *Journal of Supply Chain Management* 42, no. 1 (2006): 4–12.

33. T. Friedman, *The World Is Flat* (New York: Picador, 2007).

34. PricewaterhouseCoopers, "Partnerships Have Big Payoffs for Fast-Growth Companies," *Trendsetter Barometer*, August 26, 2002.

35. Business First, "UPS Logistics Provides Variety of Services at Local Center," April 19, 2002, www.bizjournals.com/louisville/stories/2002/04/22/story5.html?t=printable (accessed November 16, 2008).

36. Coopers & Lybrand Consulting, *Alliances* (New York: Coopers & Lybrand Consulting, 1997).

37. G. Kok and L. Widleman, "High Touch Partnering: Beyond Traditional Selection Perspectives" (white paper published by KPMG, Amsterdam, 1999).

38. B. Barringer and J. Harrison, "Walking a Tightrope: Creating Value Through Inter-organizational Relationships," *Journal of Management* 26, no. 3 (2000): 367–403.

39. F. Reichheld, "The Microeconomics of Customer Relationships," *MIT Sloan Management Review* 47, no. 2 (2006): 73–78; C. Markides, "A Dynamic View of Strategy," *Sloan Management Review* 40, no. 3 (1999): 55–63.

40. J. C. Anderson, J. A. Narus, and W. van Rossum, "Customer Value Propositions in Business Markets," *Harvard Business Review* 84, no. 3 (2006): 90–99.

41. E. Anderson and V. Onyemah, "How Right Should the Customer Be?" *Harvard Business Review* 84, no. 7/8 (2006): 58–67.

PART 3

Moving from an Idea to an Entrepreneurial Firm

MERRILL GUERRA
Founder, Merrill Guerra
MBA, Stephen M. Ross School of
Business, University of Michigan, 2007

Getting Personal

with Merrill Guerra

BEST ADVICE I'VE RECEIVED
Trust your gut instincts or that "little voice" inside you

MY BIGGEST WORRY AS AN ENTREPRENEUR
Being able to successfully surmount (survive) the latest challenge put before me

MY BIGGEST SURPRISE AS AN ENTREPRENEUR
Everything really does take longer and cost more than I thought it would

WHAT I'D LIKE TO BE DOING IN 10 YEARS
To continue making a difference in my community, serving as Founder, and exploring my artistic side

WHAT I DO WHEN I'M NOT WORKING
Read, play mom and taxi driver for my kids, hang out with close friends

HARDEST PART OF GETTING FUNDING
EVERYTHING. Surviving long enough to actually get the checks in the bank

CHAPTERSEVEN
Preparing the Proper *Ethical and Legal* Foundation

OPENING PROFILE

REALKIDZ
Getting Off to a Good Start—Ethically and Legally
www.realkidz.com

The founding and early success of RealKidz is a heartwarming story. The company was founded by Merrill Guerra, the mother of a nine-year-old plus-sized girl, who always had trouble finding clothing for her daughter. Guerra talked to other mothers who faced the same challenge. The idea behind RealKidz was to create a company that not only sold plus-sized clothes for young girls, but spoke out on their behalf and helped boost their confidence and self-esteem. Mainline clothing companies, like Old Navy and JCPenney, offered some clothes for plus-sized adolescent girls.[1] But there was no "go to" company for stylish clothing for 5- to 12-year-olds in this category. Guerra's vision was to make RealKidz that company.

In fall 2006, Guerra entered the evening MBA program at the University of Michigan. Although RealKidz was on Guerra's mind, it was still just an idea. Two experiences in her MBA program helped Guerra move RealKidz from an idea to a functioning firm. First, she received encouragement from Michigan alumnus Todd Sullivan, who sponsored her as a 2006 Marci Gani intern at his own online retail company, Spirit Shop. At Spirit Shop, which sells apparel products that have college or university logos, Guerra learned the ins and outs of Internet retailing. The second experience, which Guerra pursued at Sullivan's urging, was to take New Venture Creations, a class taught by Lecturer Jim Price. In the class, business ideas are proposed by students and area entrepreneurs, and once an idea attracts the attention of five students, the students are organized into a team to write a comprehensive business plan on the idea. Guerra proposed RealKidz to the class and attracted enough interest from her classmates to form a team. Working on the plan forced Guerra to do additional marketing research on the RealKidz idea, which resulted in her becoming even more passionate about the possibility. The business plan provided the foundation for an even more robust plan that won "runner-up" at the 2007 Michigan business plan competition. It also provided the impetus for several grants that Guerra was able to obtain to help with the start-up costs of RealKidz.

RealKidz was incorporated in February 2007, with the first line of clothing scheduled to be sold during the back-to-school season in fall 2007. The company's initial target market was 5- to 12-year-old plus-sized girls. Sales were scheduled to kick off on the Internet and via network marketing with catalog sales to follow. Network marketing is direct sales like Pampered Chef and Tupperware. Along with selling clothes, Guerra also planned to build an online community where parents of plus-sized kids could share information and ask advice from food coaches, psychologists, and other professionals.

From the start, Guerra laid a solid legal and ethical foundation for RealKidz. The "About Us" tab on the company's Web site lists its mission statement, vision statement, and values. RealKidz's mission, consistent with how the company has been put

Learning Objectives

After studying this chapter you should be ready to:

1. Describe how to create a strong ethical culture in an entrepreneurial venture.

2. Explain the importance of "leading by example" in terms of establishing a strong ethical culture in a firm.

3. Explain the importance of having a code of conduct and an ethics training program.

4. Explain the criteria important to selecting an attorney for a new firm.

5. Discuss the importance of a founders' agreement.

6. Provide several suggestions for how entrepreneurial firms can avoid litigation.

7. Discuss the importance of nondisclosure and noncompete agreements.

8. Provide an overview of the business licenses and business permits that a start-up must obtain before it starts conducting business.

9. Discuss the differences among sole proprietorships, partnerships, corporations, and limited liability companies.

10. Explain why most fast-growth entrepreneurial ventures organize as corporations or limited liability companies rather than sole proprietorships or partnerships.

together, is "To enhance children's self-esteem by providing them with clothing they look good in and are excited to wear and by providing their families with support and encouragement to incorporate healthy lifestyle choices into their daily lives." The company's values are also stipulated and are clearly evident in RealKidz's approach to its market. Although not a specific bullet point on the values statement, Guerra's number one goal for RealKidz is to be a positive influence in young people's lives.[2]

Getting the company off to a good start legally has also been a priority. In this area, Guerra has gotten more than she bargained for. The first lawyer she hired incorporated RealKidz as a C corporation. In retrospect, Guerra believes it would have been better to have started as a Subchapter S corporation. The difference triggered a larger initial tax liability than RealKidz would otherwise have paid. The second lawyer the company hired, which Guerra obtained via a referral, has been a better fit, and has built some flexibility into his fee schedule. To obtain the trademarks she needs, Guerra is working with a separate attorney. A particularly startling legal challenge Guerra experienced was contracting with a clothing designer who turned out to be a scam artist. The experience was a stark reminder of the importance of obtaining references before entering into business relationships.

Guerra is now immersed in executing RealKidz's business plan. She has experienced some setbacks raising the necessary funds to move RealKidz forward, but closed her first major round of funding on November 14, 2008. Consistent with the socially minded nature of the company, RealKidz is currently contracting with the prison system in Michigan to produce its clothing.[3]

The ethical and legal challenges involved with starting a firm are complicated. It is extremely important that entrepreneurs understand these issues and try diligently to avoid costly mistakes. This chapter begins by discussing the most important initial ethical and legal issues facing a new firm, including establishing a strong ethical organizational culture, choosing a lawyer, drafting a founders' agreement, and avoiding litigation. The chapter next discusses the different forms of business organization, including sole proprietorships, partnerships, corporations, and limited liability companies.

Chapter 12 discusses the protection of intellectual property through patents, trademarks, copyrights, and trade secrets. This topic, which is also a legal issue, is becoming increasingly important as entrepreneurs rely more on intellectual property rather than physical property as a source of a competitive advantage. Chapter 15 discusses legal issues pertaining to franchising. The chapter next discusses the licenses and permits that may be needed to launch a business, along with the different forms of business organization, including sole proprietorships, partnerships, corporations, and limited liability companies.

INITIAL ETHICAL AND LEGAL ISSUES FACING A NEW FIRM

As the opening case about RealKidz suggests, new ventures must deal with important ethical and legal issues at the time of their launching. Ethical and legal errors made early on can be extremely costly for a new venture down the road. And there is a tendency for entrepreneurs to overestimate their knowledge of the law. In fact, in one study 254 small retailers and service company owners were asked to judge the legality of several business practices.[4] A sample of the practices included in the survey is shown next. Which practices do you think are legal and which ones do you think aren't legal?

- Avoiding Social Security payments for independent contractors
- Hiring only experienced help
- Preempting potential competition with prices below costs
- Agreeing to divide a market with rivals

The first two practices are legal, while the second two are illegal. How did you do? For comparison purposes, you might want to know that the participants in the survey were wrong 35 percent of the time about these four practices. The study doesn't imply that entrepreneurs break the law intentionally or that they do not have ethical intentions. What the study does suggest is that entrepreneurs tend to overestimate their knowledge of the legal complexities involved with launching and running a business.

As a company grows, the legal environment becomes even more complex. A reevaluation of a company's ownership structure usually takes place when investors become involved. In addition, companies that go public are required to comply with a host of Securities and Exchange Commission (SEC) regulations, including regulations spawned by the Sarbanes-Oxley Act of 2002. We provide more information about the Sarbanes-Oxley Act in Chapter 10.

Against this backdrop, the following sections discuss several of the most important ethical and legal issues facing the founders of new firms.

Establishing a Strong Ethical Culture for a Firm

The single most important thing the founders of an entrepreneurial venture can do is establish a strong ethical culture for their firms. The data regarding business ethics are not encouraging. For example, 54 percent of the 2002 *Inc.* 500 CEOs surveyed thought that unethical business practices were as common among small private companies as large organizations.[5] Similarly, in 2007 the National Business Ethics Survey, conducted by the Ethics Resource Center, surveyed nearly 2,000 American workers regarding ethics-related issues. A total of 55 percent of the employees surveyed said they had observed conduct that violated company ethical standards, policy, or the law during the past year. Of the employees who observed misconduct at work, just 42 percent reported it to management.[6] The top 10 most common types of ethical misconduct observed by employees are shown in Table 7.1.

In analyzing the results of its survey, the Ethics Resource Center concluded that the most important thing an organization can do to combat the figures its study revealed is to establish a strong ethical culture. But strong ethical cultures don't emerge by themselves. It takes entrepreneurs who make ethics a priority and organizational policies and procedures that encourage ethical behavior (and punish unethical behavior) to make it happen. The following are specific steps that an entrepreneurial organization can take to build a strong ethical culture.

Lead by Example   The most important thing that any entrepreneur, or team of entrepreneurs, can do to build a strong ethical culture in their organization is to lead by example. According to the 2007 National Business Ethics Survey report, three things that are particularly important in building a strong ethical culture in a firm are:

- Leaders who intentionally make ethics a part of their daily conversations and decision making

Learning Objective

1. Describe how to create a strong ethical culture in an entrepreneurial venture.

Learning Objective

2. Explain the importance of "leading by example" in terms of establishing a strong ethical culture in a firm.

Table 7.1   Top 10 Most Common Types of Ethical Misconduct
(Based on 2007 National Business Ethics Survey)

Ethical Misconduct	Percent of Employees Who Have Observed the Misconduct in Their Companies (During the Past 12 Months)
Putting own interests ahead of organization	22%
Abusive behavior	21
Lying to employees	20
Misreporting hours worked	17
Internet abuse	16
Safety violations	15
Lying to stakeholders	14
Discrimination	13
Stealing	11
Sexual harassment	10

Source: National Business Ethics Survey, An Inside View of Private Sector Ethics (Washington, DC: Ethics Resource Center, 2007).

■ Supervisors who emphasize integrity when working with their direct reports
■ Peers who encourage each other to act ethically

In companies where these attributes are present, a stronger ethical culture exists. This finding vividly demonstrates the important role that everyone involved with a start-up plays in developing a strong ethical culture for their firm.[7]

Establish a Code of Conduct   A **code of conduct** (or code of ethics) is a formal statement of an organization's values on certain ethical and social issues.[8] The advantage of having a code of conduct is that it provides specific guidance to managers and employees regarding what is expected of them in terms of ethical

Learning Objective

3. Explain the importance of having a code of conduct and an ethics training program.

As part of building an ethical culture, many entrepreneurial firms are becoming more proactive in regard to helping address social needs. Here, Bill Gates, the chairman of Microsoft, gives a baby an oral polio drop at a community health clinic in India. Bill Gates is the driving force behind the Bill & Melinda Gates Foundation, which is now the largest charitable foundation in the world.

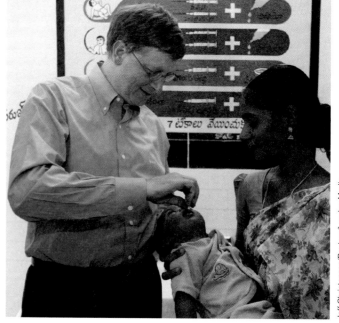

Jeff Christensen/Reuters/Landov Media

behavior. Consider what Google has done in this area. The company's informal corporate motto is "Don't be evil," but it also has a formal code of conduct, which explicitly states what is and isn't permissible in the organization. The table of contents for Google's code of conduct is shown in Table 7.2. It illustrates the

Table 7.2 TABLE OF CONTENTS OF GOOGLE'S CODE OF CONDUCT

I.   **Serve Our Users**
  a. Integrity
  b. Usefulness
  c. Privacy
  d. Responsiveness
  e. Take Action

II. **Respect Each Other**
  a. Equal Opportunity Employment
  b. Positive Environment
  c. Drugs and Alcohol
  d. Safe Workplace
  e. Dog Policy

III. **Avoid Conflicts of Interest**
  a. Personal Investments
  b. Outside Employment
  c. Outside Board Membership
  d. Friends and Relatives: Co-Worker Relationships
  e. Gifts, Entertainment and Payments
  f. Reporting

IV. **Preserve Confidentiality**
  a. Confidential Information
  b. Google Partners
  c. Competitors; Former Employees
  d. Outside Communications and Research

V.   **Protect Google's Assets**
  a. Intellectual Property
  b. Company Equipment
  c. The Network
  d. Physical Security
  e. Use of Google's Equipment and Facilities
  f. Employee Data

VI. **Ensure Financial Integrity and Responsibility**
  a. Spending Google's Money
  b. Signing a Contract
  c. Recording Transactions
  d. Reporting Financial or Accounting Irregularities
  e. Hiring Suppliers
  f. Retaining Records

VII. **Obey the Law**
  a. Export Controls
  b. Competition Laws
  c. Insider Trading Laws
  d. Anti-Bribery Laws

VIII. **Conclusion**

Source: Google Web site, http://investor.google.com/conduct.html (accessed December 6, 2008). Google Code of Conduct © Google Inc. and is used with permission.

ethical issues that Google thinks can be bolstered and better explained to employees via a written document to which they are required to adhere. A copy of Google's full code of conduct is available at http://investor.google.com/conduct.html.

In practice, some codes of conduct are very specific, like Google's. Other codes of conduct set out more general principles about an organization's beliefs on issues such as product quality, respect for customers and employees, and social responsibility. The 2007 National Business Ethics Survey, already referred to, found that employees are much more likely to report ethical misconduct in their firms when specific compliance mechanisms like codes of conduct are in place.[9]

Implement an Ethics Training Program Firms also use ethics training programs to promote ethical behavior. **Ethics training programs** teach business ethics to help employees deal with ethical dilemmas and improve their overall ethical conduct. An **ethical dilemma** is a situation that involves doing something that is beneficial to oneself or the organization, but may be unethical. Most employees confront ethical dilemmas at some point during their careers. Evidence surfacing during the global financial crisis of 2008 and 2009 suggests that a number of individuals working in a variety of firms were experiencing ethical dilemmas.

Ethics training programs can be provided by outside vendors or can be developed in-house. For example, one organization, Character Training International (CTI), provides ethics training programs for both large organizations and smaller entrepreneurial firms. The company offers a variety of ethics-related training services, including on-site workshops, speeches, a train-the-trainer curriculum, videos, and consulting services. A distinctive attribute of CTI is its focus on the moral and ethical roots of workplace behavior. In workshops, participants talk about the reasons behind ethical dilemmas and are provided practical, helpful information about how to prevent problems and how to deal appropriately with the ethical problems and temptations that do arise. The hope is that this training will significantly cut down on employee misconduct and fraud and will increase morale.[10]

In summary, ethical cultures are built through both strong ethical leadership and administrative tools that reinforce and govern ethical behavior in organizations. Building an ethical culture motivates employees to behave ethically and responsibly from the inside out, rather than relying strictly on laws that motivate

Many businesses provide their employees formal ethics training to alert them to the most likely ethics-related issues they'll encounter in their jobs. In this photo, a supervisor trains two new hires while going over an ethics-related manual.

Lockyer, Romilly/Getty Images Inc.-Image Bank

FIGURE 7.1

Potential Payoffs for
Establishing a Strong
Ethical Culture

behavior from the outside in.[11] There are many potential payoffs to organizations
that act and behave in an ethical manner. A sample of the potential payoffs
appears in Figure 7.1.

The strength of a firm's ethical culture and fortitude is put to the test when
it faces a crisis. An example of a firm that demonstrated a strong ethical culture
and fortitude in the midst of a crisis is provided in the "Savvy Entrepreneurial
Firm" feature.

Choosing an Attorney for a Firm

It is important for an entrepreneur to select an attorney as early as possible when
developing a business venture. Table 7.3 provides guidelines to consider when
selecting an attorney. It is critically important that the attorney be familiar with
start-up issues and that he or she has successfully shepherded entrepreneurs
through the start-up process before. It is not wise to select an attorney just
because she is a friend or because you were pleased with the way he prepared
your will. For issues dealing with intellectual property protection, it is essential to
use an attorney who specializes in this field, such as a patent attorney, when
filing a patent application.[12]

**Learning
Objective**

4. Explain the criteria
important to selecting
an attorney for a new
firm.

Table 7.3   HOW TO SELECT AN ATTORNEY

1. Contact the local bar association and ask for a list of attorneys who specialize in business start-ups in your area.
2. Interview several attorneys. Check references. Ask your prospective attorney whom he or she has guided through the start-up process before and talk to the attorney's clients. If an attorney is reluctant to give you the names of past or present clients, select another attorney.
3. Select an attorney who is familiar with the start-up process. Make sure that the attorney is more than just a legal technician. Most entrepreneurs need an attorney who is patient and is willing to guide them through the start-up process.
4. Select an attorney who can assist you in raising money for your venture. This is a challenging issue for most entrepreneurs, and help in this area can be invaluable.
5. Make sure your attorney has a track record of completing his or her work on time. It can be very frustrating to be prepared to move forward with a business venture, only to be stymied by delays on the part of an attorney.
6. Talk about fees. If your attorney won't give you a good idea of what the start-up process will cost, keep looking.
7. Trust your intuition. Select an attorney who you think understands your business and with whom you will be comfortable spending time and having open discussions about the dreams you have for your entrepreneurial venture.
8. Learn as much about the process of starting a business yourself as possible. It will help you identify any problems that may exist or any aspect that may have been overlooked. Remember, it's your business start-up, not your attorney's. Stay in control.

Savvy Entrepreneurial FIRM
Skype: Demonstrating a Strong Moral Fortitude by Proactively Responding to a Crisis
www.skype.com

One measure of a business's values and its ethical fortitude is how it responds to a crisis. For example, Johnson & Johnson is praised to this day for the exemplary manner in which it handled the Tylenol crisis. In 1982, someone in the Chicago area laced Extra Strength Tylenol capsules with poison, killing seven people. Johnson & Johnson quickly halted Tylenol production and advertising and issued a nationwide recall of Tylenol products, a decision that cost the company an estimated $100 million. The company also showed a great deal of concern for public safety and for those affected. In contrast, soft-drink giant Coca-Cola was slow to react when 33 Belgian school children fell ill complaining of headaches and nausea after drinking Coke. Although managers from the local Coke plant visited the school soon after, they failed to issue a total product recall for some days. Coca-Cola eventually recalled over 15 million containers of the soft drink after the Belgian Health Ministry announced a ban on the firm's drinks. In the same week, the governments of France, Netherlands, and Luxembourg also banned Coca-Cola's products, and the company had to assure British customers that the products made in its U.K. factories were safe. Coca-Cola's financial performance in Europe suffered a major setback following the crisis, which led it to rethink its marketing and management strategies to get in closer touch with Coke drinkers worldwide.

These types of crises also occur in young entrepreneurial firms, and the manner in which a firm handles the crisis sends a message to its customers regarding its values and trustworthiness.

Swedish entrepreneurs Janus Friis and Niklas Zennstrom launched Skype in 2003 with the idea of building a global company that offers phone calls for free, liberating consumers and businesses from the need to pay for talking to each other across the world. Zennstrom's idea was fueled by his dislike of overwhelming corporate power and companies that offer bad service. In August 2007, this policy was tested thoroughly when a software fault prevented registered users from accessing and making telephone calls using every version of Skype software downloaded since the company launched.

The problem had all the potential for a public relations disaster. Skype has 220 million registered users, and during the day there may be close to 6 million people connected at any one time making phone calls and sending instant messages and videos. Many small businesses have also become reliant on Skype after cancelling fixed-line telephone systems in favor of free on-Net calls.

As soon as the first problems were reported, the company quickly acknowledged that there was a problem, writing on Skype's official blog, Heartbeat-Skype: "Some of you may be having problems logging into Skype. Our engineering team has determined that it's a software issue. We expect this to be resolved within 12 to 24 hours. Meanwhile, you can simply leave your Skype client running and as soon as the issue is resolved, you will be logged in. We apologize for the inconvenience."

It also disabled downloads of the program to prevent further problems. The Skype team kept users updated with regular posts, and when the problem was eventually solved the following day, the company returned to apologize again for the inconvenience. As well as explaining how the fault happened, blaming "a software bug within the network resource algorithm," it also took the opportunity to dispel many of the conspiracy theories doing the rounds online about a viral attack or a slipup during routine site maintenance. Users were also reassured that at no time was their security compromised by the incident.

Zennstrom added a message of his own, writing, "We're back now and we're stronger."

This was the first time that Skype, which was bought by auction site eBay for $2.6 billion in 2005, was confronted with such a serious problem since it launched.

By showing contrition as well as deep concern about its users, explaining why the outage occurred, the team took an important step in restoring the trust and confidence of its customers.

Questions for Critical Thinking

1. What would have been the incorrect way for Skype to have responded to the crisis? What actions or behaviors on Skype's part would have shown a lack of moral fortitude rather than a presence of it?
2. Do you think Skype's response to its clients was sufficient? Is there more that Skype or its founder Niklas Zennstrom should have said or done to mend fences with its customers?
3. Spend some time looking at Skype's Web site. In what ways does Skype.com convey to its customers that it cares about them and intends to behave in an honest, ethical, and forthright manner?
4. Find at least one additional example of a firm that faced a crisis and explain how the firm reacted to the crisis. Comment on the degree of moral fortitude and proactivity the firm exhibited in its response to the crisis.

Source: "Skype Is on Its Way Back After Software Glitch," *eFlux Media*, August 17, 2007; "Skype Blames Two-Day Service Collapse on Software Glitch," *Information Week*, August 20, 2007.

Entrepreneurs often object to the expense of hiring an attorney when there are many books, Web sites, and other resources that can help them address legal issues on their own. However, these alternatives should be chosen with extreme caution. Many attorneys recognize that start-ups are short on cash and will work out an installment plan or other payment arrangement to get the firm the legal help it needs without starving it of cash, as was the case with Merrill Guerra, the entrepreneur profiled in this chapter's opening feature. This is particularly true if the attorney senses that the new venture has strong commercial potential and may develop into a steady client in the future. There are also ways for entrepreneurs to save on legal fees and to increase the value of their relationship with their attorney. The following are several ways for entrepreneurs to achieve these dual objectives:

■ **Group together legal matters:** It is typically cheaper to consult with an attorney on several matters at one time rather than schedule several separate meetings. For example, in one conference, a team of start-up entrepreneurs and their attorney could draft a founders' agreement, decide on a form of business organization, and discuss how to best draft nondisclosure and noncompete agreements for new employees. (We discuss these issues later in the chapter.)

■ **Offer to assist the attorney:** There are excellent resources available to help entrepreneurs acquaint themselves with legal matters. An entrepreneur could help the attorney save time by writing the first few drafts of a founders' agreement or a contract or by helping gather the documents needed to deal with a legal issue.

■ **Ask your attorney to join your advisory board:** Many start-ups form advisory boards (discussed in Chapter 9). Advisory board members typically serve as volunteers to help young firms get off to a good start. An attorney serving on an advisory board becomes a coach and a confidant as well as a paid service provider. However, entrepreneurs must be careful not to give the impression that the attorney was asked to serve on the advisory board as a way of getting free legal advice.

■ **Use nonlawyer professionals:** Nonlawyer professionals can perform some tasks at a much lower fee than a lawyer would charge. Examples include management consultants for business planning, tax preparation services for tax work, and insurance agents for advice on insurance planning.

One thing entrepreneurs should guard themselves against is ceding too much control to an attorney. While an attorney should be sought out and relied upon for legal advice, the major decisions pertaining to the firm should be made by the entrepreneurs. Entrepreneurs should also develop a good working knowledge of business law. This notion is affirmed by Constance E. Bagley, a professor at Harvard University, who wrote, "Just as a lawyer needs a sufficient understanding of how business operates and the strategies for success to be an effective partner (in an attorney–client relationship with an entrepreneur), the manager and entrepreneur need to have some knowledge of legal nomenclature and the legal principles most relevant to their business."[13]

Drafting a Founders' Agreement

Learning Objective

5. Discuss the importance of a founders' agreement.

It is important to ensure that founders are in agreement regarding their interests in the venture and their commitment to its future. It is easy for a team of entrepreneurs to get caught up in the excitement of launching a

Table 7.4   Items Included in a Founders' (or Shareholders')
Agreement

- Nature of the prospective business
- A brief business plan
- Identity and proposed titles of the founders
- Legal form of business ownership
- Apportionment of stock (or division of ownership)
- Consideration paid for stock or ownership share of each of the founders (may be cash or "sweat equity")
- Identification of any intellectual property signed over to the business by any of the founders
- Description of the initial operating capital
- Buyback clause, which explains how a founder's shares will be disposed of if she or he dies, wants to sell, or is forced to sell by court order

venture and fail to put in writing their initial agreements regarding the ownership of the firm. A **founders' agreement** (or shareholders' agreement) is a written document that deals with issues such as the relative split of the equity among the founders of the firm, how individual founders will be compensated for the cash or the "sweat equity" they put into the firm, and how long the founders will have to remain with the firm for their shares to fully vest.[14] The items typically included in a founders' agreement are shown in Table 7.4.

An important issue addressed by most founders' agreements is what happens to the equity of a founder if the founder dies or decides to leave the firm. Most founders' agreements include a **buyback clause**, which legally obligates departing founders to sell to the remaining founders their interest in the firm if the remaining founders are interested.[15] In most cases, the agreement also specifies the formula for computing the dollar value to be paid. The presence of a buyback clause is important for at least two reasons. First, if a founder leaves the firm, the remaining founders may need the shares to offer to a replacement person. Second, if founders leave because they are disgruntled, the buyback clause provides the remaining founders a mechanism to keep the shares of the firm in the hands of people who are fully committed to a positive future for the venture.

Avoiding Legal Disputes

**Learning
Objective**

6. *Provide several
suggestions for how
entrepreneurial firms
can avoid litigation.*

Most legal disputes are the result of misunderstandings, sloppiness, or a simple lack of knowledge of the law. Getting bogged down in legal disputes is something that an entrepreneur should work hard to avoid. It is important early in the life of a new business to establish practices and procedures to help avoid legal disputes. Legal snafus, particularly if they are coupled with management mistakes, can be extremely damaging to any firm, as illustrated in this chapter's "What Went Wrong?" feature.

There are several steps entrepreneurs can take to avoid legal disputes and complications, as discussed next.

Meet All Contractual Obligations   It is important to meet all contractual obligations on time. This includes paying vendors, contractors, and employees as agreed and delivering goods or services as promised. If an obligation cannot be met on time, the problem should be communicated to the affected parties

What Went WRONG?

How Legal Snafus Can Stop a Business in Its Tracks

Building a coffee chain in China, a country famous for its taste in tea, might seem a challenge for some companies, but not for global coffee giant Starbucks. However, when the Seattle-based chain decided to target the Chinese market in the late 1990s, the choice of beverage of potential customers was not the biggest problem. The challenge to its international expansion plans came from copycat chain Shanghai Xingbake, and the resultant legal row over copyright infringement embroiled the two companies in a lengthy and complex legal battle.

The row centred on the name *Xingbake*. In Chinese, *xing* means "star" and *bake* sounds very much like *bucks*. Although the American coffee company registered the name Starbucks and trademark pictures associated with it in China in 1996, it did not register the Xing Bake trademark until December 28, 1999.

While Starbucks' application for the trademark "Xing Bake" was pending, local company Shanghai Xingbake preregistered the corporate name Xing Bake and gained approval. Shanghai Xingbake's principle business was the sale of hot drinks and Western-style meals in a chain of restaurants in Shanghai, which appeared to emulate Starbucks' style of upholstered chairs and roomy seating.

To compound the potential confusion, Shanghai Xingbake printed "Starbuck Coffee" on its price list, which was hard to distinguish from the American company's trademark *Starbucks*. Shanghai Xingbake's logo, which was featured on menus, café windows, receipts, and business cards, also appeared to be copying Starbuck's distinctive logo using one small circle inside a larger one, with white characters on a green background and two stars embedded in the circles' overlapped area. The only difference was the Chinese company used a coffee cup in the circle instead of Starbucks' ubiquitous mermaid. Finally, Shanghai Xingbake used the slogan "Xing Bake Coffee" prominently on its storefront and price lists.

Although Starbucks immediately launched a legal action, Shanghai Xingbake appeared to have a strong case because it had succeeded in registering its Chinese name first. Under Chinese law, trademark rights are normally bestowed on the company that first files for a trademark. The case eventually went to court and, breaking with tradition, the Shanghai court ruled that, as a direct Chinese translation of "Starbucks," Xingbake infringed on the American coffee maker's trademark, even though the Chinese company was first to register its name. The court ruled that Shanghai Xingbake intentionally used Xingbake in its name to mislead the public, violating trademark law and basic commercial ethics of equality, honesty, and good faith. Starbucks won the exceptional ruling on the strength that it is one of the world's best-known brands and is well recognized in China too.

Shanghai Xingbake was fined 500,000 yuan (US$64,000) for infringing Starbucks' trademark and ordered to change its name and apologize publicly through a local newspaper. Despite losing subsequent appeals, Shanghai Xingbake hesitated to change its name for some time. Eventually, after the courts ordered a freezing of the defendant's assets and garnishment of its bank accounts, Shanghai Xingbake changed its name to Fangyun Coffee and agreed to pay the compensation by installments. Trademark lawsuits can be both lengthy and prohibitively expensive, and Fangyun has never fully recovered from the experience.

Questions for Critical Thinking

1. To what extent do you believe establishing a strong ethical culture could have helped Shanghai Xingbake avoid its difficulties?
2. Imagine you were given the job of writing a code of conduct for Shanghai Xingbake when the company was founded. Using the table of contents of Google's code of conduct as a guide (Table 7.1), construct a table of contents for Shanghai Xingbake's code of conduct. Make Shanghai Xingbake's code of conduct fit its industry and individual circumstances.
3. If you had been one of the entrepreneurs founding Shanghai Xingbake, what would you have done differently compared to the actions described in this feature?

as soon as possible. It is irritating to a vendor, for example, not only to not get paid on time but also to have no explanation for the delay. Commenting on this issue, David Preiser, the managing director of an investment banking company in Los Angeles, says, "Credibility and confidence are built slowly but destroyed rapidly."[16] Preiser recommends being forthright with vendors or creditors if an obligation cannot be met and providing the affected party or parties a realistic plan for repaying the money as a way of retaining their confidence.

Avoid Undercapitalization   If a new business is starved for money, it is much more likely to experience financial problems that will lead to litigation.[17] A new business should raise the money it needs to effectively conduct business or should stem its growth to conserve cash. Many entrepreneurs face a dilemma regarding this issue. It is the goal of most entrepreneurs to retain as much of the equity in their firms as possible, but equity must often be shared with investors to obtain sufficient investment capital to support the firm's growth. This issue is discussed in more detail in Chapter 10.

Get Everything in Writing   Many business disputes arise because of the lack of a written agreement or because poorly prepared written agreements do not anticipate potential areas of dispute.[18] Although it is tempting to try to show business partners or employees that they are "trusted" by downplaying the need for a written agreement, this approach is usually a mistake. Disputes are much easier to resolve if the rights and obligations of the parties involved are in writing. For example, what if a new business agreed to pay a Web design firm $5,000 to design its Web site? The new business should know what it's getting for its money, and the Web design firm should know when the project is due and when it will receive payment for its services. In this case, a dispute could easily arise if the parties simply shook hands on the deal and the Web design firm promised to have a "good-looking Web site" done "as soon as possible." The two parties could easily later disagree over the quality and functionality of the finished Web site and the project's completion date.

The experiences and perspectives of Maxine Clark, the founder of Build-A-Bear Workshop, provide a solid illustration of the practical benefits of putting things in writing, even when dealing with a trusted partner:

> While I prefer only the necessary contracts (and certainly as few pages as possible), once you find a good partner you can trust, written up-front agreements are often a clean way to be sure all discussed terms are acceptable to all parties. It's also a good idea after a meeting to be sure someone records the facts and agree-to points, and distribute them to all participants in writing. E-mail is a good method for doing this. Steps like this will make your life easier. After all, the bigger a business gets, the harder it is to remember all details about every vendor, contract, and meeting. Written records give you good notes for doing follow-up, too.[19]

One of the simplest ways to avoid misunderstandings and ultimately legal disputes is to get everything in writing.

Will & Deni McIntyre/Photo Researchers, Inc.

Nondisclosure and Noncompetition. (a) At all times while this agreement is in force and after its expiration or termination, [employee name] agrees to refrain from disclosing [company name]'s customer lists, trade secrets, or other confidential material. [Employee name] agrees to take reasonable security measures to prevent accidental disclosure and industrial espionage.

(b) While this agreement is in force, the employee agrees to use [his/her] best efforts to [describe job] and to abide by the nondisclosure and noncompetition terms of this agreement; the employer agrees to compensate the employee as follows: [describe compensation]. After expiration or termination of this agreement, [employee name] agrees not to compete with [company name] for a period of [number] years within a [number] mile radius of [company name and location]. This prohibition will not apply if this agreement is terminated because [company] violated the terms of this agreement.

Competition means owning or working for a business of the following type: [specify type of business employee may not engage in].

(c) [Employee name] agrees to pay liquidated damages in the amount of $[dollar amount] for any violation of the covenant not to compete contained in subparagraph (b) of this paragraph.

IN WITNESS WHEREOF, [company name] and [employee name] have signed this agreement.

_____

[company name]

_____

[employee's name]
Date: _____

Source: Office Depot.

FIGURE 7.2

Sample Nondisclosure and Noncompete Agreement

There are also two important written agreements that the majority of firms ask their employees to sign. A **nondisclosure agreement** binds an employee or another party (such as a supplier) to not disclose a company's trade secrets. A **noncompete agreement** prevents an individual from competing against a former employer for a specific period of time. A sample nondisclosure and noncompete agreement is shown in Figure 7.2.

Learning Objective

7. Discuss the importance of nondisclosure and noncompete agreements.

Set Standards Organizations should also set standards that govern employees' behavior beyond what can be expressed via a code of conduct. For example, four of the most common ethical problem areas that occur in an organization are human resource ethical problems, conflicts of interest, customer confidence, and inappropriate use of corporate resources. Policies and procedures should be established to deal with these issues. In addition, as reflected in the "Partnering for Success" boxed features throughout this book, firms are increasingly partnering with others to achieve their objectives. Because of this, entrepreneurial ventures should be vigilant when selecting their alliance partners. A firm falls short in terms of establishing high ethical standards if it is willing to partner with firms that behave in a contrary manner. This chapter's "Partnering for Success" feature illustrates how two firms, Patagonia and Build-A-Bear Workshop, deal with this issue.

When legal disputes do occur, they can often be settled through negotiation or mediation, rather than more expensive and potentially damaging litigation. **Mediation** is a process in which an impartial third party (usually a professional mediator) helps those involved in a dispute reach an agreement. At times, legal disputes can also be avoided by a simple apology and a sincere pledge on the part of the offending party to make amends. An example that illustrates this point is provided by Harvard Professor Constance E. Bagley, who was quoted earlier in this chapter.[20] In regard to the role a simple apology plays in resolving legal disputes, Professor Bagley refers to a *Wall Street Journal* article in which the writer commented about a jury

Partnering for SUCCESS
Patagonia and Build-A-Bear Workshop: Picking Trustworthy Partners
www.patagonia.com
www.buildabear.com

Patagonia

Patagonia sells rugged clothing and gear to mountain climbers, skiers, and other extreme-sport enthusiasts. The company is also well known for its environmental stands and its commitment to product quality. Patagonia has never owned a fabric mill or a sewing shop. Instead, to make a ski jacket, for example, it buys fabric from a mill, zippers and facings from other manufacturers, and then hires a sewing shop to complete the garment. To meet its own environmental standards and ensure product quality, it works closely with each partner to make sure the jacket meets its rigid standards.

As a result of these standards, Patagonia does as much business as it can with as few partners as possible and chooses its relationships carefully. The first thing the company looks for in a partner is the quality of its work. It doesn't look for the lowest-cost provider, who might sew one day for a warehouse outlet store such as Costco and try to sew the next day for Patagonia. Contractors that sew on the lowest-cost basis, the company reasons, wouldn't hire sewing operators of the skill required or welcome Patagonia's oversight of its working conditions and environmental standards. What Patagonia looks for, more than anything, is a good fit between itself and the companies it partners with. It sees its partners as an extension of its own business, and wants partners that convey Patagonia's own sense of product quality, business ethics, and environmental and social concern.

Once a relationship is established, Patagonia doesn't leave adherence to its principles to chance. Its production department monitors its partners on a consistent basis. The objective is for both sides to prosper and win. In fact, in describing the company's relationship with its partners, Patagonia founder Yvon Chouinard says, "We become like friends, family—mutually selfish business partners; what's good for them is good for us."

Build-A-Bear Workshop

A similar set of beliefs and actions describe Build-A-Bear Workshop. Build-A-Bear lets its customers, who are usually children, design and build their own stuffed animals, in a sort of Santa's workshop setting. Like Patagonia, Build-A-Bear is a very socially conscious organization, and looks for partners that

reflect its values. Affirming this point, Maxine Clark, the company's founder, said, "The most successful corporate partnerships are forged between like-minded companies with similar cultures that have come together for a common goal, where both sides benefit from the relationship."

Also similar to Patagonia, Build-A-Bear thinks of its partners as good friends. Reflecting on her experiences in this area, Clark said, "I tend to think of partners as good business friends—companies and people who would do everything they could to help us succeed and for whom I would do the same." In a book she wrote about founding and building Build-A-Bear into a successful company, Clark attributes having good partners to careful selection. She also likens business partnership to a marriage, which has many benefits but also takes hard work: "Good business partnerships are like successful marriages. To work, they require compatibility, trust and cooperation. Both parties need to be invested in one another's well-being and strive for a common goal."

Both Patagonia and Build-A-Bear make extensive use of partnerships and are leaders in their respective industries.

Questions for Critical Thinking

1. To what extent do you believe that Patagonia and Build-A-Bear Workshop's ethical cultures drive their views on partnering?
2. Assume you were assigned the task of writing a code of conduct for Patagonia. Write the portion of the code of conduct that deals with business partnership relationships.
3. List the similarities that you see between the partnership philosophies of Patagonia and Build-A-Bear Workshop.
4. Spend some time studying Patagonia, by looking at the company's Web site and via other Internet searches. Describe Patagonia's general approach to business ethics, social responsibility, and environmental concerns. What, if anything, can start-ups learn from Patagonia's philosophies and its experiences?

Sources: M. Clark, *The Bear Necessities of Business* (New York: Wiley, 2006); Y. Chouinard, *Let My People Go Surfing* (New York: The Penguin Press, 2005).

awarding $2.7 million to a woman who spilled scalding hot McDonald's coffee on her lap.

> A jury awarded $2.7 million to a woman who spilled scalding hot McDonald's coffee on her lap. Although this case is often cited as an example of a tort (legal) system run amok, the *Wall Street Journal* faulted McDonald's for not only failing to respond to prior scalding incidents but also for mishandling the injured woman's complaints by not apologizing.[21]

A final issue important in promoting business ethics involves the manner in which entrepreneurs and managers demonstrate accountability to their investors and shareholders. This issue, which we discuss in greater detail in Chapter 10, is particularly important given the rash of corporate scandals in the early 2000s and those that were surfacing in early 2009 as well.

OBTAINING BUSINESS LICENSES AND PERMITS

Before a business is launched, a number of licenses and permits are typically needed. What is actually needed varies by city, county, and state, as well as by type of business, so it's important for the entrepreneur to study local regulations carefully. Some licenses are difficult to get—such as liquor licenses. For example, in some states, the only way to get a liquor license is to buy a preexisting license. This stipulation often results in a bidding war when a business is willing to give up its liquor license, which increases the price.

Learning Objective

8. Provide an overview of the business licenses and business permits that a start-up must obtain before it starts conducting business.

Business Licenses

In most communities, a business needs a license to operate. A **business license** can be obtained at the city clerk's office in the community where the business will be located. If the business will be run out of the founder's home, a separate home occupation business license is often required. When a business license is applied for, the city planning and zoning departments usually check to make sure the business's address is zoned for the type of business that is being planned. If a business will be located outside a city or town's jurisdiction, the county courthouse will issue the business license.

If a business is a sole proprietorship, it can usually stop here, as far as obtaining a business license goes. If a business has employees, or is a corporation, limited liability company, or limited partnership, it will usually need a state business license in addition to its local one. There are additional state provisions that you may need to comply with. If you're starting a retail or service business, you'll need to obtain a sales tax license, which enables you to collect taxes on the state's behalf. Special licenses are needed to sell liquor, lottery tickets, gasoline, or firearms. People in certain professions, such as barbers, chiropractors, nurses, and real estate agents, must normally pass a state examination and maintain a professional license to conduct business. Certain businesses also require special state licenses. Examples of these types of businesses include child care, health care facilities, hotels, and restaurants. It's important to check to see which licenses your business needs.

A narrow group of businesses are required to have a U.S. business license, including investment advising, drug manufacturing, preparation of meat products, broadcasting, interstate trucking, and businesses that manufacture tobacco, alcohol, or firearms, or sell firearms. These licenses are obtained through the U.S. Federal Trade Commission.

Nearly all businesses are required to obtain a U.S. **employer identification number (EIN)**, also known as a tax identification number, which is used in filing various business tax returns. The only exception is sole proprietors who do not have employees. In this instance the sole proprietor uses his or her social security number as the tax identification number. A tax identification number can be obtained from the U.S. Internal Revenue Service by calling 800-829-4933.

Business Permits

Along with obtaining the appropriate licenses, some businesses may need to obtain one or more permits. The need to obtain a permit or permits depends on the nature and location of the business. For example, if you plan to sell food, either as a restaurateur or as a wholesaler to other retail businesses, you'll need a city or county health permit. If your business will be open to the public or will use flammable material, you may need a fire department permit. Some communities require businesses to obtain a permit to put up a sign. If you're occupying a building, there may also be building code requirements that need to be complied with.

All businesses that plan to use a fictitious name, which is any name other than the business owner's name, need a **fictitious business name permit** (also called a *dba* or *doing business as*). If a business is a sole proprietorship, the permit can be obtained at the city or county level. The way this works is that if your name is Justin Ryan and you apply for a business license, your business will be registered as Justin Ryan. If you want to use another name, like *Snake River Computer Consulting*, then you'll need a fictitious name permit. You'll typically need a fictitious name permit to obtain a checking account in your business's name. It's also important to have a fictitious name permit if you execute any contracts, sign any agreements, or pay bills or accept payments under your business's name. Selecting a name for a business and obtaining a fictitious business name permit if needed is an important task, not only to comply with the law but because a business's name is a critical part of its branding strategy.[22] It's also one of the first things that people associate with a business. Appendix 7.1 contains a set of guidelines and suggestions for picking a business's name. As illustrated in the appendix, it is important that a business choose a name that facilitates rather than hinders how it wants to differentiate itself in the marketplace.

Several resources are available to assist business founders in identifying the proper licenses and permits to apply for. The SBA maintains a Web site, at www.sba.gov/hotlist/license.html, that features links, which provide information on how to obtain a business license in each U.S. state. Many city governments also publish documents or maintain online resources that provide guidance for doing business in their city. Good places to look for these publications or resources are the city government's Web site, the city library's Web site, or the Web site for the local Chamber of Commerce. For example, the Dallas Public Library maintains an excellent online resource titled "Starting a Small Business in Dallas." The site is available at http://dallaslibrary.org/CGI/smallbiz.htm.

Learning Objective

9. Discuss the differences among sole proprietorships, partnerships, corporations, and limited liability companies.

CHOOSING A FORM OF BUSINESS ORGANIZATION

When a business is launched, a form of legal entity must be chosen. Sole proprietorship, partnerships, corporations, and limited liability companies are the most common legal entities from which entrepreneurs make a choice.

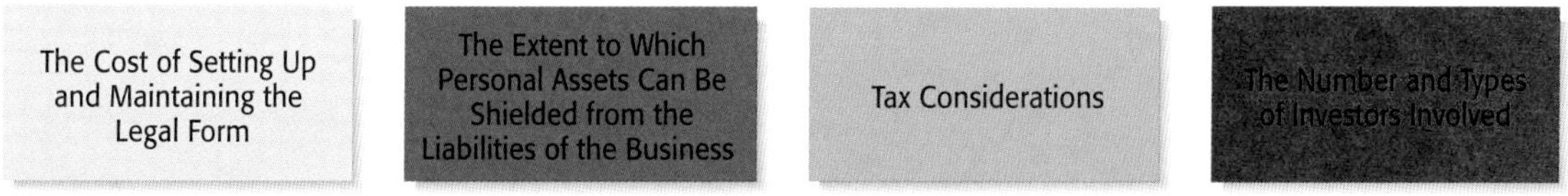

| The Cost of Setting Up and Maintaining the Legal Form | The Extent to Which Personal Assets Can Be Shielded from the Liabilities of the Business | Tax Considerations | The Number and Types of Investors Involved |

FIGURE 7.3

Factors Critical in Selecting a Form of Business Organization

Choosing a legal entity is not a one-time event. As a business grows and matures, it is necessary to periodically review whether the current form of business organization remains appropriate. In most cases, a firm's form of business entity can be changed without triggering adverse tax implications.

There is no single form of business organization that works best in all situations. It's up to the owners of a firm and their attorney to select the legal entity that best meets their needs. The decision typically hinges on several factors, which are shown in Figure 7.3. It is important to be careful in selecting a legal entity for a new firm because each form of business organization involves trade-offs among these factors and because an entrepreneur wants to be sure to achieve the founders' specific objectives.

This section describes the four forms of business organization and discusses the advantages and disadvantages of each. A comparison of the four legal entities, based on the factors that are typically the most important in making a selection, is provided in Table 7.5.

Sole Proprietorship

The simplest form of business entity is the sole proprietorship. A **sole proprietorship** is a form of business organization involving one person, and the person and the business are essentially the same. Sole proprietorships are the most prevalent form of business organization. The two most important advantages of a sole proprietorship are that the owner maintains complete control over the business and that business losses can be deducted against the owner's personal tax return.[23]

Setting up a sole proprietorship is cheap and relatively easy compared to the other forms of business ownership. The only legal requirement, in most U.S. states, is to obtain the appropriate license and permits to do business as described in the previous section of the chapter.

If the business will be operated under a trade name (e.g., Pacific Coast Consulting) instead of the name of the owner (e.g., Samuel Ryan), the owner will have to file an assumed or fictitious name certificate with the appropriate local government agency, as mentioned earlier in the chapter. This step is required to ensure that there is only one business in an area using the same name and provides a public record of the owner's name and contact information.

A sole proprietorship is not a separate legal entity. For tax purposes, the profit or loss of the business flows through to the owner's personal tax return, and the business ends at the owner's death or loss of interest in the business. The sole proprietor is responsible for all the liabilities of the business, and this is a significant drawback. If a sole proprietor's business is sued, the owner could theoretically lose all the business's assets along with personal assets. The liquidity of an owner's investment in a sole proprietorship is typically low. **Liquidity** is the ability to sell a business or other asset quickly at a price that is close to its market value.[24] It is usually difficult for a sole proprietorship to raise investment capital because the ownership of the business cannot be shared. Unlimited liability and difficulty raising investment capital are the primary reasons entrepreneurs typically form corporations or limited liability companies as opposed to sole proprietorships. Most sole proprietorships are salary-substitute or lifestyle firms (as described in Chapter 1) and are typically a poor choice for an aggressive entrepreneurial firm.

Table 7.5 Comparison of Forms of Business Ownership

Factor		Proprietorship		Corporation		Limited Liability Company
	Sole Partnership	General	Limited	C Corporation	S Corporation	
Number of owners allowed	1	Unlimited number of general partners allowed	Unlimited number of general and limited partners allowed	Unlimited	Up to 100	Unlimited number of "members" allowed
Cost of setting up and maintaining	Low	Moderate	Moderate	High	High	High
Personal liability of owners	Unlimited	Unlimited for all partners	Unlimited for general partners; limited partners only to extent of investment	Limited to amount of investment	Limited to amount of investment	Limited to amount of investment
Continuity of business	Ends at death of owner	Death or withdrawal of one partner unless otherwise specified	Death or withdrawal of general partner	Perpetual	Perpetual	Typically limited to a fixed amount of time
Taxation	Not a taxable entity; sole proprietor pays all taxes	Not a taxable entity; each partner pays taxes on his or her share of income and can deduct losses against other sources of income	Not a taxable entity; each partner pays taxes on his or her share of income and can deduct losses against other sources of income	Separate taxable entity	No tax at entity level; income/loss is passed through to the shareholders	No tax at entity level if properly structured; income/loss is passed through to the members
Management control	Sole proprietor is in full control	All partners share control equally, unless otherwise specified	Only general partners have control	Board of directors elected by the shareholders	Board of directors elected by the shareholders	Members share control or appoint manager
Method of raising capital	Must be raised by sole proprietor	Must be raised by general partners	Sale of limited partnerships, depending on terms of operating agreement	Sell shares of stock to the public	Sell shares of stock to the public	It's possible to sell interests, depending on the terms of the operating agreement
Liquidity of investment	Low	Low	Low	High, if publicly traded	Low	Low
Subject to double taxation	No	No	No	Yes	No	No

To summarize, the primary advantages and disadvantages of a sole proprietorship are as follows:

Advantages of a Sole Proprietorship

- Creating one is easy and inexpensive.
- The owner maintains complete control of the business and retains all the profits.
- Business losses can be deducted against the sole proprietor's other sources of income.
- It is not subject to double taxation (explained later).
- The business is easy to dissolve.

Disadvantages of a Sole Proprietorship

- Liability on the owner's part is unlimited.
- The business relies on the skills and abilities of a single owner to be successful. Of course, the owner can hire employees who have additional skills and abilities.
- Raising capital can be difficult.
- The business ends at the owner's death or loss of interest in the business.
- The liquidity of the owner's investment is low.

Partnerships

If two or more people start a business, they must organize as a partnership, corporation, or limited liability company. Partnerships are organized as either general or limited partnerships.

General Partnerships   A **general partnership** is a form of business organization where two or more people pool their skills, abilities, and resources to run a business. The primary advantage of a general partnership over a sole proprietorship is that the business isn't dependent on a single person for its survival and success. In fact, in most cases, the partners have equal say in how the business is run. Most partnerships have a partnership agreement, which is a legal document that is similar to a founders' agreement. A **partnership agreement** details the responsibilities and the ownership shares of the partners involved with an organization. The business created by a partnership ends at the death or withdrawal of a partner, unless otherwise stated in the partnership agreement. General partnerships are typically found in service industries. In many U.S. states, a general partnership must file a certificate of partnership or similar document as evidence of its existence. Similar to a sole proprietorship, the profit or loss of a general partnership flows through to the partner's personal tax returns. If a business has four general partners and they all have equal ownership in the business, then one-fourth of the profits or losses would flow through to each partner's individual tax return.[25] The partnership files an informational tax return only.

The primary disadvantage of a general partnership is that the individual partners are liable for all the partnership's debts and obligations. If one partner is negligent while conducting business on behalf of the partnership, all the partners may be liable for damages. Although the nonnegligent partners may later try to recover their losses from the negligent one, the joint liability of all partners to the injured party remains. It is typically easier for a general partnership to raise money than a sole proprietorship simply because more than one person is willing to assume liability for a loan. One way a general partnership can raise investment capital is by adding more partners. Investors are typically reluctant to sign on as general partners, however, because of the unlimited liability that follows each one.

In summary, the primary advantages and disadvantages of a general partnership are as follows:

Advantages of a General Partnership

■ Creating one is relatively easy and inexpensive compared to a corporation or limited liability company.

■ The skills and abilities of more than one individual are available to the firm.

■ Having more than one owner may make it easier to raise funds.

■ Business losses can be deducted against the partners' other sources of income.

■ It is not subject to double taxation (explained later).

Disadvantages of a General Partnership

■ Liability on the part of each general partner is unlimited.

■ The business relies on the skills and abilities of a fixed number of partners. Of course, similar to a sole proprietorship, the partners can hire employees who have additional skills and abilities.

■ Raising capital can be difficult.

■ Because decision making among the partners is shared, disagreements can occur.

■ The business ends at the death or withdrawal of one partner unless otherwise stated in the partnership agreement.

■ The liquidity of each partner's investment is low.

Limited Partnerships   A **limited partnership** is a modified form of a general partnership. The major difference between the two is that a limited partnership includes two classes of owners: general partners and limited partners. There are no limits on the number of general or limited partners permitted in a limited partnership. Similar to a general partnership, the general partners are liable for the debts and obligations of the partnership, but the limited partners are liable only up to the amount of their investment. The limited partners may not exercise any significant control over the organization without jeopardizing their limited liability status.[26] Similar to general partnerships, most limited partnerships have partnership agreements. A **limited partnership agreement** sets forth the rights and duties of the general and limited partners, along with the details of how the partnership will be managed and eventually dissolved.

A limited partnership is usually formed to raise money or to spread out the risk of a venture without forming a corporation. Limited partnerships are common in real estate development, oil and gas exploration, and motion picture ventures.[27]

Learning Objective

10. Explain why most fast-growth entrepreneurial ventures organize as corporations or limited liability companies rather than sole proprietorships or partnerships.

Corporations

A **corporation** is a separate legal entity organized under the authority of a government. Corporations are organized as either C corporations or subchapter S corporations. The following description pertains to C corporations, which are what most people think of when they hear the word *corporation*. Subchapter S corporations are explained later.

C Corporations   A **C corporation** is a separate legal entity that, in the eyes of the law, is separate from its owners. In most cases, the corporation shields its owners, who are called **shareholders**, from personal liability for the debts and obligations of the corporation. A corporation is governed by a board of directors, which is elected by the shareholders (more about this in Chapter 9). In most instances, the board hires officers to oversee the day-to-day management of the organization. It is usually easier for a corporation to raise investment capital than a sole proprietorship or a partnership because the shareholders are not liable beyond their investment in the firm. It is also easier to allocate partial ownership interests in a corporation through the distribution of stock. Most C corporations have two classes of stock: common and preferred. **Preferred stock** is typically issued to conservative investors who have preferential rights over common stockholders in regard to dividends and to the assets of the corporation in the event of liquidation. **Common stock** is issued more broadly than preferred stock. The common stockholders have voting rights and elect the board of directors of the firm. The common stockholders are typically the last to get paid in the event of the liquidation of the corporation, that is, after the creditors and the preferred stockholders.[28]

Establishing a corporation is more complicated than a sole proprietorship or a partnership. A U.S. corporation is formed by filing **articles of incorporation** with the secretary of state's office in the U.S. state of incorporation. The articles of incorporation typically include the corporation's name, purpose, authorized number of stock shares, classes of stock, and other conditions of operation.[29] In most states, corporations must file papers annually, and government agencies impose annual fees. It is important that a corporation's owners fully comply with these regulations. If the owners of a corporation don't file their annual paperwork, neglect to pay their annual fees, or commit fraud, a court could ignore the fact that a corporation has been established and the owners could be held personally liable for actions of the corporation. This chain of effects is referred to as "**piercing the corporate veil**."[30]

A corporation is taxed as a separate legal entity. In fact, the "C" in the title "C corporation" comes from the fact that regular corporations are taxed under subchapter C of the Internal Revenue Code. A disadvantage of corporations is that they are subject to **double taxation**, which means that a corporation is taxed on its net income and, when the same income is distributed to shareholders in the form of dividends, is taxed again on shareholders' personal income tax returns. This complication is one of the reasons that entrepreneurial firms often retain their earnings rather than paying dividends to their shareholders. The firm can use the earnings to fuel future growth and at the same time avoid double taxation. The hope is that the shareholders will ultimately be rewarded by an appreciation in the value of the company's stock.

Another advantage of corporations is the ease of transferring stock. It is often difficult for a sole proprietor to sell a business and even more awkward for a partner to sell a partial interest in a general partnership. If a corporation is listed on a major stock exchange, such as the New York Stock Exchange or the NASDAQ, an owner can sell shares at almost a moment's notice. This advantage of incorporating, however, does not extend to corporations that are not listed on a major stock exchange. There are approximately 3,200 companies listed on both the New York Stock and the NASDAQ. These firms are **public corporations**. The stockholders of these 6,400 companies enjoy a **liquid market** for their stock, meaning that the stock can be bought and sold fairly easily through an organized marketplace. It is much more difficult to sell stock in closely held or private corporations. In a **closely held corporation**, the voting stock is held by a small number of individuals and is very thinly or infrequently traded.[31] A **private corporation** is one in which all the shares are held by a few shareholders, such as management or family members, and are not publicly traded.[32] The vast majority of the corporations in the United States are private corporations. The stock in both closely held and private corporations is fairly **illiquid**, meaning that it typically isn't easy to find a buyer for the stock.

A final advantage of organizing as a C corporation is the ability to share stock with employees as part of an employee incentive plan. Because it's easy to distribute stock in small amounts, many corporations, both public and private, distribute stock as part of their employee bonus or profit-sharing plans. Such incentive plans are intended to help firms attract, motivate, and retain high-quality employees.[33] **Stock options** are a special form of incentive compensation. These plans provide employees the option or right to buy a certain number of shares of their company's stock at a stated price over a certain period of time. The most compelling advantage of stock options is the potential rewards to participants when (and if) the stock price increases.[34] Many employees receive stock options at the time they are hired and then periodically receive additional options. As employees accumulate stock options, the link between their potential reward and their company's stock price becomes increasingly clear. This link provides a powerful inducement for employees to exert extra effort on behalf of their firm in hopes of positively affecting the stock price.[35]

To summarize, the advantages and disadvantages of a C corporation are as follows:

Advantages of a C Corporation

- Owners are liable only for the debts and obligations of the corporation up to the amount of their investment.
- The mechanics of raising capital is easier.
- No restrictions exist on the number of shareholders, which differs from subchapter S corporations.
- Stock is liquid if traded on a major stock exchange.
- The ability to share stock with employees through stock option or other incentive plans can be a powerful form of employee motivation.

Disadvantages of a C Corporation

- Setting up and maintaining one is more difficult than for a sole proprietorship or a partnership.
- Business losses cannot be deducted against the shareholders' other sources of income.
- Income is subject to double taxation, meaning that it is taxed at the corporate and the shareholder levels.
- Small shareholders typically have little voice in the management of the firm.

Subchapter S Corporation   A **subchapter S corporation** combines the advantages of a partnership and a C corporation. It is similar to a partnership in that the profits and losses of the business are not subject to double taxation. The subchapter S corporation does not pay taxes; instead, the profits or losses of the business are passed through to the individual tax returns of the owners. It is also similar to a corporation in that the owners are not subject to personal liability for the behavior of the business. An additional advantage of the subchapter S corporation pertains to self-employment tax. By electing the subchapter S corporate status, only the earnings actually paid out as salary are subject to payroll taxes. The ordinary income that is disbursed by the business to the shareholders is not subject to payroll taxes or self-employment tax.

Because of these advantages, many entrepreneurial firms start as subchapter S corporations. There are strict standards that a business must meet to qualify for status as a subchapter S corporation:

■ The business cannot be a subsidiary of another corporation.

■ The shareholders must be U.S. citizens. Partnerships and C corporations may not own shares in a subchapter S corporation. Certain types of trusts and estates are eligible to own shares in a subchapter S corporation.

■ It can have only one class of stock issued and outstanding (either preferred stock or common stock).

■ It can have no more than 100 members. Husbands and wives count as one member, even if they own separate shares of stock. In some instances, family members count as one member.

■ All shareholders must agree to have the corporation formed as a subchapter S corporation.

The primary disadvantages of a subchapter S corporation are restrictions in qualifying, expenses involved with setting up and maintaining the subchapter S status, and the fact that a subchapter S corporation is limited to 100 shareholders.[36] If a subchapter S corporation wants to include more than 100 shareholders, it must convert to a C corporation or a limited liability company.

Limited Liability Company

The **limited liability company (LLC)** is a form of business organization that is rapidly gaining popularity. The concept originated in Germany and was first introduced in the United States in 1978. Along with the subchapter S corporation, it is a popular choice for start-up firms. As with partnerships and corporations, the profits of an LLC flow through to the tax returns of the owners and are not subject to double taxation. The main advantage of the LLC is that all partners enjoy limited liability. This differs from regular and limited partnerships, where at least one partner is liable for the debts of the partnership. The LLC combines the limited liability advantage of the corporation with the tax advantages of the partnership.[37] DreamWorks SKG, the movie studio started by Steven Spielberg, Jeffrey Katzenberg, and David Geffen, was an LLC until it went public in late 2004.

Some of the terminology used for an LLC differs from the other forms of business ownership. For example, the shareholders of an LLC are called "members," and instead of owning stock, the members have "interests." The LLC is more flexible than a subchapter S corporation in terms of number of owners and tax-related issues. An LLC must be a private business—it cannot be publicly traded. If at some point the members want to take the business public and be listed on one of the major stock exchanges, it must be converted to a C corporation.

The LLC is rather complex to set up and maintain, and the rules governing the LLC vary. Members may elect to manage the LLC themselves or may designate one or more managers (who may or may not be members) to run the business on a day-to-day basis. The profits and losses of the business may be allocated to the members anyway they choose. For example, if two people owned an LLC, they could split the yearly profits 50–50, 75–25, 90–10, or any other way they choose.[38]

In summary, the advantages and disadvantages of an LLC are as follows:

Advantages of a Limited Liability Company

■ Members are liable for the debts and obligations of the business only up to the amount of their investment.

■ The number of shareholders is unlimited.

■ An LLC can elect to be taxed as a sole proprietor, partnership, S corporation, or corporation, providing much flexibility.

■ Because profits are taxed only at the shareholder level, there is no double taxation.

Disadvantages of a Limited Liability Company

■ Setting up and maintaining one is more difficult and expensive.

■ Tax accounting can be complicated.

■ Some of the regulations governing LLCs vary.

■ Because LLCs are a relatively new type of business entity, there is not as much legal precedent available for owners to anticipate how legal disputes might affect their businesses.

■ Some governments levy a franchise tax on LLCs—which is essentially a fee the LLC pays the government for the benefit of limited liability.

Chapter Summary

1. The single most important thing the founders of an entrepreneurial venture can do is establish a strong ethical culture in their firms. Three important ways to do this are (1) lead by example, (2) establish a code of conduct, and (3) implement an ethics training program.

2. In the context of "leading by example," three keys to building a strong ethical culture in a firm are (1) having leaders who intentionally make ethics a part of their daily conversations and decision making, (2) supervisors who emphasize integrity when working with their direct reports, and (3) peers who encourage each other to act ethically.

3. A code of ethics and ethics training program are two techniques entrepreneurs use to promote high standards of business ethics in their firms. A code of conduct describes the general value system, moral principles, and specific ethical rules that govern a firm. An ethics training program provides employees with instructions for how to deal with ethical dilemmas when they occur.

4. The criteria important for selecting an attorney for a new firm are shown in Table 7.3. Critical issues include selecting an attorney familiar with the start-up process, selecting an attorney who can assist you in raising money, and making certain that the attorney has a track record of completing work on time.

5. It is important to ensure that a venture's founders agree on their relative interests in the venture and their commitment to its future. A founders' (or shareholders') agreement is a written document dealing with issues such as the split of equity between or among the founders of the firm, how individual founders will be compensated for the cash or the "sweat equity" they put into the firm, and how long the founders will have to stay with the firm for their shares to fully vest.

6. Suggestions for how new firms can avoid litigation include meeting all contractual obligations, avoiding undercapitalization, getting everything in writing, and promoting business ethics in the firm.

7. A nondisclosure agreement is a promise made by an employee or another party (such as a supplier) not to disclose a company's trade secrets. A noncompete agreement prevents an individual from competing against a former employer for a specific period of time.

8. Before a business is launched, a number of licenses and permits are typically needed. They vary by city, county, and province, as well as by type of business, so it's important to study local regulations carefully. In most communities, a business needs a license to operate. Along with obtaining the appropriate licenses, some businesses may need to obtain one or more permits.

9. The major differences among sole proprietorships, partnerships, corporations, and limited liability companies are shown in Table 7.5. These forms of business organization differ in terms of the number of owners allowed, cost of setting up and maintaining, personal liability of owners, continuity of the business, methods of taxation, degree of management control, ease of raising capital, and ease of liquidating investments.

10. Fast-growth firms tend to organize as corporations or limited liability companies for two main reasons: to shield the owners from personal liability for the behavior of the firm and to make it easier to raise capital.

Key Terms

articles of incorporation, **255**
business license, **249**
buyback clause, **244**
C corporation, **255**
closely held corporation, **255**
code of conduct, **238**
common stock, **255**
corporation, **254**
double taxation, **255**
employer identification
  number (EIN), **250**
ethical dilemma, **240**
ethics training programs, **240**

fictitious business name
  permit, **250**
founders' agreement, **244**
general partnership, **253**
illiquid, **256**
limited liability
  company (LLC), **257**
limited partnership, **254**
limited partnership
  agreement, **254**
liquid market, **255**
liquidity, **251**
mediation, **247**

noncompete agreement, **247**
nondisclosure agreement, **247**
partnership agreement, **253**
piercing the corporate veil, **255**
preferred stock, **255**
private corporation, **255**
public corporations, **255**
shareholders, **255**
sole proprietorship, **251**
stock options, **256**
subchapter
  S corporation, **256**

Review Questions

1. When should your friend, who is considering launching a consulting firm to provide financial services to small businesses, think about the ethical climate she wants to establish in her venture?

2. In general, do entrepreneurs tend to overestimate or underestimate their knowledge of the laws that pertain to starting a new firm? What does the answer to this question suggest that entrepreneurs do before they start a firm?

3. Why is it important for an entrepreneur to build a strong ethical culture for the firm? What are some of the specific steps that an entrepreneurial venture can take to build a strong ethical culture?

4. Describe what is meant by the terms *code of conduct* and *ethics training programs*. What is their purpose?

5. What are some of the more important criteria to consider when selecting an attorney for a new firm?

6. Describe what a founders' agreement is and why it's important for a team of entrepreneurs to have one in place when launching a venture.

7. Describe the purpose of a nondisclosure agreement and the purpose of a noncompete agreement.

8. Describe several ways entrepreneurial ventures can avoid legal disputes.

9. Explain what mediation is and how mediation is used to resolve disputes.

10. At what point, during the process of starting a firm, does a business need to focus on the business licenses and permits that it needs? Are business licenses and permits the same in all cities and provinces or do they vary?

11. Why is it important for the founders of a firm to think carefully about the name they pick for their company?

12. The following statement appears in this chapter: "Choosing a legal entity (for an entrepreneurial venture) is not a one-time event." Why isn't choosing a legal entity a one-time event? What might trigger a firm's decision to change how it is legally organized?

13. What are the advantages and disadvantages of organizing a new firm as a sole proprietorship? Is a sole proprietorship an appropriate form of ownership for an aggressive entrepreneurial firm? Why or why not?

14. Describe the differences between a general partnership and a limited partnership. Is a general partnership an appropriate form of ownership for two people pooling their resources to start a high-growth entrepreneurial firm?

15. What are the major advantages and disadvantages of a C corporation? How is a C corporation subject to double taxation?

16. What is the difference between preferred stock and common stock? Who gets paid first in the event of liquidation—the preferred stockholders or the common stockholders?

17. What is meant by the term *piercing the corporate veil*? What are the implications for the owners of a corporation if the corporate veil is pierced?

18. What are the differences between a public corporation, a closely held corporation, and a private corporation? Which type of corporation enjoys the highest level of liquidity for its stock?

19. What are stock options? Why would a corporation offer stock options to its employees?

20. What are the advantages and disadvantages of a limited liability company? Is a limited liability company an appropriate form of ownership for an aggressive entrepreneurial firm?

Application Questions

1. Assume that Merrill Guerra, the founder of RealKidz (the company focused on at the beginning of the chapter), has asked you to help her write a code of conduct for her firm. Given your understanding of RealKidz's business model and its priorities, put together a table of contents for RealKidz's code of conduct.

2. Suppose you are talking to a friend who is launching a company to manufacture and sell super energy-efficient light fixtures about how to establish an ethical culture in his firm. Your friend says to you, "I know that having a code of conduct and offering ethics training to my employees is important, but I think I'll hold off on those things initially. What's most important is the example that I set for my employees." How would you respond to your friend's statement?

3. Jason, Martin, and Marie are working on an idea for a new company, which they hope to launch within three months. Marie is pressuring Jason and Martin to accompany her to see an attorney to draw up a founders' agreement and talk about legal issues in general. Both Jason and Martin think Marie is jumping the gun and don't see the need to spend money for a founders' agreement or an attorney until the firm has been operating for a

few weeks. If you were asked to weigh in on this disagreement, would you side with Marie or Jason and Martin? Explain your decision.

4. The "You Be the VC 7.1" feature focuses on Velib, a company that is encouraging people to give up their cars in favor of pedal power with an easy-to-use, self-service, bike-for-hire system. Spend some time studying Velib. Other than the ethical and legal issues that confront all firms, what special issues do you think Velib should be particularly attentive to?

5. Kelly Peterson owns an electronics firm in Pittsburgh. He has told you that he has been suffering some cash flow problems, but has avoided having to borrow money by letting some of his bills run late and by cutting corners on meeting some of his contractual obligations. When you raised your eyebrows as he told you this, he said, "Don't worry; I'm really not nervous about it. I have some big orders coming in, and am confident I can catch up on my bills and renegotiate my contracts then." Do you think Kelly has a sound strategy? What could he be doing differently? What are the downsides to what Kelly is currently doing?

6. Nancy Wills is purchasing a business named Niagara Laser Optics near Buffalo, New York. The business has had several brushes with the law during the past several years, dealing with claims of false advertising and wrongful termination of employees. As a result, Nancy is very concerned about the ethical culture of the firm. What specific techniques could Nancy use to increase the emphasis placed on business ethics when she takes control of the firm?

7. Assume you are opening a restaurant near the college or university you attend and have decided to name it *Campus Burger, Fries, and Shakes.* Based on the location of your college or university, identify the specific business licenses and permits you would need to open your business.

8. A classmate of yours is starting a company that is designed to help high school athletes maximize their chances of obtaining a college scholarship. The company will help athletes put together highlight films of their high school accomplishments, write letters of introduction to college coaches, and manage the process of prospecting and communicating with college coaches and administrators. Based on the material in Appendix 7.1, suggest a name for the business. Explain how the name will help the company communicate its purpose and build its brand.

9. Of the "You Be the VC" features included in Chapters 1 through 7 of this book, which do you think has the best name for its business, and which do you think has the worst name? Explain your selections and the criteria you used to make your determinations.

10. Melanie Keeley, a classmate of yours, recently talked to an attorney about the issues that she should think about as she determines the form of business ownership that is most suitable for her firm. One thing the attorney told her to focus on is the extent to which the form of business ownership she chooses shields her from personal liability for her business. Melanie is not sure she fully understands this point. Clarify for Melanie specifically what the attorney was referring to and the forms of business ownership that will shield her from personal liability for her business.

11. For an entrepreneurial start-up, what situation would favor organizing as a subchapter S corporation rather than as a limited liability company? What situation would favor a limited liability company over a subchapter S corporation?

12. Brian just formed a C corporation. The shareholders of the corporation will be Brian and his wife Carrie and his father Bob, who put $35,000 of cash into the business. Brian explained to his wife and dad that he organized the business as a C corporation because of the ease of transfer of ownership of the stock. He said that if any of the three of them wanted his or her money out of the corporation, that person could simply find a buyer for the

stock, just like the shareholders of Microsoft and other large public corporations do, and transfer the ownership. Does Brian have realistic expectations regarding the ease of getting out of his investment if he wants to? Why or why not?

13. You have been approached by a close family friend who is putting together a limited liability company to purchase a condominium complex near Cocoa Beach in Florida. He is asking you along with a number of family members and friends to each invest $10,000 in his company. The condominium complex is for sale for $5 million. Your friend hopes to convince 50 people to invest $10,000 apiece, which will raise $500,000, and borrow the remaining $4.5 million to close the deal. You told your friend, "I don't mind investing the $10,000, but I'm really nervous about being on the hook for a $4.5 million loan if the deal goes bad. Your friend insists that all you will have at risk is your $10,000 and you won't be liable for anything else, no matter what happens. Is your friend right or wrong? Explain your answer.

14. Determine specifically what the requirements are for starting a limited liability company in your area. Indicate what forms need to be filed, where they can be obtained, how the filing process works, and what fees are involved.

15. Laura just took a job with Cisco Systems in San Jose, California. One of the things that attracted her to Cisco was the stock option plan that Cisco offers its employees. Explain what is meant by a stock option plan and why a company such as Cisco Systems would offer stock options to its employees.

You Be the VC 7.1

Company: Velib

www.velib.paris.fr

Business Idea: Reduce traffic congestion, air pollution, and wear and tear on the nation's highways by introducing an easy-to-use, self-service, bike-for-hire system.

Pitch: Traffic congestion is stressful, causes air pollution, and costs millions in tax revenue to keep roads in good repair. Now one company is encouraging people to give up their cars in favor of pedal power. Velib, located in Paris, France, is pioneering the concept of a public bicycle rental program.

On July 15, 2007, 10,000 bicycles were introduced to the city, along with 750 automated rental stations, which hold 15 bicycles each. Customers pay a deposit of $200 for an unlimited number of rentals and are then given a charge card, which also detaches the bikes from the cycle racks. The first half hour is free and thereafter it costs as little as $1.30 an hour, and there is unlimited access for 24 hours a day. The bike does not need to be returned to the same pick-up point. Customers can pick up one of the distinctive gray bicycles from a rack near the Eiffel Tower, cycle to the Pantheon, and leave it at the nearest Velib stand there. Twenty trucks are used each night to redistribute the bicycles to high-demand stations.

Theft is kept to a minimum by the heavy design of the bikes. The parking facilities are also secure, and the credit card deposit system deters users from "forgetting" to return the bikes, because fines can be collected directly from the card. The service is primarily aimed at people who are making short journeys, and there are currently more than 190,000 people signed up for the service, with 94 percent saying they are very satisfied. Each bicycle is used on average 30 times a day, and the average trip time is just 18 minutes. Visitors to the city can take out short-term subscriptions by simply using their credit cards directly at the cycle rack terminals.

The service is financed by family-controlled advertising company JCDecaux, which provides the bikes in return for an exclusive contract to sell outdoor advertising in prime locations around Paris. JCDecaux paid start-up costs of around $115 million and is signed up to operate and repair the bikes for 10 years.

Since the launch, the number of bicycles available for hire has doubled to 20,000, and the number of rental stations has increased to 1,450. City officials say traffic has been reduced by 5 percent in the French capital.

Q&A: Based on the material covered in this chapter, what questions would you ask the firm's founders before making your funding decision? What answers would satisfy you?

Decision: If you had to make your decision on just the information provided in the pitch and on the company's Web site, would you fund this firm? Why or why not?

You Be the VC 7.2
Company: Jaman
www.jaman.com

Business Idea: Create an online platform that provides independent filmmakers a place to post, showcase, and market their films, and allows users the opportunity to discover, watch, and enjoy independent films and movies.

Pitch: Finding a way to distribute their films is the biggest obstacle independent filmmakers confront. Even films that do well at independent film festivals find it difficult to strike distribution deals that enable their films to be seen. Jaman is an online platform that provides an alternative for independent filmmakers. Filmmakers can post their films on Jaman's Web site, and viewers from around the world can browse and select from Jaman's library of thousands of unique films and then view the firms either for free or for a fee on their PCs, Macs, televisions, or home-set-top boxes. The free films are supported by advertising and the pay-per view films are available for as low as $1.99 per week for viewing. Jaman is building a global audience for its site by reaching out to independent filmmakers and film production companies around the world to post their material. For example, Jaman has signed deals with Celestial Pictures in Hong Kong for Chinese-language films and Venevision International for Spanish-language films. Jaman is aggressively pursuing similar partnerships.

Jaman's site supports cutting-edge technology that enables users to either download movies to the devices they'll use to play them or watch them immediately on their Web browser (depending on the movie). To facilitate conversation about the independent films listed on its site, Jaman supports a forum where people can review, discuss, and recommend films to one another.

Along with making its platform available to independent filmmakers, Jaman's goal is to act as a conduit through which immigrant communities in the United States have access to films from their native countries. The three communities the site is focusing on initially are the Latino community, people from Greater China, and the Indian subcontinent. The founders of Jaman believe that these are underserved film markets in North America, and the majority of the movies from these countries (including the countries of origin for the Latino immigrant population in the United States) never get distribution in North America. Jaman makes money through a split of the advertising revenue and the pay-per-view revenue generated by the films that are posted on its site.

Q&A: Based on the material covered in this chapter, what questions would you ask the firm's founders before making your funding decision? What answers would satisfy you?

Decision: If you had to make your decision on just the information provided in the pitch and on the company's Web site, would you fund this company? Why or why not?

CASE7.1

Preparing a Proper Legal Foundation: A Start-Up Fable

Bruce R. Barringer
Oklahoma State University
R. Duane Ireland
Texas A & M University

Introduction

Jack Peterson and Sarah Jones are planning to start a business. Their plan is to locate and operate 10 kiosks in malls and other high-traffic areas to sell accessories for Apple iPods and iPhones. To complement their accessory sales, the two have created a series of short videos that help users learn how to make better use of their iPods and iPhones. The videos will be sold or used as value-added promotions and will be delivered via streaming video on Jack and Sarah's Web site. Customers will be provided access codes to retrieve the videos from the Web site, which will also sell additional iPod and iPhone accessories.

The tentative name for the business is iUser Accessories. Jack and Sarah like to use the word *tentative* because they aren't completely sold on the name. The Internet domain name, www.iuseraccessories.com, was available, so they registered it on GoDaddy.com. Part of their start-up funding will be used to hire a trademark attorney to do a formal trademark search before they use the name or do any advertising.

Jack and Sarah met in an introduction to entrepreneurship course at their local university. They hit it off while working on the initial business plan for iUser Accessories, which they completed as an assignment for the class. Their senior year, they refined the plan by working on it during a business planning class. They took first place in a university-wide business plan competition just before graduation. The win netted them $7,500 in cash and $7,500 in "in-kind" services for the business. Their plan was to use the money to establish a relationship with an accountant affiliated with the university.

Feasibility Analysis and Business Plan

As part of their business plan, Jack and Sarah completed a product feasibility analysis for iUser Accessories. They first developed a concept statement and distributed it to a total of 16 people, including professors, electronic store owners, iPod and iPhone users, and the parents of young iPod users. The responses were both positive and instructive. The idea to distribute the videos dealing with how to better use your iPod and iPhone, via streaming video over the Internet, and providing customers access codes to retrieve the videos, came directly from one of the concept statement participants. Jack and Sarah's original idea was to distribute this material in a more conventional manner. The person who came up with the idea wrote on the bottom of the concept statement, "Not only will this approach save you money (by not having to distribute actual videos) but it will drive traffic to your Web site and provide you with additional e-commerce opportunities."

Following the concept statement, Jack and Sarah surveyed 410 people in their target market, which is 15- to 35-year-olds. They did this by approaching people wherever they could and politely asking them to complete the survey. They persuaded one of their marketing professors to help them with the survey's design, to make sure it generalized to a larger population. They learned that 52 percent of the people in their target market own an iPod or iPhone or plan to get one soon. The survey also listed a total of 26 iPod and iPhone accessories, which are available through vendors that Jack and Sarah have access to. The results affirmed Jack and Sarah's notion that the vast majority of people in their target market don't realize the number of iPod and iPhone accessories that exist, let alone know where to get them. They also were pleased with the high degree of interest expressed by the survey participants in learning more about many of the accessories.

Start-Up Capital

As part of their business plan, Jack and Sarah completed one- and three-year pro forma financial statements, which demonstrate the potential viability of their business. They have commitments for $66,000 of funding from friends and family. According to their projections, they should be cash-flow positive within four months and will not need any additional infusions of cash, unless they expand the business beyond the scope of their original business plan. The projections include salaries of $32,000 per year for both Jack and Sarah, who will both work more than 40 hours a week manning the kiosks and running the business.

Jack and Sarah are fortunate in that they are able to each contribute $3,000 to the business personally and were able to gain commitments of

$30,000 each from their respective groups of friends and family. A year or so ago they participated in a class offered by their local Small Business Development Center (SBDC) about how to start a business and remembered an attorney saying that's it all right to talk to people about funding prior to talking to an attorney but don't actually accept any money until you have your legal ducks in order. As a result, other than their own money, Jack and Sarah didn't actually have the $66,000 yet. They can accumulate it within 30 days once they are confident that the business is a go.

Preparing for the Meeting with the Attorney

Jack and Sarah plan to launch their business on September 15, just two months prior to the start of the busy Christmas season. They spent some time asking around the business school and the technology incubator attached to their university to identify the name of a good small-business attorney. They identified an attorney and made the appointment. The appointment was scheduled for 2:15 P.M. on July 16 at the attorney's office.

Another take-away that Jack and Sarah gleaned from the SBDC class was to plan carefully the time you spend with an attorney, to make best use of your time and minimize expenses. As a result, prior to the meeting, Jack and Sarah planned to spend several evenings at a local Borders bookstore, looking at books that deal with forms of business ownership and other legal issues and making a concise list of issues to discuss with the attorney. They had also gone over this material in preparing their business plan. In the meeting with the attorney, they want to be as well informed as possible and actually lead the discussion and make recommendations. Sarah's dad is a real estate agent and had dealt with many attorneys during his career. One thing he told her, in helping her prepare for this meeting, is that attorneys are helpful and necessary but shouldn't make your decisions for you. Sarah shared this insight with Jack, and they were both determined to follow that advice in their upcoming meeting.

Jack and Sarah's Recommendations

To put their list on paper and get started, Jack created the document at the top of the next column.

Jack and Sarah spent the next several evenings completing this list and talking about their business. When they made the call to set up the meeting with the attorney, the attorney told them that she wasn't an intellectual property lawyer, and if it looked like the business was a go after their meeting, she could arrange for them to talk to one of her partners who specialized in patent and trademark law. As a result, Jack and Sarah knew that this meeting would focus more on forms of business ownership and general

Jack Peterson and Sarah Jones

Founders, iUser Accessories

List of Legal Issues to Discuss with Attorney

Issue	**Jack and Sarah's Recommendation**

legal issues, and they would address their intellectual property questions at another meeting.

The Day Arrives

The day for the meeting arrived, and Jack and Sarah met at the attorney's office at 2:15 P.M. They had e-mailed the attorney their list of issues along with their recommendations a week prior to the meeting. The attorney greeted them with a firm handshake and opened a file labeled "iUser Accessories, Jack Peterson and Sarah Jones." Seeing their names like that, on an attorney's file, made it seem like their company was already real. The attorney looked at both of them and placed a copy of the list they had e-mailed in front of her. The list already had a number of handwritten notes on it. The attorney smiled and said to Jack and Sarah, "Let's get started."

Discussion Questions

1. Complete Jack and Sarah's list for them, including the issues you think they will place on the list along with their recommendations. Which of the issues do you think will stimulate the most discussion with the attorney, and which issues do you think will stimulate the least?
2. Make a list of the things you think Jack and Sarah did right in preparing for their meeting with the attorney.
3. Comment on the product feasibility analysis that Jack and Sarah completed. Do you think the way Jack and Sarah approached this task was appropriate and sufficient?
4. What advantages do Jack and Sarah have starting iUser Accessories together, rather than one of them starting it as a sole entrepreneur? What challenges do you think Jack and Sarah will have keeping their partnership together?

(continued)

Application Questions

1. Suggest an alternative to iUser Accessories for the name of Jack and Sarah's firm. Check to see if the ".com" version of the Internet domain name is available. If it isn't, select another name and continue selecting names until you can match a name with an available domain name.

2. Do you think it is too early for Jack and Sarah to start laying an ethical foundation for their firm? What steps can they take now to lay a solid ethical foundation for their firm?

CASE7.2

TOMS Shoes: Combining Social Consciousness and Profits
www.tomsshoes.com

Bruce R. Barringer
Oklahoma State University
R. Duane Ireland
Texas A & M University

Introduction

If you ever wondered if you could combine an entrepreneurial itch with a social cause and make money doing it, Blake Mycoskie, the founder of TOMS Shoes, is someone you should meet. TOMS has a simple yet inspiring business model. For every pair of shoes it sells, it gives a pair away to a child in need.

Origin of TOMS

In 2005 Mycoskie, a serial entrepreneur, needed a break. After starting five companies in 12 years, he traveled to Argentina looking for some time to relax, experience the culture, and take it all in. He met some expatriates who were doing social work in villages on the outskirts of Buenos Aires and asked if he could tag along. In one village in particular, he noticed that most of the children didn't have shoes. He stopped a few of the kids to look at their feet and saw cuts, abrasions, and infections. He knew the villagers were poor and couldn't afford to buy their children shoes and wondered what he could do to help. He also knew that there was an inexpensive shoe in Argentina called the alpargata. What would be the best way to provide poor Argentinean children alpargata shoes?

Mycoskie thought about starting a charity but felt the charity model wouldn't work. He envisioned himself asking his family and friends for contributions, and knew they would contribute once, or twice, or maybe even several times. But it would be hard to continue to ask. What he needed was an approach that would sustain itself by a product that people needed to buy anyway. That's when Mycoskie came up with the idea for TOMS. In an interview with Treehugger Radio in fall 2008 Mycoskie recalls:

> The idea that day on the farm was, "I'm going to make this shoe. I'm going to make this traditional Argentine shoe that people haven't seen (in the U.S.) yet. I'm going to sell it and for every pair I sell, I'm going to give one back to these kids in Argentina until they all have shoes. I'm going to continue to do it so they always have shoes." That was the idea 2 $\frac{1}{2}$ years ago and it hasn't changed one bit since.

Creating a Business

Mycoskie returned to the United States and set up shop in Santa Monica, California. He started TOMS with no shoe industry experience. The company was originally called Shoes for Tomorrow but was quickly shortened to TOMS. The mainstay TOMS is a canvas slip-on shoe. They are made out of organic canvas and postconsumer recycled plastic, which makes them lightweight and environmentally friendly. The shoes were originally made in Argentina but are now made in several places around the world. Strict fair-labor and fair-trade practices are observed in all TOMS factories, consistent with the company's humanitarian mission. Mycoskie admits that the first year and a half TOMS was in existence he did a good job of telling the company's story but a poor job of making shoes. So he hired some folks from Nike, Asics, and Tommy Bahama and now makes good shoes.

TOMS currently has 36 employees and 30 interns working in its home office. The employees and interns are mostly people who have fallen in love with the TOMS concept. Because TOMS has such a compelling story, its message has spread primarily via word of mouth. TOMS also makes extensive use of YouTube, Facebook, and MySpace as mediums for spreading the word. In fact, take a few minutes next time you are at your computer and watch the TOMS "Shoe Drop" video on YouTube. It will tug at your heartstrings as it has thousands of other people.

TOMS involves its customers and volunteers in its activities, which is another way of keeping its message alive. Every two weeks a group of 15 TOMS volunteers travels to Argentina or another part of the world to make a "shoe drop"—which is the term TOMS uses for giving away shoes. Anyone can apply to make the trip. It's a very personal experience. Each shoe given away by the company is placed on a child by a TOMS volunteer. Volunteers pay their own travel expenses, but the trip is arranged by TOMS. TOMS has made shoe drops in the United States as well. Most of the U.S. drops have taken place in the Gulf Coast regions hardest hit by Hurricane Katrina and other storms.

Although TOMS is still a start-up it has struck licensing deals with Ralph Lauren and several department stores, and has distribution deals in place with Nordstrom, Urban Outfitters, Whole Foods, and a number of others retailers. TOMS's pledge to give away a pair of shoes for every pair it sells is prominently displayed wherever its shoes are sold.

Challenges of Mixing Philanthropy and Profits

Not everything has been smooth sailing for Mycoskie and TOMS. As of fall 2008 the company had not reached profitability. It has experienced some difficulty scaling its operations, which is not uncommon for a rapidly growing firm. According to Mycoskie's interview with Treehugger, while it's nice to distribute through a large retailer like Nordstrom, Nordstrom is used to dealing with large shoe companies like Nike and Tory Burke, which can result in frustrations. So when TOMS has trouble keeping up with a large retailer's demand, the exchange, according to Mycoskie, will go something like this:

"Dude, why can't you ship this at the right time?" We are like, "Because we have one person trying to ship to 400 stores."

Another challenge that TOMS has, which Mycoskie talks openly about, is that people may eventually tire of its shoes, regardless of how much they believe in the concept. As a result, TOMS is designing new styles of shoes, consistent with its mission. There is another Argentine shoe in the works that will come out in 2009 or 2010, which is a more year-round shoe than the alpargate shoe. TOMS just launched a new product, which is called the wrap boot. It's only for women and is very stylish. It's both a departure and a close cousin of the traditional alpargate shoe. To keep its mission fresh, TOMS may at some point reach beyond shoes. It will only do so if Mycoskie and his team find another cause that TOMS is uniquely equip to tackle.

The jury is still out regarding TOMS's ability to operate profitably. Although the company's philanthropy is the reason many of its customers buy TOMS's shoes, giving away a pair of shoes for every one its sells takes a toll on the bottom line. Because of this, Mycoskie readily admits that TOMS will probably never be "really profitable."

Discussion Questions

1. Based on what you know about TOMS, from the feature and the company's Web site, what ethical and legal issues, other than those that all firms grapple with, should TOMS be particularly attentive to? How can TOMS avoid ethical and/or legal mishaps in these areas?
2. If TOMS initiated an ethics training program, which issues do you think it would focus on the most?
3. Do you think consumers are willing to pay more for a product when they know that a portion of their purchase price will go to a good cause? If so, how important is this sentiment to TOMS? How effectively does TOMS communicate its mission and socially conscious principles to its customers?
4. What forms of business organization would be appropriate for TOMS? Explain your answer.

Application Questions

1. How should TOMS handle it if at some point it becomes economically unfeasibility to give away a pair of shoes for every pair it sells? For instance, if TOMS decided to shift to a model of giving away one pair of shoes for every two pairs that it sells, how should it communicate that decision to its stakeholders?
2. What can a business that wants to operate in a socially conscious manner, but doesn't have the mission and business model that emphasizes social consciousness or philanthropy to the extent that TOMS does, learn from TOMS's experiences?

Source: "Jason Gordon and Blake Mycoskie," Treehugger Radio Podcast (Part 1 and Part 2), September 18, 2008.

Endnotes

1. A. McConnon, "Bigger Kids Want to Dress Cool Too, *Business Week*, June 19, 2008.
2. RealKidz homepage, www.realkidz.com (accessed December 9, 2008).
3. Personal conversation with Merrill Guerra, December 5, 2008.
4. R. T. Peterson, "Small Retailers and Service Company Accuracy in Evaluating the Legality of Specified Practices," *Journal of Small Business Management* 39, no. 4 (2001): 312–19.
5. C. Caggiano, "A Strategic Misalliance," *Inc.*, October 2002.
6. *National Business Ethics Survey, An Inside View of Private Sector Ethics* (Washington, DC: Ethics Resource Center, 2007).
7. *National Business Ethics Survey*, 2007.
8. Wikipedia, "Ethical Code," www.wikipedia.org (accessed December 5, 2008).
9. *National Business Ethics Survey*, 2007.
10. Character Training International homepage, www.character-ethics.org (accessed December 8, 2008).
11. T. Friedman, *Hot, Flat, and Crowded* (New York: Farrar, Straus and Giroux, 2008).
12. T. Monosoff, *The Mom Inventors Handbook* (New York: McGraw-Hill, 2005).
13. C. E. Bagley, *Legal Aspects of Entrepreneurship: A Conceptual Framework* (Cambridge, MA: Harvard Business School Publishing, 2002).
14. B. A. Garner, Editor, *Black's Law Dictionary* (St. Paul, MN; West Group, 2002).
15. K. W. Clarkson, R. L. Miller, G. A. Jentz, and F. B. Cross, *West's Business Law* (New York: West Educational Publishing, 1998).
16. J. A. Fraser, "Cash Flow: When a Cash Crisis Strikes," *Inc.*, February 1, 1996, 104.
17. C. Sutton, "Cash Is King, Hard Lessons Some Small-Business Owners and Managers Forgot!" www.smallbusinessanswers.com (accessed July 28, 2008); A. J. Sherman, *Fast-Track Business Growth* (Washington, DC: Kiplinger Washington Editors, 2001).
18. C. Frank, "Get Everything in Writing," The Kauffman Foundation, www.entrepreneurship.org/Resources/Detail/Default.aspx?id=11328 (accessed December 12, 2008, originally posted July 1, 2000).
19. M. Clark, *The Bear Necessities of Business* (New York: Wiley, 2006), 112.
20. C. E. Bagley, *Legal Aspects of Entrepreneurship: A Conceptual Framework* (Cambridge, MA: Harvard Business School Publishing, 2002), 17.
21. A. Gerlin, "A Matter of Degree: How a Jury Decided That a Coffee Spill Is Worth $2.7 Million," *Wall Street Journal*, September 1, 1994.
22. S. Barlyn, "Name That Firm," *Wall Street Journal*, March 16, 2008, R7.
23. H. R. Cheeseman, *The Legal Environment of Business and Online Commerce* 5th ed. (Upper Saddle River, NJ: Pearson Education, 2007).
24. M. C. Ehrhardt and E. F. Brigham, *Corporate Finance* (Cincinnati: South-Western, 2003).
25. "General Partnership," TraderStatus.Com homepage, www.traderstatus.com (accessed August 5, 2006); A. J. Sherman, *The Complete Guide to Running and Growing Your Business* (New York: Random House, 1997).
26. *Black's Law Dictionary.*
27. Sherman, *The Complete Guide to Running and Growing Your Business.*
28. R. A. Brealty and S. C. Myers, *Financing and Risk Management* (New York: McGraw-Hill, 2003).
29. *Black's Law Dictionary.*
30. Clarkson et al., *West's Business Law.*
31. Investorwords.com homepage, www.investorwords.com (accessed December 8, 2008).
32. Investorwords.com homepage, www.investorwords.com (accessed December 8, 2008).
33. M. A. Williams and R. P. Rao, "CEO Stock Options and Equity Risk Incentives," *Journal of Business Finance and Accounting* 33 (2006), 26–33.
34. P. K. Zingheim and J. R. Schuster, *Pay People Right!* (San Francisco: Jossey-Bass, 2000).
35. D. O'Donnell, D. McGuire, and C. Cross, "Critically Challenging Some Assumptions in HRD," *International Journal of Training and Development* 19, no. 1 (2006): 4–16.
36. C. E. Bagley and C. E. Dauchy, *The Entrepreneur's Guide to Business Law* (New York: West Educational Publishing, 1998).
37. Ehrhardt and Brigham, *Corporate Finance.*
38. Sherman, *The Complete Guide to Running and Growing Your Business.*

Appendix 7.1   WHAT'S IN A BUSINESS NAME?: A LOT OF TROUBLE IF YOU AREN'T CAREFUL

Introduction

While at first glance naming a business may seem like a minor issue, it is an extremely important one. A company's name is one of the first things people associate with a business, and it is a word or phrase that will be said thousands or hundreds of thousands of times during the life of a firm. A company's name is also the most critical aspect of its branding strategy. A company brand is the unique set of attributes that allow consumers to separate it from its competitors. As a result, it is important that a business choose its name carefully so that it will facilitate rather than hinder how the business wants to differentiate itself in the marketplace.

If an entrepreneur isn't careful, the process of naming a business can also result in a peck of trouble. There are a number of legal issues involved in naming a business, which should be taken seriously. If a business selects a name and later finds out that it's already been legally taken, the business may have to (1) amend its articles of incorporation, (2) change its Internet domain name, (3) obtain new listings in telephone and other directories, (4) purchase new stationery and business cards, (5) redo signage and advertising, and (6) incur the expense and potential embarrassment of introducing a new name to its customers. These are complications that no entrepreneur wants to endure. The following case describes the strategies for naming a business along with the legal issues involved.

Strategies for Naming a Business

The primary consideration in naming a company is that the name should complement the type of business the company plans to be. It is helpful to divide companies into four categories to discuss this issue.

Consumer-Driven Companies

If a company plans to focus on a particular type of customer, its name should reflect the attributes of its clientele. For example, a high-end clothing store that specializes in small sizes for women is called La Petite Femme. Similarly, the company described in Case 2.1, "CarePages," helps caregivers keep relatives and friends of someone who is in the hospital up-to-date on their condition. These companies have names that were chosen to appeal specifically to their target market or clientele.

Product- or Service-Driven Companies

If a company plans to focus on a particular product or service, its name should reflect the advantages that its product or service brings to the marketplace. Examples include Jiffy Print, ServiceMaster, and 1-800-FLOWERS. These names were chosen to reflect the distinctive attributes of the product or service the company offers, regardless of the clientele.

Industry-Driven Companies

If a company plans to focus on a broad range of products or services in a particular industry, its name should reflect the category it is participating in. Examples include General Motors, Bed Bath & Beyond, and Home Depot. These companies have names that are intentionally broad and are not limiting in regard to target market or product selection.

Personality- or Image-Driven Companies

Some companies are founded by individuals who put such an indelible stamp on the company that it may be smart to name the company after the founder. Examples include Liz Claiborne, Walt Disney, Charles Schwab, The Trump Organization, and Magic Johnson Enterprises. These companies have names that benefit from a positive association with a popular or distinctive founder. Of course, this strategy can backfire if the founder falls out of favor in the public's eye.

While names come to some business owners easily, for others it's a painstaking process. It was a painstaking process for JetBlue, as described in the book *Blue Streak*, which is a chronology of the early years of JetBlue. According to Barbara Peterson, the book's author, David Neeleman, the founder of JetBlue, and his initial management team agonized over what to name the company and considered literally hundreds of names before settling on JetBlue. JetBlue was launched in 1999. Neeleman felt that a strong brand would surmount the handicap of being a new airline and believed that the company's name was the key to building its brand. A list of some of the alternative names that Neeleman and his management team seriously considered for JetBlue is shown at top of facing page. Today, it's hard to think of JetBlue as anything other than JetBlue, which illustrates the power of branding.

Names That Were Seriously Considered for JetBlue

Air Hop	Egg
Scout Air	It
Competition	Blue
Home	Fair Air
Air Taxi	Scout
Avenues	Hi! Way
Civilization Airways	True Blue

Legal Issues Involved in Naming a Business

The general rule for business names is that they must be unique. In other words, in most instances, there may not be more than one business per name per state. In addition, a business may not have a name that is confusingly similar to another business. This regulation prevents a software company from naming itself Macrosoft, for example, which Microsoft would undoubtedly claim is confusingly similar to its name.

To determine whether a name is available in a particular state, the entrepreneur must usually contact the secretary of state's office to see if a particular name is available. The inquiry can typically be accomplished over the phone or by mail. If the name is available, the next step is to reserve it in the manner recommended by the secretary of state's office. Many attorneys and incorporation services include this step in the fee-based services they offer to entrepreneurs and their ventures.

Once a name that is available has been chosen, it should be trademarked. The process for obtaining a trademark is straightforward and relatively inexpensive, given the protection it provides. A full explanation of how to obtain a trademark is provided in Chapter 12 of this book.

The entire process of naming a business is often very frustrating for entrepreneurs, because it is becoming increasingly difficult to find a name that isn't already taken. For example, if an entrepreneur was planning to open a new quick-printing service, almost every possible permutation of the word *printing* with words like *quick*, *swift*, *fast*, *rapid*, *speedy*, *jiffy*, *express*, *instant*, and so forth are taken. In addition, sometimes names that work in one culture don't work in another, which is something that should be taken into consideration. The classic example of this is the Chevy NOVA. After much advertising and fanfare, the car received a very cool reception in Mexico. It turned out that the phrase *no va* in Spanish means "Doesn't Go." Not surprisingly, the NOVA didn't sell well in Mexico.

As a result of these complications, and for other reasons, entrepreneurs use a variety of other strategies when naming their business. Some names are simply made up, because the firm wants a name that is catchy or distinctive, or because it needs to make up a name to get an Internet domain name that isn't already taken (more about this later). Examples of names that were made up include Exxon, Cingular, Verizon, eBay, Google, and Xerox. Some of these names are made up with the help of marketing research firms that use sophisticated methodologies such as an evaluation of the "linguistic properties" (will a consumer read the name properly?), the "phonetic transparency" (is it spelled as it sounds?), and the "multilingual functionality" (is it as intelligible in Japanese as in English?) of a particular name. All of these issues are potentially important. Several years ago Anderson Consulting changed its name to Accenture. The pronunciation of "Accenture" isn't obvious, which has been a problem for the firm ever since.

Internet Domain Names

A final complicating factor in selecting a name for a company is registering an Internet domain name. A domain name is a company's Internet address (e.g., www.intel.com). Most companies want their domain name to be the same as their company's name. It is easy to register a domain name through an online registration service such as GoDaddy.com (www.godaddy.com). The standard fee for registering and maintaining a domain name is about $9 per year.

Because no two domain names can be exactly the same, frustrations often arise when a company tries to register its domain name and the name is already taken. There are two reasons that a name may already be taken. First, a company may find that another company with the same name has already registered it. For example, if an entrepreneur started a company called Delta Semiconductor, it would find that the domain name www.delta.com is already taken by Delta Airlines. This scenario plays itself out every day and represents a challenge for new firms that have chosen fairly ordinary names. The firm can either select another domain name (such as www.deltasemiconductor.com) or try to acquire the name from its present owner. However, it is unlikely that Delta Airlines would give up www.delta.com for any price. The second reason that a domain name may already be taken is that it might be in the hands of someone who has registered the name with the intention of using it at a later date or of someone who simply collects domain names in hopes that someone will want to buy the name at a higher price. In addition, all of the 1,000 most common English words have been registered, along with the U.S. Census Bureau's list of the 1,219 most common male names, the 2,814 most common female names, and the 10,000 most common surnames.

Still, a little imagination goes a long was in selecting a company name and an Internet domain name. For example, we (your book's authors) made up the name iUser Accessories for the business described in Case 7.1. The Internet domain name www.iuseraccessories.com was available, which we registered on GoDaddy.com for $8.95 per year. What might we do with this Internet domain name? We aren't certain. But, another party deciding to launch an entrepreneurial venture with this name will discover that the hoped-for name is already registered.

CRAIG MARTYN
Founder, BLMA Models
BS in Communications, University of
California Riverside, Anticipated 2010

Getting Personal

with Craig Martyn

CURRENTLY IN MY IPOD
Jimmy Eat World, Relient K,
Senses Fail

BEST ADVICE I'VE RECEIVED
Moderation is everything

**WHAT I'D LIKE TO BE DOING
IN 10 YEARS**
I'd like to have a staff
of extremely talented
individuals who share my
values and strive for
excellence

**MY BIGGEST SURPRISE
AS AN ENTREPRENEUR**
Making money isn't easy?
Ha!

**MY BIGGEST WORRY
AS AN ENTREPRENEUR**
Continue to develop unique
and innovative ideas

**BEST PART OF BEING
A STUDENT**
Learning the formal way to
handle the business—why
reinvent the wheel if you
don't have to

CHAPTEREIGHT

Assessing a New Venture's *Financial Strength* and Viability

OPENING PROFILE

BLMA MODELS
Keeping a Sharp Eye on Cash Flow from the Start
www.bmlamodels.com

Craig Martyn has been interested in trains for as long as he can remember. As a 15-year-old, he made model train accessories and sold them to enthusiasts. His sales steadily increased and he started seeing model trains as a business rather than a hobby. In late 2005, Martyn launched the full-time BLMA Models and began shipping his products to distributors and dealers all over the world.

BLMA Models now sells a broad range of model train freight cars, scenery accessories, and detail parts. The company specializes in model train replicas that are referred to as HO, N, and Z Scale replicas. HO Scale is 1:87 (the most popular), N Scale is 1:160, and Z Scale is 1:220. Martyn takes numerous photographs of the trains and parts he replicates and analyzes blueprints, if available, before CAD (computer-aided design) drawings are produced and a replica is made. BLMA Models sells its products through distributors, directly to stores, and through its Web site. The model train industry is a global industry with over $1.2 billion in annual sales and 500,000 to 1 million participants worldwide.

Early on, BLMA Models sold its products as kits that required assembly on the customer's part. The pieces that went into the kits were designed by Martyn and made by contract manufacturers in the United States. The products were sold in kit form because of the high cost of assembly. By chance encounter, Martyn met an individual at a trade show who put him in contact with two Chinese-based factories that make and assemble model trains. Martyn followed the lead and 50 percent of his products are now made in China. As a result, BLMA Models now sells fully assembled products in addition to kits. The assembled products produce a larger profit margin for BLMA Models.

Cash flow management is the biggest challenge Martyn has experienced in his business. This challenge manifests itself in two ways. First, BLMA Models experiences substantial up-front expenses before a new product earns revenue. A new model freight car, for example, must be researched and designed by Martyn, who uses a contract design engineer to help with the CAD drawings. The Chinese manufacturer must then do the tooling necessary to create molds of the product and adapt its product line. These up-front costs must be paid before a product enters production. Martyn plans new projects on a timeline, so profits from existing products are available to fund the up-front costs of new products. The challenge is that the new products are not always produced on time, and Martyn doesn't have sufficient clout with his Chinese manufacturers to place penalty clauses in his contracts. This complication often causes more money to be outstanding in up-front expenses without corresponding revenue than originally planned. For example, at the time this book went to press, an order for model brass bridges, which will sell for $325 apiece, was

Learning Objectives

After studying this chapter you should be ready to:

1. Explain the two functions of the financial management of a firm.

2. Identify the four main financial objectives of entrepreneurial ventures.

3. Explain the difference between historical and pro forma financial statements.

4. Explain the purpose of an income statement.

5. Explain the purpose of a balance sheet.

6. Explain the purpose of a statement of cash flows.

7. Discuss how financial ratios are used to analyze and interpret a firm's financial statements.

8. Discuss the role of forecasts in projecting a firm's future income and expenses.

9. Explain what a completely new firm bases its forecasts on.

10. Explain what is meant by the term *percent-of-sales method*.

one year late in production. The same scenario applies to other initiatives on which BLMA Models is working. For example, BLMA is exploring the idea of expanding beyond model trains and producing miniature replicas of businesses for companies like In-N-Out Burger in California. In-N-Out Burger sells souvenirs in its stores, like T-shirts and caps that feature a picture of an In-N-Out restaurant. The idea is that BLMA could produce scale replicas of In-N-Out Burger restaurants to be sold with the other souvenir items. If BLMA succeeds and In-N-Out Burger places a large order, that's great for the long term but it will create a short-term cash flow challenge. Just like the production of model trains, substantial up-front costs will be needed to design and set up the manufacturing of the In-N-Out Burger miniatures before corresponding revenue is earned. The second way that cash flow challenges manifest themselves for BLMA Models is that once a production run for a product is complete, it must be paid in full either before it is shipped from China or shortly thereafter. It then takes a period of months for the product to be inventoried and sold.

For Martyn and his company, these challenges are not debilitating because BLMA Models is profitable, there is good demand for its products, and Martyn has obtained a loan from friends and family to provide a cushion in his cash flow. But cash flow management is an ever present concern and is something that Martyn focuses on daily. The key is to keep sufficient cash available to meet BLMA Models' routine cash needs, pay the up-front costs for new projects, and pay for finished products before they are shipped from China.

In terms of overall financial management, Martyn is comfortable with where BLMA Models stands today. He anticipates, however, that as BLMA Models grows, the company will need to prepare more sophisticated financial statements than it currently does and will need to implement more robust financial controls.[1]

In this chapter, we'll look at how new ventures manage their finances and assess their financial strength and viability. For the purposes of completeness, we'll look at how both existing firms and entrepreneurial ventures accomplish these tasks. First, we'll consider general financial management and discuss the financial objectives of a firm and the steps involved in the financial management process. **Financial management** deals with two activities: raising money and managing a company's finances in a way that achieves the highest rate of return.[2] We cover the process of raising money in Chapter 10. This chapter focuses on how a company manages its finances in an effort to increase its financial strength and earn the highest rate of return. Next, we'll examine how existing firms track their financial progress through preparing, analyzing, and maintaining past financial statements. Finally, we'll discuss how both existing firms and start-up ventures forecast future income and expenses and how the forecasts are used to prepare pro forma (i.e., projected) financial statements. Pro forma financial statements, which include the pro forma income statement, the pro forma balance sheet, and the pro forma statement of cash flows, are extremely helpful to firms in financial planning.

INTRODUCTION TO FINANCIAL MANAGEMENT

An entrepreneur's ability to pursue an opportunity and turn the opportunity into a viable entrepreneurial firm hinges largely on the availability of money. Regardless of the quality of a product or service, a company can't be viable in the long run unless it is successful financially. Money either comes from external sources (such as investors or lenders) or is internally generated through earnings. It is important for a firm to have a solid grasp of how it is doing financially. One of the most common mistakes young entrepreneurial firms make is not placing an emphasis on financial management and putting in place appropriate forms of financial controls.[3]

Entrepreneurs and those managing established companies must be aware of how much money they have in the bank and if that amount is sufficient to satisfy their firm's financial obligations. Just because a firm is successful doesn't mean that it doesn't face financial challenges.[4] For example, many of the small firms that sell their products to larger companies such as IBM, General Electric, and The Home Depot don't get paid for 30 to 60 days from the time they make a sale. Think about the difficulty this scenario creates. The small firm must buy parts, pay its employees, pay its routine bills, ship its products, and then wait for one to two months for payment. Unless a firm manages its money carefully, it is easy to run out of cash, even if its products or services are selling like hotcakes.[5] Similarly, as a company grows, its cash demands often increase to service a growing clientele. It is important for a firm to accurately anticipate whether it will be able to fund its growth through earnings or if it will need to look for investment capital or borrowing to raise needed cash.

The financial management of a firm deals with questions such as the following on an ongoing basis:

- How are we doing? Are we making or losing money?
- How much cash do we have on hand?
- Do we have enough cash to meet our short-term obligations?
- How efficiently are we utilizing our assets?
- How do our growth and net profits compare to those of our industry peers?
- Where will the funds we need for capital improvements come from?
- Are there ways we can partner with other firms to share risk and reduce the amount of cash we need?
- Overall, are we in good shape financially?

A properly managed firm stays on top of the issues suggested by these questions through the tools and techniques that we'll discuss in this chapter.

Financial Objectives of a Firm

Most entrepreneurial firms—whether they have been in business for several years or they are start-ups—have four main financial objectives: profitability, liquidity, efficiency, and stability. Understanding these objectives sets a firm on the right financial course and helps it track the answers to the previously posed questions. Figure 8.1 describes each of these objectives.

Profitability is the ability to earn a profit. Many start-ups are not profitable during their first one to three years while they are training employees and building their brands, but a firm must become profitable to remain viable and provide a return to its owners.

Liquidity is a company's ability to meet its short-term financial obligations. Even if a firm is profitable, it is often a challenge to keep enough money in the

Learning Objective

1. Explain the two functions of the financial management of a firm.

Learning Objective

2. Identify the four main financial objectives of entrepreneurial ventures.

FIGURE 8.1

Primary Financial
Objectives of
Entrepreneurial Firms

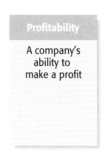

Profitability	Liquidity	Efficiency	Stability
A company's ability to make a profit	A company's ability to meet its short-term obligations	How productively a firm utilizes its assets	The overall health of the financial structure of the firm, particularly as it relates to its debt-to-equity ratio

bank to meet its routine obligations in a timely manner. To do so, a firm must keep a close watch on accounts receivable and inventories. A company's **accounts receivable** is money owed to it by its customers. Its **inventory** is its merchandise, raw materials, and products waiting to be sold. If a firm allows the levels of either of these assets to get too high, it may not be able to keep sufficient cash on hand to meet its short-term obligations.[6]

Efficiency is how productively a firm utilizes its assets relative to its revenue and its profits. Southwest Airlines, for example, uses its assets very productively. Its turnaround time, or the time that its airplanes sit on the ground while they are being unloaded and reloaded, is the lowest in the airline industry. As Southwest officials are quick to point out, "Our planes don't make any money sitting on the ground—we have to get them back into the air."[7]

Stability is the strength and vigor of the firm's overall financial posture. For a firm to be stable, it must not only earn a profit and remain liquid but also keep its debt in check. If a firm continues to borrow from its lenders and its **debt-to-equity ratio**, which is calculated by dividing its long-term debt by its shareholders' equity, gets too high, it may have trouble meeting its obligations and securing the level of financing needed to fuel its growth.

An increasingly common way that small companies improve their prospects across several of these areas is to join buying groups or co-ops, where businesses band together to attain volume discounts on products and services. Gaining access to products and services this way facilitates smaller firms' efforts to compete on more of a "level playing field" with larger, more established companies. The way buying groups work, and how they're able to help businesses cut costs without adversely affecting their competitiveness, is described in the "Partnering for Success" feature.

The Process of Financial Management

To assess whether its financial objectives are being met, firms rely heavily on analyses of financial statements, forecasts, and budgets. A **financial statement** is a written report that quantitatively describes a firm's financial health. The income statement, the balance sheet, and the statement of cash flows are the financial statements entrepreneurs use most commonly. **Forecasts** are an estimate of a firm's future income and expenses, based on its past performance, its current circumstances, and its future plans.[8] New ventures typically base their forecasts on an estimate of sales and then on industry averages or the experiences of similar start-ups regarding the cost of goods sold (based on a percentage of sales) and on other expenses. **Budgets** are itemized forecasts of a company's income, expenses, and capital needs and are also an important tool for financial planning and control.[9]

The process of a firm's financial management is shown in Figure 8.2. It begins by tracking the company's past financial performance through the preparation and analysis of financial statements. These statements organize and report the firm's financial transactions. They tell a firm how much money it is making or losing (income statement), the structure of its assets and liabilities (balance

Partnering for SUCCESS
Organizing Buying Groups to Cuts Costs and Maintain Competitiveness

One challenge that businesses confront is cutting costs in ways that don't erode their ability to remain competitive. Many cost-cutting techniques, such as scaling back on hiring, lowering marketing expenses, or reducing inventory, may save money but may also decrease a business's chances to remain competitive. One technique that can help to conserve a product-based business's financial assets without adverse side effects is to join or organize a buying group.

A buying group, or buying co-op, is a partnership that bands small businesses and start-up firms together to attain volume discounts on products and services. An example is the independent supermarket consortium Coopernic, a not-for-profit European grocery buying group that combines the buying power of retailers in Belgium, France, Switzerland, Germany, and Italy. The cost of running the organization is split among the members, as is the savings made on grocery products. A similar buying group is the U.K.-based United Aftermarket Network, which supplies its members in the vehicle trade with parts from leading motor manufacturers that have been bought at a group discount.

In Thailand, Stockbuz is another successful example of a group-buying operation, which has solved a problem for both yarn producers and manufacturers of apparel. The clothes makers forecast demand based on sales data, seasonality, and retailer feedback and buy fabrics in bulk from the yarn producers. This, in turn, helps reduce market uncertainty for the fabric producers and ensures orders are honored. There are similar buying co-ops in other industries.

The beauty of buying groups is that they generally allow businesses to obtain the exact same product for a lower price, with no undesirable impact (other than the membership fee) on the other parts of their operations. The money that's freed up can go directly to a business's bottom line or be used to invest in customer service or other methods to increase competitiveness. There is no national directory of industry buying groups. The best way to find out whether there are buying groups servicing an industry is to conduct Internet research and ask among industry participants.

Questions for Critical Thinking

1. Which of the four financial objectives of a firm—profitability, liquidity, efficiency, or stability—does participating in a buying cooperative contribute to the most?
2. Do some Internet and/or library research to discern whether there is a small business buying group or groups that New Venture Fitness Drinks, the fictitious company introduced in Chapter 3 and used as an example throughout this chapter, could benefit from. New Venture Fitness Drinks' products contain all the ingredients used to make smoothies and similar fitness drinks and shakes.
3. Identify three ways, other than buying cooperatives, that small businesses partner with other small businesses to cut costs without sacrificing their competitiveness?
4. In an effort to improve the financial position of their firms, do you think the majority of entrepreneurs spend an equal amount of time focusing on (1) cost cutting and (2) increasing revenues? If not, which of the two do you think they spend more time on and why?

sheet), and where its cash is coming from and going (statement of cash flows). The statements also help a firm discern how it stacks up against its competitors and industry norms. Most firms look at two to three years of past financial statements when preparing forecasts.

The next step is to prepare forecasts for two to three years in the future. Then forecasts are used to prepare a firm's pro forma financial statements, which, along with its more fine-tuned budgets, constitute its financial plan.

The final step in the process is the ongoing analysis of a firm's financial results. **Financial ratios**, which depict relationships between items on a firm's financial statements, are used to discern whether a firm is meeting its financial objectives and how it stacks up against its industry peers. These ratios are also used to assess trends. Obviously, a completely new venture would start at step 2 in Figure 8.2. It is important that a new venture be familiar with the entire process, however. Typically, new ventures prepare financial statements quarterly so that as soon as the first quarter is completed, the new venture will have historic financial statements to help prepare forecasts and pro forma statements for future periods.

FIGURE 8.2

The Process of
Financial Management

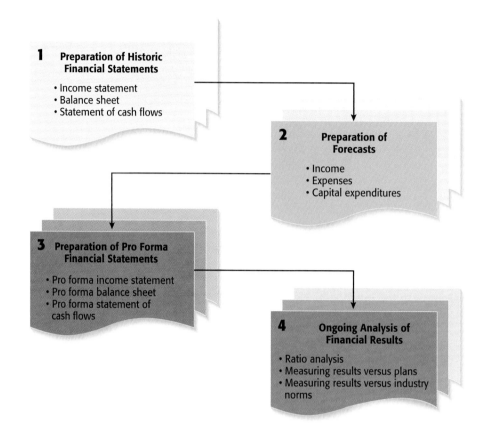

It is important for a firm to evaluate how it is faring relative to its industry. Sometimes raw financial ratios that are not viewed in context are deceiving. For example, a firm's past three years' income statements may show that it is increasing its sales at a rate of 15 percent per year. This number may seem impressive—until one learns that the industry in which the firm competes is growing at a rate of 30 percent per year, showing that the firm is steadily losing market share.

Many experienced entrepreneurs stress the importance of keeping on top of the financial management of a firm. In the competitive environments in which most firms exist, it's simply not good enough to shoot from the hip when making financial decisions. Reinforcing this point, Bill Gates, the founder of Microsoft, said,

> The business side of any company starts and ends with hard-core analysis of its numbers. Whatever else you do, if you don't understand what's happening in your business factually and you're making business decisions based on anecdotal data or gut instinct, you'll eventually pay a big price.[10]

FINANCIAL STATEMENTS AND FORECASTS

Learning Objective

3. Explain the difference between historical and pro forma financial statements.

Historical financial statements reflect past performance and are usually prepared on a quarterly and annual basis. Publicly traded firms are required by the Securities and Exchange Commission (SEC) to prepare financial statements and make them available to the public. The statements are submitted to the SEC through a number of required filings. The most comprehensive filing is the **10-K**, which is a report similar to the annual report except that it contains more detailed information about the company's business.[11] The 10-K for any publicly traded firm is available through the SEC's Web site (www.sec.gov/index.htm).

Corbis/Bettmann

The first step toward prudent financial management is keeping good records. This entrepreneur, who is the owner of an advertising agency, takes a minute during a hectic day to update her financial records. Good record keeping is essential for tax reporting and the generation of accurate financial statements.

Pro forma financial statements are projections for future periods based on forecasts and are typically completed for two to three years in the future. Pro forma financial statements are strictly planning tools and are not required by the SEC. In fact, most companies consider their pro forma statements to be confidential and reveal them to outsiders, such as lenders and investors, only on a "need-to-know" basis.

To illustrate how these financial instruments are prepared, let's look at New Venture Fitness Drinks, the fictitious sports drink company to which you were introduced in Chapter 3. New Venture Fitness Drinks has been in business for five years. Targeting sports enthusiasts, the company sells a line of nutritional fitness drinks. It opened a single location in 2005, added a second location in 2008, and plans to add a third in 2009. The company's strategy is to place small restaurants, similar to smoothie restaurants, near large outdoor sports complexes. The company is profitable and is growing at a rate of 25 percent per year.

Historical Financial Statements

Historical financial statements include the income statement, the balance sheet, and the statement of cash flows. The statements are usually prepared in this order because information flows logically from one to the next. In start-ups, financial statements are typically scrutinized closely to monitor the financial progress of the firm. On the rare occasion when a company has not used financial statements in planning, it should prepare and maintain them anyway. If a firm goes to a banker or investor to raise funds, the banker or investor will invariably ask for copies of past financial statements to analyze the firm's financial history. If a firm does not have these statements, it may be precluded from serious consideration for an investment or a loan. Let's look at each of these statements.

Income Statement   The **income statement** reflects the results of the operations of a firm over a specified period of time.[12] It records all the revenues and expenses for the given period and shows whether the firm is making a profit or is experiencing a loss (which is why the income statement if often referred to as the "profit-and-loss statement"). Income statements are typically prepared on a

Learning Objective

4. Explain the purpose of an income statement.

monthly, quarterly, and annual basis. Most income statements are prepared in a multiyear format, making it easy to spot trends.

The consolidated income statement for the past three years for New Venture Fitness Drinks is shown in Table 8.1. The value of the multiperiod format is clear. It's easy to see that the company's sales are increasing at the rate of about 25 percent per year, it is profitable, and its net income is increasing. The numbers are used to evaluate the effect of past strategies and to help project future sales and earnings.

The three numbers that receive the most attention when evaluating an income statement are the following:

- **Net sales: Net sales** consist of total sales minus allowances for returned goods and discounts.
- **Cost of sales (or cost of goods sold): Cost of sales** includes all the direct costs associated with producing or delivering a product or service, including the material costs and direct labor. In the case of New Venture Fitness Drinks, this would include the ingredients that go into the fitness drinks and the labor needed to produce them.
- **Operating expenses: Operating expenses** include marketing, administrative costs, and other expenses not directly related to producing a product or service.

One of the most valuable things that entrepreneurs and managers do with income statements is to compare the ratios of cost of sales and operating expenses to net sales for different periods. For example, the cost of sales for New Venture Fitness Drinks, which includes the ingredients for its fitness drinks and the labor needed to make them, has been 55, 49, and 46 percent of

Table 8.1 CONSOLIDATED INCOME STATEMENTS FOR NEW VENTURE FITNESS DRINKS, INC.

	December 31, 2008	December 31, 2007	December 31, 2006
Net sales	$586,600	$463,100	$368,900
Cost of sales	268,900	225,500	201,500
Gross profit	317,700	237,600	167,400
Operating expenses			
Selling, general, and administrative expenses	117,800	104,700	90,200
Depreciation	13,500	5,900	5,100
Operating income	186,400	127,000	72,100
Other income			
Interest income	1,900	800	1,100
Interest expense	(15,000)	(6,900)	(6,400)
Other income (expense), net	10,900	(1,300)	1,200
Income before income taxes	184,200	119,600	68,000
Income tax expense	53,200	36,600	18,000
Net income	131,000	83,000	50,000
Earnings per share	1.31	0.83	0.50

sales for 2006, 2007, and 2008, respectively. This is a healthy trend. It shows that the company is steadily decreasing its material and labor costs per dollar of sales. This is the type of trend that can be noticed fairly easily by looking at a firm's multiyear income statements.

One ratio of particular importance in evaluating a firm's income statements is profit margin. A firm's **profit margin**, or return on sales, is computed by dividing net income by net sales. For the years 2006, 2007, and 2008, the profit margin for New Venture Fitness Drinks has been 13.6, 17.9, and 22.3 percent, respectively. This is also a healthy trend. A firm's profit margin tells it what percentage of every dollar in sales contributes to the bottom line. An increasing profit margin means that a firm is either boosting its sales without increasing its expenses or that it is doing a better job of controlling its costs. In contrast, a declining profit margin means that a firm is losing control of its costs or that it is slashing prices to maintain or increase sales.

One ratio that will not be computed for New Venture Fitness Drinks is **price-to-earnings ratio, or P/E ratio.** New Venture Fitness Drinks is incorporated, so it has stock, but its stock is not traded on a public exchange such as the NASDAQ or the New York Stock Exchange. P/E is a simple ratio that measures the price of a company's stock against its earnings.[13] Generally, the higher a company's price-to-earnings ratio goes, the greater the market thinks it will grow. In 2008, New Venture Fitness Drinks earned $1.31 per share. If it was listed on the NASDAQ and its stock was trading at $20 per share, its P/E would be 15.3. This is what is meant when you hear that a company is selling for "15 times earnings."

The importance of looking at several years of income statements rather than just one is illustrated in this chapter's "Savvy Entrepreneurial Firm" feature.

Balance Sheet   Unlike the income statement, which covers a specified *period* of time, a **balance sheet** is a snapshot of a company's assets, liabilities, and owners' equity at a specific *point* in time.[14] The left-hand side of a balance sheet (or the top, depending on how it is displayed) shows a firm's assets, while the right-hand side (or bottom) shows its liabilities and owners' equity. The assets are listed in order of their "liquidity," or the length of time it takes to convert them to cash. The liabilities are listed in the order in which they must be paid. A balance sheet must always "balance," meaning that a firm's assets must always equal its liabilities plus owners' equity.[15]

The major categories of assets listed on a balance sheet are the following:

■ **Current assets: Current assets** include cash plus items that are readily convertible to cash, such as accounts receivable, marketable securities, and inventories.

■ **Fixed assets: Fixed assets** are assets used over a longer time frame, such as real estate, buildings, equipment, and furniture.

■ **Other assets: Other assets** are miscellaneous assets, including accumulated goodwill.

The major categories of liabilities listed on a balance sheet are the following:

■ **Current liabilities: Current liabilities** include obligations that are payable within a year, including accounts payable, accrued expenses, and the current portion of long-term debt.

■ **Long-term liabilities: Long-term liabilities** include notes or loans that are repayable beyond one year, including liabilities associated with purchasing real estate, buildings, and equipment.

■ **Owners' equity: Owners' equity** is the equity invested in the business by its owners plus the accumulated earnings retained by the business after paying dividends.

Learning Objective

5. Explain the purpose of a balance sheet.

Savvy Entrepreneurial FIRM
Know the Facts Behind the Numbers

Let's say that New Venture Fitness Drinks was interested in hiring a new chief executive officer (CEO) and was interviewing the CEOs of three small restaurant chains. To get a sense of how savvy each candidate was at managing a firm's finances, the board of directors of New Venture Fitness Drinks asked each person to submit the 2008 income statement for his or her current firm. An analysis of an abbreviated version of each firm's income statement is shown here.

	Candidate 1: CEO of New Venture Soup and Salad	Candidate 2: CEO of New Venture Beef	Candidate 3: CEO of New Venture Sea Food
Net sales	$326,400	$281,200	$486,700
Cost of sales	150,500	143,900	174,700
Gross profit	175,900	137,300	312,000
All expenses, including taxes and depreciation	114,200	112,400	150,000
Net income	61,700	24,900	162,000

By glancing at these statements, it would appear that the shrewdest financial manager of the three is the CEO of New Venture Sea Food. The company's net income is more than double that of the other two firms. In addition, New Venture Sea Food's cost of sales was 35.9 percent of net sales in 2008, compared to 46.1 percent for New Venture Soup and Salad and 51 percent for New Venture Beef. Similarly, New Venture Sea Food's expenses were 30.9 percent of sales, compared to 35.0 percent for New Venture Soup and Salad and 40 percent for New Venture Beef.

Fortunately, one of the board members of New Venture Fitness Drinks asked a series of questions during the personal interviews of the candidates and uncovered some revealing information. As it turns out, New Venture Sea Food was in the hottest segment of the restaurant industry in 2008. Seafood restaurants of comparable size produced about 1.5 times as much net income as New Venture Sea Food did. So if candidate 3 had done his job properly, his company's net income should have been in the neighborhood of $240,000 instead of $162,000. New Venture Soup and Salad was in a slow-growth area and at midyear feared that it might not meet its financial targets. So the CEO pulled several of his best people off projects and reassigned them to marketing to develop new menu items. In other words, the company borrowed from its future to make its numbers work today.

As for New Venture Beef, the CEO found herself in a market that was losing appeal. Several reports that gained national publicity were published early in the year warning consumers of the risks of eating red meat. To compensate, the CEO quickly implemented a productivity improvement program and partnered with a local beef promotion board to counter the bad press with more objective research results about beef's nutritional value. The company also participated in several volunteer efforts in its local community to raise the visibility of its restaurants in a positive manner. If the CEO of New Venture Beef hadn't moved quickly to take these actions, its 2008 performance would have been much worse.

Ultimately, New Venture Fitness Drinks decided that candidate 2, the CEO of New Venture Beef, was the best candidate for its job. This example illustrates the need to look at multiple years of an income statement rather than a single year to fairly assess how well a firm is performing financially. It also illustrates the need to look beyond the numbers and understand the circumstances that surround a firm's financial results.

Questions for Critical Thinking

1. Show the income statements for the three candidates to two or three friends who are majoring in business. Ask them to select the best CEO from among these three people on the basis of these income statements. In addition, ask your friends to explain their choices to you. Did your friends choose the same candidate? If not, what do you think caused the differences in their choices?

2. Based on material presented in this chapter, earlier chapters in this book, and your general business knowledge, where would you go to find information about the growth of the different segments of the restaurant industry? Where would you go to find information about the profitability of the restaurant industry in general?

3. What would have been the appropriate financial information to request from the three candidates for the job?

4. What are the three most important insights you gained from studying this feature? Which of these insights surprised you, and why?

Balance sheets are somewhat deceiving. First, a company's assets are recorded at cost rather than fair market value. A firm may have invested $500,000 in real estate several years ago that is worth $1 million today, but the value that is reflected on the firm's current balance sheet is the $500,000 purchase price rather than the $1 million fair market value. Second, intellectual property, such as patents, trademarks, and copyrights, receive value on the balance sheet in some cases and in some cases they don't, depending on the circumstances involved. In many cases, a firm's intellectual property will receive no value on its balance sheet even though it may be very valuable from a practical standpoint.[16] Third, intangible assets, such as the amount of training a firm has provided to its employees and the value of its brand, are not recognized on its balance sheet. Finally, the good-will that a firm has accumulated is not reported on its balance sheet, although this may be the firm's single most valuable asset.

The consolidated balance sheet for New Venture Fitness Drinks is shown in Table 8.2. Again, multiple years are shown so that trends can be easily spotted. When evaluating a balance sheet, the two primary questions are whether a firm has sufficient short-term assets to cover its short-term debts and whether it is financially sound overall. There are two calculations that provide the answer to the first question. In 2008, the **working capital** of New Venture Fitness Drinks, defined as its current assets minus its current liabilities, was $82,500. This number represents the amount of liquid assets the firm has available. Its **current ratio**, which equals the firm's current assets divided by its current liabilities, provides another picture of the relationship between its current assets and current liabilities and can tell us more about the firm's ability to pay its short-term debts.

New Venture Fitness Drink's current ratio is 3.06, meaning that it has $3.06 in current assets for every $1.00 in current liabilities. This is a healthy number and provides confidence that the company will be able to meet its current lia-bilities. The company's trend in this area is also positive. For the years 2006, 2007, and 2008, its current ratio has been 2.35, 2.26, and 3.06, respectively.

Computing a company's overall debt ratio will give us the answer to the second question, as it is a means of assessing a firm's overall financial sound-ness. A company's debt ratio is computed by dividing its total debt by its total assets. The present debt ratio for New Venture Fitness Drinks is 39.7 percent, meaning that 39.7 percent of its total assets are financed by debt and the remaining 60.3 percent by owners' equity. This is a healthy number for a young firm. The trend for New Venture Fitness Drinks in this area is also encouraging. For the years 2006, 2007, and 2008, its debt ratio has been 42.3, 37.4, and 39.7 percent, respectively. These figures indicate that, over time, the company is relying less on debt to finance its operations. In general, less debt creates more freedom for the entrepreneurial firm in terms of taking different actions.

The numbers across all the firm's financial statements are consistent with one another. Note that the $131,000 net income reported by New Venture Fitness Drinks on its 2008 income statement shows up as the difference between its 2008 and 2007 retained earnings on its 2008 balance sheet. This number would have been different if New Venture Fitness Drinks had paid dividends to its stockholders, but it paid no dividends in 2008. The company retained all of its $131,000 in earnings.

Statement of Cash Flows The **statement of cash flows** summarizes the changes in a firm's cash position for a specified period of time and details why the change occurred. The statement of cash flows is similar to a month-end bank statement. It reveals how much cash is on hand at the end of the month as well as how the cash was acquired and spent during the month.

Learning Objective

6. Explain the purpose of a statement of cash flows.

Table 8.2 CONSOLIDATED BALANCE SHEETS FOR NEW VENTURE FITNESS DRINKS, INC.

Assets	December 31, 2008	December 31, 2007	December 31, 2006
Current assets			
Cash and cash equivalents	$63,800	$54,600	$56,500
Accounts receivable, less allowance for doubtful accounts	39,600	48,900	50,200
Inventories	19,200	20,400	21,400
Total current assets	122,600	123,900	128,100
Property, plant, and equipment			
Land	260,000	160,000	160,000
Buildings and equipment	412,000	261,500	149,000
Total property, plant, and equipment	672,000	421,500	309,000
Less: accumulated depreciation	65,000	51,500	45,600
Net property, plant, and equipment	607,000	370,000	263,400
Total assets	729,600	493,900	391,500
Liabilities and shareholders' equity **Current liabilities**			
Accounts payable	30,200	46,900	50,400
Accrued expenses	9,900	8,000	4,100
Total current liabilities	40,100	54,900	54,500
Long-term liabilities			
Long-term debt	249,500	130,000	111,000
Long-term liabilities	249,500	130,000	111,000
Total liabilities	289,600	184,900	165,500
Shareholders' equity			
Common stock (100,000 shares)	10,000	10,000	10,000
Retained earnings	430,000	299,000	216,000
Total shareholders' equity	440,000	309,000	226,000
Total liabilities and shareholders' equity	729,600	493,900	391,500

The statement of cash flows is divided into three separate activities: operating activities, investing activities, and financing activities. These activities, which are explained in the following list, are the activities from which a firm obtains and uses cash:

■ **Operating activities: Operating activities** include net income (or loss), depreciation, and changes in current assets and current liabilities other than cash and short-term debt. A firm's net income, taken from its income statement, is the first line on the corresponding period's cash flow statement.

■ **Investing activities: Investing activities** include the purchase, sale, or investment in fixed assets, such as real estate, equipment, and buildings.

■ **Financing activities: Financing activities** include cash raised during the period by borrowing money or selling stock and/or cash used during the period by paying dividends, buying back outstanding stock, or buying back outstanding bonds.

Interpreting and analyzing cash flow statements takes practice. On the statement, the *uses* of cash are recorded as negative figures (which are shown by placing them in parentheses) and the *sources* of cash are recorded as positive figures. An item such as depreciation is shown as a positive figure on the statement of cash flows because it was deducted from net income on the income statement but was not a cash expenditure. Similarly, a decrease in accounts payable shows up as a negative figure on the cash flow statement because the firm used part of its cash to reduce its accounts payable balance from one period to the next.

The statement of cash flows for New Venture Fitness Drinks is shown in Table 8.3. As a management tool, it is intended to provide perspective on the following questions: Is the firm generating excess cash that could be used to pay down debt or returned to stockholders in the form of dividends? Is the firm generating enough cash to fund its investment activities from earnings, or is it relying on lenders or investors? Is the firm generating sufficient cash to pay down its short-term liabilities, or are its short-term liabilities increasing as the result of an insufficient amount of cash?

Again, a multiperiod statement is created so that trends can easily be spotted. A large increase in a firm's cash balance is not necessarily a good sign. It could mean that the firm is borrowing heavily, is not paying down its short-term liabilities, or is accumulating cash that could be put to work for a more productive purpose. On the other hand, it is almost always prudent for a young firm to have a healthy cash balance.

Table 8.3 shows the consolidated statement of cash flows for New Venture Fitness Drinks for two years instead of three because it takes three years of balance sheets to produce two years of cash flow statements. The statements show that New Venture Fitness Drinks is funding its investment activities from a combination of debt and earnings while at the same time it is slowly decreasing its accounts receivable and inventory levels (which is good—these items are major drains on a company's cash flow). It is also steadily increasing its cash on hand. These are encouraging signs for a new venture.

Ratio Analysis   The most practical way to interpret or make sense of a firm's historical financial statements is through ratio analysis. Table 8.4, on page 287, is a summary of the ratios used to evaluate New Venture Fitness Drinks during the time period covered by the previously provided financial statements. The ratios are divided into profitability ratios, liquidity ratios, and overall financial stability ratios. These ratios provide a means of interpreting the historical financial statements for New Venture Fitness Drinks and provide a starting point for forecasting the firm's financial performance and capabilities for the future.

Learning Objective

7. Discuss how financial ratios are used to analyze and interpret a firm's financial statements.

Comparing a Firm's Financial Results to Industry Norms   Comparing its financial results to industry norms helps a firm determine how it stacks up against its competitors and if there are any financial "red flags" requiring attention. This type of comparison works best for firms that are of similar size, so the results should be interpreted with caution by new firms. Many sources provide industry-related information. For example, Hoover's provides industry norms to which a new firm can compare itself and is typically free of charge if accessed from a university library that subscribes to Hoover's premium

Table 8.3 CONSOLIDATED STATEMENT OF CASH FLOWS FOR NEW VENTURE FITNESS DRINKS, INC.

	December 31, 2008	December 31, 2007
Cash flows from operating activities		
Net income	$131,000	$83,000
Additions (sources of cash)		
Depreciation	13,500	5,900
Decreases in accounts receivable	9,300	1,300
Increase in accrued expenses	1,900	3,900
Decrease in inventory	1,200	1,000
Subtractions (uses of cash)		
Decrease in accounts payable	(16,700)	(3,500)
Total adjustments	9,200	8,600
Net cash provided by operating activities	140,200	91,600
Cash flows from investing activities		
Purchase of building and equipment	(250,500)	(112,500)
Net cash flows provided by investing activities	(250,500)	(112,500)
Cash flows from financing activities		
Proceeds from increase in long-term debt	119,500	19,000
Net cash flows provided by financing activities		19,000
Increase in cash	9,200	(1,900)
Cash and cash equivalents at the beginning of year	54,600	56,500
Cash and cash equivalents at the end of each year	63,800	54,600

service. To access this information, simply go to www.hoovers.com. As shown, comparing Dell's financial ratios to industry norms, Dell is depicted in a positive light and the comparison raises no immediate red flags, other than revenue growth being below the industry median. Reliable data are harder to come by for private firms. Several suggestions for obtaining comparison data for private firms are provided in Chapter 3.

Comparison Data (2007–2008 Fiscal Year)	Dell Inc.	Industry Median[a]	Market Median[b]
Gross profit margin	18.30%	33.80%	52.60%
Net profit margin	5.90	4.40	4.70
Return on equity (ROE)	51.00	11.10	7.00
Return on assets (ROA)	9.60	3.40	0.70
12-month revenue growth	6.80	11.80	7.10

[a] Industry: computer hardware.
[b] All firms listed on the major stock exchanges.

Forecasts

As depicted in Figure 8.2, the analysis of a firm's historical financial statement is followed by the preparation of forecasts. Forecasts are predictions of a firm's future sales, expenses, income, and capital expenditures. A firm's forecasts provide the basis for its pro forma financial statements. A well-developed set of pro forma financial statements helps a firm create accurate budgets, build financial plans, and manage its finances in a proactive rather than a reactive manner.

As mentioned earlier, completely new firms typically base their forecasts on a good-faith estimate of sales and on industry averages (based on a percentage of sales) or the experiences of similar start-ups for cost of goods sold and other expenses. As a result, a completely new firm's forecast should be preceded in its business plan by an explanation of the sources of the numbers for the forecast and the assumptions used to generate them. This explanation is called an **assumptions sheet**, as mentioned in Chapter 4. Investors typically study assumptions sheets like hawks to make sure the numbers contained in the forecasts and the resulting financial projections are realistic. For example, the assumptions sheet for a new venture may say that its forecasts are based on selling 500 units of its new product the first year, 1,000 units the second year, and 1,500 units the third year and that its cost of goods sold will remain stable (meaning that it will stay fixed at a certain percentage of net sales) over the three-year period. It's up to the reader of the plan to determine if these numbers are realistic.[17] If the reader feels they are not, then the credibility of the entire plan is called into question.

Sales Forecast A **sales forecast** is a projection of a firm's sales for a specified period (such as a year), though most firms forecast their sales for two to five years into the future.[18] It is the first forecast developed and is the basis for most of the other forecasts.[19] A sales forecast for an existing firm is based on (1) its

> ### Learning Objective
>
> 8. Discuss the role of forecasts in projecting a firm's future income and expenses.

> ### Learning Objective
>
> 9. Explain what a completely new firm bases its forecasts on.

Table 8.4 RATIO ANALYSIS FOR NEW VENTURE FITNESS DRINKS, INC.

Ratio	Formula	2008	2007	2006
Profitability ratios: associate the amount of income earned with the resources used to generate it				
Return on assets	ROA = net income/average total assets[a]	21.4%	18.7%	14.7%
Return on equity	ROE = net income/average shareholders' equity[b]	35.0%	31.0%	24.9%
Profit margin	Profit margin = net income/net sales	22.3%	17.9%	13.6%
Liquidity ratios: measure the extent to which a company can quickly liquidate assets to cover short-term liabilities				
Current	Current assets/current liabilities	3.06	2.26	2.35
Quick	Quick assets/current liabilities	2.58	1.89	1.96
Overall financial stability ratio: measures the overall financial stability of a firm				
Debt	Total debt/total assets	39.7%	37.4%	42.3%
Debt to Equity	Total liabilities/owners' equity	65.8%	59.8%	73.2%

[a] Average total assets = beginning total assets + ending total assets ÷ 2.
[b] Average shareholders' equity = beginning shareholders' equity + ending shareholders' equity ÷ 2.

record of past sales, (2) its current production capacity and product demand, and (3) any factor or factors that will affect its future production capacity and product demand. To demonstrate how a sales forecast works, Figure 8.3 is a graph of the past sales and the forecasted future sales for New Venture Fitness Drinks. The company's sales increased at a rate of about 26 percent per year from 2006 to 2008 as the company became established and more people became aware of its brand. In forecasting its sales for 2009 and 2010, the company took into consideration the following factors:

■ The fitness craze in America continues to gain momentum and should continue to attract new people to try its fitness drinks.

■ The interest in intramural sports, especially football, baseball, and softball, should continue to provide a high level of traffic for its restaurants, which are located near large intramural sports complexes.

■ The company expanded from a single location in 2005 to two locations in 2008 (the second restaurant was added in November 2008), and this should increase its capacity to serve fitness drinks by approximately 50 percent. The second restaurant is smaller than the first and is located in an area where the company is not as well known. The company will be actively promoting the new restaurant but knows it will take time to win market share.

■ The general economy in the city where the company is located is flat—it is neither growing nor shrinking. However, layoffs are rumored for a larger employer near the location of the new restaurant.

The combination of these factors results in a forecast of a 40 percent increase in sales from 2008 to 2009 and a 25 percent increase in sales from 2009 to 2010. It is extremely important for a company such as New Venture Drinks to forecast future sales as accurately as possible. If it overestimates the demand for its products, it might get stuck with excess inventory and spend too much on overhead. If it underestimates the demand for its product, it might have to turn away business, and some of its potential customers might get into the habit of buying other firms' fitness drinks.

Note that sophisticated tools are available to help firms project their future sales. One approach is to use **regression analysis**, which is a statistical technique used to find relationships between variables for the purpose of predicting future values.[20] For example, if New Venture Fitness Drinks felt that its future sales were a function of its advertising expenditures, the number of people who participate in intramural sports at the sports complexes near its restaurants, and the price of its drinks, it could predict future sales using regression analysis as long as it had historical data for each of these variables. If the company used simpler logic and felt that its future sales would increase a certain percentage over its current sales, regression analysis could be used to generate a more precise estimate of future sales than was predicted from the information contained in Figure 8.3. For a new firm that has limited years of "annual data," monthly data could be used to project sales.

Learning Objective

10. Explain what is meant by the term *percent-of-sales method.*

Forecast of Costs of Sales and Other Items   Once a firm has completed its sales forecast, it must forecast its cost of sales (or cost of goods sold) and the other items on its income statement. The most common way to do this is to use the **percent-of-sales method**, which is a method for expressing each expense item as a percentage of sales.[21] For example, in the case of New Venture Fitness Drinks, its cost of sales has averaged 47.5 percent over the past two years. In 2008, its sales were $586,600 and its cost of sales was $268,900. The company's sales are forecast to be $821,200 in 2009.

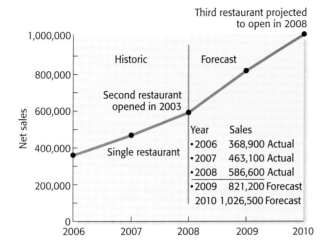

FIGURE 8.3

Historical and Forecasted Annual Sales for New Venture Fitness Drinks

Therefore, based on the percent-of-sales method, its cost of sales in 2009 will be $390,000, or 47.5 percent of projected sales. The same procedure could be used to forecast the cost of each expense item on the company's income statement.

Once a firm completes its forecast using the percent-of-sales method, it usually goes through its income statement on an item-by-item basis to see if there are opportunities to make more precise forecasts. For example, a firm can closely estimate its depreciation expenses, so it wouldn't be appropriate to use the percent-of-sales method to make a forecast for this item. In addition, some expense items are not tied to sales. For those items, reasonable estimates are made.

Obviously, a firm must apply common sense in using the percent-of-sales method. If a company is implementing cost-cutting measures, for example, it might be able to justify projecting a smaller percentage increase in expenses as opposed to sales. Similarly, if a firm hires an administrator, such as a chief financial officer, toward the end of the year and plans to pay the person $75,000 the next year, that $75,000 may have no immediate impact on sales. In this case, the firm's forecast for administrative expenses may have to be adjusted upward beyond what the percent-of-sales method would suggest.

If a firm determines that it can use the percent-of-sales method and it follows the procedure described previously, then the net result is that each expense item on its income statement (with the exception of those items that may be individually forecast, such as depreciation) will grow at the same rate as sales. This approach is called the **constant ratio method of forecasting**. This approach will be used in preparing the pro forma financial statements for New Venture Fitness Drinks in the next section.

A summary of the forecasts used to prepare the pro forma financial statements for New Venture Fitness Drinks is provided in Table 8.5.

In addition to computing sales forecasts, when a company like New Venture Fitness Drinks considers opening a new restaurant or producing a new product, it often calculates a break-even analysis to determine if the proposed initiative is feasible. The **break-even point** for a new restaurant or product is the point where total revenue received equals total costs associated with the output of the restaurant or the sale of the product.[22] In the case of opening a new restaurant, New Venture Fitness Drinks could use break-even analysis as one way of determining whether the proposed initiative is feasible. The formula for break-even analysis is as follows: Total fixed costs/(price – average variable costs). As a result, if the total fixed cost associated with opening a new restaurant is $101,000 per year, the average price for a fitness drink is $2.75, and the

Table 8.5 Forecasts Used to Prepare Pro Forma Financial Statements for New Venture Fitness Drinks, Inc.

Pro Forma Income Statements

Net sales

Historic	Average sales increase of 25% per year
2009	Increase to 40% as the result of increased brand awareness and the opening of a second service location
2010	Increase 25% as the result of increased brand awareness (a third service location will be opened late in the year)

Cost of goods sold (COGS)

Historic	Average of 47.5% of sales the past two years
2009	47.5% of sales
2010	47.5% of sales

Selling, general, and administrative expenses

Historic	Average 22% of sales the past two years
2009	Increase to 25% of sales as the result of the opening of a second service location (the increase will not be any larger as the result of increased operating efficiencies)
2010	25% of sales

Interest expense

Historic	6% to 7% of long-term debt
2009	7% of long-term debt
2010	7% of long-term debt

Other income

Historic	Licensing income of $10,900 per year
2009	Licensing income will increase to $20,000 as the result of the renegotiation of the licensing contract
2010	Licensing income will be $20,000

Pro Forma Balance Sheets

Accounts receivable

Historic	Accounts receivable have trended down to 6.8% of sales in 2008 from 13.6% of sales in 2007
2009	7% of sales
2010	7% of sales

Inventories

Historic	Inventories have trended down to 3.3% of sales in 2008 from 4.4% of sales in 2007
2009	4% of sales (reflecting slight increase over 2003 as the result of the opening of a second service location)
2010	4% of sales

Land, buildings, and equipment

2009	$100,000 in equipment purchases and capital improvements made to existing buildings
2010	$275,000 in capital improvements, including a $100,000 real estate purchase and $175,000 in buildings and equipment

Table 8.5   *(continued)*

Accounts payable

Historic	Accounts payable have trended down to 5.1% of sales in 2008 from 13.6% of sales in 2007 because of the implementation of more effective collection methods (a slightly higher level of accounts payable will be projected for the future)
2009	7% of sales
2010	7% of sales

Long-term debt

2009	$75,000 reduction in long-term debt from earnings
2010	$150,000 will be borrowed to finance $275,000 to acquire land, equipment, and buildings (the balance of the acquisition costs will be funded from earnings)

variable cost for each drink is $1.10, then the break-even point for the new restaurant is as follows:

$101,000 (total fixed costs)/($2.75 − $1.10) or $1.65 = 61,212 units

The number means that the new restaurant will have to sell 61,212 "units" or fitness drinks per year to "break even" at the current price of the drinks. That number breaks down to the sale of 170 fitness drinks per day, on average, based on a 360-day year. To determine whether opening the new restaurant is feasible, the managers of New Venture Fitness Drinks would compare this number against the historic sales figures for their other restaurants, making adjustments as appropriate (e.g., the new restaurant may have a better or worse location than the existing restaurants). If selling 170 fitness drinks per day seems unrealistic, then the managers of New Fitness Drinks might opt to not open the new restaurant, or find ways to lower fixed or variable costs or increase revenues. An obvious way to increase revenues is to raise the price of the fitness drinks, if that option is realistic given the competitive nature of the marketplace.

In the context of lowering costs, one thing a new venture should guard itself against is becoming overly optimistic about cutting costs by switching to a supplier that promises to deliver the same quality at a lower cost or by buying supplies through a B2B (business-to-business) exchange. Often, these tactics represent false hopes for cost savings, as illustrated in this chapter's "What Went Wrong?" feature.

PRO FORMA FINANCIAL STATEMENTS

A firm's pro forma financial statements are similar to its historical financial statements except that they look forward rather than track the past. New ventures typically offer pro forma statements, but well-managed established firms also maintain these statements as part of their routine financial planning process and to help prepare budgets. The preparation of pro forma statements also helps firms rethink their strategies and make adjustments if necessary. For example, if the pro forma statements predict a downturn in profitability, a firm can make operational changes, such as increasing prices or decreasing expenses, to help prevent the decrease in profitability from actually happening.[23]

What Went WRONG?
B2B Exchanges: A False Hope for Cost Savings?

A B2B (business-to-business) exchange is an online marketplace that connects the buyers and the sellers in an industry. The goal of these connections is to improve the efficiency of the supply chain and save money for everyone. ChemConnect is an example of a B2B exchange. ChemConnect helps companies that purchase chemicals locate the suppliers they need and negotiate a favorable price. True to the nature of an effective online exchange, ChemConnect has helped many companies find suppliers for the raw materials they need and buyers for the products they sell that they would never reach otherwise. In fact, as of late 2008, ChemConnect's international community of members included more than 9,000 companies from over 150 countries worldwide.

In the early days of e-commerce, experts predicted that B2B exchanges would change the way companies interacted with their buyers and suppliers. Unfortunately, the majority of online exchanges have not worked out as well as ChemConnect. In fact, a study conducted by George Day, Adam Fein, and Gregg Ruppersberger tracked the number of B2B exchanges from 1,500 in 2001 to fewer than 700 in 2002 to an estimated 180 in 2003. The study notes that this kind of shakeout has occurred in new technology markets before, but usually over a 20- to 30-year period. Although the number of B2B exchanges is higher today than in 2003, the numbers are still well below initial expectations. So what went wrong, so fast, with B2B exchanges?

Well, several things. First, even though many B2B exchanges were proficient in helping firms find the supplier with the lowest price, price isn't everything. Most suppliers want to establish a relationship with the companies they sell to rather than make a one-time sale motivated strictly by price. In fact, many advisers counsel firms to limit the number of their suppliers to develop trusting relationships and ensure the delivery of high-quality products or parts. B2B exchanges encourage just the opposite by emphasizing price as the most important buying criterion.

Second, rather than seeing B2B exchanges as making the supply chain more efficient, many firms see the exchanges as adding one more layer of cost. Once a supplier and seller get together and start doing business with each other, they can easily avoid the exchange and eliminate the exchange's commission. As Art Jahnke, writing in *CIO* magazine, put it,

Neither (the buyer and the seller) is prepared to dance to the tune of an intermediary who had a bright idea a few years back, and who wants to sit back and take a percentage forever.

Third, the technology involved with B2B exchanges seldom lived up to the promise. A common complaint from both buyers and sellers was the functionality of B2B Web sites.

Although some exchanges, such as ChemConnect, are doing well, the jury is still out on the future of B2B exchanges. The majority of the exchanges have not been able to overcome the obstacles described here and, in the end, have represented a false hope for cost savings.

Questions for Critical Thinking

1. Choose two companies in your community with which you are familiar. Make an appointment with a top-level manager in each company. Ask the managers to describe the criteria they deem most important when working with their suppliers. Is price the most important criterion for the people you are interviewing? If so, why? If not, are relationships important? If relationships are important to your interviewees, how do they go about establishing and maintaining those relationships?

2. Given the knowledge you've acquired from studying this book as well as from other academic courses and work experience, develop a list of advantages and disadvantages associated with entrepreneurs deciding to rely on B2B transactions. For entrepreneurs, do the advantages of B2B transactions outweigh the disadvantages, or is the reverse true, and why?

3. What would you anticipate the attributes are of the B2B exchanges that have survived?

4. List some ways, other than B2B exchanges, that entrepreneurs are leveraging the power of the Internet to cut costs.

Sources: ChemConnect homepage, www.chemconnect.com (accessed December 12, 2008); H. Min, J. Caltagirone, and A. Serpico, "Life After a Dot-Com Bubble," *International Journal of Information Technology and Management* 7, no. 1 (2008): 21–35; G. S. Day, A. J. Fein, and G. Ruppersberger, "Shakeouts in Digital Markets: Lessons from B2B Exchanges," *California Management Review* 45, no. 2 (2003): 131–50; and A. Jahnke, "What Was Wrong with B2B Exchanges?" *CIO*, June 20, 2002.

A firm's pro forma financial statements should not be prepared in isolation. Instead, they should be created in conjunction with the firm's overall planning activities. The following sections explain the development of pro forma financial statements for New Venture Fitness Drinks.

Pro Forma Income Statement

Once a firm forecasts its future income and expenses, the creation of the **pro forma income statement** is merely a matter of plugging in the numbers. Table 8.6 shows the pro forma income statement for New Venture Fitness Drinks. Recall that net sales for New Venture Fitness Drinks are forecast to increase by 40 percent from 2008 to 2009 and by 25 percent from 2009 to 2010 and that its cost of sales has averaged 47.5 percent of net sales. In the pro forma income statement, the constant ratio method of forecasting is used to forecast the cost of sales and general and administrative expense, meaning that these items are projected to remain at the same percentage of sales in the future as they were in the past (which is the mathematical equivalent of saying that they will increase at the same rate of sales). Depreciation, other income, and several other items that are not directly tied to sales are figured separately—using reasonable estimates. The most dramatic change is "other income," which jumps significantly from 2008 to 2009. New Venture Fitness

Table 8.6   Pro Forma Income Statement for New Venture Fitness Drinks, Inc.

	2008 Actual	2009 Projected	2010 Projected
Net sales	$586,600	$821,200	$1,026,500
Cost of sales	268,900	390,000	487,600
Gross profit	317,700	431,200	538,900
Operating expenses			
Selling, general, and administrative expenses	117,800	205,300	256,600
Depreciation	13,500	18,500	22,500
Operating income	186,400	207,400	259,800
Other income			
Interest income	1,900	2,000	2,000
Interest expense	(15,000)	(17,500)	(17,000)
Other income (expense), net	10,900	20,000	20,000
Income before income taxes	184,200	211,900	264,800
Income tax expense	53,200	63,600	79,400
Net income	131,000	148,300	185,400
Earnings per share	1.31	1.48	1.85

The preparation of pro forma financial statements shouldn't be viewed as a drudgery. Well-developed pro forma financial statements help a firm rethink its strategies, make adjustments where necessary, and plan for the future.

Gary Connor/PhotoEdit Inc.

Drinks anticipates a significant increase in this category as the result of the renegotiation of a licensing agreement for one of its fitness drinks that is sold by another company.

Pro Forma Balance Sheet

The **pro forma balance sheet** provides a firm a sense of how its activities will affect its ability to meet its short-term liabilities and how its finances will evolve over time. It can also quickly show how much of a firm's money will be tied up in accounts receivable, inventory, and equipment. The pro forma balance sheet is also used to project the overall financial soundness of a company. For example, a firm may have a very aggressive set of pro forma income statements that project rapidly increasing growth and profitability. However, if this rapid growth and profitability push the firm's debt ratio to 75 percent (which is extremely high), investors may conclude that there is too much risk involved for the firm to be an attractive investment.

The pro forma balance sheet for New Venture Fitness Drinks is shown in Table 8.7. Note that the company's projected change in retained earnings each year is consistent with its projected net income for the same period on its pro forma income statements. The same approach was used to construct the pro forma balance sheets as the pro forma income statements. For each item listed under current assets and current liabilities, the item's historical percentage of sales was used to project its future percentage of sales. Several of the numbers were adjusted slightly upward, such as inventory levels and accounts payable, to reflect the potential impact of the opening of the second restaurant.

In regard to property, plant, and equipment, New Venture Fitness Drinks plans to invest $100,000 in 2009 and $275,000 in 2010. The pro forma balance sheet shows a corresponding increase in valuation in this category for 2009 and 2010, respectively. The company's projected long-term debt for 2009 and 2010 reflects changes resulting from principal reductions from cash flow and increased borrowing to fund the property, plant, and equipment purchases just mentioned. These transactions are reflected in the pro forma statement of cash flows for New Venture Fitness Drinks.

Table 8.7   PRO FORMA BALANCE SHEETS FOR NEW VENTURE FITNESS DRINKS, INC.

Assets	December 31, 2008	Projected 2009	Projected 2010
Current assets			
Cash and cash equivalents	$63,800	$53,400	$80,200
Accounts receivable, less allowance for doubtful accounts	39,600	57,500	71,900
Inventories	19,200	32,900	41,000
Total current assets	122,600	143,800	193,100
Property, plant, and equipment			
Land	260,000	260,000	360,000
Buildings and equipment	412,000	512,000	687,000
Total property, plant, and equipment	672,000	772,000	1,047,000
Less: accumulated depreciation	65,000	83,500	106,000
Net property, plant, and equipment	607,000	688,500	941,000
Total assets	729,600	832,300	1,134,100
Liabilities and shareholders' equity			
Current liabilities			
Accounts payable	30,200	57,500	71,900
Accrued expenses	9,900	12,000	14,000
Total current liabilities	40,100	69,500	85,900
Long-term liabilities			
Long-term debt	249,500	174,500	274,500
Total long-term liabilities	249,500	174,500	274,500
Total liabilities	289,600	244,000	360,400
Shareholders' equity			
Common stock (100,000 shares)	10,000	10,000	10,000
Retained earnings	430,000	578,300	763,700
Total shareholders' equity	440,000	588,300	773,700
Total liabilities and shareholders' equity	729,600	832,300	1,134,100

Pro Forma Statement of Cash Flows

The **pro forma statement of cash flows** shows the projected flow of cash into and out of the company during a specified period. The most important function of the pro forma statement of cash flows is to project whether the firm will have sufficient cash to meet its needs. As with the historical statement of cash flows, the pro forma statement of cash flows is broken into three activities: operating activities, investing activities, and financing activities. Close attention is typically paid to the section on operating activities because it shows how changes in the company's accounts receivable, accounts payable, and inventory levels affect the cash that it has available for investing and finance activities. If any of these items increases at a rate that is faster than the company's annual increase in sales, it typically raises a red flag. For example, an increase in accounts receivable, which is money that is owed to a company by its customers, decreases the amount of cash that it has available for investment or finance activities. If accounts receivable gets out of hand, it may jeopardize a company's ability to fund its growth or service its debt.

The pro forma consolidated statement of cash flows for New Venture Fitness Drinks is shown in Table 8.8. The figures appearing on the statement come directly, or are calculated directly, from the pro forma income statement and the pro forma balance sheet. The one exception is that the last line of each statement of cash flows, which reflects the company's cash balance at the end of the period, becomes the first line of the company's balance sheet for the next period. The pro forma statement of cash flows for New Venture Fitness Drinks shows healthy cash balances at the end of each projected period and shows that investment activities are being funded more by earnings than by debt. This scenario reflects a company that is generating sufficient cash flow to fund the majority of its growth without overly relying on debt or investment capital.

In regard to dividends, the pro forma statement of cash flows shows that New Venture Fitness Drinks is not planning to pay a dividend to its stockholders in 2009 and 2010. Recall that New Venture Fitness Drinks is incorporated and has

Table 8.8 Pro Forma Statement of Cash Flows for New Venture Fitness Drinks, Inc.

	December 31, 2008	Projected 2009	Projected 2010
Cash flows from operating activities			
Net income	$131,000	$148,300	$185,400
Changes in working capital			
Depreciation	13,500	18,500	22,500
Increase (decrease) in accounts receivable	9,300	(17,900)	(14,400)
Increase (decrease) in accrued expenses	1,900	2,100	2,000
Increase (decrease) in inventory	1,200	(13,700)	(8,100)
Increase (decrease) in accounts payable	(16,700)	27,300	14,400
Total adjustments	9,200	16,300	16,400
Net cash provided by operating activities	140,200	164,600	201,800
Cash flows from investing activities			
Purchase of building and equipment	(250,500)	(100,000)	(275,000)
Net cash flows provided by investing activities	(250,500)	(100,000)	(275,000)
Cash flows from financing activities			
Proceeds from increase in long-term debt	119,500	—	100,000
Principle reduction in long-term debt		(75,000)	
Net cash flows provided by financing activities			
Increase in cash	9,200	(10,400)	26,800
Cash and cash equivalents at the beginning of the year	54,600	63,800	53,400
Cash and cash equivalents at the end of the year	63,800	53,400	80,200

stockholders even though it is not traded on an organized exchange. If New Venture Fitness Drinks were planning to pay a dividend, the projected dividend payments would show up under financing activities and would reduce the amount of cash available for investing and financing activities. It is common for a new firm to invest the majority of its cash in activities that fund its growth, such as property, plant, and equipment purchases, rather than pay dividends.

Ratio Analysis

The same financial ratios used to evaluate a firm's historical financial statements should be used to evaluate the pro forma financial statements. This work is completed so the firm can get a sense of how its projected financial performance compares to its past performance and how its projected activities will affect its cash position and its overall financial soundness.

The historical financial ratios and projected ratios for New Venture Fitness Drinks are shown in Table 8.9. The profitability ratios show a slight decline from the historical period to the projected. This indicates that the projected increase in assets and corresponding sales will not produce income quite as efficiently as has been the case historically. Still, the numbers are strong, and no dramatic changes are projected.

The liquidity ratios show a consistently healthy ratio of current assets to current liabilities, suggesting that the firm should be able to cover its short-term liabilities without difficulty. The overall financial stability ratios indicate promising trends. The debt ratio drops from an actual of 39.7 percent in 2008 to a projected 31.8 percent in 2010. The debt-to-equity ratio shows an even more dramatic drop, indicating that an increasing portion of the firm's assets is being funded by equity rather than debt.

In summary, it is extremely important for a firm to understand its financial position at all times and for new ventures to base their financial projections on solid numbers. As mentioned earlier, regardless of how successful a firm is in other areas, it must succeed financially to remain strong and viable.

Table 8.9 RATIO ANALYSIS OF HISTORICAL AND PRO FORMA FINANCIAL STATEMENTS FOR NEW VENTURE FITNESS DRINKS, INC.

	Historical			Projected	
Ratio	2006	2007	2008	2009	2010
Profitability ratios					
Return on assets	14.7%	18.7%	21.4%	19.0%	18.9%
Return on equity	24.9%	31.0%	35.0%	28.9%	27.2%
Profit margin	13.6%	17.9%	22.3%	18.1%	18.1%
Liquidity ratios					
Current	2.35	2.26	3.05	2.07	2.24
Quick	1.96	1.89	2.58	1.60	1.78
Overall financial stability ratios					
Debt	42.3%	37.4%	39.7%	29.3%	31.8%
Debt to equity	73.2%	59.8%	65.8%	41.5%	46.6%

Chapter Summary

1. Financial management deals with two activities: raising money and managing a company's finances in a way that achieves the highest rate of return.
2. Profitability, liquidity, efficiency, and stability are the four main financial objectives of entrepreneurial firms.
3. Historical financial statements reflect past performance. Pro forma financial statements are projections for expected performance in future periods.
4. An income statement reflects the results of a firm's operations over a specified period of time. It records all the revenues and expenses for the given period and shows whether the firm is making a profit or is experiencing a loss.
5. A balance sheet is a snapshot of a company's assets, liabilities, and owners' equity.
6. A statement of cash flows summarizes the changes in a firm's cash position for a specified period of time.
7. Financial ratios depict relationships between items on a firm's financial statement and are used to discern if a firm is meeting its financial objectives and how it stacks up against its competitors.
8. Forecasts are predictions of a firm's future sales, expenses, income, and capital expenditures. A firm's forecasts provide the basis for its pro forma financial statements.
9. Completely new firms typically base their forecasts on a good-faith estimate of sales and on industry averages (based on a percentage of sales) or the experiences of similar start-ups for cost of goods sold and other expenses.
10. Once a firm has completed its sales forecast, it must forecast its costs of sales as well as the other items on its income statement. The most common way to do this is to use the percent-of-sales method, which is a method for expressing each expense item as a percentage of sales.

Key Terms

10-K, **278**
accounts receivable, **276**
assumptions sheet, **287**
balance sheet, **281**
break-even point, **289**
budgets, **276**
constant ratio method
    of forecasting, **289**
cost of sales, **280**
current assets, **281**
current liabilities, **281**
current ratio, **283**
debt-to-equity ratio, **276**
efficiency, **276**
financial management, **274**
financial ratios, **277**

financial statement, **276**
financing activities, **285**
fixed assets, **281**
forecasts, **276**
historical financial
    statements, **278**
income statement, **279**
inventory, **276**
investing activities, **285**
liquidity **275**
long-term liabilities, **281**
net sales, **280**
operating activities, **284**
operating expenses, **280**
other assets, **281**
owners' equity, **281**

percent-of-sales method, **288**
price/earnings (P/E) ratio, **281**
pro forma balance sheet, **294**
pro forma financial
    statements, **279**
pro forma income
    statement, **293**
pro forma statement
    of cash flows, **295**
profit margin, **281**
profitability, **275**
regression analysis, **288**
sales forecast, **287**
stability, **276**
statement of cash flows, **283**
working capital, **283**

Review Questions

1. What are the two primary functions of the financial management of a firm?
2. What are the four main financial objectives of a firm?
3. Why is it important for a company to focus on its liquidity? What special challenges do entrepreneurial firms have in regard to remaining liquid?

4. What is meant by the term *efficiency* as it relates to the financial management of a firm?
5. What is meant by the term *stability* as it relates to the financial management of a firm?
6. What is the purpose of a forecast? What factors does a firm use to create its forecasts of future income and expenses?
7. On what factors or conditions do completely new firms base their forecasts?
8. What is the purpose of an income statement? What are the three numbers that receive the most attention when evaluating an income statement? Why are these numbers important?
9. How does a firm compute its profit margin? What is the significance of this ratio?
10. How does a firm compute its price-to-earnings ratio? Why does a high price-to-earnings ratio indicate that the stock market thinks the firm will grow?
11. What is the purpose of a balance sheet?
12. What are the major categories of assets and liabilities on a balance sheet? Briefly explain each category.
13. What is meant by the term *working capital*? Why is working capital an important consideration for entrepreneurial firms?
14. How does a firm compute its current ratio? Is this a relatively important or unimportant financial ratio? Explain your answer.
15. What is the purpose of a statement of cash flows?
16. What are the three separate categories of activities that are reflected on a firm's statement of cash flows? Briefly explain the importance of each activity.
17. What is the purpose of financial ratios? Why are financial ratios particularly useful in helping a firm interpret its financial statements?
18. What is the purpose of an assumptions sheet?
19. Describe why a firm's sales forecast is the basis for most of the other forecasts.
20. Explain what is meant by the percent-of-sales method as it relates to forecasts.

Application Questions

1. Refer to the opening feature, which focuses on BLMA Models, a company that designs and sells model trains and accessories to the model train community. Make a list of the things that you believe Craig Martyn, the founder of BLMA, has done "right" in regard to the financial management of the company.
2. Kirsten, a friend of yours, plans to open a fashion boutique that will sell women's clothing and accessories. She told you that she leafed through several books on how to prepare forecasts and pro forma financial statements but that the books were geared toward existing firms that have several years of historical financial statements on which to base their projections. If Kirsten asked you your advice for how to prepare forecasts for a completely new women's fashion boutique, what would you tell her?
3. Suppose a friend of yours showed you the pro forma income statements for his start-up and exclaimed excitedly that during the first three years of operations his firm will make a net income of $150,000 per year, which is just the amount of money ($450,000) the firm will need to pay off a three-year loan. Explain to your friend why he might not actually have $450,000 in cash, even though his pro forma income statements say that he will earn that amount of money.
4. Kate Snow just retired from a career with Wal-Mart, cashing out a sizable retirement fund at the time of doing so. To start a second career, she is looking at the possibility of buying three different businesses. She has three years' historical financial statements for each business and has been pouring over the numbers. She was puzzled when she read the following

statement in a book about small business financial management, "Be careful when looking at balance sheets to fully understand what you're looking at. In some respects balance sheets are very revealing, and in other respects they can be very deceiving." What do you think the author of the book meant by that statement?

5. Tim Phillips, who owns a digital photography start-up in Sioux Falls, South Dakota, plans to expand his business in two to three years by servicing clients in Minneapolis, Minnesota, and Des Moines, Iowa. He hopes to get a bank loan to fund the expansion, so he wants to do everything he can to strengthen his financial statements before he applies for a loan. One thing that he read recently is that banks focus intently on a firm's current ratio and its overall debt/asset ratio when considering loan requests. Explain to Tim why these two ratios are critical indicators of the financial strength of a business. What can Tim do to improve those ratios for his company?

6. Chipotle Mexican Grill is a publicly traded company. Calculate the firm's price-to-earnings ratio (P/E). What does Chipotle's P/E ratio tell you about investors' expectations regarding the company's growth?

7. Jarrett Baker is the founder of an enterprise software company located in Philadelphia. By looking at the income statements for Jarrett's business over the past three years, you see that its working capital has declined from $42,400 in 2006 to $17,900 in 2007 to $3,100 in 2008. If this trend continues, in what ways could it jeopardize the future of Jarrett's business?

8. Jorge Martinez is thinking about buying an existing printing business and has been carefully studying the records of the business to get a good handle on its historical financial performance. Jorge heard that you are taking a class in entrepreneurship and asks you, "What suggestions do you have for me to make the best use of this financial information (i.e., three years of audited income statements, balance sheets, and statements of cash flow)?" What suggestions would you give Jorge for making the maximum use of the financial statements?

9. Casey Cordell is the owner of a digital photography service in Madison, Wisconsin. The company has been profitable every year of its existence. Its debt ratio is currently 68 percent, its current ratio is 1.1, and its debt-to-equity ratio is 72.2 percent. Do these financial numbers cause any reason to be concerned? Why or why not?

10. Spend some time studying Radar Golf, the subject of the "You Be the VC 8.1" feature. Given the nature of its business, what financial management issues should Radar Golf be most attentive to and why?

11. Go to Hoover's (www.hoovers.com) and analyze how the financials of Panera Bread, the company that is the focus of Case 5.1, compare to other firms in the restaurant industry in the same manner as Dell Inc. was compared to other firms in the computer industry in this chapter. Evaluate the financial performance of Panera Bread as it compares to industry norms.

12. Suppose a colleague of yours is gearing up to write a business plan for a business she intends to start. She told you she plans to prepare the financial statements first, to get that job out of the way before she tackles the rest of the plan. Explain to your colleague the flaw in her approach.

13. Refer to "You Be the VC 5.1" feature, which focuses on Expresso Fitness, the company that produces high-end exercise bikes. If the founders of Expresso Fitness asked you to help them complete a break-even analysis for their business, how would you go about it?

14. Josh Lee has owned a fitness center for the past four years. He has historical financial statements but has never put together a set of pro forma financial statements. He just applied for a bank loan and has been told he needs a set of pro forma financial statements for the next two years. If Josh asked you to help him, how would you tell him to proceed?

15. Brenda Wilson owns a restaurant chain named Rhapsody Cuisine. She is planning to expand her chain from 9 restaurants to 15. Brenda is now working to put together a set of pro forma financial statements for an investor who expressed interest in her expansion project. Brenda used a combination of common sense and industry norms to project her future income and expenses. Shortly after she submitted the financial statements, she received them back with a handwritten note from the investor, who wrote, "I'm comfortable with your sales forecasts but think you would be on firmer ground if you used the percent-of-sales method to forecast expenses. Please redo the statements." If Brenda asked you what the investor was talking about, what would you tell her?

You Be the VC 8.1

Company: Radar Golf

www.radargolf.com

Business Idea: Develop a tiny electronic tag to put inside golf balls to make them easy to find when lost.

Pitch: What is more frustrating than losing a ball during a round of golf? Not only does a lost ball cost a player a two-stroke penalty but looking for a ball slows down play on a golf course. Slow play is frustrating for all and reduces everyone's enjoyment of the game.

Radar Golf offers a solution to these problems. The company has developed a small electronic tag that can be built into a golf ball during the manufacturing process. The tagged ball looks, feels, and performs like a regular golf ball. When a ball is difficult to find, the golfer pulls out a handheld unit (that has also been developed by Radar Golf), turns it on, points it in the direction of interest, and is led toward the ball. Depending on the terrain, it works for up to 100 feet away. By moving the unit from left to right, a pulsed audio tone (from the handheld unit) provides information on ball location and distance. The golfer quickly walks in the direction of the ball, allowing it to be located within seconds. The system can be adapted to any brand of golf ball. Rather than manufacture its own balls, Radar Golf plans to license its technology to golf ball manufacturers.

Radar Golf's system is intended to speed up play, improve the golfer's score, and provide an exciting new product to the $44 billion worldwide golf industry. It may also relieve a little of the frustration that most golfers experience on the golf course.

Q&A: Based on the material covered in this chapter, what questions would you ask the firm's founders before making your funding decision? What answers would satisfy you?

Decision: If you had to make your decision on just the information provided in the pitch and on the company's Web site, would you fund this company? Why or why not?

You Be the VC 8.2

Company: Virgin Galactic

www.virgingalactic.com

Business Idea: Offer suborbital spaceflights and later orbital spaceflights to the paying public.

Pitch: This company is no spoof. It is deadly serious—and has very credible people behind it. Virgin Galactic is a company that was launched by Sir Richard Branson's Virgin Group and plans to start offering spaceflights in the foreseeable future.

Designs for the spaceship that will carry the company's passengers are progressing at a facility led by Burton Rutan, the visionary behind the maiden voyage of *SpaceShipOne* in 2004. Recall that *SpaceShipOne* successfully traveled to suborbital space and back twice in late 2004, reaching an altitude of over 67 miles. The company is now deeply involved in comprehensive and detailed R&D efforts. The purpose of these efforts is

(continued)

to take what was learned from *SpaceShipOne*'s trips to space and create a new, more robust spaceship called *Virgin Galactic.* Sir Richard's vision to build a space tourism business and Burt Rutan's technical knowledge and passion for the future of manned spaceflight create an ideal combination to launch an entrepreneurial venture. Articulating his personal passion for Virgin Galactic, Richard Branson is quoted on the company's Web site as saying: "We hope to create thousands of astronauts over the next few years and bring alive their dreams of seeing the majestic beauty of our planet from above, the stars in all their glory and the amazing sensation of weightlessness and space flight."

The mechanics of how this product will work are interesting. The Virgin Galactic spacecraft will be carried under the belly of a large plane until around 52,000 feet, where it will be released and will then rocket into space. The entire flight will take around 2.5 hours. The suborbital portion of the flight will last for approximately 6 minutes. Passengers will be able to release themselves from their seats and float around the cabin. There are several videos posted on YouTube (simply type in "Virgin Galactic") that depict how this experience will unfold.

After departing space, the spaceship will glide back to earth and will land at its point of departure. Safety is being emphasized in every aspect of the ship's design, to create a robust, reusable craft that inspires confidence. The spacecraft will be flown by a crew of two pilots, and passengers will need about one week of training before the flight. Although seats on the first flight have been sold at a premium (starting at $200,000 for the first 100), after the initial 500 passengers, seats will be booked with a deposit of $20,000.

To illustrate how much confidence serious people have in Virgin Galactic's ability to turn its dream into a reality, the U.S. state of New Mexico recently committed $200 million in order to build a spaceport in the southern part of the state. Virgin Galactic has agreed to locate its world headquarters and mission control in New Mexico, the place from which the flights will originate.

Q&A: Based on the material covered in this chapter, what questions would you ask the firm's founders before making your funding decision? What answers would satisfy you?

Decision: If you had to make your decision on just the information provided in the pitch and on the company's Web site, would you fund this firm? Why or why not?

CASE8.1

Heartache and Financial Failure: What Happens When Financial Challenges Become Overwhelming
www.coldstonecreamery.com

Bruce R. Barringer
Oklahoma State University
R. Duane Ireland
Texas A & M University

Introduction

When a business struggles financially, not only is its budget stressed but the people who own and operate the business are often stressed as well. That's why it's so important that a business practice prudent financial management. While most people launch a business to satisfy a consumer need, they also do it to improve their lives and to achieve financial security. The worst-case scenario is to work hard to launch a business and invest a lot of money only to have the business deteriorate your quality of life and leave you worse off financially than you were before.

Cold Stone Creamery

Cold Stone Creamery was founded in 1988 by Susan and Donald Sutherland. The couple liked ice cream that was neither hard-packed nor soft-serve, and opened the first Cold Stone Creamery in Tempe, in the U.S. state of Arizona. The "Cold Stone" name comes from the frozen granite stone used to mix "mix-ins" like candy, Oreo cookies, nuts, or other edibles into ice cream in Cold Stone stores. In 1995, Cold Stone opened its first franchise in Tucson, Arizona, and grew quickly through the late 1990s and early to mid-2000s. At its peak it had around 1,400 franchise stores in the United States and several foreign countries. The number of stores doubled from 2003 to 2005 alone.

In June 2008, a *Wall Street Journal* article, by Richard Gibson, examined the unusually high number of Cold Stone Creamery franchises that had closed or been put up for sale by their owners, many of whom had suffered severe financial losses and emotional distress. The article lays out both sides of the story—including the claims made by disgruntled Cold Stone franchisees and the company's counterclaims. While the article examines the financial plight of a number of Cold Stone franchisees it makes a larger point. The Cold Stone Creamery story illustrates the financial and emotional hardships that beset business owners if their costs are too high relative to their revenues and/or they're trying to sell a premium-priced product in a tough economy. It also illustrates some of the most important financial issues that business founders should be mindful of when setting up a new business.

Challenges Facing Cold Stone Creamery Franchisees

The following are the financial challenges confronting Cold Stone Creamery franchisees:

1. High prices in a tough economy. It's hard to sell enough $4.00 scoops of ice cream in a difficult economy to support the overhead of a business that has a high overhead. Many Cold Stone Creamery franchises are located in the food courts of enclosed malls or high-traffic strip malls. Rent alone can exceed $7,000 per month. When you add the franchisee fees and other expenses, it requires a franchisee to sell a lot of scoops of ice cream per day just to break even.
2. Saturated market. Cold Stone expanded rapidly and many franchisees complain that the stores are too close together. Its competitors also expanded in the 1990s and early to mid-2000s. Combine the growing number of ice cream shops with the increased availability of premium ice cream (like Häagen-Dazs and Ben & Jerry's) in grocery stores, and it makes for a crowded market.

3. Believing the hype. Many Cold Stone franchisees bought in when the buzz surrounding the company was the strongest. At one time Cold Stone was a hot franchise and was frequently talked up in the press. While it's exciting to hear about a successful business concept, it's important to maintain a healthy sense of skepticism, particularly for a business that relies on a healthy economy to generate significant sales.
4. Franchisor control. In regard to specific financial issues, Cold Stone Creamery franchisees have complained about the way they are required to operate their businesses. An example is a Cold Stone franchisee who complained in a blog post that he recently saw twenty-four 24-ounce Pepsi bottles at Sam's Club for $14.21, but as a franchisee was required to buy Pepsi products from an approved distributor, and ended up paying $21.65 for twenty 20-ounce bottles. Another franchisee argued in an article published in *The Gazette*, the local newspaper in Colorado Springs, Colorado, that Cold Stone didn't allow him to do his own advertising, but was forced to honor $40,000 in two-for-one coupons mailed out by the corporate office.

The cumulative result of these points is that many current and former Cold Stone franchisees say that it's extremely difficult to make money owning and operating a Cold Stone Creamery franchise. Some go so far as to say that the company's business model is "broken." According to the *Wall Street Journal* article mentioned previously, 100 Cold Stone Creamery stores closed in 2007 (up from 60 in 2006), and one Cold Stone Web site recently had 303 stores up for sale. Cold Stone's president, Chris Prasifka, acknowledges in the article that the "inventory of stores for sale now is higher than it has been." But a company spokeswoman characterized the for-sale number as "at par with industry expectations."

Emotional and Financial Toll

A Web search will produce many articles and blog posts from former Cold Stone Creamery franchisees who talk about both the financial toll and the emotional toll that losing their Cold Stone franchise has imposed on their lives. As of fall 2008, there were still more than 1,000 Cold Stone Creamery stores open, and the company continues to sell franchises. The company argues that the ultimate success of an individual store depends on how well it's operated.

(continued)

Discussion Questions

1. If you were thinking about buying a franchise, like a Cold Stone Creamery store, what financial information would you look at and analyze before you completed the purchase? Be specific.
2. After reading the case, do you sympathize with the disgruntled Cold Stone franchisees, or do you believe the company's explanations?
3. Do you think that some businesses that have financial trouble might never have had a chance to begin with? If so, what can a business owner (including a franchisor of a Cold Store Creamery) do ahead of time to make sure the business is financially feasible? Use the concepts conveyed in this chapter and Chapter 3 to formulate your answer.
4. At some point in your career, could you see yourself buying a franchise? If so, what type of franchise do you think you'd enjoy owning?

Application Questions

1. What lessons, regardless of the type of business involved, can a prospective business owner learn by reading this case?
2. Do some Internet research to see what the status of Cold Stone Creamery and its franchisees are today. Has the business environment for Cold Stone Creamery franchisees improved or are a number of them still going out of business? Make a list of the business and environmental factors working for and factors working against Cold Stone Creamery franchisees.

Sources: R. Gibson, "The Inside Scoop," *Wall Street Journal*, June 12, 2008; M. Cassutt, "Cooling Business," *The Gazette*, May 3, 2008.

CASE8.2

Dell Inc.: How Its Business Model Sweetens Its Financial Statements

www.dell.com

Bruce R. Barringer
Oklahoma State University
R. Duane Ireland
Texas A & M University

Introduction

As we've mentioned in other chapters, there are many reasons that Dell Inc.'s sales approach was so successful for many years. One of the most profound reasons revolves around the effect that selling directly to the end user has had on Dell's financial structure. Conventionally, a business forecasts its demand and then schedules its production. The sales forecast that it sets reverberates throughout the supply chain. Historically at least, a company such as Hewlett-Packard (HP) shared its forecasts with its component manufacturers, which set their production schedules accordingly. With this approach, if sales fall short of projections, everyone gets stuck with inventory that's hard to unload. In fact, an often-told joke in the PC industry is that unsold inventory is like unsold vegetables—it spoils quickly. If sales go better than expected, everyone has to scramble to meet demand. Think of the financial implications that this way of doing business has for computer manufacturers and their suppliers. Forecasting, inventory levels, and unsold, obsolete products are just some of the challenges.

Financial Advantages of Dell's Business Model

Dell's business model (which was quite innovative when first introduced) sidesteps these problems through its direct-sales approach. Building to order (BTO) means producing a unit after the customer's order is transmitted to the factory floor. There's not much forecasting to do because the tempo of sales is determined in real time. Component suppliers who also build to order get information electronically from Dell as customers place orders. They deliver parts that Dell quickly places into production. Shippers, such as UPS and FedEx, cart the products away as soon as they exit the production process. This process compresses the amount of time it takes from order to delivery and forces everyone in the supply chain to be extremely efficient. In addition, an average computer manufacturer pays its suppliers 30 days before a computer is shipped to a store, bought by a consumer, and paid for. Dell's BTO model allows it to receive payment from its customers immediately. It then waits 36 days to pay its suppliers. That means that Dell has achieved a cash-conversion cycle (i.e., time between an outlay of cash for parts and the collection of payments for goods made from them) of negative 36 days. Some analysts have observed that the net result of this process is that Dell's customers and suppliers essentially finance its operations.

As an added benefit, Dell's model significantly improves its inventory turnover, which is an important financial metric for an assembly company. Inventory turnover is determined by the following formula:

$$\text{Inventory Turnover} = \frac{\text{Cost of Good Sold}}{\text{Average Inventories}}$$

A high inventory turnover means that a company is converting its inventory into cash quickly. According to an article in *Fast Company*, Dell turns its inventory over 107 times per year, which provides it a significant advantage over HP and IBM, which flip their inventories 8.5 and 17.5 times per year, respectively. This advantage enables Dell to generate a tremendous amount of cash that it uses to fund its growth. It also enables Dell to introduce new technology more quickly than many of its rivals, which use slower-moving, indirect distribution channels.

Along with crunching numbers, savvy managers assess the impact of their financial strategies on their overall goals and levels of customer satisfaction. Ultimately, it doesn't matter that a company has pretty financial statements if its customers are starting to go elsewhere. Dell's business model shines in this area too. Because it turns its inventory over quickly, it offers its customers the latest technologies rather than saddling them with products that are soon-to-be outdated. It can also pass along the advantages of falling component costs quicker than its competitors can. Dell's business model is shifting some, and a portion of its computers are now sold through retail outlets. The

vast majority of its sales, however, still take place via the Internet or over the phone.

It's hard to quantify how much long-term benefit a firm receives by passing along advantages to its customers. Positive "buzz" is a hard thing to put a price tag on. If you were the CEO of HP or Lenovo, it would also be hard to know how to respond. Companies such as HP can't simply scrap unsold inventory just because it's getting a little outdated.

The Downside of Pushing Cost Savings Too Far

Although the majority of the decisions that Dell has made have both sweetened its financial statements and pleased its customers, Dell is learning the hard way that cost savings can be pushed too far. In the early 1990s, partly in response to the challenges imposed by its rapid growth, Dell started outsourcing the majority of its call center activities to low-wage countries in Asia and Central America. This strategy led to a chorus of growing complaints about long wait times for customer service calls and poor postsales support. In response, Dell has spent over $100 million to revive its customer service, including an effort to increase the percentage of full-time Dell employees who man customer service support lines and reduce its use of part-time and contract workers. The jury is still out on whether Dell has done enough to stem the tide of customer dissatisfaction. Another downside is that Dell pushes its suppliers hard. While most suppliers respond positively, it's hard to gauge the long-term impact in supplier relations by assuming the role of "taskmaster," as Dell does, in its relationships with its suppliers.

Discussion Questions

1. Investigate the financial ratio of inventory turnover. Find current information about Dell (www.hoovers.com is a good starting place) and report whether its inventory turnover is still as impressive as the number mentioned in the case. How does Dell's current inventory turnover ratio compare to that of its competitors?

2. Locate Dell's most recent 10-K report and either locate or compute what you believe are the three most important financial ratios for Dell. Are the ratios impressive or do they provide you reason for concern?

3. If you were the CEO of HP, how would you respond to Dell's direct approach to selling?

4. What lessons can a young entrepreneurial firm learn from Dell's experiences?

(continued)

Application Questions

1. Do some Internet research to see if Dell has successfully stemmed the tide of customer complaints regarding its call center management and after-sales support. What long-term adverse affect, if any, do you think that Dell's decision to cut costs by outsourcing the majority of its call center operations in the early 1990s will have on the firm's reputation and level of customer satisfaction?

2. Look at the most recent 10-K report of Hewlett-Packard. Study the report carefully, and comment on any statements or claims that HP is making

regarding how it is improving the efficiency of its supply chain. Also, do an Internet search to see if others have written about HP's efforts to improve its supply chain. Based on your investigation, do you think HP is making meaningful strides in "catching up" to Dell in terms of supply chain management? If so, how is HP doing this?

Sources: B. Breen, "Living in Dell Time," *Fast Company,* December 19, 2007. 10-K report submitted to the Securities and Exchange Commission, filed March 31, 2008.

Endnotes

1. Personal conversation with Craig Martyn, January 7, 2009.
2. S. B. Block, G. A. Hirt, and B. Danielsen, *Foundations of Financial Management* (New York: McGraw-Hill, 2009).
3. S. Shane, *The Illusions of Entrepreneurship* (New Haven, CT: Yale University Press, 2008).
4. C. Leach and R. W. Melicher, *Entrepreneurial Finance,* 3rd ed. (Mason, OH: Cengage South-Western, 2009); P. Adelman and A. Marks, *Entrepreneurial Finance,* 4th ed. (Upper Saddle River, NJ: Prentice Hall, 2007).
5. J. D. Ryan and G. Hiduke, *Small Business: An Entrepreneur's Business Plan,* 8th ed. (Mason, OH: Cengage South-Western, 2009).
6. N. Huyghebaert and L. M. Van de Gucht, "The Determinants of Financial Structure: New Insights from Business Start-Ups," *European Financial Management* 13, no. 1 (2007): 101–133; R. Stutely, *The Definitive Guide to Managing the Numbers* (New York: Financial Times Prentice Hall, 2003).
7. J. H. Gittell, *The Southwest Airlines Way* (New York: McGraw-Hill, 2003), 7.
8. W. B. Gartner and M. G. Bellamy, *Creating the Enterprise* (Mason, OH: Cengage South-Western, 2009).
9. K. G. Palepu and P. M. Healy, *Business Analysis and Valuation: Using Financial Statements,* 4th ed. (Mason, OH: Cengage South-Western, 2008).
10. B. Gates, *Business @ the Speed of Thought* (New York: Time Warner, 1999), 214.
11. SEC homepage, www.sec.gov (accessed December 12, 2008).
12. D. Kuratko and J. Hornsby, *New Venture Management* (Upper Saddle River, NJ: Prentice Hall, 2008).
13. J. K. Shim, *Dictionary of Business Terms* (Mason, OH: Thomson Higher Education, 2006).
14. Kuratko and Hornsby, *New Venture Management.*
15. C. H. Bigson, *Financial Reporting and Analysis: Using Financial Accounting Information,* 10th ed. (Mason, OH: Cengage South-Western, 2007); A. Damodaran, *Applied Corporate Finance* (New York: John Wiley & Sons, 2006).
16. A. K. Arrow, "Managing IP Financial Assets," in *From Ideas to Assets,* ed. B. Berman (New York: John Wiley & Sons, 2002), 111–37.
17. J. E. Lange, A. Mollov, M. Pearlmutter, S. Singh, and W. D. Bygrave, "Pre-Start-Up Formal Business Plans and Post-Start-Up Performance: A Study of 116 New Ventures," *Venture Capital* 9, no. 4 (2007): 237–56; W. Lasher, *The Perfect Business Plan Made Simple* (New York, Broadway Books, 2005).
18. B. B. Lichtenstein, N. M. Carter, K. J. Dooley, and W. B. Gartner, "Complexity Dynamics of Nascent Entrepreneurship," *Journal of Business Venturing* 22, no. 2 (2007): 236–61.
19. M. Schindehutte, M. H. Morris, and L. F. Pitt, *Rethinking Marketing: The Entrepreneurial Imperative* (Upper Saddle River, NJ: Prentice Hall, 2009).

20. D. R. Anderson, D. J. Sweeney, and T. A. Williams, *Statistics for Business and Economics*, 10th ed. (Cincinnati: South-Western College Publishing, 2008).

21. E. F. Brigham and J. F. Houston, *Fundamentals of Financial Management, Concise Edition* (Cincinnati: South-Western College Publishing, 2008).

22. A. Damodaran, *Applied Corporate Finance* (New York: John Wiley & Sons, 2006).

23. Adelman and Marks, *Entrepreneurial Finance.*

JORDAN GOLDMAN
Founder, Unigo
BA, Wesleyan University, 2004

Getting Personal

with Jordan Goldman

CURRENTLY IN MY IPOD
Menomena

**MY BIGGEST SURPRISE
AS AN ENTREPRENEUR**
How much fun it is to learn
new things every day

**WHAT I'D LIKE TO BE DOING
IN 10 YEARS**
Helping Unigo become
a global company

**BEST PART OF BEING
A STUDENT**
Being constantly
surrounded by smart
people with great ideas

**MY ADVICE FOR NEW
ENTREPRENEURS**
Recognize what you don't
know, and reach out to
smart people who can
help you learn

**WHAT I DO WHEN
I'M NOT WORKING**
Watch movies, hang out
around New York City

CHAPTERNINE
Building a *New-Venture* Team

OPENING PROFILE

UNIGO

Hitting the Ground Running

www.unigo.com

Jordan Goldman has a talent for drawing advice from others. After graduating from Wesleyan University in the United States in 2004, he spent two years in England and then returned to America. With no money or business contacts, he started investigating a business idea. The idea revolved around the challenge of choosing a college. When Goldman was 18, he created a series of student-written guidebooks called the *Students' Guide to Colleges*, published by Penguin Books. One thing that troubled Goldman about the books is that each college only got a small number of pages, and there were no photos, videos, or interactivity. What if a Web site could be created, Goldman reasoned, where vast amounts of information about colleges could be included? With the cost of obtaining a four-year degree at some colleges reaching $250,000, it seemed to Goldman that students and parents would want all the information they could get about the colleges they were considering.

To get advice on how to proceed, Goldman accessed the Wesleyan alumni database and looked for people who worked in finance and who graduated 10 or more years before he did. He e-mailed about 500 people and just said: "Look, I have this idea. What do I do now? What comes next?"[1] About 50 Wesleyan alums answered his message. One of the replies was from Frank Sica, a former president of Soros Private Funds Management. Soros agreed to meet with Goldman at a diner where he had breakfast every morning. By the time breakfast was over that day, Sica was on the way to becoming Goldman's first investor.

Goldman's company, named Unigo, was launched in late 2007, and the Web site went live in September 2008. The up-front work involved hiring an editorial team to write profiles for the initial colleges to be featured on the site, and recruiting students on each campus to provide content and encourage other students to join in. Unigo is a free platform that allows college students to share photos, videos, and reviews of their schools. Because it's online, it doesn't have the space limitations that traditional college guides, like the Princeton Review, have. Unigo's mission is to provide high school students and their parents a candid, behind-the-scenes look at a college—from a student's point of view. The only content provided by Unigo is the written profiles. For instance, at the time this book went to press, the University of Florida had 101 reviews, 15 photos, 22 videos, and 4 documents posted on Unigo's Web site. The review and videos covered a wide range of students talking about their experiences inside and outside the classroom at the University of Florida. The site also allows a user to sort by major. So a high school student, who is interested in political science, can look at all the reviews and videos posted by political science majors at the University of Florida.

Goldman's knack for drawing advice from others is reflected in how he's built Unigo's new venture team. Unigo has 15 employees—5 of which are part of the top management team. In making hiring decisions, Goldman looks for passion and adaptability. He's also

Learning Objectives

After studying this chapter you should be ready to:

1. Identify the primary elements of a new-venture team.

2. Explain the term *liability of newness.*

3. Discuss the difference between heterogeneous and homogeneous founding teams.

4. Identify the personal attributes that strengthen a founder's chances of successfully launching an entrepreneurial venture.

5. Describe how to construct a "skills profile" and explain how it helps a start-up identify gaps in its new-venture team.

6. Describe a board of directors and explain the difference between inside directors and outside directors.

7. Identify the two primary ways in which the nonemployee members of a start-up's new- venture team help the firm.

8. Describe the concept of signaling and explain its importance.

9. Discuss the purpose of forming an advisory board.

10. Explain why new ventures use consultants for help and advice.

not reluctant to surround himself with people who have more experience in specific areas than he does. His top management team includes a chief financial officer (CFO) and chief technical officer (CTO), individuals who have deep amounts of experience in their expertise.

In terms of getting outside advice, Goldman has a board of advisers and a board of directors. The five-person board of advisers includes Tom Rogers, the CEO of TiVo, Bob Chase, the president of the National Education Association, and Don Ross, the president of Bankrate, Inc. The board of directors consists of founders and investors. Goldman calls on individual members of his board of advisers when he needs advice in specific areas. His board of directors meets once a month, either in person or via a conference call. Goldman also provides his board of directors biweekly updates on Unigo's key activities.

When asked how he assembled such an impressive group of advisers, Goldman is quick to say that he simply cold-called the majority of them. Goldman feels that his youth is an advantage, and that experienced businesspeople enjoy helping young people get started. The keys to a successful working relationship between a young entrepreneur and seasoned advisers, in Goldman's experience, is to act professionally, respect their time, and be prepared for meetings, so they are as substantive and productive as possible.

Unigo is expected to quickly gain momentum as the number of colleges and universities featured on its Web site grows. One thing that can be expected from Goldman is a continued propensity to reach out to others for advice as Unigo grows and faces future challenges.[2]

In this chapter, we'll focus on how the founders of an entrepreneurial venture build a new-venture team as well as the importance of the team to the firm's overall success.[3] A **new-venture team** is the group of founders, key employees, and advisers that move a new venture from an idea to a fully functioning firm. Usually, the team doesn't come together all at once. Instead, it is built as the new firm can afford to hire additional personnel. The team also involves more than paid employees. Many firms have a board of directors, a board of advisers, and other professionals on whom they rely for direction and advice.

In this chapter's first section, we discuss the role of an entrepreneurial venture's founder or founders and emphasize the substantial effect that founders have on their firm's future. We then turn our attention to a discussion about how the founders build a new-venture team, including the recruitment and selection of key employees and the forming of a board of directors. The chapter's second section examines the important role of advisers and other professionals in shaping and rounding out a new-venture team.

As we note throughout this book, new ventures have a high propensity to fail. The high failure rate is due in part to what is known as the **liability of newness**, which refers to the fact that companies often falter because the people who start them aren't able to adjust quickly enough to their new roles and because the firm lacks a "track record" with outside buyers and suppliers.[4] Assembling a talented and experienced new-venture team is one path firms can take to overcome these limitations. Indeed, experienced management teams that get up to speed quickly are much less likely to make a novice's mistakes. In addition, firms able to persuade high-quality individuals to join them as directors or advisers quickly gain legitimacy with a variety of individuals, such as some of those working inside the venture as well as some people outside the venture (e.g., suppliers, customers, and investors). In turn, legitimacy opens doors that otherwise would be closed.

Another way entrepreneurs overcome the liability of newness is by attending entrepreneurship-focused workshops, speaker series, boot camps, and similar events. These types of activities are often sponsored by local universities, small business development centers, and economic development commissions.

CREATING A NEW-VENTURE TEAM

Those who launch or found an entrepreneurial venture have an important role to play in shaping the firm's business concept. Stated even more directly, it is widely known that a well-conceived business plan cannot get off the ground unless a firm has the leaders and personnel to carry it out. As one expert put it, "People are the one factor in production . . . that animates all the others."[5] Often, several start-ups develop what is essentially the same idea at the same time. When this happens, the key to success is not the idea but rather the ability of the initial founder or founders to assemble a team that can execute the idea better than anyone else.

The way a founder builds a new-venture team sends an important signal to potential investors, partners, and employees. Some founders like the feeling of control and are reluctant to involve themselves with partners or hire managers who are more experienced than they are. In contrast, other founders are keenly aware of their own limitations and work hard to find the most experienced people available to bring on board. Similarly, some new firms never form an advisory board, whereas others persuade the most important (and influential) people they can find to provide them with counsel and advice. In general, the way to impress potential investors, partners, and employees is to put together as strong a team as possible.[6] Investors and others know that experienced personnel and access to good-quality advice contributes greatly to a new venture's success.

The elements of a new-venture team are shown in Figure 9.1. It's important that each element, or group of people, that constitutes the team have a common vision for the new venture and that everyone's role is clearly spelled out. Breakdowns in these areas can lead to the failure of an otherwise promising new venture, as illustrated in the "What Went Wrong?" feature.

Learning Objective

1. Identify the primary elements of a new-venture team.

Learning Objective

2. Explain the term *liability of newness*.

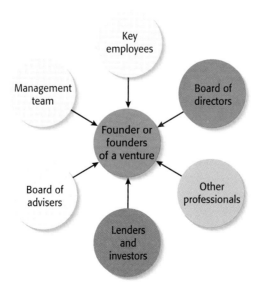

FIGURE 9.1

Elements of a New-Venture Team

What Went WRONG?

Monitor110: How a Lack of Consensus and a Clear Leader Can Damage a New-Venture Team

Jeff Stewart and Roger Ehrenberg launched Monitor110 in 2005. The idea was to help hedge fund managers and professional investors make better investment decisions by identifying and tracking the most insightful information being put out on the Internet every day. Because hedge fund managers and professional investors are busy and are always looking for an edge, the idea was that they'd pay someone to help them sort through the deluge of information posted on the Internet and identify, in real-time, the information most pertinent to their investment priorities and strategies.

Monitor110's idea was compelling and it attracted substantial investment capital. Unfortunately, however, in July 2008, it failed. One of Monitor110's cofounders, Roger Ehrenberg, wrote a lengthy blog post reflecting on the company's failure. He believes that Monitor110 committed "Seven Deadly Sins" that contributed to its failure:

1. The lack of a single, "the buck stops here" leader until too late in the game.
2. No separation between the technology organization and the product organization.
3. Too much PR, too early (raising expectations to unrealistic levels).
4. Too much money (which allowed the company to repeat mistakes).
5. Not close enough to the customer.
6. Slow to adapt to market realities.
7. Disagreement on strategy both within the company and with the board.

Three of the seven reasons listed above deal with new-venture team issues. This, is more than any other category of reasons, illustrates the importance of a firm's new-venture team and how well it functions to a new venture's success.

In regard to number 1, "The lack of a single, 'the buck stops here' leader until too late in the game," as Monitor100 took shape, a problematic relationship developed between the company's cofounders. Jeff Stewart had technology experience and Roger Ehrenberg had experience on Wall Street, so Stewart focused on technology and product development and Ehrenberg focused on fund-raising, HR, and client access. On paper, the arrangement made perfect sense. But when it came time to make tough decisions, there wasn't a clear decision maker or leader. Because Monitor100 was ultimately a technology company, technology tended to dominate the discussions and carried the most weight, resulting in products that the business side wasn't happy with and found difficult to sell. Neither Stewart nor Ehrenberg had the power to change things, and the board didn't intervene until it was too late.

Number 2, "No separation between the technology organization and product organization," was also problematic. Technology and product management were effectively bundled together with the same decision makers for both. Instead of having a staff of product managers as advocates for the customer, technology was running the show. This structure allowed the technology guys to build a full set of features into a product prior to a release (slowing the release date), rather than releasing products more quickly and allowing the product managers to interact with customers, listen to their feedback, and incorporate their feedback into the final product.

Finally, in regard to number 7, "Disagreement on strategy both within the company and with the board," there were disagreements both within the management team and with the board of directors on a number of important issues. For example, similar to number 2, there were people in the company advocating that the best possible technological solution should be found to mine data on the Web. By insisting on the best solution, enormous effort was dedicated to building the company's technological back-end. Ultimately, the back-end may have been too complex, and the data provided to the customers wasn't commensurate with the effort being made to collect it.

The Monitor110 story illustrates the importance of making sure that everyone on a new venture's management team (including the board of directors) is in agreement regarding the company's priorities and its direction. It also illustrates the importance of making sure a decision-making structure is in place that doesn't result in a stalemate if the founders (or other key members of the new-venture team) disagree on important strategic decisions.

Questions for Critical Thinking

1. If two or more people start a company together, how can they work out an arrangement for decision making that avoids the lack of a single "the buck stops here" leader that was problematic for Monitor110?
2. According to the feature, Monitor110 saw itself as a "technology" company. In what ways was this "self-image" problematic?
3. How could Monitor110's board of directors have played a more positive role in helping the company avoid the problems illustrated in the feature?
4. What lessons can start-ups learn from this feature to help them set up and manage their new-venture teams?

Source: R. Ehrenberg, "Monitor110: A Post Mortem," www.informationarbitrage.com (accessed September 16, 2008). Used with permission of Roger Ehrenberg.

We'll look at each of these elements in the next section. While reading these descriptions, remember that entrepreneurial ventures vary in how they use the elements.

The Founder or Founders

A founder's or founders' characteristics and their early decisions have a significant effect on the way an entrepreneurial venture is received and the manner in which the new-venture team takes shape. The size of the founding team and the qualities of the founder or founders are the two most important issues in this matter.

Size of the Founding Team   The first decision that most founders face is whether to start a firm on their own or whether to build an initial **founding team**. Studies show that more than one individual starts 50 to 70 percent of all new firms.[7] It is generally believed that new ventures started by a team have an advantage over those started by an individual because a team brings more talent, resources, ideas, and professional contacts to a new venture than does a sole entrepreneur.[8] In addition, the psychological support that cofounders of a new business can offer one another is an important element in the firm's success.[9]

Several factors affect the value of a team that is starting a new firm. First, teams that have worked together before, as opposed to teams that are working together for the first time, have an edge. If people have worked together before and have decided to partner to start a firm together, it usually means that they get along personally and trust one another.[10] They also tend to communicate with one another more effectively than people who are new to one another.[11] Second, if the members of the team are **heterogeneous**, meaning that they are diverse in terms of their abilities and experiences, rather than **homogeneous**, meaning that their areas of expertise are very similar to one another, they are likely to have different points of view about technology, hiring decisions, competitive tactics, and other important activities. Typically, these different points of view generate debate and constructive conflict among the founders, reducing the likelihood that decisions will be made in haste or without the airing of alternative points of view.[12] A founding team can be too big, causing communication problems and an increased potential for conflict. A founding team larger than four people is typically too large to be practical.[13]

There are two potential pitfalls associated with starting a firm as a team rather than as a sole entrepreneur. First, the team members may not get along. This is the reason investors favor teams consisting of people who have worked together before. It is simply more likely that people who have gotten along with one another in the past will continue to get along in the future. Second, if two or more people start a firm as "equals," conflicts can arise when the firm needs to establish a formal structure and designate one person as the chief executive officer (CEO). If the firm has investors, the investors will usually weigh in on who should be appointed CEO. In these instances, it is easy for the founder that wasn't chosen as the CEO to feel slighted. This problem is exacerbated if multiple founders are involved and they all stay with the firm. At some point, a hierarchy will have to be developed, and the founders will have to decide who reports to whom. Some of these problems can be avoided through the development of a founders' agreement, which was described in Chapter 7.

Qualities of the Founders   The second major issue pertaining to the founders of a firm is the qualities they bring to the table. The past several chapters have illustrated the importance that investors and others place on the strength of the firm's founders and initial management team. One reason the founders are so important is that in the early days of a firm, their knowledge, skills, and experiences are

Learning Objective

3. Discuss the difference between heterogeneous and homogeneous founding teams.

Learning Objective

4. Identify the personal attributes that strengthen a founder's chances of successfully launching an entrepreneurial venture.

the most valuable resource the firm has. Because of this, new firms are judged largely on their "potential" rather than their current assets or current performance. In most cases, this results in people judging the future prospects of a firm by evaluating the strength of its founders and initial management team.

Several features are thought to be significant to a founder's success. The level of a founder's education is important because it's believed that entrepreneurial abilities such as search skills, foresight, creativity, and computer skills are enhanced through obtaining a college degree. Similarly, some observers think that higher education equips a founder with important business-related skills, such as math and communications. In addition, specific forms of education, such as engineering, computer science, management information systems, physics, and biochemistry, provide the recipients of this education an advantage if they start a firm that is related to their area of expertise.[14]

Prior entrepreneurial experience, relevant industry experience, and networking are other attributes that strengthen the chances of a founder's success. Indeed, the results of research studies somewhat consistently suggest that **prior entrepreneurial experience** is one of the most consistent predictors of future entrepreneurial performance.[15] Because launching a new venture is a complex task, entrepreneurs with prior start-up experience have a distinct advantage. The impact of **relevant industry experience** on an entrepreneur's ability to successfully launch and grow a firm has also been studied.[16] Entrepreneurs with experience in the same industry as their current venture will have a more mature network of industry contacts and will have a better understanding of the subtleties of their respective industries.[17] The importance of this factor is particularly evident for entrepreneurs who start firms in technical industries such as biotechnology. The demands of biotechnology are sufficiently intense that it would be virtually impossible for someone to start a biotech firm while at the same time learning biotechnology. The person must have an understanding of biotechnology prior to launching a firm through either relevant industry experience or an academic background. Some entrepreneurs, who come from a nonbusiness background, fear that a lack of business experience will be their Achilles' heel. There are several steps or techniques that entrepreneurs can utilize to overcome a lack of business experience. These steps are highlighted in the "Savvy Entrepreneurial Firm" feature.

A particularly important attribute for founders or founding teams is the presence of a mature network of social and professional contacts.[18] Founders

One quality that's particularly important for business founders is the ability to network, or to build relationships with people who might be helpful to a new firm. Here, a group of young business founders informally network with one another at an outdoor café.

Bill Bachmann/PhotoEdit Inc.

Savvy Entrepreneurial FIRM
Overcoming a Lack of Business Experience

Many people who start businesses do not have prior business experience. This is often a worry to people who fit this description. They know that people with experience in accounting, finance, and management generally have a leg up on those who are tackling these challenges for the first time.

There are three steps or techniques that people without prior business experience can take to compensate for a lack of experience.

Find a Partner

As explained in this chapter, taking on one or more partners is a step that many business founders take to bolster the experience and expertise available to launch their venture. The ideal partnership brings together people with complementary skills. As a result, a software engineer who has developed a new software product may want to seek a partner who has business experience to create a better-rounded team. This scenario played out for Kabir Shahani and Chris Hahn, the cofounders of Appature, a software company that targets the health care industry. In this instance, Hahn sought out Shahani to create a partnership in which their respective skills complement each other's. Shahani recalls:

> He (Hahn) had a lot of faith in my skills, and I feel really fortunate that he did. I'll never forget that conversation. We were sitting in a Thai restaurant in the International district (of Seattle), and he said, 'Look, I can build anything, and I think you can sell anything, so let's do it.'"

Get Help

There are many places for business founders to get management advice and help. The Small Business Development Center (SBDC), for example, is a government agency that provides free management assistance and coaching to business owners. You can find your local SBDC at www.sba.gov/sbdc. Another good choice is the Service Corps of Retired Executives (SCORE), which is a nonprofit organization that provides free consulting services to small businesses. You can find your local SCORE chapter at www.score.org. There are also organizations that provide coaching, advice, and support to specific groups of business owners and tailor their offerings to fit the groups. An example is Ladies Who Launch (www.ladieswholaunch.com), an organization that sponsors workshops and provides materials that encourage and support female business owners.

If you're looking for a support group in your area and can't find one, check the Meetup Web site. Meetup (www.meetup.com) is an online platform that allows individuals to organize local groups via the Internet.

Once a group is formed, its members "meet up" on a regular basis off-line. Simply follow the directions on Meetup's home page to discover if there is a small business or entrepreneurship Meetup group in your area. The following is a sample of small business Meetup groups that were meeting when this book went to press:

- Memphis Small Business and Entrepreneur Meetup Group
- New Iowa Entrepreneurs' Coalition
- Chicago Small Business Progress Report Group
- Cleveland Small Business Meetup Group
- Women in Business Meetup Group (Casselberry, FL)

Participate in Online Forums

There are a growing number of online forums that have been developed to provide business owners support and advice. An example is StartupNation (www.startupnation.com), which sponsors online forums that cover topics such as selecting a business for yourself, business planning, hiring, partnering and mentoring, and accounting and financial management. It also features open-ended forums such as "coffee talk," where small business owners can chat with one another about any topic that is on their minds. The general tone of the forums tends to be supportive and upbeat, which is exactly what business owners with limited experience need. A small business forum that is more specific is the Small Business Computing and E-Commerce Forum (www.smallbusinesscomputing.com). This forum is similar to the one just described but focuses strictly on technology issues.

Questions for Critical Thinking

1. If you were thinking about starting a business and were looking for a business partner, what types of skills and experiences would you look for in the person you partnered with?
2. Identify three sources of business help or advice, particularly useful to someone who's starting a business without prior business experience, not mentioned in the feature.
3. How valuable do you believe that online forums, like those mentioned previously, can be to someone who's trying to learn the "business" aspect of starting a business?
4. What other techniques, not mentioned previously, can people who don't have prior business experience utilize to compensate for their lack of experience?

Source: nPost homepage, www.npost.com (accessed September 25, 2008). Used with permission of *nPost.com*.

Table 9.1 PREFERRED ATTRIBUTES OF THE FOUNDER OR FOUNDERS
OF AN ENTREPRENEURIAL VENTURE

Attribute	Explanation
Firm started by a team	New ventures that are started by a team can provide greater resources, a broader diversity of viewpoints, and a broader array of other positive attributes than ventures started by individuals.
Higher education	Evidence suggests that important entrepreneurial skills are enhanced through higher education.
Prior entrepreneurial experience	Founders with prior entrepreneurial experience are familiar with the entrepreneurial process and are more likely to avoid costly mistakes than founders new to the rigors of the entrepreneurial process.
Relevant industry experience	Founders with experience in the same industry as their new venture will most likely have better-established professional networks and more applicable marketing and management expertise than founders without relevant industry experience.
Broad social and professional network	Founders with broad social and professional networks have potential access to additional know-how, capital, and customer referrals.

must often "work" their social and personal networks to raise money or gain access to critical resources on behalf of their firms.[19] **Networking** is building and maintaining relationships with people whose interests are similar or whose relationship could bring advantages to a firm. The way this might play out in practice is that a founder calls a business acquaintance or friend to ask for an introduction to a potential investor, business partner, or customer. For some founders, networking is easy and is an important part of their daily routine. For others, it is a learned skill.

Table 9.1 shows the preferred attributes of the founder or founders of a firm. Start-ups that have founders or a team of founders with these attributes have the best chances of early success.

Recruiting and Selecting Key Employees

Once the decision to launch a new venture has been made, building a management team and hiring key employees begins. Start-ups vary in terms of how quickly they need to add personnel. In some instances, the founders work alone for a period of time while the business plan is being written and the venture begins taking shape. In other instances, employees are hired immediately.

One technique available to entrepreneurs to help prioritize their hiring needs is to maintain a skills profile. A **skills profile** is a chart that depicts the most important skills that are needed and where skills gaps exist. A skills profile for New Venture Fitness Drinks, the fictitious company introduced in Chapter 3, is shown in Figure 9.2. Along with depicting where a firm's most important skills gaps exist, a skills profile should explain how current skills gaps are being dealt with. For example, two of New Venture Fitness Drink's skills gaps are being covered (on a short-term basis) by members of the board of advisers and the third skills gap does not need to be filled until the firm initiates a franchising program, which is still three to five years in the future.

Evidence suggests that finding good employees today is not an easy task. Consider the results of a recent survey by PricewaterhouseCoopers (PWC) as evidence of this. In the PWC survey, the CEOs of 245 rapid-growth firms were asked if finding qualified workers was a concern. A total of 40 percent of the CEOs, in the first quarter of 2008, reported that a lack of qualified workers is a potential barrier to growth for their firms over the next 12 months.[20] A study conducted by the

Learning Objective

5. Describe how to construct a "skills profile" and explain how it helps a start-up identify gaps in its new-venture team.

FIGURE 9.2

Skills Profile for New Venture Fitness Drinks

	Executive Leadership	Store Operations	Supply Chain Management	Marketing and Sales	HR/Recruiting	Accounting and Finance	Community Relations	Information Systems	Franchise Operations
Jack Petty	X								
Peggy Wells		X				X			
Jill Petersen				X					
Cameron Ivey			X						
Gap 1					O				
Gap 2							O		
Gap 3									O

X = position filled
O = position vacant

Council for Entrepreneurial Development, which is an organization that supports entrepreneurship in the Research Triangle area of North Carolina, resulted in a similar finding. When asked to rank the key factors in growing an entrepreneurial company, entrepreneurs in the Research Triangle area selected "Availability of Qualified Technical and Non-Technical Workers" as the number one factor.[21]

Founders differ in their approach to the task of recruiting and selecting key employees. Some founders draw on their network of contacts to identify candidates for key positions. Others ask their existing employees for referrals. Safilo USA, a luxury eyewear company, pays its employees for referrals. An employee who refers someone who joins the company gets $500 after the new hire has been with Safilo for six months and another $500 after a year.[22] Many companies use interns to help fill personnel needs. TOMS, the socially conscious shoe company described in Case 7.2, has about 60 employees—half of which are interns. Other companies rely on job search Web sites like Monster.com or PartnerUp (www.partnerup.com), a site dedicated to helping entrepreneurs find partners and employees.

Many founders worry about hiring the wrong person for a key role. Because most new firms are strapped for cash, every team member must make a valuable contribution, so it's not good enough to hire someone who is well intended but who doesn't precisely fit the job. Alisa Nessler, the founder of Lane15, a software start-up, emphasizes this point in the following remarks:

One of the first things you learn in a start-up is that it's very expensive to make a bad hire. In a large company, people sometimes tend to think that when you have somebody who fits into the bucket labeled "Heart's in the right place," or the one labeled "Good attitude but just not getting it done," you can work around it. Maybe it's because in an established organization, it's easier to lose sight of the contributions each individual is making. In a start-up, you simply can't do that. Everyone is important. Every team member's work has to have a direct impact on value, or the person has to go.[23]

On some occasions, key hires work out perfectly and fill the exact roles that the founders of the firm need. For example, Dave Olsen was one of the first hires made by Starbucks founder Howard Schultz. At the time of his hiring, Olsen was the owner of a popular coffeehouse in the university district of Seattle, the city where Starbucks was launched. In his autobiography, Schultz recalls the following about the hiring of Olsen:

> On the day of our meeting, Dave and I sat on my office floor and I started spreading the plans and blueprints out and talking about my idea. Dave got it right away. He had spent ten years in an apron, behind a counter, serving espresso drinks. He had experienced firsthand the excitement people can develop about espresso, both in his café and in Italy. I didn't have to convince him that this idea had big potential. He just knew it in his bones. The synergy was too good to be true. My strength was looking outward: communicating the vision, inspiring investors, raising money, finding real estate, designing the stores, building the brand, and planning for the future. Dave understood the inner workings: the nuts and bolts of operating a retail café, hiring and training baristas (coffee brewers), ensuring the best quality coffee.[24]

Dave Olsen went on to become a key member of the Starbucks new-venture team and remains with the company today, where he serves as the senior vice president for culture and leadership development.

One attribute investors value in founders is a willingness to be flexible and assume the role that makes the most sense for them in their venture rather than insisting on being the CEO. This is a difficult task for some founders who become entrepreneurs to "be their own boss" or put their distinctive stamp on a firm. Founders who do remain flexible, however, often have an easier time obtaining financing or funding. The way many founders look at this issue is that it is better to be the vice president of a $100-million firm than the CEO of a $10-million firm.

The Roles of the Board of Directors

Learning Objective

6. Describe a board of directors and explain the difference between inside directors and outside directors.

If a new venture organizes as a corporation, it is legally required to have a **board of directors**—a panel of individuals who are elected by a corporation's shareholders to oversee the management of the firm.[25] A board is typically made up of both inside and outside directors. An **inside director** is a person who is also an officer of the firm. An **outside director** is someone who is not employed by the firm. A board of directors has three formal responsibilities: (1) appoint the firm's officers (the key managers), (2) declare dividends, and (3) oversee the affairs of the corporation. In the wake of corporate scandals such as Enron and WorldCom and others, the emphasis on the board's role in making sure the firm is operating in an ethical manner continues to become stronger. One outcome of this movement is a trend toward putting more outsiders on boards of directors, because people who do not work for the firm are usually more willing to scrutinize the behavior of management than insiders who work for the company. Most boards meet formally three or four times a year. Large firms pay their directors for their service. New ventures are more likely to pay their directors in company stock or ask them to serve without direct compensation—at least until the company is profitable. The boards for publicly traded companies are required by law to have audit and compensation committees. Many boards also have nominating committees to select stockholders to run for vacant board positions.

If handled properly, a company's board of directors can be an important part of its new-venture team. Providing expert guidance and legitimacy in the eyes of others (e.g., customers, investors, and even competitors) are two ways a board of directors can help a new firm get off to a good start and develop what, it is hoped, will become a sustainable competitive advantage.

Provide Guidance   Although a board of directors has formal governance responsibilities, its most useful role is to provide guidance and support to the firm's managers.[26] Many CEOs interact with their board members frequently and obtain important input. The key to making this happen is to pick board members with needed skills and useful experiences who are willing to give advice and ask insightful and probing questions. The extent to which an effective board can help shape a firm and provide it a competitive advantage in the marketplace is expressed by Ram Charan, an expert on the role of boards of directors in corporations:

> They (effective boards) listen, probe, debate, and become engaged in the company's most pressing issues. Directors share their expertise and wisdom as a matter of course. As they do, management and the board learn together, a collective wisdom emerges, and managerial judgment improves. The on-site coaching and consulting expand the mental capacity of the CEO and the top management team and give the company a competitive edge out there in the marketplace.[27]

Because managers rely on board members for counsel and advice, the search for outside directors should be purposeful, with the objective of filling gaps in the experience and background of the venture's executives and the other directors. For example, if two computer programmers started a software firm and neither one of them had any marketing experience, it would make sense to place a marketing executive on the board of directors. Indeed, a board of directors has the foundation to effectively serve its organization when its members represent many important organizational skills (e.g., manufacturing, human resource management, and financing) involved with running a company.

Lend Legitimacy   Providing legitimacy for the entrepreneurial venture is another important function of a board of directors. Well-known and respected board members bring instant credibility to the firm. For example, just imagine the positive buzz a firm could generate if it could say that Eric Schmidt of Google or Steven Jobs of Apple had agreed to serve on its board of directors. This phenomenon is referred to as **signaling**. Without a credible signal, it is difficult for potential customers, investors, or employees to identify high-quality start-ups. Presumably, high-quality individuals would be reluctant to serve on the board of a low-quality firm because that would put their reputation at risk. So when a high-quality individual does agree to serve on a board of a firm, the individual is in essence "signaling" that the company has potential to be successful.[28]

Achieving legitimacy through high-quality board members can result in other positive outcomes. Investors like to see new-venture teams, including the board of directors, that have people with enough clout to get their foot in the door with potential suppliers and customers. Board members are also often instrumental in helping young firms arrange financing or funding. As we will discuss in Chapter 10, it's almost impossible for an entrepreneurial venture's founders to get the attention of an investor without a personal introduction. One way firms deal with this challenge is by placing individuals on their boards who are acquainted with people in the investment community.

A list of the most desirable qualities in a board of directors and the most desirable qualities in individual board members is provided in Table 9.2.

Learning Objective

7. Identify the two primary ways in which the nonemployee members of a start-up's new-venture team help the firm.

Learning Objective

8. Describe the concept of signaling and explain its importance.

Table 9.2   ATTRIBUTES OF EFFECTIVE BOARDS OF DIRECTORS AND EFFECTIVE BOARD MEMBERS

Attributes of Effective Boards of Directors

- Strong communication with the CEO
- Customer-focused point of view
- Complementary mix of talents
- Decisiveness
- Mutual respect and regard for each other and the management team of the firm
- Ability and willingness to stand up to the CEO and top managers of the firm
- Strong ethics

Attributes of Strong Board Members

- Strong personal and professional networks
- Respected in their field
- Willingness to make personal introductions on behalf of the firm
- Strong interpersonal communication skills
- Pattern recognition skills
- Investment and/or operating experience
- Ability and willingness to mentor the CEO and the top managers of the firm

ROUNDING OUT THE TEAM: THE ROLE OF PROFESSIONAL ADVISERS

Along with the new-venture team members we've already identified, founders often rely on professionals with whom they interact for important counsel and advice. In many cases, these professionals become an important part of the new-venture team and fill what some entrepreneurs call "talent holes."

Next, we discuss the roles that boards of advisers, lenders, investors, and other professionals play in rounding out new-venture teams.

Entrepreneurs often meet with a member of their advisory board on a personal basis to obtain valuable business advice. With a carefully selected advisory board, entrepreneurs can tap into a wide range of experience and expertise.

Todd B. Powell/Creative Eye/MIRA.com

Board of Advisers

Some start-up firms are forming advisory boards to provide them direction and advice.[29] An **advisory board** is a panel of experts who are asked by a firm's managers to provide counsel and advice on an ongoing basis. Unlike a board of directors, an advisory board possesses no legal responsibility for the firm and gives nonbinding advice.[30] As a result, more people are willing to serve on a company's board of advisers than on its board of directors because it requires less time and no legal liability is involved. A board of advisers can be established for general purposes or can be set up to address a specific issue or need. For example, some start-ups set up customer advisory boards shortly after they are founded to help them fine-tune their initial offerings. Similar to a board of directors, the main purpose of a board of advisers is to provide guidance and lend legitimacy to a firm. Both of these attributes are seen in the advisory board set up by Laura Udall, the entrepreneur who started ZUCA, a company mentioned previously in this book. When asked about the type of advice she gets from her board of directors and board of advisers, Udall said:

> The company (ZUCA) has a board of directors, but I also have created a board of volunteer advisors that has been very helpful with tactical and strategic decisions. The advisory board has evolved over the years as a result of my network. I asked each of the members to join as a result of their specific expertise. It now includes a CFO/COO of a prominent corporation, an executive in the luggage industry, a mom inventor who has founded several successful companies, a product designer, and a manufacturing expert.[31]

Imagine the type of advice and support Udall gleans from this group of advisers. An example of a firm that set up a customer advisory board for a different reason, to help develop its initial product, is highlighted in the "Partnering for Success" feature.

Most boards of advisers have between 5 and 15 members. Companies typically pay the members of their board of advisers a small honorarium for their service either annually or on a per-meeting basis. Boards of advisers interact with each other and with a firm's managers in several ways. Some advisory boards meet three or four times a year at the company's headquarters or in another location. Other advisory boards meet in an online environment. In some cases, a firm's board of advisers will be scattered across the country, making it more cost-effective for a firm's managers to interact with the members of the board on the telephone or via e-mail rather than to bring them physically together. In these situations, board members don't interact with each other at all on a face-to-face basis yet still provide high levels of counsel and advice.

The fact that a start-up has a board of directors does not preclude it from having one or more board of advisers. For example, Coolibar, a maker of sun protective clothing, has a board of directors and a medical advisory board. According to Coolibar, its medical advisory board "provides advice to the company regarding UV radiation, sunburn, and the science of detecting, preventing, and treating skin cancer and other UV-related medical disorders, such as lupus.[32] The board currently consists of six medical doctors, all with impressive credentials. Similarly, Intouch Technologies, a medical robotics company, has a board of directors along with a business and strategy advisory board, an applications and clinical advisory board, and a scientific and technical advisory board. A total of 15 individuals serve on these respective boards.[33]

VisualCV, the subject of the "You Be the VC 9.1" feature in this chapter, is a start-up that is attempting to replace the traditional paper résumé with a

Learning Objective

9. Discuss the purpose of forming an advisory board.

Partnering for SUCCESS
Need Help with Product Development? Consider Setting Up a Customer Advisory Board

Although most firms that have a customer advisory board set them up after their firm is started, primarily to assess customer satisfaction and brainstorm new product ideas, customer advisory boards can be useful before a firm has customers as well. An example of a firm that did this is iConclude, an IT solutions company that was recently acquired by Opsware (www.opsware.com). iConclude was founded to help other companies troubleshoot mission critical software and hardware problems, but when it came to producing an actual product, the company wasn't exactly sure what its product should look like. To make sure it didn't stumble and produce a product that wasn't what its clients needed, the company decided to form a customer advisory board to dig deep into its future customers' problems and discern the exact features its product should include. Reflecting on the nature of the customer advisory board that was set up, and what the effort accomplished, Sunny Gupta, iConclude's founder, recalls:

> We were very upfront with all of the companies we spoke with. We realized we needed real customer input in order for us to really get the right product into the market. That led us to form a customer advisory board of 7 to 8 of these (firms with large IT departments) companies mostly out of Seattle. They met with us every second week and really tried to hone down on exactly what their problems were and what would be the ideal solution from

their perspective. This got them on board much, much earlier with us which was pretty instrumental because we identified real requirements which enabled us to build the right product."

Ultimately, iConclude built a successful product and was acquired shortly after by a much larger firm.

Questions for Critical Thinking

1. Why do you think iConclude was able to persuade other companies to serve on its customer advisory board?
2. What insight or insights do you believe that iConclude gained by assembling a customer advisory board before rather than after its product was fully developed? What benefits, other than getting good quality advice, did iConclude glean from putting together a customer advisory board?
3. How do you think iConclude utilized its customer advisory board after its product was launched?
4. Look at Fitbit (www.fitbit.com), the focus of the "You Be the VC 9.2" feature. What type of advisory board or advisory boards would make the most sense for Fitbit?

Source: nPost, "Sunny Gupta, CEO of iConclude," www.npost.com (accessed June 22, 2007). Used with permission of *nPost.com.*

virtual résumé that resides on the Web, and allows a job seeker to include all the items in a standard résumé along with a video introduction, visuals depicting accomplishments, links to letters of recommendation, and similar material. VisualCV has a 13-member board of advisers. Each of the company's board members has a VisualCV on the company's Web site. The following is a short list, including credentials, of some of the members of VisualCV's board of advisers:

- ■ James Collins—Recruiting Manager for VeriSign Inc. Collins has more than 10 years of experience in progressive full-life-cycle recruiting and the management of recruiting teams. He has success working with start-ups and publicly held companies in the technology, bio-tech, and health care sectors.
- ■ Brad Phillips—Cofounder and Partner of the Heiden Group. Phillips has played a crucial role in building the Heiden Group (which is a recruiting service for venture-backed companies) from no revenue to just under $3 million in revenue in less than three years. Prior to cofounding the Heiden Group, Phillips spent 14 years in consulting.
- ■ Guy Kawasaki—Founding Partner of Garage Technology Ventures and Cofounder of Nononina (the owner of Alltop.com and Truemors.com).

Kawasaki is the author of eight books including *The Art of the Start*. Previously, he was an Apple Fellow at Apple Computer.

■ Catherine King—President and CEO of HRPLUS, an international provider of background screening and drug testing services. King is a recruitment, staffing, HRO, and professional services expert. King is driving the future direction of HRPLUS, including the development of new products and technology.

■ Dr. Terrence LaPier—Cofounder and Senior Partner at Pierpont Group. The Pierpont Group is a strategic advisory and private equity firm. Dr. LaPier is also an adjunct faculty member at the University of Pennsylvania's Wharton School of Business where he teaches courses in entrepreneurship leadership, venture initiation, and international business.[34]

This example provides an illustration of the breadth of talent and expertise that a firm can have available when it creates a board of advisers. Imagine the combined network of friends and business acquaintances that VisualCV's board of advisers has and the number of referrals they can make to people who are in a position to help VisualCV become successful.

There are several guidelines to organizing a board of advisers. First, a board of advisers should not be organized just so a company can boast of it. Advisers will become quickly disillusioned if they don't play a meaningful role in the firm's development and growth. Second, a firm should look for board members who are compatible and complement one another in terms of experience and expertise. Unless the board is being set up for a specific purpose, a board that includes members with varying backgrounds is preferable to a board of people with similar backgrounds. Third, when inviting a person to serve on its board of advisers, a company should carefully spell out to the individual the rules in terms of access to confidential information.[35] Some firms ask the members of their advisory board to sign nondisclosure agreements, which are described in Chapter 7. Finally, firms should caution their advisers to disclose that they have a relationship with the venture before posting positive comments about it or its products on blogs or in Internet chat rooms. A potential conflict of interest surfaces when a person says positive things about a company without disclosing an affiliation with the firm, particularly if there is a financial stake in the company. This issue has become more important as participation in Internet blogging has skyrocketed.[36]

Although having a board of advisers is widely recommended in start-up circles, most start-ups do not have one. As a result, one way a start-up can make itself stand out is to have one or more boards of advisers.

Lenders and Investors

As emphasized throughout this book, lenders and investors have a vested interest in the companies they finance, often causing them to become very involved in helping the firms they fund. It is rare that a lender or investor will put money into a new venture and then simply step back and wait to see what happens. In fact, the institutional rules governing banks and investment firms typically require that they monitor new ventures fairly closely, at least during the initial years of a loan or an investment.[37]

The amount of time and energy a lender or investor dedicates to a new firm depends on the amount of money involved and how much help the new firm needs. For example, a lender with a well-secured loan may spend very little time with a client, whereas a venture capitalist may spend an enormous amount of time helping a new venture refine its business model, recruit management personnel, and meet with current and prospective customers and suppliers. In fact, evidence suggests that an average venture capitalist is likely to visit each company in a portfolio multiple times a year.[38] This number denotes a high level of involvement and support.

As with the other nonemployee members of a firm's new-venture team, lenders and investors help new firms by providing guidance and lending legitimacy and assume the natural role of providing financial oversight.[39] In some instances, lenders and investors also work hard to help new firms fill out their management teams. Sometimes this issue is so important that a new venture will try to obtain investment capital not only to get access to money but also to obtain help hiring key employees.

For example, during its beginning stages, eBay's partners, Pierre Omidyar and Jeff Skoll, decided to recruit a CEO. They wanted someone who was not only experienced but also had the types of credentials that Wall Street investors value. They soon discovered that every experienced manager they tried to recruit asked if they had venture capital backing—which at that time they did not. For a new firm trying to recruit a seasoned executive, venture capital backing is a sort of seal of legitimacy. To get this valuable seal, Omidyar and Skoll obtained funding from Benchmark Venture Capital, even though eBay didn't really need the money. Writer Randall Stross recalls this event as follows:

> eBay was an anomaly: a profitable company that was able to self-fund its growth and that turned to venture capital solely for contacts and counsel. No larger lesson can be drawn. When Benchmark wired the first millions to eBay's bank account, the figurative check was tossed into the vault—and there it would sit, unneeded and undisturbed.[40]

This strategy worked for eBay. Soon after affiliating with Benchmark, Bob Kagle, one of Benchmark's general partners, led eBay to Meg Whitman, an executive who had experience working for several top firms, including Procter & Gamble, Disney, and Hasbro. In March 2008, Whitman stepped down as eBay's president and CEO (John Donahoe replaced her in these roles). However, Whitman continues serving as a member of the firm's board of directors.

Experienced investors can also assist new ventures in the hiring process by helping them structure compensation packages that are fair to both the firm and the new hires. An illustration of this advantage is provided by Alisa Nessler, CEO of Lane15, a firm backed by venture capital:

> If you're looking to recruit that all-important CEO, investors can be a particular boon. They know how much a CEO should earn, cash- and stock-wise. They can help you negotiate a package that fits your capital and equity structures, while also motivating the CEO to build a world-class company.[41]

Bankers also play a role in establishing the legitimacy of new ventures and their initial management teams. Research evidence rather consistently suggests that the presence of bank loans is a favorable signal to other capital providers.[42] Investors often take a seat on the boards of directors of the firms they fund to provide oversight and advice. For example, Fitbit, the subject of the "You Be the VC 9.2" feature, received $2 million in funding in October 2008. At the same time, Doug Levin, the company's angel investor, joined Fitbit's board of directors. It is less common for a banker to take a seat on the board of directors of an entrepreneurial venture, primarily because bankers provide operating capital rather than large amounts of investment capital to new firms.

There are additional ways that lenders and investors add value to a new firm beyond financing and funding. These roles are highlighted in Table 9.3.

Table 9.3 BEYOND FINANCING AND FUNDING: WAYS LENDERS AND INVESTORS ADD VALUE TO AN ENTREPRENEURIAL VENTURE

- Help identify and recruit key management personnel
- Provide insight into the industry and markets in which the venture intends to participate
- Help the venture fine-tune its business model
- Serve as a sounding board for new ideas
- Provide introductions to additional sources of capital
- Recruit customers
- Help to arrange business partnerships
- Serve on the venture's board of directors or board of advisers
- Provide a sense of calm in the midst of the emotional roller-coaster ride that many new-venture teams experience

Other Professionals

At times, other professionals assume important roles in a new venture's success. Attorneys, accountants, and business consultants are often good sources of counsel and advice. The role of lawyers in helping firms get off to a good start is discussed in Chapter 7, and the role of accountants is discussed in Chapter 8. So here, let's take a look at the role a consultant may play.

Consultants A **consultant** is an individual who gives professional or expert advice. New ventures vary in terms of how much they rely on business consultants for direction. In some ways, the role of the general business consultant has diminished in importance as businesses seek specialists to get advice on complex issues such as patents, tax planning, and security laws. In other ways, the role of general business consultant is as important as ever; it is the general business consultant who conducts in-depth analyses on behalf of a firm, such as preparing a feasibility study or an industry analysis. Because of the time it would take, it would be inappropriate to ask a member of a board of directors or board of advisers to take on one of these tasks on behalf of a firm. These more time-intensive tasks must be performed by the firm itself or by a paid consultant.

Learning Objective

10. Explain why new ventures use consultants for help and advice.

Those leading an entrepreneurial venture often turn to consultants for help and advice because while large firms can afford to employ experts in many areas, new firms typically can't. If a new firm needs help in a specialized area, such as building a product prototype, it may need to hire an engineering consulting firm to do the work. The fees that consultants charge are typically negotiable. If a new venture has good potential and offers a consulting firm the possibility of repeat business, the firm will often be willing to reduce its fee or work out favorable payment arrangements.

Consultants fall into two categories: paid consultants and consultants who are made available for free or at a reduced rate through a nonprofit or government agency. The first category includes large international consulting firms, such as Bearing Point (formerly KPMG), Accenture, IBM Global Services, and Bain & Company. These firms provide a wide array of services but are beyond the reach of most start-ups because of budget limitations. But there are many smaller, localized firms. The best way to find them is to ask around for a referral.

Consultants are also available through nonprofit or government agencies. SCORE, for example, is a nonprofit organization that provides free consulting services to small businesses. SCORE currently has over 10,500 volunteers with about 1,300 of these individuals serving as e-counselors—people who answer

Many entrepreneurs establish relationships with SBDC or SCORE advisers and rely on these individuals to plug gaps in their new-venture teams until they can afford to hire additional personnel. In this photo, a SCORE adviser, who is a retired CPA, is helping an entrepreneur set up an accounting system for her business.

David Young-Wolff/PhotoEdit Inc.

questions via the Internet. Commonly, SCORE volunteers are retired business owners who counsel in areas as diverse as finance, operations, and sales.[43] And the U.S. Small Business Administration, a government agency, provides a variety of consulting services to small businesses and entrepreneurs, primarily through its network of Small Business Development Centers (SBDC), which are spread throughout the United States. There is evidence that these centers are effective in providing advice and helping entrepreneurial ventures get off to a good start. For example, one study found that the rates of survival, growth, and innovation of SBDC-counseled firms are higher than the population of start-ups in general.[44]

In summary, putting together a new-venture team is one of the most critical activities that a founder or founders of a firm undertake. Many entrepreneurs suffer by not thinking broadly enough or carefully enough about this process. Ultimately, people must make any new venture work. New ventures benefit by surrounding themselves with high-quality employees and advisers to tackle the challenges involved with launching and growing an entrepreneurial firm.

Chapter Summary

1. A new-venture team is the group of people who move a new venture from an idea to a fully functioning firm. The primary elements of a new-venture team are the company founders, key employees, the board of directors, the board of advisers, lenders and investors, and other professionals.

2. The liability of newness refers to the fact that entrepreneurial ventures often falter or even fail because the people who start them can't adjust quickly enough to their new roles and because the firm lacks a "track record" with customers and suppliers. These limitations can be overcome by assembling a talented and experienced new-venture team.

3. A heterogeneous founding team has members with diverse abilities and experiences. A homogeneous founding team has members who are very similar to one another.

4. The personal attributes that affect a founder's chances of launching a successful new firm include level of education, prior entrepreneurial experience, relevant industry experience, and the ability to network. Networking is building and maintaining relationships with people who are similar or whose friendship could bring advantages to the firm.
5. A skills profile is a chart that depicts the most importance skills that are needed in a new venture and where skills gaps exist.
6. The two primary ways in which the nonemployee members of a start-up's new-venture team help the firm are by providing guidance and lending legitimacy.
7. A board of directors is a panel of individuals who is elected by a corporation's shareholders to oversee the management of the firm. It is typically made up of both inside and outside directors. An inside director is a person who is also an officer of the firm. An outside director is someone who is not employed by the firm.
8. When a high-quality individual agrees to serve on a company's board of directors, the individual is in essence expressing an opinion that the company has potential (why else would the individual agree to serve?). This phenomenon is referred to as signaling.
9. An advisory board is a panel of experts who are asked by the management of a firm to provide counsel and advice on an ongoing basis.
10. The primary reason that new ventures turn to consultants for help and advice is that while large firms can afford to employ experts in many areas, new firms typically can't. Consultants can be paid or can be part of a nonprofit or government agency and provide their services for free or for a reduced rate.

Key Terms

advisory board, **321**
board of directors, **318**
consultant, **325**
founding team, **313**
heterogeneous, **313**
homogeneous, **313**
inside director, **318**

liability of newness, **310**
networking, **316**
new-venture team, **310**
outside director, **318**
prior entrepreneurial
 experience, **314**

relevant industry experience,
 314
signaling, **319**
skills profile, **316**

Review Questions

1. What is a new-venture team? Who are the primary participants in a start-up's new-venture team?
2. What is liability of newness? What can a new venture do to overcome the liability of newness?
3. Do new ventures started by a team have an advantage over new ventures started by a sole entrepreneur, or is the opposite the case?
4. Describe the difference between a heterogeneous and a homogeneous founding team.
5. Describe the two potential pitfalls of using a team to start a firm.
6. What are the personal attributes that affect a founder's chances of launching a successful new firm? In your judgment, which of these attributes are the most important? Why?

7. Explain why having relevant industry experience helps the founder of a firm.

8. Define the term *networking*. Why is it important for an entrepreneur to have a vibrant social and professional network?

9. What are the reasons for completing a skills profile for a new firm?

10. What is a board of directors? What is the difference between inside and outside directors?

11. Describe the three formal responsibilities of a board of directors.

12. Explain why recruiting a well-known and highly respected board of directors lends legitimacy to a firm.

13. Define the term *signaling*.

14. Discuss the purpose of forming an advisory board. If you were the founder of an entrepreneurial firm, would you set up an advisory board? Why or why not?

15. Describe the different ways that advisory boards meet and conduct their business.

16. Describe several of the guidelines to setting up a board of advisers.

17. In what ways do lenders and investors lend legitimacy to a firm?

18. Explain why new ventures often turn to consultants for advice.

19. Describe the purpose of SCORE. What type of advice and counsel do SCORE volunteers provide?

20. As noted in the chapter, SBDCs (Small Business Development Centers) seem to contribute positively to the launch of an entrepreneurial venture. In your opinion, what accounts for this positive relationship? If you were launching an entrepreneurial venture today, would you seek the services of an SBDC? Why or why not?

Application Questions

1. Reread the opening case. What factors did Jordan Goldman have working in his favor, and what factors did he have working against him as the founder of Unigo?

2. Jennifer Snell works for REI, a retailer of outdoor gear, equipment, and clothing. Jennifer is thinking about leaving REI to start an e-commerce company that specializes in selling hiking and camping gear. Jennifer's background is in marketing, sales, and customer service. What qualities should she look for in a potential partner or "cofounder" for her new company?

3. Neil Frasier, a friend of your family, is a very proficient accountant. He's 61 and has spent his entire career working at the Sears Holdings Corp. headquarters in Chicago. He just got a call from a high school buddy that still lives in the small town in Wisconsin that they both grew up in. Neil's buddy tells him that the sole accountant in town is retiring and has his business for sale. Neil has always wanted to return to his home town. He thinks about it for a few minutes and then tells his buddy, "As much as I'd absolutely love to come back home, I don't have any business experience and I'm 61 years old. Those are two strikes against me—I'll have to pass on buying the business." Is Neil's thinking sound? What would tell Neil if he asked you for your advice?

4. According to the chapter, prior entrepreneurial experience, relevant industry experience, and networking are attributes that strengthen a person's chances of launching a successful venture. Think about the type of company

that you might launch someday. Which of these attributes do you currently possess? What steps can you take now to build strengths in each of these areas?

5. Spend some time looking at the "Management Team" section of VisualCV's Web site (under the "About Us" tab). On a scale of 1 to 10 (10 is high), rate the management team's ability to operate and grow VisualCV.

6. Imagine you're talking to a friend who is developing a line of innovative accessories for Apple iPhone users. You asked your friend if she's thought about establishing a board of advisers and she said, "The iPhone accessories industry is moving so fast the last thing I need is a group of people giving me advice. I need to be nimble and quick to market." What are the flaws in your friend's thinking?

7. Justin Campbell, who lives in Nashville, is setting up a board of advisers for his start-up. He feels a little let down because the three most suitable people to serve on his board live in Memphis, Dallas, and Oklahoma City. Justin is reluctant to ask these people to serve on his board of advisers because he can't afford to pay their airfare and hotel accommodations to attend board meetings in Nashville. What advice would you give Justin that would be helpful?

8. Three days ago Peggy Armstrong sent a lengthy e-mail message to a long-time business acquaintance, asking the acquaintance if she'd consider cofounding a tutoring service with her. Peggy attached a first draft of her business plan. The acquaintance just replied to Peggy's message and said that she'd be interested under three conditions. After reading the conditions, Peggy thought to herself, "Boy did I make the right decision approaching her. These conditions are tough but smart." Speculate on what the conditions might have been.

9. Look at Table 9.2. What do you think is the most important attribute of an effective board of directors and the single most important attribute of an individual board member? Explain your answers.

10. Look at this chapter's "Savvy Entrepreneurial Firm" feature. Name at least two online social networks that have the potential to be helpful to entrepreneurs that were not mentioned in the feature. Explain the purpose of each of the social networks.

11. Early in the chapter, under the section titled "Creating a New Venture Team," a quote is provided that reads as follows: "People are the one factor in production . . . that animates all others." In the context of everything you know and have learned about entrepreneurship, what does this quote mean to you?

12. Reneé Coombs, a professional investor, was having lunch with a colleague recently and said, "Do you remember Phil Moore, the entrepreneur we met the other day, who has invented a new kind of computer keyboard? I checked up on him, and he has all the right personal attributes to be a successful entrepreneur." Reneé's dinner companion said, "Really, tell me about him." What do you think Reneé would say if she were describing a person who had all the right personal attributes to be a successful entrepreneur?

13. Jim Lane is an executive with General Motors. A former coworker of his recently started a company and raised $3 million from a well-known investor even though he didn't need the money to launch the business. Jim thinks his friend is foolish and can't think of one reason to take money from an investor if you don't need it. If you were talking to Jim, what would you tell him about this situation?

14. Melanie Atkins is preparing to launch a software firm near Minneapolis. She is very capable but is worried about the amount of money she'll

need to spend paying consultants to help her launch and grow her business. Does Melanie have to rely strictly on paid consultants to help her launch and grow her business? If not, what alternatives does Melanie have?

15. What type of networking opportunities are available via your college or university, or entrepreneurial-minded organizations in the city or town that you live in, that could be helpful to you in your entrepreneurial career?

You Be the VC 9.1
Company: VisualCV
www.visualcv.com

Business Idea: Replace the traditional paper résumé with a virtual résumé that resides on the Web, and allows a job seeker to include all the items in a standard résumé, along with a video introduction, visuals depicting accomplishments, a sample of one's work, links to letters of recommendation, and similar material.

Pitch: VisualCV is very much like a regular résumé, but it takes advantage of the Web by allowing job seekers to add short videos, samples of their work, visuals (such as a chart showing surpassed sales targets), links, and similar materials to their résumés. Once a job seeker completes a VisualCV, it can be kept private, shared with potential employers on a case-by-case basis, or made public on the Internet. Most VisualCVs include a video greeting from the job seekers (less than two minutes), which allows them to display their personality, talk briefly about their qualifications, and show their enthusiasm for a particular job or career. Other common items include video recommendations, samples of one's work (think of an architect showing pictures of the buildings that she's designed), and verifications of past recognition or awards (such as pictures of awards or plaques). It's also common for job seekers to place links within their résumés. For example, if a job seeker listed three years of work experience with a small company in Virginia, a link can be provided to the company's Web site. A job seeker can place his or her VisualCV on any online résumé or job-posting site, such as Monster.com or CareerBuilder.

VisualCV also allows companies to create their own interactive pages to communicate with job seekers. Similar to the manner in which a job seeker sets up his or her site, a company can provide a video introduction to the firm, post video testimonials from satisfied employees, provide revenue numbers, number of employees, and similar information if desired, and post information about salary ranges and benefits. Many companies also create a video or text-based Q&A component to their VisualCV site, to address questions like "what are the advantages of working for this company?" "what is the culture like?" and "what does it take to get a promotion?"

VisualCV can be used for purposes other than seeking a job. Anyone can set up a VisualCV and use it as a professional profile to distribute before meetings, send to potential clients, or post on their Web site.

VisualCV is free for individuals and the basic functionality is free for companies. VisualCV will make money by selling premium services to corporations and recruiters. An example of a premium service, for a company, will be the ability to create "binders" of the VisualCVs of the applicants who have been short-listed for a particular job, and then route the binders to the appropriate hiring managers within the company, who can make comments and annotations on the individual VisualCVs. VisualCV will also customize or "white label" (i.e., brand) an individual company's VisualCV, on a fee basis, so that it is distinctive and seamlessly integrates with the company's other recruitment and selection efforts.

Q&A: Based on the material covered in this chapter, what questions would you ask the firm's founders before making your funding decision? What answers would satisfy you?

Decision: If you had to make your decision on just the information provided in the pitch and on the company's Web site, would you fund this company? Why or why not?

You Be the VC 9.2

Company: Fitbit

www.fitbit.com

Business Idea: Create an ultra-compact wireless wearable device that automatically tracks data about a person's exercise and health-related activities.

Pitch: Most people know that they need to exercise to first improve and then maintain their health. But simply buying a pair of running shoes or a bicycle is rarely the answer. People must be motivated to stay committed to an exercise plan. One thing that sports psychologists have found helps people stay committed is to keep track of their daily progress. It's also very motivating to people to graphically see the results of their exercise efforts and to be able to share their progress with family, friends, and people who are trying to achieve the same objectives. Exercise and weight loss are serious issues. Studies show that 60 percent of Americans are overweight.

Fitbit has developed an ultra-compact wireless sensor that can be clipped to a person's clothing called the Fitbit Tracker. The device automatically tracks and records data about a person's activities, such as calories burned, sleep quality, steps, and distance. The collected data is wirelessly uploaded to a Web site where users can see their data and track their progress toward personal goals. Users can also share their progress with others and compare themselves against people with similar goals. Nutrition, weight, and other health information can be manually entered at the site,

to provide users a holistic view of their exercise and health-related activities and accomplishments.

The Fitbit Tracker is as small as a pack of matches, and contains a motion sensor like the ones found in the Nintendo Wii. The Tracker uses motion-sensing technology to capture all of a person's physical activities throughout the day and night. To measure sleep quality, a user slides the Fitbit Tracker onto a wristband at bedtime. As you fall in and out of REM sleep, your wrist experiences tiny tremors, which enables the Tracker to measure how long it takes you to fall asleep, how many times you wake up during the night, and how many hours a night you sleep (opposed to lying awake).

To add a bit of levity to its Web site, Fitbit displays a user's progress toward their goals in the form of an avatar that changes (i.e., gets thinner or fatter) as a user advances toward or falls behind their goals. The initial price is $99.00.

Q&A: Based on the material covered in this chapter, what questions would you ask the firm's founders before making your funding decision? What answers would satisfy you?

Decision: If you had to make your decision on just the information provided in the pitch and on the company's Web site, would you fund this company? Why or why not?

CASE 9.1

How a "Key Hire" Can Place an Entrepreneurial Firm on the Right Track

www.1800petmeds.com
www.google.com

Bruce R. Barringer
Oklahoma State University
R. Duane Ireland
Texas A & M University

Introduction

As entrepreneurial firms assemble their new-venture teams, there is often a pivotal "key hire" that the founders make that fills a key competency

gap or allows the firm to get over an important hurdle. The key hire might be someone with specific technical expertise, might be someone with experience raising money, or might be a

(continued)

person with experience building a business. If the key hire isn't made, a young firm can often struggle to gain momentum.

The following are examples of two firms that made a "key hire" early on that significantly improved their prospects for moving forward.

1-800-PetMeds

1-800-PetMeds is America's largest pet pharmacy. It sells prescription and nonprescription pet medications and nutritional supplements for dogs, cats, and horses at a substantial cost savings to the customer. Founded in 1996, the company purchases its products at wholesale prices and ships directly to customers. About 70 percent of the company's sales are for nonprescription items like flea and tick medications and nutritional supplements. The other 30 percent of sales are for prescription medications. When an order for a prescription medication is received, 1-800-PetMeds verifies the order by calling the veterinarian who wrote the prescription. As soon as the verification is in hand, 1-800-PetMeds bills the customer and sends out the order.

Sound easy? It is today but getting started was tough. Pause for a moment and think to yourself, "What's the biggest challenge with making this business model work?" The answer: getting veterinarians to cooperate. Vets sell pet medications. So why would they cooperate? Why would they take 1-800-PetMeds' phone calls and verify the prescriptions? Here's what happened.

1-800-PetMeds was started in 1996 by Dr. Marc Puleo, an anesthesiologist. He got the idea to start a mail-order pharmacy for pets after listening to a nurse complain about the high price her veterinarian charged for antibiotics for her dog. Consumers loved 1-800-PetMeds, but veterinarians hated it. They often refused to write a prescription if they knew a client was going to have it filled by 1-800-PetMeds. They also complained to pharmacy regulators that PedMeds' in-house veterinarians were prescribing drugs for pets without seeing them. These activities caused problems for 1-800-PetMeds, and the company struggled to get past them. By 2001, the company was losing more than $50,000 a week and was under investigation in 10 U.S. states.

To correct these problems, Puleo hired Menderes Akdag as 1-800-PetMeds' new CEO. Akdag was the former president of Lens Express, one of the first companies to sell contact lens on the Internet. (Lens Express is now 1-800-CONTACTS.) Early on, Lens Express faced the exact same problem that 1-800-PetMeds was experiencing. Optometrists, who made money selling contact lenses, would often make it difficult for their patients to get a copy of their prescription to pass along to Lens Express. Akdag played tough and led the contact lens industry through a series of legal maneuvers that resulted in regulations that clearly gave patients a right to their prescriptions. Optometrists were forced to comply, and Lens Express took off.

At 1-800-PetMeds Akdag took on the same challenge with a modified approach. He cancelled 1-800-PetMeds' "Alternative Veterinarian Program" (the program that allowed 1-800-PetMeds' veterinarians to prescribe medications without seeing an animal), which was a major sticking point with veterinarians. He also used board hearings and the media to educate consumers and remind veterinarians about the laws. Consumers had a clear right to have their pets' prescriptions filled by a mail-order pharmacy. The tactics worked, and the veterinarians eventually backed off.

Today, 1-800-PetMeds is closing in on $200 million in annual sales. Over 2 million consumers purchased dog, cat, and horse medications from 1-800-PetMeds between 2007 and 2008.

Google

Google's start-up story is well known. Larry Page and Sergey Brin, two computer science graduate students at Stanford, launched Google in 1998. The two met in 1995 and by 1996 started collaborating on a search engine technology. In September 1998 Google formally opened its doors in Menlo Park, California, in a small office attached to the garage of a friend. Page and Brin's search engine technology quickly gained a following. Today, Google has over $5 billion in annual sales, 20,000 employees, and conducts nearly 65 percent of all Web searches in the United States.

In the late 1990s, John Doerr, one of Google's venture capitalists, urged Eric Schmidt to talk to Page and Brin about the company's CEO position. Schmidt was reluctant, but Doerr pressed telling Schmidt "Go look at Google. This is a little jewel that needs help scaling it."

According to Silicon Valley lore, Page and Brin weren't anxious to hire a CEO, but Google's investors were insisting. So far their $25 million investment in Google had netted them nothing, and they were adamant that Page and Brin hire someone more experienced and older than them who could grow the company and be its public face when it came time for an IPO. Google's investors also wanted Page and Brin to focus on what they did best—think about intriguing problems. Why not let an experienced hand endure the mundane tasks of managing the day-to-day operations of the company?

The interview with Schmidt was finally arranged. Schmidt was the CEO of Novell and former chief technology officer at Sun Microsystems. Although he wasn't looking for a new job, he knew he would need one soon after Novell completed a merger that was in the works. The interview, again according to Silicon Valley lore, went well and the three clicked. Page and Brin liked Schmidt's temperament and pedigree. Besides being an experienced CEO, he was a computer scientist, with a PhD from Cal Berkley and an undergraduate degree from Princeton. He also had a credential that not all interviewers would appreciate but Page and Brin liked. He had failed at something. While at Sun Microsystems, he had challenged Microsoft by leading the development of Java, an independent programming language, and had led the company's Internet strategy. Although the Internet portion of Sun's effort mainly failed, it showed Page and Brin that Schmidt had the mettle to take on Bill Gates and try to give consumers a choice.

Schmidt agreed to become Google's CEO in January 2001, and to show his commitment invested $1 million of his personal funds in Google preferred stock. He finished up his work at Novell and joined Google permanently in July. When he arrived, he found a company that was being run by technologists and scientists, who had enormous passion for products and end users but little management experience. He set out to build a business infrastructure. According to David A. Vise, author of *The Google Story*, Schmidt had the "right sensibility and touch with Larry and Sergey." Reflecting on the seemingly ideal match between Schmidt's experience and Page and Brin's vision and culture, Vise wrote:

> The more time he (Schmidt) spent at Google, the more impressed he became with the culture they (Page and Brin) had created, and the clarity and sense of shared mission that pervaded the company. They had a broad vision. His (Schmidt's) job was to put that vision into a framework that would give

it the best chance to produce tangible financial results.

Schmidt was the "key hire" at Google. One can only speculate where Google would be today without an experienced and steady hand to build its infrastructure and guide its growth.

Discussion Questions

1. Why was Menderes Akdag the ideal choice to lead 1-800-PetMeds? What do you think would have happened if Dr. Marc Puleo, 1-800-PetMeds' founder, would have remained at the helm of the company himself?

2. If 1-800-PetMeds had put together a board of advisers when the company was founded, what type of people should it have asked to participate?

3. Why was Eric Schmidt the ideal choice to lead Google? What do you think would have happened if Page and Brin had refused to hire a CEO?

4. Look at Table 9.1. Of the five attributes listed in the table, how many did Page and Brin have at the time they founded Google? How did the absence of these limit their ability to build Google into a large company? How many of the attributes that Page and Brin didn't have did Eric Schmidt have when he joined Google?

Application Questions

1. In what ways did both Dr. Marc Puleo's and Larry Page and Sergey Brin's lack of business experience show in their early management of their respective new ventures?

2. Look at the "You Be the VC 9.2" feature. What type of new-venture team should Fitbit be assembling? Make up a simulated new-venture team for Fitbit that would be capable of growing the company.

Sources: D. A. Vise, *The Google Story* (New York: Bantam Dell, 2005); 1-800-PetMeds homepage, www.1800petmeds.com (accessed October 21, 2008); "PetMed Express," *Business Week*, May 25, 2006.

CASE9.2

Zappos: Making Human Resources the Key to Customer Service

www.zappos.com

Bruce R. Barringer
Oklahoma State University
R. Duane Ireland
Texas A & M University

Introduction

Zappos.com is an online shoe retailer that has built a strong brand and has shown impressive sales growth since its founding. The company had zero sales in 1990, $370 million in 2005, and over $1 billion in 2008. It's also profitable. Zappos's formula for success is seemingly simple. It acquires customers through word-of-mouth and search engine marketing (SEM) and then wows them with customer service that keeps them coming back. The popular press often touts Zappos as the classic example of what can be accomplished through exemplary customer service.

But what's really behind Zappos's extraordinary success? Its prices are slightly on the high end. Its Web site isn't fancy. And it sells shoes for crying out loud! How does Zappos consistently deliver such a high level of customer service that people are willing to buy shoes online to the tune of $1 billion per year? Read on.

Why Shoes?

Zappos was founded by Nick Swinmurn. Swinmurn had such a hard time finding shoes that he started an e-commerce company to help people just like himself. He was turned away by investors who thought it was crazy to think that people would buy shoes online. Seriously—who buys shoes without trying them on first? Swinmurn persevered, heartened by the fact that over $2 billion in shoes are sold via mail order catalogs every year—so people do buy shoes without trying them on. Selling shoes is also a fundamentally good business. You don't need to educate people about the product—people know shoes. The brands are strong, and the margins are good. The average order on Zappos.com is over $100, and the margin is 50 percent. That leaves a lot of room for profit. It's also possible to run an effective SEM campaign for shoes. Try this: Search Google for "Nike shoes," "Reebok shoes," and "kid's shoes," one by one. How many times do you see search engine ads for Zappos to the right of the results? Many. Zappos also has an effective affiliate program. Over 17,000 affiliates drive traffic to Zappos's online store. Today, Zappos features a selection of over 90,000 styles of shoes from 500 brands.

Customer Service

According to reliable reports, customer service is what makes Zappos special. Call center employees don't use scripts and aren't pressed to keep calls short. Shipping and returns are free. The warehouse is open 24/7 so customers can place an order as late as 11 P.M. and still get quick delivery. Behind the scenes, most orders are upgraded to next-day delivery so customers are pleasantly surprised when their order arrives before expected. Normally, the early arrival is accompanied by an e-mail message from Zappos saying that the order was upgraded to next-day delivery because they are a "valued customer."

Zappos also has a very liberal return policy. It will take returns for up to 365 days no questions asked. When a customer is on the phone with a Zappos employee and is struggling with which pair of shoes to buy, the Zappos employees will suggest that the customer buy both pairs, and simply return the less desirable shoes. If Zappos's warehouse is out of a pair of shoes a customer wants, Zappos will e-mail the customer links to other Web sites where the shoes are for sale. Zappos also does little things to help its customers out. For example, its toll-free phone number is listed at the top of every page on its Web site. It also has the fastest site on the Web. According to Gomez, a Web research firm, in September 2006 Zappos's site took 0.879 seconds to load on a broadband-connected Internet site, the fastest of the top 50 Web retailers. Zappos has pretty much held that position since 2006.

What all this effort has gotten Zappos is a loyal customer base and word-of-mouth advertising. Approximately 50 percent of Zappos's orders come from existing customers, and an additional 20 percent are from new customers who were referred by existing customers. Of Zappos's 8.5 million customers, 3.7 million are customers who've bought something in the last 12 months.

Tony Hsieh

CEO Tony Hsieh is at the center of everything Zappos does. In his early 20s, Hsieh started a company called LinkExchange, which let small companies barter for banner ads. Hsieh insisted that every e-mail coming into the company was answered promptly and politely. In college, Hsieh made money by selling pizzas out of his Harvard dorm room. A classmate, Alfred Lin, bought whole pizzas from Hsieh and resold them piece by piece, making more money. Hsieh sold LinkExchange to Microsoft for $265 million in 1998 and he and Lin started an angel investment fund. Zappos's founder Nick Swinmurn pitched Hsieh and Lin, trying to raise money. Hsieh was so impressed with Zappos's market opportunity that he invested in the firm and briefly served as Zappos's co-CEO with Swinmurn. It wasn't long before Hsieh and Lin were running Zappos. Hsieh became Zappos's CEO and Lin became the CFO in the early 2000s.

Human Resources

While exemplary customer service may be what keeps Zappos's customers coming back, the root of the company's competitive advantage is its human resource management policies. The company is fiercely protective of its culture, which has been crafted to facilitate its high level of customer service. Every new employee, regardless of their assignment, spends four weeks as a customer service rep at Zappos's Las Vegas headquarters and a week in its Kentucky warehouse, where the new hire is immersed in Zappos's culture, strategy, and obsession with customer service. All 1,700 employees get a free lunch every day. Health insurance is 100 percent paid (although employees do pay for their dependents). Employees are given wide latitude to use their judgment to delight customers.

That's not all. After just a week into the orientation period, each new hire is given what Zappos calls "the offer." The company says to each new hire, "If you quit today, we'll pay you for the amount of time you've worked, plus $2,000." Why would Zappos do this? Because they want employees to quit if they don't like the Zappos culture. The $2,000 payoff is small potatoes, Hsieh and his top management team believe, opposed to having a half-hearted employee on the payroll.

Another distinctive aspect of Zappos is its use of Twitter.com. Twitter is a hybrid that's part instant messaging and part social networking. The way it works is that you sign up for a Twitter account (which is free), then you begin by entering short messages, no more than 140 characters long—sort of an online diary. You're not writing these messages for anyone in particular—you're just talking about what you're doing or sharing a thought. Many of

Zappos's 1,700 employees, including the CEO, have Twitter accounts, and comment throughout the day about what they're doing. Anyone can read the updates. Give it a try. You can access Tony Hsieh's Zappos account at http://twitter.com/zappos. Go to the site and read Hsieh's updates for the day. In his posts, Hsieh frequently refers to something Zappos is doing or a change it has made in its Web site and asks, "What do you think about this?" The replies he gets are from Zappos employees, customers, and others. Hsieh's use of Twitter and his willingness to allow employees to post about work-related issues is emblematic of the open and transparent culture that Zappos is building.

What Lies Ahead

Two main challenges lie ahead for Zappos. First is the competition in the online shoe industry. Zappos's success hasn't gone unnoticed. Major online competitors include Endless.com, Shoebuy.com, JCPenny.com, and Amazon.com. Footlocker and Wal-Mart, which sell both online and through their retail stores, are also in the mix. All are trying to emulate Zappos and add a little extra to win market share. For example, Endless.com offers free overnight shipping, free return shipping, 365-day returns, and a 100 percent price guarantee. Sound familiar? The 100 percent price guarantee is a one-up on Zappos, which doesn't provide the same guarantee.

The second challenge is whether Zappos will be able to maintain its unique culture as it continues to grow. Zappos sees itself as a customer service company rather than a shoe company and has ambitions to grow beyond shoes. It's already added clothing, bags, and accessories. Tony Hsieh remarked that someday, if things continue to go well, there may be a Zappos airline. Hsieh's vision is to leverage Zappos's unique approach to human resource management and customer service to ambitious heights.

Discussion Questions

1. Explain why Tony Hsieh was a good choice to take over Zappos and form the nucleus of the company's new-venture team when he joined Zappos in the early 2000s.

2. What advantages did Tony Hsieh and Alfred Li have in working together at Zappos? Together, do they make for a more compelling nucleus to Zappos's new-venture team than either one would as an individual?

3. To what extent do you believe the story that Zappos excels because of customer service and its customer service excels because of savvy human resource management? If you believe the

(continued)

story, what can other entrepreneurs learn from Zappos's experiences?

4. There is no information in the case about Zappos's board of directors. Based on what you know about Zappos and CEO Tony Hsieh, speculate on the role that Zappos's board of directors played in the company's development.

Application Questions

1. Do you believe that Zappos will be able to leverage its expertise in human resources management and customer service well beyond shoes? If so, how much upside potential do you think Zappos has?

Do you think there will be a Zappos airline someday? Why or why not?

2. Spend a couple of days following Tony Hsieh's Twitter account. Describe your reaction to what you read.

Sources: Zappos homepage, www.zappos.com (accessed November 17, 2008) N. Gabbay, "Zappos.com Case Study: Why Shoes Are Great for E-Commerce . . . Yes, Really." Startup Review, www.startup-review.com (accessed November 17, 2008, originally posted on September 17, 2006); *Business Week*, "A Shine on Their Shoes," http://www.businessweek.com/print/magazine/content/05_49/b3962118.htm?chan=gl (accessed November 17, 2008, originally posted on December 5, 2005).

Endnotes

1. J. Dee, "The Tell-All Campus Tour," *New York Times*, September 21, 2008.
2. Personal Interview with Jordan Goldman, December 8, 2008.
3. D. A. Harper, "Towards a Theory of Entrepreneurial Teams," *Journal of Business Venturing* 23, no. 6 (2008): 613–26.
4. M. Hager, J. Galaskiewicz, W. Bielefeld, and J. Pins, "Takes From the Grave: Organizations' Accounts of Their Own Demise," *American Behavioral Scientist* 39, no. 8 (2006): 975–94; A. Stinchcombe, "Social Structure and Organization," in *Handbook of Organizations*, ed. James G. March (Chicago: Rand McNally, 1965), 142–93.
5. C. Read, J. Ross, J. Dunleavy, D. Schulman, and J. Bramante, *eCFO* (Chichester, UK: John Wiley & Sons, 2001), 117.
6. P. G. Klein, "Opportunity Discovery, Entrepreneurial Action, and Economic Organization," *Strategic Entrepreneurship Journal* 2, no. 3 (2008): 175–90.
7. L. He, "Do Founders Matter? A Study of Executive Compensation, Governance Structure and Firm Performance," *Journal of Business Venturing* 23, no. 3 (2008): 257–79.
8. C. E. Shalley and J. E. Perry-Smith, "The Emergence of Team Creative Cognition: The Role of Diverse Outside Ties, Sociocognitive Network Centrality, and Team Evolution," *Strategic Entrepreneurship Journal* 2, no. 1 (2008): 23–41; D. P. Forbes, P. S. Borchert, M. E. Zellmer-Bruhn, and H. J. Sapienza, "Entrepreneurial Team Formation: An Exploration of New Member Addition," *Entrepreneurship Theory and Practice* 30, no. 3 (2006): 225–48.
9. A. Lockett, D. Ucbasaran, and J. Butler, "Opening Up the Investor-Investee Dyad: Syndicates, Teams, and Networks," *Entrepreneurship Theory and Practice* 30, no. 2 (2006): 117–30.
10. K. Eisenhardt and C. Schoonhoven, "Organizational Growth: Linking Founding Team, Strategy, Environment, and Growth Among U.S. Semiconductor Ventures, 1978–1988," *Administrative Science Quarterly* 35 (1990): 504–29.
11. T. Zenger and B. Lawrence, "Organizational Demography: The Differential Effects of Age and Tenure Distribution on Technical Communication," *Academy of Management Journal* 32 (1989): 353–76.
12. Eisenhardt and Schoonhoven, "Organizational Growth."
13. B. Clarysee and N. Moray, "A Process Study of Entrepreneurial Team Formation: The Case of a Research-Based Spin-Off," *Journal of Business Venturing* 19 (2004): 55–79.
14. D. Ravasi and C. Turati, "Exploring Entrepreneurial Learning: A Comparative Study of Technology Development Projects," *Journal of Business Venturing* 20 (2005): 137–64; A. C. Cooper, F. J. Gimeno-Gascon, and C. Y. Woo, "Initial Human and Financial Capital as Predictors of New Venture Performance," *Journal of Business Venturing* 9, no. 5 (1994): 371–95.
15. D. B. Audretsch, W. Bonte, and M. Keilbach, "Entrepreneurial Capital and Its Impact on Knowledge Diffusion and Economic Performance," *Journal of Business Venturing* 23, no. 6 (2008): 687–98; D. Politis, "The Process of Entrepreneurial

Learning: A Conceptual Framework," *Entrepreneurship Theory and Practice* 29, no. 4 (2005): 399–424.

16. Claysee and Moray, "A Process Study of Entrepreneurial Team Formation."

17. K. Foss and N. J. Foss, "Understanding Opportunity Discovery and Sustainable Advantage: The Role of Transaction Costs and Property Rights," *Strategic Entrepreneurship Journal* 2, no. 3 (2008): 191–207; C. Hienerth and A. Kessler, "Measuring Success in Family Businesses: The Concept of Configurational Fit," *Family Business Review* 19, no. 2 (2006): 115–34.

18. T. E. Stuart and O. Sorenson, "Strategic Networks and Entrepreneurial Ventures," *Strategic Entrepreneurship Journal* 1, nos. 3 and 4 (2008): 211–27; D. M. DeCarolis and P. Saparito, "Social Capital, Cognition, and Entrepreneurial Opportunities: A Theoretical Framework," *Entrepreneurship Theory and Practice* 30, no. 1 (2006): 41–56.

19. F. Welter and D. Smallbone, "Exploring the Role of Trust in Entrepreneurial Activity," *Entrepreneurship Theory and Practice* 30 (2006): 465–75.

20. Trendsetter Barometer Business Outlook 3Q 2008, www.barometersurveys.com/production/barsurv.nsf/Barometer_Trendsetter, Fall 2008 (accessed November 15, 2008).

21. Council of Entrepreneurial Development, "Entrepreneurial Satisfaction Survey Report" (Raleigh-Durham, NC, 2007).

22. M. Henricks, "A Look Ahead," *Entrepreneur*, January 2007, 70–76.

23. R. Adams, *A Good Hard Kick in the Ass* (New York: Crown Business, 2002), 240.

24. H. Schultz, *Pour Your Heart into It* (New York: Hyperion, 1997), 82.

25. R. H. Lester, A. Hillman, A. Zardkoohi, and A. A. Cannella, Jr., "Former Government Officials as Outside Directors: The Role of Human and Social Capital," *Academy of Management Journal* 51, no. 5 (2008): 999–1013.

26. A. J. Hillman, C. Shropshire, and A. A. Cannella, Jr., "Organizational Predictors of Women on Corporate Boards," *Academy of Management Journal* 50, no. 4 (2007): 941–952.

27. R. Charan, *Boards at Work* (San Francisco: Jossey-Bass Publishers, 1998), 3.

28. L. W. Busenitz, J. O. Fiet, and D. D. Moesel, "Signaling in Venture Capitalist–New Venture Team Funding Decisions: Does It Indicate Long-Term Venture Outcomes?" *Entrepreneurship Theory and Practice* 29, no. 1 (2005): 1–12.

29. P. Devorak, "Board of Advisers Can Help Steer Small Firms to Right Track," *Wall Street Journal*, March 3, 2008, B4.

30. A. Sherman, *Fast-Track Business Growth* (Washington, DC: Kiplinger Books, 2001).

31. "Featured Mom Investors: Laura Udall," Mom Inventors, www.mominventors.com (accessed November 17, 2008).

32. Coolibar homepage, www.coolibar.com (accessed November 17, 2008).

33. Intouch Technologies homepage, www.intouchhealth.com (accessed November 18, 2008).

34. VisualCV homepage, www.visualcv.com (accessed November 16, 2008).

35. S. Schmidt and M. Brauer, "Strategic Governance: How to Assess Board Effectiveness in Guiding Strategy Execution," *Corporate Governance: An International Review* 14 (2006): 13–22.

36. R. Buckman, "Blog Buzz on High-Tech Start-Up Causes Some Static," *Wall Street Journal*, February 9, 2006, B4.

37. D. Dimov and D. De Clercq, "Venture Capital Investment Strategy and Portfolio Failure Rate: A Longitudinal Study," *Entrepreneurship Theory and Practice* 30 (2006): 207–23; J. Lerner, "Venture Capitalists and the Oversight of Private Firms," *Journal of Finance* 50, no. 1 (1995): 301–18.

38. Y. Li, "Duration Analysis of Venture Capital Staging: A Real Options Perspective," *Journal of Business Venturing* 23, no. 5 (2008): 497–512.

39. A. Davila, G. Foster, and M. Gupta, "Venture Capital Financing and the Growth of Startup Firms," *Journal of Business Venturing* 18 (2004): 689–708.

40. R. Stross, *eBoys* (New York: Crown Books, 2000), 29.

41. Adams, *A Good Hard Kick in the Ass*, 173.

42. D. Cumming, "Adverse Selection and Capital Structure: Evidence from Venture Capital," *Entrepreneurship Theory and Practice* 30 (2006): 155–83.

43. SCORE homepage, www.score.org (accessed December 12, 2008).

44. J. J. Chrisman and W. E. McMullan, "A Preliminary Assessment of Outsider Assistance as a Knowledge Resource: The Longer-Term Impact of New Venture Counseling," *Entrepreneurship Theory and Practice* 24, no. 1 (2000): 37–53.

ANDY TABAR
Founder, Bizooki
BS, Entrepreneurship, Belmont University, expected 2010

Getting Personal

with Andy Tabar

CURRENTLY IN MY IPOD
Joe Satriani

MY BIGGEST WORRY AS AN ENTREPRENEUR
Not meeting my own expectations

HARDEST PART OF GETTING FUNDING
The years of work that lead up to it

BEST ADVICE I'VE RECEIVED
Focus. Success requires hard work, but not overwork

WHAT I DO WHEN I'M NOT WORKING
Play guitar, travel frequently, being with friends and family

FIRST ENTREPRENEURIAL EXPERIENCE
Competing against my family members at garage sales

CHAPTER TEN
Getting *Financing* or Funding

OPENING PROFILE

BIZOOKI
Raising Money Through a Variety of Sources
www.bizooki.com

In 2008 Andy Tabar, a student at Belmont University, was tweaking his start-up, Bizooki, a Web-based company that helps businesses become more efficient by utilizing global talent. The idea behind Bizooki is that many businesses need technical projects completed more efficiently, like the preparation of Web sites, interactive CD-ROMs, or marketing research, but don't have in-house expertise. By outsourcing the task to the most efficient global provider, the task can be completed inexpensively and on time. Bizooki acts as a matchmaker—bringing together businesses that need these types of tasks completed with a network of global providers. Although Bizooki didn't take a large sum of money to launch, the way Tabar has funded Bizooki is instructive for aspiring entrepreneurs. Rather than trying to raise money from investors or bankers, he has relied on a combination of bootstrapping, loans from friends and family, and creative sources of financing.

Tabar's experience raising and managing money started at an early age. As a high school student, he built Web sites, strictly on a cash basis. He didn't need much money because he was essentially selling his time. When he graduated from high school, he brushed up on his knowledge of how to obtain credit, knowing that at some point he'd need external funding. The first step he took was to obtain an ExxonMobil credit card—not because he needed the credit but to start establishing a credit history.

Tabar, who grew up in Ohio, chose Belmont University in Nashville primarily because of its entrepreneurship program. He experimented with a number of business ideas before settling on Bizooki. Along the way, he utilized several techniques to either raise money or gain access to resources in creative ways. One example is that as a freshman, he applied for membership to the university's Practicing Student Entrepreneur Program (also called the "hatchery"). Through the hatchery, Tabar and about 70 of his classmates gained access to desks, computers, phones, fax machines, and copy machines, along with the opportunity to brainstorm business ideas with one another. Another example, which is becoming increasingly popular among student entrepreneurs, is that he entered several business plan competitions. He won Belmont's top award in 2006 and 2008, netting $5,000 in cash both times. He also won $5,000 in the University of Evansville's competition in 2008.

The cost savings and money generated by these techniques helped Tabar flesh out his idea for Bizooki and get the company off the ground. He borrowed several small amounts of money from an interesting source: Rather than going through a bank, he registered with Prosper.com, a peer-to-peer lending network. Prosper is an online auction Web site that matches people who want to borrow money with people who are willing to make loans. Tabar obtained several loans of around $5,000 apiece through Prosper, but he used Prosper as a platform to obtain loans primarily from friends and family rather than outsiders. Prosper provides a convenient, formal, and legitimate

Learning Objectives

After studying this chapter you should be ready to:

1. Explain why most entrepreneurial ventures need to raise money during their early life.

2. Identify the three sources of personal financing available to entrepreneurs.

3. Provide examples of how entrepreneurs bootstrap to raise money or cut costs.

4. Identify the three steps involved in properly preparing to raise debt or equity financing.

5. Discuss the difference between equity funding and debt financing.

6. Explain the role of an elevator speech in attracting financing for an entrepreneurial venture.

7. Describe the difference between a business angel and a venture capitalist.

8. Explain why an initial public offering (IPO) is an important milestone in an entrepreneurial venture.

9. Discuss the SBA Guaranteed Loan Program.

10. Explain the advantages of leasing for an entrepreneurial venture.

format for people to loan money to one another, even if they know one another before the loan is made. Although Tabar hasn't tried it yet, he is also considering utilizing Zopa.com, which is a similar online peer-to-peer lending network.

Looking forward, Tabar anticipates needing additional sources of funds as Bizooki grows or to launch additional ventures. He has met a number of angel investors, primarily through the entrepreneurship program at Belmont. But he hasn't taken any of their offers, which he believes will work to his advantage in the long run. He believes that moving cautiously, and only taking money from an investor when the timing is right to grow the investment, builds credibility and trust in the investment community. He also continues to build his credit history if bank financing becomes an attractive alternative.[1]

In general, start-ups often have difficulty raising money because they are unknown and untested. Founders must frequently use their own money, try to secure grants, or go to friends and family for help. This effort is often a grueling endeavor. Many entrepreneurs hear "no" many times before they match up successfully with a banker or investor.

In this chapter, we focus on the process of getting financing or funding. We begin by discussing why firms raise capital. We follow this with a description of personal financing and the importance of personal funds, capital from friends and family, and bootstrapping in the early life of a firm. We then turn to the different forms of equity, debt, and creative financing available to entrepreneurial ventures. We also emphasize the importance of preparing to secure these types of financing.

THE IMPORTANCE OF GETTING FINANCING OR FUNDING

Few people deal with the process of raising investment capital until they need to raise capital for their own firm. As a result, many entrepreneurs go about the task of raising capital haphazardly because they lack experience in this area and because they don't know much about their choices.[2] This shortfall may cause a business owner to place too much reliance on some sources of capital and not enough on others.[3] Entrepreneurs need to have as full an understanding as possible of the alternatives that are available in regard to raising money. And raising money is a balancing act. Although a venture may need to raise money to survive, its founders usually don't want to deal with people who don't understand or care about their long-term goals.

The need to raise money catches some entrepreneurs off-guard in that many of them launch their firms with the intention of funding all their needs internally. Commonly, though, entrepreneurs discover that operating without investment capital or borrowed money is more difficult than they anticipated. Because of this, it is important for entrepreneurs to understand the role of investment capital in the survival and subsequent success of a new firm.

Why Most New Ventures Need Funding

Learning Objective

1. Explain why most entrepreneurial ventures need to raise money during their early life.

There are three reasons that most entrepreneurial ventures need to raise money during their early life: cash flow challenges, capital investments, and lengthy product development cycles. These reasons are laid out in Figure 10.1. Let's look at each reason so we can better understand their importance.

Cash Flow Challenges As a firm grows, it requires an increasing amount of cash to operate as the foundation for serving its customers. Often, equipment must be purchased and new employees hired and trained before the increased customer base generates additional income. The lag between spending to generate revenue and earning income from the firm's operations creates cash flow challenges, particularly for new, often small, ventures as well as for ventures that are growing rapidly.

If a firm operates in the red, its negative real-time cash flow, usually computed monthly, is called its burn rate. A company's **burn rate** is the rate at which it is spending its capital until it reaches profitability. Although a negative cash flow is sometimes justified early in a firm's life—to build plants and buy equipment, train employees, and establish its brand—it can cause severe complications. A firm usually fails if it burns through all its capital before it becomes profitable. This is why inadequate financial resources is one of the primary reasons new firms fail.[4] A firm can simply run out of money even if it has good products and satisfied customers.

To prevent their firms from running out of money, most entrepreneurs need investment capital or a line of credit from a bank to cover cash flow short-falls until their firms can begin making money. It is usually difficult for a new firm to get a line of credit from a bank (for reasons discussed later). So new ventures often look for investment capital, bootstrap their operations, or try to arrange some type of creative financing.

Capital Investments Firms often need to raise money early on to fund capital investments. Although it may be possible for the venture's founders to fund its initial activities, it becomes increasingly difficult for them to do so when it comes to buying property, constructing buildings, purchasing equipment, or investing in other capital projects. Many entrepreneurial ventures are able to delay or avoid these types of expenditures by leasing space or co-opting the resources of alliance partners. However, at some point in its growth cycle, the firm's needs may become specialized enough that it makes sense to purchase capital assets rather than rent or lease them.

Lengthy Product Development Cycles In some industries, firms need to raise money to pay the up-front costs of lengthy product development cycles. For example, it typically takes about two years and at least $4 million to develop an electronic game.[5] In the biotech industry, the path to commercial licensing

Cash Flow Challenges	Capital Investments	Lengthy Product Development Cycles
Inventory must be purchased, employees must be trained and paid, and advertising must be paid for before cash is generated from sales.	The cost of buying real estate, building facilities, and purchasing equipment typically exceeds a firm's ability to provide funds for these needs on its own.	Some products are under development for years before they generate earnings. The up-front costs often exceed a firm's ability to fund these activities on its own.

FIGURE 10.1

Three Reasons Start-Ups Need Funding

Being an entrepreneur in the biotech industry requires a lot of determination and drive. The path to getting a new drug approved takes 8 to 14 years. This "tortoise-like pace" of new product development normally takes a substantial up-front investment before a payoff is realized.

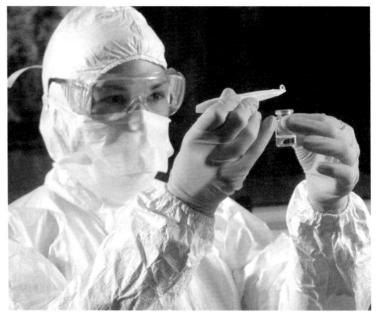

Chris Barry/Phototake NYC

takes 8 to 14 years.[6] This tortoise-like pace of product development requires substantial up-front investment before the anticipated payoff is realized. While the biotech industry is an extreme example, lengthy product development cycles are the realities ventures face in many industries.

Although most new ventures need funding at some point during their launch or development, it is generally unhealthy for a start-up to have access to too much money too fast. This scenario played out for Webvan, a potentially promising start-up. The speed of its expansion, made possible by an overabundance of start-up funds, turned out to be its undoing, as illustrated in the "What Went Wrong?" feature.

Sources of Personal Financing

Learning Objective

2. Identify the three sources of personal financing available to entrepreneurs.

Typically, the seed money that gets a company off the ground comes from the founders' own pockets. There are three categories of sources of money in this area: personal funds, friends and family, and bootstrapping. These sources are depicted in Figure 10.2 and are explained next.

Personal Funds   The vast majority of founders contribute personal funds along with sweat equity to their ventures.[7] In fact, in a Kauffman Foundation survey of nearly 5,000 new business owners, just 10 percent used external sources of funds their first year of operation.[8] The numbers change some but

FIGURE 10.2

Sources of Personal Financing

Personal Funds	Friends and Family	Bootstrapping
Involves both financial resources and sweat equity. Sweat equity represents the value of the time and effort that a founder puts into a firm.	Often comes in the form of loans or investments, but can also involve outright gifts, foregone or delayed compensation, or reduced or free rent.	Finding ways to avoid the need for external financing through creativity, ingenuity, thriftiness, cost-cutting, obtaining grants, or any other means.

What Went WRONG?

Webvan: How Having Too Much Money Can Be Just as Harmful as Having Too Little

There's a saying in investment circles that the worst thing you can do to a start-up is give it too much money. Too much money can enable a start-up to spend money carelessly, expand too quickly, and operate unprofitably for too long. In contrast, if a start-up is on a tight budget, it has to spend its money wisely, learn to be self-reliant, and develop a mind-set of frugality to survive.

Webvan had too much money in spades. The company, which was launched in the late 1990s, delivered grocery store items to customers' homes. The basic idea behind Webvan's plan was that the company could lower the costs of selling groceries by storing and sorting groceries in huge warehouses and making home deliveries rather than incurring the costs involved with running traditional grocery stores. The company reasoned that consumers would flock to its service because it relieved them of the time-intensive task of grocery shopping. On the allure of this pitch, Webvan was able to raise more than $1 billion of venture capital and investor funding in the late 1990s.

Flush with cash, Webvan plowed full steam ahead. The sensible approach to rolling out its service would have been to build a few facilities and work out all the bugs before going nationwide. Instead, Webvan embarked on a 26-city expansion plan. Because of the speed of the plan, it wasn't able to take the lessons it learned in one location and incorporate them into the next, because the next location was already coming online. For example, Webvan built elaborate on-site butcher operations in every warehouse, only to later determine it was more efficient to buy prepared meat and have it delivered to the warehouses (making the butcher facilities obsolete). Similarly, the company built separate fresh vegetable and fruit operations in each warehouse, only to later determine it was better to combine them.

There's more: The simultaneous rollout of the company's service in multiple locations forced it to adopt a single approach to servicing customers, which ignored local demographic and shopping patterns. As a result, its standard service was more popular in some locations than others. In San Francisco, which is densely populated and has a lot of people who don't own cars, it did well. In Atlanta,

which is more suburban and most people own cars, it did poorly. The lower than expected demand in many locations worked against Webvan's need to capture large economies of scale and resulted in blatant inefficiencies. For example, in some locations, Webvan's drivers would have to drive 30 miles to make a single delivery.

The results from these actions are not desirable. Just two years after it made its first delivery Webvan collapsed, with no money and investors who had no appetite to invest additional funds. As a postscript, although the online grocery market is still in its infancy, it does have successes. An example is FreshDirect, an online grocer that delivers to residences, offices, and commuter rail stops in the New York City area. Unlike Webvan, the company's expansion has been slow, and since its opening in 2002, it has added product lines and widened the area it covers around New York City rather than opened new facilities. The company employs 2,000 people and has sales around $200 million.

Questions for Critical Thinking

1. Why do you think Webvan's investors didn't do a better job of supervising its growth?
2. The "You Be the VC 10.2" feature focuses on Crushpad, a company that plans to build urban wineries in cities across the United States. What lessons can Crushpad learn from Webvan's experiences?
3. Spend some time investigating FreshDirect, the New York City online grocer mentioned in the feature. Make a list of the things that you believe FreshDirect is doing to grow in a healthy manner. In what ways could FreshDirect get itself in trouble if it received a large infusion of funds and decided to expand aggressively.
4. Describe what you believe would have been a more reasonable money-raising plan and expansion plan for Webvan.

Sources: P. Carroll and C. Mui, *Billion-Dollar Lessons* (New York: Penguin Group, 2008); Hoover's, "FreshDirect," www.hoovers.com (accessed September 15, 2008).

not as much as you might think as firms get older. Results from a number of studies that have examined firms that have been in business for just a few years up to a total of eight years show that close to 50 percent of the firms received no external funding—the money came strictly from the personal funds of the founders and the profits of the firms.[9] **Sweat equity** represents the value of the time and effort that a founder puts into a new venture. Because many founders do not have a substantial amount of cash to put into their ventures, it is often the sweat equity that makes the most difference.

Friends and Family   Friends and family are the second source of funds for many new ventures. This type of contribution often comes in the form of loans or investments but can also involve outright gifts, foregone or delayed compensation (if a friend or family member works for the new venture), or reduced or free rent. For example, Cisco Systems, the giant producer of Internet routers and switches, started in the house of one of its cofounder's parents. Similarly, Ted Waitt, the founder of Gateway Computer, got his start with a $10,000 loan from his grandmother.

There are three rules of thumb that entrepreneurs should follow when asking friends and family members for money. First, the request should be presented in a businesslike manner, just like one would deal with a banker or investor. The potential of the business along with the risks involved should be carefully and fully described. Second, if the help the entrepreneur receives is in the form of a loan, a promissory note should be prepared, with a repayment schedule, and the note should be signed by both parties. Stipulating the terms of the loan in writing reduces the potential of a misunderstanding and protects both the entrepreneur and the friend or family member providing the funding. Third, financial help should be requested only from those who are in a legitimate position to offer assistance. It's not a good idea to ask certain friends or family members, regardless of how much they may have expressed a willingness to help, for assistance if losing the money would cripple them financially. Entrepreneurs who are unable to repay a loan to a friend or family member risk not only damaging their business relationship with them but their personal relationship as well.[10]

Virgin Money helps structure arrangements between business owners and friends or family members. The company offers two plans. The Handshake Basic, which costs $99, is for loans of less than $10,000. Virgin Money provides the parties involved with the documents needed to execute a loan agreement. A more formal plan, the Business Builder, is for loans between $25,000 and $100,000, and includes more elaborate forms of documentation. The cost is more than $199, depending on the nature of the agreement.[11] Accountants, attorneys, and bankers can also help people structure loan agreements.[12]

Bootstrapping   A third source of seed money for a new venture is referred to as bootstrapping. **Bootstrapping** is finding ways to avoid the need for external financing or funding through creativity, ingenuity, thriftiness, cost-cutting, or any means necessary.[13] (The term comes from the adage "pull yourself up by your bootstraps.") It is the term attached to the general philosophy of minimizing start-up expenses by aggressively pursuing cost-cutting techniques and money-saving tactics. There are many well-known examples of entrepreneurs who bootstrapped to get their companies started. Legend has it that Steve Jobs and partner Steve Wozniak sold a Volkswagen van and a Hewlett-Packard programmable calculator to raise $1,350, which was the initial seed capital for Apple Computer.

An illustration of how adept some entrepreneurs are at bootstrapping is provided by Michelle Madhok, the founder of SheFinds, a company that helps busy women (through a twice-weekly e-mail newsletter) keep in touch with fashion trends and find good values on the Internet. In describing how she combined her personal savings with bootstrapping to start her company, Madhok said:

> I financed SheFinds myself and have spent about $5,000 of my own money to get the business off the ground. The most expensive items were forming the LLC, legal costs and public relations. My [Web] site was built for about $250 by a guy in the

Table 10.1   EXAMPLES OF BOOTSTRAPPING METHODS

- Buy used instead of new equipment
- Coordinate purchases with other businesses
- Lease equipment instead of buying
- Obtain payments in advance from customers
- Minimize personal expenses
- Avoid unnecessary expenses, such as lavish office space or furniture
- Buy items cheaply but prudently through discount outlets or online auctions such as eBay, rather than at full-price stores
- Share office space or employees with other businesses
- Hire interns

Ukraine who I found on craigslist (www.craigslist.org). My photos were done for barter and I got a good deal on the illustrations on my site because the artist had downtime. I work with many independents—my lawyer is an independent, because I don't see the value in paying for a big, fancy firm. And I look for discount resources on the Internet—if you search around, you can find companies that will make quality color copies for about 20 cents a copy.[14]

There are many ways entrepreneurs bootstrap to raise money or cut costs. Some of the more common examples of bootstrapping are provided in Table 10.1.

Learning Objective

3. Provide examples of how entrepreneurs bootstrap to raise money or cut costs.

Preparing to Raise Debt or Equity Financing

Once a start-up's financial needs exceed what personal funds, friends and family, and bootstrapping can provide, debt and equity are the two most common sources of funds. The most important thing an entrepreneur must do at this point is determine precisely what the company needs and the most appropriate source to use to obtain those funds. A carefully planned approach to raising money increases a firm's chance of success and can save an entrepreneur considerable time.

The steps involved in properly preparing to raise debt or equity financing are shown in Figure 10.3 and are discussed next.

Step 1   **Determine precisely how much money the company needs**
Constructing and analyzing documented cash flow statements and projections for needed capital expenditures are actions taken to complete this step. This information should already be in the business plan, as described in Chapter 4.

Knowing exactly how much money to ask for is important for at least two reasons. First, a company doesn't want to get caught short, yet it doesn't want to pay for capital it doesn't need. Second, entrepreneurs talking to a potential lender or investor make a poor impression when they appear uncertain about the amount of money required to support their venture.

Learning Objective

4. Identify the three steps involved in properly preparing to raise debt or equity financing.

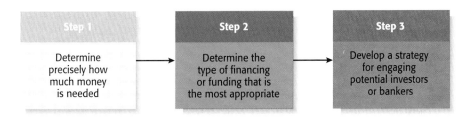

Step 1	Step 2	Step 3
Determine precisely how much money is needed	Determine the type of financing or funding that is the most appropriate	Develop a strategy for engaging potential investors or bankers

FIGURE 10.3

Preparation for Debt or Equity Financing

Learning
Objective

5. Discuss the difference
between equity funding
and debt financing.

Step 2 Determine the most appropriate type of financing or funding
Equity and debt financing are the two most common alternatives for raising money. **Equity financing** (or funding) means exchanging partial ownership in a firm, usually in the form of stock, for funding. Angel investors, private placement, venture capital, and initial public offerings are the most common sources of equity funding (we discuss all these sources later in the chapter). Equity funding is not a loan—the money that is received is not paid back. Instead, equity investors become partial owners of the firm. Some equity investors invest "for the long haul" and are content to receive a return on their investment through dividend payments on their stock. More commonly, equity investors have a three- to five-year investment horizon and expect to get their money back, along with a substantial capital gain, through the sale of their stock. The stock is typically sold following a **liquidity event**, which is an occurrence that converts some or all of a company's stock into cash. The three most common liquidity events for a new venture are to go public, find a buyer, or merge with another company.

Because of the risks involved, equity investors are very demanding and fund only a small percentage of the business plans they consider.[15] An equity investor considers a firm that has a unique business opportunity, high growth potential, a clearly defined niche market, and proven management to be an ideal candidate. In contrast, businesses that don't fit these criteria have a hard time getting equity funding. Many entrepreneurs are not familiar with the standards that equity investors apply and get discouraged when they are repeatedly turned down by venture capitalists and angel investors. Often, the reason they don't qualify for venture capital or angel investment isn't because their business proposal is poor, but because they don't meet the exacting standards equity investors usually apply.[16]

Debt financing is getting a loan. The most common sources of debt financing are commercial banks and Small Business Administration (SBA) guaranteed loans. The types of bank loans and SBA guaranteed loans available to entrepreneurs are discussed later in this chapter. In general, banks lend money that must be repaid with interest. Banks are not investors. As a result, bankers are interested in minimizing risk, properly collateralizing loans, and repayment, as opposed to return on investment and capital gains. The ideal candidate for a bank loan is a firm with a strong cash flow, low leverage, audited financial statements, good management, and a healthy balance sheet. A careful review of these criteria demonstrates why it's difficult for start-ups to receive bank loans. Most start-ups are simply too early in their life cycle to have the set of characteristics bankers want.

Table 10.2 provides an overview of three common profiles of new ventures and the type of financing or funding that is appropriate for each one. This table illustrates why most start-ups must rely on personal funds, friends and family, and bootstrapping at the outset and must wait until later to obtain equity or debt financing. Indeed, most new ventures do not have the characteristics required by bankers or investors until they have proven their product or service idea and have achieved a certain measure of success in the marketplace.

Learning
Objective

6. Explain the role of an
elevator speech in
attracting financing
for an entrepreneurial
venture.

Step 3 Developing a strategy for engaging potential investors or bankers There are three steps to developing a strategy for engaging potential investors or bankers. First, the lead entrepreneurs in a new venture should prepare an **elevator speech (or pitch)**—a brief,

Table 10.2 MATCHING AN ENTREPRENEURIAL VENTURE'S CHARACTERISTICS WITH THE APPROPRIATE FORM OF FINANCING OR FUNDING

Characteristics of the Venture	Appropriate Source of Financing or Funding
The business has high risk with an uncertain return:	Personal funds, friends, family, and other forms of bootstrapping
Weak cash flow	
High leverage	
Low-to-moderate growth	
Unproven management	
The business has low risk with a more predictable return:	Debt financing
Strong cash flow	
Low leverage	
Audited financials	
Good management	
Healthy balance sheet	
The business offers a high return:	Equity
Unique business idea	
High growth	
Niche market	
Proven management	

carefully constructed statement that outlines the merits of a business opportunity. Why is it called an elevator speech? If an entrepreneur stepped into an elevator on the 25th floor of a building and found that by a stroke of luck a potential investor was in the same elevator, the entrepreneur would have the time it takes to get from the 25th floor to the ground floor to try to get the investor interested in the business opportunity. Most elevator speeches are 45 seconds to 2 minutes long.[17]

There are many occasions when a carefully constructed elevator speech might come in handy. For example, many university-sponsored centers for entrepreneurship hold events that bring investors and entrepreneurs together. Often, these events include social hours and refreshment breaks designed specifically for the purpose of allowing entrepreneurs looking for funding to mingle with potential investors. An outline for a 60-second elevator speech is provided in Table 10.3.

The second step in developing a strategy for engaging potential investors or bankers is more deliberate and requires identifying and contacting the best prospects. First, the new venture should carefully assess the type of financing or funding it is likely to qualify for, as depicted in Table 10.2. Then, a list of potential bankers or investors should be compiled. If venture capital funding is felt to be appropriate, for example, a little legwork can go a long way in pinpointing likely investors. A new venture should identify the venture funds that are investing money in the industry in which it intends to compete and target those firms first. To do this, look to the venture capital firms' Web sites. These reveal the industries in which the firms have an interest. Sometimes, these sites also provide a list of the companies the

Table 10.3 GUIDELINES FOR PREPARING AN ELEVATOR SPEECH

The elevator speech is a very brief description of your opportunity, product idea, qualifications, and market. Imagine that you step into an elevator in a tall building and a potential investor is already there; you have about 60 seconds to explain your business idea.

Step 1	Describe the opportunity or problem that needs to be solved	20 seconds
Step 2	Describe how your product or service meets the opportunity or solves the problem	20 seconds
Step 3	Describe your qualifications	10 seconds
Step 4	Describe your market	10 seconds
Total		60 seconds

firm has funded. For an example, access Sequoia Capital's Web site (www.sequoiacap.com), a well-known venture capital firm.

A cardinal rule for approaching a banker or an investor is to get a personal introduction. Bankers and investors receive many business plans, and most of them end up in what often becomes an unread stack of paper in a corner in their offices. To have your business plan noticed, find someone who knows the banker or the investor and ask for an introduction. This requirement is explained in blunt terms by Randall Stross, the author of *eBoys*, a book about the venture capital industry. Stross spent two years observing the day-to-day activities at Benchmark Venture Capital, a prominent Silicon Valley venture capital firm. According to Strauss,

The business plan that comes in from a complete stranger, either without the blessing of someone the venture capital firm knows well or without professional recommendations that render an introduction superfluous, is all but certain not to make the cut. In fact, knowing that this is the case becomes a tacit requirement from the perspective of a venture guy: Anyone whom I don't know who approaches me directly with a business plan shows me they haven't passed Entrepreneurship 101.[18]

The third step in engaging potential investors or bankers is to be prepared to provide the investor or banker a completed business plan and make a presentation of the plan if requested. We looked at how to present a business plan in Chapter 4. The presentation should be as polished as possible and should demonstrate why the new venture represents an attractive endeavor for the lender or investor.

Because the process of raising money is complicated, it is important to obtain as much advice as possible for how to navigate the funding process. One approach is to find a mentor, as illustrated in the "Partnering for Success" feature.

SOURCES OF EQUITY FUNDING

The primary disadvantage of equity funding is that the firm's owners relinquish part of their ownership interest and may lose some control. The primary advantage is access to capital. In addition, because investors become partial owners of the firms in which they invest, they often try to help those firms by offering their expertise and assistance. Unlike a loan, the money received from an equity investor doesn't have to be paid back. The investor receives a return on the investment through dividend payments and by selling the stock.

The three most common forms of equity funding are described next.

Partnering for SUCCESS
Want Help Navigating the Process of Raising Money? Find a Mentor

Raising money isn't easy. It is a complex and painstaking process, where experience helps. This reality puts first-time entrepreneurs at a disadvantage. While there are many good books about raising money and SBDC and SCORE counselors can be helpful, what many first-time business owners find most helpful is to find a mentor to guide them through the process.

A mentor is someone who is more experienced than you are and is willing to be your counselor, confidant, and go-to person for advice. There are two ways to find a mentor. First is to work your network of acquaintances—professors, business owners, accountants, attorneys—to determine if there is someone available that you trust, has experience raising money, and is willing to become your mentor. Many first-time entrepreneurs are surprised by how many people are eager to share their expertise and enter into a mentoring relationship. The second way is to utilize one of the growing number of Web sites that help match business founders with people who are willing to become mentors. One site is MicroMentor.org, which is a nonprofit that matches business founders with mentors. You can go to the site and fill out a profile about yourself and your goals, and then search profiles of potential mentors who match your needs. Once a match is made, the mentoring can take place through e-mail, instant messaging, Web conferencing, or over the phone. There is a tab on MicroMentor's Web site that provides access to "success stories" of business founders who have had excellent results using its service. A similar service is iMantri—a for-profit organization where mentors charge for their services. iMantri makes money by taking a cut of the fees.

There are also Web sites geared toward helping entrepreneurs raise money with that also provide a mentor-matching service. Examples include GoBigNetwork.com and Jumpstart's IdeaCrossing.org. These sites offer online ads for mentors.

The ideal situation is to find a mentor in your own community so you can meet face-to-face. Still, the online options provide business founders a wide range of mentors to choose from, which may result in a better match. Online mentoring and counseling relationships are becoming increasingly common. Nearly 40 percent of all the counseling and mentoring done by SCORE counselors is now done online.

Similar to any relationship, a business founder should be careful and only share private information with a mentor once a trusting relationship has been established.

Questions for Critical Thinking

1. If you were starting a business, would you check out one of the online mentoring sites? Why or why not?
2. To what degree do you believe that having a mentor can make the difference between an entrepreneur succeeding or failing? In what areas of the entrepreneurial process do you think mentors are called upon the most?
3. What are some of the traditional, off-line sources of mentoring for entrepreneurs? Which of these could you take advantage of if you decided to launch a firm? How large a role have these organizations played in the growth and success of entrepreneurship?
4. Spend some time experimenting with one of the mentoring Web sites mentioned previously. Is the site easy to navigate? After spending some time looking at the site, would you be more likely or less likely to use it if you were in the process of starting a company?

Source: Wall Street Journal (Eastern Edition) by K. Sports. Copyright 2008 by Dow Jones & Company, Inc.

Business Angels

Business angels are individuals who invest their personal capital directly in start-ups. The term *angel* was first used in connection with finance to describe wealthy New Yorkers who invested in Broadway plays. The prototypical business angel, who invests in entrepreneurial start-ups, is about 50 years old, has high income and wealth, is well educated, has succeeded as an entrepreneur, and invests in companies that are in the region where he or she lives.[19] These investors generally invest between $10,000 and $500,000 in a single company and are looking for companies that have the potential to grow 30 to 40 percent per year before they are acquired or go public.[20] Jeffrey Sohl, the director of the University of New Hampshire's Center for Venture Research, estimates that

Learning Objective

7. Describe the difference between a business angel and a venture capitalist.

only 10 to 15 percent of private companies meet that criterion.[21] Many well-known firms have received their initial funding from one or more business angels. For example, Apple Computer received its initial investment capital from Mike Markkula, who obtained his wealth as an executive with Intel. In 1977, Markkula invested $91,000 in Apple and personally guaranteed another $250,000 in credit lines. When Apple went public in 1980, his stock in the company was worth more than $150 million.[22] Similarly, in 1998 Google received its first investment from Sun Microsystems' cofounder Andy Bechtolsheim, who gave Larry Page and Sergey Brin (Google's cofounders) a check for $100,000 after they showed him an early version of Google's search engine.[23] Can you image what Bechtolsheim's investment was worth when Google went public in 2005?

The number of angel investors in the United States alone, which is estimated to be around 258,200, has increased dramatically over the past decade.[24] The rapid increase is due in part to the high returns that some angels report. In 2007, angels invested $26.0 billion in 57,120 small companies.[25] By comparison, during that same period, venture capital funds invested about $29.9 billion in 2,648 deals.[26] Software accounted for the largest share of angel investments, with 27 percent of total investment in 2007, followed by health care services/medical devices and equipment (19 percent), biotech (12 percent), industrial/energy (8 percent), retail (6 percent), and media (5 percent).[27] In exchange for their investment, angels expect a rather hefty annual return—usually in the neighborhood of 35 to 40 percent.[28] They also usually fill a seat on the board of directors of the firms in which they invest and provide varying levels of managerial input.

Business angels are valuable because of their willingness to make relatively small investments. This gives access to equity funding to a start-up that needs just $50,000 rather than the $1 million minimum investment that most venture capitalists require. Many angels are also motivated by more than financial returns; they enjoy the process of mentoring a new firm. Oron Strauss is a 1995 Dartmouth College graduate who received angel funding. Recalling an experience with his angel investor, Strauss said,

> About a year ago, when I was having a particularly bad week, I fired off a long, heartfelt e-mail message to my angel. I explained, in great detail, the difficulties I faced and my thoughts about them. His response was succinct: "All sounds normal. You're handling it well. Keep up the good work." My first reaction was disappointment over what struck me as a curt response. Then I realized that the angel had given me the best possible response. He understood that what I was going through was normal and that I would make it.[29]

Most angels remain fairly anonymous and are matched up with entrepreneurs through referrals. To find a business angel investor, an entrepreneur should discretely work a network of acquaintances to see if anyone can make an appropriate introduction. An advantage that college students have in regard to finding business angels is that many angels judge college- or university-sponsored business plan competitions. The number of organized groups of angels continues to grow. Typically, each group consists of 10 to 150 angel investors in a local area that meet regularly to listen to business plan presentations. While some groups focus on a specific industry, most groups are open to a variety of areas and select those markets with which some of their members have expertise. The Angel Capital Education Foundation provides a list of angel groups in Canada and the United States on its Web site (www.angelcapitaleducation.org). In many areas, local governments and nonprofit organizations are active in trying to bring entrepreneurs and angel investors together.

It's important to be fully prepared and look sharp before meeting with a business angel. This team of entrepreneurs is taking one last look at its PowerPoint presentation before presenting its business plan to an angel investor.

Venture Capital

Venture capital is money that is invested by venture capital firms in start-ups and small businesses with exceptional growth potential.[30] In the United States alone, there are about 650 venture capital firms, which provide funding to about 2,600 firms per year. As mentioned, in 2007, venture capital firms invested $29.9 billion in just over 2,600 companies.[31] The peak year for venture capital investing was 2000, when $106.6 billion was invested at the height of the e-commerce craze. A distinct difference between angel investors and venture capital firms is that angels tend to invest earlier in the life of a company, whereas venture capitalists come in later. The majority of venture capital money goes to follow-on funding for businesses originally funded by angel investors, government programs (which are discussed later in the chapter), or by some other means.

Venture capital firms are limited partnerships of money managers who raise money in "funds" to invest in start-ups and growing firms. The funds, or pools of money, are raised from wealthy individuals, pension plans, university endowments, foreign investors, and similar sources. A typical fund is $75 million to $200 million and invests in 20 to 30 companies over a three- to five-year period.[32] The venture capitalists who manage the fund receive an annual management fee in addition to 20 to 25 percent of the profits earned by the fund. The percentage of the profits the venture capitalists get is called the **carry**. So if a venture capital firm raised a $100 million fund and the fund grew to $500 million, a 20 percent carry means that the firm would get, after repaying the original $100 million, 20 percent of the $400 million in profits, or $80 million. The investors in the fund would get the remainder. Venture capitalists shoot for a 30 to 40 percent or more annual return on their investment and a total return over the life of the investment of 5 to 20 times the initial investment.[33] Some venture capital "funds" invest in specific areas. For example, in 2008 Kleiner Perkins Caufield & Byers launched a $100 million fund to finance companies building new applications, services, and components for Apple Inc.'s iPhone and iPod Touch. The managers of the fund indicated that they planned to make investments ranging from $100,000 of seed capital to $15 million of expansion capital for qualifying companies.[34]

Because of the venture capital industry's lucrative nature and because in the past venture capitalists have funded high-profile successes such as Google, Cisco Systems, eBay, and Yahoo!, the industry receives a great deal of attention. But actually, venture capitalists fund very few entrepreneurial ventures in comparison to business angels and relative to the number of firms needing funding. Remember, venture capitalists fund about 2,600 companies per year, compared to 57,000 funded by business angels. As mentioned earlier in this chapter, many entrepreneurs become discouraged when they are repeatedly rejected for venture capital funding, even though they may have an excellent business plan. Venture capitalists are looking for the "home run." This target causes venture capitalists to reject the majority of the proposals they consider.

Venture capitalists know that they are making risky investments and that some investments won't pan out. In fact, most venture firms anticipate that about 15 to 25 percent of their investments will be home runs, 25 to 35 percent will be winners, 25 to 35 percent will break even, and 15 to 25 percent will fail.[35] The home runs must be sensational to make up for the break-even firms and the failures.

Still, for the firms that qualify, venture capital is a viable alternative to equity funding. An advantage to obtaining this funding is that venture capitalists are extremely well connected in the business world (by this we mean that they have a large number of useful contacts with customers, suppliers, government representatives, and so forth) and can offer a firm considerable assistance beyond funding. Firms that qualify typically obtain their money in stages that correspond to their own stage of development. Once a venture capitalist makes an investment in a firm, subsequent investments are made in **rounds** (or stages) and are referred to as **follow-on funding**. Table 10.4 shows the various stages in the venture capital process, from the seed stage to buyout financing.

An important part of obtaining venture capital funding is going through the **due diligence** process, which refers to the process of investigating the merits of a potential venture and verifying the key claims made in the business plan. Firms that prove to be suitable for venture capital funding should conduct their own due diligence of the venture capitalists with whom they are working to ensure that they are a good fit. An entrepreneur should ask the following

Table 10.4   STAGES (OR ROUNDS) OF VENTURE CAPITAL FUNDING

Stage or Round	Purpose of the Funding
Seed funding	Investment made very early in a venture's life to fund the development of a prototype and feasibility analysis.
Start-up funding	Investment made to firms exhibiting few if any commercial sales but in which product development and market research are reasonably complete. Management is in place, and the firm has completed its business model. Funding is needed to start production.
First-stage funding	Funding that occurs when the firm has started commercial production and sales but requires additional financing to ramp up its production capacity.
Second-stage funding	Funding that occurs when a firm is successfully selling a product but needs to expand both its production capacity and its markets.
Mezzanine financing	Investment made in a firm to provide for further expansion or to bridge its financing needs before launching an IPO or before a buyout.
Buyout funding	Funding provided to help one company acquire another.

questions and scrutinize the answers to them before accepting funding from a venture capital firm:

- Do the venture capitalists have experience in our industry?
- Do they take a highly active or passive management role?
- Are the personalities on both sides of the table compatible?
- Does the firm have deep enough pockets or sufficient contacts within the venture capital industry to provide follow-on rounds of financing?
- Is the firm negotiating in good faith in regard to the percentage of our firm they want in exchange for their investment?

Along with traditional venture capital, there is also **corporate venture capital**. This type of capital is similar to traditional venture capital except that the money comes from corporations that invest in start-ups related to their areas of interest.

Initial Public Offering

Another source of equity funding is to sell stock to the public by staging an **initial public offering (IPO)**. An IPO is the first sale of stock by a firm to the public. Any later public issuance of shares is referred to as a **secondary market offering**. When a company goes public, its stock is typically traded on one of the major stock exchanges. Most entrepreneurial firms that go public trade on the NASDAQ, which is weighted heavily toward technology, biotech, and small-company stocks.[36] An IPO is an important milestone for a firm.[37] Typically, a firm is not able to go public until it has demonstrated that it is viable and has a bright future.

Learning Objective

8. Explain why an initial public offering (IPO) is an important milestone in an entrepreneurial venture.

Firms decide to go public for several reasons. First, it is a way to raise equity capital to fund current and future operations. Second, an IPO raises a firm's public profile, making it easier to attract high-quality customers, alliance partners, and employees. Third, an IPO is a liquidity event that provides a mechanism for the company's stockholders, including its investors, to cash out their investments. Finally, by going public, a firm creates another form of currency that can be used to grow the company. It is not uncommon for one firm to buy another company by paying for it with stock rather than with cash.[38] The stock comes from "authorized but not yet issued stock," which in essence means that the firm issues new shares of stock to make the purchase.

Although there are many advantages to going public, it is a complicated and expensive process and subjects firms to substantial costs related to SEC reporting requirements. Many of the most costly requirements were initiated by the U.S. **Sarbanes-Oxley Act** of 2002. The Sarbanes-Oxley Act is a law that was passed in response to corporate accounting scandals involving prominent corporations, like Enron and WorldCom. This wide-ranging act established a number of new or enhanced reporting standards for public corporations.

The first step in initiating a public offering is for a firm to hire an investment bank. An **investment bank** is an institution that acts as an underwriter or agent for a firm issuing securities.[39] The investment bank acts as the firm's advocate and adviser and walks it through the process of going public. The most important issues the firm and its investment bank must agree on are the amount of capital needed by the firm, the type of stock to be issued, the price of the stock when it goes public (e.g., $12 per share), and the cost to the firm to issue the securities. Although not fully known as this book went to press, the effects of the global financial crisis that surfaced in late 2008 on investment banks could be quite substantial. At a minimum, early indications are that the transactions of investment banks will be more heavily regulated in countries throughout the world.

There are a number of hoops the investment bank must jump through to assure the Securities and Exchange Commission (SEC) that the offer is legitimate. During the time the SEC is investigating the potential offering, the investment bank issues a **preliminary prospectus** that describes the offering to the general public. The preliminary prospectus is also called the "red herring." After the SEC has approved the offering, the investment bank issues the **final prospectus**, which sets a date and issuing price for the offering.

In addition to getting the offering approved, the investment bank is responsible for drumming up support for the offering. As part of this process, the investment bank typically takes the top management team of the firm wanting to go public on a **road show**, which is a whirlwind tour that consists of meetings in key cities where the firm presents its business plan to groups of investors.[40] Until December 1, 2005, the presentations made during these road shows were seen only by the investors physically present in the various cities; an SEC regulation went into effect at that time requiring that road show presentations be taped and made available to the public. Road show presentations can now be viewed online at www.retailroadshow.com. If enough interest in a potential public offering is created, the offering will take place on the date scheduled in the prospectus. If it isn't, the offering will be delayed or canceled.

Timing and luck play a role in whether a public offering is successful. For example, a total of 332 IPOs raised about $50 billion in 1999, the height of the Internet bubble. When the bubble burst in early 2001, the IPO marketplace all but dried up, particularly for technology and telecom stocks. Since then, the market has recovered some, although it is still not robust, and most firms cannot count on an IPO to raise capital or as an exit strategy. There were 205 IPOs in 2005, 230 in 2006, 237 in 2007, and 43 in 2008. The vitality of the IPO market hinges largely on the state of the overall economy and the mood of the investing public, as evidenced by the sharp downturn in numbers in 2008, a bad year for the U.S. economy. Early evidence suggested that 2009's IPO activity might be less than 2008's. However, even when facing a strong economy and a positive mood toward investing, an entrepreneurial venture should guard itself against becoming caught up in the euphoria and rushing its IPO.

A variation of the IPO is a **private placement**, which is the direct sale of an issue of securities to a large institutional investor. When a private placement is initiated, there is no public offering, and no prospectus is prepared.

SOURCES OF DEBT FINANCING

Debt financing involves getting a loan or selling corporate bonds. Because it is virtually impossible for a new venture to sell corporate bonds, we'll focus on obtaining loans.

There are two common types of loans. The first is a **single-purpose loan**, in which a specific amount of money is borrowed that must be repaid in a fixed amount of time with interest. The second is a **line of credit**, in which a borrowing "cap" is established and borrowers can use the credit at their discretion. Lines of credit require periodic interest payments.

There are two major advantages to obtaining a loan as opposed to equity funding. The first is that none of the ownership of the firm is surrendered—a major advantage for most entrepreneurs. The second is that interest payments on a loan are tax deductible in contrast to dividend payments made to investors, which aren't.

There are two major disadvantages of getting a loan. The first is that it must be repaid, which may be difficult in a start-up venture in which the entrepreneur is focused on getting the company off the ground. Cash is typically "tight" during a new venture's first few months and sometimes for a year or more. The second is that lenders often impose strict conditions on loans and insist on ample collateral to fully protect their investment. Even if a start-up is incorporated, a lender may require that an entrepreneur's personal assets be collateralized as a condition of the loan.

The three common sources or categories of debt financing available to entrepreneurs are described next.

Commercial Banks

Historically, commercial banks have not been viewed as practical sources of financing for start-up firms.[41] This sentiment is not a knock against banks; it is just that banks are risk averse, and financing start-ups is risky business. Instead of looking for businesses that are "home runs," which is what venture capitalists seek to do, banks look for customers who will reliably repay their loans. As shown in Table 10.2, banks are interested in firms that have a strong cash flow, low leverage, audited financials, good management, and a healthy balance sheet. Although many new ventures have good management, few have the other characteristics, at least initially. But banks are an important source of credit for small businesses later in their life cycles.

There are two reasons that banks have historically been reluctant to lend money to start-ups. First, as mentioned previously, banks are risk averse. In addition, banks frequently have internal controls and regulatory restrictions prohibiting them from making high-risk loans. So when an entrepreneur approaches a banker with a request for a $250,000 loan and the only collateral the entrepreneur has to offer is the recognition of a problem that needs to be solved, a plan to solve it, and perhaps some intellectual property, there is usually no practical way for the bank to help. Banks typically have standards that guide their lending, such as minimum debt-to-equity ratios that work against start-up entrepreneurs.

The second reason banks have historically been reluctant to lend money to start-ups is that lending to small firms is not as profitable as lending to large firms, which have historically been the staple clients of commercial banks. If an entrepreneur approaches a banker with a request for a $50,000 loan, it may simply not be worth the banker's time to do the due diligence necessary to determine the entrepreneur's risk profile. Considerable time is required to digest a business plan and investigate the merits of a new firm. Research shows that a firm's size is an important factor in determining its access to debt capital.[42] The $50,000 loan may be seen as both high risk and marginally profitable (based on the amount of time it would take to do the due diligence involved), making it doubly uninviting for a commercial bank.[43]

Despite these historical precedents, some banks are starting to engage start-up entrepreneurs—although the jury is still out regarding how significant these lenders will become. When it comes to start-ups, some banks are rethinking their lending standards and are beginning to focus on cash flow and the strength of the management team rather than on collateral and the strength of the balance sheet. Entrepreneurs should follow developments in this area closely.

SBA Guaranteed Loans

Approximately 50 percent of the 9,000 banks in the United States participate in the country's **SBA Guaranteed Loan Program**. The most notable SBA program available to small businesses is the **7(A) Loan Guaranty Program**. This program accounts for 90 percent of the SBA's loan activity. The program operates through private-sector lenders who provide loans that are guaranteed by the SBA. The

Learning Objective

9. Discuss the SBA Guaranteed Loan Program.

The SBA Guaranteed Loan program is a viable source of financing for many U.S. entrepreneurs. Approximately 50 percent of the 9,000 banks in the United States participate in the program.

loans are for small businesses that are unable to secure financing on reasonable terms through normal lending channels. The SBA does not currently have funding for direct loans, nor does it provide grants or low-interest-rate loans for business start-ups or expansion.

Almost all small businesses are eligible to apply for an SBA guaranteed loan. The SBA can guarantee as much as 85 percent (debt to equity) on loans up to $150,000 and 75 percent on loans of over $150,000. In most cases, the maximum guarantee is $1.5 million. A guaranteed loan can be used for working capital to expand a new business or start a new one. It can also be used for real estate purchases, renovation, construction, or equipment purchases. To obtain an SBA guaranteed loan, an application must meet the requirements of both the SBA and the lender. Individuals must typically pledge all of their assets to secure the loan.[44]

Although SBA guaranteed loans are utilized more heavily by existing small businesses than start-ups, they should not be dismissed as a possible source of funding. Since its inception, the SBA has helped make $280 billion in loans to nearly 1.3 million businesses—more money than any other source of financing.[45] Diane Nelson, the woman who built Kazoo & Company into a successful business and is the subject of Case 4.1, got her start through a $500,000 SBA guaranteed loan. John and Caprial Pence, who own several businesses in Portland, Oregon, have relied on the SBA guaranteed loan program twice for funding. The Pences' story, which is related in the "Savvy Entrepreneurial Firm" feature, illustrates the important role that the SBA loan program plays in funding small businesses and entrepreneurs. The Pences' own the types of businesses that typically don't qualify for equity funding. In their case, the SBA program enabled them to build the thriving businesses that they own today.

Other Sources of Debt Financing

There are a variety of other avenues business owners can pursue to borrow money. Getting loans from friends and family, discussed earlier, is a popular choice. Credit card debt, although easy to obtain, should be used sparingly. One channel for borrowing funds that is getting quite a bit of attention is Prosper.com, the peer-to-peer lending network that Andy Tabar utilized, as described in the opening profile. Prosper is an online auction Web site that

Savvy Entrepreneurial FIRM

John and Caprial Pence: How the SBA Guaranteed Loan Program Helped Two Entrepreneurs Get the Financing They Needed

www.caprialandjohnskitchen.com

John and Caprial Pence are two of Portland, Oregon's, finest cooks and busiest entrepreneurs. The two run a growing number of ventures in the Portland area, all focused around fine food. A distinctive aspect of their story is the role that the SBA Guaranteed Loan Program has played in their success. The Pences have utilized the SBA loan program twice, and it has been instrumental in helping them build their businesses.

John and Caprial grew up on opposite coasts and met at the Culinary Institute of America in Hyde Park, NY, where they were both attending school to become chefs. In the mid-1980s, following graduation, they moved to Seattle, where they launched their careers. In 1990, Caprial won the 1990 James Beard Award for Best Chef in the Pacific Northwest. At the same time, she was working on her first cookbook, teaching classes, and appearing on local TV. By 1992, the Pences were able to write their own ticket, and they moved to Portland.

In Portland, the Pences bought the old West-moreland Bistro with private financing and renamed it Caprial's Bistro. In 1998, they decided to remodel and expand the Bistro when space became available next door. The Pences considered several options for financing. The most realistic alternative, based on the advice of their banker, was an SBA guaranteed loan. The Pences agreed, and the bank facilitated a $260,000, seven-year SBA guaranteed loan. The loan enabled the couple to expand the seating capacity of their restaurant from 26 to 70.

Following the expansion of their restaurant, the Pences decided to diversify and leverage their cooking expertise by opening a cooking school and cookware shop. A second SBA guaranteed loan, for an identical amount as the first one ($260,000), made these objectives a reality. All three locations, the restaurant, the school, and the shop, are located near one another, making it easy for their customers to visit more than one location in a single trip. The addition of the cooking school and the cookware shop has tripled the Pences' annual revenue.

The future for the Pences and their ventures looks bright. The restaurant initially brought in around $1,000 a day, but now brings in $4,000 to $5,000 on an average weekday. The cooking school offers classes and demonstrations nearly every evening, where participants pay from $35 to $135 for hands-on classes or to view special cooking demonstrations. Just recently, the Pences started broadcasting a television show from the cooking school, and Caprial celebrated the printing of her eighth cookbook. Commenting on their experiences borrowing money to fund their growing operations, John Pence remarked, "We learned to get into this business (cooking) at the lowest debt level and have a cushion of working capital."

Questions for Critical Thinking

1. When the Pences decided to expand and remodel their restaurant in 1998, what sources of funding or financing were realistically available to them?
2. Do some research to find out what it takes to qualify for an SBA guaranteed loan. What criteria do the SBA and the participating lenders typically apply when evaluating candidates for loans?
3. Based on the material provided here, any additional information you can garner from the Pences' Web site, and your general knowledge of entrepreneurship, write a short analysis of why you think the Pences have been successful.
4. Do you think the Pences would be where they are today if they hadn't been made aware of the SBA Guaranteed Loan Program? Do you think most entrepreneurs are aware of the program?

Sources: Caprial and John's Kitchen homepage, www. caprialandjohnskitchen.com (accessed December 16, 2008); S. Herochik, "Restaurateurs Fit More on Their Plate with Help of Loan Program," *Bizjournals*, www.bizjournals.com/sba/1 (accessed January 31, 2006).

matches people who want to borrow money with people who are willing to make loans. Most of the loans made via Prosper are fairly small ($25,000) but might be sufficient to meet a new business's needs.[46] There are also organizations that lend money to specific demographic groups. For example, Count Me In, an advocacy group for female business owners, provides loans of $500 to $10,000 to women starting or growing a business.[47] Make Mine a Million $ Business, which is aligned with Count Me In and American Express, lends up to $50,000 to female-owned start-ups that have been in business for at least two years and have $250,000 or more in annual revenue.

Some lenders specialize in microfinance, which are very small loans. For example, ACCION USA gives $500 credit-builder loans to people with no credit history. While $500 might not sound like much, it could be enough to open a home-based business.[48]

CREATIVE SOURCES OF FINANCING AND FUNDING

Because financing and funding are difficult to obtain, particularly for start-ups, entrepreneurs often use creative ways to obtain financial resources. Even for firms that have financing or funding available, it is prudent to search for sources of capital that are less expensive than traditional ones. The following sections discuss three of the more common creative sources of financing and funding for entrepreneurial firms.

Leasing

Learning Objective

10. Explain the advantages of leasing for an entrepreneurial venture.

A **lease** is a written agreement in which the owner of a piece of property allows an individual or business to use the property for a specified period of time in exchange for payments. The major advantage of leasing is that it enables a company to acquire the use of assets with very little or no down payment. Leases for facilities and leases for equipment are the two most common types of leases that entrepreneurial ventures undertake.[49] For example, many new businesses lease computers from Dell Inc. or other PC manufacturers. The advantage for the new business is that it can gain access to the computers it needs with very little money invested up-front.

There are many different players in the leasing business. Some vendors, such as Dell, lease directly to businesses. As with banks, the vendors look for lease clients with good credit backgrounds and the ability to make the lease payments. There are also **venture-leasing firms** that act as brokers, bringing the parties involved in a lease together. These firms are acquainted with the producers of specialized equipment and match these producers with new ventures that are in need of the equipment. One of the responsibilities of these firms is conducting due diligence to make sure that the new ventures involved will be able to keep up with their lease payments.

Most leases involve a modest down payment and monthly payments during the duration of the lease. At the end of an equipment lease, the new venture typically has the option to stop using the equipment, purchase it at fair market value, or renew the lease. Lease deals that involve a substantial amount of money should be negotiated and entered into with the same amount of scrutiny as when getting financing or funding. Leasing is almost always more expensive than paying cash for an item, so most entrepreneurs think of leasing as an alternative to equity or debt financing. Although the down payment is typically lower, the primary disadvantage is that at the end of the lease, the lessee doesn't own the property or equipment.[50] Of course, this may be an advantage if a company is leasing equipment, such as computers or copy machines that can rather quickly become technologically obsolete.

SBIR and STTR Grant Programs

The Small Business Innovation Research (SBIR) and the Small Business Technology Transfer (STTR) programs are two important sources of early stage funding for technology firms. These programs provide cash grants to entrepreneurs who are working on projects in specific areas. The main difference between the SBIR and the STTR programs is that the STTR program requires the participation of researchers working at universities or other research institutions. For the purpose of the program, the term *small business* is defined as an American-owned for-profit business with fewer than 500 employees. The principle researcher must also be employed by the business.[51]

The **SBIR Program** is a competitive grant program that provides over $1 billion per year to small businesses for early stage and development projects. Each year, 11 U.S. departments and agencies are required by the SBIR to reserve a portion of their research and development funds for awards to small businesses. The agencies that participate, along with the types of areas that are funded, are shown in Table 10.5. Guidelines for how to apply for the grants are provided on each agency's Web site, along with a description of the types of projects the agencies are interested in supporting. The SBIR is a three-phase program, meaning that firms that qualify have the potential to receive more than one grant to fund a particular proposal. These three phases, along with the amount of funding available for each phase, are as follows:

■ **Phase I** is a six-month feasibility study in which the business must demonstrate the technical feasibility of the proposed innovation. Funding available for Phase I research ranges from $75,000 to $100,000, depending on the agency involved.

■ **Phase II** awards are made for up to $750,000 for as long as two years to successful Phase I companies. The purpose of a Phase II grant is to develop and test a prototype of Phase I innovations. The funding that is available for Phase II research ranges from $300,000 to $750,000, depending on the agency involved. Some agencies have **fast-track programs** where applicants can simultaneously submit Phase I and Phase II applications.

■ **Phase III** is the period during which Phase II innovations move from the research and development lab to the marketplace. No SBIR funds are involved. At this point, the business must find private funding or financing to commercialize the product or service. In some cases, such as with the U.S. Department of Defense, the government may be the primary customer for the product.

Table 10.5 SMALL BUSINESS INNOVATION RESEARCH: THREE-PHASE PROGRAM

Phase	Purpose of Phase	Duration	Funding Available (Varies by Agency)
Phase I	To demonstrate the proposed innovation's technical feasibility	Up to 6 months	Up to $100,000
Phase II	Available to successful Phase I companies. The purpose of a Phase II grant is to develop and test a prototype of the innovation validated in phase I.*	Up to 2 years	Up to $750,000
Phase III	Period in which Phase II innovations move from the research and development lab to the marketplace.	Open	No SBIR funding available, however, U.S. agencies may award non-SBIR funded follow-on grants or contracts for products or processes that meet the mission needs of those agencies, or for further R&D.

*Some agencies have a fast-track program where applicants can submit Phase I and Phase II applications simultaneously. U.S. Government agencies that participate in this program include the following: Department of Agriculture, Department of Commerce, Department of Defense, Department of Education, Department of Energy, Department of Health and Human Services, Department of Homeland Security, Department of Transportation, Environmental Protection Agency, NASA, National Institutes of Health, and National Science Foundation.

Historically, less than 15 percent of all Phase I proposals are funded, and about 30 percent of all Phase II proposals are funded. The payoff for successful proposals, however, is high. The money is essentially free. It is a grant, meaning that it doesn't have to be paid back and no equity in the firm is at stake. The recipient of the grant also retains the rights to the intellectual property developed while working with the support provided by the grant. The real payoff is in Phase III if the new venture can commercialize the research results.

The **STTR Program** is a variation of the SBIR for collaborative research projects that involve small businesses and research organizations, such as universities or U.S. laboratories. More information about the STTR program can be obtained from the SBA.

Other Grant Programs

There are a limited number of other grant programs available to entrepreneurs. Obtaining a grant takes a little detective work. Granting agencies are by nature low-key, so they normally need to be sought out. A typical scenario of a small business that received a grant is provided by Rozalia Williams, the founder of Hidden Curriculum Education, a for-profit company that offers college life skills courses. To kick-start her business, Williams received a $72,500 grant from Miami-Dade Empowerment Trust, a granting agency in Dade County, Florida. The purpose of the Miami-Dade Empowerment Trust is to encourage the creation of businesses in disadvantaged neighborhoods of Dade County. The key to Williams's success, which is true in most grant-awarding situations, is that her business fit nicely with the mission of the granting organization, and she was willing to take her business into the areas the granting agency was committed to improving. After being awarded the grant and conducting her college prep courses in four Dade County neighborhoods over a three-year period, Williams received an additional $100,000 loan from the Miami-Dade Empowerment Trust to expand her business. There are also private foundations that grant money to both existing and start-up firms. These grants are usually tied to specific objectives or a specific project, such as research and development in a specific area.

The U.S. government has grant programs beyond the SBIR and STTR programs described previously. The full spectrum of grants available is listed at www.grants.gov. U.S. state and local governments, private foundations, and philanthropic organizations also post grant announcements on their Web sites. Finding a grant that fits your business is the key. This is no small task. It is worth the effort, however, if you can obtain some or all of your start-up costs through a granting agency.

One thing to be careful of is grant-related scams. Business owners often receive unsolicited letters or e-mail messages from individuals or organizations that assure them that for a fee they can help the business gain access to hundreds of business-related grants. The reality is that there aren't hundreds of business-related grants that fit any one business. Most of these types of offers are a scam.

Strategic Partners

Strategic partners are another source of capital for new ventures.[52] Indeed, strategic partners often play a critical role in helping young firms fund their operations and round out their business models.

Biotechnology companies, for example, rely heavily on partners for financial support. Biotech firms, which are typically fairly small, often partner with larger drug companies to conduct clinical trials and bring products to market.

Most of these arrangements involve a licensing agreement. A typical agreement works like this: A biotech firm licenses a product that is under development to a pharmaceutical company in exchange for financial support during the development of the product and beyond. This type of arrangement gives the biotech firm money to operate while the drug is being developed. The downside to this approach is that the larger firm ultimately markets the drug and retains a large share of the income for itself. Sometimes strategic partnerships take on a different role in helping biotech firms take products to market and allows them to keep a larger share of the income than licensing arrangements permit.

Finally, many partnerships are formed to share the costs of product or service development, to gain access to a particular resource, or to facilitate speed to market.[53] In exchange for access to plant and equipment and established distribution channels, new ventures bring an entrepreneurial spirit and new ideas to these partnerships. These types of arrangements can help new ventures lessen the need for financing or funding.

Chapter Summary

1. For three reasons—cash flow challenges, capital investment needs, and the reality of lengthy product development cycles—most new firms need to raise money at some point during the early part of their life.

2. Personal funds, friends and family, and bootstrapping are the three sources of personal financing available to entrepreneurs.

3. Entrepreneurs are often very creative in finding ways to bootstrap to raise money or cut costs. Examples of bootstrapping include minimizing personal expenses and putting all profits back into the business, establishing partnerships and sharing expenses with partners, and sharing office space and/or employees with other businesses.

4. The three steps involved in properly preparing to raise debt or equity financing are as follows: Determine precisely how much money is needed, determine the type of financing or funding that is most appropriate, and develop a strategy for engaging potential investors or bankers.

5. An elevator speech is a brief, carefully constructed statement outlining a business opportunity's merits.

6. Equity funding involves exchanging partial ownership in a firm, which is usually in the form of stock, for funding. Debt financing is getting a loan.

7. Business angels are individuals who invest their personal capital directly in start-up ventures. These investors tend to be high-net-worth individuals who generally invest between $25,000 and $150,000 in a single company. Venture capital is money that is invested by venture capital firms in start-ups and small businesses with exceptional growth potential. Typically, venture capitalists invest at least $1 million in a single company.

8. An initial public offering (IPO) is an important milestone for a firm for four reasons: It is a way to raise equity capital, it raises a firm's public profile, it is a liquidity event, and it creates another form of currency (company stock) that can be used to grow the company.

9. The main SBA program available to small businesses is referred to as the 7(A) Loan Guaranty Program. This program operates through private-sector lenders providing loans that are guaranteed by the SBA. The loans are for small businesses that are unable to secure financing on reasonable terms through normal lending channels.

10. A lease is a written agreement in which the owner of a piece of property allows an individual or business to use the property for a specified period of time in exchange for payments. The major advantage of leasing is that it enables a company to acquire the use of assets with very little or no down payment.

Key Terms

7(A) Loan Guaranty
    Program, **355**
bootstrapping, **344**
burn rate, **341**
business angels, **349**
carry, **351**
corporate venture capital, **353**
debt financing, **346**
due diligence, **352**
elevator speech (or pitch), **346**
equity financing, **346**
fast-track programs, **359**

final prospectus, **354**
follow-on funding, **352**
initial public offering
    (IPO), **353**
investment bank, **353**
lease, **358**
line of credit, **354**
liquidity event, **346**
preliminary prospectus, **354**
private placement, **354**
road show, **354**
rounds, **352**

Sarbanes-Oxley Act, **353**
SBA Guaranteed Loan
    Program, **355**
SBIR Program, **359**
secondary market offering, **353**
single-purpose loan, **354**
STTR Program, **360**
sweat equity, **343**
venture capital, **351**
venture-leasing firm, **358**

Review Questions

1. What are the three most common reasons most entrepreneurial ventures need to raise money in their early life?
2. What is meant by the term *burn rate*? What are the consequences of experiencing a negative burn rate for a relatively long period of time?
3. What is meant by the term *sweat equity*?
4. To what extent do entrepreneurs rely on their personal funds and funds from friends and families to finance their ventures? What are the three rules of thumb that a business owner should follow when asking friends and family members for start-up funds?
5. What is bootstrapping? Provide several examples of how entrepreneurs bootstrap to raise money or cut costs. In your judgment, how important is the art of bootstrapping for an entrepreneurial venture?
6. Describe the three steps involved in properly preparing to raise debt or equity financing.
7. Briefly describe the difference between equity funding and debt financing.
8. Describe the most common sources of equity funding.
9. Describe the most common sources of debt financing.
10. What is the purpose of an elevator speech? Why is preparing an elevator speech one of the first things an entrepreneur should do in the process of raising money?
11. Why is it so important to get a personal introduction before approaching a potential investor or banker?
12. Describe the three steps required to effectively engage potential investors or bankers.
13. Identify the three most common forms of equity funding.
14. Describe the nature of business angel funding. What types of people typically become business angels, and what is the unique role that business angels play in the process of funding entrepreneurial firms?
15. Describe what is meant by the term *venture capital*. Where do venture capital firms get their money? What types of firms do venture capitalists commonly want to fund? Why?
16. Describe the purpose of an initial public offering (IPO). Why is an initial public offering considered to be an important milestone for an entrepreneurial firm?
17. What is the purpose of the investment bank in the initial public offering process?
18. In general, why are commercial banks reluctant to loan money to start-ups?

19. Briefly describe the SBA's 7(A) Loan Guaranty Program. Do most start-up firms qualify for an SBA guaranteed loan? Why or why not?

20. What is a Small Business Innovation Research (SBIR) grant? Why would a firm want to apply for such a grant if it so qualified?

Application Questions

1. Write a 60-second elevator speech for Solix Biofuels, which is the "You Be the VC 10.1" feature in this chapter.

2. Pamela Smith, a friend of yours, was recently telling you about a company that her father is starting in the solar power industry. One thing her father is particularly excited about, according to Pamela, is that he's already received offers from several angel investors, and feels that he'll be able to raise more money than he actually needs to launch his company. Pamela was surprised when you seemed a little skeptical and said, "You know, there are several potential disadvantages to raising more money than what's needed." Pamela asked you to expand on your remarks. What would you say?

3. Jim Carter, a classmate of yours, is preparing to launch an e-commerce company to sell home repair guidebooks, tools, how-to videos, and related material for home repair and remodeling projects. He just told you that he talked to his paternal grandmother over the weekend, and she has agreed to lend him $25,000 to launch the firm. When you asked Jim what arrangements he has made with his grandmother to formalize the loan, he look puzzled and said, "She plans to send me a check in a week or so—she just needs to get the money out of her savings account." Jim seemed concerned by the worried look on your face and said, "Tell me what you're thinking. I really want to do the right thing here." What would you say to Jim?

4. John Baker is in the midst of starting a computer hardware firm and thinks he has identified a real problem that his company will be able to solve. He has put together a management team and has invested $150,000 of his own money in the project. Because John feels that time is of the essence, he has decided to try to obtain venture capital funding. Is John on the right track? How should he go about obtaining venture capital funding?

5. One criticism of the venture capital industry is that the majority of the money is invested in a small number of geographic areas in the United States. In fact, historically, over 50 percent of venture capital investments have been made in just two U.S. states. Do some research on the venture capital industry, and determine which two states are the perennial leaders for venture capital funding. How much of a disadvantage do you believe that entrepreneurs who live in very small states like North Dakota and Wyoming have just because of their distance from the majority of venture capital firms?

6. Study the two "You Be the VC" features at the end of Chapter 9 and the two "You Be the VC" features at the end of this chapter. In your judgment, which of the four firms is the better candidate for venture capital funding? Which is the poorest candidate? Justify your answers.

7. A handful of business schools are experimenting with giving their students the opportunity to run venture capital funds with real money. Identify one or more of these business schools, and describe the nature of its student-run venture capital fund. Would you enjoy participating in running a student-run venture capital fund? What do you think you'd learn from the experience?

8. Cathy Mills has spent the past five years bootstrapping a very successful consumer software company. Her company now has strong cash flow and a healthy balance sheet, and she has put together an impressive management team. Cathy has decided to branch out into business software and needs $175,000 to start her new division. Given Cathy's situation, what type of funding or financing do you think she would be eligible for? Explain your answer.

9. According to information in the chapter, the three areas that receive the most funding from business angels are software, health care services/ medical devices and equipment, and biotech. Why do you think business angels are attracted to start-ups in these areas? Why wouldn't someone starting a new soup and salad restaurant, for example, be equally interesting to business angels?

10. Patricia Rob is the CEO of a medical equipment company that is on the verge of going public. She recently decided to write an e-mail message to her entire workforce to explain the reasons the company was going public. If you were Patricia, what would you include in the message? Explain your answer.

11. Imagine you invented a new type of car seat for children, which is lighter and safer than the car seats currently on the market. You have a business plan and have won two business plan contests based on your idea. You also have a working prototype. You'd like to find an angel investor to fund the launch of your firm. Describe how you'd go about finding an angel investor in the area in which you live. Make a list of the specific steps you'd take, and the specific people you'd talk to, to try to locate an appropriate angel investor.

12. In early 2006, Chipotle Mexican Grill (www.chipotle.com) launched a very successful public offering. This is despite the fact that the market for IPOs was not particularly robust at that time. Study Chipotle Mexican Grill and determine why Chipotle was a good candidate for launching a public offering. Do you think Chipotle could launch an equally successful initial public offering today?

13. Ed Sayers just returned from a meeting with his banker with a frustrated look on his face. He tosses his keys on the kitchen counter and tells his wife, "I just can't understand where my banker is coming from. I have a great idea for a new firm, but the bank isn't interested in helping me with a loan. Tomorrow, I'm going to visit a couple of other banks to see if I have better luck." Do you think Ed will have any better luck with the second and third banks he visits? Why or why not?

14. Mary Sherman, who lives near Houston, Texas, is in the process of setting up a manufacturing facility that will produce highly specialized equipment for the oil drilling industry. The high cost of equipment is an issue with which Mary is struggling. She has talked to several investors who have balked at funding the equipment. Mary has thought about leasing instead of buying but isn't quite sure if leasing is the way to go. If Mary asked you your advice, what would you tell her? What other alternatives does Mary have?

15. Alex Gondolas is in the early stages of developing a new laser optics technology that may be of interest to the U.S. Department of Defense. Alex recently attended a seminar for start-ups and was advised to apply for a Small Business Innovation Research grant to fund his project. Alex thought about applying for the grant but decided it was too much hassle and paperwork. If you were advising Alex, would you tell him to rethink his decision? Why or why not?

You Be the VC 10.1

Company: Solix Biofuels

www.solixbiofuels.com

Business Idea: Create a commercially viable biodiesel fuel using algae as the central ingredient.

Pitch: With gasoline and diesel fuel selling at or near record high prices, there is a robust need for alternative sources of fuel to power cars, trucks, and industrial equipment. Solix Biofuels, operating from the campus of Colorado State University, is addressing this issue by developing systems to convert algae into biodiesel.

Algae can be found almost everywhere—oceans, lakes, ponds, and swimming pools. While not technically a plant, algae has the same photosynthetic ability to convert sunshine into energy that plants do. For some species of algae, the chemical energy is in the form of oils very similar to vegetable oil. What's the big deal? The big deal is that these oils can be processed and used to produce biodiesel. And algae's growth and productivity is potentially 30 to 100 times higher than crops like soybeans.

Algae have other advantages. Producing algae uses less water than conventional agriculture (like corn and soybeans), and can be located on nonproductive land. In addition, since the entire algae organism converts sunlight into oil, according to Solix's estimates, algae can produce more oil in an area the size of a two-car garage than soybeans can in an area equivalent to a football field.

Solix is an R&D intensive start-up, which has sorted through strains of algae from around the world to identify the best strains for biodiesel production. To make algae-based biodiesel production viable, the next steps are to find the most economical and efficient ways to grow the algae, harvest the oil, and convert the oil into biodiesel. Algae is not picky about the area of the country in which it's grown, which is a big plus. Experts estimate that an acre of algae production could yield 8,000 to 10,000 gallons of oil per year, compared to 50 or 60 gallons per year for soybeans, 20 gallons for corn, and 150 gallons using canola or rapeseeds. One of the biggest remaining hurdles to initiating algae-based biodiesel production is growing algae in controlled settings. Although algae grow seemingly uninhibited in pools, lakes, and ponds, if it's placed under stress, which is what happens if it's grown in a controlled environment, it won't reproduce. Solix is at the forefront of solving this and similar problems that will enable it to move forward with algae-based biodiesel production.

Producing biodiesel represents both a commercial and an environmental opportunity. Algae-based biodiesel has the potential to be the perfect fuel—abundant, renewable, nonreliant on fossil fuels, and suitable to be produced in currently nonproductive areas.

Q&A: Based on the material covered in this chapter, what questions would you ask the firm's founders before making your funding decision? What answers would satisfy you?

Decision: If you had to make your decision on just the information provided in the pitch and on the company's Web site, would you fund this company? Why or why not?

You Be the VC 10.2

Company: Crushpad

www.crushpadwine.com

Business Idea: Enable wine enthusiasts to create their own wines using grapes from California's most renowned vineyards, and provide an Internet platform for wine enthusiasts to create groups to produce wine and to interact with each other in other ways.

Pitch: There are two million wine enthusiasts across the United States who regularly buy high-end wine. Regardless of how passionate these people are, they have no way of creating their own wines, short of buying a winery. Crushpad's mission is to change this by opening urban wineries that allow wine enthusiasts

(continued)

to create their own wines. The company's first winery is in San Francisco, with plans to open four to five additional wineries during the next several years. Crushpad has two distinct target markets. The first market is affluent individuals, who have the capital and interest to create their own wines. These individuals work with Crushpad, and can be involved in as little or as much of the process of making their individual wines as they desire. If they opt for a high level of involvement, they can follow a process called the Crushpad 30, which allows the customer to participate in all of the technical decisions regarding the production of their wine. They can also come into the winery and watch their wine being made. Crushpad's second target market is entrepreneurs who want to create their own branded wines to resell to the public. In this category, Crushpad has customers who are producing lots of wine as small as 50 cases a year to as large as 1,200.

In addition to helping its clients produce wine, Crushpad has set up a social networking environment, called Crushnet, to allow its customers to interact with each other and create wines as groups.

The groups can then share the cost of producing the wine and distribute the finished product among the community. They can also have a lot of fun along the way, from collectively selecting the grapes that will be used to create their wine to utilizing online tools to create their packaging.

Crushpad's launch comes at a time when interest in wine is at an all-time high in the United States and elsewhere. The sale of premium wines is now a $3 billion dollar a year industry in the United States, and is growing at a rate of 11 percent per year. Crushpad is creating a new segment in the industry by allowing individuals and entrepreneurs to create small lots of their own wines.

Q&A: Based on the material covered in this chapter, what questions would you ask the firm's founders before making your funding decision? What answers would satisfy you?

Decision: If you had to make your decision on just the information provided in the pitch and on the company's Web site, would you fund this company? Why or why not?

CASE10.1

Dogster: Pursuing a Patient and Confident Part to Funding
www.dogster.com

Bruce R. Barringer
Oklahoma State University
R. Duane Ireland
Texas A & M University

Introduction

Dogster is a social networking site for dog owners. Like its sister site, Catster, it is a warm, devoted community site that provides its members the ability to create customizable Web pages for their dogs, connect with other dog owners, leave little treats for other dogs (via the purchase of virtual currency), and participate in contests. Many people chuckled when they first saw the site, which was launched in 2004. It was a social networking site for dog owners after all! How much potential could it have?

The Beginnings of Dogster and Catster

Dogster was started by Ted Rheingold. Rheingold was making a living designing Web sites, and

wasn't making much money at it. His wife liked dogs and he noticed that she sought out Web sites, like animal rescue sites, just to look at pictures of dogs. He thought "why not create a site where anyone could post pictures of dogs?"

Rheingold's initial ambitions were not grandiose. He dubbed the site Dogster and figured he could make enough on online advertising to pay his $500 monthly rent. In early 2004, the site caught on and Rheingold increasingly saw it as a promising business. Catster was added to provide a social network for cat enthusiasts.

Financial Values and Attitudes About Funding

From the outset Rheingold ran Dogster and Catster in a lean manner. His initial developers worked on a spec basis—they would only get paid if the site made money. The sites were bootstrapped from 2004 until mid-2006. During this time Rheingold wanted to prove to the investment community, and to himself, that his business was real and had good long-term potential. Having observed the Internet boom and bust just a few years earlier, Rheingold had no appetite for venture capital funding. His philosophy was that if a company took venture capital funding it had to have big goals, and if the goals didn't work out it had to find other big goals to meet its investors' expectations. Rheingold preferred to build Dogster and Catster organically and experiment with both little and big goals. He was also getting good feedback from users, the sites were growing, and he was attracting good quality advertisers, all on his own. His advertisers included Disney, Target, PetSmart, and Gap, which liked the demographic that Dogster was attracting. By mid-2006, just two years after the site launched, it had 250,000 registered users (across both sites) and its demographic was 80 percent women between the ages of 20 and 40.

Turning Points—In Terms of Profitability and Funding

In 2005, Dogster and Catster turned a profit. It was still small (less than 10 employees), was lean and fit, had taken no money from investors or bankers, and was growing at the pace that its profits permitted. Rheingold and his team focused intently on two things—customer service and monetizing Dogster and Catster in a healthy

manner. They answered all member e-mails, frequently solicited feedback about things they were trying, and immersed themselves in building healthy online communities. One thing that Rheingold found, and frequently mentions when interviewed, is that social networks don't run themselves. He and his team frequently placed posts on the sites to keep discussions lively and moving forward and intervened if spats between users developed. Rheingold once said that Dogster and Catster were like "gardens [that needed to be] watched over every day."

In September 2006, Rheingold announced that Dogster and Catster, for the first time, were taking money from investors. It was $1 million from a group of angel investors. The following diagram illustrates the rationale for the timing of the investment. Dogster and Catster were at the end of the introduction stage of the typical organizational life cycle. The main goals of the introduction stage, for a well-managed start-up, are to get off to a good start, find out what works and what doesn't work, lay the groundwork for building a larger organization, and gain momentum in the marketplace. Dogster and Catster had met these goals and achieved profitability to boot. It was now time to grow the company at a more accelerated rate.

When people find out about Dogster and Catster and marvel at their seemingly quick success, Rheingold likes to quip that it takes three to four years to create an overnight success. What he's referring to is the 2003–2006 timeframe when he and his team worked tirelessly with little money to build Dogster and Catster's brand and lay the foundation for future growth.

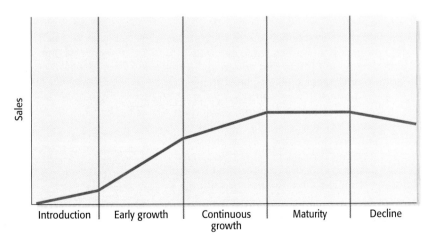

Organizational Life Cycle

(continued)

Plans for the $1 Million Investment

When Rheingold accepted the $1 million in September 2006, he was both transparent and guarded about what he planned to do with the money. In an interview with ZDNet, a tech blog and news site, Rheingold said:

> The investment allows us to test how big Dogster and Catster can become, and to invest in more pet properties, such as horses, fish, birds, reptiles—all kinds of critters. We feel confident with our foundation and rounding out our pet offerings. We can take advantage of our head start and then start with non-pet topics.

He was not forthcoming on what non-pet "passions" the company would pursue, but said that dating is not one of them.

Rheingold's statement to ZDNet was consistent with what businesses normally do when they enter the growth stage of their life cycle, which is where Dogster and Catster were at. At this point a company is normally still focused on building the market share of its initial product or service but has related products in the works. To bring related products online normally takes investment in the form of additional infrastructure and personnel. This is why financing or funding is often necessary at this point.

Dogster and Catster Today and in the Future

As this book went to press, Dogster and Catster were still growing. The company is 5 1/2 years old (4 1/2 since the launch of the Web site), has 17 employees, and has not accepted additional funding. In October 2008, it achieved one million page views (over the two sites), a milestone of which the company was clearly proud. Its sites are becoming more interactive and engaging as new technologies become available (such as streaming video), and Rheingold continues to talk about adding additional sites and leveraging Dogster and Catster's good brand in nonpet areas. As for venture capital funding, Rheingold said that when a VC round is right for his company he's all for it. But waxing philosophical, he went on to say that if you love what you do and don't think you can execute on the plan that a VC investment would require, it's best to wait until a better time.

To assess Dogster and Catster's future potential, spend some time looking at Dogster.

com. It reflects the core competencies that Rheingold and his team possess. If you want a firsthand view of what Dogster's members are up to, I (Bruce Barringer, coauthor of this book) invite you to visit my dog Aimee's Dogster page at www.dogster.com/dogs/902263. Aimee is a young Cavalier King Charles Spaniel. She has many Dogster friends (as you'll see on her Web page), belongs to several Dogster play groups, and has been left quite a few virtual bones by Dogster friends.

Discussion Questions

1. Do you think Rheingold has grown Dogster and Catster too slowly? What were the potential upsides and potential downsides of growing the company more rapidly in the early years?
2. Look at Table 10.2. When Dogster was first launched, what type of financing or funding would it have been qualified to receive?
3. Spend some time looking at Dogster's Web site. Why do you think the company has been successful? From the case and from any additional material you can find, make of list of 10 things that Rheingold has done "right" in bringing Dogster to the point where it is today.
4. What lessons can other start-ups learn from Dogster's experiences?

Application Questions

1. Describe how Rheingold avoided needing funding or financing to build Dogster until September 2006.
2. What do you think the future holds for Dogster, Catster, and Rheingold's initiatives in general? How do you think Rheingold will continue to grow his company (or companies), and do you think he will need to raise additional rounds of funding to accomplish his objectives?

Sources: Dogster homepage, www.dogster.com (accessed November 15, 2008); A. Stern, "Interview with the Top Dog, Ted Rheingold, CEO Dogster," CenterNetworks blog post, www.centernetworks.com/interview-ted-rheingold-ceo-dogster (accessed November 15, 2008, posted September 20, 2006); D. Farber, "Dogster Plans to Embrace All Critters," ZDNet blog post, http://blogs.zdnet.com/BLF/?=3609 (accessed November 15, 2008, posted September 13, 2006).

CASE 10.2

Zazzle: Will the Company Disappoint or "Dazzle" Its Investors?
www.zazzle.com

Bruce R. Barringer
Oklahoma State University
R. Duane Ireland
Texas A & M University

Introduction

Zazzle is an online service that allows its customers to upload images that can be printed on T-shirts, stamps, posters, cards, coffee mugs, and a variety of other items. In addition, customers can choose from Zazzle's library of over 500,000 images, including 3,500 pictures of 130 characters from The Walt Disney Company. Zazzle's expansive library also includes historical images from the Library of Congress in Washington, D.C., the California State Library, the Boston Public Library, and similar institutions.

Zazzle also allows the creators of digital images to place their images on its Web site. If someone buys the image, the creator of the image is paid a 10 percent royalty. The royalty jumps to 17 percent if the buyer of the image was referred to Zazzle by its creator.

This service provides a marketplace for artists, freelance photographers, and photo hobbyists to sell their work.

In spring 2005, Zazzle raised $16 million in venture capital (VC) funding from Kleiner Perkins Caufield & Byers and Sherpalo Ventures. While the venture capitalists that led the funding, John Doerr at Kleiner Perkins and Ram Shriram at Sherpalo Ventures, expressed confidence in Zazzle's future, a number of journalists and bloggers were puzzled by the investment. "What's so unique about Zazzle?" and "How can a company that sells T-shirts get $16 million in funding?" were common observations.

We tell the Zazzle story in the following paragraphs. Eventually, will the venture capitalists or the critics of their investment be proven correct? Read about Zazzle, and then you decide!

Zazzle's Start-Up Story

Zazzle was founded in 1999 by Bobby and Jeff Beaver, two Stanford University students. Their father, Robert Beaver, was a serial entrepreneur (a serial entrepreneur is a person who launches one entrepreneurial venture after another). While at Stanford, the two brothers became interested in the Internet, which was all the buzz at the time, and

decided to start an Internet company of their own when they graduated. Their goal was to identify an online opportunity that wasn't currently being pursued, was meaningful, and was something they could build a real business around. For a number of reasons, they started talking about the printed apparel industry. Printed apparel, which includes products like Mickey Mouse T-shirts and Boston Red Sox and New York Yankees' sweaters, is a $25 billion to $30 billion industry. At the time, there was no dominant Internet company servicing the industry. As a result, the Beavers decided to focus their efforts on starting a company in the Internet printed apparel industry.

The reason there wasn't an Internet company focused on the printed apparel industry, the Beavers soon learned, is that the industry was plagued by antiquated technology. The only effective way to make high-quality printed T-shirts, and other apparel products, was through a process called silk-screening. Although silk-screening produces a high-quality product, it is very labor-intensive. As a result, to justify the cost, most manufacturers must make lots of 100 or more of the same product. An alternative is to iron on designs. Although quicker, iron-on designs are not of high quality.

The vision that the Beavers fashioned was to create a company that could print T-shirts one at a time at an affordable price. The idea was to create an "on-demand" (one at a time) printing company where a customer could send the company a digital picture of a newborn baby, for example, and order just a few shirts with the baby's picture to distribute to family and friends. In addition, the Beavers wanted to guarantee 24-hour delivery, so the shirts could be distributed by the new parents right away. Another piece of the Beavers' vision was to provide aspiring artists, freelance photographers, and photo hobbyists a marketplace to sell their work. Most of these folks never got their work on a T-shirt or a sweater because they would have to make 100 or more of them at a time and store the product as inventory. Some images may sell only a few T-shirts or

(continued)

sweaters, let alone 100, making the prospects impractical.

The Beavers set out to make this happen and named their company Zazzle. Their dad, who joined the firm, had good connections in the Silicon Valley. He relied on these connections to help his sons put together a small team of people to tackle the technological challenge of printing T-shirts and other apparel products on demand at an affordable price. It took three years of bootstrapping and painstaking work to do it, but the small Zazzle team persevered. They developed a proprietary way of reengineering the silk-screening process to automate it and drive down the costs, making producing a high-quality individual T-shirt or other apparel product on demand practical.

The Zazzle Web site was launched in 2003. Orders quickly began flowing to the company, with the pace quickening as more people learned about the service. Financially, the company never ran large deficits, as did many start-ups. In fact, it teetered on profitability from the beginning. Zazzle's business model was very similar to Dell's. It had essentially no inventory costs, except for the physical disk space needed to store digital images and a supply of paper and ink. Its customers paid by credit card before an order was processed and shipped. And its suppliers, the independent artists and companies that placed images on Zazzle's site, didn't get paid until Zazzle did.

Enter the VCs

Incredibly, a year or so after Zazzle's Web site was up and running, the company was contacted by a venture capital firm. The founders remember being "shocked, humbled, and thrilled" that a venture capital firm would be interested in their business. As luck would have it, one of Zazzle's first key hires, Matt Wilsey, knew Brook Byers, a partner at Kleiner Perkins, through their kids, who went to the same school. Byers became interested in what Zazzle was doing and encouraged his partners to check it out. This initial overture caused the Beavers to do their own due diligence on the venture capital process, and they discussed funding with several firms. Kleiner Perkins and Sherpalo offered to invest $16 million, so the decision boiled down to whether Zazzle wanted to accept the VCs' terms if they were to accept the money.

The Pros and Cons of Accepting the Money

As is typically the case with a relationship between an entrepreneurial venture and a venture capitalist, there were pros and cons to accepting the money. On the pro side, partnering with two prestigious venture capital firms would lend Zazzle tremendous credibility. The founders also liked the two lead venture capitalists, John Doerr and Ram Shriram. Both were early investors in Google and had successful track records. The Zazzle team also felt comfortable with their potential investors. They shared a common vision for the future of Zazzle, and both Doerr and Shriram had reputations for being "hands-on" investors.

Zazzle could also grow much more quickly with $16 million available to build its infrastructure, hire more employees, and build the firm's brand. The major con or disadvantage to accepting the money was that Zazzle would be forced into a fast-growth mode. The founders knew that anytime a company accepts venture capital funding the pace of activity quickens, overhead gets bigger, larger returns are expected, and scrutiny is increased. They would also be giving up in exchange for the money a sizable piece of the company that they had spent four long years building.

In the end, Zazzle took the money, thinking that the opportunity to take the company to the next level, and the opportunity to partner with two prestigious venture capital firms, was just too good to pass up. Commenting on why the investment made sense, Bobby Beaver, one of Zazzle's founders said,

> Their (Kleiner Perkins and Sherpalo Ventures) support will help us expand our marketplace, as we drive to provide all individuals with an outlet where they can create and share products limited only by imagination.

In a *Seattle Times* article that was written shortly after the funding was announced, John Doerr, the venture capitalist, expressed nothing short of wild enthusiasm for Zazzle's future. "This will be a smash success" he predicted. Commenting on Zazzle's founders, Bobby and Jeff Beaver, Doerr said "They are Googlesque in their energy and their ability to think big."

The Aftermath

After Zazzle's funding was announced, several bloggers and journalists weighed in, discussing the merits of the investments. One blogger, Jason Ball, who is a London-based venture capitalist and writes a blog called TechBytes, wrote:

> A $16 million Series A round for a T-shirt site? With all due respect to KPCB (Kleiner Perkins), because they deserve it, an investment of this size in this space baffles me. From a London perspective, it looks like they're partying like it's 1999 all over again in California.

Similar comments were posted expressing surprise that Zazzle was able to raise so much money from its venture capitalists.

For its part, Zazzle's growth has accelerated as a result of the funding, and the company continues to expand its partnership and its business. The company claims that its online galleries now contain hundreds of thousands of totally unique, user-submitted photos, along with a growing library of photos from sources as diverse as Build-A-Bear Workshop and Twentieth-Century Fox's *Family Guy* television series. Zazzle was recognized by *TechCrunch* as 2007's "Best Business Model" in its first annual "Crunchies" awards. It has also been noted by industry experts, such as B. Joseph Pine, for its easy-to-use technology.

Discussion Questions

1. So what do you think? Do you think Kleiner Perkins and Sherpalo Ventures made a wise decision investing $16 million in Zazzle? Three years from now, do you think that Zazzle will have disappointed or dazzled its investors? Why?

2. Look at Table 10.2 in the chapter. At the time that Zazzle raised venture capital funding, to what extent did it resemble the ideal candidate for venture capital funding as stipulated by the materials in the table?

3. Evaluate Jason Ball's (the blogger's) criticism of Kleiner Perkins's investment in Zazzle. Do you think Ball makes some good points or do you think his arguments are off-base? Explain your answer.

4. What do you think is Zazzle's exit strategy? How will Kleiner Perkins and Sherpalo Ventures recoup their investment?

Application Questions

1. One of the criticisms of Zazzle is that its service is almost identical to a similar venture-backed company called Café Press. Look at Zazzle's and Café Press's (www.cafepress.com) Web sites. What points of differentiation, if any, do you see between Café Press and Zazzle?

2. Spend some time on Zazzle's Web site creating a T-shirt (you don't have to actually buy it). Did you find the site to be easy to navigate and Zazzle's product offering appealing? What is it that you liked about the experience and what did you not like? Did your experience influence your perception of the wisdom of Kleiner Perkins's and Sherpalo's investment in Zazzle?

Sources: R. Beaver and J. Beaver, Stanford Technology Ventures Program, Entrepreneurial Thought Leaders Podcast, December 2005; "Why Zazzle Dazzles John Doerr," *Business Week*, July 2005; M. Liedtke, "Early Investors in Google Expect Zazzle to Dazzle," *Seattle Times*, July 2005; J. Ball, TechBytes Blog, April 19, 2005.

Endnotes

1. Personal interview with Andy Tabar, December 22, 2008.
2. A. Schwienbacher, "A Theoretical Analysis of Optimal Financing Strategies for Different Types of Capital-Constrained Entrepreneurs," *Journal of Business Venturing* 22, no. 6, 2007: 753–81; J. W. Mullins and D. Forlani, "Missing the Boat or Sinking the Boat: A Study of New Venture Decision Making," *Journal of Business Venturing* 20 (2005): 47–69.
3. D. Cumming, "Adverse Selection and Capital Structure: Evidence from Venture Capital," *Entrepreneurship Theory and Practice* 30 (2006): 155–83.
4. N. Huyghebaert and L. M. Van de Gucht, "The Determinants of Financial Structure: New Insights from Business Start-Ups," *European Financial Management* 13, no. 1 (2007): 101–33; K. Soufani, D. Vrontis, and P. Poutziouris, "Private Equity for Small Firms: A Conceptual Model of Adaptation Versus Standardisation Strategy," *International Journal of Entrepreneurship and Small Business* 3 (2006): 498–515.
5. F. Alpert, "Entertainment Software: Suddenly Huge, Little Understood," *Asia Pacific Journal of Marketing and Logistics* 19, no. 1 (2007): 87–100; G. Keighley, "Could This Be the Next Disney?" *Business 2.0*, December 2002, 110–18.
6. G. Binder and P. Bashe, *Science Lessons* (Boston, MA: Harvard Business Press, 2008).
7. S. Shane, *The Illusions of Entrepreneurship* (New Haven, CT: Yale University Press, 2008).
8. J. Ballou, T. Barton, D. DesRoches, F. Potter, E. J. Reedy, A. Robb, S. Shane, and Z. Zhao, *The Kauffman Firm Survey* (Kansas City, MO: The Kauffman Foundation), March 2008.

9. P. Reynolds and S. White, *The Entrepreneurial Process: Economic Growth, Men, Women, and Minorities* (Westport, CT: Greenwood, 1997).

10. B. Barringer, *The Truths About Starting a Business* (Upper Saddle River, NJ: Financial Times Press, 2009).

11. Virgin Money homepage, www.virginmoney.com (accessed December 15, 2008).

12. C. DeBaise, "The Family Plan," *Wall Street Journal*, November 26, 2007, R3.

13. J. Cornwall, *Bootstrapping* (Upper Saddle River, NJ: Prentice Hall, 2009).

14. "Meet Michelle Madhok," Ladies Who Launch homepage, www.ladieswholaunch.com (accessed December 16, 2008).

15. A. Winton and V. Yerramilli, "Entrepreneurial Finance: Banks Versus Venture Capital," *Journal of Financial Economics* 88, no. 1 (2008): 51–79; A. Lockett, D. Ucbasaran, and J. Butler, "Opening Up the Investor–Investee Dyad: Syndicates, Teams, and Networks," *Entrepreneurship Theory and Practice* 30 (2006): 117–30.

16. M. G. Jacobides and S. G. Winter, "Entrepreneurship and Firm Boundaries: The Theory of a Firm," *Journal of Management Studies* 44, no. 7 (2007): 1213–41; J. Florin, "Is Venture Capital Worth It? Effects on Firm Performance and Founder Returns," *Journal of Business Venturing* 20 (2005): 113–35.

17. B. Barringer, *Preparing Effective Business Plans* (Upper Saddle River, NJ: Prentice Hall, 2008).

18. R. Stross, *eBoys* (New York: Crown Business, 2000), 25.

19. D. Politis, "Business Angels and Value Added: What Do We Know and Where Do We Go?" *Venture Capital* 10, no. 2 (2008): 127–47; Angel Capital Education Foundation, www.angelcapitaleducation.org/dir_resources/for_entrepreneurs.aspx (accessed December 16, 2008).

20. J. Melloan, "Angels with Angels," *Inc.*, July 2005.

21. Melloan, "Angels with Angels."

22. G. Thoma, "Striving for a Large Market: Evidence from a General Purpose Technology in Action," *Industrial and Corporate Change* 18 (2009): 107–38; "ASAP," *Forbes*, June 1, 1998, 24.

23. J. Battelle, *The Search* (New York: Portfolio, 2005).

24. Center for Venture Research, *The Angel Investor Market in 2007: Mixed Signs of Growth* (Durham: University of New Hampshire, 2007).

25. Center for Venture Research, *The Angel Investor Market in 2007*.

26. Dow Jones VentureSource homepage, www.venturesource.com (accessed December 16, 2008).

27. Center for Venture Research, *The Angel Investor Market in 2007*.

28. PricewaterhouseCoopers, "The Second Key: Writing the Business Plan," www.pwcglobal.com (accessed July 30, 2006).

29. O. Strauss, "Touched by an Angel," *Entrepreneur's Byline*, www.entreworld.org (accessed March 20, 2003).

30. D. Cumming, D. Schmidt, and U. Walz, "Legality and Venture Capital Governance Around the World," *Journal of Business Venturing* (2008), Investorwords, www.investorwords.com, doi:10.1016/j.jbusvent.2008.07.001 (accessed Aug. 27, 2008).

31. Dow Jones VentureSource homepage, www.venturesource.com (accessed December 16, 2008).

32. PricewaterhouseCoopers, *Three Keys to Obtaining Venture Capital* (New York: PricewaterhouseCoopers, 2001).

33. PricewaterhouseCoopers, *Three Keys to Obtaining Venture Capital*.

34. Kleiner Perkins Caufield & Byers, www.kpcb.com/initiatives/ifund (accessed December 16, 2008).

35. D. Laurie, *Venture Catalyst* (Cambridge, MA: Perseus, 2001).

36. J. M. Nelson, "Intangible Assets, Book-to-Market, and Common Stock Returns," *Journal of Financial Research* 29 (2006): 21–41.

37. C. M. Daily, S. T. Certo, and D. R. Dalton, "Investment Bankers and IPO Pricing: Does Prospectus Information Matter?" *Journal of Business Venturing* 20 (2005): 93–111.

38. M. A. Hitt, R. D. Ireland, and R. E. Hoskisson, *Strategic Management: Competitiveness and Globalization*, 8th ed. (Mason, OH: South-Western College Publishing, 2009).

39. B. M. Barber, R. Lehavy, and B. Trueman, "Comparing the Stock Recommendation Performance of Investment Banks and Independent Research Firms," *Journal of Financial Economics* 85, no. 2 (2007): 490–517; Investorwords, www.investorwords.com (accessed December 24, 2008).

40. F. Lipman, *The Complete Going Public Handbook* (Roseville, CA: Prima Publishing, 2000).
41. T. R. Vanacker and S. Manigart, "Pecking Order and Debt Capacity Considerations for High-Growth Companies Seeking Financing," *Small Business Economics* (2008): forthcoming.
42. G. Haines and L. Riding, "Loan Guarantee Programs for Small Firms: Recent Canadian Experience on Risk, Economic Impacts, and Incrementality," *Frontiers of Entrepreneurship Research* 16 (1995): 422–36.
43. V. Bruns, D. V. Holland, D. A. Shepherd, and J. Wiklund, "The Role of Human Capital in Loan Officers' Decision Policies," *Entrepreneurship Theory and Practice*, 32 (2008): 485–506.
44. SBA homepage, www.sba.gov (accessed July 20, 2006).
45. G. Bounds, "Fed Fund," *Wall Street Journal*, November 29, 2004.
46. Prosper homepage, www.prosper.com (accessed December 17, 2008).
47. Count Me In homepage, www.countmein.org (accessed December 17, 2008).
48. ACCION homepage, www.accion.org (accessed December 17, 2008).
49. J. Nesheim, *High Tech Start Up: The Complete Handbook for Creating Successful New High Tech Companies* (New York: Free Press, 2000).
50. A. Sherman, *Raising Capital* (Washington, DC: Kiplinger Books, 2000).
51. SBA homepage, www.sba.gov (accessed July 20, 2006).
52. S. A. Alvarez, R. D. Ireland, and J. J. Reuer, "Entrepreneurship and Strategic Alliances," *Journal of Business Venturing* 21 (2006): 401–404.
53. B. Barringer and J. Harrison, "Walking a Tightrope: Creating Value Through Interorganizational Relationships," *Journal of Management* 26 (2000): 367–403.

PART 4

Managing and Growing an Entrepreneurial Firm

Getting Personal

with Misa Chien

**MY BIGGEST WORRY
AS AN ENTREPRENEUR**
Maintaining a healthy
balance in my life

**MY ADVICE FOR NEW
ENTREPRENEURS**
Failure is just as valuable
as success, you learn from
your mistakes

**BEST PART OF BEING
A STUDENT**
Being surrounded by and
meeting so many other
inspiring, talented, and
amazing people

**WHAT I'D LIKE TO BE
DOING IN 10 YEARS**
Running a successful
company that I am
passionate about

**MY BIGGEST SURPRISE
AS AN ENTREPRENEUR**
The amazing support
and encouragement I have
received from friends, family,
and other entrepreneurs

BEST ADVICE I'VE RECEIVED
Follow your passion, and the
income will come

MISA CHIEN
Founder, Miss Misa
BA, Global Studies and French,
UCLA, 2008

CHAPTERELEVEN
Unique *Marketing* Issues

OPENING PROFILE
MISS MISA
Creating a New Brand in the Jewelry Industry
www.missmisa.com

If you were shopping for jewelry and found Miss Misa, an online seller of one-of-a-kind jewelry products, you'd never guess the company was started in a small dorm room in Los Angeles, California. Miss Misa, which is the name of the company, is the creation of Misa Chien, a 2008 graduate of UCLA with a degree in global studies and French. Chien uses vintage and retro charms, chains, and semiprecious stones to create one-of-a-kind jewelry products. The products are sold through her Web site, www.missmisa.com, and through other online venues.

Miss Misa was launched in 2003 when Chien was just a freshman. During her four years at UCLA, she licensed the business, set up a Web site, designed jewelry, found a manufacturer in China, and got the business up and running. She also participated in several study abroad programs, which helped shape Miss Misa in several ways. During a study abroad program in Shanghai, China, she studied jewelry manufacturing and made contacts that assisted her in finding the Chinese manufacturer that now makes her products. During a similar program in France, she studied French culture. Chien has a special affection for France and much of her jewelry is fashioned after French art and architecture.[1]

Chien has always had a knack for designing and making jewelry. At 18 she opened an eBay account, where she not only sold jewelry but learned the jewelry business by following auctions and watching what sold and what didn't sell on eBay. Since that time, she has used eBay as her testing ground for what's likely to sell and what isn't likely to sell on her own Web site. If she designs a piece of jewelry and it sells well on eBay, she knows it will sell well on her own Web site if she places a large order with her manufacturer.

At the outset, Chien tried to draw attention to her Web site through traditional advertising techniques, like print advertising, which were expensive and produced only mixed results. Recently, partly as a result of reading *The Tipping Point* by Malcolm Gladwell, Chien has transitioned to advertising primarily via Facebook. *The Tipping Point* talks about how momentum for change begins, and can be applied to how businesses create buzz and interest in their products. One thing Chien is doing with Facebook is asking select people to list her Web site as one of their "favorite" Web sites on the front page of their Facebook pages. In some instances she's compensating people for doing this by providing them free jewelry samples. One of the people she's asked has over 1,500 friends on her Facebook page—people who will see Miss Misa prominently displayed as a "favorite" Web site on the page.

In terms of the traditional elements of the marketing mix, Miss Misa's products are aimed at 15- to 40-year-old women. Over time, Chien has reduced, rather than increased, the number of products she sells to make her Web site easier to navigate. Her products are affordable and are described as having whimsical designs. According to Chien, her jewelry is not made from expensive components. Her value added is

Learning Objectives

After studying this chapter you should be ready to:

1. Explain the purpose of market segmentation.

2. Describe the importance of selecting a target market.

3. Explain why it is important for a start-up to establish a unique position in its target market.

4. Describe the importance of the ability to position a company's products on benefits rather than features.

5. Illustrate the two major ways in which a company builds a brand.

6. Identify the four components of the marketing mix.

7. Explain the difference between a core product and an actual product.

8. Contrast cost-based pricing and value-based pricing.

9. Explain the differences between advertising and public relations.

10. Weigh the advantages and disadvantages of selling direct versus selling through intermediaries.

her innovative designs. In terms of distribution, the majority of Miss Misa's products are sold through its Web site and on Shopflick.com. Shopflick.com is an online retailer that sells a variety of fashion items. One thing the site does is film short videos of the vendors who sell products through its site. The videos feature the vendors describing their products and talking about the reasons they're passionate about what they sell. Chien credits Shopflick for helping her better understand how to position and talk about her product. In terms of price, Chien takes the price she pays to produce a piece of jewelry and marks it up six to seven times. While that sounds like a large markup, she benefits by using inexpensive components and utilizing a Chinese manufacturer to make the jewelry. As a result, she's able to price her products competitively, even with the markup. In terms of promotion, along with the Facebook campaign, Chien has a press kit, which was prepared by freelancers she found on www.elance.com, and has distributed the kit to magazines that cover the jewelry industry. She's hopeful that this initiative will draw positive attention to her business. The most pressing marketing issue that Chien is currently facing is whether to find a distributor and start selling Miss Misa jewelry through fashion boutiques and retail stores.[2]

In this chapter, we'll look at the marketing challenges confronting entrepreneurial firms. Marketing involves a range of issues, from promotions to selecting a target market to managing distribution channels. Marketing is a broad subject, and there are many books dedicated to marketing and its subfields. However, in this chapter, we zero in on the marketing challenges that are most pressing for young entrepreneurial firms. The reason for doing this is that marketing is an essential component to the success of a start-up firm.[3]

We begin this chapter by discussing how firms define and select their target markets. Next, we discuss two issues that are particularly important for new firms—selling benefits rather than features and establishing a brand. The chapter concludes by discussing the four key facets of marketing as they relate to young entrepreneurial firms. These four facets, commonly referred to as the "4Ps" of marketing, are product, price, promotion, and place (or distribution).

SELECTING A MARKET AND ESTABLISHING A POSITION

In order to succeed, a new firm must address this important question: Who are our customers, and how will we appeal to them?[4] A well-managed start-up uses a three-step approach to answer these questions: segmenting the market, selecting or developing a niche within a target market, and establishing a unique position in the target market. These steps are shown in Figure 11.1. In each step, the entrepreneurial venture must answer an important question that will help it pinpoint its market and determine how to attract customers in that market. Gary Heavin, the founder of Curves, a fitness center exclusively for women described in Case 5.2, addressed these issues when he crafted the initial strategy for his company.

FIGURE 11.1

The Process of Selecting a Target Market and Positioning Strategy

When asked about the importance of having a clearly defined target market in the fitness industry, he said:

> There are so many fitness companies that it is dog-eat-dog in the general fitness industry. The only hope for the average small fitness provider is that they focus on something and do that better than anything else.[5]

As noted in Chapter 3, a firm's **target market** is the limited group of individuals or businesses that it goes after or to which it tries to appeal. It is important that a firm first choose its target market and position itself within its target market because virtually all its marketing decisions hinge on these critical initial choices. If other marketing decisions are made first, such as choosing an advertising campaign, there is a danger the firm will not send a clear message to its target customers.

Segmenting the Market

The first step in selecting a target market is to study the industry in which the firm intends to compete and determine the different potential target markets in that industry. This process is called **market segmentation**, as explained in Chapter 4. Market segmentation is important because a new firm typically has only enough resources to target one market segment, at least initially.[6] Markets can be segmented in a number of different ways, including product type, price point, and customers served.[7] For example, the computer industry can be segmented by product type (i.e., handheld computers, laptops, PCs, minicomputers, and mainframes) or customers served (i.e., individuals, businesses, schools, and government).[8] A firm typically selects the segment that represents the best prospects for entry, as discussed in Chapter 3, and that is the most compatible with its core competencies. There are several important objectives an entrepreneurial venture should try to accomplish as part of its market segmentation process:[9]

Learning Objective

1. Explain the purpose of market segmentation.

■ The process should identify one or more relatively homogeneous groups of target customers within the industry the firm plans to enter in regard to their wants and needs.

■ Differences within the segment the firm chooses should be small compared to differences across segments.

■ The segment should be distinct enough so that its members can be easily identified. Once identified, advertising and promotional campaigns can be established to appeal specifically to the target market.

■ It should be possible to determine the size of the segment so that a firm knows how large its potential market is before it aggressively moves forward. A firm's growth can quickly plateau if its market segment is too small—even if the people in its segment are very satisfied with its product or service.

As mentioned previously, markets can be segmented in a number of ways, including by product type, price point, distribution channels used, and customers served. Sometimes a firm will segment its market on more than one dimension to drill down to a specific market niche that it thinks it is uniquely capable of serving. Curves segments its market first on customers serviced and second on price (it is less expensive to join than most fitness centers). Following the lead of Curves, there are now firms serving other previously underserved segments of the fitness market. An example is My Gym Children's Fitness Center, a franchise organization designed to help children 6 weeks to 13 years old develop physically, cognitively, and emotionally.[10]

Despite the importance of market segmentation, it is a process entrepreneurs commonly overlook. Overlooking this important activity can result in a faulty assessment of the size of the potential market for a new product or service. For example, U.S. businesses spend approximately $680 billion on information and communications technology per year.[11] If a start-up planned to introduce a new information or communications technology product to the market, it would be incorrect to say that the total market potential for the product is $680 billion. Obviously, the market opportunity needs to be better defined. The start-up needs to identify the different segments in the $680 billion U.S. market for information and communications technology so it can target the segment it feels it is uniquely capable of serving.[12]

Selecting a Target Market

Learning Objective

2. *Describe the importance of selecting a target market.*

Once a firm has segmented the market, the next step is to select a target market. As discussed in previous chapters, the market must be sufficiently attractive, and the firm must be able to serve it well. Typically, a firm (especially a start-up venture) doesn't target an entire segment of a market because many market segments are too large to target successfully. Instead, most firms target a niche market within the segment. For example, within the broad cell phone market there are several small niche markets that are targeted by different companies. A **niche market** is a place within a market segment that represents a narrow group of customers with similar interests. As mentioned in Chapter 2, two recent start-ups in the cell phone industry target specific niche markets. GreatCall produces a cell phone called the Jitterbug, which is designed specifically for older users. Another company, Firefly Mobile, is selling a cell phone designed specifically for tweens, ages 8 to 12. By focusing on a clearly defined market, a firm can become an expert in that market and then be able to provide its customers with high levels of value and service. This advantage is one of the reasons why Philip Kotler, a world-renowned marketing expert, says that "there are riches in niches."[13]

Sometimes firms make the mistake of selecting a market and then rushing forward without fully understanding that market or its customers, as discussed in Chapter 3. Other times, firms try to appeal to multiple markets simultaneously and spread themselves too thin, not becoming an expert in any specific market. Firms that determine and then focus on a single niche have a better chance of becoming experts in that market and reaping the accompanying rewards.

The biggest challenge a new firm faces when selecting a target market is choosing a market that is attractive enough to be interesting but is different enough that the firm isn't just another face in the crowd. A firm's choice of target markets must also be in sync with its business model and the backgrounds and skills of its founders and other personnel. A firm must also continually monitor the attractiveness of its target market. Societal preferences change, a fact that sometimes causes a target market to lose its attractiveness for a firm and the product or service it has to offer customers.

Establishing a Unique Position

After selecting a target market, the firm's next step is to establish a "position" within it that differentiates it from its competitors. As we discussed in Chapter 5, position is concerned with how the firm is situated relative to competitors. In a sense, a position is the part of a market or of a segment of the market the firm is claiming as its own. A firm's market position can be understood by studying the features of its goods or services. For example, BMW's position (luxury) in the automobile market differs from Chevrolet's position (functional). Clearly, these products differ from each other in substantial ways. Even within the luxury automobile market, BMW's position (more sports-driving oriented) differs from that of Lexus (more luxury-features oriented). Today, automobile manufacturers are seeking different positions in the fuel-efficient markets. Current examples of these positions include hybrids (e.g., Toyota's Prius) and electric plug-ins (e.g., Chevrolet's Volt). The term *differentiation* was introduced in Chapter 6, where we emphasized that a firm's position in the marketplace determines how it is situated relative to its competitors. From a marketing perspective, this translates into the image of the way a firm wants to be perceived by its customers and answers the question, "Why should someone in our target market buy our product or service instead of our competitors'?"[14] Of course, once a firm positions itself in a certain way, it must be able to follow through with a product or service offering that lives up to the image it has created. However, no amount of positioning will help when customers have tried the firm's product or service and are dissatisfied with their experience.

Once a company has identified its position and primary points of differentiation, a helpful technique is to develop a **product attribute map**, which illustrates a firm's positioning strategy relative to its major rivals. A product attribute map for Curves International, the fitness center for women, is shown in Figure 11.2. The map is based on the two primary attributes that people look for in a fitness center—range of amenities provided and the extent to which the center is tailored to meet their specific needs. The point is to assess Curves' strengths and/or weaknesses in each of these categories and plot it on the map. The same is done for Curves' major competitors. The results are shown in Figure 11.2. While Curves does not rank high in terms of amenities provided (it features a single 30-minute workout), it outranks its competitors by a wide

Learning Objective

3. Explain why it's important for a start-up to establish a unique position in its target market.

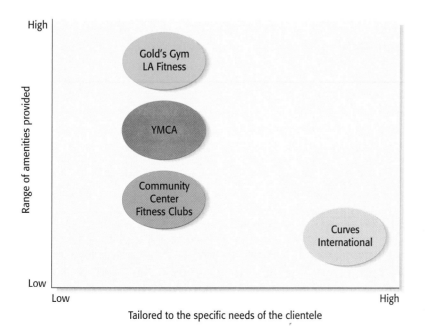

FIGURE 11.2

Product Attribute Map for Curves International

Table 11.1 MATCH THE COMPANY TO ITS TAGLINE

Company	Tagline
Minted	Turn your words into action
FLAVORx	We know what makes you sweat
CarePages	We make medicine a lot less yucky
RealKidz	Reinventing the résumé
Yelp	Marketing with a taste
Sure Girl	Real people. Real reviews.
VisualCV	Welcome to a community of hope
Jott	Lifestyles for everybody
First Flavor	The freshest designs on paper

margin in terms of being tailored to its target market's specific needs. Since Curves was founded in 1992, a realization of its position relative to its rivals has been reflected in all of its advertising and promotions. It emphasizes that it's "just for women" to leverage its strength and deemphasizes the importance of amenities (most of its competitors' strength) by reinforcing the notion that its speedy workouts (a member can walk in, work out, and walk out, all in just over half an hour) fits into the busy lifestyles of its members. It also counters the importance of amenities by advertising its low price. Any firm can develop a similar product attribute map to illustrate its position in an industry and help direct its marketing plan.

Firms often develop a **tagline**—a phrase that is used consistently in a company's literature, advertisements, promotions, stationery, and even invoices and thus becomes associated with that company—to reinforce the position they have staked out in their market. An example is Nike's familiar "Just do it." The Nike tagline, which was introduced in 1988, implies that people don't need to be told they should exercise—they already know that. The challenge is to "Just do it." The beauty of this simple three-word expression is that it applies equally to a 21-year-old triathlete and a 65-year-old mall walker. This clever tagline, along with Nike's positioning strategy, helped the firm expand its product line beyond running shoes to athletic products for all age groups.[15]

Table 11.1 is a short matching quiz that asks you to match companies featured in this book with their taglines. A company has created a successful tagline if the message makes you think of its products or services and the position it has established in its market.

KEY MARKETING ISSUES FOR NEW VENTURES

There are indeed many marketing issues with which entrepreneurial ventures must grapple. However, the selling of benefits rather than features and establishing a brand are very critical to a new venture's early success. A lack of attention to either of these issues can cripple a firm's marketing efforts by sending confusing messages to the firm's intended customers.

Selling Benefits Rather Than Features

Many entrepreneurs make the mistake of positioning their company's products or services on features rather than benefits. A positioning or marketing strategy that focuses on the features of a product, such as its technical merits, is usually much less effective than a campaign focusing on the merits of what the product can do.[16] Consider a cell phone manufacturer that claims, "Our cell phones are equipped with sufficient memory to store 1,000 phone numbers." The ability to store 1,000 phone numbers is a feature rather than a benefit. While features are nice, they typically don't entice someone to buy a product. A better way for the manufacturer to market the same cell phone would be to say, "Our cell phone lets you store up to 1,000 phone numbers, giving you the phone numbers of your family, your friends, and people you only phone once a year right at your fingertips." This statement focuses on benefits. It tells prospects how buying the product will enhance their lives.

One of the most successful advertising campaigns ever launched by McDonald's contained ads that featured the jingle, "You deserve a break today—at McDonald's." McDonald's could have stressed the cleanliness of its stores or the speed of its service, both of which are features. Instead, it struck a chord with people by focusing on one of the biggest benefits of eating at McDonald's—not having to cook. Although not as obvious in today's society, not having to cook a meal at home was a major advantage when McDonald's started using this tagline.

The same rationale can be applied to any product or service. Consider the ZUCA rolling backpack. In her initial attempts to get the ZUCA noticed, Laura Udall could have talked about the ZUCA's durable aluminum frame, its over-sized silent wheels, the washable nature of the bag, and the number of colors that were available. All of these are features of the ZUCA rolling backpack. It's much more likely that she focused on the benefits of the product—the fact that it relieves back pain and is durable enough that a child can sit on it while waiting for the school bus. (The ZUCA includes a foldout seat.) These are the benefits or the value that the ZUCA delivers to its users—and will most likely resonate with parents, the ultimate purchasers of backpacks for their children.

Learning Objective

4. Describe the importance of the ability to position a company's products on benefits rather than features.

Getty Images - Stockbyte, Royalty Free

When marketing a product, it's important to focus on benefits rather than features. While the cell phone the woman in this picture is talking on may have many attractive features, the reason she bought it is to keep in touch with family, friends, and business associates, which are benefits. This is why Nokia's tagline is "Connecting People."

Establishing a Brand

Learning Objective

5. Illustrate the two major ways in which a company builds a brand.

A **brand** is the set of attributes—positive or negative—that people associate with a company. These attributes can be positive, such as trustworthy, innovative, dependable, or easy to deal with. Or they can be negative, such as cheap, unreliable, arrogant, or difficult to deal with. The customer loyalty a company creates through its brand is one of its most valuable assets. Lending support to this sentiment, Russell Hanlin, the CEO of Sunkist Growers, said, "An orange is an orange . . . is an orange. Unless . . . that orange happens to be a Sunkist, a name 80 percent of consumers know and trust."[17] By putting its name on an orange, Sunkist is making a promise to its customers that the orange will be wholesome and fresh. It is important that Sunkist not break this promise. Some companies monitor the integrity of their brands through **brand management**, which is a program used to protect the image and value of an organization's brand in consumers' minds. This means that if Sunkist discovered that some of its oranges weren't fresh, it would take immediate steps to correct the problem.

Table 11.2 lists the different ways people think about the meaning of a brand. All the sentiments expressed in the table are similar, but they illustrate the multifaceted nature of a company's brand.

Start-ups must build a brand from scratch, which starts with selecting the company's name, as described in Chapter 7's Appendix. One of the keys to effective branding is to create a strong personality for a firm, designed to appeal to the chosen target market.[18] Southwest Airlines, for example, has created a brand that denotes fun. This is a good fit for its target market: people traveling for pleasure rather than business. Similarly, Starbucks and Barnes & Noble have each created a brand that denotes an experience framed around warmth and hospitality, encouraging people to linger and buy additional products. A company ultimately wants its customers to strongly identify with it—to see themselves as "Southwest Airlines flyers" or "Starbucks coffee drinkers." People won't do this, however, unless they see a company as being different from competitors in ways that create value for them.

So how does a new firm develop a brand? On a philosophical level, a firm must have meaning in its customers' lives. It must create value—something for which customers are willing to pay. Imagine a father shopping for airline tickets so that he can take his three children to see their grandparents for Christmas. If Southwest Airlines can get his family to their destination for $75 per ticket cheaper than its competitors, Southwest has real meaning in the father's life. Similarly, if a teenage boy buys *Madden NFL*, and playing the game with

Table 11.2   WHAT'S A BRAND? DIFFERENT WAYS OF THINKING
ABOUT THE MEANING OF A BRAND

- A brand is a promise.
- A brand is a guarantee.
- A brand is a pledge.
- A brand is a reputation.
- A brand is an unwritten warrantee.
- A brand is an expectation of performance.
- A brand is a presentation of credentials.
- A brand is a mark of trust and reduced risk.
- A brand is a collection of memories.
- A brand is a handshake between a company and its customers.

Source: Adapted from *Emotional Branding* by Daryl Travis, copyright © 2000 by Daryl Travis. Used by permission of Pima Publishing, a division of Random House, Inc.

classmates results in lasting friendships, then *Madden NFL* will have a special place in his heart. Firms that create meaning in their customers' lives stand for something in terms of benefits, whether it is low prices, fun, fashion, quality, friendliness, dependability, or something else. This meaning creates a bond between a company and its customers.

On a more practical level, brands are built through a number of techniques, including advertising, public relations, sponsorships, support of social causes, and good performance. A firm's name, logo, Web site design, and even its letterhead are part of its brand. It's important for start-ups, particularly if they plan to sell to other businesses, to have a polished image immediately so that they have credibility when they approach their potential customers. Affirming all of these points, Dan Byrne, the CEO of Byrne Specialty Gases, a company that provides specialized gases to laboratories, sums up what his company has done to build a strong brand during its 20 years of existence:

> It is all based on trust, reliability, responsiveness, quality, etc. It is all these infinitesimal details that drive a company's brand. We have the attitude that everything matters. We lost a large customer once that went to a discount provider. Three months later the customer called us back almost hat in hand. Our level of service reinforces our brand and keeps customers coming back to us.[19]

Most experts warn against placing an overreliance on advertising to build a firm's brand. A more affordable approach is to rely on word of mouth, the media, and ingenuity to create positive buzz about a company. Creating **buzz** means creating awareness and a sense of anticipation about a company and its offerings.[20] This process can start during feasibility analysis, when a company shows its concept statement or product prototype to prospective buyers or industry experts. Unless a company wants what it is doing to be kept secret (to preserve its proprietary technology or its first-mover advantage), it hopes that people start talking about it and its exciting new product or service. This is certainly the case for movie production studios as they hope that people talking about a movie they enjoyed watching will encourage others to visit their local theaters.[21] In addition, newspapers, magazines, and trade journals are always looking for stories about interesting companies. In fact, receiving a favorable review of its products or services in a magazine or a trade journal lends a sense of legitimacy to a firm that would be hard to duplicate through advertisements.

Focusing too much on the features and benefits of their products is a common mistake entrepreneurs make when trying to gain attention from the media. Journalists are typically skeptical when entrepreneurs start talking about how great their products are relative to those of their competitors. What journalists usually prefer is a human interest story about why a firm was started or a story focused on something that's distinctly unique about the start-up. For example, 1-800-GOT-JUNK?, the focus of Case 13.1, removes junk from people's homes and businesses. To generate positive buzz, Brian Scudamore, the company's founder, wanted to get on *The Oprah Winfrey Show*, so he sent a letter to the show's producers asking to be featured on any segment having to do with home renovation, a popular topic among the show's viewers. Scudamore hoped to show how 1-800-GOT-JUNK? can help people remove debris during a home renovation project. After getting no response, he pitched the show several more times but to no avail. Finally, he got a call from an *Oprah* producer who told Scudamore to be in Los Angeles in three days for a guest appearance on a show about a woman who was hoarding junk in her house. The point of this illustration is that *Oprah*'s producers weren't interested in featuring 1-800-GOT-JUNK? just to help Scudamore get free publicity. What finally sparked their interest was how 1-800-GOT-JUNK? could help a desperate person reclaim her home (and life) from junk. Since the *Oprah* appearance, Scudamore has landed similar spots on *Dr. Phil* and *The View* with Barbara Walters.[22]

It is important that a firm establishes a strong brand image. This photo features Zappos's founder and CEO Tony Hsieh. Hsieh wants Zappos's brand to stand for competitive pricing, strong customer service, and a pleasant shopping experience.

Brad Swonetz/Redux Pictures

Ultimately, a strong brand can be a very powerful asset for a firm. Over 50 percent of consumers say that a known and trusted brand is a reason to buy a product.[23] As a result, a brand allows a company to charge a price for its products that is consistent with its image. A successful brand can also increase the market value of a company by 50 to 75 percent.[24] This increased valuation can be very important to a firm if it is acquired, merges with another firm, or launches an initial public offering. **Brand equity** is the term that denotes the set of assets and liabilities that are linked to a brand and enable it to raise a firm's valuation.[25] It is important for firms to understand brand equity and how to use it to create value. As explained in this chapter's "What Went Wrong" feature, companies sometimes fail to effectively execute when it comes to this activity.

Although the assets and liabilities that make up a firm's brand equity will vary from context to context, they usually are grouped into the following five categories:

■ Brand loyalty
■ Name recognition
■ Perceived quality (of a firm's products and services)
■ Brand associations in addition to quality (e.g., good service)
■ Other proprietary assets, such as patents, trademarks, and high-quality partnerships

THE 4Ps OF MARKETING FOR NEW VENTURES

Learning Objective

6. Identify the four components of the marketing mix.

Once a company decides on its target market, establishes a position within that market, and establishes a brand, it is ready to begin planning the details of its marketing mix. A firm's **marketing mix** is the set of controllable, tactical marketing tools that it uses to produce the response it wants in the target market.[26] Most marketers organize their marketing mix into four categories: product, price, promotion, and place (or distribution). For an obvious reason, these categories are commonly referred to as the 4Ps.

What Went WRONG?

Quaker Oats' Botched Acquisition of Snapple: The Price of Failing to Understand the Real Meaning of a Company's Brand

www.snapple.com

Many entrepreneurial firms are acquired at some point during their corporate lives, or the founders leave or retire and turn over the day-to-day management of the company to a new management team. On these occasions, it is important that the new owners or the new managers of the company fully understand the meaning of the company's brand. If they don't, they can make decisions that inadvertently diminish the value of the brand. There is no better story to illustrate this point than Quaker Oats' failed acquisition of Snapple.

Snapple was created in 1972 by Leonard Marsh, Hyman Golden, and Arnold Greenberg, three beverage entrepreneurs. From the outset, Snapple was positioned as a quirky, fashionable alternative to standard soft-drink brands. Its flavors, which over time grew to include teas, diet drinks, juice drinks, and lemonades, included stylish and eccentric names, such as Lime Green Tea, Diet Cranberry Raspberry, and Super Sour Lemonade. The company's slogan—"Made from the best stuff on earth"—referred to its all-natural ingredients. In the early 1990s, the company hired Rush Limbaugh and Howard Stern as celebrity endorsers. In 1993, Wendy Kauffman, one of Snapple's employees, was recruited to be the commercial spokesperson for the brand. Kauffman had taken it upon herself to answer letters that were coming into the company with questions about the product. The quirky ads centered on Kauffman reading letters out loud and delivering comical responses. The commercials were so popular that Kauffman became affectionately known as the "Snapple Lady."

In 1994, food giant Quaker Oats bought Snapple for $1.7 billion. In 1997, just three short years later, the company sold Snapple to a private investment group for $300 million, losing an astounding $1.4 billion in the process. What went wrong? As many observers have written, plenty—starting with branding.

The consensus view among those who observed Quaker Oats' handling of Snapple is that the company simply didn't understand the Snapple brand. From the outset, Quaker saw Snapple as an all-around sports drink, similar to Gatorade, rather than the eclectic drink it was. This perception led to two strategic marketing blunders.

Blunder 1: Distribution. Prior to the Quaker Oats' acquisition, Snapple was sold primarily through small shops and gas stations. This distribution approach made Snapple a drink that had to be sought out or was available as a "treat" for travelers. Once Quaker Oats got hold of Snapple, it mainlined Snapple into its mass merchandise channels and suddenly it was available everywhere. This switch took the uniqueness away from Snapple. It was now just another beverage among dozens of others on grocery store shelves.

Blunder 2: Promotion. Quaker Oats did away with Snapple's celebrity endorsers and silenced Wendy Kaufman, the Snapple Lady. In their place, Quaker launched an advertising campaign boasting that Snapple would be happy to be third behind Coca-Cola and Pepsi in the beverage market. The ads fell flat.

The combined impact of these blunders was a rapid erosion of Snapple's once strong brand. Prior to the acquisition, Snapple's brand stood for fun, quirkiness, uniqueness, and good nutrition. Snapple was a treat to be savored and enjoyed. Quaker Oats did nothing to support those elements of Snapple's appeal. Instead, it in effect "rebranded" Snapple into a mainline brand. The result was a continuous slide in sales, until Quaker eventually gave up and sold Snapple to Triarc in 1997. Triarc returned Snapple to its roots by reintroducing Wendy Kauffman (the Snapple Lady) in its promotions and reinvigorating the positive attributes of Snapple's original positioning strategy and brand. Gradually, Snapple's original customers returned and the brand increased in value. In 2000, Cadbury Schweppes bought Snapple for $1 billion, and Snapple is now almost fully restored after its rocky ride.

Questions for Critical Thinking

1. Why do you think Snapple was successful prior to its acquisition by Quaker Oats?
2. Why do you think Quaker Oats didn't work harder to more fully understand the nature of Snapple's brand before it made the changes described here?
3. How would you describe Snapple's positioning strategy before the Quaker Oats' acquisition? How would you describe the way that Quaker Oats tried to position Snapple?
4. Provide an example of what you think is a very cleverly branded product. What has the company that makes the product done to make its branding distinctive and effective?

Sources: Snapple homepage, www.snapple.com (accessed December 1, 2008); M. Haig, *Brand Failures* (London: Kogan Page, 2003).

The way a firm sells and distributes its product dramatically affects a company's marketing program. This effect means that the first decision a firm has to make is its overall approach to selling its product or service. Even for similar firms, the marketing mix can vary significantly, depending on the way the firms do business. For example, a software firm can sell directly through its Web site or through retail stores, or it can license its product to another company to be sold under that company's brand name. A start-up that plans to sell directly to the public would set up its promotions program in a much different way than a firm planning to license its products to other firms. A firm's marketing program should be consistent with its business model and its overall business plan.

Let's look more closely at the 4Ps. Again, these are broad topics on which entire books have been written. In this section, we focus on the aspects of the 4Ps that are most relevant to entrepreneurial ventures.

Product

A firm's **product**, in the context of its marketing mix, is the good or service it offers to its target market. Technically, a product is something that takes on physical form, such as an Apple iPod, an electronic game, or a laptop computer. A **service** is an activity or benefit that is intangible and does not take on a physical form, such as an airplane trip or advice from an attorney. But when discussing a firm's marketing mix, both products and services are lumped together under the label "product."

Determining the product or products to be sold is central to the firm's entire marketing effort. As stressed throughout this book, the most important attribute of a product is that it adds value in the minds of its target customers. Let's think about this by comparing vitamins with pain pills, as articulated by Henry W. Chesbrough, a professor at Harvard University:

> We all know that vitamins are good for us and that we should take them. Most of us, though, do not take vitamins on a regular basis, and whatever benefits vitamins provide do not seem to be greatly missed in the short term. People therefore pay relatively very little for vitamins. In contrast, people know when they need a pain killer. And they know they need it now, not later. They can also tell quite readily whether the reliever is working. People will be willing to pay a great deal more for a pain reliever than they pay for a vitamin. In this context, the pain reliever provides a much stronger value proposition than does a vitamin—because the need is felt more acutely, the benefit is greater and is perceived much more quickly.[27]

This example illustrates at least in part why investors prefer to fund firms that potentially have breakthrough products, such as a software firm that is working on a product to eliminate e-mail spam or a biotech firm that is working on a cure for a disease. These products are pain pills rather than vitamins because their benefits would be felt intensely and quickly. In contrast, a new restaurant start-up or a new retail store may be exciting, but these types of firms are more akin to a vitamin than a pain pill. The benefits of these businesses would not be felt as intensely.

As the firm prepares to sell its product, an important distinction should be made between the core product and the actual product. While the core product may be a CD that contains an antivirus software program, the actual product, which is what the customer buys, may have as many as five characteristics: a quality level, features, design, a brand name, and packaging.[28] For example, the Norton antivirus program is an actual product. Its name, features, warranty, ability to upgrade, packaging, and other attributes have all been carefully combined to deliver the benefits of the product: protecting computers

Learning Objective

7. Explain the difference between a core product and an actual product.

and their contents against damage and protecting computer users against work interruption. When first introducing a product to the market, an entrepreneur needs to make sure that more than the core product is right. Attention also needs to be paid to the actual product—the features, design, packaging, and so on that constitute the collection of benefits that the customer ultimately buys. Anyone who has ever tried to remove a product from a frustratingly rigid plastic container knows that the way a product is packaged is part of the product itself. The quality of the product should not be compromised by missteps in other areas.

The initial rollout is one of the most critical times in the marketing of a new product. All new firms face the challenge that they are unknown and that it takes a leap of faith for their first customers to buy their products. Some start-ups meet this challenge by using reference accounts. A **reference account** is an early user of a firm's product who is willing to give a testimonial regarding his or her experience with the product. For example, imagine the effect of a spokesperson for Apple Inc. saying that Apple used a new computer hardware firm's products and was pleased with their performance. A testimonial such as this would pave the way for the sales force of this new firm's hardware, and the new firm could use it to reduce fears that it was selling an untested and perhaps ineffective product.

To obtain reference accounts, new firms must often offer their product to an initial group of customers for free or at a reduced price in exchange for their willingness to try the product and for their feedback. There is nothing improper about this process as long as everything is kept aboveboard and the entrepreneur is not indirectly "paying" someone to offer a positive endorsement. Still, many entrepreneurs are reluctant to give away products, even in exchange for a potential endorsement. But there are several advantages to getting a strong set of endorsements: credibility with peers, noncompany advocates who are willing to talk to the press, and quotes or examples to use in company brochures and advertisements.

Price

Price is the amount of money consumers pay to buy a product. It is the only element in the marketing mix that produces revenue; all other elements represent

There is a difference between a company's core product and its actual product. The core product is the product itself, while the actual product includes the product along with its quality level, features, design, a brand name, and packaging. Consumers buy the actual product rather than the core product. Here, two entrepreneurs are designing the boxes that their product will be packaged in.

Getty Images Inc. - Stone Allstock

costs.[29] Price is an extremely important element of the marketing mix because it ultimately determines how much money a company can earn. The price a company charges for its products also sends a clear message to its target market. For example, Oakley positions its sunglasses as innovative, state-of-the art products that are both high quality and visually appealing. This position in the market suggests the premium price that Oakley charges. If Oakley tried to establish the position described previously and charged a low price for its products, it would send confusing signals to its customers. Its customers would wonder, "Are Oakley sunglasses high quality or aren't they?" In addition, the lower price wouldn't generate the sales revenue Oakley requires to continuously differentiate its sunglasses from competitors' products in ways that create value for customers.

Most entrepreneurs use one of two methods to set the price for their products: cost-based pricing or value-based pricing.

Learning Objective

8. Contrast cost-based pricing and value-based pricing.

Cost-Based Pricing   In **cost-based pricing**, the list price is determined by adding a markup percentage to a product's cost. The markup percentage may be standard for the industry or may be arbitrarily determined by the entrepreneur. The advantage of this method is that it is straightforward, and it is relatively easy to justify the price of a good or service. The disadvantage is that it is not always easy to estimate what the costs of a product will be. Once a price is set, it is difficult to raise it, even if a company's costs increase in an unpredicted manner. In addition, cost-based pricing is based on what a company thinks it should receive rather than on what the market thinks a good or service is worth. It is becoming increasingly difficult for companies to dictate prices to their customers, given customers' ability to comparison shop on the Internet to find what they believe is the best bargain for them.[30]

Value-Based Pricing   In **value-based pricing**, the list price is determined by estimating what consumers are willing to pay for a product and then backing off a bit to provide a cushion. What a customer is willing to pay is determined by the perceived value of the product and by the number of choices available in the marketplace. Sometimes, to make this determination, a company has to work backwards by testing to see what its target market is willing to pay. A firm influences its customers' perception of the value through positioning, branding, and the other elements of the marketing mix. Most experts recommend value-based pricing because it hinges on the perceived value of a product or service rather than cost-plus markup, which, as stated previously, is a formula that ignores the customer.[31] A gross margin (a company's net sales minus its costs of goods sold) of 60 to 80 percent is not uncommon in high-tech industries. An Intel chip that sells for $300 may cost $50 to $60 to produce. This type of markup reflects the perceived value of the chip. If Intel used a cost-based pricing method instead of a value-based approach, it would probably charge much less for its chips and earn less profit.

Most experts also warn entrepreneurs to resist the temptation to charge a low price for their products in the hopes of capturing market share. This approach can win a sale but generates little profit. In addition, most consumers make a **price-quality attribution** when looking at the price of a product. This means that consumers naturally assume that the higher-priced product is also the better-quality product.[32] If a firm charges a low price for its products, it sends a signal to its customers that the product is low quality regardless of whether it really is.

A vivid example of the association between price and quality is provided by SmugMug, an online photo-sharing site that charges a $40-per-year base subscription fee. SmugMug, which is growing rapidly, has 300,000 paying customers and more than 425 million photos stored. What's interesting about the company is that most of its competitors, including Shutterfly and Flickr, offer a similar service for free. Ostensibly, the reason SmugMug is able to charge a fee is that it offers higher levels of customer service and has a more user-friendly interface (in terms of how you view your photos online) than its competitors. But the owners of SmugMug feel that its ability to charge goes beyond these obvious points. Some of the free sites have closed abruptly, and their users have lost photos. SmugMug, because it charges, is seen as more reliable and dependable for the long term. (Who wants to lose their photos?) In addition, the owners believe that when people pay for something, they innately assign a higher value to it. As a result, SmugMug users tend to treat the site with respect, by posting attractive, high-quality photos that are in good taste. SmugMug's users appreciate this facet of the site, compared to the free sites, where unseemly photos often creep in.[33]

The overarching point of this example is that the price a company is able to charge is largely a function of (1) the objective quality of a product or service and (2) the perception of value that you create in the minds of your customers relative to competing products in the marketplace. These are issues a firm should consider when developing its positioning and branding strategies.

Promotion

Promotion refers to the activities the firm takes to communicate the merits of its product to its target market. Ultimately, the goal of these activities is to persuade people to buy the product. There are a number of these activities, but most start-ups have limited resources, meaning that they must carefully study promotion activities before choosing the one or ones they'll use. Let's look at the most common activities entrepreneurs use to promote their products.

Advertising   **Advertising** is making people aware of a product in hopes of persuading them to buy it. Advertising's major goals are to do the following:

Learning Objective

9. Explain the differences between advertising and public relations.

- Raise customer awareness of a product
- Explain a product's comparative features and benefits
- Create associations between a product and a certain lifestyle

These goals can be accomplished through a number of media, including direct mail, magazines, newspapers, radio, the Internet, television, and billboard advertising. The most effective ads tend to be those that are memorable and support a product's brand. However, advertising has some major weaknesses, including the following:

- Low credibility
- The possibility that a high percentage of the people who see the ad will not be interested
- Message clutter (meaning that after hearing or reading so many ads, people simply tune out)
- Relative costliness compared to other forms of promotions
- The perception that advertising is intrusive[34]

Because of these weaknesses, most start-ups do not advertise their products broadly. Instead, they tend to be very frugal and selective in their advertising efforts or engage in hybrid promotional campaigns that aren't advertising per se but are designed to promote a product or service. An illustration of a hybrid promotional campaign is Unilever's partnership with *Sofia's Diary* to promote the Sure Girl teen antiperspirant. Rather than simply advertise on the show or

Partnering for SUCCESS

Sofia's Diary: Building Awareness of Major Brands Among a Key Segment of Young Consumers Through a Multichannel Campaign

Sofia's Diary, an online teen drama, was launched in Portugal in 2003 and has become a worldwide phenomenon with versions in the United Kingdom, Germany, the United States, and Vietnam. Under the name *Sufie's Diary*, it has generated millions of fans in China and Hong Kong, where it is also shown on TV screens in airports, buses, and subway stations. Owned by Sony Pictures Television International, it was originally envisaged as an experimental Web and mobile service, but evolved into an important marketing tool for branded-content partners.

The idea is to follow the day-to-day life of teenager Sofia, in real time. Online polls and phone voting empower viewers to make decisions for Sofia while she adjusts to various life problems, driving the plotlines in three-minute online video Webisodes. The buzz behind the youth drama has seen multinational companies vie to sign six-figure sponsorship deals, relishing the opportunity to get closer to the youth audience, a notoriously difficult market to target. So far Clinique, Golddigga, Unilever, and Pearl Drops are just some of the companies to get their products in the show.

The tie-up is more than mere product placement, too. Unilever, for example, sponsored the U.K. version screened on the Bebo Web site to promote its newly launched Sure Girl teen antiperspirant, utilizing the connection in several ways. As well as Sofia characters using the product, the online audience was encouraged to open up a dialogue with other viewers on a dedicated Unilever/Sure Girl homepage on Bebo. They could submit articles on themes like "What makes you sweat?" and potentially win a cameo role in the drama.

Another tie-up, with Golddigga, involved a number of different elements over and above the characters simply wearing the urban clothing brand. Viewers were invited by Golddigga to join *Sofia*-themed online

competitions by describing their "ultimate girls night out," for example.

The format has been hailed as a breakthrough in making money out of interactive TV and has proven to be a highly effective way to target and engage the tech-savvy youth market. The level of interaction achieved with brand sponsors is hard to replicate in a traditional television format.

Questions for Critical Thinking

1. Why do you think Unilever didn't elect to direct viewers to its own Web site to obtain more information about the Sure Girl teen antiperspirant, rather than partnering with *Sofia's Diary* and basing all its competition activity on the Bebo Web site?
2. Consider a well-known youth consumer brand, which regularly advertises on television in your area. Could it do the same thing that Unilever and Golddigga did? What would be the most effective way to target its audience? Would interactive TV work well for a brand that has already established credibility on traditional channels?
3. Look at the advantages and disadvantages of advertising listed in the chapter. Which of the advantages of advertising did Unilever capture through its approach to promoting its product through *Sofia's Diary*, and which of the disadvantages of advertising did it minimize or avoid?
4. What can start-up firms that operate in completely different industries than Unilever and Golddigga learn from this feature?

Source: "Sofia's Diary Opens Up to Product Placement," *Mad.co.uk*, March 27, 2008; "Sony Bags Another Ad-Funded TV Hit," *Marketing-interactive.com*, February 19, 2009.

stick to product placement, Unilever partnered with *Sofia's Dairy* in a way that drove significant traffic to interact with its brand. An explanation of how Unilever accomplished this objective is provided in the "Partnering for Success" feature.

Along with engaging in hybrid promotional campaigns, many start-ups advertise in trade journals or utilize highly focused pay-per-click advertising provided by Google, Yahoo!, or another online firm to economize the advertising dollars. Pay-per-click advertising represents a major innovation in advertising and has been embraced by firms of all sizes. Google has two pay-per-click programs—AdWords and AdSense. AdWords allows an advertiser to buy keywords on Google's homepage (www.google.com), which triggers text-based ads to the side (and sometimes above) the search results when the keyword is used. So, if you type "football ball" into the Google search bar, you will see ads that have been paid for by companies that have footballs to sell. Many advertisers report impressive

Table 11.3 DESCRIPTION OF GOOGLE ADWORDS AND ADSENSE PROGRAMS FOR ADVERTISERS AND WEB SITE OWNERS

AdWords	AdSense
Allows advertisers to buy keywords on the Google homepage	Allows advertisers to buy ads that will be shown on other Web sites instead of Google's homepage.
Triggers text-based ads to the side (and sometimes above) search results when the keyword is used.	Google selects sites of interest for the advertiser's customers.
Advertisers are charged on a pay-per-click basis.	Advertisers are charged on a pay-per-click or per-thousand-impression basis.
The program includes local, national, and international distribution.	Advertisers are not restricted to text-based ads. Choices include text, image, and video advertisements.
Advertisers specify the maximum amount they are willing to pay per click. The ordering of the paid listings on the search results depends on other advertisers' bids and the historical click-through rates of all ads shown for a given search.	Advertisers benefit because their ads are seen as less intrusive than most banner ads, because the content of the ad is often relevant to the Web site.
Advertisers have the option of enabling their ads to be displayed on Google's partner network. This network includes AOL, Ask.com, and Netscape.	Web site owners benefit by using the service to monetize their Web sites.
Advertisers benefit because they are able to place their ads in front of people who are already searching for information about their product.	A companion to the regular AdSense program, AdSense for Search lets Web site owners place the Google search box on their Web site. Google shares any ad revenues it makes from those searches.

results utilizing this approach, presumably because they are able to place their ads in front of people who are already searching for information about their product. Google's other pay-per-click program is called AdSense. It is similar to AdWords, except the advertiser's ads appear on other Web sites instead of Google's homepage. For example, an organization that promotes football might allow Google to place some of its client's ads on its Web site. The advertiser pays on a pay-for-click basis when its ad is clicked on the football organization's site, just like it does with AdWords. Google shares the revenue generated by the advertisers with the sponsoring site. Table 11.3 provides a summary of the Google AdWords and Google AdSense programs. Yahoo! and Microsoft's programs, which are very similar to Google's, are called Yahoo! Search Marketing and Microsoft adCenter, respectively.

As an aside, the Google AdSense program, as discussed in Chapter 6, allows people who know a lot about a particular topic to launch a Web site, populate it with articles, tips, videos, and other useful information and make money online by essentially selling access to the people attracted to the Web site. For example, Tim Carter, a well-known columnist on home repair, has a Web site named Ask the Builder (www.askthebuilder.com). Information and instructions on all types of home building projects and repair are available on this Web site, as are links to areas that focus on specific topics, like air conditioning, cabinets, deck construction, and plumbing. Clicking any one of these areas brings up AdSense ads that deal with that specific area. All together, the site has hundreds of AdSense ads. Carter is able to do this and still attract large numbers of visitors because the information he provides is good and helpful. He might also believe that his ads, in a certain respect, add valuable content to the site. If someone is looking at the portion of his site that deals with how to construct a deck, he or she might actually appreciate seeing ads that point to Web sites where books and blueprints for building decks are available.

FIGURE 11.3

Steps Involved in
Putting Together an
Advertisement

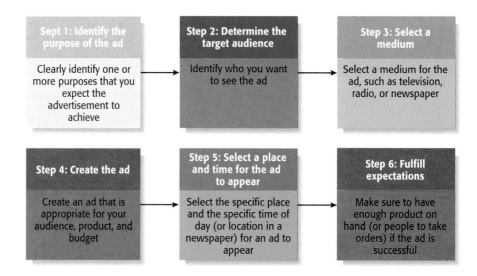

Sept 1: Identify the purpose of the ad	Step 2: Determine the target audience	Step 3: Select a medium
Clearly identify one or more purposes that you expect the advertisement to achieve	Identify who you want to see the ad	Select a medium for the ad, such as television, radio, or newspaper

Step 4: Create the ad	Step 5: Select a place and time for the ad to appear	Step 6: Fulfill expectations
Create an ad that is appropriate for your audience, product, and budget	Select the specific place and the specific time of day (or location in a newspaper) for an ad to appear	Make sure to have enough product on hand (or people to take orders) if the ad is successful

The steps involved in putting together an advertisement are shown in Figure 11.3. Typically, for start-up firms, advertisements are the most effective if they're part of a coordinated marketing campaign.[35] For example, a print ad might feature a product's benefits and direct the reader to a Web site for more information. The Web site might offer access to coupons or other incentives if the visitor fills out an information request form (which asks for name, address, and phone number). The names collected from the information request form could then be used to make sales calls. Some companies also benefit by hiring celebrities to endorse their products. This alternative is illustrated in Case 11.2, which focuses on Proactiv, a company that sells acne prevention cream. Proactiv has made very effective use of celebrity endorsers, although this approach is expensive and is appropriate on a case-by-case basis. Another alternative that is illustrated in the Proactiv case is the use of infomercials. An **infomercial** is a television commercial that runs as long as a television show and usually includes a pitch selling an item directly to the public.[36] Infomercials can be very effective in specialized cases, as illustrated in the Proactiv example.

Entrepreneurs should be aware that a poorly crafted ad runs the risk of irritating the firm's target audience. In fact, in direct response to advertising, negative terms such as *junk mail*, *spam*, and *telemarketing* (which is not in itself a negative word, although many people associate it with being interrupted) have become part of our standard language. The "mute" button on a television remote was designed primarily to silence ads. There are no easy ways for advertisers to meet these challenges, but they point out the importance of making sure that an advertisement is carefully crafted, that it is consistent with the brand image a firm wants to convey, and that it is geared to its target market.

Public Relations   One of the most cost-effective ways to increase the awareness of the products a company sells is through public relations. **Public relations** refer to efforts to establish and maintain a company's image with the public. The major difference between public relations and advertising is that public relations is not paid for—directly. The cost of public relations to a firm is the effort it makes to network with journalists and other people to try to interest them in saying or writing good things about the company and its products. Several techniques fit the definition of public relations, as shown in Table 11.4.

Many start-ups emphasize public relations over advertising primarily because it's cheaper and helps build the firm's credibility. In their book *The Fall of Advertising and the Rise of PR*, Al and Laura Ries argue that in launching a new product, it is better to start with public relations than advertising because people

Table 11.4 PUBLIC RELATIONS TECHNIQUES

Technique	Description
Press release	An announcement made by a firm that is circulated to the press. Start-ups typically circulate a press release when something positive happens, such as the launch of a new product or the hiring of a new executive.
Media coverage	Any coverage in print or broadcast media. In most cases, start-ups try to cultivate media coverage, as long as it is positive.
Articles in industry press and periodicals	Articles in industry press and periodicals are particularly coveted because they are read by people already interested in the industry in which the start-up is participating.
Blogging	A blog is a type of Web site where entries (similar to journal or diary entries) are displayed in reverse chronological order (with the most recent entries first). There are blogs that cover most industries. Outwardly talking about the merits of one's own products or services is considered spamming but making thoughtful and substantive contributions to a blog is a public service. When you sign (i.e., identify yourself online) your entry, include your company's Web site address so people who are interested in your contributions can refer back to you and your company.
Monthly newsletter	Many companies stay in touch with their potential target audience by producing and distributing a monthly or quarterly newsletter. Along with containing updates on a firm's products and services, the newsletter should contain more general information of interest to the reader. Companies should avoid sending out newsletters that simply brag about their products. These types of newsletters are often seen as too self-serving.
News conference	A news conference is the live dissemination of new information by a firm to invited media. A start-up might call a news conference to announce a breakthrough new product or service innovation.
Civic, social, and community involvement	Start-ups often try to create a positive image of their organization by sponsoring local events or asking their employees to be involved in civic clubs such as the Chamber of Commerce or the Rotary Club.

view advertising as the self-serving voice of a company that's anxious to make a sale. Advertising, according to the authors, is largely discounted. In contrast, public relations allows a firm to tell its story through a third party, such as a magazine or a newspaper. If a magazine along the lines of *Inc.* or *Business Week* publishes a positive review of a new company's products, consumers are likely to believe that those products are at least worth a try. They think that because these magazines have no vested interest in the company, they have no reason to stretch the truth or lie about the usefulness or value of a company's products.[37]

There are many ways in which a start-up can enhance its chances of getting noticed by the press. One technique is to prepare a **press kit**, which is a folder that contains background information about the company and includes a list of its most recent accomplishments. The kit is normally distributed to journalists and made available online. Another technique is to be present at industry trade shows and other events. A **trade show** is an event at which the goods or services in a specific industry are exhibited and demonstrated. Members of the media often attend trade shows to get the latest industry news. For example, the largest trade show for consumer electronics is International CES, which is held in Las Vegas every January. Many companies wait until this show to announce their most exciting new products. They do this in part because they have a captive media audience that is eager to find interesting stories to write about. A recent International CES show is pictured in Chapter 5.

Other Promotion-Related Activities   There are many other activities that help a firm promote and sell its products. Some firms, for example, give away free samples of their products. This technique is used by pharmaceutical companies that give physicians free samples to distribute to their patients as appropriate. Many food companies distribute free samples in grocery and discount stores. A similar technique is to offer free trials such as a three-month subscription to a magazine or a two-week membership to a fitness club to try to hook potential customers by exposing them directly to the product or service.

Another technique is event sponsorships. Many firms sponsor sporting events, enter floats in parades, or sponsor civic events, such as a concert series, to align their names with something of interest to their target markets. Whether these types of techniques are cost-effective is usually unclear; it's difficult to determine how much a firm gains from sponsoring a Little League baseball team or a concert series.

A fairly new technique that has received quite a bit of attention is **viral marketing**, which facilitates and encourages people to pass along a marketing message about a particular product. The most well-known example of viral marketing is Hotmail. When Hotmail first started distributing free e-mail accounts, it put a tagline on every message sent out by Hotmail users that read "Get free e-mail with Hotmail." Within less than a year, the company had several million users. Every e-mail message that passed through the Hotmail system was essentially an advertisement for Hotmail. The success of viral marketing depends on the pass-along rate from person to person. Very few companies have come close to matching Hotmail's success with viral marketing. However, the idea of designing a promotional campaign that encourages a firm's current customers to recommend its product to future customers is well worth considering.

A technique related to both viral marketing and creating buzz, which was referred to earlier in the chapter, is guerrilla marketing. **Guerrilla marketing** is a low-budget approach to marketing that relies on ingenuity, cleverness, and surprise rather than traditional techniques. The point is to create awareness of a firm and its products, often in unconventional and memorable ways. The term was first coined and defined by Jay Conrad Levinson in the 1984 book *Guerrilla Marketing*. Guerrilla marketing is particularly suitable for entrepreneurial firms, which are often on a tight budget but have creativity, enthusiasm, and passion to draw from. Firms often use very entertaining and engaging guerilla marketing techniques to build awareness for their products and services, as illustrated in the "Savvy Entrepreneurial Firm" feature.

Place (or Distribution)

Place, or distribution, encompasses all the activities that move a firm's product from its place of origin to the consumer. A **distribution channel** is the route a product takes from the place it is made to the customer who is the end user.

The first choice a firm has to make regarding distribution is whether to sell its products directly to consumers or through intermediaries such as wholesalers or distributors. Within most industries, both choices are available, so the decision typically depends on how a firm believes its target market wants to buy its product. For example, it would make sense for a recording company that is targeting the teen market to produce digital recordings and sell the recordings directly over the Web. Most teens have access to a computer and know how to download music. In contrast, it wouldn't make nearly as much sense for a recording company targeting retirees to use the same distribution channel to sell its music offerings. A much smaller percentage of the retiree market has access to computers and knows how to download music from the Web. In this instance, it would make more sense to produce CDs and partner with wholesalers or distributors to place them in retail outlets where retirees shop.

Savvy Entrepreneurial FIRM

Utilizing Guerrilla Marketing Techniques to Create Product Awareness in Entertaining, Clever, and Effective Ways

One thing most successful businesses do is try to create "awareness" or a sense of excitement around their new product or service. Creating positive "awareness" is the goal of all guerrilla marketing campaigns. But how is awareness created, particularly if a company is on a tight budget? How do companies get people talking about their products and services?

An increasing popular approach is to create entertaining and clever video spots, which can be shown on YouTube and similar Web sites. For example, Steve Spangler, the owner of Spangler Science, a Web site that sells science kits and experiments, gained national attention after a video of himself demonstrating the explosive effects of dropping Mentos into 2-liter bottles of soda spread across the Internet. If you haven't seen the video, go to YouTube.com and type in "the original Mentos geyser video." The awareness created by the video raised Spangler's visibility, and his company is now reportedly generating more than $5 million in annual sales. A similar example is Blendtec's "Will It Blend?" series. Blendtec sells high-end blenders that people use in their kitchens. To demonstrate the strength of its blenders, the company produced a series of short videos with a geeky-looking company scientist, dressed in a white lab coat, blending the Apple iPod, the Apple iPhone, the Wii Remote, and similar items. The first videos, which blended more common items like marbles and golf balls, cost $50 apiece to create. The result: The videos have been watched more than 60 million times (6 million the first week), and Blendtec's sales are up 20 percent. It's possible for business-to-business companies to pursue a similar approach. For example, TIBCO, a service-oriented architecture (SOA) company, has an entertaining series of short YouTube videos called "Greg the Architect." The videos follow the trials and tribulations of a young software architect (played by an action figure) as he tries to make sense of the same types of problems that TIBCO's real-life customers struggle with.

There are many ways that companies create awareness off-line, and the methods are only limited by a company's imagination. Red Bull generated buzz or awareness when it entered into the United States (it started in Australia) through the unique design of its bottles and by offering free samples of its energy drinks in sports clubs, on beaches, and in other places where sports enthusiasts congregate. When the product finally hit the store shelves, it sold quickly. Similarly, Jones Soda asks its customers to submit photos of themselves (or anything else they feel is interesting) and

selects a sample to place on their labels. The company has kept the buzz alive by supporting a chat room, where customers can talk about the ever-changing labels, and by sponsoring contests. For example, at the time this book went to press, the company had just completed a contest for the chance to become the 10,000th picture to be placed on a Jones Soda bottle. The winner was Erik Carlson from Schaumburg, Illinois, who submitted a picture of the Chicago skyline. Erik received 1,180 votes from Jones Soda customers who cared enough to log onto the company's Web site to look at the various entries and vote.

Guerrilla marketing campaigns are a little tricky, and a company has to make sure its campaign is consistent with its brand and the overall image it wants to convey. But much can be done to get people talking about a product or service through ingenuity and a creative mind-set.

Questions for Critical Thinking

1. Look at the Web site of Steve Spangler Science at www.stevespanglerscience.com. Do you think Steve Spangler Science would be generating more than $5 million in annual sales if the Mentos geyser video had never been made? How much money would Spangler have had to spend on print and media advertising to create the same level of name recognition that he created through the Mentos geyser videos?
2. Aside from their corny appeal, do you think the Blendtec videos are effective? In other words, do the videos convince you that buying a Blendtec blender would be a good choice?
3. Relate an example of guerilla marketing that you've observed. Explain the purpose and effectiveness of the campaign. If you're not familiar with a guerilla marketing campaign, do some Internet or library research to become familiar with one.
4. The "You Be the VC 11.1" feature focuses on First Flavor, a company that is creating print ads that can be licked by consumers so they can get a sense of a product's taste. Suggest a guerilla marketing campaign to raise First Flavor's awareness.

Sources: R. Brunner and S. Emery, *Do You Matter: How Great Design Will Make People Love Your Company* (Upper Saddle River, NJ: FT Press, 2009); C. Li and J. Bernoff, *Groundswell* (Boston, MA: Harvard Business Press, 2008); Business-Opportunities homepage, www.business-opportunities.biz/2007/08/27/attracting-customers-with-a-blog (accessed September 17, 2008).

FIGURE 11.4

Selling Direct Versus
Selling Through
Intermediaries

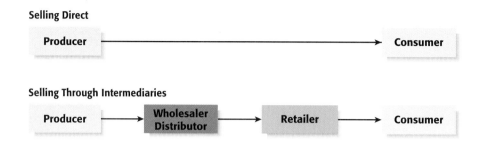

Figure 11.4 shows the difference between selling direct and selling through an intermediary. Let's look at the strengths and weaknesses of each approach.

Selling Direct   Many firms sell direct to customers. Being able to control the process of moving their products from their place of origin to the end user instead of relying on third parties is a major advantage of direct selling. Examples of companies that sell direct are Abercrombie & Fitch, which sells its clothing exclusively through company-owned stores, and Fitbit, which sells its exercise and sleep monitoring device strictly through its Web site.

The disadvantage of selling direct is that a firm has more of its capital tied up in fixed assets because it must own or rent retail outlets, must maintain a sales force, or must support an e-commerce Web site. It must also find its own buyers rather than have distributors that are constantly looking for new outlets for the firm's products.

The advent of the Internet has changed how many companies sell their products. Many firms that once sold their products exclusively through retail stores are now also selling directly online. The process of eliminating layers of middlemen, such as distributors and wholesalers, to sell directly to customers is called **disintermediation**. This is a tricky process, particularly if a firm wants to sell online and through its traditional distribution channels simultaneously. For example, if a firm has traditionally sold its products through electronics stores and is now offering the same products for sale online, the electronics stores may refuse to stock the products or may insist that they be sold online for the same price offered in the stores. This problem is referred to as channel conflict. **Channel conflict** occurs when two or more separate marketing channels (e.g., online sales and retail sales) are in conflict over their roles in selling a firm's products.

Selling Through Intermediaries   Firms selling through intermediaries typically pass off their products to wholesalers or distributors who place them in retail outlets to be sold. An advantage of this approach is that the firm does not need to own as much of the distribution channel. For example, if a company makes MP3 players and the players are sold through retail outlets such as Best Buy and Wal-Mart, the company avoids the cost of building and maintaining retail outlets. It can also rely on its wholesalers to manage its relationship with Best Buy and Wal-Mart and to find other retail outlets to sell its products. The trick to utilizing this approach is to find wholesalers and distributors that will represent a firm's products. A start-up must often pitch wholesalers and distributors much like it pitches an investor for money to win their support and cooperation.

The disadvantage of selling through intermediaries is that a firm loses a certain amount of control of its product. Even if a wholesaler or distributor places a firm's products with a top-notch retailer like Best Buy or Wal-Mart, there is no guarantee that Best Buy or Wal-Mart's employees will talk up the firm's products as much as it would if it had its own stores. Selling via distributors and wholesalers can also be expensive, so it is best to carefully weigh all options. For example, a firm that sells an item for $100 on its Web site and makes $50 (after expenses) may only make $10 if the exact same item is placed by a distributor into a retail store. The $40 difference represents the profits taken by the distributor and the retailer.

Learning Objective

10. Weigh the advantages and disadvantages of selling direct versus selling through intermediaries.

Some firms enter into exclusive distribution arrangements with channel partners. **Exclusive distribution arrangements** give a retailer or other intermediary the exclusive rights to sell a company's products. The advantage to giving out an exclusive distribution agreement is to motivate a retailer or other intermediary to make a concerted effort to sell a firm's products without having to worry about direct competitors. For example, if Nokia granted AT&T the exclusive rights to sell a new type of cell phone, AT&T would be more motivated to advertise and push the phone than if many or all cell phone companies had access to the same phone.

One choice that entrepreneurs are confronted with when selling through intermediaries is how many channels to sell through. The more channels a firm sells through, the faster it can grow. But there are two problems associated with selling through multiple channels, particularly early in the life of a firm. First, a firm can lose control of how its products are being sold. For example, the more retailers through which Liz Claiborne sells its clothing, the more likely it is that one or more retailers will not display the clothes in the manner the company wants. Second, the more channels a firm sells through, the more opportunity there is for channel conflict. If a trendy store in a mall is selling Liz Claiborne clothes and a discount outlet at the edge of town starts selling the same clothes for half the price, do you think the store in the mall will be upset?

Chapter Summary

1. The first step in selecting a target market is to study the industry in which the firm intends to compete and determine the different potential target markets within that industry. This process is called market segmentation. Markets can be segmented in a number of ways, including product type, price point, distribution channels used, and customers served.

2. After a firm has selected its target market, the next step is to establish a "position" within it that differentiates it from its competitors. The term *position* was introduced in Chapter 5, where it was emphasized that a firm's position in the marketplace determines how it is situated relative to its competitors. From a marketing perspective, this translates into the image of the way a firm wants to be perceived by its customers. Importantly, position answers the question, "Why should someone in our target market buy our good or service instead of our competitors?"

3. A product attribute map illustrates a firm's position in its industry relative to its major rivals. It is used as a visual illustration of a firm's positioning strategy and helps a firm develop its marketing plan.

4. Many entrepreneurs make the mistake of creating a strategy that focuses on the features of a product, such as its technical merits. This approach is usually less effective than a campaign focusing on the benefits of owning the product, such as convenience or being able to keep in better touch with family or friends.

5. A company's brand is the set of attributes people associate with it. On a philosophical level, a firm builds a brand by having it create meaning in customers' lives. It must create value. On a more practical level, brands are built through advertising, public relations, sponsorships, supporting social causes, and good performance.

6. A firm's marketing mix is the set of controllable, tactical marketing tools that it uses to produce the response it wants in its target market. Most marketers organize their marketing mix around the 4Ps: product, price, promotion, and place (or distribution).

7. The product itself is a firm's core product, such as the CD that contains an antivirus program. The actual product, which is what the customer buys, is

more encompassing. It may have as many as five characteristics: a quality level, features, design, a brand name, and packaging.

8. In cost-based pricing, the list price is determined by adding a markup percentage to the product's cost. In value-based pricing, the list price is determined by estimating what consumers are willing to pay for a product and then backing off a bit to provide a cushion.

9. Advertising is making people aware of a good or service in hopes of persuading them to buy it. Public relations refers to efforts to establish and maintain a company's image with the public. The major difference between the two is that advertising is paid for, and public relations isn't—at least directly. The cost of public relations to a firm is the effort it makes to network with journalists and other people to try to interest them in saying and/or writing good things about the company.

10. The first choice a firm must make regarding distribution is whether to sell its products directly to consumers or through intermediaries (e.g., wholesalers and retailers). An advantage of selling direct is that it allows a firm to maintain control of its products rather than relying on third parties. The disadvantage is that it ties up more capital in fixed assets because the firm must own (or rent) retail outlets or must field a sales force to sell its products. An advantage of selling through intermediaries is that a firm doesn't have to own much of its distribution channel (e.g., trucks and retail outlets). A disadvantage of this approach is that a firm loses some control of its product in that there is no guarantee that the retailers it sells through will talk up and push its products as much as the manufacturer would if it had its own stores.

Key Terms

advertising, **391**
brand, **384**
brand equity, **386**
brand management, **384**
buzz, **385**
channel conflict, **398**
cost-based pricing, **390**
disintermediation, **398**
distribution channel, **396**
exclusive distribution
    arrangements, **399**

guerilla marketing, **396**
infomercial, **394**
market segmentation, **379**
marketing mix, **386**
niche market, **380**
place, **396**
press kit, **395**
price, **389**
price-quality attribution, **390**
product, **388**

product attribute map, **381**
promotion, **391**
public relations, **394**
reference account, **389**
service, **388**
tagline, **382**
target market, **379**
trade show, **395**
value-based pricing, **390**
viral marketing, **396**

Review Questions

1. What is a target market? Why is it important for a firm to choose its target market early in the process of launching its venture?
2. Explain the importance of market segmentation. Describe several ways in which markets can be segmented.
3. How should a firm go about constructing a product attribute map?
4. What is a niche market? Provide examples of niche markets in the women's clothing industry.
5. Describe what is meant by a firm's positioning strategy.
6. What is a tagline? What is your favorite tagline? Why?
7. Why is it important for firms to sell the benefits of its products rather than the features?
8. What is a brand? Provide an example of a brand that you buy frequently and describe the mental image that pops into your mind when you hear or see the brand's name.

9. What is the purpose of brand management?
10. What is meant by creating "buzz" for a company? Provide an example of a firm that has created effective buzz for its product or service.
11. What is meant by the term *brand equity*?
12. Identify and briefly describe the four elements of a firm's "marketing mix."
13. Describe the difference between a core product and an actual product.
14. What is a reference account? How can having a reference account help a new firm?
15. Contrast cost-based pricing and value-based pricing.
16. What is meant by the phrase "price-quality attribution"? How does an understanding of this phrase help an entrepreneur know how to price a product?
17. What is meant by the term *guerilla marketing*? Provide an example of guerilla marketing not provided in the chapter.
18. Contrast the roles of advertising and public relations in promoting a firm and its products.
19. What is the purpose of a press release?
20. Contrast the advantages of selling direct versus the advantages of selling through an intermediary.

Application Questions

1. Reread the Opening Profile. After doing this, make a list of all the things that you think that Misa Chien has done right in building Miss Misa's marketing program.
2. Paul Bustamante is in the process of opening a music store in Tallahassee, Florida. After touring the store, a friend asked him, "Who's your target market?" Paul shrugged and said, "Kids who go to Florida State I guess, but I haven't given it much thought." What could Paul gain by thinking more carefully about his target market and how important would those insights be?
3. If you decided to start a small-business consulting service in Columbus, Ohio, how would you approach the following topics: market segmentation, selecting a target market, and developing a positioning strategy?
4. Reread the "You Be the VC 2.2" feature, which focuses on Mariah Power. How do you think Mariah Power segmented the wind-generated power industry? Describe Mariah Power's positioning strategy.
5. Imagine you're opening a new pizza, sub, and sandwich restaurant near the campus of the college or university you are attending. Suggest six ways to market your restaurant that don't include newspaper, radio, or television advertising.
6. Assume that you just invented a new type of computer printer that can be easily folded up and carried like a laptop computer. You have decided to start a company to produce the printer. Select a name and a tagline for your new company.
7. Derek Smith just opened a new restaurant that focuses on healthy food, such as salads, soups, and smoothie drinks, made from natural ingredients. He named the restaurant Derek's Health Escape. The jingle that Derek wrote for his first ad is "Fiber, nutrition, vitamins, and low-fat, that's what Derek's Health Escape is all about." Do you like Derek's jingle? If so, explain why. If not, suggest an alternative and explain why your jingle is better than Derek's.
8. Suggest some guerilla marketing that Derek Smith could utilize to create awareness about Derek's Health Escape.
9. Spend some time looking at Red Bull's Web site (the U.S. site). Comment on each element of Red Bull's marketing mix (product, price, promotion, and place in terms of distribution and sales). If you need additional information, conduct Internet or library research to obtain it. On a scale of 1 to 10

(10 is high), rate the strength of Red Bull's overall marketing plan. Justify your ratings.

10. The "You Be the VC 11.1" feature focuses on First Flavor, a company that is creating print ads that can be licked by consumers so they get a sense of a product's taste. Consider each of the 4Ps and comment on the most important issues for First Flavor to consider in each area.

11. Shannon has developed a new type of space heater that is quieter and safer than previous generations of space heaters and is particularly geared to people who live in small spaces, such as apartments or dorm rooms. Shannon doesn't know how to price this product. Describe to Shannon the two most common methods of pricing, and give her your recommendation for how to price the product.

12. Skip ahead to Case 15.1, which focuses on Snap Fitness. Snap Fitness is a franchise organization that is opening neighborhood fitness clubs that are open 24/7 so people can exercise at the time of day that works best for them. Make a list of the types of public relations activities that the owners of Snap Fitness and their franchisees could engage in to promote the company.

13. Kelly Andrews has developed a new line of jewelry that has created some positive buzz among friends and some business stores in her local community. When asked by a reporter, "Where do you plan to sell your jewelry?" Kelly said, "Hopefully everywhere—jewelry stores, Target, Wal-Mart, gift shops, online, through catalogs, and a dozen other places." Write a critique of Kelly's approach.

14. Peter Sanders is interested in iPods and for some time has supported a Web site that provides information for iPod enthusiasts. Although Peter thoroughly enjoys running the site, it has become a financial burden, and he is thinking about shutting it down. Provide some suggestions to Peter for ways to avoid shutting down the site for financial reasons.

15. Nate Jones, a friend of yours, is in the early stages of conducting a feasibility analysis for an e-commerce Web site, which will focus on the sale of products for extreme sports, such as snowboarding, rock climbing, mountain biking, and hang gliding. Nate is familiar with the concept of branding, and knows that because his company is new he'll have to build a brand from scratch. Compose a 100- to 200-word e-mail message to Nate providing him suggestions for how to approach this task.

You Be the VC 11.1

Company: First Flavor

www.firstflavor.com

Business Idea: Create ads that can be licked by consumers so they get a sense of a product's taste.

Pitch: In February 2008, Welch's grape juice took out a full-page print ad that gave readers a chance to sample its grape juice by licking the ad. The front of the ad showed a huge bottle of the juice, while the back had a smaller picture of the juice and a peel-off strip. The instructions next to the strip read, "For a TASTY fact, remove & LICK."

The peel-off strip in the ad was provided by First Flavor, via its groundbreaking Peel 'n Taste technology. While scent technologies, used to create scratch-and-sniff ads and fragrant ink, have been around for some time, lickable ads are new, and First Flavor is at the forefront. The company is capable of making lickable strips that cover a wide range of tastes, from soy milk to cheese pizza to children's cold medicines. In some cases, the lickable strips are made with a small amount of the actual product, and in other cases they're made with artificial ingredients. The ads are completely safe and meet safety requirements laid out by the Food and Drug Administration. In addition, they come individually packaged in tamper-evident, easy-to-open sachets.

There are several reasons that lickable ads are appealing to advertisers. A product company, like Welch's, can introduce the taste of a product to consumers without the expense and aggravation of a sampling campaign. Sampling campaigns are popular because marketers have found that 90 percent of shoppers are likely or somewhat likely to buy a product that they have sampled and liked. If a marketer can achieve the same result through a less expensive lickable ad campaign, costs are reduced. In terms of print advertising, once an ad is placed in a newspaper or magazine, getting people to use multiple senses to process it is a good thing. The more involved people become in interacting with an ad the more likely they are to remember it.

Finally, since the average consumer is exposed to more than 2,000 marketing messages a day, anything an advertiser can do to stand out is to its advantage. A positive experience with a lickable ad will drive a product's sales and brand awareness.

First Flavor has a large potential market for its lickable ad technology. Lickable ads can be used in print advertisements, direct mail, in-store coupon dispensers, product-in-product cross promotions, and special advertising and promotional events.

Q&A: Based on the material covered in this chapter, what questions would you ask the firm's founders before making your funding decision? What answers would satisfy you?

Decision: If you had to make your decision on just the information provided in the pitch and on the company's Web site, would you fund this company? Why or why not?

You Be the VC 11.2

Company: WebVet

www.webvet.com

Business Idea: Create a Web site that provides pet owners a one-stop destination for information regarding pet health issues.

Pitch: If you're looking for reliable information about human medical conditions, you can quickly turn to WebMD or a similar Web site, which contains useful and authoritative information about any medical issue. But what if your dog stops eating or your cat starts losing its hair? Or what if you're browsing through a pet supply store and see vitamins for dogs, and wonder which dogs need vitamins and whether they are really necessary? You'll probably worry and do a Google search, and peck around the Web trying to find relevant information.

WebVet was founded to help pet owners answer just these types of questions. It is the WebMD for pets, and includes a comprehensive collection of articles and information. The four main components of the site include explore, health topics, news flash, and hot topics. Explore connects visitors with general information about pets, such as pet care and wellness, diet and exercise, and holistic care (such as home remedies for common dog ailments). Health topics deals with common pet maladies and diseases, such as allergies, open wound care, kennel cough, and Lyme disease. News flash includes current news events involving pets, such as interesting pet rescue stories. Hot topics include topical issues pertaining to pets like how to

keep pets safe during a particularly hot stretch of summer. The purpose of having such a current and rich mix of information is to encourage pet owners to visit the site regularly rather just when their pets are having a problem.

All the information posted on WebVet is written by a qualified staff and is reviewed annually by a panel of veterinarians. Like WebMD for human health, the site does not diagnose, suggest treatment, or take positions of whether one form of treatment for a pet disease is better than another. Instead, the site provides objective information, access to all points of view, and urges its visitors to consult with their veterinarians on the best course of action for their individual pet. WebVet also provides a forum for pet owners to interact and discuss pet-related issues with one another. Forum topics include how to handle a new pet, grieving the loss of a pet, and inspirational pet stories. WebVet makes money by selling sponsorships and advertising on its Web site.

Q&A: Based on the material covered in this chapter, what questions would you ask the firm's founders before making your funding decision? What answers would satisfy you?

Decision: If you had to make your decision on just the information provided in the pitch and on the company's Web site, would you fund this company? Why or why not?

CASE 11.1

eBags: The 4Ps of a Successful Online Retailer
www.ebags.com

Bruce R. Barringer
Oklahoma State University
R. Duane Ireland
Texas A & M University

Introduction

In 1998, Jon Nordmark left an executive position at Samsonite and cofounded eBags, an online retailer of luggage, handbags, backpacks, and other types of bags. Through frugal management and good customer service, eBags weathered the dot-com storm and is not only an Internet survivor, but an exemplar of how to conduct business profitably online. In fact, although the company is privately held and does not release financial results, it is thought to be profitable and growing at about 30 percent per year.

Since the company was founded, a large percentage of its effort has been devoted to its marketing program. The 4Ps—product, price, promotion, and place—are as important for Internet companies as brick-and-mortar retailers. In fact, a discussion of each of the Ps provides a sense of the attributes that have led to eBags' success, and the challenges that the company faces in the future.

Product

In its four years, eBags has grown from a few hundred products to offer more than 36,000 products from 520 brands. It carries products from all the major brands, including Samsonite, Nike, North Face, and JanSport. In a single day, more than 100,000 visitors use its Web site.

As with most Internet retailers, eBags takes advantage of the virtually unlimited space offered by the virtual world. A disadvantage that regular stores have in carrying luggage is that it takes up so much floor space. "Why is most luggage black? Because people (can't) afford the floor space to sell different colors," Bob Kagle, one of the venture capitalists who funded eBags, once observed. Echoing this theme, Bob Cobb, an eBags cofounder, said, "We got one popular (bag) that comes in three colors. The number one color is red. People love the fact that they can see their luggage coming off the baggage carousel."

eBags has a very deep selection of products in its most popular categories. For example, it carries over 200 brands and 12,000 different women's handbags. So a woman may browse at lunch while she's having a brown bag at her desk and casually sort through a broad selection of handbags. To enhance the shopping experience for handbags eBags has an area called "On the Streets," where emerging handbag designers pitch their products in a video format. In the videos the designers talk about how they got their start, where their inspiration comes from, and how their bags are different from everyone else's.

In 2004, eBags expanded into footwear by buying Shoedini.com, but after three years abandoned the effort and sold the site to Zappos.com. The company feels the purchase was a mistake and has resharpened its focus on bags.

Price

Although it's not exactly known how eBags prices its products (price is usually a trade secret), it is aggressive in its pricing, one of the factors that lures shoppers to its Web site. Just recently, the company has become ever-more aggressive in this area by offering lowest-price guarantees and a completely free return policy.

In all areas of its marketing mix, eBags tests its practices before they are implemented. For example, before it implemented its lowest-price guarantee, it conducted a test in which half of the visitors to its Web site were offered the 110 percent price guarantee and the other half weren't. The test showed a 10 percent increase in the sales conversion rate (people who shopped and then made a purchase) for the visitors who were offered the guarantee as opposed to those who weren't.

Promotion

In regard to promotions, eBags has not done a lot of advertising. Instead, it has relied largely on public relations and word of mouth to drive traffic to its Web site. In addition, eBags has a clean, easy-to-navigate Web site to make shopping at eBags a satisfying experience. For example, if a shopper conducts a search for backpacks, he or she will be prompted to choose a brand or price range, after which the site will display extensive details on products within the chosen category. The company also uses its Web site to help customers shop for specialized items. For example, eBags has a "laptop bag finder" on its

Web site, where you key in the laptop you own and it displays all the bags that fit your laptop.

In late 2002, eBags launched a catalog to complement its Web site. The catalog is attractive and provides eBags another means of placing its products in front of potential customers. Special catalogs are produced to promote specific categories of items. For example, in 2008 the company sent out 750,000 back-to-school catalogs to households that had purchased backpacks within the last several years. Maintaining an effective catalog campaign is a challenge. Rising costs are making catalogs more expensive to produce and ship. In addition, because a catalog may sit on someone's coffee table for several months before they see something they like and place an order on eBags' Web site, it's hard to know how much business a particular catalog creates.

To spur word-of-mouth advertising, eBags tries to be scrappy and quick. In mid-2008, for example, the TSA started allowing certain laptop bags to go through airport security without the laptop being taken out of the bag. CODi made the first approved bags. eBags was the first company to offer the bag for sale online, and posted a video showing how the bag works. eBags also put out a press release to tell the world that the bag was approved and that it was for sale on eBags.

eBags also makes extensive use of customer reviews. It has over 1.5 million reviews on its site that come from people who have purchased, used, and have taken the time to provide feedback on a product. For example, at the time this book went to press, the JanSport Superbreak Backpack (SKU-T501) had 5,556 reviews. A total of 5,306 of the reviewers (96 percent) said they would buy the product again. The overall satisfaction rating was 9 on a 10-point scale. The reviews not only help shoppers make informed decisions but provide important feedback to the manufacturers of products sold via eBags.

Place (or Distribution)

One of the keys to eBags' success is its distribution strategy. Normally, offering the number of products that eBags does would cost a fortune in warehousing. It would also require eBags to assume the risk of trying to anticipate customer demand. To keep its costs down and to avoid this risk, eBags uses a simple yet innovative strategy to maintain its inventory. It has none. Instead, eBags employs a strategy called drop shipping. With drop shipping, eBags and other online merchants maintain little or no inventory. Instead, they rely on manufacturers and wholesalers to ship products directly to consumers. Profit margins on

drop-shipped items tend to be lower because the retailer shares the profits on the sale with the manufacturer or distributor. But for eBags drop shipping has been a great deal.

Here's how it works: eBags takes an order that is then electronically transmitted to the appropriate shipper, such as North Face. North Face then packages and ships the item, usually in a day or so. The product is shipped in a box with eBags' logo and name, and the buyer never knows the difference. The practice turned eBags—instantly and with little risk—into a "category killer" almost overnight. A category killer is a firm that concentrates on one product and offers such a wide selection that it becomes difficult for firms that offer only a small selection of the product to compete. An example is Home Depot in the hardware industry. eBags sees itself as a category killer in the bags industry. "It's probably one of the most important reasons why we survived," Cobb said.

Discussion Questions

1. Describe eBags' positioning strategy. Do you think the strategy is effective? Why or why not?
2. In a short paragraph, describe eBags' brand. Comment on the strengths and/or weaknesses of the brand.
3. What steps has eBags taken to energize its customers? How has eBags turned its customers into advocates for eBags and the products it sells?
4. What is the difference between eBags' core product and its actual product? Describe its actual product and your assessment of whether the actual product provides an attractive or an unattractive mix of characteristics.

Application Questions

1. Draw a product attribute map for eBags.
2. Compare and contrast eBags and Zappos (the subject of Case 9.2). Why do you think Zappos doesn't drop ship like eBags does? What would eBags gain and what would it lose if it adopted Zappos's approach to warehousing and distributing products?

Sources: C. Li and J. Bernoff, *Groundswell* (Boston, MA: Harvard Business Press, 2008); J. Keenan, "A Chat with October's Profile, Peter Cobb, Co-founder/Senior Vice President, eBags," *Catalogue Success*, www.catalog-success.com/story/print.bsp?sid=176422&var=story (accessed October 2008); D. Fuscaldo, "How Can Online Retailers Carry So Many Products? eSecret Is 'Drop Shipping,'" *Wall Street Journal*, April 28, 2003.

CASE11.2

Proactiv: How Three Critical Marketing Decisions Shaped a New Venture's Future

www.proactiv.com

Bruce R. Barringer
Oklahoma State University
R. Duane Ireland
Texas A & M University

Introduction

In 1995, two dermatologists, Dr. Katie Rodan and Dr. Kathy Fields, developed what they believed was a medical breakthrough in fighting acne. Their mission: to help millions of people rid themselves of acne and acne-related problems. They named their product Proactiv Solutions. This name was chosen because the product could heal existing blemishes and *proactively* help prevent new ones from forming.

Today, Proactiv is the number 1 selling acne product in the United States, even though it's not available in most stores. It's sold primarily through infomercials, the company's Web site, a subscription service called the "Proactiv Solution Clear Skin Club," and in select upscale boutiques and kiosks. The way Proactiv reached the point it currently occupies is an interesting story. Early in its life, Proactiv was shaped by three critical marketing decisions, from which the company has not wavered, even to this day. This case recounts these decisions and discusses how the decisions shaped this entrepreneurial venture's future.

How It Started

Katie Rodan and Kathy Fields met while they were working summer jobs at a cardiovascular research lab in Los Angeles. The lab was developing a drug to treat post–heart attack patients. Both Rodan and Fields enjoyed the exciting pace of the work as well as the camaraderie they shared with the lab's researchers and doctors. After earning their college degrees, they both went to medical school and became dermatologists. They stayed in touch and often shared with one another how surprised they were at the number of acne patients they were seeing. At the time, the medical research said that only 3 percent of the adult population had acne, but Rodan and Fields became convinced that the number was higher. They were each seeing acne patients on a daily basis, and they weren't just seeing teenagers. They were seeing women in their 20s, 30s, 40s, and even in their 50s who were suffering from acne and acne-related problems.

Rodan and Fields decided to form a partnership to investigate the acne issue further. They started by talking to their patients, asking them a wide range of acne-related questions. What they found was that the vast majority of their patients hated the acne products on the market. The most common complaints were that the products were very drying and they were very irritating. Worst of all, patients told Rodan and Fields, the available products did not work. At this point, the two physicians started thinking there might be an opportunity for them to create a better product.

Rodan and Fields spent the next couple of years thoroughly investigating the acne products on the market. After testing many of the products on their patients, they made what they believed was a shocking discovery. All of the products on the market were designed to spot-treat a pimple—none were designed to stop the pimple from forming in the first place. This just didn't make sense to the two dermatologists—from both a practical and a medical standpoint. By the time you see a pimple, whatever treatment you administer, it's too little too late. In their judgment, not taking steps to prevent acne from developing was akin to not brushing your teeth and going to the dentist to fill cavities. Why not brush your teeth and floss and try to prevent the cavities from developing in the first place?

This revelation motivated Rodan and Fields to start working on a product of their own—one that would be more proactive in preventing acne and acne-related problems. They hired a chemist, and the three worked together for another couple of years. Finally, they had a product they were happy with and that seemed to work and to satisfy their patients.

Important Revelations

To get ideas about how to market and develop their product, which didn't have a name yet, Rodan hosted dinner parties at her house and conducted brainstorming sessions with the guests. The guests included business executives, market researchers, marketing consultants, an FDA regulatory attorney, the chief financial officer of a major company, and others. One of the things the participants in these sessions stressed to Rodan and Fields was the importance of marketing research. In particular, the group urged Rodan and Fields to hire an unbiased third party to validate their findings. Rodan and Fields took this advice to heart and hired an outside consultant. In focus groups that the consultant led, Rodan and Fields learned two important things about older women. First, many women who medically *do* have acne refuse to believe it. Second, people don't like to talk about their acne with others. Rodan and Fields also learned that their product still needed work. There were several aspects of the product that needed improvement, a need that Rodan and Fields fully intended to take care of.

Three Critical Marketing Decisions That Shaped the Future of the Firm

Critical Marketing Decision 1: We're a Skin Care Company After Rodan and Fields reformulated the product again, they hired another marketing consultant to advise them as to how they should proceed to successfully market their product. The first piece of advice they got from the consultant was to think of their product as a skin care rather than as an acne product. At the time, the acne market in the United States was about $250 million a year, a low number by consumer products standards. In contrast, the skin care market was several billion dollars a year, making it much more attractive. The consultant told Rodan and Fields to think of their product as a skin care system that just happens to treat acne, rather than an acne medication alone. This recommendation obviously caused Rodan and Fields to have a much broader vision for the scope of the market for their product.

Critical Marketing Decision 2: Our Name Is Proactiv After Rodan and Fields started thinking of their product as part of the skin care market, they got advice from a marketing specialist about what to name their product. The name the

specialist recommended was Proactiv (proactive without the e). Looking back, Rodan and Fields admit that initially they didn't get the reason for this recommendation. They were hoping for a more cosmetic-sounding name, like Dermo-Beautiful. The name Proactiv turned out to be perfect. It captured the essence of what Rodan and Fields were trying to accomplish—to create a product that would be *proactive* (rather than *reactive*) in dealing with acne and acne-related issues. In other words, the name Proactiv captured the entrepreneurs' interest in signaling to customers that their product was intended to prevent the occurrence of additional acne-related problems for them.

Critical Marketing Decision 3: Infomercials To get their product on the market, Rodan and Fields initially tried to raise investment capital. They were repeatedly turned down. The biggest objection they encountered was the sentiment that if their product was so good and so obvious, why hadn't Procter & Gamble or Johnson & Johnson already thought of it? Surely they must have dermatologists on their advisory boards telling them what to do, was the comment repeatedly expressed to Rodan and Fields as they talked to those with investment capital. After giving up on raising capital, Rodan and Fields approached Neutrogena to try to get a licensing deal. Neutrogena passed on the deal but did make a suggestion that resonated with Rodan and Fields. Neutrogena said that the most effective way to sell the product would be via infomercials. Initially, Rodan and Fields were shocked, because they had a fairly low opinion of infomercials. But there was one company, according to the folks at Neutrogena, named Guthy-Renker that made high-quality infomercials for professional products like Proactiv. Rodan and Fields also got to thinking that an infomercial might be the best way to educate people about their product. The following table lays out the points in favor of using infomercials to sell a product in which Rodan and Fields had a great deal of confidence.

Why Infomercials Have Worked for Proactiv (Infomercials Are 30–60 Minute Programs That Are Paid for by an Advertiser)

- People need to be reeducated about how to treat acne.
- The reeducation can't be done in a 30-second or 60-second television commercial, or in a print ad.
- Acne is an embarrassing problem, so people will be most open to learning about it in the privacy of their homes.
- The demographic group that spends the most time watching infomercials, women in their 20s, 30s, and 40s, are Proactiv's market.
- Infomercials provide Proactiv the opportunity to show heartfelt testimonials of people who have used the product. Showing "before" and "after" pictures of people who have used the product and have experienced dramatic results has been a particularly persuasive tactic.

Guthy-Renker

After being turned down by Neutrogena, Rodan and Fields were about ready to throw in the towel when they met, simply by chance, a person who introduced them to Guthy-Renker, the infomercial

company that people at Neutrogena recommended highly. After several meetings, Guthy-Renker offered to license Proactiv and to create an infomercial to sell the product. It also put up the money to buy the media time needed for the infomercial to be

(continued)

televised. The initial infomercial was targeted toward women in the age group most ignored by the present providers of acne products. The 30-minute spot carefully explained what acne is, how it can affect older women, and how Proactiv was the only product available that potentially prevented acne from occurring. It also offered a complete money-back guarantee. The first infomercial sold twice as much Proactiv as expected, and Guthy-Renker and Proactiv remain close partners today.

It was also Guthy-Renker's idea to get celebrity endorsements for Proactiv. The first celebrity endorser was Judith Light. Light was followed by Vanessa Williams, and now a number of other celebrities (including Elle Macpherson) endorse the product.

Proactiv Today

Today, Proactiv is strong. The first Guthy-Renker infomercial ran in 1994, and the product has steadily gained market share since. Proactiv is now being sold in Europe and Asia as well as in the United States. Neither the product nor the sales strategy has changed since Proactiv was first introduced. The three marketing decisions described here set the direction for the company, and the company remains fully committed to taking only the actions suggested by these decisions.

Discussion Questions

1. Does Proactiv sell features or benefits? Provide evidence from the case to support your conclusion.
2. Discuss the things that Rodan and Fields learned, prior to meeting Guthy-Renker, that

persuaded them that infomercials were the best way to sell Proactiv. If Proactiv hadn't developed infomercials in partnership with Guthy-Renker, do you think Proactiv would be in existence today? Describe why infomercials were a better choice than print or media advertising for Proactiv when the company was first being introduced.
3. Describe Proactiv's positioning strategy. To what extent did the three critical marketing decisions discussed in the case shape the evolution of Proactiv's positioning strategy?
4. What is the difference between Proactiv's core product and its actual product? Describe its actual product and your assessment of whether the actual product provides an attractive mix of characteristics.

Application Questions

1. In your judgment, why doesn't Proactiv sell through mainline retail stores along with the direct-to-consumers channel? Make your answer as thoughtful and substantive as possible.
2. Use materials included in Chapter 1 to identify the characteristics of successful entrepreneurs you see in Katie Rodan and Kathy Fields. To what extent do you believe these characteristics have contributed to Proactiv's success?

Sources: Proactiv homepage, www.proactiv.com (accessed May 10, 2006); K. Rodan, Stanford Technology Ventures Entrepreneurial Thought Leaders Podcast, April 2006.

Endnotes

1. "Back to Business," *Entrepreneur,* May 2007.
2. Personal Conversation with Misa Chien, November 18, 2008.
3. D. F. Kuratko and J. S. Hornsby, *New Venture Management* (Upper Saddle River: Pearson/Prentice Hall, 2009); J. Nesheim, *The Power of Unfair Advantage* (New York: Free Press, 2005).
4. M. Schindehutte, M. H. Morris, and L. F. Pitt, *Rethinking Marketing: The Entrepreneurial Imperative* (Upper Saddle River: Pearson/Prentice Hall, 2009); R. McKanna, *Relationship Marketing: Strategies for the Age of the Customer* (New York: Basic Books, 2006).
5. P. Kufahl, "Get into the Niche," *Club Industry,* December 1, 2002.
6. D. L. Rainey, *Product Innovation* (Cambridge, UK: Cambridge University Press, 2005).
7. C. P. Blocker and D. J. Flint, "Customer Segments as Moving Targets: Integrating Customer Value Dynamism into Segment Instability Logic," *Industrial Marketing Management* 36, no. 6 (2007): 810–22; A. Weinstein, "A Strategic Framework for Defining and Segmenting Markets," *Journal of Strategic Marketing* 14, no. 2 (2006): 115–27.
8. S. K. Fixson and J.-K. Park, "The Power of Integrality: Linkages Between Product Architecture, Innovation, and Industry Structure," *Research Policy* 37, no. 8 (2008): 1296–1316; J. Kurtzman and G. Rifkin, *Startups That Work* (New York: Portfolio, 2005).
9. O. Walker, H. Boyd, J. Mullins, and J. Larreche, *Marketing Strategy: A Decision-Focused Approach* (Boston: McGraw-Hill, 2003).

10. My Gym homepage, www.mypgym.com (accessed December 2, 2008).

11. A. Loten. "Study: Business IT Spending to Grow," *Inc.*, August 11, 2008.

12. S. F. Slater, G. T. M. Hult, and E. M. Olson, "On the Importance of Matching Strategic Behavior and Target Market Selection to Business Strategy in High-Tech Markets," *Journal of the Academy of Marketing Science* 35, no. 1 (2007): 5–17; R. W. Price, *Roadmap to Entrepreneurial Success* (New York: AMACOM, 2004).

13. P. Kotler, *Marketing Insights from A to Z* (New York: John Wiley & Sons, 2003), 65.

14. K. J. Clancy and P. C. Krieg, *Counterintuitive Marketing: Achieve Great Results Using Uncommon Sense* (New York: Free Press, 2000).

15. A. Venkatesh and L. A. Meamber, "Arts and Aesthetics: Marketing and Cultural Production," *Marketing Theory* 6, no. 1 (2006): 11–39; S. Bedbury, *A New Brand World* (New York: Penguin, 2002).

16. B. Y. Shine, J. Park, and R. S. Wyer, Jr., "Brand Synergy Effects in Multiple Brand Extensions," *Journal of Marketing Research* 44, no. 4 (2007): 663–70; F. Reichheld, "Microeconomics of Customer Relationships," *MIT Sloan Management Review* 47, no. 2 (2006): 73–78.

17. Kotler, *Marketing Insights from A to Z,* 65.

18. M. J. Kay, "Strong Brands and Corporate Brands," *European Journal of Marketing* 40, nos. 7 & 8 (2006): 742–60.

19. N. C. Kaiser, "Dan Byrne, CEO of Byrne Specialty Gases," nPost.com (www.nPost.com), from the nscript of an interview conducted April 29, 2004.

20. R. D. Ahuja, T. A. Michels, M. M. Walker, and M. Weissbuch, "Teen Perceptions of Disclosures in Buzz Marketing," *Journal of Consumer Marketing* 24, no. 3 (2007): 151–59; D. Debelak, *Bringing Your Product to Market in Less Than a Year,* 2nd ed. (New York: John Wiley & Sons, 2005).

21. I. Mohr, "Buzz Marketing for Movies," *Business Horizons* 50, no. 5 (2007): 395–403; E. Rosen, *The Anatomy of Buzz* (New York: Random House, 2000).

22. B. Nelson, Forbes.com, www.1800gotjunk.com/us_en/about/gotjunk_forbes.aspx (accessed December 1, 2008).

23. J. Blasberg, V. Vishwanath, and J. Allen, "Tools for Converting Consumers Into Advocates," *Strategy & Leadership* 36, no. 2 (2008): 16–23; N. J. Hicks, "From Ben Franklin to Branding: The Evolution of Health Services Marketing," in *Branding Health Services,* ed. G. Bashe, N. J. Hicks and A. Ziegenfuss (Gaithersburg, MD: Aspen Publishers, 2000), 1–18.

24. Hicks, "From Ben Franklin to Branding."

25. S. Sriram, S. Balachander, and M. U. Kalwani, "Monitoring the Dynamics of Brand Equity Using Store-Level Data," *Journal of Marketing* 71, no. 2 (2007): 61–78; B. B. Stern, "What Does *Brand* Mean? Historical Analysis Method and Construct Definition," *Journal of the Academy of Marketing Science* 34 (2006): 216–23.

26. P. Kotler and G. Armstrong, *Principles of Marketing* 12th ed. (Upper Saddle River, NJ: Prentice Hall, 2008).

27. H. W. Chesbrough, *Open Innovation* (Boston: Harvard Business School Press, 2003).

28. Kotler and Armstrong, *Principles of Marketing.*

29. Kotler and Armstrong, *Principles of Marketing.*

30. M. J. Silverstein, *Treasure Hunt* (New York: Portfolio, 2006).

31. R. Minhas and J. C. Moon, "The Office of Fair Trading Report: A Prescription for Value-Based Drug Pricing," *Journal of the Royal Society of Medicine* 100, no. 5 (2007): 216–18; J. H. Boyett and J. T. Boyett, *The Guru Guide to Marketing* (New York: John Wiley & Sons, 2003).

32. E. Gamliel and R. Herstein, "The Effect of Framing on Willingness to Buy Private Brands," *Journal of Consumer Marketing* 24, no. 6 (2007): 334–39.

33. D. MacAskill, CEO of SmugMug, nPost homepage, www.npost.com (accessed December 1, 2008, originally posted January 16, 2007).

34. R. A. Nykiel, *Marketing Your Business: A Guide to Developing a Strategic Marketing Plan* (New York: Best Business Books, 2003).

35. R. Ferguson, "Word of Mouth and Viral Marketing: Taking the Temperature of the Hottest Trends in Marketing," *Journal of Consumer Marketing* 25, no. 3 (2008): 179–82; B. Barton, "Integrating Advertising with Other Campaigns," in *Business: The Ultimate Resource* (New York: Bloomsbury Publishing, 2003).

36. American Marketing Association, Dictionary of Marketing Terms, www.marketingpower.com (accessed August 10, 2006).

37. A. Ries and L. Ries, *The Fall of Advertising and the Rise of PR* (New York: HarperBusiness, 2002).

EBEN BAYER
Cofounder, Ecovative Design
BS College of Engineering, Rensselaer Polytechnic
Institute, 2007

GAVIN McINTYRE
Cofounder, Ecovative Design
BS College of Engineering, Rensselaer Polytechnic
Institute, 2007

Getting Personal

with Eben Bayer

CURRENTLY IN MY IPOD
Firecracker, Red Hot
Valentines

**MY ADVICE FOR NEW
ENTREPRENEURS**
Go for it!

**WHAT I DO WHEN
I'M NOT WORKING**
Read, run, play music

BEST ADVICE I'VE RECEIVED
Dream big

**BEST PART OF BEING
A STUDENT**
Scheduling your own time

**MY BIGGEST SURPRISE
AS AN ENTREPRENEUR**
It's not magic, just a lot
to learn

CHAPTERTWELVE
The Importance of *Intellectual* Property

OPENING PROFILE
ECOVATIVE DESIGN
The Key Role of Intellectual Property in Its Early Success
www.ecovativedesign.com

In spring 2007, Eben Bayer and Gavin McIntyre, two engineering students at Rensselaer Polytechnic Institute (RPI), enrolled in the Inventor's Studio class. The class, which is taught by RPI lecturer Burt Swersey, helps seniors use the technical knowledge they learned in their other classes to develop new product ideas. Bayer and McIntyre formed a team and set out investigating product ideas. Among the requirements of the class is that an idea must be patentable and it must serve a socially responsible purpose. In the photo, Bayer is pictured on the left and McIntyre is on the right.

Bayer and McIntyre decided to run with an idea that Bayer had conceived prior to the beginning of the class. Bayer grew up on a maple syrup farm in Vermont and had the idea of creating an organic building insulation from mushrooms. As a kid, he'd hunted for mushrooms, knew their root systems, and thought that the way a mushroom's root system grows might be harnessed to bond materials together. As the class progressed, McIntyre literally grew mushroom samples under his bed to study their properties.[1] The idea was further vetted and was deemed to be technically feasible. To see if it was patentable, Bayer and McIntyre looked through about 800 existing patents, studied academic journals, and learned how to use the U.S. Patent and Trademark Office's (USPTO) search engines to see if an identical technology had been patented. They found that they'd hit on a truly original idea. While many companies sell "green" building products such as recycled fiberboard and plant-based paints, no one was doing exactly what they were proposing. Unlike many green building products, Bayer and McIntyre's product, which they named "Greensulate," isn't made from preexisting materials and takes very little energy or expense to produce because it's grown from organic materials.

In May 2007, Bayer and McIntyre graduated from RPI. Both had jobs lined-up—Bayer with a defense contractor and McIntyre with National Labs. Incredibly, both quit their jobs, Bayer on his first day, to start a company to further investigate the merits of Greensulate.

Bayer and McIntyre named their company Ecovative Design. They received a $250,000 grant from the U.S. state of New York and combined that money with other bootstrapping techniques to get started. Here's a layman's version of how Greensulate is made: A mixture of water, mineral particles, cellulose, and hydrogen peroxide are poured into molds and then injected with living mushroom cells. Placed in a dark environment, the mushroom cells start to grow, digesting the cellulose as food and sprouting thousands of root-like cellular strands. A couple of weeks later, a one-inch-thick panel of foam like insulation is fully grown. The insulation can be used in various building materials. The biggest potential for Greensulate is to replace Styrofoam, which is used as insulation in constructing homes and other buildings. Greensulate is just as cost effective as Styrofoam and is sturdier and more environmentally friendly.[2]

After Ecovative Design was launched, Bayer and McIntyre developed a second product called "Negative Volume," which is a packaging material produced using

Learning Objectives

After studying this chapter you should be ready to:

1. Define the term *intellectual property* and describe its importance.

2. Specify the rules of thumb for determining whether a particular piece of intellectual property is worth the time and expense of protecting.

3. Discuss the four major forms of intellectual property: patents, trademarks, copyrights, and trade secrets.

4. Describe the six-step process for obtaining a patent.

5. Identify the four types of trademarks.

6. Identify the types of material that are eligible for copyright protection.

7. Discuss the legal environment that facilitates trade secret protection.

8. Identify the most common types of trade secret disputes.

9. Describe some of the physical measures that firms take to protect their trade secrets.

10. Explain the two primary reasons for conducting an intellectual property audit.

agricultural by-products. The product will be used in the shipping of large items like television sets and windows. Unlike Styrofoam, which mostly ends up in landfills, Negative Volume is so environmentally friendly that it can literally be placed in a garden and used for fertilizer after it's no longer needed for shipping.

One thing that Bayer and McIntyre have been particularly careful to do, as they've developed their products, is to apply for patents on the key elements of their technologies. They have also utilized other forms of intellectual property. Both Greensulate and Negative Volume are trademarked. Much of Ecovative Design's printed material is copyrighted. As is the case with many savvy start-ups, however, not all of its intellectual property is legally protected. Some of the projects that Bayer, McIntyre, and their team are working on are trade secrets, and aren't protected by patents, copyrights, or trademarks, partly to keep them secret. The people who are privy to these projects sign nondisclosure agreements, promising to keep the information confidential.

Ecovative Design received a big boost in late 2008 when it won the coveted Picnic Green Challenge Prize in Amsterdam, Holland. The prize was 500,000 euros, which is approximately $750,000. The five-judge panel endorsed Ecovative's vision that Greensulate has the potential to revolutionize an entire industry and significantly decrease carbon emissions on a globally significant scale. As an insulating material, Greensulate is just as good as existing products while consuming five times less energy to produce, and generating 10 times lower CO_2 emissions.[3]

Ecovative Design is now moving forward as a business with its intellectual property securely intact. The firm hopes to begin manufacturing products in 2009 and introduce them into the marketplace in 2010.

Many entrepreneurial firms have valuable intellectual property. In fact, virtually all businesses, including start-ups, have knowledge, information, and ideas that are critical to their success.

For at least three reasons, it is important for businesses to recognize what intellectual property is and how to protect it. First, the intellectual property of a business often represents its most valuable asset.[4] Think of the value of the Google trademark, the Nike "swoosh" logo, or the Microsoft Windows operating system. All of these are examples of intellectual property, and because of intellectual property laws, they are the exclusive properties of the firms that own them. Second, it is important to understand what intellectual property is and how to protect it to avoid unintentional violations of intellectual property laws. For example, imagine the hardship facing an entrepreneurial start-up if it selected a name for its business, heavily advertised that name, and was later forced to change the name because it was infringing on a trademark. Finally, intellectual property can be licensed or sold, providing valuable licensing income.

We begin this chapter by defining intellectual property and exploring when intellectual property protection is warranted. There are costs involved with legally protecting intellectual property, and the costs sometimes outweigh the benefits, at least in the short term. Next, we discuss the four key forms of intellectual property. The chapter ends with a discussion of the importance of conducting an intellectual

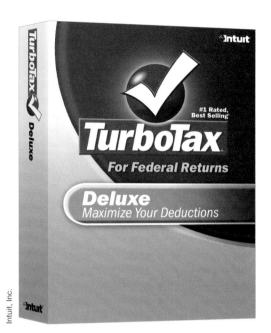

Intuit, Inc.

If you purchase the latest version of TurboTax, the $75 or so you pay is not for the CD-ROM and disks themselves. The value you are paying for is the access you now have to the intellectual property contained on the disk.

property audit, which is a proactive tool an entrepreneurial firm can use to catalog the intellectual property it owns and determine how its intellectual property should be protected.

THE IMPORTANCE OF INTELLECTUAL PROPERTY

Intellectual property is any product of human intellect that is intangible but has value in the marketplace. It is called "intellectual" property because it is the product of human imagination, creativity, and inventiveness.[5] Traditionally, businesses have thought of their physical assets such as land, buildings, and equipment, as their most important assets. Increasingly, however, a company's intellectual assets are the most valuable.[6] In the case of Ecovative Design, intellectual property consists of intangible assets such as an invention, a business's logo, and a company's Internet domain name. All these assets can provide a business with a competitive advantage in the marketplace, and the loss of such assets can be just as costly (if not more so) to a business as the loss of physical property or equipment.

Not all firms are as intellectual property savvy as Ecovative Design. In fact, common mistakes that entrepreneurial firms make are not properly identifying all their intellectual property, not fully recognizing the value of their intellectual property, not using their intellectual property as part of their overall plan of success, and not taking sufficient steps to protect it. These challenges are presented in Figure 12.1. It can be difficult, however, to determine what qualifies as intellectual property and whether it should be legally protected. Every facet of a company's operations probably owns intellectual property that should be protected. To illustrate this point, Table 12.1 provides examples of the intellectual property that typically resides within the departments of midsize entrepreneurial firms.

The USPTO feels that small businesses are particularly susceptible to not being diligent enough in protecting intellectual property because they frequently lack the resources and expertise available to large firms. As a result, the USPTO has set up a Web site, www.uspto.gov/smallbusiness, to provide

Learning Objective

1. Define the term *intellectual property* and describe its importance.

FIGURE 12.1

Common Mistakes
Firms Make in Regard
to Intellectual Property

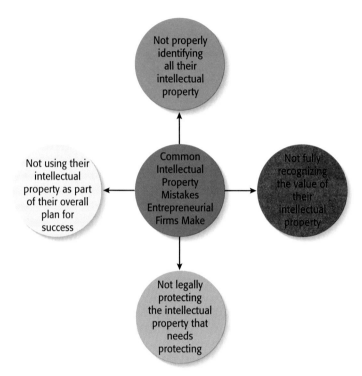

small businesses with information about intellectual property protection. If you currently have what you believe may be a patentable idea, go to this Web site to learn more about actions you may take to investigate this possibility.

Intellectual property is also an important part of our nation's economy and its competitive advantage in the world marketplace. "It's a huge issue," U.S. Commerce Secretary Carlos Gutierrez said. "There is so much of our economy that is linked to branded products, patented products, copyrights. So much of our economy thrives on creativity."[7]

Table 12.1   EXAMPLES OF INTELLECTUAL PROPERTY THAT TYPICALLY RESIDES WITHIN A MIDSIZED ENTREPRENEURIAL FIRM'S DEPARTMENTS

Department	Forms of Intellectual Property Typically Present	Usual Methods of Protection
Marketing	Names, slogans, logos, jingles, advertisements, brochures, pamphlets, ad copy under development, customer lists, prospect lists, and similar items	Trademark, copyright, and trade secret
Management	Recruiting brochures, employee handbooks, forms and checklists used by recruiters in qualifying and hiring candidates, written training materials, and company newsletters	Copyright and trade secret
Finance	Contractual forms, PowerPoint slides describing the company's financial performance, written methodologies explaining how the company handles its finances, and employee pay records	Copyright and trade secret
Management information systems	Web site design, Internet domain names, company-specific training manuals for computer equipment and software, original computer code, e-mail lists name registry	Copyright, trade secret, and Internet domain
Research and development	New and useful inventions and business processes, improvements to existing inventions and processes, and laboratory notes documenting invention discovery dates and charting the progress on various projects	Patent and trade secret

Determining What Intellectual Property to Legally Protect

Learning Objective

2. Specify the rules of thumb for determining whether a particular piece of intellectual property is worth the time and expense of protecting.

There are two primary rules of thumb for deciding if intellectual property protection should be pursued for a particular intellectual asset. First, a firm should determine if the intellectual property in question is directly related to its competitive advantage. For example, Amazon.com has a business method patent on its "one-click" ordering system, which is a nice feature of its Web site and is arguably directly related to its competitive advantage. Similarly, when Dogster launched a social networking Web site specifically designed for dog owners, it would have been foolish for the company not to trademark the Dogster name. In contrast, if a business develops a product or business method or produces printed material that isn't directly related to its competitive advantage, intellectual property protection may not be warranted.

The second primary criterion for deciding if intellectual property protection should be pursued is to determine whether an item has value in the marketplace. A common mistake that young companies make is to invent a product, spend a considerable amount of money to patent it, and find that the market for the product does not exist or that the existing market is too small to be worthy of pursuit. As discussed in Chapter 3, business ideas should be properly tested before a considerable amount of money is spent developing and legally protecting them. Owning the exclusive right to something no one wants is of little value. Similarly, if a company develops a logo for a special event, it is probably a waste of money to register it with the USPTO if there is a good chance the logo will not be used again.

On other occasions, obtaining intellectual property protection is crucial because if appropriate forms of protection are not obtained, the value of the intellectual property can be lost. This scenario played out for Dippin' Dots, a maker of ice cream treats. Curt Jones, Dippin' Dots' founder, invented a way of flash freezing ice cream mix in a manner that produces small beads of ice cream. The small beads of ice cream, which Dippin' Dots calls "Ice Cream of the Future," are flavorful and fun. Unfortunately, as illustrated in the "What Went Wrong?" feature, Dippin' Dots' patent on its unique way of producing ice cream was recently invalidated, and now the company has two new competitors that are producing ice cream treats very similar to what Dippin' Dots offers. Dippin' Dots' experience is a vivid reminder that a firm must follow the absolute letter of the law in obtaining intellectual property protection or the protection can be lost.

The Four Key Forms of Intellectual Property

Learning Objective

3. Discuss the four major forms of intellectual property: patents, trademarks, copyrights, and trade secrets.

Patents, trademarks, copyrights, and trade secrets are the four key forms of intellectual property. We discuss each form of intellectual property protection in the following sections. Intellectual property laws exist to encourage creativity and innovation by granting individuals who risk their time and money in creative endeavors exclusive rights to the fruits of their labors for a period of time. Intellectual property laws also help individuals make well-informed choices. For example, when a consumer sees a Panera Bread restaurant, she knows exactly what to expect because only Panera Bread is permitted to use the Panera Bread trademark for soups, signature sandwiches, and bakery products.

One special note about intellectual property laws is that it is up to entrepreneurs to take advantage of them and to safeguard their intellectual property once it is legally protected. Police forces and fire departments are available to quickly respond if an entrepreneur's buildings or other physical assets are threatened, but there are no intellectual property police forces or fire departments in existence. The courts prosecute individuals and companies that break

What Went WRONG?

Dippin' Dots: Why the USPTO Invalidated Its Patent and It Now Has Two New Competitors

www.dippindots.com

Dippin' Dots is an ice cream snack, sold by Dippin' Dots franchises in the food courts of malls and similar locations. The company was founded in 1987 by Curt Jones, a microbiologist. Jones pioneered the process of cryogenic encapsulation, which is a fancy way of saying he flash froze ice cream mix in a way that produced small beads of ice cream. The small beads of ice cream, which Dippin' Dots calls "Ice Cream of the Future," are flavorful, light, and fun. Simply buying a Dippin' Dots cup of ice cream is part of the experience. The ice cream beads are literally "poured" into a cup and are often described as "tingly and almost crunchy" when consumed.

Although Dippin' Dots is still going strong, the company experienced a major setback in 2007 when its patent was invalidated by the USPTO. Specifically, on February 9, 2007, the Federal Circuit Court ruled that Dippin' Dots' method of making frozen ice cream pellets was invalid because it was obvious. The ruling resulted from a lawsuit that Dippin' Dots filed against Mini Melts, a competitor that started selling a beaded ice cream treat, alleging trade dress infringement on the shape of its multicolored ice cream bits. The suit, *Dippin' Dots, Inc. v. Frosty Bites Distribution, LLL aka Mini Melts,* was unsuccessful. One of the arguments that Mini Melts used in undermining Dippin' Dots was that the company committed patent fraud by not disclosing that it had sold its ice cream product one year prior to applying for its patent. Technically, an inventor of a new product (or process) is required to apply for a patent within one year of inventing the product or the product is considered to be "public art" and the right to file for a patent is forfeited. An exception is made for sales made for testing or experimental purposes (such as in a feasibility test). But the sales must be made for one of these two purposes, and not for commercial purposes.

It turns out that Dippin' Dots and its founder Curt Jones sold novelty ice cream products to over 800 customers using a process very similar to the process that was eventually patented, and the sales took place more than one year before the filing of the patent. Mini Melts argued that the sales invalidated Dippin' Dots' patent, so Dippin' Dots had no right to sue it for trade dress infringement (for making a similar ice cream product).

The jury agreed with Mini Melts, and the District Court for the Northern District of Texas entered a judgment in favor of Mini Melts, finding that Dippin' Dots' patent was invalid. Dippin' Dots appealed to the Federal Circuit Court, which affirmed the lower court's decision. The result was—with a patent no longer protecting the exclusivity of its product—Dippin' Dots has two new competitors, Mini Melts and MolliCoolz, which are producing ice cream treats very similar to what Dippin' Dots offers.

This case is a stark reminder that not only the spirit, but the absolute letter of the law must be followed regarding intellectual property issues. More narrowly, it is a reminder for inventors and entrepreneurs to be particularly aware of the one-year rule for filing a patent application following the invention of a product or process.

Questions for Critical Thinking

1. In what ways could Dippin' Dots be hurt by its patent being invalidated? To what degree was Dippin' Dots' patent an important part of its competitive advantage?
2. How can an entrepreneur be sure that the "letter of the law" is followed when filing a patent application?
3. Look at the Web sites of Mini Melts and MolliCoolz. How similar are their products to what Dippin' Dots introduced to the marketplace? If Dippin' Dots' patent was solid, do you think the company would have solid grounds to sue Mini Melts and MolliCoolz for infringing on its patent?
4. How can Dippin' Dots differentiate itself from its competitors now that it can't stop its competitors from selling a product that is similar to what it sells?

Source: T. F. Zuber, S. J. Lazaris, "Protecting Your Process Patent: How Dippin' Dots May Make It More Difficult to Secure Process Patents After Prior Sales," www.zuberlaw.com (accessed September 16, 2008). Thomas F. Zuber, Esq. is the Managing Partner of Zuber & Taillieu LLP, practicing intellectual property protection and exploitation from its Los Angeles office. Spyros J. Lazaris, Esq. is a Counsel in the Los Angeles office of Zuber & Taillieu LLP, and the head of its patent and trademark prosecution department. The biographies of both attorneys may be viewed at www.zuberlaw.com.

intellectual property laws. However, the individual entrepreneur must understand intellectual property laws, safeguard intellectual property assets, and initiate litigation if intellectual property rights are infringed upon or violated.

There is a government-sponsored Web site, www.stopfakes.gov, that provides information about how to file a complaint if a business feels that a "knock off" product is infringing on its intellectual property. Increasingly, counterfeit goods are a problem for firms that have spent considerable resources to brand their products in ways that create value for customers. Counterfeit Callaway golf clubs and "fake" Louis Vuitton purses are examples of goods that counterfeiters target.

PATENTS

A **patent** is a grant from the government conferring the rights to exclude others from making, selling, or using an invention for the term of the patent.[21] The owner of the patent is granted a legal monopoly for a limited amount of time. However, a patent does not give its owner the right to make, use, or sell the invention; it gives the owner only the right to exclude others from doing so. This is a confusing issue for many entrepreneurs. If a company is granted a patent for an item, it is natural to assume that it could start making and selling the item immediately. But it cannot. A patent owner can legally make or sell the patented invention only if no other patents are infringed on by doing so.[22] For example, if an inventor obtained a patent on a computer chip and the chip needed technology patented earlier by Intel to work, the inventor would need to obtain permission from Intel to make and sell the chip. Intel may refuse permission or ask for a licensing fee for the use of its patented technology. Although this system may seem odd, it is really the only way the system could work. Many inventions are improvements on existing inventions, and the system allows the improvements to be patented, but only with the permission of the original inventors, who usually benefit by obtaining licensing income in exchange for their consent.[23]

Patent protection has deep roots in U.S. history and is the only form of intellectual property right expressly mentioned in the original articles of the U.S. Constitution. The first patent was granted in 1790 for a process of making potash, an ingredient in fertilizer. Patents are important because they grant inventors temporary, exclusive rights to market their inventions. This right gives inventors and their financial backers the opportunity to recoup their costs and earn a profit in exchange for the risks and costs they incur during the invention process. If it weren't for patent laws, inventors would have little incentive to invest time and money in new inventions. "No one would develop a drug if you didn't have a patent," Dr. William Haseltine, the CEO of Human Genome Sciences, a biotech firm, once said.[24]

Since the first patent was granted in 1790, the USPTO has granted over 7 million patents. Some inventors, and companies, are very prolific and have multiple patents. There is increasing interest in patents, as shown in Table 12.2,

Table 12.2   GROWTH IN PATENT APPLICATIONS IN THE UNITED STATES

	2006	2007	2008
Applications received	445,613	468,330	496,762
Patents issued	183,187	184,376	182,556
Total patents pending	1,003,884	1,112,517	1,208,076
Average time for approval	31.1 months	31.9 months	32.2 months

Source: United States Patent and Trademark Office, *Performance and Accountability Report for Fiscal Year 2008.*

as advances in technology spawn new inventions. The USPTO, the sole entity responsible for granting patents in the United States, is strained. At the end of 2008, there were 1,208,076 patent applications pending, and it took an average of 32.2 months to get a patent application approved. The USPTO has 6,055 full-time patent examiners to handle its patent caseload.

Types of Patents

There are three types of patents: utility patents, design patents, and plant patents. As shown in Figure 12.2, there are three basic requirements for a patent to be granted: The subject of the patent application must be (1) useful, (2) novel in relation to prior arts in the field, and (3) not obvious to a person of ordinary skill in the field.

Utility patents are the most common type of patent and cover what we generally think of as new inventions. Patents in this category may be granted to anyone who "invents or discovers any new and useful process, machine, manufacture, or composition of matter, or any new and useful improvement thereof."[25] The term of a utility patent is 20 years from the date of the initial application. After 20 years, the patent expires, and the invention falls into the public domain, which means that anyone can produce and sell the invention without paying the prior patent holder. Consider the pharmaceutical industry. Assume a drug produced by Pfizer is prescribed for you and that, when seeking to fill the prescription, your pharmacist tells you there is no generic equivalent available. The lack of a generic equivalent typically means that a patent owned by Pfizer protects the drug and that the 20-year term of the patent has not expired. If the pharmacist tells you there is a generic version of the drug available, that typically means the 20-year patent has expired and other companies are now making a drug chemically identical to Pfizer's. The price of the generic version of the drug is generally lower because the manufacturer of the generic version of the drug is not trying to recover the costs Pfizer (in this case) incurred to develop the product (the drug) in question.

A utility patent cannot be obtained for an "idea" or a "suggestion" for a new product or process. A complete description of the invention for which a utility patent is sought is required, including drawings and technical details. In addition, a patent must be applied for within one year of when a product or process was first offered for sale, put into public use, or was described in any printed publication, as illustrated in the Dippin' Dots case, or the right to obtain a patent is forfeited. The requirement that a patent application must be filed within one year of the milestones referred to previously is called the **one year after first use deadline**.

Recently, utility patent law has added business method patents, which have been of particular interest to Internet firms. A **business method patent** is a patent that protects an invention that is or facilitates a method of doing business. Patents for these purposes were not allowed in the United States until 1998, when a federal circuit court issued an opinion allowing a patent for a business method, holding that business methods, mathematical algorithms,

FIGURE 12.2

Three Basic Requirements for a Patent

The subject of the patent application, whether it is an invention, design, or business method, must be . . .

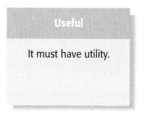

Useful	Novel	Not Obvious
It must have utility.	It must be different from what has come before (i.e., not in the "prior art").	It must be not obvious to a person of ordinary skill in the field.

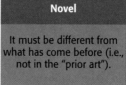

and software are patentable as long as they produce useful, tangible, and concrete results. This ruling opened a Pandora's box and has caused many firms to scramble to try to patent their business methods. Since 1998, the most notable business method patents awarded have been Amazon.com's one-click ordering system, Priceline.com's "name-your-price" business model, and Netflix's method for allowing customers to set up a rental list of movies they want mailed to them. Activities associated with a business method patent can be an important source of competitive advantage for a firm.

Design patents are the second most common type of patent and cover the invention of new, original, and ornamental designs for manufactured products.[26] A design patent is good for 14 years from the grant date. While a utility patent protects the way an invention is used and works, a design patent protects the way it looks. As a result, if an entrepreneur invented a new version of the computer mouse, it would be prudent to apply for a utility patent to cover the way the mouse works and for a design patent to protect the way the mouse looks. Although all computer mice perform essentially the same function, they can be ornamentally designed in an infinite number of ways. As long as each new design is considered by the USPTO to be novel and nonobvious, it is eligible for design patent protection. This is not a trivial issue in that product design is increasingly becoming an important source of competitive advantage for many firms producing many different types of products. Hewlett-Packard, for example, is emphasizing unique designs for its personal computers as a way to "personalize" what is essentially a commodity-like product.

Plant patents protect new varieties of plants that can be reproduced asexually. Such plants are reproduced by grafting or crossbreeding rather than by planting seeds. The new variety can be different from previous plants in its resistance to disease or drought or in its scent, appearance, color, or productivity. Thus, a new color for a rose or a new type of hybrid vegetable would be eligible for plant patent protection. The term for plant patent protection is 20 years from the date of the original application.

Table 12.3 provides a summary of the three forms of patent protection, the types of inventions the patents cover, and the duration of the patents.

Who Can Apply for a Patent?

Only the inventor of a product can apply for a patent. If two or more people make an invention jointly, they must apply for the patent together. Someone who simply heard about the design of a product or is trying to patent something that is in the public domain may not apply for a patent.

There are notable exceptions to these rules. First, if an invention is made during the course of the inventor's employment, the employer typically is

Table 12.3 SUMMARY OF THE THREE FORMS OF PATENT PROTECTION, THE TYPES OF INVENTIONS THE PATENTS COVER, AND THE DURATION OF THE PATENTS

Type of Patent	Types of Inventions Covered	Duration
Utility	New or useful process, machine, manufacture, or composition of material or any new and useful improvement thereof	20 years from the date of the original application
Design	Invention of new, original, and ornamental designs for manufactured products	14 years from the date of the original application
Plant	Any new varieties of plants that can be reproduced asexually	20 years from the date of the original application

assigned the right to apply for the patent through an **assignment of invention agreement** signed by the employee as part of the employment agreement. A second exception is that the rights to apply for an invention can be sold. This option can be an important source of revenue for entrepreneurial firms. If a firm has an invention that it doesn't want to pursue on its own, the rights to apply for a patent on the invention can be sold to another party.

The Process of Obtaining a Patent

Learning Objective

4. Describe the six-step process for obtaining a patent.

Obtaining a patent is a six-step process, as illustrated in Figure 12.3 and as we discuss here. The costs involved, which vary depending on the complexity of the device, range from between $4,000 to $6,500 to patent a relatively simple device, like a new type of paper clip, to between $9,000 and $12,000 to patent a moderately complex device, like a power hand tool, to $25,000 or more to patent a medical device. The costs involved include attorney fees and USPTO filing fees. Costs go up substantially when trying to patent a highly complex product.[27]

Step 1   **Make sure the invention is practical.** As mentioned earlier, there are two rules of thumb for making the decision to patent. Intellectual property that is worth protecting typically is directly related to the competitive advantage of the firm seeking the protection or has independent value in the marketplace.

Step 2   **Document when the invention was made.** Put together a set of documents clearly stating when the invention was first thought of, dates on which experiments were conducted in perfecting it, and the date it was first used and found to operate satisfactorily. Inventors should get in the habit of filling out an "invention logbook" on a daily basis to record their activities. An **invention logbook** documents the dates and activities related to the development of a particular invention. As soon as an inventor has an idea for an invention, a complete description of the invention should be written down, sketches should be made of it, and how it works should be described in detail. The inventor should then sign and date the documents and indicate that he or she is the inventor. If possible, a notary or another party without a financial interest in the invention should witness the inventor's signature. This step is important because if two inventors independently develop essentially the same invention, the right to apply for the patent belongs to the person who came up with it first. Some countries, including the United States, adhere to the **first-to-invent rule** rather than the first-to-file rule, meaning that the first person to invent an item or process is given preference

FIGURE 12.3

The Process of Obtaining a Patent

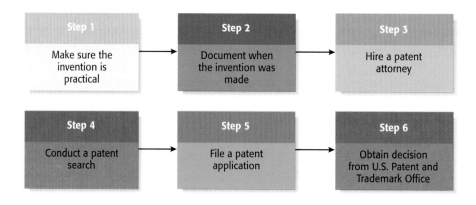

over another person who is first to file a patent application. If there is a dispute regarding who was first to invent a product, the dispute is resolved in an administrative proceeding known as an **interference** that a judge at the USPTO presides over.

Step 3   **Hire a patent attorney.** It is highly recommended that an inventor work with a patent attorney. Even though there are "patent-it-yourself" books and Web sites on the market, it is generally naïve for an entrepreneur to think that the patent process can be successfully navigated without expert help. As an indication of the difficulty of writing a patent application, the USPTO requires all attorneys and agents to pass a tough exam before they can interact with the agency on behalf of a client.

Step 4   **Conduct a patent search.** To be patentable, an invention must be novel and different enough from what already exists. A patent attorney typically spends several hours searching the USPTO's database (which is available online at www.uspto.gov) to study similar patents. After the search is completed and the patents that are similar to the invention in question have been carefully studied, the patent attorney renders an opinion regarding the probability of obtaining a patent on the new invention.

Step 5   **File a patent application.** The fifth step, if the inventor decides to proceed, is to file a patent application with the USPTO in Washington, D.C. Unlike copyright and trademark applications, which can be prepared and filed easily by their owners, patent applications are highly technical and almost always require expert assistance. Approximately 80 percent of inventors retain patent attorneys or agents to prepare and file their patent applications.[28]

Step 6   **Obtain a decision from the USPTO.** When the USPTO receives a patent application, it is given a serial number, assigned to an examiner, and then waits to be examined. The patent examiner investigates the application and issues a written report ("Office Action") to the applicant's patent attorney, often asking for modifications to the application. Most of the interactions that applicants have with the USPTO are by mail. Occasionally, an inventor and a lawyer will meet face to face with a patent examiner to discuss the invention and the written report. There is room to negotiate with the patent office to try to make an invention patentable. Eventually, a yes-or-no decision will be rendered. A rejected application can be appealed, but appeals are rare and expensive.

One provision of patent law that is particularly important to entrepreneurs is that the USPTO allows inventors to file a **provisional patent application** for utility patents, pending the preparation and filing of a complete application. A provisional patent application provides the means to establish an early effective filing date for a nonprovisional patent application, and allows the term "Patent Pending" to be applied.

In some instances, entrepreneurs license their patents to larger firms, which have nationwide distribution channels to market a product. In fact, consumer products companies, like Kraft and General Mills, which at one time relied strictly on their own scientists to develop new products, now have formal programs for inventors and entrepreneurs to submit product ideas, as illustrated in the "Partnering for Success" feature. One requirement most large firms make is that an idea must be patented or a patent must be applied for before they will consider evaluating it.

Partnering for SUCCESS
Entrepreneurs and Large Firms: Partnering to Bring Patented Products to Market

A common problem that inventors and entrepreneurs have is achieving distribution of their products. Gary Schwartzberg is a case in point. Schwartzberg, along with a partner, developed a new type of bagel. Dubbed the "Bageler," the bagel was tube-shaped and filled with cream cheese. Schwartzberg was able to get the product into supermarkets and schools in South Florida, where he lived, but couldn't achieve wider distribution. He finally mailed Kraft a box of his cream-cheese-filled bagels with a proposal. He picked Kraft because he wanted to use Philadelphia Cream Cheese (a Kraft product) to fill the bagel.

By coincidence, Kraft had been working on a similar product but couldn't get it right. Schwartzberg had a patented process for "encapsulating" the cream cheese in the center of the bagel without the cream cheese escaping during the baking process. Kraft bit and after some back and forth, Schwartzberg and Kraft hammered out a deal. Schwartzberg told the *Wall Street Journal* that he can't discuss the details of the deal because of a confidentiality agreement with Kraft, but says it's structured as a strategic alliance and he "has skin in the game." Schwartzberg's product, which is now called Bagel-fuls, is sold nationwide by Kraft Foods.

Entrepreneurs and inventors are finding that large consumer products companies are increasingly interested in what they have to offer. For example, in 2006, Kraft launched a program and Web site at http://brands.kraftfoods.com/innovatewithkraft that actively seeks out small businesses and inventors as partners for product development. The company gets 40 to 50 submissions per month. Dozens of new ideas, resulting from the site, have become new products or enhancements to existing products, the company says. Kraft says it looks at new ideas on a case-by-case basis, and agreements may be structured as strategic partnerships, licensing agreements, or joint developments.

General Mills has a program similar to Kraft's called the General Mills Worldwide Innovation Network, or

G-Win, at www.generalmills.com/corporate/open_innovation/index.aspx. Like Kraft, General Mills is getting a consistent stream of new ideas, and says that 300 percent more ideas have come into the company since it launched the Web site, which includes an online submission form. Procter & Gamble also has a well-developed idea submission program available at www.pgconnectdevelop.com.

Prior to approaching a company like Kraft or General Mills, an inventor or an entrepreneur should have intellectual property protection on the product they're trying to interest the large firm in. Some large companies, like General Mills and Procter & Gamble, require that a submission be covered by an existing patent or that a patent-pending application has been filed before they'll consider an idea.

Questions for Critical Thinking

1. For an inventor or entrepreneur, what are the upsides to working with a company like Kraft or General Mills? What, if any, are the downsides?
2. Why do you think Kraft, General Mills, and similar companies seek ideas from independent entrepreneurs? Why not bolster their own research and development departments and develop ideas in-house?
3. Look at the idea submission Web sites for the three companies mentioned in this feature. What are the similarities and what are the differences among these Web site? Which site is the easiest to navigate and why?
4. In most cases, do you think inventors and entrepreneurs get a fair shake when they license a product to a large firm? What steps should entrepreneurs take to make sure they are getting a fair deal?

Source: Wall Street Journal (Eastern Edition) by S. Coval. Copyright 2005 by Dow Jones & Company.

Patent Infringement

Patent infringement takes place when one party engages in the unauthorized use of another party's patent. A typical example of an infringement claim was that initiated by Alacritech, a start-up firm, which claimed that Microsoft violated two of its patents on technology used to speed the performance of computers connected to networks. According to court documents, Alacritech showed its technology to Microsoft in 2003, hoping that Microsoft would license it. But Microsoft passed on the offer and later announced a surprisingly similar technology, called Chimney. Alacritech again offered to license the technology to

Microsoft but was rebuffed. In response, Alacritech filed suit against Microsoft in 2004. Microsoft claimed that its technology was developed independently.[29] In April 2005, the U.S. District Court in San Francisco sided with Alacritech and filed a preliminary injunction against Microsoft, preventing it from shipping products that contained the contested technology. In mid-2005, the suit was settled out of court, with Microsoft agreeing to license Alacritech's technology.[30]

The tough part about patent infringement cases is that they are costly to litigate, which puts start-up firms and their entrepreneurs at quite a disadvantage. While there is no way of knowing how much it cost Alacritech to sue Microsoft, a typical patent-infringement suit, according to *Fortune Small Business*, costs each side at least $500,000 to litigate.[31] The number of patent infringement cases in the United States alone has doubled in the last 10 years. Today, nearly 3,000 U.S. cases are filed a year.[32] This statistic suggests that all firms should constantly protect their intellectual property.

TRADEMARKS

A **trademark** is any word, name, symbol, or device used to identify the source or origin of products or services and to distinguish those products or services from others. All businesses want to be recognized by their potential clientele and use their names, logos, and other distinguishing features to enhance their visibility. Trademarks also provide consumers with useful information. For example, consumers know what to expect when they see an Abercrombie & Fitch store in a mall. Think of how confusing it would be if any retail store could use the name Abercrombie & Fitch.

As is the case with patents, trademarks have a rich history. Archaeologists have found evidence that as far back as 3,500 years ago, potters made distinctive marks on their articles of pottery to distinguish their work from others. But consider a more modern example. The original name that Jerry Yang and David Filo, the cofounders of Yahoo!, selected for their Internet directory service was "Jerry's Guide to the World Wide Web." Not too catchy, is it? The name was later changed to Yahoo!, which caught on with early adopters of the Internet and now is one of the most recognizable trademarks in America.

Noah Berger/Bloomberg News/Landov

This flag, which depicts Cisco Systems' trademark, flies in front of the company's headquarters in San Jose, California. Companies like Cisco Systems fiercely protect their trademarks, which are the most compelling aspects of their brands. To be thorough, Cisco Systems has separately trademarked its name and its familiar rendition of the Golden Gate Bridge, which appears below its name on the flag. Cisco Systems has also trademarked its tagline, which is "Empowering the Internet Generation."

The Four Types of Trademarks

Learning Objective

5. Identify the four types of trademarks.

There are four types of trademarks: trademarks, service marks, collective marks, and certification marks (see Table 12.4). Trademarks and service marks are of the greatest interest to entrepreneurs.

Trademarks, as described previously, include any word, name, symbol, or device used to identify and distinguish one company's products from another's. Trademarks are used in the advertising and promotion of tangible products, such as Nokia for cell phones, Nike for athletic shoes, and Electronic Arts for electronic games.

Service marks are similar to ordinary trademarks, but they are used to identify the services or intangible activities of a business rather than a business's physical product. Service marks include *The Princeton Review* for test prep services, eBay for online auctions, and AT&T for cell phone service.

Collective marks are trademarks or service marks used by the members of a cooperative, association, or other collective group, including marks indicating membership in a union or similar organization. The marks belonging to the American Bar Association, The International Franchise Association, and the Entrepreneurs' Organization are examples of collective marks.

Finally, **certification marks** are marks, words, names, symbols, or devices used by a person other than its owner to certify a particular quality about a product or service. The most familiar certification mark is the UL mark, which certifies that a product meets the safety standards established by Underwriters Laboratories. Other examples are the Good Housekeeping Seal of Approval, Stilton Cheese (a product from the Stilton region in England), and 100% Napa Valley (from grapes grown in the Napa Valley of northern California).

Table 12.4 SUMMARY OF THE FOUR FORMS OF TRADEMARK PROTECTION, THE TYPE OF MARKS THE TRADEMARKS COVER, AND THE DURATION OF THE TRADEMARKS

Type of Trademark	Type of Marks Covered	Duration
Trademark	Any word, name, symbol, or device used to identify and distinguish one company's goods from another	Renewable every 10 years, as long as the mark remains in use
	Examples: *Apple, Starbucks, FitBit, Sprig Toys, Netflix, TOMS*	
Service mark	Similar to trademarks; are used to identify the services or intangible activities of a business, rather than a business's physical products	Renewable every 10 years, as long as the mark remains in use
	Examples: *1-800-FLOWERS*; *Ameritrade, Amazon.com, Clean Air Lawn Care, eBay, Overstock.com, ZENhome*	
Collective mark	Trademarks or service marks used by the members of a cooperative, association, or other collective group	Renewable every 10 years, as long as the mark remains in use
	Examples: *Information Technology Industry Council, International Franchise Association, Rotary International*	
Certification mark	Marks, words, names, symbols, or devices used by a person other than its owner to certify a particular quality about a good or service	Renewable every 10 years, as long as the mark remains in use
	Examples: *100% Napa Valley, Florida Oranges, National Organic Program, Underwriters Laboratories*	

What Is Protected Under Trademark Law?

Trademark law, which falls under the **Lanham Act**, passed in 1946, protects the following items:

■ **Words:** All combinations of words are eligible for trademark registration, including single words, short phrases, and slogans. Ready Solar, Activate Drinks, and the National Football League are examples of words and phrases that have been registered as trademarks.

■ **Numbers and letters:** Numbers and letters are eligible for registration. Examples include 3M, MSNBC, and AT&T. Alphanumeric marks are also registerable, such as 1-800-FREE-411.

■ **Designs or logos:** A mark consisting solely of a design, such as the Golden Gate Bridge for Cisco Systems or the Nike swoosh logo, may be eligible for registration. The mark must be distinctive rather than generic. As a result, no one can claim exclusive rights to the image of the Golden Gate Bridge, but Cisco Systems can trademark its unique depiction of the bridge. Composite marks consist of a word or words in conjunction with a design. An example is the trademark for Zephyrhill's bottled water, which includes Zephyrhill's name below a picture of mountain scenery and water.

■ **Sounds:** Distinctive sounds can be trademarked, although this form of trademark protection is rare. The most recognizable examples are the MGM's lion's roar, the familiar four-tone sound that accompanies "Intel Inside" commercials, and the Yahoo! yodel.

■ **Fragrances:** The fragrance of a product may be registerable as long as the product is not known for the fragrance or the fragrance does not enhance the use of the product. As a result, the fragrance of a perfume or room deodorizer is not eligible for trademark protection, whereas stationery treated with a special fragrance in most cases would be.

■ **Shapes:** The shape of a product, as long as it has no impact on the product's function, can be trademarked. The unique shape of the Apple iPod has received trademark protection.[33] The Coca-Cola Company has trademarked its famous curved bottle. The shape of the bottle has no effect on the quality of the bottle or the beverage it holds; therefore, the shape is not functional.

■ **Colors:** A trademark may be obtained for a color as long as the color is not functional. For example, Nexium, a medicine pill that treats acid reflux disease, is purple and is marketed as "the purple pill." The color of the pill has no bearing on its functionality; therefore it can be protected by trademark protection.

■ **Trade dress:** The manner in which a product is "dressed up" to appeal to customers is protectable. This category includes the overall packaging, design, and configuration of a product. As a result, the overall look of a business is protected as its trade dress. In a famous case in 1992, *Two Pesos, Inc., v. Taco Cabana International Inc.*, the U.S. Supreme Court protected the overall design, colors, and configuration of a chain of Mexican restaurants from a competitor using a similar decor.[34]

Trademark protection is very broad and provides many opportunities for businesses to differentiate themselves from one another. The key for young entrepreneurial firms is to trademark their products and services in ways that draw positive attention to them in a compelling manner.

Exclusions from Trademark Protection

There are notable exclusions from trademark protection that are set forth in the U.S. Trademark Act:

- **Immoral or scandalous matter:** A company cannot trademark immoral or scandalous matter, including profane words.
- **Deceptive matter:** Marks that are deceptive cannot be registered. For example, a food company couldn't register the name "Fresh Florida Oranges" if the oranges weren't from Florida.
- **Descriptive marks:** Marks that are merely descriptive of a product or service cannot be trademarked. For example, an entrepreneur couldn't design a new type of golf ball and try to obtain trademark protection on the words *golf ball*. The words describe a type of product rather than a brand of product, such as Titleist or MaxFli, and are needed by all golf ball manufacturers to be competitive. This issue is a real concern for the manufacturers of very popular products. Recently, Xerox was in danger of losing trademark protection for the Xerox name because of the common use of the word *Xerox* as a verb (e.g., "I am going to Xerox this").
- **Surnames:** A trademark consisting primarily of a surname, such as Anderson or Smith, is typically not protectable. An exception is a surname combined with other wording that is intended to trademark a distinct product, such as William's Fresh Fish or Smith's Computer Emporium.

The Process of Obtaining a Trademark

As illustrated in Figure 12.4, selecting and registering a trademark is a three-step process. Once a U.S. trademark has been used in interstate commerce, it can be registered with the USPTO for a renewable term of 10 years and can theoretically remain registered forever as long as the trademark stays in use.

Technically, a trademark does not need to be registered to receive protection and to prevent other companies from using confusingly similar marks. Once a mark is used in commerce, such as in an advertisement, it is protected. There are several distinct advantages, however, in registering a trademark with the USPTO: Registered marks are allowed nationwide priority for use of the mark, registered marks may use the U.S. trademark registration symbol (®), and registered marks carry with them the right to block the importation of infringing goods into the United States. The right to use the trademark registration symbol is particularly important. Attaching the trademark symbol to a product (e.g., My Yahoo!®) provides notice of a trademark owner's registration. This posting allows an owner to recover damages in an infringement action and helps reduce an offender's claim that it didn't know that a particular name or logo was trademarked.

There are three steps in selecting and registering a trademark:

Step 1 Select an appropriate mark. There are several rules of thumb to help business owners and entrepreneurs select appropriate trademarks. First, a mark, whether it is a name, logo, design, or

FIGURE 12.4

The Process of Obtaining a Trademark

fragrance, should display creativity and strength. Marks that are inherently distinctive, such as the McDonald's Golden Arches; made-up words, such as *Google* and *eBay*; and words that evoke particular images, such as *Double Delight Ice Cream*, are strong trademarks. Second, words that create a favorable impression about a product or service are helpful. A name such as *Safe and Secure Childcare* for a day care center positively resonates with parents.

Step 2 **Perform a trademark search.** Once a trademark has been selected, a trademark search should be conducted to determine if the trademark is available. If someone else has already established rights to the proposed mark, it cannot be used. There are several ways to conduct a trademark search, from self-help searches to hiring a firm specializing in trademark clearance checks. The search should include both national and regional and local searches in any locales in which business will be conducted. If the trademark will be used overseas, the search should also include the countries where the trademark will be used.

Although it is not necessary to hire an attorney to conduct a trademark search, it is probably a good idea to do so. Self-searches can also be conducted. A simple-to-use search engine is available at the USPTO's Web site (www.uspto.org). Using this Web site, a person can check the agency's database of three million registered, abandoned, canceled, and expired marks and pending applications. Adopting a trademark without conducting a trademark search is risky. If a mark is challenged as an infringement, a company may have to destroy all its goods that bear the mark (including products, business cards, stationery, signs, and so on) and then select a new mark. The cost of refamiliarizing customers with an existing product under a new name or logo could be substantial.

Step 3 **Create rights in the trademark.** The final step in establishing a trademark is to create rights in the mark. In the United States, if the trademark is inherently distinctive (think of Starbucks, iTunes, or Nokia), the first person to use the mark becomes its owner. If the mark is descriptive, such as BUFFERIN for buffered aspirin, using the mark merely begins the process of developing a secondary meaning necessary to create full trademark protection. **Secondary meaning** arises when, over time, consumers start to identify a trademark with a specific product. For example, the name CHAP STICK for lip balm was originally considered to be descriptive, and thus not afforded trademark protection. As people started to think of CHAP STICK as lip balm, it met the threshold of secondary meaning and was able to be trademarked.

There are two ways that the USPTO can offer further protection for firms concerned about maintaining the exclusive rights to their trademarks. First, a person can file an **intent-to-use trademark application**. This is an application based on the applicant's intention to use a trademark. Once this application is filed, the owner obtains the benefits of registration. The benefits are lost, however, if the owner does not use the mark in business within six months of registration. Further protection can be obtained by filing a formal application for a trademark. The application must include a drawing of the trademark and a filing fee (ranging from $275 to $375, depending on how the application is filed). After a trademark application is filed, an examining attorney at the USPTO determines if the trademark can be registered.

COPYRIGHTS

A **copyright** is a form of intellectual property protection that grants to the owner of a work of authorship the legal right to determine how the work is used and to obtain the economic benefits from the work.[35] The work must be in a tangible form, such as a book, operating manual, magazine article, musical score, computer software program, or architectural drawing. If something is not in a tangible form, such as a speech that has never been recorded or saved on a computer disk, copyright law does not protect it.

Businesses typically possess a treasure trove of copyrightable material, as illustrated earlier in Table 12.1. A work does not have to have artistic merit to be eligible for copyright protection. As a result, things such as operating manuals, advertising brochures, and training videos qualify for protection. The Copyright Revision Act of 1976 governs copyright law in the United States. Under the law, an original work is protected automatically from the time it is created and put into a tangible form whether it is published or not. The first copyright in the United States was granted on May 31, 1790, to a Philadelphia educator named John Barry for a spelling book.

What Is Protected by a Copyright?

Learning Objective

6. Identify the types of material that are eligible for copyright protection.

Copyright laws protect "original works of authorship" that are fixed in a tangible form of expression. The primary categories of material that can be copyrighted follow:

■ **Literary works:** Anything written down is a literary work, including books, poetry, reference works, speeches, advertising copy, employee manuals, games, and computer programs. Characters found in literary works are protectable if they possess a high degree of distinctiveness. A character that looks and acts like Garfield, the cartoon cat, would infringe on the copyright that protects Garfield.

■ **Musical compositions:** A musical composition, including any accompanying words, that is in a fixed form (e.g., a musical score, cassette tape, CD, or an MP3 file) is protectable. The owner of the copyright is usually the composer and possibly a lyricist. **Derivative works**, which are works that are new renditions of something that is already copyrighted, are also copyrightable. As a result of this provision, a musician who performs a unique rendition of a song written and copyrighted by Lil Wayne, Beyonce, or the Jonas Brothers, for example, can obtain a copyright on his or her effort. Of course, each of these artists would have to consent to the infringement on its copyright of the original song before the new song could be used commercially, which is a common way that composers earn extra income.

■ **Computer software:** In 1980, the United States passed the **Computer Software Copyright Act**, which amended previous copyright acts. Now, all forms of computer programs are protected.

■ **Dramatic works:** A dramatic work is a theatrical performance, such as a play, comedy routine, newscast, movie, or television show. An entire dramatic work can be protected under a single copyright. As a result, a dramatic work such as a television show doesn't need a separate copyright for the video and audio portions of the show.

■ **Pantomimes and choreographic works:** A pantomime is a performance that uses gestures and facial expressions rather than words to communicate a situation. Choreography is the arrangement of dance movements. Copyright laws in these areas protect ballets, dance movements, and mime works.

■ **Pictorial, graphic, and sculptural works:** This is a broad category that includes photographs, prints, art reproductions, cartoons, maps, globes, jewelry, fabrics, games, technical drawings, diagrams, posters, toys, sculptures, and charts.

Other categories of items covered by copyright law include motion pictures and other audiovisual works, sound recordings, and architectural works.

As can be seen, copyright law provides broad protection for authors and the creators of other types of copyrightable work. The most common mistake entrepreneurs make in this area is not thinking broadly enough about what they should copyright.

Exclusions from Copyright Protection

There are exclusions from copyright protection. The main exclusion is that copyright laws cannot protect ideas. For example, an entrepreneur may have the idea to open a football-themed restaurant. The idea itself is not eligible for copyright protection. However, if the entrepreneur writes down specifically what the football-themed restaurant will look like and how it would operate, that description is copyrightable. The legal principle describing this concept is called the **idea–expression dichotomy**. An idea is not copyrightable, but the specific expression of an idea is.

Other exclusions from copyright protection include facts (e.g., population statistics), titles (e.g., *Introduction to Entrepreneurship*), and lists of ingredients (e.g., recipes).

How to Obtain a Copyright

As mentioned, copyright law protects any work of authorship the moment it assumes a tangible form. Technically, it is not necessary to provide a copyright notice or register work with the U.S. Copyright Office to be protected by copyright legislation. The following steps can be taken, however, to enhance the protection offered by the copyright statutes.

First, copyright protection can be enhanced for anything written by attaching the copyright notice, or "**copyright bug**" as it is sometimes called. The bug—a "c" inside a circle—typically appears in the following form: © [first year of publication] [author or copyright owner]. Thus, the notice at the bottom of a magazine ad for Dell Inc.'s computers in 2009 would read © 2009 Dell Inc. By placing this notice at the bottom of a document, an author (or company) can prevent someone from copying the work without permission and claiming that they did not know that the work was copyrighted. Substitutes for the copyright bug include the word "Copyright" and the abbreviation "Copr."

Second, further protection can be obtained by registering a work with the U.S. Copyright Office. Filing a simple form and depositing one or two samples of the work with the U.S. Copyright Office completes the registration process. The need to supply a sample depends on the nature of the item involved. Obviously, one could not supply one or two samples of an original painting. The current cost of obtaining a copyright is $30 per item. Although the $30 fee seems modest, in many cases it is impractical for a prolific author to register everything he or she creates. In all cases, however, it is recommended that the copyright bug be attached to copyrightable work and that registration be contemplated on a case-by-case basis. A copyright can be registered at any time, but filing promptly is recommended and makes it easier to sue for copyright infringement.

Copyrights last a long time. According to current law, any work created on or after January 1, 1978, is protected for the life of the author plus 70 years. For works made for hire, the duration of the copyright is 95 years from publication or 120 years from creation, whichever is shorter. For works created before 1978, the duration times vary, depending on when the work was created. After a copyright expires, the work goes into the public domain, meaning it becomes available for anyone's use.

Copyright Infringement

Copyright infringement is a growing problem around the world, with estimates of the costs to owners at more than $20 billion per year. For example, less than a week after the film was released in the United States, bootleg video discs of the original Harry Potter movie were reported to be for sale in at least two Asian countries. The Black Crowes recently sued Gretchen Wilson (and two other parties) claiming that Wilson's song "Work Hard, Play Harder" was a "little too similar to their song 'Jealous Again.'"[36] **Copyright infringement** occurs when one work derives from another, is an exact copy, or shows substantial similarity to the original work. To prove infringement, a copyright owner is required to show that the alleged infringer had prior access to the copyrighted work and that the work is substantially similar to the owner's.

There are many ways to prevent infringement. For example, a technique frequently used to guard against the illegal copying of software code is to embed and hide in the code useless information, such as the birth dates and addresses of the authors. It's hard for infringers to spot useless information if they are simply cutting and pasting large amounts of code from one program to another. If software code is illegally copied and an infringement suit is filed, it is difficult for the accused party to explain why the (supposedly original) code included the birth dates and addresses of its accusers. Similarly, some publishers of maps, guides, and other reference works will deliberately include bits of phony information in their products, such as fake streets, nonexistent railroad crossings, and so on, to try to catch copiers. Again, it would be pretty hard for someone who copied someone else's copyrighted street guide to explain why the name of a fake street was included.[37]

Current law permits limited infringement of copyrighted material. Consider **fair use**, which is the limited use of copyrighted material for purposes such as criticism, comment, news reporting, teaching, or scholarship. This provision is what allows textbook authors to repeat quotes from magazine articles (as long as

The rampant illegal downloading and sharing of music—copyright infringement—is a major challenge the music industry is trying to overcome. Hackers are always looking for a new way to skirt the law.

Peter Arnold, Inc./KM-71-05-05.JPG

the original source is cited), movie critics to show clips from movies, and teachers to distribute portions of newspaper articles. The reasoning behind the law is that the benefit to the public from such uses outweighs any harm to the copyright owner. Other situations in which copyrighted material may be used to a limited degree without fear of infringement include parody, reproduction by libraries, and making a single backup copy of a computer program or a digital music file for personal use.

There are limits, however, to the extent that fair use can be legitimately claimed, as illustrated in the "Savvy Entrepreneurial Firm" feature.

Copyrights and the Internet

Every day, vast quantities of material are posted on the Internet and can be downloaded or copied by anyone with a computer. Because the information is stored somewhere on a computer or Internet server, it is in a tangible form and probably qualifies for copyright protection. As a result, anyone who downloads material from the Internet and uses it for personal purposes should be cautious and realize that copyright laws are just as applicable for material on the Internet as they are for material purchased from a bookstore or borrowed from a library. Because the Internet is still fairly new, the courts have been busy sorting out Internet-related copyright issues.

Copyright laws, particularly as they apply to the Internet, are sometimes difficult to follow, and it is easy for people to dismiss them as contrary to common sense. For example, say that a golf instructor in Phoenix posted a set of "golf tips" on his Web site for his students to use as they prepare for their lessons. Because the notes are on a Web site, anyone can download the notes and use them. As a result, suppose that another golf instructor, in Dallas, ran across the golf tips, downloaded them, and decided to distribute them to his students. Under existing law, the second golf instructor probably violated the intellectual property rights of the first. Arguably, he should have gotten permission from the first golf instructor before using the notes even if the Web site didn't include any information about how to contact the first instructor. To many people, this scenario doesn't make sense. The first golf instructor put his notes on a public Web site, didn't include any information about how to obtain permission to use them, and didn't even include information about how he could be contacted. In addition, he made no attempt to protect the notes, such as posting them on a password-protected Web page. Still, intellectual property rights apply, and the second instructor runs the risk of a copyright infringement suit.

There are a number of techniques available for entrepreneurs and Webmasters to prevent unauthorized material from being copied from a Web site. Password protecting the portion of a site containing sensitive or proprietary information is a common first step. In addition, there are a number of technical protection tools available on the market that limit access to or the use of online information, including selected use of encryption, digital watermarking (hidden copyright messages), and digital fingerprinting (hidden serial numbers or a set of characteristics that tend to distinguish an object from other similar objects).

TRADE SECRETS

Most companies, including start-ups, have a wealth of information that is critical to their success but does not qualify for patent, trademark, or copyright protection. Some of this information is confidential and needs to be kept secret to help a firm maintain its competitive advantage. An example is a company's customer list. A company may have been extremely diligent over time tracking the preferences

Savvy Entrepreneurial FIRM

Protecting Intellectual Property: Elvis's Memory, and Intellectual Property, Live On

www.elvis.com

Savvy owners of intellectual property are always on the lookout for people who infringe on their intellectual property and take legal action when necessary. In 2003, this scenario played out in a dispute involving a company named Passport Video and the copyright holders of music and videos produced by the late Elvis Presley.

Elvis, affectionately known as "The King" of rock and roll, was a musical icon for more than 20 years, until his death on August 16, 1977. During his career, Elvis was very prolific, and a wide variety of people own the copyrights to his music, videos, and films. In the early 2000s, Passport Video, a video production company, produced a video documentary of Elvis's life, named *The Definitive Elvis*. The documentary, which included 16 one-hour episodes, focused on every aspect of Elvis's life, and was priced at $99.00. Each episode contained shots of Elvis performing—many of which were taken from sources that are copyrighted and owned by Elvis Presley Enterprises or others. Passport did not get permission to use the material. As a result, the copyright holders, who caught wind of the production of the video, got together and in August 2003 decided to sue Passport for copyright infringement.

Passport mounted a defense, claiming that its use of the copyrighted material was fair use and that it had spent over $2 million producing and marketing the documentary. Fair use is a doctrine in U.S. copyright law that allows limited use of copyrighted material without requiring permission from the copyright holder. In general, the following uses are protected under this doctrine:

- Quotation of the copyrighted work for review or criticism or in a scholarly or technical work
- Use in a parody or satire
- Brief quotation in a news report
- Reproduction by a teacher or a student of a small part of the work to illustrate a lesson
- Incidental reproduction of a work in a newsreel or broadcast of an event being reported
- Reproduction of a work in a legislative or judicial proceeding

After listening to both sides, the U.S. District Court ruled in favor of the plaintiffs, saying that fair use didn't apply and Passport should have obtained the appropriate copyright permissions.

Passport persisted, appealing the decision to the Ninth Circuit Court of Appeals, arguing that its documentary of Elvis's life constituted scholarly research and should therefore be protected under fair use. The U.S. District Court disagreed and affirmed the ruling of the lower court. In its ruling, the court said, "The King is dead. His legacy, and those that wish to profit from it, remain very much alive." The court found that Passport's documentary was for commercial use rather than scholarly research, although the commercial nature of the project was not the deciding factor. Instead, the extent to which the copyrighted material was used tipped the decision for the court, which referred to the lower court's original assessment in its ruling. In its decision, the Ninth Circuit Court of Appeals, quoting from the decision of the lower court, said:

Passport's use of clips from television appearances, although in most cases of short duration, were repeated numerous times throughout the tapes. While using a small number of clips to reference an event for biographical purposes seems fair, using a clip over and over will likely no longer serve a biographical purpose. Additionally, some of the clips were not short in length. Passport's use of Elvis' appearance on The Steve Allen Show *plays for over a minute and many more clips play for more than just a few seconds.*

The ruling prevented Passport from moving forward with the sale of its documentary.

In this case, the copyright law did exactly what it is designed to do: protect the legal owners of Elvis's material from copyright infringement.

Questions for Critical Thinking

1. Do you agree with the Ninth Circuit Court's ruling? Why or why not?
2. Why do you think the copyright holders of Elvis's work objected to Passport's video?
3. What can the founder or founders of an entrepreneurial firm learn from this case?
4. Do you think Passport Video acted ethically and honestly and believed that its production was protected by fair use, or do you think the firm was simply using fair use as a way of avoiding paying royalties for the copyrighted material it was using?

Sources: H. R. Cheeseman, The Legal Environment of Business and Online Commerce, 5th ed. (Upper Saddle River, NJ: Prentice Hall, 2007); Ruling by the United States District Court for the Central District of California in the case of Elvis Presley Enterprises v. Passport Video, November 6, 2004.

and buying habits of its customers, helping it fine-tune its marketing message and target past customers for future business. If this list fell into the hands of one or more of the company's competitors, its value would be largely lost, and it would no longer provide the firm a competitive advantage over its competitors.

A **trade secret** is any formula, pattern, physical device, idea, process, or other information that provides the owner of the information with a competitive advantage in the marketplace. Trade secrets include marketing plans, product formulas, financial forecasts, employee rosters, logs of sales calls, and laboratory notebooks. The medium in which information is stored typically has no impact on whether it can be protected as a trade secret. As a result, written documents, computer files, audiotapes, videotapes, financial statements, and even an employee's memory of various items can be protected from unauthorized disclosure.

Unlike patents, trademarks, and copyrights, there is no single government agency that regulates trade secret laws. Instead, in the United States, for example, trade secrets are governed by a patchwork of various state laws. The U.S. **Economic Espionage Act**, passed in the United States in 1996, does criminalize the theft of trade secrets. The **Uniform Trade Secrets Act**, which a special commission drafted in the United States in 1979, attempted to set nationwide standards for trade secret legislation. Although the majority of U.S. states have adopted the act, most revised it, resulting in a wide disparity among states in regard to trade secret legislation and enforcement.

Learning Objective

7. Discuss the legal environment that facilitates trade secret protection.

What Qualifies for Trade Secret Protection?

Not all information qualifies for trade secret protection. In general, information that is known to the public or that competitors can discover through legal means doesn't qualify for trade secret protection. If a company passes out brochures at a trade show that are available to anyone in attendance, nothing that is in the brochure can typically qualify as a trade secret. Similarly, if a secret is disclosed by mistake, it typically loses its trade secret status. For example, if an employee of a company is talking on a cell phone in a public place and is overheard by a competitor, anything the employee says is generally exempt from trade secret protection. Simply stated, the general philosophy of trade secret legislation is that the law will not protect a trade secret unless its owner protects it first.

Companies can maintain protection for their trade secrets if they take reasonable steps to keep the information confidential. In assessing whether reasonable steps have been taken, courts typically examine how broadly the information is known inside and outside the firm, the value of the information, the extent of measures taken to protect the secrecy of the information, the effort expended in developing the information, and the ease with which other companies could develop the information. On the basis of these criteria, the strongest case for trade secret protection is information that is characterized by the following:

- ■ Is not known outside the company
- ■ Is known only inside the company on a "need-to-know" basis
- ■ Is safeguarded by stringent efforts to keep the information confidential
- ■ Is valuable and provides the company a compelling competitive advantage
- ■ Was developed at great cost, time, and effort
- ■ Cannot be easily duplicated, reverse engineered, or discovered.

Trade Secret Disputes

Learning Objective

8. Identify the most common types of trade secret disputes.

Trade secret disputes arise most frequently when an employee leaves a firm to join a competitor and is accused of taking confidential information along. For example, a marketing executive for one firm may take a job with a competitor and create a marketing plan for the new employer that is nearly identical to the plan being worked on at the previous job. The original employer could argue that the marketing plan on which the departed employee was working was a company trade secret and that the employee essentially stole the plan and took it to the new job. The key factor in winning a trade secret dispute is that some type of theft or misappropriation must have taken place. Trade secrets can be lawfully discovered. For example, it's not illegal for one company to buy another company's products and take them apart to see how they are assembled. In fact, this is a relatively common practice, which is another reason companies continuously attempt to innovate as a means of trying to stay at least one step ahead of competitors.

A company damaged by trade secret theft can initiate a civil action for damages in court. The action should be taken as soon after the discovery of the theft as possible. In denying the allegation, the defendant will typically argue that the information in question was independently developed (meaning no theft took place), was obtained by proper means (such as with the permission of the owner), is common knowledge (meaning it is not subject to trade secret protection), or was innocently received (such as through a casual conversation at a business meeting). Memorization is not a defense. As a result, an employee of one firm can't say that "all I took from my old job to my new one was what's in my head" and claim that just because the information conveyed wasn't in written form, it's not subject to trade secret protection. If the courts rule in favor of the firm that feels its trade secret has been stolen, the firm can stop the offender from using the trade secret and obtain substantial financial damages.

Trade Secret Protection Methods

Aggressive protection of trade secrets is necessary to prevent intentional or unintentional disclosure. In addition, one of the key factors in determining whether something constitutes a trade secret is the extent of the efforts to keep it secret. Companies protect trade secrets through physical measures and written agreements.

Learning Objective

9. Describe some of the physical measures that firms take to protect their trade secrets.

Physical Measures   There are a number of physical measures firms use to protect trade secrets, from security fences around buildings, to providing employees access to file cabinets that lock, to much more elaborate measures. The level of protection depends on the nature of the trade secret. For example, although a retail store may consider its inventory control procedures to be a trade secret, it may not consider this information vital and may take appropriate yet not extreme measures to protect the information. In contrast, a biotech firm may be on the cusp of discovering a cure for a disease and may take extreme measures to protect the confidentiality of the work being conducted in its laboratories.

The following are examples of commonly used physical measures for protecting trade secrets:

- **Restricting access:** Many companies restrict physical access to confidential material to only the employees who have a "need to know." For example, access to a company's customer list may be restricted to key personnel in the marketing department.
- **Labeling documents:** Sensitive documents should be stamped or labeled "confidential," "proprietary," "restricted," or "secret." If possible, these documents should be secured when not in use. Such labeling should be restricted to particularly sensitive documents. If everything is labeled

"confidential," there is a risk that employees will soon lose their ability to distinguish between slightly and highly confidential material.

■ **Password protecting confidential computer files:** Providing employees with clearance to view confidential information by using secure passwords can restrict information on a company's computer network, Web site, or intranet. Companies can also write-protect documents to ensure that employees can read but not modify certain documents.

■ **Maintaining logbooks for visitors:** Visitors can be denied access to confidential information by asking them to sign in when they arrive at a company facility, wear name badges that identify them as visitors, and always be accompanied by a company employee.

■ **Maintain logbooks for access to sensitive material:** Many companies maintain logbooks for sensitive material and make their employees "check out" and "check in" the material.

■ **Maintaining adequate overall security measures:** Commonsense measures are also helpful. Shredders should be provided to destroy documents as appropriate. Employees who have access to confidential material should have desks and cabinets that can be locked and secured. Alarms, security systems, and security personnel should be used to protect a firm's premises.

Some of these measures may seem extreme. However, unfortunately we live in a world that is not perfect, and companies need to safeguard their information against both inadvertent disclosure and outright theft. Steps such as shredding documents may seem like overkill at first glance but may be very important in ultimately protecting trade secrets. Believe it or not, there have been a number of cases in which companies have caught competitors literally going through the trash bins behind their buildings looking for confidential information.

Written Agreements   It is important for a company's employees to know that it is their duty to keep trade secrets and other forms of confidential information secret. For the best protection, a firm should ask its employees to sign nondisclosure and noncompete agreements, as discussed in Chapter 7.

Intellectual property, and the problems that underlie the need for intellectual property to be created, are important enough that firms have been started strictly for the purpose of helping companies solve problems and obtain the intellectual property that they need.

CONDUCTING AN INTELLECTUAL PROPERTY AUDIT

The first step a firm should take to protect its intellectual property is to complete an intellectual property audit. This is recommended for all firms, regardless of size, from start-ups to mature companies. An **intellectual property audit** is conducted to determine the intellectual property a company owns.

The following sections describe the reasons for conducting an intellectual property audit and the basic steps in the audit process. Some firms hire attorneys to conduct the audit, whereas others conduct the audit on their own. Once an audit is completed, a company can determine the appropriate measures it needs to take to protect the intellectual property that it owns and that is worth the effort and expense of protecting.

Why Conduct an Intellectual Property Audit?

Learning Objective

10. Explain the two primary reasons for conducting an intellectual property audit.

There are two primary reasons for conducting an intellectual property audit. First, it is prudent for a company to periodically determine whether its intellectual property is being properly protected. As illustrated in Table 12.5, intellectual property resides in every department in a firm, and it is common for firms to simply overlook intellectual property that is eligible for protection.

The second reason for a company to conduct an intellectual property audit is to remain prepared to justify its value in the event of a merger or acquisition. Larger companies purchase many small, entrepreneurial firms primarily because the larger company wants the small firm's intellectual property. When a larger company approaches, the smaller firm should be ready and able to justify its valuation.

The Process of Conducting an Intellectual Property Audit

The first step in conducting an intellectual property audit is to develop an inventory of a firm's existing intellectual property. The inventory should include the firm's present registrations of patents, trademarks, and copyrights. Also included should be any agreements or licenses allowing the company to use someone else's intellectual property rights or allowing someone else to use the focal company's intellectual property.

The second step is to identify works in progress to ensure that they are being documented in a systematic, orderly manner. This is particularly important in research and development. As mentioned earlier, if two inventors independently develop essentially the same invention, the right to apply for the patent belongs to the person who invented the product first. Properly

Table 12.5 TYPES OF QUESTIONS TO ASK WHEN CONDUCTING AN INTELLECTUAL PROPERTY AUDIT

Patents	Copyrights
• Are products under development that require patent protection?	• Is there a policy in place regarding what material needs the copyright bug and when the bug is to be put in place?
• Are current patent maintenance fees up to date?	• Is there a policy in place regarding when copyrightable material should be registered?
• Do we have any business methods that should be patented?	• Is proper documentation in place to protect the company's rights to use the material it creates or pays to have created?
• Do we own any patents that are no longer consistent with our business plan that could be sold or licensed?	• Are we in compliance with the copyright license agreements into which we have entered?
• Do our scientists properly document key discovery dates?	

Trademarks	Trade Secrets
• Are we using any names or slogans that require trademark protection?	• Are internal security arrangements adequate to protect the firm's intellectual property?
• Do we intend to expand the use of trademarks in other countries?	• Are employees who do not have a "need to know" routinely provided access to important trade secrets?
• Do we need additional trademarks to cover new products and services?	• Is there a policy in place to govern the use of nondisclosure and noncompete agreements?
• Is anyone infringing on our trademarks?	• Are company trade secrets leaking out to competitors?

dated and witnessed invention logbooks and other documents help prove the date an invention was made.

The third step of the audit is to specify the firm's key trade secrets and describe how they are being protected. Putting this information in writing helps minimize the chance that if a trade secret is lost, someone can claim that it wasn't really a trade secret because the owner took no specific steps to protect it.

Chapter Summary

1. Intellectual property is any product of human intellect that is intangible but has value in the marketplace. It is called intellectual property because it is the product of human imagination, creativity, and inventiveness.

2. Patents, trademarks, copyrights, and trade secrets are the major forms of intellectual property. A common mistake companies make is not thinking broadly enough when identifying their intellectual property assets. Almost all companies, regardless of size or age, have intellectual property worth protecting. But to protect this property, firms must first identify it.

3. There are two rules of thumb for determining whether intellectual property is worth the time and expense of protecting. First, a firm should determine whether the intellectual property in question is directly related to its current competitive advantage or could facilitate the development of future competitive advantages. Second, it's important to know whether the intellectual property has independent value in the marketplace.

4. Obtaining a patent is a painstaking, six-step process that usually requires the help of a patent attorney. A patent can be sold or licensed, which is a common strategy for entrepreneurial firms.

5. Trademarks, service marks, collective marks, and certification marks are the four types of trademarks. Trademark law is far-reaching, helping businesses be creative in drawing attention to their products and services. Examples of marks that can be protected include words, numbers and letters, designs and logos, sounds, fragrances, shapes, and colors. Immoral or scandalous matter, deceptive matter, descriptive marks, and surnames are ineligible for trademark protection.

6. Copyright law protects original works of authorship that are fixed in a tangible form of expression. This is a broad definition and means that almost anything a company produces that can be written down, recorded, or videotaped or that takes a tangible form itself (such as a sculpture) is eligible for copyright protection. Examples of copyrightable material include literary works, musical compositions, dramatic works, and pictorial, graphic, and sculptural works.

7. Unlike patents, trademarks, and copyrights, there is not a single government agency that regulates trade secret laws. Instead, in the United States, trade secrets are governed by a patchwork of various state laws. The U.S. Economic Espionage Act, for example, does criminalize the theft of trade secrets.

8. Trade secret disputes arise most frequently when an employee leaves a firm to join a competitor and is accused of taking confidential information along. Firms protect their trade secrets through both physical measures and written agreements.

9. Firms use a number of physical measures to protect their trade secrets. These include restricting access, labeling documents, password protecting

computer files, maintaining logbooks for visitors, and maintaining adequate overall security measures.

10. There are two primary reasons for conducting an intellectual property audit. First, it is prudent for a company to periodically assess the intellectual property it owns to determine whether it is being properly protected. Second, a firm should conduct a periodic intellectual property audit to remain prepared to justify its value in the event of a merger or acquisition.

Key Terms

assignment of invention agreement, **420**
business method patent, **418**
certification marks, **424**
collective marks, **424**
Computer Software Copyright Act, **428**
copyright, **428**
copyright bug, **429**
copyright infringement, **430**
derivative works, **428**
design patents, **419**
Economic Espionage Act, **433**

fair use, **430**
first-to-invent rule, **420**
idea–expression dichotomy, **429**
intellectual property, **413**
intellectual property audit, **435**
intent-to-use trademark application, **427**
interference, **421**
invention logbook, **420**
Lanham Act, **425**
one year after first use deadline, **418**

patent, **417**
patent infringement, **422**
plant patents, **419**
provisional patent application, **421**
secondary meaning, **427**
service marks, **424**
trademark, **423**
trade secret, **433**
Uniform Trade Secrets Act, **433**
utility patents, **418**

Review Questions

1. What distinguishes intellectual property from other types of property, such as land, buildings, and inventory? Provide several examples of intellectual property and describe its importance to a firm.
2. What are the two primary rules for determining whether intellectual property protection should be pursued for a particular intellectual asset?
3. Search the USPTO database and find three patents issued to Donald E. Weder of Highland Park, Illinois. Describe the patents. In what areas are most of Mr. Weder's patents?
4. What are the major differences between utility patents and design patents? Provide an example of each.
5. What is a business method patent? Provide an example of a business method patent and explain how having such a patent can provide a firm a competitive advantage in the marketplace.
6. Give an example of a design patent. Explain how having a design patent can provide a firm a competitive advantage in the marketplace.
7. Describe the purpose of an assignment of invention agreement. Is it a good idea for firms to ask their employees to sign assignment of invention agreements?
8. What are the six steps in applying for a patent? Make your answer as thorough as possible.
9. What is a trademark? Provide several examples of trademarks, and describe how they help a firm establish a competitive advantage in the marketplace.
10. What are the three steps involved in selecting and registering a trademark?
11. What is meant by the term *trade dress*?
12. What is a copyright?

13. In the context of copyright law, what is meant by the term *derivative work*? Provide an example of when this concept is important for the creators of copyrightable material.

14. If an entrepreneur has an idea for a themed restaurant based on television game shows is the idea itself eligible for copyright protection? Why or why not?

15. What is a copyright bug? Where would one expect to find the bug, and how is it used?

16. What is meant by the phrase *copyright infringement*? Would you characterize copyright infringement as a minor or as a major problem around the world? Explain.

17. What is a trade secret? Provide an example of a trade secret, and describe how it helps a firm establish a competitive advantage in the marketplace.

18. What information does not qualify for trade secret protection? Make your answer as thorough as possible.

19. What types of physical measures do firms take to protect their trade secrets?

20. What are the two primary purposes of conducting an intellectual property audit? What risks does a company run if it doesn't periodically conduct an intellectual property audit?

Application Questions

1. Amy Rozinski owns a small optics firm named Northland Optics. About 11 months ago, the company invented a new product that has sold extremely well to consumers in a localized area. Amy has decided to wait a year to see how the product does and will then apply for a patent if the product appears to have a good future. Is this a good approach for Amy to follow? Why or why not?

2. Spend some time studying Cyber-Rain, the subject of the "You Be the VC 12.1" feature. Make a list of the forms of intellectual property protection that Cyber-Rain should have to properly protect itself. Be as specific as possible in compiling your list.

3. Search the USPTO database and find three patents issued to Donald E. Weder of Highland Park, Illinois. Describe the patents. In what areas are most of Mr. Weder's patents?

4. Tyler Simms just invented a new product that he is convinced is unique and will make him wealthy. The product is a toothbrush with a tube of toothpaste attached to the handle. Tyler is anxious to file a patent application on the product, but when he tells you about the idea, you say—"whoa, let's do a preliminary patent application search first to see if someone else has already patented this idea." What do you find when you help Tyler with the preliminary search?

5. Spend some time studying Wakoopa, the subject of the "You Be the VC 12.2" feature. Do you think Wakoopa's unique method of establishing a social network for software users to make it easier to track, share, and find software is suitable for a business method patent? If so, if you were the founder of Wakoopa would you spend the money to try to obtain a business method patent? Why or why not?

6. On January 8, 2008, the USPTO granted Apple Inc. a trademark for the three-dimensional shape of its iPod media player. Why would Apple Inc. go to the trouble of applying for a trademark on the shape of the iPod?

7. Pam Tarver just opened an information technology consulting company and has thought for a long time about what to name it. She finally settled on the fictitious name Infoxx. Search the USPTO database to determine if the name Infoxx is available. Is it? If it is available, describe how Pam would go about obtaining a trademark on Infoxx or any other name.

8. Rick Sanford lives in a small community in northern Minnesota. He is planning to open the only fried chicken restaurant in his area and would like to trademark the words *fried chicken.* Because of his special circumstances, can he do this?

9. Ken and Jackie Smith just purchased a small winery in the Napa Valley of northern California. One thing they noticed when they were investigating the winery is that the owners never placed the "100% Napa Valley" certification mark on their bottles. Now that they own the winery Ken and Jackie are looking into using the mark. Investigate what is required to place the "100% Napa Valley" certification mark on a bottle of wine. If Ken and Jackie's winery qualifies, should they use the mark?

10. Maggie Simpson has always admired her Grandmother Thompson's cooking and has considered putting together a cookbook titled *Grandma Thompson's Favorite Recipes.* Some of Grandma's recipes are truly original, and before she writes the book, Maggie would like to copyright several of the most original ones. Can she do this?

11. Jason Scott is the CEO of a small graphic design company in Orlando, Florida. Several months ago, he spent an entire day searching the Web site of Dolphin Graphics, a larger graphics design firm in Miami. From its Web site, Jason was able to put together a list of Dolphin's major customers and is using the list to prospect new customers for his firm. After discovering what he is doing, Dolphin has threatened to sue Jason if he doesn't stop using its customer list, which it claims is a trade secret. Is Jason infringing on Dolphin's trade secrets?

12. Melanie Hays owns a firm near Austin, Texas. Her firm, Health Care Technologies, makes disk drives for computers that are used in the health care industry. Recently, Melanie found out that her largest competitor (1) bought several of her disk drives and took them apart to see how they were manufactured, (2) has spent considerable time on her Web site seeing how her products are marketed, and (3) consistently picks up brochures at her booth at trade shows. Melanie is confident that her competitor is smart enough to not violate any of her patents, trademarks, or copyrights, but is upset because some of her best ideas might be lost anyway. Is there anything that Melanie can do to stop her competitor from doing what it's doing?

13. Suppose you were asked by the founders of Cyber-Rain to advise them on protecting their trade secrets. Assume the company operates out of a single facility where it manufactures its current products and is in the process of developing new products. Make a list of recommendations for the company.

14. Two years ago, Mike Carini opened a restaurant called Mike's Italian. To his horror, Mike just found out that several disgruntled customers have launched a Web site with the Internet address www.avoidmikesitalian.com. The site contains testimonials by people who have eaten at Mike's and have not been satisfied. Is there anything that Mike can do to shut down the Web site?

15. Refer to Case 11.2, which focused on Proactiv, the maker of acne prevention medication. If you were hired to conduct an intellectual property audit for Proactiv, list 10 specific things you would check (or audit) to make sure that Proactiv is doing exactly what it should be doing regarding the intellectual property that it owns.

You Be the VC 12.1

Company: Cyber-Rain

www.cyber-rain.com

Business Idea: Create a device that utilizes online weather forecasts to regulate the amount of water that a home owner's sprinkler system dispenses.

Pitch: Have you ever driven by a home and seen its sprinkler system operating during a rainstorm? If so, you probably shook your head and thought, "what a waste." Not only does watering make little sense when it's raining, but it is costly to home owners. In addition, it's hard on lawns and shrubs and strains municipalities that are struggling to maintain a proper water supply.

Cyber-Rain wants to change this scenario. The company has built a hardware device that, once installed, monitors the weather so that a home owner's sprinkler system lets up when it rains, is threatening to rain, or has rained recently. The installation process is simple. The home owner simply swaps out his or her current sprinkler system controller for the Cyber-Rain controller, and then loads Cyber-Rain's software onto a home computer. A Cyber-Rain transmitter, which is plugged into one of the computer's USB slots, allows the computer and the controller to wirelessly communicate. The system, which is very flexible, is then ready for use. Independent zones can be programmed based on individual soil type, plant type, and even landscape slope to ensure that the right amount of

water is dispensed based on weather conditions. Because the Cyber-Rain device interfaces directly with your home computer, there are no monthly fees. The system will even give you a monthly report on the amount of water you're saving.

Nationally, home owners with traditional sprinkler controllers spend an average of $1,500 a year in water costs and an untold amount in plant replacement costs. By keeping an eye on the weather, the Cyber-Rain system dispenses on average 30 to 70 percent less water, saving the home owner money and paying for itself in just several months. It also results in healthier lawns, helps municipalities conserve water, and minimizes environmental damage caused by excessive water runoff.

Q&A: Based on the material covered in this chapter, what questions would you ask the firm's founders before making your funding decision? What answers would satisfy you?

Decision: If you had to make your decision on just the information provided in the pitch and on the company's Web site, would you fund this company? Why or why not?

You Be the VC 12.2

Company: Wakoopa

www.wakoopa.com

Business Idea: To establish a social network for software users to make it easier to track, share, and find software.

Pitch: Buying computer software online or from a store is often a tricky task, and keeping up to date with the latest releases can be confusing. There are thousands of new software programs every year and dozens of different operating systems. It can be difficult to get a completely impartial view. Although there are many online Web sites and magazines offering software reviews, there is no way of knowing how long the reviewer has used the program and what kind of program he or she usually likes.

Wakoopa was founded by two Dutch bloggers, Robert Gaal and Wouter Broekhof, to solve these problems and create a social network for software users.

Wakoopa's sign-up process is very simple: Users provide a user name and password and then are given a page with the download links for the Wakoopa tracking software. They then install a small application on their PC or Mac that works by performing a check every 15 minutes to track what software they use for a range of applications such as music players, office software, and photo editing, and how long they use it for. The information gathered can then be shared with friends, and personal profiles are

(continued)

automatically updated with any news, updates, or reviews on each specific application. It helps people decide whether or not to spend money on a program, because they can check out the statistics beforehand and see if the program is a one-hit wonder, or if it has proved its value to many users in the long term.

The Wakoopa site features a list of the current programs running with user reviews and a list of new versions of software. There is also a "software I might like" section, which provides recommendations based on current software usage.

In the first six months following its launch in April 2007, 17,000 people downloaded the Wakoopa tracking program. In the following year, that sum doubled again, helping to generate some 250 million hours of unique and useful data about software, including lists of the most popular and most used software applications on a year-by-year basis. Early adopters of the site are primarily tech-savvy software

developers and gamers, although there is evidence that the service is being used more widely by consumers who are happy to see their own desktop behavior become public. The payback is a lively social network for software and the opportunity to test the pulse of what are the most popular and unpopular new Web applications.

Gaal and Broekhof have ambitious plans for Wakoopa and want the site to become the place for software information and will achieve this by adding in more features and supporting more operating systems.

Q&A: Based on the material covered in this chapter, what questions would you ask the firm's founders before making your funding decision? What answers would satisfy you?

Decision: If you had to make your decision on just the information provided in the pitch and on the company's Web site, would you fund this firm? Why or why not?

CASE 12.1

You Make the Call: Can a Company Patent How It Makes a Peanut Butter and Jelly Sandwich?
www.smuckers.com
www.albies.com

Bruce R. Barringer
Oklahoma State University
R. Duane Ireland
Texas A & M University

Introduction

Here's a question that a panel of judges recently decided: Can a company patent how it makes a peanut butter and jelly sandwich? More specifically, in this instance, judges considered whether J. M. Smucker's method of making Uncrustables—which is a crustless peanut butter and jelly sandwich sealed inside soft bread—is worthy of legal protection against imitators. While the nature of this case is interesting, the legal rulings resulting from the case have broader implications. At stake is how generous the patent office should be in awarding patents—an issue with solid arguments on both sides.

There were actually two cases leading up to the case that resulted in the final verdict. The three cases are designated Round 1, Round 2,

and Round 3 of Smucker's battle to patent the peanut butter and jelly sandwich.

The case involves Smucker's Uncrustables sandwich. Uncrustables are found in the frozen food section of most grocery stores. They are 2-ounce peanut butter and jelly pockets that come in two flavors—grape and strawberry—and are sealed inside soft bread. They come in boxes of 4, 10, or 18 sandwiches per box. To make an Uncrustables ready to eat, the customer simply needs to let it thaw for 30–60 minutes after being taken out of the freezer.

The Uncrustables was developed in 1995 by David Geske, of Fargo, North Dakota, and Len Kretchman, of Fergus Falls, Minnesota. The two started mass-producing them for Midwestern schools. Smucker's took note of their success and bought Geske and Kretchman's company in 1999. The purchase of the company included a general patent on crustless peanut butter and jelly sandwiches (Patent No. 6,004,596) that Geske and Kretchman had obtained.

Round 1: Smucker's Versus Albie's Foods

It wasn't long before Smucker's was defending its turf. In 2001, Smucker's ordered a much smaller firm, Albie's Foods, to stop selling its own crustless peanut butter and jelly sandwich. Albie's was selling the sandwich to a local school district. Albie's fought back, and the case was eventually dismissed. In its arguments, Albie's contended that the "pasty"—a meat pie with crimped edges, which the company saw its crustless peanut butter and jelly sandwich as a variation of—had been a popular food in northern Michigan since the immigration of copper and iron miners from England in the 1800s.

Round 2: Smucker's and the Patent Office

Stung by its experience with the case it brought against Albie's, Smucker's returned to the USPTO to try to get its general patent on crustless peanut butter and jelly sandwiches broadened as a means of being able to better defend the Uncrustables. The patent office rejected the application. The gist of Smucker's argument was that its sandwich's sealed edge is unique and its layering approach, which keeps the jelly in the middle of the sandwich, is one-of-a-kind, and as such, should be protected by law. The patent office disagreed with this view. It said that the crimped edge, which was one of the things Smucker's argued was unique about its sandwich, is similar to the crimped edges in ravioli and pie crusts. In addition, the patent office determined that putting jelly in the middle of a peanut butter and jelly sandwich is hardly unique, and as evidence cited a 1994 *Wichita* (Kansas) *Eagle* newspaper article on back-to-school tips that suggested just this approach.

Round 3: Smucker's Appeals

Smucker's appealed the patent office's decision to the U.S. Court of Appeals. During the court hearings the attorney representing Smucker's argued that the method for making the Uncrustables is unique because the two slices of bread are sealed by compression but are not "smashed" as they are in tarts or ravioli. (Recall, the patent office's original decision compared the process of making Uncrustables to that of making ravioli.) Smucker's further argued that it wouldn't be fair to let other

companies simply copy the Uncrustables and benefit from the hard work of Smucker's scientists and the money that the company had invested to produce what it believed was a unique product. The Uncrustables is also a big seller for Smucker's. According to a *Wall Street Journal* article, the product generated sales of $27.5 million in 2004.

Broader Issues Involved

The Smucker's case was watched closely because of the broader issues involved. Critics of the U.S. patent process contend that the USPTO is too generous when awarding patents—a generosity that they say stifles innovation and drives up the cost for consumers. Close to 500,000 patents are filed each year, and nearly 65 percent of them are granted. In the Smucker's case, the critics would argue that Smucker's shouldn't get the patent, because it will deter other food companies from making their own versions of peanut butter and jelly sandwiches, which will keep the price of the Uncrustables high. Advocates of the U.S. patent process argue the opposite—that patents motivate a company like Smucker's to invest in new-product innovation, and that absent patent protection, a company like Smucker's would have no incentive to develop a product like the Uncrustables.

The Court's Ruling

In mid-April 2005, after listening to all the arguments, the U.S. Court of Appeals ruled on whether Smucker's should get the patent it was requesting. Which way do you think the court ruled?

Discussion Questions

1. Go to the USPTO's Web site (www.uspto.gov) to look up Patent No. 6,004,596. Read the patent. After reading the patent, are you more inclined or less inclined to side with the Smucker's point of view?
2. Type "Uncrustables" into the Google search engine and look at the Uncrustables sandwich. Spend a little time reading about the Uncrustables on Smucker's Web site. Again, after looking over the Web site, are you more inclined or less inclined to side with the Smucker's point of view?
3. In regard to the arguments espoused by the "critics" of the U.S. patent system and the "advocates" of the U.S. patent system, which of the points of view do you agree with? Thinking as an entrepreneur, use your own words to state why you think the critics or the advocates have a stronger point of view.

(continued)

4. So what do you think happened? Do you think Smucker's did or didn't get the patent it was requesting?

Application Questions

1. What would be the impact, if any, on the entrepreneurial sector of the U.S. economy if patents became increasingly hard to get? Would it help or hurt the majority of entrepreneurial companies? Why?

2. Based on the material in the chapter, are there facets of the U.S. patent system and, in particular, the operations of the USPTO that you think need to be improved or changed? What are these facets? Using the perspective of an entrepreneur, what changes do you believe should be made?

Source: Wall Street Journal (Eastern Edition) by S. Munzo. Copyright 2005 by Dow Jones & Company, Inc.

CASE 12.2

A Classic Trademark Dispute: Harley-Davidson Versus The Hog Farm

www.harley-davidson.com
www.the-hog-farm.com

Bruce R. Barringer
Oklahoma State University
R. Duane Ireland
Texas A & M University

Introduction

If you live near Buffalo, New York, and own a motorcycle that needs to be fixed, you're in luck. Just down the road, in West Seneca, New York, you'll find The Hog Farm, a business that is owned by Ron Grottanelli. All the repairs you might want are available from this store. Ron, who likes to be called "Grott," opened The Hog Farm in 1969. From the beginning, the business serviced all makes and models of motorcycles and even built "custom bikes." The custom bikes, according to Grott, have always been particularly special, especially in the early days. They had fancy paint, long front ends, and lots of chrome and were affectionately called "hogs."

As time passed, The Hog Farm grew, becoming a place for motorcycle enthusiasts to gather and enjoy one another's company. To facilitate this, The Hog Farm started hosting a series of yearly events, including flea markets and celebrations over holiday weekends. To brand its events, the company started using the word hog more and more often. For example, it began hosting a "Hog Holiday" in July and a "Hog Labor Day Holiday" in September. It also started attaching the word hog to many of its products. For example, the company sells an engine degreaser called "Hog Wash."

Of course, from the early days of its existence, Harley-Davidson was one of the motorcycle brands on which The Hog Farm personnel worked the most. Grott remembers the bleakest days in Harley-Davidson's history, during the late 1960s and the early 1970s, when it looked as though the company might go under. During this period, Grott helped keep his customers fired up about motorcycles and feels like he helped keep the Harley-Davidson flame alive. Harley-Davidson recovered, reestablishing itself as a premier motorcycle manufacturer.

As motorcycles continued to gain popularity in the United States, everything was looking good for the Grottanellis and their business until a series of events took place that landed them and The Hog Farm in court opposite, of all companies, Harley-Davidson. In the 1980s, Harley started taking control of the word hog, including registering it as a trademark in 1987. Following the registration, Harley started scouring the country looking for shops and companies that used the word when referring to motorcycles. To Harley-Davidson, a hog was a Harley, and no one else was entitled to use that name when referring to a motorcycle. When Harley finally caught up with The Hog Farm, it asked that it change its name and quit using the "hog" when referring to motorcycles or related products.

The Trial

Rather than giving in, however, Grott decided to fight, and a classic trademark dispute took shape. "You certainly have a memory lapse," Grott wrote to the company when it started demanding that he stop using the "hog." "In the 50s, 60s, and 70s, you wanted no association [with the word *hog*]," he wrote. "You cringed whenever Harleys were included in discussions about motorcycles called hogs by the people that rode them; they were a means of escape from the square world." Harley didn't back down, and the case came to a head in a U.S. district court near Buffalo. The courtroom was quite a scene and on opening day was packed with bikers supporting The Hog Farm's right to keep its operations as they had been established. To try to diffuse the image of a big corporation trying to squash the little guy, a Harley attorney, in an interview outside the courtroom, said, "Harley-Davidson is not trying to hurt these people. All they are trying to do is protect their trademark." The trial, which went on for several days, basically boiled down to Harley's assertion that, by virtue of its trademark, it has exclusive rights to the word *hog* in reference to motorcycles. Grott argued that Harley's assertion was unreasonable because "hog" had been used to refer to motorcycles long before Harley trademarked it in 1987.

The Court's Decision

In announcing its decision, the court reviewed the trial and related the following facts. First, the court found that several periodicals and books have used the term *hog* to refer to motorcycles. The earliest source was a 1935 issue of *Popular Mechanics* that used "Hog Heaven" in the caption of a picture of some large motorcycles. Similarly, in 1965, a *Newsweek* article noted that the motorcycle gang Hell's Angels used the word *hog* to refer to big motorcycles. Further, the court pointed out that several American dictionaries and slang dictionaries defined the word *hog* as a form of large motorcycle.

In addition, the court found that throughout the 1970s and 1980s, many motorcycle enthusiasts began using the word *hog* when referring to Harley-Davidson motorcycles. Initially, Harley attempted to distance itself from any association of that word with its products. It was not until 1981 that Harley-Davidson began to use the word *hog* in its promotions and advertisements. The court found that Harley-Davidson itself recognized that the word referred in a generic sense to large motorcycles before it trademarked the word in 1987. The court therefore concluded that Harley-Davidson couldn't prevent The Hog Farm from using the word *hog* in connection with motorcycles. In essence, the court ruled that Harley-Davidson couldn't appropriate a term that was already in the public domain and turn it into its own private property.

The Hog Farm Lives to See Another Day

So, The Hog Farm lives to see another day, and the Hog Holidays sponsored by the Grottanellis and their company continue without a name change. However, Grott remains irritated with the Harley-Davidson company and the actions it took against his firm. His anger and disappointment are suggested by the following comment, which recently appeared on his firm's Web site: "The Hog Farm celebrates 100 years of the Harley-Davidson motorcycle we love, and the company we hate!" This case provides an important lesson in trademark law, particularly as it pertains to the protection of generic names from becoming the exclusive property of a single company.

Discussion Questions

1. Do you agree or disagree with the court's decision? Why or why not?
2. To what extent do you believe that The Hog Farm would have been harmed if it had lost the decision? If you were Ron Grottanelli and the decision had gone against you, how would you have rebranded your company?
3. What can other companies as well as entrepreneurs who are interested in trademark law learn from the case of Harley-Davidson versus The Hog Farm?
4. For a company like Harley-Davidson, how important a factor is its intellectual property in enabling it to maintain a sustainable competitive advantage? How about The Hog Farm?

Application Questions

1. List several examples of names that are currently controlled by companies that you think are becoming "generic" enough that their trademark protection may be in jeopardy. What can a company do to prevent this from happening?
2. The "You Be the VC 12.1" feature in this chapter focuses on Cyber-Rain, the company that is starting a business with the purpose of helping homeowners in their efforts to more efficiently water their lawns. Write a short intellectual property protection plan for this company. Include in the plan all facets of Cyber-Rain and its operations that should be protected, and the form of intellectual property protection that should be used in each instance.

Sources: The Hog Farm homepage, www.the-hog-farm.com (accessed May 15, 2006); M. Beebe, "Hog Farm Trial Less Than Easy Ride," *Buffalo News*, October 27, 1996, B1; R. Grottanelli, "History of the Hog Farm," www.the-hog-farm. com (accessed January 28, 2002 and July 21, 2004).

Endnotes

1. K. Beamon, "Around the House," *This Old House,* www.thisoldhouse.com (accessed October 2007).

2. J. Pasko, "Mushrooms Become Source for Eco-Building," *Washingtonpost.com,* July 24, 2007.

3. "Ecovative Wins 500,000 Euro Prize (750,000 USD)!" Ecovative Design Blog, http://ecovativedesign.blogspot.com (accessed December 3, 2008, originally posted on October 2, 2008).

4. H. R. Cheesman, *The Legal Environment of Business and Online Commerce,* 5th ed. (Upper Saddle River, NJ: Prentice Hall, 2007).

5. R. Ramcharan, "Singapore's Emerging Knowledge Economy: Role of Intellectual Property and Its Possible Implications for Singaporean Society," *The Journal of World Intellectual Property* 9, no. 3 (2006): 316–43; D. E. Bouchoux, *Intellectual Property* (New York: AMACOM Books, 2001).

6. R. Shapiro and N. Pham, "Economic Effects of Intellectual Property—Intensive Manufacturing in the U.S.," *County Business Pattern,* U.S. Census Bureau, www.the-value-of-ip.org/ip_report.pdf (accessed July 2007).

7. A. Murray, "Protecting Ideas Is Crucial for U.S. Businesses," *Wall Street Journal,* November 9, 2005, A2.

8. *Baxter Intern., Inc. v. COBE Laboratories Inc.,* 88 F.3d 1054, 1060 (Fed.Cir. 1996).

9. *Chemithon Corp. v. Procter & Gamble Co.,* 287 F.Supp. 291 (D.C.Md. 1968) (citing 35 U.S.C.A. § 102(b)).

10. 714 F.2d 1144 at 1148 (*See also Invitrogen Corp. v. Biocrest Mfg.,* 424 F.3d 1374, 1382 (Fed.Cir.2005) (citing *Metallizing Eng'g Co. v. Kenyon Bearing & Auto Parts Co.,* 153 F.3d 516, 520 (2d Cir.1946) (Learned Hand, J.))).

11. 476 F.3d 1337 as 1343 (citing *LNP Eng'g Plastics, Inc. v. Miller Waste Mills, Inc.,* 275 F.3d 1347, 1353 (Fed.Cir.2001)).

12. *Lough v. Brunswick Corp.,* 86 F.3d 1113, 1120 (Fed.Cir.1996).

13. 476 F.3d 1337 at 1344 (referring to *In re Smith,* 714 F.2d 1127, 1135 (Fed.Cir.1983) ("The experimental use exception . . . does not include market testing where the inventor is attempting to gauge consumer demand for his claimed invention.")).

14. 476 F.3d 1337 at 1344.

15. 476 F.3d 1337 at 1343 (citing *C.R. Bard, Inc. v. M3 Sys., Inc.,* 157 F.3d 1340, 1351 (Fed.Cir.1998).

16. *Id.* at 1344 (citing *Alza Corp. v. Mylan Labs., Inc.,* 464 F.3d 1286, 1291 (Fed.Cir.2006).

17. *Id.* (citing *Graham v. John Deere Co.,* 383 U.S. 1, 17 (1966)).

18. 476 F.3d 1337 at 1344.

19. *Id.*

20. 287 F.Supp. 291 at 308.

21. U.S. Patent and Trademark Office, "What Are Patents, Trademarks, Servicemarks, and Copyrights?" www.uspto.gov (accessed December 6, 2008); A. Esteve, "Patent Protection of Computer-Implemented Inventions Vis-À-Vis Open Source Software," *The Journal of World Intellectual Property* 9, no. 3 (2006): 276–300.

22. H. J. Knight, "Intellectual Property '101,'" in *From Ideas to Assets,* ed. B. Berman (New York: John Wiley & Sons, 2002), 3–25.

23. Knight, "Intellectual Property '101.'"

24. G. Wolff, *The Biotech Investor's Bible* (New York: John Wiley & Sons, 2001).

25. U.S. Patent and Trademark Office, www.uspto.gov (accessed January 10, 2002).

26. D. Bouchoux, *Intellectual Property: The Law of Trademarks, Copyrights, Patents, and Trade Secrets for the Paralegal* (New York: Delmar Cengage Learning, 2008).

27. G. Quinn, "Costs of Obtaining a Patent," IPWatchdog homepage, www.ipwatchdog.com (accessed November 16, 2008).

28. Bouchoux, *Intellectual Property.*

29. P. Thurrott, "Start-Up Cleans Microsoft's Chimney in Court," *WindowsITPro,* April 14, 2005.

30. A. Gilbert, "Microsoft Settles Infringement Suit," *ZDNet,* July 14, 2005.

31. "Protection Money," *Fortune Small Business,* October 2005.

32. J. Mendelson, "Interesting Patent Statistics," Mendelson's Musings Blog, www.jasonmendelson.com/blog/archives/2008/09/interesting-pat.php.php, (accessed November 22, 2008, originally posted on September 5, 2008).

33. D. Orozco and J. Conley, "Shape of Things to Come," *Wall Street Journal*, May 12, 2008, R6.

34. G. Gelb and B. Gelb, "When Appearances Are Deceiving," *Wall Street Journal*, December 1, 2007, B1.

35. InvestorWords.com, "Definition of Copyright," www.investorwords.com (accessed December 6, 2008); C. E. Bagley and C. E. Dauchy, *The Entrepreneur's Guide to Business Law*, 2nd ed. (Cincinnati: South-Western College Publishing, 2002).

36. E. R. Danton, "Black Crowes Accuse Gretchen Wilson of Copyright Infringement," *Hartford Courant*, www.blogs.courant.com (accessed August 1, 2008); *Los Angeles Times*, November 20, 2001.

37. *Wired*, November 11, 2005.

Getting Personal

with Jon Goodman

CURRENTLY IN MY IPOD
Jay-Z

HARDEST PART OF GETTING FUNDING
Writing a solid business plan

MY BIGGEST SURPRISE AS AN ENTREPRENEUR
Realizing how much work it actually is

MY ADVICE FOR NEW ENTREPRENEURS
Make it happen

FIRST ENTREPRENEURIAL EXPERIENCE
Lemonade stand

WHAT I DO WHEN I'M NOT WORKING
Watching football or movies

JON GOODMAN
Founder, JGoods
BS, Business Administration, Saint John's University, expected 2009

CHAPTERTHIRTEEN

Preparing for and *Evaluating* the Challenges of Growth

OPENING PROFILE

JGOODS
Preparing for Growth Cautiously
www.thejgcustoms.com

If you're watching a video by rapper Jay-Z or Cam-Ron, or seeing a great catch by Joe Mauer of the Minnesota Twins, and you notice their artistically adorned Nike shoes, it's a good bet the shoes were customized by Jon Goodman, a young entrepreneur who specializes in customizing shoes. These are just a few of Goodman's clients.

Goodman started customizing sneakers when he was in high school, first for himself and then for others. He spent quite a bit of time finding the paints and other materials that worked best for sneakers and other leather shoes. The idea behind "customizing" shoes is to give them a special look or identity—just like people customize clothing, jewelry, or anything else. You can see examples of Goodman's work on his Web site, www.thejgcustoms.com. For example, the sneakers he customized for Cam-Ron had horizontal stripes in almost-black purple, royal purple, gray, and white, with a heel that fades from the deep purple to the brighter shade. The pair of shoes he customized for Memphis Bleek, another rapper, has horizontal stripes in red, black, gray, and white.[1] The pair he customized for Pharrell Williams, who has his own shoe/clothing brand called "Ice Cream," looks like the inside of a traditional ice cream store.

In 2003, Goodman converted his hobby into a business and launched JGoods Customs, LLC. He has been slowly growing the business ever since—splitting his time between JGoods and his studies at St. John's University in Minnesota. JGoods sells two products—customized shoes, like those referred to previously, and a $44.95 kit for customizing shoes at home. The kit includes paint, brushes, and other materials needed to customize shoes, along with a 26-page step-by-step guide written by Goodman. The company also sells a variety of paints beyond those included in the kit. The 1/2-ounce containers of paint sell for $24.95. Two things Goodman has working in his favor are the high priority that many people place on shoes and the trend toward customization in all areas. Nike, for example, has an initiative called Nike iD, where customers can customize the Nike shoes they buy in select stores. Web sites like Zazzle and Café Press allow individuals to customize T-shirts, sweaters, caps, and a variety of other products.

Goodman is scheduled to graduate from St. John's in 2009 and is contemplating the best ways to grow his business. One alternative is to hire employees and grow the customized shoe side of the business. Goodman still customizes each pair of shoes he sells himself. While they sell for an average of $900, it is a time-consuming and specialized process. The biggest challenge that Goldman sees in ramping up this side of the business is finding and training the craftspeople he'd need. There is a potentially large and profitable market for customized shoes. For example, one market the

Learning Objectives

After studying this chapter you should be ready to:

1. Explain the term *sustained growth.*

2. Describe how firms can properly prepare for growth.

3. Discuss the six most common reasons firms pursue growth.

4. Explain the importance of knowing the stages of growth.

5. Describe the most important factors for firms to focus on during each stage of growth.

6. Describe the managerial capacity problem and how it inhibits firm growth.

7. Discuss the challenges for firm growth imposed by adverse selection and moral hazard.

8. Discuss the day-to-day challenges of growing a firm.

9. Explain why "cash flow management" is a challenge for growing a firm.

10. Explain how "quality control" can become a challenge for growing a firm.

Learning Objective

1. Explain the term *sustained growth.*

company is presently exploring is the market for customized baby shoes. To test this category, Goodman recently released a one-of-a-kind Nike Air VXTII kids shoe called "Baby Goods." These shoes are priced at about $450 a pair.

The second alternative for growing JGoods is to expand the kit and accessories part of the business. Goodman does not produce the kits himself—they are made by a contract manufacturer. A distributor has approached Goodman and expressed interest in distributing his kits. They would be placed in shoe boutiques and craft retailers like Michaels. The trick to getting boutiques and retailers to sign on is to prove that the kits will sell. Craft stores, in particular, are risk averse and will only take new products if they have a track record of selling in other venues. Goodman's confident that his current manufacturer can grow with his business and manufacture the number of kits that he needs. A key to growing this side of the business, however, will be to find an initial group of stores to sell through and establish a track record of success.

Goodman is sensitive to the fact that growth takes money and resources. He's willing to grow JGoods at a measured rate. So far, JGoods has not required investment capital to grow. Goodman believes the key to growing JGoods successfully will be finding the right people to facilitate the growth, whether it is employees, distributors, investors, or someone else.[2]

The JGoods case is encouraging in that the company has gotten off to a good start and has achieved growth in a well-executed manner. Its true test will be whether it is able to achieve **sustained growth**, which is growth in both revenues and profits over a sustained period of time. Evidence shows that relatively few firms generate sustained, profitable growth.[3] For example, normally only one in three businesses that make *Inc.* magazine's list of the 500 fastest growing private firms in America repeats the following year.[4] In addition, a recent study found that only 3 percent of all firms are "gazelles" or rapid growth firms at any given time. Still, these firms are important to the economy and account for nearly all new private sector job and sales growth.[5] As a result, studying firm growth is important to help individual firms understand how to achieve sustained growth and for a national economy.

Although challenging, most entrepreneurial ventures try to grow and see it as an important part of their ability to remain successful.[6] This sentiment was expressed by Hewlett-Packard (HP) cofounder David Packard, who wrote that while HP was being built, he and cofounder Bill Hewlett had "speculated many times about the optimum size of a company." The pair "did not believe that growth was important for its own sake" but eventually concluded that "continuous growth was essential" for the company to remain competitive.[7] When HP published a formal list of its objectives in 1996, one of the seven objectives was growth.[8] For HP, acquiring Compaq Computer Corporation contributed to the firm's continuing commitment to growth. Although a controversial strategic decision, acquiring Compaq seems to have provided HP with the breadth and depth it needed to improve its ability to compete against strong computer competitors such as Dell Inc. In fact, HP now holds the largest percentage of the global market for personal computers.

The first part of the chapter focuses on preparing for growth, including a discussion of three specific areas that a firm can focus on to equip itself for growth. The second part of the chapter focuses on reasons for growth. Although sustained growth is almost always the result of deliberate intentions, a firm can't always choose its pace of growth. This section lists the seven primary reasons that motivate and stimulate business growth. The chapter's third section focuses on managing growth, which centers on knowing and managing the stages of growth. The final section of the chapter looks at the challenges of growth, including the managerial capacity problem and the day-to-day challenges of growing a firm.

PREPARING FOR GROWTH

Most entrepreneurial firms want to grow. Especially in the short term, growth in sales revenue is an important indicator of an entrepreneurial venture's potential to survive today and be successful tomorrow. Growth is exciting and for most businesses is an indication of success. Many entrepreneurial firms have grown quickly and have produced impressive results for their employees and owners: Consider Starbucks, Zappos, and Google, among others, as examples of this.

While there is some trial and error involved in starting and growing any business, the degree to which a firm prepares for its future growth has a direct bearing on its level of success.[9] This section focuses on three important things a business can do to prepare for growth.

Learning Objective

2. Describe how firms can properly prepare for growth.

Appreciating the Nature of Business Growth

The first thing that a business can do to prepare for growth is to appreciate the nature of business growth. Growing a business successfully takes preparation, good management, and an appreciation of the issues involved. The following are issues about business growth that entrepreneurs should appreciate.

Not All Businesses Have the Potential to Be Aggressive Growth Firms   The businesses that have the potential to grow the fastest over a sustained period of time are ones that solve a significant problem or have a major impact on their customers' productivity or lives. This is why the lists of fast-growing firms are often dominated by health care, technology, and entertainment companies. These companies can potentially have the most significant impact on their customers' businesses or lives. This point is affirmed by contrasting the sporting goods store industry with the biotechnology and the video game industries. From 2007 to 2008, the average sporting goods store in the United States alone grew by 2.6 percent while firms in biotechnology and video games grew by 12.9 percent and 9.5 percent, respectively.[10] While there is nothing wrong with starting and owning a sporting goods store, it's important to have a realistic outlook of how fast the business will likely grow. Even though an individual sporting goods store might get off to a fast start, as its gets larger, its annual growth will normally start to reflect its industry norm.

A Business Can Grow Too Fast   Many businesses start fast and never let up, which stresses a business financially and can leave its owners emotionally drained. This sentiment is affirmed by Vipin Jain, the CEO of Retrevo, a consumer electronics company. Jain has started several companies. When asked what lessons he's learned as a serial entrepreneur, Jain replied:

> I think one thing (I've) learned is to not get carried away. Building a startup not only takes a good vision and a good market that you want to go after, but it also requires systematic execution. You can only run at a certain pace. Don't try to overrun yourself. Be conservative in your spending. Don't burn all the cash you have, because you need that. You need to be very, very conscientious about how your business grows and what kind of expenses you have to support your growth.[11]

Sometimes businesses grow at a measured pace and then experience a sudden upswing in orders and have difficulty keeping up. This scenario can transform a business with satisfied customers and employees into a chaotic workplace with people scrambling to push the business's product out the door as quickly as possible. The way to prevent this from happening is to recognize when to put the brakes on and have the courage to do it. This set of circumstances played out early in the life of The Pampered Chef, a company that sells kitchen utensils through home parties. Just about the time the company was gaining serious momentum, it realized that it didn't have enough inventory to serve the busy Christmas season. This reality posed a serious dilemma. It couldn't instantly increase its inventory (its vendors were all low and the company was small, so it couldn't make extraordinary demands), yet it didn't want to discourage its home consultants from making sales or signing up new consultants. One option was to institute a recruiting freeze (on new home consultants), which would slow the rate of sales. Doris Christopher, the company's founder, remembers asking others for advice. Most advised against instituting a recruiting freeze, arguing that the lifeblood of any direct sales organization is to sign up new recruits. In the end, the company decided to institute the freeze and slowed its sales enough to fill all orders on time during the holiday season. The freeze was lifted the following January, and the number of The Pampered Chef recruits soared. Reflecting on the decision, Doris Christopher later wrote:

> Looking back, the recruiting freeze augmented our reputation with our sales force, customers, and vendors. People saw us as an honest company that was trying to do the right thing and not overestimating our capabilities.[12]

Other businesses have faced similar dilemmas and have sometimes made the right call and sometimes haven't. The overarching point is that growth must be handled carefully. A business can only grow as fast as its infrastructure allows, as will be emphasized throughout this chapter. Table 13.1 provides a list of 10 warning signs that a business is growing too fast.

Business Success Doesn't Always Scale Unfortunately, the very thing that makes a business successful might suffer as the result of growth. This is what business experts often mean when they say growth is a "two edged sword." For example, businesses that are based on providing high levels of individualized service often don't grow or scale well. For example, an investment brokerage service that initially provided high levels of personalized attention can quickly evolve into providing standard or even substandard service as it adds customers and starts automating its services. Its initial customers might find it harder to get individualized service than it once was and start viewing the company as just another ordinary business.

There is also a category of businesses that sell high-end or specialty products that earn high margins. These businesses typically sell their

Table 13.1   10 WARNING SIGNS THAT A BUSINESS IS GROWING
TOO FAST

- Borrowing money to pay for routine operating expenses
- Extremely tight profit margins
- Over-stretched staff
- Declining product quality
- E-mail starts going unanswered
- Customer complaints are up
- Employees dread coming to work
- Productivity is falling
- Operating in a "crisis" mode becomes the norm rather than the exception
- The business's accountants are starting to worry

products through venues where customers prioritize quality over price. These businesses can grow but only at a measured pace. If they grow too quickly, they can lose the "exclusivity" they are trying to project or can damage their special appeal. Fashion clothing boutiques often limit the number of garments they sell in a certain size or color for a similar reason. Even though they know they could sell more of a particular blouse or dress, they deliberately limit their sales so their customers don't see each other wearing identical items.

An example of a business that didn't scale well because it had difficulty growing beyond a single location is provided in the "What Went Wrong?" feature. Meetro was a location-aware instant message platform that grew successfully in Chicago, but the founders encountered problems growing the business beyond its home market. Meetro eventually failed because its founders just couldn't grow it successfully.

Staying Committed to a Core Strategy

The second thing that a business can do to prepare for growth is to stay committed to a core strategy. As discussed in Chapter 6, an important part of a firm's business model is its core strategy, which defines how it competes relative to its rivals. A firm's core strategy is largely determined by its core competencies, or what it does particularly well. While this insight might seem self-evident, it's important that a business not lose sight of its core strategy as it prepares for growth. If a business becomes distracted or starts pursuing every opportunity for growth that it's presented, it can easily stray into areas where it finds itself at a competitive disadvantage. Remember that as we explained in Case 11.1, eBags exited the shoe business by selling the site it acquired (Shoedini.com) to Zappos after only three years. eBags' executives decided that the shoe business was too far of a stretch from the firm's core business. Amazon.com also strayed into other businesses early in its life. Just months after it announced that it intended to become "a place where you can buy anything from anyone," Amazon laid off 15 percent of its workforce and started eliminating product lines under the slogan "Get the Crap Out." The company quickly realized that it was competing in areas that were not well-matched with its core strategy and its distinctive competencies, and its competitors had a decided advantage.

The way most businesses typically evolve is to start by selling a product or service that is consistent with their core strategy and increase sales by incrementally moving into areas that are different from, but are related to, their core

What Went WRONG?

Meetro: Sometimes Businesses Just Don't Scale

Meetro was a location-aware instant messaging platform. Launched on June 1, 2005, it could determine the user's physical location and inform the user of Meetro users in the same vicinity. So, if you were walking across campus and had Meetro running on your cell phone, you could tell if anyone near you was a Meetro user, look at their profile page, and if you felt you had anything in common could instant message (IM) the person and try to hook up. Unlike other instant messaging platforms, you could IM other Meetro users who were nearby instantly, even if you weren't on their approved "friend" list. For privacy reasons, Meetro never revealed the exact location of another user. Once you contacted a Meetro user, it was up to the user to decide whether to respond. The user could ignore the message or say, "I'm at the coffee shop on Broadway and Fifth Street." Meetro used clever technology to make its service work. Toward the end of 2006, to enhance its service, Meetro introduced features to display businesses that were nearby (in addition to people), such as restaurants, cafés, and shops. Despite all this, Meetro failed. What went wrong?

Several things. First, it was too hard to build a large enough critical mass of people, beyond the company's home base, using the service to make it worthwhile. The service launched in Chicago, and the founders worked hard to get their friends and acquaintances to sign up. Meetro even got nice write-ups in the Chicago papers, which motivated additional adoptions. But the founders couldn't be present in every city, and the company didn't have the money for a massive advertising campaign. So the service didn't scale. If you signed up for Meetro in Boise, Idaho, or even New York City, chances are you would look at Meetro and there wouldn't be anyone else on the service nearby. The extent of the location problem became even more evident to the founders when they moved Meetro from Chicago to the Silicon Valley. Because the founders and their team weren't in Chicago anymore to push the service, organize events, and stoke the press, Meetro did okay but never grew as fast as it did when the founders were physically present.

The second problem with Meetro is that if someone wasn't online when you were online, you couldn't locate or reach them. Although most people have their cell phones and computers on 24/7 today, that wasn't necessarily the case when Meetro launched in 2005. A final problem was that Meetro required its users to download software. As people became more acquainted with Web 2.0 applications, which normally don't require the user to download software (think YouTube and Facebook), the fact that Meetro's software had to be downloaded was a deterrent. In the end, Meetro was a service that worked and gained traction in a single location, but the founders could never envision a way to grow the firm and create the scale necessary to make it successful.

Questions for Critical Thinking

1. Are there ways that the founders of Meetro could have more effectively grown or scaled the business?
2. Did the founders of Meetro seem to have a very detailed or coherent growth-related plan?
3. How could Meetro have used partnerships to help grow or scale its business?
4. In what ways would Meetro's business be easier to start today?

Sources: P. Bragiel, "Meetro," www.techcrunch.com (accessed September 17, 2008); Wikipedia, "Meetro," www.wikipedia.org (accessed September 17, 2008).

strengths and capabilities. This is what Zappos, the subject of Case 9.2, is doing. The company started by selling shoes and has gradually expanded into clothing, bags, and accessories. The success of its new product lines will be determined largely by whether the company's existing core competencies are sufficient to profitably sell these items. If they aren't, then Zappos will have to develop or acquire additional core competencies, or it is likely to struggle to effectively manage its growth.

A parable that helps affirm why sticking to a core strategy is so important is provided by Jim Collins in his book *Good to Great*. In the book, Collins retells the fable of the fox and the hedgehog, which was originally told by Isaiah Berlin. According to the fable, because he is sly, cunning, and strong, everyone thinks the fox is better than the hedgehog. All the lowly hedgehog knows how to do is one thing—curl up in a ball, with its spikes out, to deter intruders. The ironic thing is that whatever the fox does, and no matter how many of its 100 tricks it tries to use, the hedgehog always wins, because it knows how to do one thing well—roll up and stick its spikes out. In *Good to Great*, Collins says businesses that are successful over the long haul are more like hedgehogs than foxes. Rather than moving swiftly in all directions, like foxes, successful businesses keep their heads down and do one thing particularly well. Like the hedgehog, they see what is essential and ignore the rest.[13]

Planning for Growth

The third thing that a firm can do to prepare for growth is to establish growth-related plans.[14] This task involves a firm thinking ahead and anticipating the type and amount of growth it wants to achieve.

The process of writing a business plan, covered in Chapter 4, greatly assists in developing growth-related plans. A business plan normally includes a detailed forecast of a firm's first three to five years of sales along with an operations plan that describes the resources the business will need to meet its projections. Even though a business will undoubtedly change during its first three to five years, it's still good to have a plan. Many businesses periodically revise their business plans and allow them to help guide their growth-related decisions.

It's also important for a business to determine, as early as practical, the strategies for growth that it will try to employ. For example, Proactiv, the acne medicine company and focus of Case 11.2, is a single-product company and has grown by steadily increasing its domestic sales, introducing its products into foreign countries, and by encouraging nontraditional users of acne medicine, like adult males, to use its product. Proactiv's decision to stick with one product and to avoid growing through initiatives like acquisitions and licensing has allowed the company to focus on marketing and building its brand. Similarly, Green Plug, the subject of the "You Be the VC 13.1" feature, has developed technology that makes it possible for a consumer to use a single recharger to recharge multiple electronic devices, such as cell phones, laptop computers, digital cameras, and cordless power tools. The company, however, does not manufacture rechargers. Instead, it sells a chip, called the Green Plug Universal Power Protocol, to existing recharger manufacturers. Green Plug's decision to sell the technology that

It's important that a business establish growth-related plans and objectives. Here, a female entrepreneur is leading a discussion with her new-venture team about the specific steps that will be required for the business to meet its growth objectives.

makes recharges more efficient and universal rather than the rechargers themselves has an impact on its growth plans.

On a more personal level, a business owner should step back and measure the company's growth plans against his or her personal goals and aspirations. The old adage, "Be careful what you wish for," is as true in business as it is in other areas of life. For example, if a business has the potential to grow rapidly, the owner should know what to expect if the fast-growth route is chosen. Fast-growth normally implies a quick pace of activity, a rapidly rising overhead, and a total commitment in terms of time and attention on the part of the business owners. The upside is that if the business is successful, the owner will normally do very well financially. The trade-offs implied by this scenario are acceptable to some business owners and aren't to others.

REASONS FOR GROWTH

Although sustained, profitable growth is almost always the result of deliberate intentions and careful planning, a firm can't always choose its pace of growth. A firm's **pace of growth** is the rate at which it is growing on an annual basis. Sometimes firms are forced into a high-growth mode sooner than they would like. For example, when a firm develops a product or service that satisfies a need for many customers such that orders roll in very quickly, it must adjust quickly or risk faltering. In other instances, a firm experiences unexpected competition and must grow to maintain its market share.

This section examines the six primary reasons firms try to grow to increase their profitability and valuation, as depicted in Figure 13.1.

Learning Objective

3. Discuss the six most common reasons firms pursue growth.

Capturing Economies of Scale   **Economies of scale** arc generated when increasing production lowers the average cost of each unit produced. This phenomenon occurs for two reasons. First, if a company can get a discount by buying component parts in bulk, it can lower its variable costs per unit as it grows larger. **Variable costs** are the costs a company incurs as it generates sales. Second, by increasing production, a company can spread its fixed costs over a greater number of units. **Fixed costs** are costs that a company incurs whether it sells something or not. For example, it may cost a company $10,000 per month to air-condition its factory. The air-conditioning cost is fixed; cooling the factory will cost the same whether the company produces 10 or 10,000 units per month.

A related reason firms grow is to make use of unused labor capacity or other resources. For example, a firm may need exactly 2.5 full-time salespeople to fully cover its trade area. Because a firm obviously can't hire 2.5 salespeople, it may hire 3 salespeople and expand its trade area.[15]

Capturing Economies of Scope   Economies of scope are similar to economies of scale, except the advantage comes through the scope (or range) of a firm's operations rather than from its scale of production. For example, a company's sales

FIGURE 13.1

Appropriate Reasons for Firm Growth

- Economies of scale
- Economies of scope
- Market leadership
- Influence, power, and survivability
- Need to accommodate the growth of key customers
- Ability to attract and retain talented employees

Some entrepreneurial firms grow quickly to capture enough business to realize economies of scale in their operations. Here, a worker sorts books in an Amazon.com warehouse. Amazon.com gains efficiencies through its large scale of operations.

Marilyn Newton/The New York Times

force may be able to sell 10 items more efficiently than 5, because the cost of travel and the salesperson's salary is spread out over 10 products rather than 5. Similarly, a company like Dell Inc. captures economies of scope in its advertising when the same advertisements advertise computers along with printers, other computer-related accessories, and extended warranty plans.

Market Leadership   **Market leadership** occurs when a firm holds the number one or the number two position in an industry or niche market in terms of sales volume. Many firms work hard to achieve market leadership, to realize economies of scale and economies of scope, and to be recognized as the brand leader. Being the market leader also permits a firm to use slogans such as "Number 1 Electronic Games Producer in America" in its promotions, helping it win customers and attract talented employees as well as business partners.

Influence, Power, and Survivability   Larger businesses usually have more influence and power than smaller firms in regard to setting standards for an industry, getting a "foot in the door" with major customers and suppliers, and garnering prestige. In addition, larger businesses can typically make a mistake yet survive more easily than entrepreneurial ventures. Commenting on this issue, Jack Welch, GE's former CEO, once said, "Size gives us another big advantage; our reach and resources enable us to go to bat more frequently, to take more swings, to experiment more, and unlike a small company, we can miss on occasion and get to swing again."[16]

A firm's capacity for growth affects its survival in additional ways. For example, a firm that stays small and relies on the efforts and motivation of its founder or a small group of people is vulnerable to the loss of their skills or interest in the firm, as evidenced in the ProtectMyPhotos feature in Chapter 1. ProtectMyPhotos failed to grow larger because the founders lost their passion for the business. Once a firm grows, however, and has a larger staff and more products and services to offer, it usually gains momentum and is no longer as dependent on the efforts and motivations of a small number of founders or employees.

Need to Accommodate the Growth of Key Customers   Sometimes firms are compelled to grow to accommodate the growth of a key customer. For example, if Intel has a major account with an electronics firm buying a large number of its semiconductor chips and the electronics firm is growing at a rate of 20 percent per year, Intel may have to add capacity each year to accommodate the growth of its customer or else risk losing some or all of its business.

Ability to Attract and Retain Talented Employees   The final reason that firms grow is to attract and retain high-quality personnel. It is natural for talented employees to want to work for a firm that can offer opportunities for promotion, higher salaries, and increased levels of responsibility. Growth is a firm's primary mechanism to generate promotional opportunities for employees, while failing to retain key employees can be very damaging to a firm's growth efforts. High turnover is expensive, and in knowledge-based industries in particular, such as biotechnology and film production, a company's number one asset is the combined talent, training, and experience of its employees. In less knowledge-intensive settings, turnover may not be as critical, but it is still costly. Based on estimates from Merck & Company, Hewlett-Packard, and *Fortune* magazine, the average cost of turnover is 1.5 times the employee's salary.[17] Entrepreneurial ventures rarely have the excess financial capital needed to support the unfavorable relationship between employee hiring and turnover. However, when talented individuals leave a large company either voluntarily or through layoffs, entrepreneurial ventures have opportunities to hire people with skills the venture did not pay for them to develop.

Although each of the reasons for growth just discussed are important, a firm should be careful to grow prudently. Establishing a relationship with Wal-Mart or Costco might seem like a dream come true for a consumer products firm, but the relationship might cripple the firm if it isn't a good fit or the large retailer captures the majority of the venture's profits. This scenario played itself out at Timbuk2, a manufacturer of urban shoulder bags. Timbuk2 forged a relationship with CompUSA to carry its bags. Timbuk2 quickly realized it had made a mistake and exited the relationship, as described in this chapter's "Savvy Entrepreneurial Firm" boxed feature.

MANAGING GROWTH

Many businesses are caught off guard by the challenges involved with growing their companies. One would think that if a business got off to a good start, steadily increased its sales, and started making money, it would get progressively easier to manage the growth of a firm. In many instances just the opposite happens. As a business increases its sales, its pace of activity quickens, its resource needs increase, and the founders often find that they're busier than ever. Major challenges can also occur. For example, a business might project its next year's sales and realize it will need more people and additional equipment to handle the increased workload. The new equipment might need to be purchased and the new people hired and trained before the increased business generates additional income. It's easy to imagine serious discussions among the members of a new venture's management team trying to figure out how that will all work out.

The reality is that a company must actively and carefully manage its growth for it to expand in a healthy and profitable manner. As a business grows and becomes better known, there are normally more opportunities that present themselves, but there are more things that can go wrong too. Many potential problems and heartaches can be avoided by prudently managing the growth

Savvy Entrepreneurial FIRM
Timbuk2: Bagging the Right Customers Rather Than the Biggest Ones
www.timbuk2.com

In early 2003, Mark Dwight, the CEO of Timbuk2, was on top of the world. Timbuk2, the San Francisco–based manufacturer of urban shoulder bags, had just inked a deal with CompUSA to carry its bags. "I thought it was our big break," Dwight recalls.

Yet just three months later, Dwight had second thoughts. It wasn't the sales. Sales were booming. But financially, Timbuk2 was being squeezed by the relationship. CompUSA's slim margins and high-volume demand were difficult for Timbuk2 to cope with. In addition, Dwight feared that selling through a mainstream retailer like CompUSA would change how consumers viewed his company. He wanted to see his company increase sales, but he didn't want it to lose its quirkiness and unique appeal either.

So Dwight cancelled the CompUSA deal and refocused Timbuk2. In refocusing the company, he compared Timbuk2 to Coach, which is a billion-dollar company but sells primarily through specialty stores. Specialty stores, like the Discovery Channel Store and the Apple Computer Store, appeal to consumers who prioritize quality and brand image over price. This attribute of specialty stores allows vendors like Timbuk2 to earn higher margins (than they would earn at a big-box retailer like CompUSA), which compensates for lower-volume sales. Selling simultaneously through specialty stores and big-box retailers is difficult for a firm like Timbuk2. The large retailers invariably insist on a lower price point than the specialty retailers, which forces the vendor to either undercut the sales price of the specialty retailers or enhance the product sold through the large retailers in some way to increase the price. In Timbuk2's case, the bags it sold through CompUSA were bundled with extra accessories to avoid undercutting the sales prices of its other retailers.

The results of Dwight's decision have been impressive. Timbuk2's sales are strong, and the company has an increasingly attractive product line, which is sold both online and through specialty stores throughout the United States. Ironically, in 2007 CompUSA closed the majority of its stores, and in early 2008 its remaining stores and e-commerce operations were acquired by Systemax Inc. There are now just a handful of CompUSA stores open in Florida, Texas, and Puerto Rico.

Questions for Critical Thinking

1. Do you think Timbuk2 made the right decision in canceling the deal with CompUSA? What were the pluses and minuses of making this decision? To what degree could Timbuk2 have been hurt when CompUSA closed the majority of its stores?
2. According to the feature, Timbuk2's CEO Mark Dwight worried that selling through CompUSA would change the way consumers viewed his company. Describe, in more detail, what you think Dwight was worried about in this area. Do you think Dwight's worries were justified?
3. Which of the six reasons for firm growth are the most motivating for Timbuk2?
4. Identify another consumer products firm that sells primarily through specialty retailers rather than big-box stores like Costco, Wal-Mart, and Target. Briefly describe whether you think the retailer would be hurt by selling through a big-box store.

Sources: Timbuk2 homepage, www.timbuk2.com (accessed on November 16, 2008); A. Tilin, "Bagging the Right Customers," *Business 2.0*, May 2005, 56–57.

---

process. This section focuses on knowing and managing the stages of growth. The final section in this chapter focuses on a related topic—the challenges of growth.

Knowing and Managing the Stages of Growth

The majority of businesses go through a discernable set of stages referred to as the organizational life cycle.[18] The stages, pictured in Figure 13.2, include introduction, early growth, continuous growth, maturity, and decline. Each stage must be managed differently. It's important for a business owner to be familiar with these stages, along with the unique opportunities and challenges that each stage entails.

Learning Objective

4. Explain the importance of knowing the stages of growth.

FIGURE 13.2

Organizational Life
Cycle

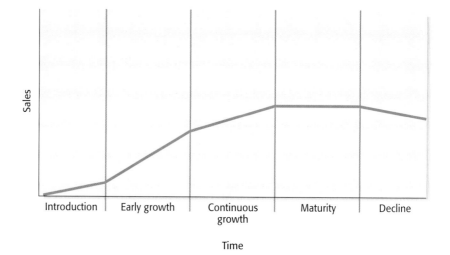

Introduction Stage   This is the start-up phase where a business determines what its core strengths and capabilities are and starts selling its initial product or service. It's a very "hands-on" phase for the founder or founders who are normally involved in every aspect of the day-to-day life of the business. The business is typically very nonbureaucratic with no (or few) written rules or procedures. The main goal of the business is to get off to a good start and to try to gain momentum in the marketplace.

The main challenges for a business in the introduction stage are to make sure the initial product or service is right and to start laying the groundwork for building a larger organization. It's important to not rush things. This sentiment is affirmed by April Singer, the founder of Rufus Shirts, a company that makes high-end shirts for men. Before growing her business beyond the introduction stage, Singer made sure that her unique approach for making men's shirts worked and that it resonated in the marketplace:

> Before growing too much too fast, I wanted to spend two seasons making sure that the concept worked, that I shipped well, and that consumers liked the product. They did.[19]

This affirmation gave Singer the confidence to expand her business and move into a more aggressive growth mode. In regard to laying the groundwork to build a larger organization, many businesses use the introduction stage to try different concepts to see what works and what doesn't, recognizing that trial and error gets harder as a business grows. It's important to document what works and start thinking about how the company's success can be replicated when the owner isn't present or when the business expands beyond its original location.

Early Growth Stage   A business's early growth stage is generally characterized by increasing sales and heightened complexity. The business is normally still focused on its initial product or service but is trying to increase its market share and might have related products in the works. The initial formation of policies and procedures takes place, and the process of running the business will start to consume more of the founder's or founders' time and attention.

For a business to be successful in this stage, two important things must take place. First, the founder or owner of the business must start transitioning from his or her role as the hands-on supervisor of every aspect of the business to a more managerial role. As articulated by Michael E. Gerber in his excellent book *The E-Myth Revisited*, the owner must start working "on the business" rather than "in the business."[20] The basic idea is that early in

**Learning
Objective**

5.   *Describe the most
important factors for
firms to focus on during
each stage of growth.*

the life of a business, the owner typically is directly involved in building the product or delivering the service that the business provides. As the business moves into the early growth stage, the owner must let go of that role and spend more time learning how to manage and build the business. If the owner isn't willing to make this transition or doesn't know it needs to be made, the business will never grow beyond the owner's ability to directly supervise everything that takes place, and the business's growth will eventually stall.

The second thing that must take place for a business to be successful in the early growth stage is that increased formalization must take place. The business has to start developing policies and procedures that tell employees how to run it when the founders or other top managers aren't present. This is how franchise restaurants run so well when they're staffed by what appears to be a group of teenagers. The employees are simply following well-documented policies and procedures. This task was clearly on the mind of Emily Levy, the founder of EBL Coaching, a tutoring service for children who are struggling in school or trying to overcome disabilities, when she was asked by Ladies Who Launch (a support network for female entrepreneurs) early in the life of her business about her growth plans:

> My future goals include continuing to spread EBL Coaching's programs nationally, using our proprietary materials and self-contained multisensory methods. I have already developed a series of workbooks, called "Strategies for Success," addressing specific study skills strategies, that are being used in a number of schools across the country. The real challenge will be figuring our how to replicate our programs while maintaining our high quality of teaching and personalized approach.[21]

Continuous Growth Stage   As a business moves beyond its early growth stage and its pace of growth accelerates, the need for structure and formalization increases. The resource requirements of the business are usually a major concern, along with the ability of the owner and manager to take the firm to the next level. Often the business will start developing new products and services and will expand to new markets. Smaller firms may be acquired, and the business might start more aggressively partnering with other firms. When handled correctly, the business's expansion will be in areas that are related to its core strengths and capabilities, or it will develop new strengths and capabilities to complement its activities.

The toughest decisions are typically made in the continuous growth stage. One tough decision is whether the owner of the business and the current management team has the experience and ability to take the firm any further. This scenario played out for Rachel Ashwell, the founder of Shabby Chic, a home furnishing business. Ashwell expanded her company to five separate locations, inked a licensing deal with Target, wrote five how-to books related to her business, and hosted her own television show on the Style Network before concluding that her business had stalled. Her choice was to continue running the business or find more experienced management to grow it further. She opted for the latter, and Shabby Chic is growing again.[22] Another example is provided in Case 9.1, which focuses on 1-800-PetMeds and Google. Both of the companies replaced their founders with professional CEOs at critical junctures in the growth of their respective firms.

The importance of developing policies and procedures increases during the continuous growth stage. It's also important for a business to develop a formal organizational structure and determine clear lines of delegation throughout the business. Well-developed policies and procedures lead to order, which typically makes the process of growing a business more organized and successful.

Maturity   A business enters the maturity stage when its growth slows. At this point, the firm typically focuses more intently on efficiently managing the products and services it has rather than expanding in new areas. Innovation slows. Formal policies and procedures, although important, can become an impediment if they are too rigid and strict.[23] It's important that the firm continues to adapt and that the founders, managers, and employees remain passionate about the products and services that are being sold. If this doesn't happen, a firm can easily slip into a no-growth situation.

A well-managed firm that finds its products and services are mature often looks for partnering or acquisition opportunities to breathe new life into the firm. For example, PepsiCo and Coca-Cola, two firms in the maturity stage of their life cycles, are aggressively acquiring small beverage companies. They're doing this to combine fresh new products with their staple products to maintain some upward momentum, even though their staple products are mature. Recently, Coca-Cola paid $4.1 billion to acquire vitaminwater maker Glacéau while PepsiCo purchased the juice business of Russia's Lebedyansky for $1.4 billion.

If a company does grow organically while in the maturity stage, it normally focuses on the "next generation" of products it already sells rather than invest in new or related products or services.

Decline   It is not inevitable that a business enter the decline stage and either deteriorate or die. Many American businesses have long histories and have thrived by adapting to environmental change and by selling products that remain important to customers. Eventually all business's products or services will be threatened by more relevant and innovative products. When this happens, a business's ability to avoid decline depends on the strength of its leadership and its ability to appropriately respond.

A firm can also enter the decline stage if it loses its sense of purpose or spreads itself so thin that it no longer has a competitive advantage in any of its markets. A firm's management team should be aware of these potential pitfalls and guard against allowing them to happen.

CHALLENGES OF GROWTH

There is a consistent set of challenges that affect all stages of a firm's growth. The challenges typically become more acute as a business grows, but a business's founder or founders and managers also become more savvy and experienced with the passage of time. The challenges illustrate that no firm grows in a competitive vacuum. As a business grows and takes market share away from rival firms, there will be a certain amount of retaliation that takes place. This is an aspect of competition that a business owner needs to be aware of and plan for. Competitive retaliation normally increases as a business grows and becomes a larger threat to its rivals.

This section is divided into two parts. The first part focuses on the managerial capacity problem, which is a framework for thinking about the overall challenge of growing a firm. The second part focuses on the four most common day-to-day challenges of growing a business.

Managerial Capacity

Learning Objective

6. Describe the managerial capacity problem and how it inhibits firm growth.

In her thoughtful and seminal book *The Theory of the Growth of the Firm*, Edith T. Penrose argues that firms are collections of productive resources that are organized in an administrative framework.[24] As an administrative framework, the primary purpose of a firm is to package its resources together with resources acquired outside the firm for the production of products and services at a profit. As a firm goes about its routine activities, the management team becomes better acquainted with the firm's resources and its markets. This knowledge leads to the expansion of a firm's **productive opportunity set**, which is the set of opportunities the firm feels it's capable of pursuing. The opportunities might include the introduction of new products, geographic expansion, licensing products to other firms, exporting, and so on. The pursuit of these new opportunities causes a firm to grow.

Penrose points out, however, that there is a problem with the execution of this simple logic. The firm's administrative framework consists of two kinds of services that are important to a firm's growth—entrepreneurial services and managerial services. **Entrepreneurial services** generate new market, product, and service ideas, while **managerial services** administer the routine functions of the firm and facilitate the profitable execution of new opportunities. However, the introduction of new product and service ideas requires substantial managerial services (or managerial "capacity") to be properly implemented and supervised. This is a complex problem because if a firm has insufficient managerial services to properly implement its entrepreneurial ideas, it can't quickly hire new managers to remedy the shortfall. It is expensive to hire new employees, and it takes time for new managers to be socialized into the firm's culture, acquire firm-specific skills and knowledge, and establish trusting relationships with other members of their firms.[25] When a firm's managerial resources are insufficient to take advantage of its new product and services opportunities, the subsequent bottleneck is referred to as the **managerial capacity problem**. James Vincent, former CEO of Biogen Inc., an entrepreneurial biotech firm, has argued convincingly in interviews that this capacity issue is his firm's number one growth constraint.[26]

As the entrepreneurial venture grows, it encounters the dual challenges of adverse selection and moral hazard. **Adverse selection** means that as the number of employees a firm needs increases, it becomes increasingly difficult for it to find the right employees, place them in appropriate positions, and provide adequate supervision.[27] The faster a firm grows, the less time managers have to evaluate the suitability of job candidates and the higher the chances are that an unsuitable candidate will be chosen. Selecting "ineffective" or "unsuitable" employees increases the venture's costs. **Moral hazard** means that as a firm grows and adds personnel, the new hires typically do not have the same ownership incentives as the original founders, so the new hires may not be as motivated as the founders to put in long hours or may even try to avoid hard work. To make sure the new hires are doing what they are employed to do, the firm will typically hire monitors (i.e., managers) to supervise the employees. This practice creates a hierarchy that is costly and isolates the top management team from its rank-and-file employees.

The basic model of firm growth articulated by Penrose is shown in Figure 13.3, and Figure 13.4 shows the essence of the growth-limiting managerial capacity problem.[28] Figure 13.4 indicates that the ability to increase managerial services is not friction free. It is constrained or limited by (1) the time required to socialize new managers, (2) how motivated entrepreneurs and/or managers are to grow their firms, (3) adverse selection, and (4) moral hazard.

One way firms deal with the managerial capacity problem is to partner with other firms and in essence co-opt a portion of their resources. An example is a recent partnership that Zazzle, the subject of Case 10.2, struck with MySpace. As described in the "Partnering for Success" feature, Zazzle has opened a new market for its products not by significantly increasing its own managerial capacity, but by piggybacking on the infrastructure and managerial capacity of a partner.

The reality of the managerial capacity problem is one of the main reasons that entrepreneurs and managers worry so much about growth. Growth is a generally positive thing, but it is easy for a firm to overshoot its capacity to manage growth in ways that will diminish the venture's sales revenues and profits.

Learning Objective

7. Discuss the challenges for firm growth imposed by adverse selection and moral hazard.

FIGURE 13.3

Basic Model of Firm Growth

Day-to-Day Challenges of Growing a Firm

Learning Objective

8. Discuss the day-to-day challenges of growing a firm.

Learning Objective

9. Explain why "cash flow management" is a challenge for growing a firm.

Along with the overarching challenges imposed by the managerial capacity problem, there are a number of day-to-day challenges involved with growing a firm. The following is a discussion of the four most common challenges.

Cash Flow Management As discussed in Chapters 8 and 10, as a firm grows, it requires an increasing amount of cash to service its customers. In addition, a firm must carefully manage its cash on hand to make sure it maintains sufficient liquidity to meet its payroll and cover its other short-term obligations. There are many colorful anecdotes about business founders who have had to rush to a bank and get a second mortgage on their houses to cover their business's payroll. This usually occurs when a business takes on too much work, and its customers are slow to pay. A business can literally have $1 million in accounts receivable but not be able to meet a $25,000 payroll. This is why almost any book you pick up about growing a business stresses the importance of properly managing your cash flow.

Growth usually increases rather than decreases the challenges involved with cash flow management because an increase in sales means that more cash will be flowing into and out of the firm. Some firms deal with potential cash flow shortfalls by establishing a line of credit at a bank or by raising investment capital. Other firms deliberately restrict the pace of their growth to avoid cash flow challenges. The latter option is preferred by Dave Schwartz, the founder of Rent-A-Wreck, a discount car rental company, who grew his firm through earnings rather than debt or investment capital. Commenting on this issue, Schwartz said:

> One of the main things I tell people starting out is not to grow too quickly. Often it's better to grow slowly, and when you do expand, try to grow with cash flow.[29]

FIGURE 13.4

The Impact of Managerial Capacity

Source: Based on material in E. T. Penrose, *The Theory of the Growth of the Firm* (Oxford: Basil Blackwell, 1959).

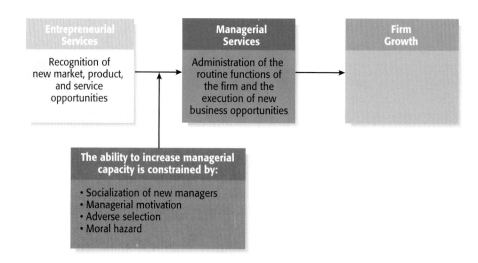

Partnering for SUCCESS

Zazzle: Addressing the Managerial Capacity Problem by Leveraging the Resources of MySpace

www.zazzle.com

www.myspace.com

Zazzle, the subject of Case 10.2, is an online service that allows its customers to upload images that can be printed on T-shirts, stamps, mouse pads, coffee mugs, skateboards, key chains, and a variety of other items. Like all young firms, Zazzle has resource constraints, and can only grow as fast as it can raise (or earn) money, hire employees, and socialize its employees into the culture of the firm.

An alternative that firms like Zazzle have, to get around the need to grow their resources at the same pace as their growth, is to partner with other firms and tap into their resources. Zazzle is doing this through a partnership with MySpace. As of mid-2007, musicians with MySpace pages were able to create virtual stores for T-shirts, posters, and other merchandise, and will be able to customize the material to their preference. The stores will be set up using a Zazzle widget, and Zazzle will manage the stores and fulfill orders, splitting the profits with the owners of the stores. The customization that Zazzle offers goes beyond what most music fans are accustomed to. For example, a customer may like a particular poster of a band, but like one band member in particular. Zazzle can isolate the face of that one band member and place it on a poster, T-shirt, or any other item. Zazzle also guarantees that all merchandise will be manufactured and shipped within 24 hours of being ordered.

Instead of entering into this partnership with MySpace, Zazzle could have hired a sales force and approached each musician and band that has a MySpace page, asking if they could help them set up an online store on their individual Web site. It would have taken time and money to hire a sales force, train the salespeople, and accumulate the new hires into Zazzle's culture. Instead, by partnering with MySpace, Zazzle was able to move quickly and by building online stores for musicians on top of MySpace's existing infrastructure, Zazzle didn't need significant additional resources or managerial capacity to reach a wide audience of potential new customers.

Questions for Critical Thinking

1. What other types of partnerships could Zazzle enter into to diminish the impact of the managerial capacity problem?
2. In what ways does a band or musician elevate part of its managerial capacity problem by allowing Zazzle to set up a virtual storefront on its MySpace page?
3. Look at Takkle, the subject of the "You Be the VC 13.2" feature. What type of partnership is Takkle utilizing to diminish the impact of the managerial capacity problem?
4. How can firms use partnerships to help avoid entering the maturity or decline stages of the organizational life cycle?

Source: Wall Street Journal (Eastern Edition) by Smith, E. Copyright 2007 by Dow Jones & Company, Inc.

Price Stability If firm growth comes at the expense of a competitor's market share, price competition can set in. For example, if an entrepreneur opens a video store near a Blockbuster that begins to erode Blockbuster's market share, Blockbuster will probably fight back by running promotions or lowering prices. This type of scenario places a new firm in a difficult predicament and illustrates why it's important to start a business by selling a differentiated product to a clearly defined target market. There is no good way for a small firm to compete head-to-head against a much larger rival on price. The best thing for a small firm to do is to avoid price competition by serving a different market and by serving that market particularly well.

Quality Control One of the most difficult challenges that businesses encounter as they grow is maintaining high levels of quality and customer service. As a firm grows, it handles more service requests and paperwork and contends with an increasing number of prospects, customers, vendors, and other stakeholders. If a business can't build its infrastructure fast enough to handle the increased activity, quality and customer service will usually suffer. What happens to many

Learning Objective

10. Explain how "quality control" can become a challenge for growing a firm.

There are few things more stressful for an entrepreneur than dealing with cash flow challenges. In this photo, the owner of a sporting goods store is diligently managing his cash flow to make sure he has sufficient funds coming in to pay his vendors, pay his employees, and cover his routine expenses.

Chuck Savage/Savage Productions Inc.

businesses is that they run into the classic chicken-or-egg quandary. It's hard to justify hiring additional employees or leasing more office space until the need is present, but if the business waits until the need is present, it usually won't have enough employees or office space to properly service new customers.

There is no easy way to resolve this type of quandary other than to recognize that it may take place and to plan for it in the best way possible. Many businesses find innovative and inexpensive ways to expand their capacity to try to avoid shortfalls in quality control or customer service. An example is eBags, the online merchant of bags and the focus of Case 11.1. eBags utilizes drop shipping rather than maintaining its own inventory, which simplifies the range of quality control issues that must be managed.

Capital Constraints Although many businesses are started fairly inexpensively, the need for capital is typically the most prevalent in the early growth and continuous growth stages of the organizational life cycle. The amount of capital required varies widely among businesses. Some businesses, like restaurant chains, might need considerable capital to hire employees, construct buildings, and purchase equipment. If they can't raise the capital they need, their growth will be stymied.

Most businesses, regardless of their industry, need capital from time to time to invest in growth-enabling projects. Their ability to raise capital, whether it's through internally generated funds, through a bank, or from investors, will determine in part whether their growth plans proceed.

Chapter Summary

1. Sustained growth is defined as growth in both revenues and profits over an extended period of time.
2. Growing a business successfully takes preparation, good management, and an appreciation of the issues involved. The three primary things that a business can do to prepare for growth are appreciating the nature of business growth, staying committed to a core strategy, and planning for growth.
3. Growth is not a random or chance event. It is something firms pursue deliberately. The six most common reasons that firms grow in an effort to

increase their profitability and valuation are as follows: to capture economies of scale; to capture economies of scope; to achieve market leadership; to maintain influence, power, and survivability; to accommodate the growth of key customers; and to maintain an ability to attract and retain talented employees.

4. Many businesses are caught off guard by the challenges involved with growing their companies. As a business increases its sales, its pace of activity quickens, its resource needs increase, and the founders often find that they're busier than ever.

5. The majority of businesses go through a discernable set of stages referred to as the organizational life cycle. The stages include introduction, early growth, continuous growth, maturity, and decline.

6. The introduction phase is where a business determines what its core strengths and capabilities are and starts selling its initial product or service. The business is typically very nonbureaucratic with no (or few) written rules or procedures. The main goal of the business is to get off to a good start and try to gain momentum in the marketplace.

7. A business's early growth stage is characterized by increasing sales and heightened complexity. For a business to succeed in this stage (1) the founder or owner of the business must start transforming from his or her role as the hands-on supervisor of every aspect of the business to a more managerial role, and (2) increased formalization must take place.

8. The toughest decisions are typically made in the continuous growth stage. One tough decision is whether the owner of the business and the current management team has the experience and ability to take the firm any further.

9. The managerial capacity problem suggests that firm growth is limited by the managerial capacity (i.e., personnel, expertise, and intellectual resources) that firms have available to implement new business ideas. The basic idea is that it does a firm little good to have exciting ideas about growth when it lacks the managerial capacity to implement its ideas.

10. The day-to-day challenges of managing growth include cash flow management, price stability, quality control, and capital constraints.

Key Terms

adverse selection, **463**	managerial capacity	pace of growth, **456**
economies of scale, **456**	problem, **463**	productive opportunity
entrepreneurial	managerial services, **463**	set, **463**
services, **463**	market leadership, **457**	sustained growth, **450**
fixed costs, **456**	moral hazard, **463**	variable costs, **456**

Review Questions

1. What is sustained growth? Why is it important?
2. Are most firms rapid-growth firms? Explain your answer.
3. What are the potential downsides to firm growth?
4. Explain why not all businesses have the potential to be aggressive-growth firms.
5. Is it possible for a firm to grow too fast? If so, what are the potential downsides?
6. Why is it difficult for some firms to grow or scale?
7. What are the benefits of planning for growth?

8. Describe economies of scale and economies of scope as rationales for firm growth.
9. List three reasons firms work hard to achieve market leadership.
10. How does a firm's growth rate affect its ability to attract and retain talented employees?
11. Briefly describe each of the five stages in the organizational life cycle.
12. Give a brief overview of the managerial capacity problem.
13. Explain what is meant by adverse selection.
14. Explain what is meant by moral hazard.
15. What is meant by the statement in the chapter that reads, "The reality of the managerial capacity problem is one of the main reasons that entrepreneurs and managers worry so much about growth"?
16. Explain why cash flow management is an important issue for a firm entering a period of rapid growth.
17. How do rapid growth firms deal with potential cash flow shortfalls?
18. Explain why price stability is an important issue for a firm entering a period of rapid growth.
19. According to the chapter, one of the most difficult challenges involved with rapid growth is quality control. Why is this so?
20. In what stage or stages of the organizational life cycle are capital constraints most prevalent?

Application Questions

1. Pete Martin just purchased a copy of *Inc.* magazine's annual issue that ranks the top 500 fastest-growing privately owned companies in America. Pete was amazed by some of the stories in the article and is more encouraged than ever to start his own art restoration firm. Pete believes his firm can grow 100 percent or more per year. He is ready to cash out his savings and get started. Is Pete starting this venture with realistic expectations? If not, what should his expectations be?
2. Twelve months ago, Brittany Nelson launched a chain of stores that sell accessories for wireless communications devices. Her first store was in Memphis, and she is now expanding into northern Mississippi and western Tennessee. Brittany's company has grown quickly from 1 store to 5, and she hopes to add 10 to 20 stores per year during the next five years. Recently, a friend told Brittany that perhaps she should slow down a bit because a company can grow "too fast." Brittany brushed the suggestion aside, simply noting that things were going fine and that growth was "no problem." Do you think Brittany should think again about her friend's advice? What are the pitfalls of growing too quickly?
3. Patty Stone owns an industrial equipment company named Get Smart Industrial that sells three products in the oil services industry. Get Smart's products are sold via a direct sales force. Patty wants to grow the firm by adding new products but has run into resistance from her chief financial officer (CFO), who argues that adding new products will increase inventory costs and place a strain on the company's cash flow. While Patty is sensitive to her CFO's concerns, what arguments can she make in favor of adding new products as a way of effectively growing her firm?
4. Brian Willard, who lives near Philadelphia, just read a lengthy article about 1-800-GOT-JUNK?, the subject of Case 13.1. He's thinking about starting a junk removal franchise company similar to 1-800-GOT-JUNK? in the northeastern and southern part of the United States. Brian has some seed money and is confident he can match 1-800-GOT-JUNK?'s 300 franchises in his first year. There are many areas in the northeast and south where

1-800-GOT-JUNK? doesn't have a presence yet, and Brian plans to target those areas first. Comment on Brian's ambitions and strategy.

5. Three years ago, Chris Dees launched a medical products company that specializes in providing products for people with diabetes. His company is number one in its industry. Recently, a couple of competitors have entered the picture, and Chris is wondering if it is worth the fight to remain number one. In terms of firm growth, what advantages are there to being the market leader?

6. Troy Milton owns a successful consumer products firm in Oakland, California. The firm has a number of talented employees who have contributed significantly to the company's success. The company has stalled in terms of growth. Curiously, Troy doesn't seem to be concerned, and a couple of his top employees have even observed that Troy seems to be enjoying the slower pace. In terms of his ability to retain his most talented employees, what risks does Troy run by letting his firm stall in terms of growth?

7. Ian Khalid lives in Tallahassee, Florida, and has owned a fiber-optics company for 5 years. He spends 12 hours a day at work micromanaging every aspect of his business, yet he still can't get the business to grow. Talk to Ian about what needs to take place for his business to move from the early growth stage to the continuous growth stage of its organizational life cycle.

8. Take a second look at WIN Detergent, the subject of the "You Be the VC 4.1" feature. Imagine you just read an article that said that the founders of WIN Detergent have decided to expand beyond detergent, and will add to their limited product line a full line of home-cleaning products along with pet shampoo and a detergent for commercial car washes. Comment on the wisdom of this strategy.

9. Meredith Colella is a food products engineer who has developed an innovative approach for the packaging of meat. Her approach will extend the shelf life of most meat products by about 30 percent. Meredith is getting ready to try to sell the idea to investors. What could Meredith tell the investors that would give them confidence that she is prepared to cope with the challenges of rapid growth?

10. Spend some time studying Green Plug, the subject of the "You Be the VC 13.1" feature. In what ways does Green Plug's business model help minimize the managerial capacity problem?

11. Stacey Williams owns a medical products firm in Durham, North Carolina. She just attended a seminar where one of the speakers said, "Participating in business partnerships can help firms lessen the impact of the managerial capacity problem." Stacey's not sure what the speaker meant by that statement. Can you help Stacey understand how participating in business partnerships can help firms lessen the impact of the managerial capacity problem?

12. Doug Rypien owns a small electronics firm in central Ohio. He is thinking about trying to grow the firm outside its immediate trade area. He is even thinking about approaching some customers in Cincinnati, believing that he has a good chance of making some sales. What are some of the day-to-day challenges that Doug will probably experience if he tries to grow his company? Given the nature of Doug's business, which of the challenges do you think will be the most demanding, and why?

13. Imagine you have a friend who has created a new board game. A prototyping lab in the College of Engineering where your friend goes to college made him a prototype of the game, which he took to a trade show and got an enthusiastic response. He even obtained orders for 2,000 copies of the game. When you asked your friend how he plans to pay for the initial production run of the game, he said that he plans to bootstrap his company and will pay for everything from his profits. Does your friend have a good sense of the financial implications of launching a new product into the marketplace?

14. Spend some time familiarizing yourself with Takkle, the subject of the "You Be the VC 13.2" feature. Which of the day-to-day challenges of growing a firm do you think will test Takkle's new-venture team the most as it tries to acquire more users and expands its offerings? Explain your answer.

15. Look at the Web site of Scuba Toys (www.scubatoys.com). As you'll see, this firm makes a wide range of products for all types of water sports. Spend some time familiarizing yourself with Scuba Toys' products and its business model. Scuba Toys is about to launch an aggressive growth strategy. Write a one-page set of recommendations for Scuba Toys that outlines some of the issues it should be aware of as it launches its growth initiative.

You Be the VC 13.1

Company: Green Plug

www.greenplug.us

Business Idea: To enable the production of a battery recharger that recharges any electronic device.

Pitch: Have you ever gone on a trip and had to carry several different battery rechargers? Or do you have a place on your kitchen counter or desk where there is a tangle of rechargers—one for your laptop, one for your cell phone, one for your iPod, and so on? It's a mess isn't it? Why hasn't someone designed a recharger that will work with all electronic devices?

Green Plug has done just that. Through the use of Green Plug technology, it's now possible for a consumer to use a single recharger to recharge multiple electronic devices. Here's how it works: Green Plug sells a chip, called the Green Plug Universal Power Protocol, to recharger manufacturers. The chip allows a manufacturer to create a "Green Plug Power Hub," which will recognize and recharge any Green Plug–enabled electronic device. Green Plug then gives away software, called GreenTalk, to electronic device manufacturers to make their devices Green Plug enabled. So, as a consumer, when you plug your iPod into a Green Plug Power Hub, the hub will recognize it as an iPod and recharge it. You can plug your cell phone, laptop, digital picture frame, and any other DC-powered electronic device into the same hub, and as long as the devices are Green Plug enabled, they will be safely recharged. An added benefit of the Green Plug Power Hub is that it will only pull enough electricity from your wall socket to fully recharge each device. Currently, if you plug your cell phone's recharger into your wall socket at night, the recharger will draw energy from the socket, even after your cell phone is fully recharged. Even if you detach your cell phone from its recharger in the morning, the recharger will continue to draw energy from your wall socket if it remains plugged in. A Green Plug Power Hub

is smarter than this, and only uses the electricity that's necessary.

To further improve the way electronic devices are recharged, Green Plug is also encouraging electronic device manufacturers to adopt a universal power connector. Every AC-powered device, such as a lamp, a vacuum cleaner, or a television set, uses a common cable and connector to obtain electricity, at least on a countrywide basis. Yet DC-power devices, like cell phones and iPods, use device-specific cables and rechargers. Green Plug plans to create a groundswell of support for the adoption of its universal power supply and the adoption of universal cables and connectors for DC-powered devices.

Green Plug's approach also eliminates the persistent throwing away of rechargers, which is wasteful and environmentally unsound. It is estimated that over 470 million rechargers and electronic power supplies are thrown away every year in the United States. Green Plug's approach stands to change this practice. Now, if you switch from a Green Plug–enabled AT&T cell phone to a Green Plug–enabled Verizon cell phone, you'll no longer need to throw away your old recharger and start using a new one if you plug your devices into a Green Plug Power Hub.

Q&A: Based on the material covered in this chapter, what questions would you ask the firm's founders before making your funding decision? What answers would satisfy you?

Decision: If you had to make your decision on just the information provided in the pitch and on the company's Web site, would you fund this company? Why or why not?

You Be the VC 13.2

Company: Takkle

www.takkle.com

Business Idea: Create an online platform for the athletes and fans of high school sports, where athletes can create profiles, upload videos and pictures, see key stats, participate in contests, and show their passion for their favorite sport.

Pitch: Takkle provides a forum for high school athletes to increase their visibility and interact with fans and other athletes. Athletes can create profiles that include a variety of information, including their hometown, school, graduation year, height, weight, most impressive accomplishments, and more. Once a profile is created, an athlete can invite his or her friends, teammates, coaches, and family members to join. Participants can also create and/or join groups on Takkle. Some of the popular groups are Takkle Recruits, Gridiron Warriors, and Soccer Life. There are also forums where athletes, coaches, parents, and fans can talk about all aspects of high school sports.

Takkle is singularly focused on high school sports, which differentiates it from other sports social networking sites. For the athlete, it appeals to the basic human desire to be noticed and to highlight one's talents and accomplishments. There is a section for rankings, such as the 100 top boys lacrosse players in the United States, which are voted on by the Takkle community. Takkle also sponsors user-created challenges (called Takkle Throwdowns and Takkle Battles), such as who can make the most three-point shots in a row or which school has the best cheerleading routine. A high school

basketball player, for example, recently posted a video of himself making 19 three-point shots in a row. Beat that—is the challenge. Through an alliance with *Sports Illustrated*, Takkle gives athletes the chance to be featured in *Sports Illustrated*'s "Faces in the Crowd" (which is a feature on high school athletes) by uploading highlight videos and getting their friends to vote on their profile. Takkle rewards participation by offering its users virtual trophies for reaching certain milestones. Athletes can win trophies for adding 500 friends, uploading 250 pictures, and for similar levels of participation. To further differentiate its site, Takkle is currently negotiating rights to provide live streaming video of select high school sporting events.

Takkle makes money through sponsorships and online advertising. The company has been able to attract high-quality advertisers, including Gatorade, Champs, and Nike. If the company broadcasts live and/or on-demand high school sporting events, it will most likely be on a pay-per-view basis.

Q&A: Based on the material covered in this chapter, what questions would you ask the firm's founders before making your funding decision? What answers would satisfy you?

Decision: If you had to make your decision on just the information provided in the pitch and on the company's Web site, would you fund this company? Why or why not?

CASE13.1

Brian Scudamore and 1-800-GOT-JUNK?:

Succeeding by Growing Carefully and Methodically

www.1800gotjunk.com

Bruce R. Barringer
Oklahoma State University
R. Duane Ireland
Texas A & M University

Introduction

Brian Scudamore remembers the exact moment of inspiration that led to starting his company. It was three days before his 19th birthday and he was

waiting his turn in a McDonald's drive-through lane. Just ahead of him was a beat-up old pickup truck filled with old tires and twisted bicycle frames. The hand-painted sign on the door read

(continued)

MARK'S HAULING. Scudamore thought, "I could do that." He figured he could buy a beat-up old truck and haul junk for people as a way of paying for his college education.

Fast-forward to today. 1-800-GOT-JUNK? advertises itself as the "world's largest junk removal business." It has over 300 franchise locations across the United States and four countries. If you have junk that needs to be removed from your home or business, all you have to do is call the company's toll-free number and if you're in one of the markets it serves you can schedule an appointment for the junk to be removed. A shiny blue and white truck, with 1-800-GOT-JUNK? embossed on the side, will show up on time. The employees, who are required to wear navy slacks, a royal-blue golf shirt (tucked in) with logo, a baseball cap, belt, and boots, will haul away your junk for a prearranged fee.

Think this business happened overnight? Think again. To get 1-800-GOT-JUNK? to where it is today, Scudamore built it step-by-step adding and subtracting along the way. The following is a chronology of 1-800-GOT-JUNK?'s growth story and a description of the challenges it faces today.

1989—The Beginning

Scudamore's inspiration to start a junk removal business, waiting in line for a burger and fries at McDonald's that night, was motivated by a simple desire to earn some extra money. Summer work in his hometown, Vancouver, Canada, was tight that year, so he was thinking about ways to make money. He bought a truck for $700, painted his phone number on the side (738-JUNK), and set off with the slogan "We'll stash your trash in a flash." (No kidding.) He named the business The Rubbish Boys, and started out by driving up and down alleys looking for stuff that garbage crews wouldn't take and offering to haul it away for a small fee. He made enough to enroll in college the following fall and continued operating the business part time.

1993 and 1994—Incorporation, Setting Up Shop, and Michael Gerber

Still operating out of his parents' basement, Scudamore formally incorporated his business in 1993. In 1994, short of graduating from college, he decided to concentrate on The Rubbish Boys full time. He moved out of his parents' home and into a small office. He paid $500 a month rent and purchased four used trucks for $1,000 each from a paving company that had gone out of business. By now, he had three trucks running

full time, 11 employees, and annual sales of $100,000, all in Vancouver.

An avid reader, Scudamore was inspired by Michael Gerber's book, *The E-Myth: Why Most Small Businesses Don't Work and What to Do About It,* first published in 1977. (This book was mentioned earlier in the chapter.) The gist of Gerber's book, along with all the books in his E-Myth series, is that businesses are more successful if they adopt a franchise model for systemizing their business, regardless of whether they plan to franchise or not. The way to go about this, according to Gerber, is to break a business down into identifiable components and then create systems to manage each component. This is how fast-food restaurants, like McDonald's, run so well when they're staffed by what appears to be a group of teenagers. The employees are simply executing a well-thought-out system. Scudamore thought hard about the systems that would be needed to expand The Rubbish Boys and allow others to replicate what he was doing. He also took advantage of several programs in the Vancouver area to sharpen his basic business skills.

In late 1994, heeding more of Michael Gerber's advice, Scudamore started shifting his emphasis from working *in* his business to working *on* the business. He implemented The Rubbish Boys' first "system" by setting up a call center to take orders and dispatch trucks.

1995 to 1997—More Systems, the Company Changes Names, and Student Franchisees

In 1995, Scudamore developed Junkware, a proprietary software program that systematized The Rubbish Boys' administrative and accounting procedures. Thinking the company was ready to grow beyond Vancouver, Scudamore expanded to Victoria, British Columbia, and hired a manager and four student employees to run the business. It was not a positive experience. Scudamore felt the manager lacked the drive he expected from a full-time employee. Shifting gears, Scudamore decided to adopt a student franchise model for growing the company patterned after College Pro Painters, a franchise organization he was familiar with. College Pro Painters sold franchises to college students to help them organize groups of students to paint houses during the summer months. Although Scudamore sold some The Rubbish Boys franchises utilizing this concept, it never gained traction. It did, however, provide him exposure to the advantages of growing The Rubbish Boys via franchising.

As he started thinking more about conventional franchising, Scudamore dropped The Rubbish Boys name and switched to 1-800-GOT-JUNK? Making the new name work was touch and go at the outset. The problem was that the corresponding phone number (1-800-468-5865) was already taken by the Idaho Department of Transportation. According to Scudamore, he called the agency 60 times asking them to give up the number and telling them how important it was to his business. He got 59 no responses before finally getting a yes, which is all he needed.

In 1997, Scudamore launched JunkNet, an intranet system that linked all his student franchisees and employees to 1-800-GOT-JUNK?'s internal computers. The system, which was built from scratch, has evolved over the years, and today 1-800-GOT-JUNK? franchisees, all over the world, log onto the JunkNet system every morning to see their daily schedules. At the end of the day, they use the same system to report their receipts and expenses.

1998 to 2000—1-800-GOT-JUNK? Starts Selling Franchises and Gains Momentum

In 1998, convinced that 1-800-GOT-JUNK? was suitable for conventional franchising, and confident that adequate systems were in place to support franchisees, Scudamore sold the company's first franchise to a former employee in Toronto, Canada. In 1999, seven more franchises opened in Canada and another 14 in the United States. Plenty of tweaking took place. For example, the one-time initial franchise fee was set at $28,000 but was quickly dropped to $10,000 to elicit more interest. In 2000, the company caught a break when it was named one of the "Top Ten Hottest New Franchises" by *Success* magazine. Scudamore recalls that the prospective franchisees who contacted 1-800-GOT-JUNK? as a result of that piece were exactly the types of franchisees the company was trying to attract.

2002 to 2006—Oprah, Continued Growth, and International Expansion

To gain visibility and spur additional growth, Scudamore developed strong media relations. He estimates that between 2002 and 2005 1-800-GOT-JUNK? was profiled in more than 2,000 newspaper and magazine articles, which greatly increased the company's exposure for prospective customers and franchisees. In March 2003, Scudamore appeared on *Oprah*, an objective he had been pursuing for some time. It paid off—the one appearance generated more than 30,000 calls from people interested in using 1-800-GOT-JUNK?'s service. In 2005, with its North American operations running smoothly, the company expanded internationally by opening a corporate-owned operation in Sydney, Australia. Scudamore didn't want to take a chance on selecting a franchisee for 1-800-GOT-JUNK?'s first foray into international markets, so it was manned by select 1-800-GOT-JUNK? employees. The Sydney operation did well and in 2006 the company started selling traditional franchises overseas.

2009 and Beyond

The challenge now facing Scudamore and 1-800-GOT-JUNK? is whether to maintain its current pace of steady growth or whether to accelerate its growth in the United States and abroad. It currently has approximately 300 franchises across the United States and four countries.

Discussion Questions

1. Make a list of 10 things that you think Scudamore has done "right" in growing 1-800-GOT-JUNK?.
2. On a scale of 1 to 10 (10 is high), how good of a job has Scudamore done "preparing" 1-800-GOT-JUNK? for growth? Justify your answer.
3. What stage of the organizational life cycle is 1-800-GOT-JUNK? currently in? Is Scudamore doing the right things to properly manage 1-800-GOT-JUNK? during this stage of the life cycle?
4. In what ways is Scudamore lessening the impact of the managerial capacity problem for 1-800-GOT-JUNK?.

Application Questions

1. What related product areas could 1-800-GOT-JUNK? move into to further accelerate its growth? Comment on whether you believe the firm is prepared to evolve in this manner.
2. Spend some time looking at 1-800-GOT-JUNK?'s Web site and do some additional reading about the company. Make a list of what you believe are some of the firm's strengths and weaknesses. In addition, briefly describe what an average day would be like for a 1-800-GOT-JUNK? franchisee.

Sources: 1-800-GOT-JUNK? homepage (accessed October 4, 2008); "1-800-GOT-JUNK?: Branding Professionalism," Industry Canada, www.ic.gc.ca/eic/site/mfbs-gprea.nsf/eng/lu00060.html (accessed November 2006).

CASE13.2

Captivate Networks: How Four Critical Decisions Shaped One Firm's Path to Growth

www.captivate.com

Bruce R. Barringer
Oklahoma State University
R. Duane Ireland
Texas A & M University

Introduction

In 1996, Michael DiFranza, a young technology executive, was restless. He had just gone through a program at Harvard, which caused him to think about starting his own firm. He would often jot down business ideas, but for one reason or another, would then rule them out. One morning, after returning from the West Coast on a red-eye flight, he stopped by his office in downtown Boston. As usual, he looked at the people already there as he stepped into the elevator and the door closed. They were fidgeting, looking at their shoes, staring at the floor numbers as they lit up, and glancing at their watches. He thought—what if you put flat-screen displays inside elevators so people had something to watch while waiting to reach their destination? Would this work? Is this a viable business idea?

After spending some time thinking about his idea, DiFranza decided to proceed and founded Captivate Networks. Today, Captivate (get it?—people are "captive" when they are in elevators) has more than 6,600 wireless, digital screens located in the elevators of premier office towers in 21 of North America's top markets. The company estimates that its screens are seen by over two million people every day. Although very successful today, Captivate's future and success were anything other than certain in the company's early days. The founders were faced with a number of critical decisions that shaped the future direction of the company. Here, we focus on four critical decisions that DiFranza and his team faced.

Critical Decision 1: Are We a Technology Company or a Media Company?

Prior to starting Captivate Networks, DiFranza worked for Mentor Graphics, a company that makes software that helps engineers design and test electronic components. One thing that DiFranza learned from his colleagues at Mentor is that it's not enough for a company to focus on

technology. A company must also focus on how its technology creates value for the end user.

The reason this issue was important for Captivate is because the leaders of the company had to find the answer to a fundamental question: At its core, was Captivate a technology company or a media company? The answer to the question made a difference. If Captivate was a technology company, its efforts should focus intently on the technology, with hopes of eventually licensing the technology to an elevator company like Otis. If Captivate was a media company, than a different set of priorities would take precedence. The company would need to clearly define its audience. It would also have to assemble sufficient data to persuade building owners to install flat-panel displays in their elevators and advertisers to pay to run ads on the displays.

DiFranza and his team decided to be a media company. The essence of the company's vision was to place ads and other programming on flat-panel displays in elevators—the technology was simply a means to an end. Although the company still had the challenge of creating the flat-panel displays and the technology needed to support them, from that point forward, Captivate was thought of as a media company first and foremost.

Critical Decision 2: Should We Hire Nielsen Media or Do Our Own Market Research?

Using its own preliminary research, Captivate identified that its audience, people riding elevators in large office buildings, had an average income of $100,000, compared to $54,000 for the general population. The demographic was professional, split 50-50 between males and females, managerial, and difficult to reach through traditional media.

Its advertisers would also catch people when they were making decisions to buy, during the heart of the business day, when it is difficult to get these people's attention otherwise.

Based on these findings, DiFranza and his team felt that it would be a no-brainer for many advertisers to try out Captivate's service.

But there was a catch: No one had ever placed flat-panel displays in elevators before, so no one knew for sure how effective the advertising would be. Because of this, DiFranza and his team approached Nielsen Media to see how much they would charge to conduct a market research study of the concept. Nielsen wanted $200,000, which was a lot of money for a start-up. The idea behind having Nielsen do the work is that it would validate the data it collected. DiFranza's fear was that if Captivate collected the data itself it would appear to be self-serving and be less believable to its potential customers—building owners and potential advertisers.

Ultimately, DiFranza and his team hired Nielsen to do the research, and the data it collected was compelling. According to the research, the average person in a large office building takes six elevator trips per day, with each trip averaging a minute. As a result, the average person was spending 120 minutes a month in elevators, or 24 hours a year. This data, along with other data Nielsen collected, armed DiFranza and his team with verified, unbiased data to support their business concept.

Critical Decision 3: Should We Take Otis's Offer?

When Captivate started installing its flat-panel displays in elevators, the first displays went into Otis elevators. Otis was so impressed with the technology that it asked Captivate to be an exclusive provider of flat-screen displays for its elevators. This offer would mean that Captivate had Otis in its corner. However, the potential downside to this arrangement was that Captivate was not allowed to install its systems in any other elevators.

It was a tough decision, but DiFranza and his team decided to pass. Although Otis was the largest elevator company in the world, the firm had only a 25 percent market share. Captivate didn't want 25 percent of the market, it wanted all of the market (or as much as it could get). In addition, because Captivate thought of itself as a media company, it saw building owners and advertisers as its primary customers, rather than elevator companies. Still, Otis's offer was hard to pass up at the time. In reflecting on this decision, DiFranza is quoted in the book *Startups That Work* by Joel Kurtzman as saying:

Here we were. We had no revenue, very little funding, a cool technology, and an idea. And

here's the largest elevator company in the world that wants to partner with us, and we said, "No."

Critical Decision 4: Should We Give the Building Owners a Cut of the Profits?

The fourth critical decision that Captivate faced was the development of its business model, and specifically how much of its revenue it should share with its partners. The most important piece of the equation was the building owners. On the one hand, Captivate could make the case that it was providing building owners a service and not offer them any revenue-sharing agreement. In addition, at the time that Captivate was rolling out its service, there was a lot of consolidation going on in the office building industry. Major owners, like Equity Office Properties and Boston Properties, were accumulating lots of buildings. Captivate felt that it could help these owners "brand" their properties by having Captivate flat panels in their elevators. On the other hand, Captivate wanted building owners to feel like they were a participant in its business rather than just bystanders. DiFranza and his team instinctually knew if building owners were offered a cut of the profits, when a problem occurred with a display, the building owners would see it as a problem that they should help fix, rather than just call Captivate or ignore the problem all together.

Ultimately, Captivate decided to offer the building owners a cut of the profits, along with several other amenities. For example, some building owners used the flat-panel displays to make announcements to their tenants, like when fire drills would be held.

Present-Day Growth Path

Captivate's service is now more popular than ever, and the demand for flat-panel displays in elevators is strong. The tragic events of September 11, 2001, have increased demand even further, as building owners look for additional ways to pass safety information along to occupants in times of emergency. Captivate's flat-panel displays are now featured in some of the most famous buildings in the world, including the Prudential Tower in Boston, the Sears Building in Chicago, and the Empire State Building in New York City. Captivate was purchased by Gannett in 2004, affirming the company's decision to become a media rather than a technology company. It now operates independently as a wholly owned subsidiary of Gannett.

(continued)

Discussion Questions

1. Which of the four decisions discussed in the case do you think was the most critical? What would have happened to Captivate if it had made the opposite decision in this circumstance?
2. Why do you think that Captivate has been able to sustain its growth? What, if anything, will eventually slow the growth of the company?
3. Of the day-to-day challenges of managing growth discussed in the chapter, which of the challenges do you think were the most difficult for Captivate to deal with during the firm's early years?
4. Why do you think Gannett purchased Captivate?

Application Questions

1. How do you think Captivate would have evolved if DiFranza and his team had seen the company as a technology company rather than a media company? Make your answer as detailed and substantive as possible.
2. Think of your professional life as a student or as an employee, if you currently have a job. List four major decisions that you made that have put you on the track that you're currently on. Reflecting back, would you change any of the decisions that you made? If so, why?

Sources: Captivate Networks homepage, www.captivate.com (accessed May 4, 2006); J. Kurtzman, *Startups That Work* (New York: Penguin Group, 2005).

Endnotes

1. M. Kadrmas, "A Shoe-In for Fashion," www.mndaily.com/2007/03/01/shoe-fashion (accessed December 16, 2008, published March 1, 2007).
2. Personal conversation with Jon Goodman, December 15, 2008.
3. Z. Acts, W. Parsons, and S. Tracy, "High Impact Firms: Gazelles Revisited," *Small Business Research Summary* (Washington, DC: SBA Office of Advocacy, June 2008).
4. D. McGinn, "Why Size Matters," *Inc.*, Fall 2004, 33.
5. Acts, Parsons, and Tracy, "High Impact Firms."
6. W. J. Baumol and R. J. Strom, "Entrepreneurship and Economic Growth," *Strategic Entrepreneurship Journal* 1, nos. 3–4 (2007): 233–38; R. W. Price, *Roadmap to Entrepreneurial Success: Powerful Strategies for Building a High-Profit Business* (New York: AMACOM, 2004).
7. D. Packard, *The HP Way: How Bill Hewlett and I Built Our Company*, ed. D. Kirby with Karen Lewis (New York: HarperBusiness, 1996).
8. Packard, *The HP Way.*
9. D. Tatum, *No Man's Land* (New York: Portfolio, 2007).
10. IBISWorld homepage, www.ibisworld.com (accessed November 18, 2008).
11. nPost homepage, www.npost.com (accessed November 19, 2008).
12. D. Christopher, *The Pampered Chef* (New York: Doubleday, 2005).
13. J. Collins, *Good to Great* (New York: Collins Books, 2001).
14. A. Rubinfeld, *Built for Growth* (Upper Saddle River: NJ, Wharton School Publishing, 2005).
15. A. Macpherson and R. Holt, "Knowledge, Learning and Small Firm Growth: A Systematic Review of the Evidence," *Research Policy* 36, no. 2 (2007): 172–92; E. Garnsey, E. Stam, and P. Heffernan, "New Firm Growth: Exploring Processes and Paths," *Industry and Innovation* 13, no. 1 (2006): 1–20; A. V. Bhide, *The Origin and Evolution of New Businesses* (Oxford: Oxford University Press, 2000).
16. J. Welch, "Growth Initiatives," *Executive Excellence* 16, no. 6 (1999): 8–9.
17. "Strategic HR Intelligence Key to Employee Retention," *The Biotech HR Pulse* 1, no. 14 (November 12, 2003): 1–4.
18. R. Phelps, R. Adams, and J. Bessant, "Life Cycles of Growing Organizations: A Review with Implications for Knowledge and Learning," *International Journal of Management Reviews* 9, no. 1 (2007): 1–30; R. Quinn and K. Cameron, "Organizational Life Cycle and Shifting Criteria of Effectiveness: Some Preliminary Evidence," *Management Science* 29, no. 1 (1982): 33–51.
19. Ladies Who Launch, http://applications.ladieswholaunch.com/featuredlady.cfm/featureid/76 (accessed November 17, 2008).

20. M. Gerber, *The E-Myth Revisited* (New York: HarperCollins, 2004).
21. Ladies Who Launch.
22. Entrepreneur, "When Success Isn't Enough," www.entrepreneur.com/magazine/ entrepreneur/2007/november/185574.html (accessed November 19, 2008, originally posted November 2007).
23. A. Nair and W. R. Boulton, "Innovation-Oriented Operations Strategy Typology and Stage-Based Model," *International Journal of Operations and Production Management* 28 no. 8 (2008): 748–71; J. Walsh and R. Dewar, "Formalization and the Organizational Life Cycle," *Journal of Management Studies*, 24 (1987): 215–31.
24. E. T. Penrose, *The Theory of the Growth of the Firm*, 3rd ed. (Oxford: Oxford University Press, 1995).
25. E. T. Penrose, *The Theory of the Growth of the Firm* (New York: John Wiley & Sons, 1959).
26. C. Zook, *Profit from the Core* (Boston: Harvard Business School Press, 2001).
27. J. J. Reuer and R. Ragozzino, "Adverse Selection and M&A Design: The Roles of Alliances and IPOs," *Journal of Economic Behavior and Organization* 66, no. 2 (2008): 195–212; D. Cumming, "Adverse Selection and Capital Structure: Evidence from Venture Capital," *Entrepreneurship Theory and Practice* 30, no. 2 (2006): 155–83.
28. Penrose, *The Theory of the Growth of the Firm* (1959).
29. D. Bartholomew, "The Perfect Pitch," *Priority*, December/January, 2004.

Getting Personal

with Sarah Schupp

CURRENTLY IN MY IPOD
Michael Franti and Spearhead

MY ADVICE FOR NEW ENTREPRENEURS
Be passionate, flexible, and pleasantly persistent

WHAT I DO WHEN I'M NOT WORKING
Skiing, hiking with my dogs—Stella and Ivan

FIRST ENTREPRENEURIAL EXPERIENCE
Selling Airheads candy on my school bus in fourth grade for a huge markup

MY BIGGEST SURPRISE AS AN ENTREPRENEUR
How quickly overhead adds up

SARAH SCHUPP
Founder, University Parent Media
BS, Leeds School of Business, University of Colorado, 2004

CHAPTERFOURTEEN
Strategies for *Firm Growth*

UNIVERSITY PARENT MEDIA
Gradually Pursuing Additional Strategies for Growth
www.universityparent.com

As a college student at the University of Colorado (CU), in Boulder, Colorado, Sarah Schupp invited her parents to visit her a couple of times a year to see where she was living and see the campus and its various attractions. Although she enjoyed her parents' visits, one challenge she always encountered was helping them plan their stay and make it enjoyable. As a dormitory resident, she wasn't familiar with the hotels and motels in Boulder, and didn't know a lot about the restaurants in different parts of town. After muddling through helping her parents plan several visits, it occurred to Schupp that what CU needed was a magazine that would provide parents a directory of hotels, motels, restaurants, and shops to help them plan their trips to Boulder.[1]

At the same time that Schupp started thinking about this idea, she enrolled in a business plan course taught by Frank Moyes, a lecturer at the Leeds School of Business at CU. The class required students to break up into teams, think of a business idea, and prepare a business plan to describe how the idea would be turned into a commercial reality. Schupp became part of a five-person team and persuaded her teammates to help her flesh out her parent magazine business idea. The class cumulated with a business plan competition—which Schupp and her teammates won.

After the class concluded, Schupp became increasingly convinced that her idea for a parent-focused university magazine was viable. In talking with the staff of the Office of Parent Relations at CU, she learned that because it is a public entity, the university can't publish a guide that endorses specific businesses. However, university personnel told Schupp that if she put together a magazine or guide that was helpful to parents, CU would make it available to parents at university events. After kicking around the idea with her professors at CU and other people as well, she started a company, named University Parent, to produce an advertising-supported guide for CU parents. She was able to sell ads to both Boulder-area businesses and national advertisers, such as Apple Inc.

University Parent's first issue was published in October 2003 and was distributed during parents' weekend. The issue contained a directory of local motels, restaurants, and shops, along with a calendar of events and articles of interest to college students and their parents. University Parent's first issue was an immediate success, causing CU to invite Schupp to produce three magazines a year—one to be distributed during orientation, one during the fall semester, and the other during the spring semester.

Schupp graduated from CU in spring 2004 and decided to try to replicate University Parent's success on other campuses. The first additional universities to sign on were Colorado State University, Southern Methodist University, Miami University of Ohio, University of Denver, and Kansas State University. University Parent grew slowly but steadily through 2005, 2006, and 2007, and at the end of 2007 was publishing customized versions of its magazine on 13 campuses with another 7 campuses committed to begin in 2008. During this period, it bolstered its Internet offerings, and now offers an online

Learning Objectives

After studying this chapter you should be ready to:

1. Explain the difference between internal growth strategies and external growth strategies.

2. Identify the keys to effective new product development.

3. Explain the common reasons new products fail.

4. Discuss a market penetration strategy.

5. Explain what an "international new venture" is and describe its importance to entrepreneurial ventures.

6. Discuss the objectives a company can achieve by acquiring another business.

7. Identify a promising acquisition candidate's characteristics.

8. Explain "licensing" and how it can be used as a growth strategy.

9. Explain "strategic alliances" and describe the difference between technological alliances and marketing alliances.

10. Explain "joint ventures" and describe the difference between a scale joint venture and a link joint venture.

Learning Objective

1. Explain the difference between internal growth strategies and external growth strategies.

service called University Parent Connection. The service places the magazines it publishes online and offers additional content for students and parents at the universities it services. This extension of its print magazine provides the company the opportunity to further engage its clients and generate additional revenue via online advertising.

University Parent, which Schupp renamed University Parent Media to reflect its online presence, has moved beyond the start-up stage and is now in a growth mode. At the end of 2007, the company obtained a line of credit from a bank with the intention of scaling up the number of universities it services. It ended 2008 with approximately 80 universities committed to publishing its magazine, utilizing its online services, or both. Although the company has focused primarily on organic growth, several external growth strategies are being pursued. An example is a partnership that the company recently struck with one of the largest job-placement Web sites. University Parent Media and the job-placement site will exchange content, which will allow both companies to provide richer online material to its clients.

Picking the most appropriate strategies for growth will play an important role in University Parent Media's future success. It has identified approximately 520 colleges and universities that are good candidates for its combined magazine and Internet services. These institutions have a sufficient proportion of out-of-state students and 18- to 23-year-old undergraduates, therefore, a guide for parents is likely to be well-received. The company is also contemplating a suite of appropriate online offerings for the larger number of small and commuter-oriented colleges and universities in the United States.[2]

University Parent Media is a typical young entrepreneurial firm. As it picks up momentum as a company, it is starting to use additional methods to leverage its core competencies and accelerate its growth. This chapter discusses the most common strategies firms use to grow. The growth strategies are divided into internal strategies for growth and external strategies for growth, as shown in Figure 14.1.

INTERNAL GROWTH STRATEGIES

Internal growth strategies involve efforts taken within the firm itself, such as new product development, other product-related strategies, and international expansion, with the purpose of increasing sales revenue and profitability. Many businesses, such as Cranium, eBags, and Zappos, are growing through internal growth strategies. The distinctive attribute of internally generated growth is that a business relies on its own competencies, expertise, business practices, and employees. Internally generated growth is often called **organic growth** because it does not rely on outside intervention. Almost all companies grow organically during the early stages of their organizational life cycles.

Effective though it can be, there are limits to internal growth. As a company enters the middle and later stages of its life cycle, it becomes more difficult to sustain growth strictly through internal means. This is the challenge facing companies such as Starbucks, which recently closed over 600 of its retail outlets and plans to close even more units. As Starbucks continued to blanket the United

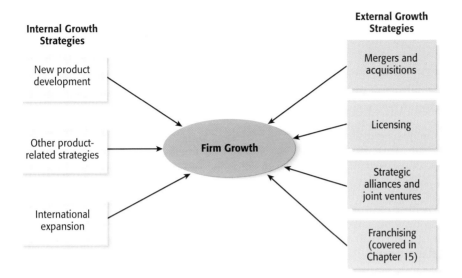

FIGURE 14.1

Internal and External Growth Strategies

States with coffee shops, it was becoming less picky about store locations, and stores were starting to cannibalize one another. These factors, along with a souring United States economy, led to the store closings and some changes in the firm's product offerings.[3] Starbucks pushed organic growth too far and in the future may rely on partnerships with companies like Dryers, which produces a Starbucks-branded ice cream, and PepsiCo, which distributes Starbucks ready-to-drink coffee products, to fuel its growth.

Table 14.1 lists the distinct advantages and disadvantages of internal growth strategies.

New Product Development

New product development involves designing, producing, and selling new products (or services) as a means of increasing firm revenues and profitability. In many fast-paced industries, new product development is a competitive necessity. For example, the average product life cycle in the computer software industry is 14 to 16 months, at the most. Because of this, to remain competitive, software companies must always have new products in their pipelines. For some companies, continually developing new products is the essence of their existence.

Although developing new products can result in substantial rewards, it is a high-risk strategy. The key is developing innovative new products that aren't simply "me-too" products that are entering already crowded markets. A PricewaterhouseCoopers survey reported that the chief executive officers (CEOs) from two-thirds of America's fastest-growing companies say that innovation is an organization-wide priority, and almost all say it has had a significant, positive impact on their business. Over the past five years, the more innovative firms in the survey have increased revenues by an average of 346 percent, versus only 138 percent for all others.[4]

When developing new products is properly executed, there is tremendous upside potential. Many biotech and pharmaceutical companies, for example, have developed products that not only improve the quality of life for their customers but also provide reliable revenue streams. In many cases, the products are patented, meaning that no one else can make them, at least until the patents expire. Successful new products can also provide sufficient cash flow to fund a company's operations and provide resources to support developing additional new products. For example, Amgen, a large and historically profitable biotech company has two stellar pharmaceutical products, Epogen and Neupogen. Epogen is used for the treatment of anemia associated with

Learning Objective

2. Identify the keys to effective new product development.

Table 14.1 ADVANTAGES AND DISADVANTAGES OF INTERNAL GROWTH STRATEGIES

Advantages	Disadvantages
Incremental, even-paced growth. A firm that grows at an even pace can continually adjust to changing environmental conditions to fine-tune its strategies over time. In contrast, a firm that doubles its size overnight through a merger or acquisition is making a much larger commitment at a single point in time.	**Slow form of growth.** In some industries, an incremental, even-paced approach toward growth does not permit a firm to develop competitive economies of scale fast enough. In addition, in some industries, it may not be possible for a firm to develop sufficient resources to remain competitive. A high level of merger and acquisition activity typically characterizes these industries.
Provides maximum control. Internal growth strategies allow a firm to maintain control over the quality of its products and services during the growth process. In contrast, firms that grow through collaborative forms of growth, such as alliances or joint ventures, must share the oversight function with their business partners.	**Need to develop new resources.** Some internal growth strategies, such as new product development, require a firm to be innovative and develop new resources. While internal innovation has many positive attributes, it is typically a slow, expensive, and risky strategy.
Preserves organizational culture. Firms emphasizing internal growth are not required to blend their organizational culture with another organization. As a result, the venture can grow under the auspices of a clearly understood, unified corporate culture.	**Investment in a failed internal effort can be difficult to recoup.** Internal growth strategies, such as new product development, run the risk that a new product or service idea may not sell, making it difficult to recoup the development cost the firm incurred.
Encourages internal entrepreneurship. Firms that grow via internal growth strategies are looking for new ideas from within the business rather than from outside stakeholders. This approach encourages a climate of internal entrepreneurship and innovation.	**Adds to industry capacity.** Some internal growth strategies add to industry capacity, and this can ultimately help force industry profitability down. For example, a restaurant chain that grows through geographic expansion may ultimately force industry profitability down by continuing to open new restaurants in an already crowded market.
Allows firms to promote from within. Firms emphasizing internal growth strategies have the advantage of being able to promote within their own organizations. The availability of promotional opportunities within a firm is a powerful tool for employee motivation.	

chronic renal failure in dialysis patients, and Neupogen helps prevent infection in cancer patients undergoing certain types of chemotherapy. These products have provided the company sufficient revenue to cover its overhead, fund new product development, and generate profits for an extended period of time.[5]

The keys to effective new product and service development, which are consistent with the material on opportunity recognition (Chapter 2) and feasibility analysis (Chapter 3) follow:

- ■ **Find a need and fill it:** Most successful new products fill a need that is presently unfilled. "Saturated" markets should be avoided. For example, in most developed countries, consumers have a more-than-adequate selection of appliances, tires, credit cards, and cell phone plans. These are crowded markets with low profit margins. The challenge for entrepreneurs is to find unfilled needs in attractive markets and then find a way to fill those needs.

- ■ **Develop products that add value:** In addition to finding a need and filling it, the most successful products are those that "add value" for customers in some meaningful way.

- ■ **Get quality and pricing right:** Every product represents a balance between quality and pricing. If the quality of a product and its price are not compatible, the product may fail and have little chance for recovery.

To put this in slightly different terms, customers are willing to pay higher prices for higher-quality products and are willing to accept lower quality when they pay lower prices.

■ **Focus on a specific target market:** Every new product and service should have a specific target market in mind, as we have highlighted throughout this book. This degree of specificity gives the innovating entrepreneurial venture the opportunity to conduct a focused promotional campaign and select the appropriate distributors. The notion that "it's a good product, so somebody will by it" is a naïve way to do business and often contributes to failure.

■ **Conduct ongoing feasibility analysis:** Once a product or service is launched, the feasibility analysis and marketing research should not end. The initial market response should be tested in focus groups and surveys, and incremental adjustments should be made when appropriate.

There is also a common set of reasons that new products fail. These include inadequate feasibility analysis, overestimation of market potential, bad timing (i.e., introducing the product at the wrong time), inadequate advertising and promotion, and poor service.

This discussion is a reminder that to achieve healthy growth, whether via new product development or another means, a firm must sell a product or service that legitimately creates value and has the potential to produce profits along with sales. Regrettably, Sock Shop, a rapidly growing retailer of apparel products, failed as a result of deficiencies in these key categories, as illustrated in the "What Went Wrong?" feature.

Learning Objective

3. Explain the common reasons new products fail.

Other Product-Related Strategies

Along with developing new products, firms grow by improving existing products or services, increasing the market penetration of an existing product or service, or pursuing a product extension strategy.

Improving an Existing Product or Service Often, a business can increase its revenue by **improving an existing product or service**—enhancing quality, making it larger or smaller, making it more convenient to use, improving its durability, or making it more up-to-date. Improving an item means increasing its value and price potential from the customer's perspective. For example, many companies that sell flat irons that are used to straighten women's hair have upgraded to ceramic irons because they allow for a more even distribution of heat. Similarly, software firms routinely increase revenues by coming out with "updated" versions of an existing software product.

A mistake many businesses make is not remaining vigilant enough regarding opportunities to improve existing products and services. It is typically much less expensive for a firm to modify an existing product or service and extend its life than to develop a new product or service from scratch. For example, many women have set aside the flat irons that they've used for years and bought a ceramic flat iron because they're safer and do a better job. Selling "improved" flat irons is a much less expensive way for curling iron manufacturers to grow sales than to develop a completely new product.

Increasing the Market Penetration of an Existing Product or Service A **market penetration strategy** involves actions taken to increase the sales of a product or service through greater marketing efforts or through increased production capacity and efficiency. An increase in a product's market share is typically accomplished by increasing advertising expenditures, offering sales

Learning Objective

4. Discuss a market penetration strategy.

What Went WRONG?

Sock Shop: How Focusing More on Growth Than Profitability and Creating Value Sank a Popular Retail Chain

Sock Shop was launched in 1983 as a shop that only sold tights, stockings, and socks and became the United Kingdom's retail phenomenon of the 1980s, before going bust after just seven years. Founders Sophie Mirman and Richard Ross initially struggled to get backing for their niche retail business, but when they finally opened their first shop in London's Knightsbridge, Sock Shop took $915 on its first day of trading, which was three times what they had expected. The idea was to use brightly colored booths, with attractive displays of merchandise carefully grouped by categories and price. The key ingredient was location, because high-volume consumer traffic was essential. Sites in or near railway stations did particularly well, because travelers with time to kill are prone to make impulse purchases of low-cost items. Price points were carefully selected to entice a range of customers, with basic socks and tights at just $2.25 and exclusive designs at $15.

New stores were added at a breathtaking pace. In 1987, Sock Shop was floated on the Unlisted Securities Market of the London Stock Exchange, with an issue price that valued the company, with 43 stores, at $42 million. The share offer was oversubscribed 53 times, and trading was frantic. Then, there was a slight, but crucial, shift in strategy. Larger shops were increasingly located in prime high street sites, rather than the high commuter traffic places such as stations, which added considerably to the cost of the leases. More than $19.8 million in capital expenditure was spent in just over a year, opening new offices, stores, and warehouses and adding new stock control systems.

Then came the fateful decision to "crack" the U.S. market. The team had not realized it was not possible to set up outlets in the New York subway, and the stores that they opened on the streets of Manhattan were plagued by drug-related crime and huge staffing costs.

In the United Kingdom, things were not much better. Abnormally high temperatures in 1988 and 1989 reduced the demand for socks and tights, and then a prolonged series of one-day train strikes meant Sock

Shop, which still had around a third of its outlets in stations, saw revenues plunge. Sock Shop had built a house of cards and with a recession just beginning to bite, property prices collapsing, and interest rates rising, the rush for growth in large and unsuitable sites meant the company could not keep up.

In February 1990, the company reported a pretax loss of nearly $6.1 million and announced its U.S. operation would close with massive losses. Almost immediately, the bank pulled the plug, the company went into administration, and shares were suspended at 51 cents. Sock Shop is now being run as an Internet-only operation and has no connection with the original founders.

Questions for Critical Thinking

1. Using materials from this chapter and Chapter 13 make a list of things that Sock Shop could have done to better prepare for growth and to better manage its growth.
2. The feature indicates that Sock Shop had been "building a house of cards." Expand the rationale for this statement. In what ways had Sock Shop built a house of cards?
3. Think about the consistent themes expressed throughout this book regarding why some entrepreneurial firms succeed and others don't. Thinking about Sock Shop from this broad perspective, write a 100- to 200-word commentary on why you think the company failed.
4. The "You Be the VC 14.1" feature focuses on Adrenalina, a company that is currently growing by opening retail stores in different locations across the United States. What can Adrenalina learn from Sock Shop's failures?

Sources: "Sock Shop Heritage and History," www.sockshop.co.uk (accessed March 10, 2009); "Business Is Child's Play for Sophie Mirman," http://business.timesonline.co.uk, March 22, 2008.

promotions, lowering the price, or increasing the size of the sales force. Consider Proactiv, the skin-care company that is the focus of Case 11.2. Since its inception in 1994, Proactiv has relied on celebrity endorsers to demonstrate and promote its product. Judith Light and Vanessa Williams were the firm's first celebrity endorsers. Over the years, the company has added additional celebrity endorsers, including Anthony Robbins, Jessica Simpson, and Jane Seymour, to appeal to a broader and more diverse clientele. Dr. Katie Rodan, a cofounder of Proactiv, points to the celebrity endorser program as one of the savviest actions the company has taken to build market share.[6]

Another example is the prepaid card, like the Starbucks Card, that almost all restaurants and retailers now offer. By making it more convenient for customers

A very common way that companies grow is by selling products that are related to their staple product. Here, a Starbucks employee is selling a customer coffee beans to be brewed at home. Along with selling brewed coffees, Starbucks has grown by selling coffee beans, coffee mugs, CDs, and other related products.

to purchase its products, restaurants and retailers boost their revenues. Prepaid cards also make it easier to give a restaurant's or retailer's offering as a gift. Think of how many people buy Target, Starbucks, or Home Depot prepaid (gift) cards as birthday or holiday gifts. A benefit to those receiving these cards is the opportunity to use them to buy a product that fulfills a true need.

Increased market penetration can also occur through increased capacity or efficiency, which permits a firm to have a greater volume of product or service to sell. In a manufacturing context, an increase in product capacity can occur by expanding plant and equipment or by outsourcing a portion of the production process to another company. **Outsourcing** is work that is done for a company by people other than the company's full-time employees, which is a practice that two-thirds of consumer product companies participate in; and some believe this percentage may increase in the foreseeable future.[7] For example, a firm that previously manufactured and packaged its product may outsource the packaging function to another company, and as a result free up factory space to increase production of the basic product.

Extending Product Lines   A **product line extension strategy** involves making additional versions of a product so that it will appeal to different clientele or making related products to sell to the same clientele. For example, a company may make another version of a low-end product, which is a little better, and then make another version of it that represents the top of the line to appeal to different clientele. This is a strategy that allows a firm to take one product and extend it into several products without incurring significant additional development expense. Computer manufacturers provide a good example of how to execute a product line extension strategy. Each manufacturer sells several versions of its desktop and laptop computers. The different versions of the same computer typically represent good, better, and best alternatives based on processor speed, memory capacity, monitor size, graphic capabilities, and other features. In regard to making related products to sell to the same clientele, many firms start by offering one product or service and then expand into related areas. For example, SmartSense, the subject of the "You Be the VC 3.2" feature, started out with a wireless patient monitoring system, which transmits vital information directly to health practitioners, for hospitals. It is now expanding into consumer versions for home use.[8]

Firms also pursue product extension strategies as a way of leveraging their core competencies into related areas. For example, Abercrombie & Fitch has applied the expertise it developed through its Abercrombie & Fitch and Hollister stores to the launching of RUEHL, a chain of stores aimed at customers 22 to 30 years old who have outgrown Abercrombie & Fitch and Hollister, and Abercrombie Kids, a chain of stores targeted at boys and girls ages 7 to 14 who are too young for Abercrombie & Fitch and Hollister. An account of the history of Oracle, a computer database software company, provides a particularly interesting example of the potential payoff of a product extension strategy. The example demonstrates that product extension strategies can take time and patience to pay off but can lead to breakthrough growth strategies:

> As Ellison [Oracle's CEO] recognized that he had sold a database to almost every one of the biggest companies in the world, he knew he would need new products to sell. That is how he came up with the idea of applications. Oracle applications would sit on top of and use Oracle databases to perform functions such as inventory management, personnel record keeping, and sales tracking. The proof of his thinking took almost seven years, but by 1995, the company generated nearly $300 million in license revenues from application products and an additional $400 million in applications-related services.[9]

Geographic Expansion   **Geographic expansion** is another internal growth strategy. Many entrepreneurial businesses grow by simply expanding from their original location to additional geographic sites. This type of expansion is most common in retail settings. For example, a small business that has a successful retail store in one location may expand by opening a second location in a nearby community. Gap Inc., Walgreens, and Chipotle are examples of firms that have grown through geographic expansion. Of course, McDonald's, which now has over 31,300 worldwide locations, is the classic example of incredibly successful growth through geographic expansion. The keys to successful geographic expansion follow:

■ **Perform successfully in the initial location:** Additional locations can learn from the initial location's success.

■ **Establish the legitimacy of the business concept in the expansion locations:** For example, a particular type of fitness center may be well accepted in its original location because it has been there a long time and has a loyal clientele. However, potential clientele in a neighboring community may be completely unfamiliar with its unique products and services. A common mistake an entrepreneurial venture makes when it expands from one community to another is to assume that if something works in one community, it will automatically work in another.

■ **Don't isolate the expansion location:** Sometimes the employees in an expansion location feel isolated and that they are not receiving adequate training and oversight from the headquarters location. It is a mistake to believe that an expansion location can excel without the same amount of attention and nurturing that it took to build the business in the original location.

International Expansion

International expansion is another common form of growth for entrepreneurial firms.[10] According to a PricewaterhouseCoopers's survey of rapid-growth entrepreneurial firms, 46 percent of the 350 firms surveyed sell in international markets.[11] A look at the world's population and purchasing power statistics affirms the importance of international markets for growth-minded firms. Approximately 95 percent of the world's population and two-thirds of its total purchasing power are located outside the United States. Influenced by these data, an increasing number of the new firms launched around the globe today are international new ventures.

International new ventures are businesses that, from inception, seek to derive significant competitive advantage by using their resources to sell products or services in multiple countries.[12] From the time they are started, these firms, which are sometimes called "global start-ups," view the world as their marketplace rather than confine themselves to a single country. Amazon.com, for example, was an international firm from its inception and now generates 46 percent of its sales from international markets. Other new firms are not international from the start, but choose to enter international markets shortly after they gain product acceptance in the United States. For example, Slingbox, which makes a product that lets people watch TV on their computers while they are away from home, was founded in 2004. Having gained favorable reaction to its product in the United States, the company started testing a beta version of its product in Europe in 2006. It now sells its product in 11 countries.[13]

Although there is vast potential associated with selling overseas, it is a fairly complex form of firm growth. Of course, alert entrepreneurs should carefully observe any changes in purchasing power among the world's societies that may result from a financial crisis like the one that started in late 2008 and continued into the early parts of 2009. Let's look at the most important issues that entrepreneurial firms should consider in pursuing growth via international expansion.

Learning Objective

5. Explain what an "international new venture" is and describe its importance to entrepreneurial ventures.

Assessing a Firm's Suitability for Growth Through International Markets
Table 14.2 provides a review of the issues that should be considered, including management/organizational issues, product and distribution issues, and financial and risk management issues, when a venture considers expanding into international markets. If these issues can be addressed successfully, growth through international markets may be an excellent choice for an entrepreneurial firm. The major impediment in this area is not fully appreciating the challenges involved.

Foreign Market Entry Strategies   The majority of entrepreneurial firms first enter foreign markets as exporters, but firms also use licensing, joint ventures, franchising, turnkey projects, and wholly owned subsidiaries to start international expansion.[14] These strategies, along with their primary advantages and disadvantages, are explained in Table 14.3.

Selling Overseas   Many entrepreneurial firms first start selling overseas by responding to an unsolicited inquiry from a foreign buyer. It is important to handle the inquiry appropriately and to observe protocols when trying to serve the needs of customers in foreign markets. Following are several rules of thumb for selling products in foreign markets:

■ Answer requests promptly and clearly. Do not ignore a request just because it lacks grammatical clarity and elegance. Individuals using a non-native language to contact a business located outside their home nation often are inexperienced with a second language.

■ Replies to foreign inquires, other than e-mail or fax, should be communicated through some form of airmail or overnight delivery. Ground delivery is slow in some areas of the world.

■ A file should be set up to retain copies of all foreign inquiries. Even if an inquiry does not lead to an immediate sale, the names of firms that have made inquiries will be valuable for future prospecting.

Table 14.2 EVALUATING A FIRM'S OVERALL SUITABILITY FOR GROWTH THROUGH INTERNATIONAL MARKETS

Management/Organizational Issues

Depth of management commitment. A firm's first consideration is to test the depth of its management commitment to entering international markets. Although a firm can "test the waters" by exporting with minimal risk, other forms of internationalization involve a far more significant commitment. A properly funded and executed international strategy requires top management support.

Depth of international experience. A firm should also assess its depth of experience in international markets. Many entrepreneurial firms have no experience in this area. As a result, to be successful, an inexperienced entrepreneurial firm may have to hire an export management company to familiarize itself with export documentation and other subtleties of the export process. Many entrepreneurial firms err by believing that selling and servicing a product or service overseas is not that much different than doing so at home. It is.

Interference with other firm initiatives. Learning how to sell in foreign markets can consume a great deal of entrepreneurs' or managers' time. Overseas travel is often required, and selling to buyers who speak a different language and live in a different time zone can be a painstaking process. Overall, efforts must be devoted to understanding the culture of the international markets the venture is considering. Thus, a firm should weigh the advantages of involvement in international markets against the time commitment involved and the potential interference with other firm initiatives.

Product and Distribution Issues

Product issues. A firm must first determine if its products or services are suitable for overseas markets. Many pertinent questions need to be answered to make this determination. For example, are a firm's products subject to national health or product safety regulations? Do the products require local service, supplies, or spare parts distribution capability? Will the products need to be redesigned to meet the specifications of customers in foreign markets? Are the products desirable to foreign customers? All these questions must have suitable answers before entering a foreign market is advisable. A firm can't simply "assume" that its products are salable and easily serviceable in foreign countries.

Distribution issues. How will the product be transported to a foreign country? Is the transportation reliable and affordable? Can the product be exported from the venture's home operation, or will it have to be manufactured in the country of sale?

Financial and Risk Management Issues

Financing export operations. Can the foreign initiative be funded from internal operations, or will additional funding be needed? How will foreign customers pay the firm? How will the firm collect bad debts in a foreign country? These questions must obtain appropriate answers before initiating overseas sales.

Foreign currency risk. How will fluctuations in exchange rates be managed? If the entrepreneurial firm is located in America and it sells to a buyer in Japan, will the American firm be paid in U.S. dollars or in Japanese yen?

- Keep promises. The biggest complaint from foreign buyers is failure to ship on time (or as promised). The first order is the most important. It sets the tone for the ongoing relationship.
- All correspondence should be personally signed. Form letters are offensive in some cultures.
- Be polite, courteous, friendly, and respectful. This is simple common sense, but politeness is particularly important in many cultures. In addition, avoid the use of business slang that is indigenous to a nation, meaning that the slang terms lack meaning in many other cultures. Stated simply, be sensitive to cultural norms and expectations.
- For a personal meeting, always make sure to send an individual who is equal in rank to the person with whom he or she will be meeting. In some cultures, it would be seen as inappropriate for a salesperson from a domestic company to meet with the vice president or president of a foreign firm.

Table 14.3 PRIMARY ADVANTAGES AND DISADVANTAGES OF VARIOUS FOREIGN-MARKET ENTRY STRATEGIES

Foreign-Market Entry Strategy	Primary Advantage	Primary Disadvantage
Exporting. Exporting is the process of producing a product at home and shipping it to a foreign market. Most entrepreneurial firms begin their international involvement as exporters.	Exporting is a relatively inexpensive way for a firm to become involved in foreign markets.	High transportation costs can make exporting uneconomical, particularly for bulky products.
Licensing. A licensing agreement is an arrangement whereby a firm with the proprietary rights to a product grants permission to another firm to manufacture that product for specified royalties or other payments. Proprietary services and processes can also be licensed.	The licensee puts up most of the capital needed to establish the overseas operation.	A firm in effect "teaches" a foreign company how to produce its proprietary product. Eventually, the foreign company will probably break away and start producing a variation of the product on its own.
Joint ventures. A joint venture involves the establishment of a firm that is jointly owned by two or more otherwise independent firms. Fuji-Xerox, for example, is a joint venture between an American and a Japanese firm.	Gaining access to the foreign partner's knowledge of local customs and market preferences.	A firm loses partial control of its business operations.
Franchising. A franchise is an agreement between a franchisor (the parent company that has a proprietary product, service, or business method) and a franchisee (an individual or firm that is willing to pay the franchisor a fee for the right to sell its product, service, and/or business method). U.S. firms can sell franchises in foreign markets, with the reverse being true as well.	The franchisee puts up the majority of capital needed to operate in the foreign market.	Quality control.
Turnkey projects. In a turnkey project, a contractor from one country builds a facility in another country, trains the personnel that will operate the facility, and *turns* over the *keys* to the project when it is completed and ready to operate.	Ability to generate revenue.	It is usually a one-time activity, and the relationships that are established in a foreign market may not be valuable to facilitate future projects.
Wholly owned subsidiary. A firm that establishes a wholly owned subsidiary in a foreign country has typically made the decision to manufacture in the foreign country and establish a permanent presence.	Provides a firm total control over its foreign operations.	The cost of setting up and maintaining a manufacturing facility and permanent presence in a foreign country can be high.

EXTERNAL GROWTH STRATEGIES

External growth strategies rely on establishing relationships with third parties, such as mergers, acquisitions, strategic alliances, joint ventures, licensing, and franchising. Thus, joint ventures, licensing, and franchising are strategic options entrepreneurial firms use to both enter foreign markets (as explained previously) and accomplish external growth. Each of these strategic options is discussed in the following sections, with the exception of franchising, which we consider separately in Chapter 15.

An emphasis on external growth strategies results in a more fast-paced, collaborative approach toward growth than the slower-paced internal strategies, such as new product development and expanding to foreign markets. External growth strategies level the playing field between smaller firms and larger companies.[15] For example, Pixar, the small animation studio that produced the animated hits *Toy Story*, *Finding Nemo*, and *Wall-E*, had a number of key strategic alliances with Disney, before it was acquired by Disney in 2006. By partnering with Disney, Pixar effectively co-opted a portion of Disney's management savvy, technical expertise, and access to distribution channels. The relationship with Disney helped Pixar grow and enhance its ability to effectively compete in the marketplace, to the point where it became an attractive acquisition target. Similarly, by acquiring other companies, relatively young firms such as Pixar can gain access to patents and proprietary techniques that take larger firms years to develop on their own.

There are distinct advantages and disadvantages to emphasizing external growth strategies, as shown in Table 14.4.

Table 14.4 ADVANTAGES AND DISADVANTAGES OF EMPHASIZING EXTERNAL GROWTH STRATEGIES

Advantages	Disadvantages
Reducing competition. Competition is lessened when a firm acquires a competitor. This step often helps a firm establish price stability by eliminating the possibility of getting in a price war with at least one competitor. By turning potential competitors into partners and through alliances and franchises, the firm can also reduce the amount of competition it experiences.	**Incompatibility of top management.** The top managers of the firms involved in an acquisition, an alliance, a licensing agreement, or a franchise organization may clash, making the implementation of the initiative difficult.
Getting access to proprietary products or services. Acquisitions or alliances are often motivated by a desire on the part of one firm to gain legitimate access to the proprietary property of another.	**Clash of corporate cultures.** Because external forms of growth require the combined effort of two or more firms, corporate cultures often clash, resulting in frustration and subpar performance.
Gaining access to new products and markets. Growth through acquisition, alliances, or franchising is a quick way for a firm to gain access to new products and markets. Licensing can also provide a firm an initial entry into a market.	**Operational problems.** Another problem that firms encounter when they acquire or collaborate with another company is that their equipment and business processes may lack full compatibility.
Obtaining access to technical expertise. Sometimes, businesses acquire or partner with other businesses to gain access to technical expertise. In franchise organizations, franchisors often receive useful tips and suggestions from their franchisees.	**Increased business complexity.** Although the vast majority of acquisitions and alliances involve companies that are in the same or closely related industries, some entrepreneurial firms acquire or partner with firms in unrelated industries. This approach vastly increases the complexity of the combined business. The firm acquiring a brand or partnership with another company to gain access to its brand may subsequently fail to further develop its own brand and trademarks. This failure can lead to an increased dependency on acquired or partnered brands, reducing the firm's ability to establish and maintain a unique identity in the marketplace.
Gaining access to an established brand name. A growing company that has good products or services may acquire or partner with an older, more established company to gain access to its trademark and name recognition.	
Economies of scale. Combining two or more previously separate firms, whether through acquisition, partnering, or franchising, often leads to greater economies of scale for the combined firms.	**Loss of organizational flexibility.** Acquiring or establishing a partnership with one firm may foreclose the possibility of acquiring or establishing a partnership with another one.
Diversification of business risk. One of the principal driving forces behind all forms of collaboration or shared ownership is to diversify business risk.	**Antitrust implications.** Acquisitions and alliances are subject to antitrust review. In addition, some countries have strict antitrust laws prohibiting certain business relationships between firms.

Mergers and Acquisitions

Many entrepreneurial firms grow through mergers and acquisitions. A **merger** is the pooling of interests to combine two or more firms into one. An **acquisition** is the outright purchase of one firm by another. In an acquisition, the surviving firm is called the **acquirer**, and the firm that is acquired is called the **target**. This section focuses on acquisitions rather than mergers because entrepreneurial firms are more commonly involved with acquisitions than mergers. According to a recent Trendsetter Barometer Survey, plans for mergers and acquisitions are on the rise, at least among fast-growth firms. A total of 35 percent of the 286 fast-growth firms in the survey are planning an acquisition or merger over the next five years, which is a higher percentage than previous periods.[16] However, the realities of the recent global financial crisis could affect the viability of these firms' merger and acquisition intentions.

Acquiring another business can fulfill several of a company's needs, such as expanding its product line, gaining access to distribution channels, achieving economies of scale, or expanding the company's geographic reach. In most cases, a firm acquires a competitor or a company that has a product line or distinctive competency that it needs. For example, eBay acquired PayPal in 2002 to gain control of the electronic payment system that was preferred by its customers. Similarly, Google acquired YouTube in 2006 to gain access to its online video streaming technology and to provide another platform for its online ads.

Although it can be advantageous, the decision to grow the entrepreneurial firm through acquisitions should be approached with caution.[17] Many firms have found that the process of assimilating another company into their current operation is not easy and can stretch finances to the brink.

Finding an Appropriate Acquisition Candidate   If a firm decides to grow through acquisition, it is extremely important for it to exercise extreme care in finding acquisition candidates. Many acquisitions fail not because the companies involved lack resolve, but because they were a poor match to begin with. There are typically two steps involved in finding an appropriate target firm. The first step is to survey the marketplace and make a "short list" of promising candidates. The second is to carefully screen each candidate to

Learning Objective

6. Discuss the objectives a company can achieve by acquiring another business.

eBay has engaged in a number of acquisitions to fuel its growth. Two of its largest and perhaps most important acquisitions have been PayPal and Skype. Former eBay CEO Meg Whitman and Skype cofounder and CEO Niklas Zennstrom share a light moment at Skype's headquarters in London, England.

Getty Images, Inc.

determine its suitability for acquisition. The key areas to focus on in accomplishing these two steps are as follows:

Learning Objective

7. Identify a promising acquisition candidate's characteristics.

■ The target firm's openness to the idea of being acquired and its ability to obtain key third-party consent. The third parties from whom consent may be required include bankers, investors, suppliers, employees, and key customers.

■ The strength of the target firm's management team, its industry, and its physical proximity to the acquiring firm's headquarters.

■ The perceived compatibility of the target company's top management team and its corporate culture with the acquiring firm's top management team and corporate culture.

■ The target firm's past and projected financial performance.

■ The likelihood that the target firm will retain its key employees and customers if it is acquired.

■ The identification of any legal complications that could impede the purchase of the target firm and the extent to which it has protected its intellectual property through patents, trademarks, and copyrights.

■ The extent to which the acquiring firm understands the business and industry of the target firm.

The screening should be as comprehensive as possible to provide the acquiring firm sufficient data to determine realistic offering prices for the firms under consideration. A common mistake among acquiring firms is to pay too much for the businesses they purchase. Firms can avoid this mistake by basing their bids on hard data rather than on guesses or intuition.

Steps Involved in an Acquisition   Completing an acquisition is a nine-step process, as illustrated in Figure 14.2:

Step 1   **Meet with the target firm's top management team:**   The acquiring firm should have legal representation at this point to help structure the initial negotiations and help settle any legal issues. The acquiring firm should also have a good idea of what it thinks the acquisition target is worth.

FIGURE 14.2

The Process of Completing the Acquisition of Another Firm

Source: Wall Street Journal (Eastern Edition) by C. DeBaise. Copyright 2007 by Dow Jones & Company Inc.

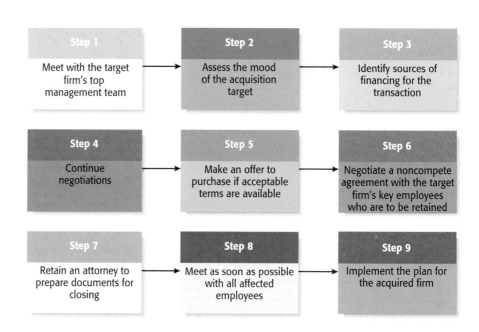

Step 2 **Assess the mood of the acquisition target:** If the target is in a "hurry to sell," it works to the acquiring firm's advantage. If the target starts to get cold feet, the negotiations may become more difficult.

Step 3 **Identify sources of financing for the transaction:** The acquiring firm should be financially prepared to complete the transaction if the terms are favorable.

Step 4 **Continue negotiations:** If a purchase is imminent, obtain all necessary shareholder and third-party consents and approvals.

Step 5 **Make an offer to purchase if acceptable terms are available:** Both parties should have the offer reviewed by attorneys and certified public accountants that represent their interests. Determine how payment will be structured.

Step 6 **Negotiate a noncompete agreement with the target firm's key employees who are to be retained:** This agreement, as explained in Chapter 7, limits the rights of the key employees of the acquired firm to start the same type of business in the acquiring firm's trade area for a specific amount of time.

Step 7 **Retain an attorney to prepare the documents for closing:** Complete the transaction.

Step 8 **Meet as soon as possible with all affected employees:** A meeting should be held as soon as possible with the employees of both the acquiring firm and the target firm. Articulate a vision for the combined firm and ease employee anxiety where possible.

Step 9 **Implement the plan for the acquired firm:** In some cases, the acquired firm is immediately assimilated into the operations of the acquiring firm. In other cases, the acquired firm is allowed to operate in a relatively autonomous manner.

Along with acquiring other firms to accelerate their growth, entrepreneurial firms are often the targets of larger firms that are looking to enter a new market or acquire proprietary technology. Sometimes selling out to a larger firm is a difficult choice for the founders of a small company, who may have started the company as an "antiestablishment" firm that vowed to not do what the large firms were doing. This decision confronted Seth Goldman, the founder of Honest Tea, an organic tea company that was established as a healthy alternative to the sugared beverages sold by PepsiCo and Coca-Cola. Goldman recently sold a large stake in Honest Tea to Coca-Cola, of all companies, which angered many of Honest Tea's loyal customers. As illustrated in the "Savvy Entrepreneurial Firm" feature, Goldman's rationale for selling to Coca-Cola is that Honest Tea will be able to actually accelerate its mission and place its wholesome products in front of more people by becoming part of the larger firm than it could as an independent company.

Licensing

Licensing is the granting of permission by one company to another company to use a specific form of its intellectual property under clearly defined conditions. Virtually any intellectual property a company owns that is protected by a patent, trademark, or copyright can be licensed to a third party. Licensing can be a very effective way of earning income, particularly for intellectual

Learning Objective

8. Explain "licensing" and how it can be used as a growth strategy.

Savvy Entrepreneurial FIRM

Honest Tea: Accelerating Its Growth and Mission Through Being Acquired by Coca-Cola

www.honesttea.com

In early 2008 when Honest Tea announced that it had sold a large stake of the company to Coca-Cola, many of its most loyal customers were outraged. Honest Tea was the antiestablishment company that had pioneered the organic bottled tea market. Its customers relied on its integrity, pioneering spirit, and independence from corporate America to provide them a line of wholesome, pure, organic beverages. Now it looked like Seth Goldman, Honest Tea's cofounder and chief evangelist, was selling out. Was it true—were Honest Tea's founders and investors abandoning their principles and independence in exchange for a big payday?

Seth Goldman says no—he says it as often as he can. He sees Honest Tea's new affiliation with Coca-Cola as a way of accelerating its growth and bringing its wholesome beverages to more people than the company could have ever done on its own. Coca-Cola purchased 40 percent of Honest Tea, making it Honest Tea's largest shareholder. But Honest Tea will keep its current management team, maintain its brand, and have three of the five board seats, making it largely autonomous. It also modeled its acquisition by Coca-Cola after a partnership forged between Groupe Danone (a large European food company) and Stonyfield Farm, a mission-driven organic yogurt, ice cream, and milk company similar in many ways to Honest Tea. Groupe Danone purchased 80 percent of Stonyfield, but the company has remained independent, has stuck to its mission, and its entrepreneurial spirit has stayed alive. One major difference between Stonyfield and Honest Tea's deals is that after three years, Coca-Cola will have the option to completely purchase Honest Tea. While that caveat caused some people within Honest Tea to pause, Coca-Cola has a reputation for leaving things that are successful alone, and even if Coca-Cola buys the remaining shares of Honest Tea, all indications are that the management of Honest Tea will remain independent for many years to come.

Goldman sees two big advantages to becoming part of Coca-Cola. First, Honest Tea will now have access to Coca-Cola's immense distribution network. Honest Tea has struggled to expand its reach beyond fitness clubs, specialty shops, and natural food groceries like Whole Foods. Now, the company's products will be available to a vast number of people, which Goldman sees as furthering Honest Tea's mission of providing a healthy alternative to traditional sugared beverages. Second, Goldman hopes that Honest Tea's values and its commitment to wholesomeness will rub off on Coca-Cola. Honest Tea will be the first organic beverage loaded on either a PepsiCo or a Coca-Cola truck. While Honest Tea's shelf space and sales will still be dwarfed by Coke, Diet Coke, and Coca-Cola's other beverages, it's a start. The large cola companies are coming to the realization that there is a growing and vibrant market for alternatives to their standard fare.

While only time will tell, Honest Tea's bet is that its growth and mission will be accelerated rather than diminished via its acquisition by Coca-Cola.

Questions for Critical Thinking

1. Do you believe that Honest Tea will be able to maintain its mission and continue to sell wholesome beverages as part of Coca-Cola? If so, how successful do you think Honest Tea will be in selling that message to its existing customers?
2. Along with the points made in the feature, why do you think Coca-Cola was interested in acquiring Honest Tea?
3. If you had been advising Seth Goldman at the time he was negotiating with Coca-Cola, what concessions (other than those mentioned in the feature) would you have asked for?
4. Is Honest Tea easy to find where you live? If so, do you buy Honest Tea? If not, will you be more likely to try Honest Tea if it starts showing up in places where Coca-Cola is sold, like supermarkets and convenience stores?

Sources: J. Del Rey, "Honest Tea's New Deal with Coke: 'Just a Tad Sweet,' " *Inc.*, February 11, 2008; "For Honest Tea, Coke Is It," http://blog.inc.com/the-mission-driven-business/2008/08/for_ honest_tea_coke_is_it.html (accessed September 17, 2008, posted August 22, 2008).

property–rich firms, such as software and biotech companies. Smaller firms also benefit by licensing trademarks or other forms of intellectual property from larger companies. For example, C-Life Group, a T-shirt manufacturer, sold around $10 million in products in the late 1990s. To increase its sales, it started licensing popular characters, like Spider-Man and G.I. Joe, to place on its shirts. In 2008, C-Life Group will surpass $100 million in sales. Commenting on the importance of licensing agreements, Hymie Shamah, C-Life Group's president, said:

> Without the brands and properties we [license] today, we would be irrelevant to the market. Every day, we come to work knowing that our relationships with our licensors and retailers are the key to our success.[18]

The terms of a license are spelled out through a **licensing agreement**, which is a formal contract between a licensor and a licensee. The **licensor** is the company that owns the intellectual property. The **licensee** is the company purchasing the right to use it. A license can be exclusive, nonexclusive, for a specific purpose, and for a specific geographic area.[19] In almost all cases, the licensee pays the licensor an initial payment plus an ongoing royalty for the right to use the intellectual property. There is no set formula for determining the amount of the initial payment or the royalties—these are issues that are part of the process of negotiating a licensing agreement.[20] Entrepreneurial firms often press for a relatively large initial payment as a way of generating immediate cash to fund their operations.

There are two principal types of licensing: technology licensing and merchandise and character licensing.

Technology Licensing **Technology licensing** is the licensing of proprietary technology that the licensor typically controls by virtue of a utility patent. This type of licensing agreement typically involves one of two scenarios. First, firms develop technologies to enhance their own products and then find noncompetitors to license the technology to spread out the costs and risks involved. Second, companies that are tightly focused on developing new products pass on their new products through licensing agreements to companies that are more marketing oriented and that have the resources to bring the products to market. This is the approach taken by Green Plug, the subject of the "You Be the VC 13.1" feature. Recall, Green Plug has developed a technology that makes it possible for a consumer to use a single recharger to recharge multiple electronic devices. Green Plug licenses its technology to other companies that manufacture rechargers.

Striking a licensing agreement with a large firm can involve tough negotiations. An entrepreneur should carefully investigate potential licensees to make sure they have a track record of paying licensing fees on time and are easy to work with. To obtain this information, it is appropriate to ask a potential licensee for references. It is also important that an entrepreneur not give away too much in regard to the nature of the proprietary technology in an initial meeting with a potential licensee. This challenge means finding the right balance of piquing a potential licensee's interest without revealing too much. Nondisclosure agreements, described in Chapter 7, should be used in discussing proprietary technologies with a potential licensee.

Merchandise and Character Licensing **Merchandise and character licensing** is the licensing of a recognized trademark or brand that the licensor typically controls through a registered trademark or copyright. For example, Harley-Davidson licenses its trademark to multiple companies that place the Harley trademark on T-shirts, jackets, collectibles, gift items, jewelry, watches, bike accessories, and so on. By doing this, Harley not only generates licensing income but also promotes the sale of Harley-Davidson motorcycles. Similarly, entrepreneurial firms such as eBay and Starbucks license their trademarks not only to earn licensing income but also to promote their products or services to a host of current and potential customers.

The key to merchandise and character licensing is to resist the temptation to license a trademark too widely and to restrict licensing to product categories that

Character licensing represents a major source of income and growth for a film company like Pixar, which is now a division of Walt Disney Corporation. Familiar characters from the film, including Marlin (left) and Dory (right), now adorn products as varied as T-shirts, dinner plates, lunch bags, and children's bedspreads.

Supplied by: Globe Photos

have relevance and that appeal to a company's customers. If a company licenses its trademark too broadly, it can lose control of the quality of the products with which its trademark is identified. This outcome can diminish the strength of a company's brand. For example, a company such as Liz Claiborne might license its trademark to a watch manufacturer that is interested in producing a line of "Liz Claiborne" men's and women's watches. Liz Claiborne would want to make sure that the watches bearing its trademark were fashionable, were of similar quality to its clothing, and were appealing to its clientele. Liz Claiborne can enforce these standards through the terms of its licensing agreements.

Strategic Alliances and Joint Ventures

The increase in the popularity of strategic alliances and joint ventures has been driven largely by a growing awareness that firms can't "go it alone" and succeed.[21] As with all forms of firm growth, strategic alliances and joint ventures have advantages and disadvantages. We present these points in Table 14.5.

Learning Objective

9. Explain "strategic alliances" and describe the difference between technological alliances and marketing alliances.

Strategic Alliances   A **strategic alliance** is a partnership between two or more firms that is developed to achieve a specific goal. Various studies show that participation in alliances can boost a firm's rate of patenting,[22] product innovation,[23] and foreign sales.[24] Alliances tend to be informal and do not involve the creation of a new entity (such as in a joint venture). An example of a firm that has made informal alliances a central portion of its growth strategy is Zlio.com, as illustrated in this chapter's "Partnering for Success" boxed feature.

Technological alliances and marketing alliances are two of the most common forms of alliances.[25] **Technological alliances** feature cooperation in research and development, engineering, and manufacturing. Research-and-development alliances often bring together entrepreneurial firms with specific technical skills and larger, more mature firms with experience in development and marketing. By pooling their complementary assets, these firms can typically produce a product and bring it to market faster and cheaper than either firm could alone.[26] Pfizer's blockbuster drug Celebrex, for example, was created via a technological alliance. Celebrex is a prescription arthritis medicine. **Marketing alliances** typically match a company with a distribution system with a company that has a product to sell in order to increase sales of a product or service. For example, an American food company may initiate an alliance with

Table 14.5 ADVANTAGES AND DISADVANTAGES OF PARTICIPATING IN STRATEGIC ALLIANCES AND JOINT VENTURES

Advantages	Disadvantages
Gain access to a particular resource. Firms engage in strategic alliances and joint ventures to gain access to a particular resource, such as capital, employees with specialized skills, or modern production facilities.	**Loss of proprietary information.** Proprietary information can be lost to a partner who is already a competitor or will eventually become one. This is a common worry.
Economies of scale. In many industries, high fixed costs require firms to find partners to expand production volume as a means of developing economies of scale.	**Management complexities.** Because strategic alliances and joint ventures require the combined effort of two or more firms, managing them can be challenging. Frustrations and costly delays often occur as a result.
Risk and cost sharing. Strategic alliances and joint ventures allow two or more firms to share the risk and cost of a particular business endeavor.	**Financial and organizational risks.** The failure rate for strategic alliances and joint ventures is high.
Gain access to a foreign market. Partnering with a local company is often the only practical way to gain access to a foreign market.	**Risk becoming dependent on a partner.** A power imbalance arises if one partner becomes overly dependent on the other. This situation increases the potential for opportunism on the part of the stronger partner. Opportunistic behavior takes advantage of a partner.
Learning. Strategic alliances and joint ventures often provide the participants the opportunity to "learn" from their partners.	**Partial loss of decision autonomy.** Joint planning and decision making may result in a loss of decision autonomy.
Speed to market. Firms with complementary skills, such as one firm being technologically strong and another having strong market access, partner to increase speed to market in hopes of capturing first-mover advantages.	**Partners' cultures may clash.** The corporate cultures of alliance partners may clash, making the implementation and management of the alliance difficult.
Neutralizing or blocking competitors. Through strategic alliances and joint ventures, firms can gain competencies and market power that can be used to neutralize or block a competitor's actions.	**Loss of organizational flexibility.** Establishing a partnership with one firm may foreclose the possibility of establishing a partnership with another firm.

Source: Adapted from B. R. Barringer and J. S. Harrison, "Walking a Tightrope: Creating Value Through Interorganizational Relationships," *Journal of Management* 26, no. 3 (2002): 367–403. Reprinted with permission of SAGE Publications.

Nestlé (a Swiss food company) to gain access to Nestlé's distribution channels in Europe. The strategic logic of this type of alliance for both partners is simple. By finding more outlets for its products, the partner that is supplying the product can increase economies of scale and reduce per unit cost. The partner that supplies the distribution channel benefits by adding products to its product line, increasing its attractiveness to those wanting to purchase a wide array of products from a single supplier.

Both technological and marketing alliances allow firms to focus on their specific area of expertise and partner with others to fill their expertise gaps. This approach is particularly attractive to entrepreneurial firms, which often don't have the financial resources or time to develop all the competencies they need to bring final products to market quickly. Michael Dell describes the early years of Dell Inc.:

> As a small start-up, we didn't have the money to build the components [used to make up a PC] ourselves. But we also asked, "Why should we want to?" Unlike many of our competitors, we actually had an option: to buy components from the specialists, leveraging the investments they had already made and allowing us to focus on what we did best—designing and delivering solutions and systems directly to customers. In forging these early alliances with suppliers, we created exactly the right strategy for a fast-growing company.[27]

Partnering for SUCCESS
Zlio.com: 250,000 Partners and Growing
www.zlio.com

Paris-based Zlio.com allows people to set up their own online stores for free. Using the service, users can choose a name, address, and template for the store they want to create, build it in under five minutes, and then open for business displaying their wares from iPods to T-shirts. Once signed up, a new shopkeeper can choose to sell any one of more than 3 million products offered by 360 merchants worldwide, including Apple, Littlewoods, and The Gap.

Zlio is the brainchild of entrepreneur Jeremie Berrebi, who launched the site in France in 2006 and in the United Kingdom and the United States in 2008. The shops, opening at a rate of 1,000 a day, have been dubbed the online equivalent of a Tupperware party because they are a way of recommending products to friends and relatives in return for a small commission. More than 35 percent of new would-be shopkeepers have signed up via a viral campaign among existing users. When a member recommends Zlio to someone else, they make 10 percent of their future revenues for life.

After setting up their sites, people pick the goods they wish to display from any of the participating merchants. The shopkeeper does not even have to handle the transactions themselves because buyers are referred to the merchants' own pages, and they don't need to worry about shipping orders because the companies take care of that too.

Zlio's members are awarded a small commission of anything between 1 to 15 percent, depending on the product sold. On goods such as high-tech equipment, where margins are notoriously tight, the commission is just 1 or 2 percent, whereas in cosmetics where markups are higher, the commission can go into double figures. Zlio takes a 35 percent slice of the commission, but, even so, members usually turn over an average of $300 a month in commission. Top sellers have been known to make as much as $3,000 per month.

The Web site capitalizes on the growing trend for "social shopping" online, and a number of other established companies such as Amazon.com are also building up recommendation services. Although still in its infancy, social shopping is growing rapidly with 1 percent of online sales now said to come from some kind of affiliate marketing where consumers are referred to other sites. Many of the Zlio stores are created around themes or hobbies; for example, one is devoted to all things red, while another sells only hot sauce.

In 2007, Zlio generated $12 million in sales for the companies with which it has tie-ups. Berrebi's vision is to roll the concept out internationally and allow people to sell products all over the world from online catalogs.

Questions for Critical Thinking

1. All parties to a strategic alliance, such as those Zlio has formed with merchants like Apple and The Gap, must possess desirable attributes or skills. What does Zlio "bring to the table" that is attractive to it partners? Prepare as comprehensive a list as possible to answer this question.
2. Study the details of Zlio's affiliate program. Does the program seem fair to all the parties involved? If you were thinking about becoming a Zlio shopkeeper, what additional questions would you ask?
3. What risks does Zlio run by having a model that includes over 1 million shopkeeper members?
4. Ask several of your friends if they have used Zlio and, if so, to relate their experiences. As customers, were they satisfied? If so, why? If not, what aspects of the firm's service disappointed your friends as customers, and what could Zlio do to avoid those problems in the future?

Source: Zlio.com homepage, www.zlio.com (accessed December 8, 2008).

Joint Ventures A **joint venture** is an entity created when two or more firms pool a portion of their resources to create a separate, jointly owned organization.[28] An example is Beverage Partners Worldwide, which is a joint venture between Coca-Cola and Nestlé that was created in 2001. The joint venture markets ready-to-drink chilled teas based on green tea and black tea in more than 40 countries worldwide.

A common reason to form a joint venture is to gain access to a foreign market.[29] In these cases, the joint venture typically consists of the firm trying to reach a foreign market and one or more local partners. Joint ventures created for reasons other than foreign market entry are typically described as either scale or link joint ventures.[30] In a **scale joint venture**, the partners collaborate at a single point in the value chain to gain economies of scale in production or distribution. This type of joint venture can be a good vehicle for developing new products or services. In a **link joint venture**, the position of the parties is not symmetrical, and the objectives of the partners may diverge. For example, many of the joint ventures between American and Canadian food companies provide the American partner with access to Canadian markets and distribution channels and the Canadian partner with the opportunity to add to its product line.

A hybrid form of joint venture that some larger firms utilize is to take small equity stakes in promising young companies. In these instances, the large companies act in the role of corporate venture capitalists, as explained in Chapter 10. Intel officially established a venture capital program in the early 1990s, named Intel Capital. Investing in private companies, this program seeks to help start-up ventures grow from their initial stages to a point of either issuing an initial public offering or being acquired. Notable investments include Red Hat, Research In Motion (maker of the popular BlackBerry), and WebMD.[31] Firms typically make investments of this nature in companies with the potential to be either suppliers or customers in the future. The equity stake provides the large company a "say" in the development of the smaller firm. On occasion, the larger firm that has a small equity stake will acquire the smaller firm. These transactions are called **spin-ins**. The opposite of a spin-in is a **spin-out**, which occurs when a larger company divests itself of one of its smaller divisions and the division becomes an independent company. Hewlett-Packard, for example, spun off its test-and-measurement equipment division in 1999, which became Agilent Technologies.

Learning Objective

10. Explain "joint ventures" and describe the difference between a scale joint venture and a link joint venture.

Chapter Summary

1. Internal growth strategies rely on efforts generated within the firm itself, such as new product development, other product-related strategies, international expansion, and Internet-driven strategies. External growth strategies rely on establishing relationships with third parties, such as mergers, licensing, strategic alliances, joint ventures, and franchising.

2. The keys to effective new product development are as follows: find a need and fill it, develop products that add value, get quality and pricing right, focus on a specific target market, and conduct an ongoing feasibility analysis.

3. The reasons that new products fail include an inadequate feasibility analysis, overestimation of market potential, bad timing (i.e., introducing a product at the wrong time), inadequate advertising and promotion, and poor service.

4. A market penetration strategy seeks to increase the sales of a product or service through greater marketing efforts or through increased production capacity and efficiency.

5. International new ventures are businesses that, from inception, seek to derive significant competitive advantage from the use of resources and the sale of outputs in multiple countries.

6. Acquiring another business can fulfill several of a company's needs, such as expanding its product line, gaining access to distribution channels, achieving competitive economies of scale, or expanding the company's geographic reach.

7. A promising acquisition candidate has the following characteristics: operates in a growing industry, has proprietary products and/or processes, has a

well-defined and established market position, has a good reputation, is involved in very little, if any, litigation, is open to the idea of being acquired by another firm, is positioned to readily obtain key third-party consent to an acquisition, and is located in a geographic area that is easily accessible from the acquiring firm's headquarters location.

8. Licensing is the granting of permission by one company to another company to use a specific form of its intellectual property under clearly defined conditions. Virtually any intellectual property a company owns can be licensed to a third party. Licensing can be a very effective way of earning income, particularly for intellectual property-rich firms, such as software and biotech companies.

9. A strategic alliance is a partnership between two or more firms that is developed to achieve a specific objective or goal. Technological alliances involve cooperating in areas such as research and development, engineering, and manufacturing. Marketing alliances typically match one firm with a partner's distribution system that is attractive to the company trying to increase sales of its products or services.

10. A joint venture is an entity that is created when two or more firms pool a portion of their resources to create a separate, jointly owned organization. In a scale joint venture, the partners collaborate at a single point in the value chain to gain economies of scale in production or distribution by combining their expertise. In a link joint venture, the position of the parties is not symmetrical and the objectives of the partners may diverge.

Key Terms

Review Questions

1. Describe the difference between an internal and an external growth strategy. Provide examples of each strategy and how each one contributes to firm growth.
2. Describe the keys to effective new product and service development.
3. Describe some of the common reasons new products fail.
4. What is a market penetration strategy? Provide an example of a market penetration strategy, and describe how using it effectively might increase a firm's sales.
5. What is a product line extension strategy? Provide an example of a product line extension strategy, and describe how its effective use might increase a firm's sales.
6. What is a geographic expansion strategy, and what are the keys to implementing a successful geographic expansion strategy for an entrepreneurial firm?

7. What is an international new venture? Explain why it might be to the benefit of an entrepreneurial start-up to position itself as an international new venture from the outset.

8. What are the six foreign-market entry strategies? Briefly describe each strategy.

9. What are several rules of thumb to follow for selling products overseas?

10. Describe the difference between a merger and an acquisition. In what ways can acquisitions help firms fill their needs?

11. What are the characteristics of a promising acquisition candidate?

12. What is the difference between a licensor and a licensee?

13. What does the term *licensing* mean? How can licensing be used to increase a firm's revenues?

14. Describe the purpose of a licensing agreement. In a licensing agreement, which party is the licensor, and which is the licensee?

15. Describe the difference between technology licensing and merchandise and character licensing. Provide examples of both types of licensing and how they can increase a firm's sales.

16. Over the past several years, why have strategic alliances and joint ventures become increasingly prevalent growth strategies? Make your answer as thoughtful and as thorough as possible.

17. Describe the difference between technological alliances and market alliances. Provide examples of both types of alliances and how they can increase a firm's sales.

18. What is a joint venture?

19. How does a joint venture differ from a strategic alliance?

20. Describe the difference between a scale joint venture and a link joint venture. Provide examples of both types of joint venture and how their effective use can increase a firm's sales.

Application Questions

1. Spend some time studying Dreamerz, the focus of the "You Be the VC 14.2" feature. Is it more likely that Dreamerz will grow through internal or external growth strategies? Provide suggestions of internal growth strategies and external growth strategies that make sense for Dreamerz.

2. As mentioned in the chapter, Starbucks has closed a large number of its coffee restaurants. Do you think Starbucks had a faulty growth strategy or do you think it is merely the victim of an economic downturn? If you believe the former, comment on where you think Starbucks went astray.

3. Jessica Martin, a classmate of yours, just returned from an entrepreneurship boot camp, which was sponsored by her university's technology incubator and consisted of three days of intense focus on how to successfully launch a firm. You overheard Jessica telling another classmate that the boot camp was extremely helpful and she's already signed up for another three-day boot camp that will focus on how to successfully grow a firm. The classmate looked at Jessica and said, "How in the world can you spend three days talking about how to successfully grow a firm?" Jessica opened her notebook and showed the classmate the 10-item agenda for the upcoming three-day boot camp. What do you think the 10 items consist of? (Consider the material in Chapter 13 and this chapter in formulating your answer.)

4. Karen Paulsen has developed a new piece of computer hardware that she is convinced is a sure hit. She can't imagine that the product could fail. She just remembered that you are taking a course in entrepreneurship, however, and calls you on your cell phone. Her question is, "Is there a common set of reasons that cause products to fail? If there is, I'd like to

know them so I can make sure to avoid them before I pitch my new product to anyone." What would you tell her?

5. Chad Caldwell manufactures cookware that is sold to restaurants. He isn't really interested in developing new products but has been wondering lately about the options he has for increasing his sales. What advice would you give Chad if he asked you if there are any "product-related strategies short of developing new "products" that he could utilize to increase his sales?

6. Spend some time studying Urban Outfitters and describe its overall approach to growth. Many people have questioned the launch of Terrain, Urban Outfitters' new chain of stores. Terrain sells home and garden products, targeting an affluent clientele. Speculate on why some observers have questioned the wisdom of adding Terrain to the Urban Outfitters family of brands.

7. Refer to Fitbit, the subject of the "You Be the VC 9.2" feature. Which of the foreign market entry strategies described in Table 14.3 make sense for Fitbit? If you were the founder of Fitbit, which strategy would you pursue first if you decided to grow via international expansion?

8. Google has been on a buying spree in recent years and has acquired a number of smaller companies. Why would a company like Google, which employs hundreds of software engineers and computer programmers, decide to buy other firms to acquire technology and add to its product line, rather than developing the technology and new products in-house?

9. Dr Pepper Snapple recently acquired Big Red, Inc. (www.bigredltd.com), a small maker of peach, pineapple, and other flavored soft-drink brands. Why do you think Dr Pepper Snapple acquired Big Red, Inc., and why do you think Big Red, Inc., allowed itself to be acquired?

10. Brian Brunner is an entrepreneur who has invented several devices that are used in the telecommunications industry. He has patented the devices and manufactures them in a job shop in St. Louis. Brian sells the devices directly to AT&T and Sprint. Last week, Brian got a certified letter in the mail from Motorola, indicating that firm's interest in licensing the technology that is represented in one of his devices. Brian doesn't know anything about licensing and has turned to you for help. What would you tell Brian about licensing, and how would you suggest that he respond to Motorola's letter?

11. A friend of yours owns a chain of five fitness centers in suburban Atlanta. The fitness centers cater primarily to young professions, ages 21 to 40. Your friend is worried because his centers have declined in terms of overall membership. Your friend told you that he's interested in pursuing strategic alliances to rev up the growth of his centers but is having trouble thinking about the types of companies he can partner with. Provide your friend with some suggestions.

12. Peter Cook owns an e-commerce Web site that sells camping and boating supplies. He spends a lot of time on the Internet and sees the phrase "affiliate program" periodically but has never really figured out what an affiliate program is all about. Explain to Peter what an affiliate program is and how he could set up an affiliate program to drive traffic to his Web site.

13. Spend some time studying Adrenalina, the focus of the "You Be the VC 14.1" feature. Suppose the company hired you to investigate how licensing could spur its growth. How would you approach the investigation? Are the licensing opportunities limited or plentiful? What types of licensing deals do you think would be appropriate for Adrenalina?

14. Study the popular social networking site MySpace.com. What growth strategies has the company employed? Make recommendations for appropriate growth strategies for the future.

15. Which of the growth strategies discussed in the chapter are the most risky? Which are the least risky? What role should risk play in a company's decision to pursue a particularly growth strategy?

You Be the VC 14.1
Company: Adrenalina
www.adrenalinastore.com

Business Idea: Launch a premier extreme sports store that combines retail sales with a great in-store entertainment experience.

Pitch: Adrenalina is a brightly lit, roomy, extreme sports store that carries a full line of extreme sports apparel and equipment. In addition, each store features a FlowRider wave machine. The FlowRider is a cutting-edge wave ramp machine that uses compact wave technology to create in-store surfing and boarding experiences for patrons. Anyone who buys a ticket ($20 for a half-hour session) can try their hand at wakeboarding (a version of surfing) right in the store while other customers watch from behind floor-to-ceiling windows. It's a real attention grabber and a lot of fun. To watch how it works, go to YouTube and type in "FlowRider." Adrenalina is the first company to place a FlowRider in a retail store. They are normally used in theme parks and on cruise ships.

Adrenalina (Spanish for "adrenaline") stocks a full line of popular and hard-to-find extreme sports products for sports enthusiasts. The store includes equipment for almost every extreme sport including skateboarding, BMX, mountain biking, surfing, wakeboarding, kitesurfing, paintball, and more. Its popular and hard-to-find lines of sportswear include Billabong, Roxy, Crocs, Quick Silver, Reef, and Fox Racing. The purpose of the FlowRider is to drive traffic to the store and to connect customers with the extreme sports culture. The FlowRider also makes Adrenalina a destination store, which not only increases its traffic but the traffic for surrounding stores. This aspect of Adrenalina's offering increases its bargaining power with mall landlords.

To build interest in extreme sports, Adrenalina's store not only caters to extreme sports enthusiasts, but to people who are interested in extreme sports and want to learn more about them. To facilitate this objective, the store is partitioned into areas that are dedicated to specific extreme sports, so people can collect information, look at the clothing and equipment that's available, and talk to salespeople who are knowledgeable about those specific sports.

Adrenalina's pilot store opened in the Florida Mall in Orlando, Florida, and the company has a number of additional stores on the drawing boards. Adrenalina's long-term plans include expanding to others countries and developing in-store sports experiences, similar to the FlowRider experience, that reflect the most popular sports in its host countries.

Q&A: Based on the material covered in this chapter, what questions would you ask the firm's founders before making your funding decision? What answers would satisfy you?

Decision: If you had to make your decision on just the information provided in the pitch and on the company's Web site, would you fund this company? Why or why not?

You Be the VC 14.2
Company: Dreamerz
www.dreamerz.com

Business Idea: Formulate a line of all-natural sleep products, which are consumed at bedtime, that help people relax and get a better night's sleep naturally and safely.

Pitch: People who get a good night's sleep have more energy, are more creative, and generally have more passion for life. But many people have trouble falling asleep and sleeping through the night. Dreamerz, which makes sleep products that are taken at bedtime, is passionate about helping people sleep. The company makes three all-natural categories of products: Dreamerz Herbal Fruit-Flavored Mix, Dreamerz Soothing Dairy, and Dreamerz Chocolate Pillows. The products come in attractive packages and are intended to be taken within one hour of going to sleep. The ingredients, which include lactium, PharmaGABA, and melatonin, promote relaxation and restful sleep. Each ingredient is natural, has been scientifically tested, and improves the overall quality of sleep without unwanted side effects. Melatonin is a staple used in all of Dreamerz's products. It is a hormone naturally secreted at night to help cue your body to go to sleep. It is known as the "sleep hormone" and helps regulate your sleep and wake cycles.

(continued)

Dreamerz has completed an independent in-home use test with 89 people. Results for the test showed that its products significantly improved sleep among users. Clinical studies completed at MIT and elsewhere have validated the sleep-aiding properties of melatonin and other ingredients in Dreamerz's products.

Dreamerz's products come in a mix form, and are added to 4 to 6 ounces of water or milk until the mix dissolves. Each mix is between 30 and 100 calories, is caffeine free, and can be taken hot or cold. The small packages of Dreamerz mix are easy to take on trips. Most people are pleasantly surprised by their good taste. Each category of Dreamerz's products comes in several flavors. Dreamerz Herbal Fruit-Flavored Mix's options

include Peaches & Dreams, Rock-a-bye Berry, and Pomegranate Pillows. Dreamerz's sleep aids are not intended to be taken every night. Most people take them when they've had a particularly stressful day, are suffering from jet lag, or are having trouble falling to sleep.

Q&A: Based on the material covered in this chapter, what questions would you ask the firm's founders before making your funding decision? What answers would satisfy you?

Decision: If you had to make your decision on just the information provided in the pitch and on the company's Web site, would you fund this company? Why or why not?

CASE 14.1

Cranium: Growing Aggressively but Carefully

www.cranium.com

Bruce R. Barringer
Oklahoma State University
R. Duane Ireland
Texas A & M University

Introduction

Cranium was founded in 1998 by two former Microsoft executives, Whit Alexander and Richard Tait. While working together at Microsoft, they discovered that they shared a passion for entrepreneurship and set out to start a firm together. They thought about starting an Internet company but decided the market space was too crowded. Then one day, after spending a weekend playing board games with his wife and friends, Tait started talking about creating a new type of board game. He noticed that different board games favored people with different skills. He was a particularly good Pictionary player, for example, but was only average at Scrabble. What if a game could be created that offered so much variety that everyone looked good when playing it? He shared his idea and his enthusiasm with Alexander, and the two decided to develop just such a game.

The result of Tait and Alexander's efforts was Cranium, a board game for adults. To provide the game a unique position in the marketplace, they decided to engineer it around the "moment," specifically the moment when players feel smart and funny around their family and friends. As a result, they designed Cranium around four decks of cards: Worm Wood, Data Head, Star Performer, and Creative Cat. The game is played by rolling

dice (there are two people per team) and going around the board. On each square on which it lands, a team is required to draw a card and either answer the question or perform the activity that's required by the card before the timer runs out. The activities included in the four decks of cards range widely, from unscrambling words, to humming a tune, to answering trivia questions, to playing charades, to sculpting. The idea is that everyone is good at something, so the game makes people feel good about themselves when they complete the task at which they have some skill.

The Company's Origins

Rather than trying to convince toy stores and retailers like Wal-Mart and Target to carry the Cranium board game, the founders (who lived in Seattle) talked Starbucks into featuring the game in its restaurants, which built just the kind of initial buzz that the founders wanted. Soon after, Barnes & Noble (which had never sold a game before) and Amazon.com signed on. They also "seeded" interest in the game by borrowing a trick they learned from the makers of Trivial Pursuit. For $15,000, they recruited 100 radio stations around the country to have their DJs read Cranium questions over the air. The callers who phoned in the correct answers got a copy of the game as a prize.

9. F. M. Stone, *The Oracle of Oracle* (New York: AMACOM Books, 2002), 125.

10. Y. Yamakawa, M. W. Peng, and D. L. Deeds, "What Drives New Ventures to Internalize from Emerging to Developed Economies?" *Entrepreneurship Theory and Practice* 32, no. 1 (2008): 59–82; R. Richmond, "More Small Firms Expand Abroad," *Wall Street Journal*, July 3, 2007, A2.

11. PricewaterhouseCoopers, "Fast-Growth CEOs Set Revenue Target and Investment Plans Higher, PricewaterhouseCoopers's Finds," *Trendsetter Barometer*, August 23, 2005.

12. J. P. Mathews, "Dragon Multinationals: New Players in 21st Century Globalization," *Asia Pacific Journal of Management* 23, no. 1 (2006): 5–27; B. M. Oviatt and P. P. McDougall, "Defining International Entrepreneurship and Modeling the Speed of Internationalization," *Entrepreneurship Theory and Practice* 29 (2005): 537–53.

13. Slingbox homepage, www.slingbox.com (accessed November 18, 2008).

14. J. W. Lu and P. W. Beamish, "Partnering Strategies and Performance of SMEs' International Joint Ventures," *Journal of Business Venturing* 21 (2006): 461–86.

15. S. A. Alvarez, R. D. Ireland, and J. J. Reuer, "Entrepreneurship and Strategic Alliances," *Journal of Business Venturing* 21 (2006): 401–04.

16. PricewaterhouseCoopers, "Plans for M&A Activity on the Rise for Fast Growth Private Companies," *Trendsetter Barometer*, January 24, 2007.

17. P. Nijkamp and J. V. Ommeren, "Drivers of Entrepreneurial Location as an Innovative Act," *International Journal of Entrepreneurship and Innovation Management* 6 (2006): 256–64.

18. S. Needleman, "Hitched to a Star," *Wall Street Journal*, August 11, 2008, R6.

19. D. H. B. Welsh, I. Alon, and C. M. Falbe, "An Examination of International Retail Franchising in Emerging Markets," *Journal of Small Business Management*, 44, no. 1 (2006): 130–49.

20. S. Shane, "Introduction to the Focused Issue on Entrepreneurship," *Management Science* 52, no. 2 (2006): 155–59.

21. J. Wiklund and D. A. Shepherd, "The Effectiveness of Alliances and Acquisitions: The Role of Resource Combination Activities," *Entrepreneurship Theory and Practice* 33, no. 1 (2009): 193–212.

22. S. A. Moskalev and R. B. Swensen, "Joint Ventures Around the Globe from 1990–2000: Forms, types, industries, countries and ownership 'patterns,' *Review of Financial Economics* 16, no. 1 (2007): 29–67.

23. F. T. Rothaermel and D. L. Deeds, "Alliance Type, Alliance Experience and Alliance Management Capability in High-Technology Ventures," *Journal of Business Venturing* 21 (2006): 429–60.

24. M. J. Leiblein and J. J. Reuer, "Building a Foreign Sales Base: The Roles of Capabilities and Alliances for Entrepreneurial Firms," *Journal of Business Venturing* 19 (2004): 285–307.

25. A. Tiwana and M. Keil, "Does Peripheral Knowledge Complement Control? An Empirical Test in Technology Outsourcing Alliances," *Strategic Management Journal* 28, no. 6 (2008): 623–34.

26. E. V. Karniouchina, L. Vitorino, and R. Verma, "Product and Service Innovation: Ideas for Future Cross-Disciplinary Research," *Journal of Product Innovation Management* 23 (2006): 274–87.

27. M. Dell, *Direct from Dell* (New York: HarperBusiness, 1999), 50.

28. Y. Luo, "Are Joint Ventures Partners More Opportunistic in a More Volatile Environment?" *Strategic Management Journal* 28, no. 1 (2007): 39–60; A. Madhok, "How Much Does Ownership Really Matter? Equity and Trust Relations in Joint Venture Relationships," *Journal of International Business Studies* 37 (2006): 4–11.

29. B. S. Javorcik, "To Share or Not to Share: Does Local Participation Matter for Spillovers from Foreign Direct Investment," *Journal of Development Economics* 85, nos. 1 and 2 (2008): 194–217; R. M. Salomon, "Spillovers to Foreign Market Participants: Assessing the Impact of Export Strategies on Innovative Productivity," *Strategic Organization* 4 (2006): 135–64.

30. N. Pangarkar, "Survival During a Crisis: Alliances by Singapore Firms," *British Journal of Management* 18, no. 3 (2008): 209–23.

31. Intel Capital homepage, www.intel.com/capital (accessed November 20, 2008).

Getting Personal

with Joseph Keeley

CURRENTLY IN MY IPOD
Amos Lee

HARDEST PART OF GETTING FUNDING
Having a new person to "answer" to

MY ADVICE FOR NEW ENTREPRENEURS
Ask for advice early and often

WHAT I DO WHEN I'M NOT WORKING
Time at home

FIRST ENTREPRENEURIAL EXPERIENCE
Custom car washing service

MY BIGGEST SURPRISE AS AN ENTREPRENEUR
The many areas that one must be good at or willing to learn

JOSEPH KEELEY
Founder, College Nannies & Tutors
BS, Entrepreneurship, St. Thomas University, 2003

CHAPTERFIFTEEN
Franchising

OPENING PROFILE
COLLEGE NANNIES & TUTORS
Franchising as a Form of Business Ownership and Growth

www.collegenannies.com

Joseph Keeley grew up in a small town in the U.S. state of North Dakota. After graduating from high school in 2000, he moved to St. Paul, Minnesota, to attend St. Thomas University. One of Keeley's passions was hockey, which he fulfilled as a member of St. Thomas's varsity hockey team. While playing hockey, he became acquainted with a couple who had two young boys and a girl. As the summer following his freshman year approached, the couple asked him if he'd be interested in watching their kids as a full-time summer job. Keeley jumped at the chance. While his two roommates spent the summer digging pools for a local contractor, Keeley engaged in fun activities with the children while acting as their nanny and role model.

The summer job got Keeley to thinking about how young kids could benefit from being around positive role models and how college students are uniquely capable of filling that role. The idea was so compelling that during his sophomore year he launched a company called Summer College Nannies. Matching college students with families that needed part-time or full-time nanny services was the firm's core service. Early on he viewed himself more as a matchmaker than as a potential franchisor and thought of his business primarily as a way to earn extra cash. But as time went on, two things struck Keeley. First, rather than just a means of earning extra money, he started to see real potential in the college nanny idea. For many parents, a service wasn't available to help them find a safe and reliable nanny. He also liked the idea of making a positive difference in the lives of families and young children. Second, he found that working on a "real" business enhanced his classroom experiences. "I feel I had 10 times the education that anyone else did because I had a working, living project everyday," Keeley said, reflecting on this point.[1]

As the business picked up steam, St. Thomas provided Keeley with office space, and he turned Summer College Nannies into a self-made internship. To get advice, he started dropping in on St. Thomas entrepreneurship professors, who urged him to enroll in the entrepreneurship program—which he did. As time went on, Keeley entered and won several business plan competitions with the Summer College Nannies business idea. He also won the 2003 Global Student Entrepreneurship Award, which is presented by the Entrepreneurs' Organization and included a $20,000 prize. At the awards ceremony, Keeley met Peter Lytle, an angel investor and well-known Minneapolis entrepreneur. Although he had interviewed for traditional jobs, by this time Keeley had decided that he would devote his time and energy to his own business venture after graduating with his college degree. Lytle was so impressed with Keeley and his business idea that he offered to invest, and Keeley accepted the offer. At this point, Lytle helped Keeley expand his vision for the business to include tutors, and College Nannies & Tutors was born.

Following graduation, the money Lytle invested provided Keeley the time and resources to more fully develop the College Nannies & Tutors business idea. The company started generating some buzz, primarily through media coverage and word

Learning Objectives

After studying this chapter you should be ready to:

1. Explain franchising and how it differs from other forms of business ownership.

2. Describe the differences between a product and trademark franchise and a business format franchise.

3. Explain the differences among an individual franchise agreement, an area franchise agreement, and a master franchise agreement.

4. Describe the advantages of establishing a franchise system as a means of firm growth.

5. Identify the rules of thumb for determining when franchising is an appropriate form of growth for a particular business.

6. Discuss the factors to consider in determining if owning a franchise is a good fit for a particular person.

7. Identify the costs associated with buying a franchise.

8. Discuss the advantages and disadvantages of buying a franchise.

9. Identify the common mistakes franchise buyers make.

10. Describe the purpose of the Franchise Disclosure Document.

of mouth. One of the things that interested the media was the fact the Keeley, a male and a recent college graduate, was starting a company in an industry—childcare—that traditionally females dominated. The first College Nannies & Tutors center was opened in Wayzata, a suburb of Minneapolis. In college, Keeley took a class in franchising and learned about the potential of this form of business. As Keeley and Lytle fine-tuned their business idea over two long years of testing and planning, it became clear that College Nannies & Tutors could be a viable franchise. Interestingly, part of the firm's franchising process included proprietary ways for screening nannies through background checks, interviews, and psychological assessments and matching them with families. Commenting on the suitability of College Nannies & Tutors for franchising, Keeley remarked, "[And] there's value there as a franchise because we've figured it out. You (a potential franchisee) don't have to go through the learning curve."[2]

College Nannies & Tutors currently has approximately 40 franchise locations across several states. The company's goal is to have 200 locations in three years.[3]

As with College Nannies & Tutors, many retail and service organizations find franchising to be an attractive form of business ownership and growth. In some industries, such as restaurants, hotels, and automobile service, franchising is a dominant business ownership form. Franchising is less common in other industries, although it is used in industries as diverse as Internet service providers, furniture restoration, massage therapy, and senior care.

There are instances in which franchising is not appropriate. For example, new technologies are typically not introduced through franchise systems, particularly if the technology is proprietary or complex. Why? Because by its nature, franchising involves sharing of knowledge between a franchisor and its franchisees; in large franchise organizations, thousands of people may be involved in doing this. The inventors of new technologies typically involve as few people as possible in the process of rolling out their new products or services because they want to keep their trade secrets secret. They typically reserve their new technologies for their own use or license them to a relatively small number of companies, with strict confidentiality agreements in place.[4]

Still, franchising is a common method of business expansion and is growing in popularity. In 2005 (the most recent year reliable statistics are available), nearly 910,000 individual franchise outlets were operating in the United States. These operations accounted for 1.1 million jobs and a combined payroll of $276.6 billion.[5] You can even go to a Web site (www.franchising.com) to examine the array of franchises available for potential entrepreneurs to consider. This Web site groups franchising opportunities by industry, location, high investment, low cost, home based, and several other criteria. These categorizations highlight the breadth of franchising opportunities now available for consideration.[6]

Unfortunately, not all the news about franchising is positive. Because many franchise systems operate in competitive industries and grow quickly, the failure rate is relatively high. In one highly regarded study, 45 percent of all retail franchises included in the study failed in their first four to seven years.[7] Plus, despite its proliferation, franchising is a relatively poorly understood form of business ownership and growth. While most students and entrepreneurs generally know what franchising is and what it entails, the many subtle aspects of franchising can be learned only through experience or careful study.

We begin this chapter, which is dedicated to franchising as an important potential path to entrepreneurship and subsequent venture growth, with a description of franchising and when to use it. We then explore setting up a franchise system from the franchisor's perspective and buying a franchise from the franchisee's point of view. Next, we look at the legal aspects of franchising. We close this chapter by considering a few additional topics related to the successful use of franchising.

WHAT IS FRANCHISING AND HOW DOES IT WORK?

Franchising is a form of business organization in which a firm that already has a successful product or service (**franchisor**) licenses its trademark and method of doing businesses to other businesses (**franchisees**) in exchange for an initial franchise fee and an ongoing royalty.[8] Some franchisors are established firms; others are first-time enterprises that entrepreneurs are launching (this is the case for College Nannies & Tutors). This section explores the origins of franchising and how franchising works.

Learning Objective

1. Explain franchising and how it differs from other forms of business ownership.

What Is Franchising?

The word *franchise* comes from an old dialect of French and means "privilege" or "freedom." Franchising has a long history. In the Middle Ages, kings and lords granted franchises to specific individuals or groups to hunt on their land or to conduct certain forms of commerce. In the 1840s, breweries in Germany granted franchises to certain taverns to be the exclusive distributors of their beer for the region. Shortly after the U.S. Civil War, the Singer Sewing Machine Company began granting distribution franchises for its sewing machines and pioneered the use of written franchise agreements. Many of the most familiar franchises in the United States, including Kentucky Fried Chicken (1952), McDonald's (1955), Burger King (1955), Midas Muffler (1956), and H&R Block (1958), started in the post–World War II era of the 1940s and 1950s.

The franchise organization Comfort Keepers demonstrates how franchises are started. A year before the company was founded, Kristina Clum, a registered nurse, noticed that her parents were having trouble with ordinary daily chores. She wanted someone to come into their home to help them but was unable to find people willing to do so. So Kristina and her husband Jerry founded a business dedicated to helping seniors cope with everyday nonmedical tasks, such as meal preparation, light housekeeping, grocery shopping, laundry, and errands. The first Comfort Keepers office was opened in Springfield, Ohio, in March 1998, and the second was opened in Dayton a year later.

Comfort Keepers is a timely idea that addresses a need for a particular target market. As we've discussed in earlier chapters, having a solid business idea is critical to achieving firm growth. In mid-2005, there were 36.8 million people in the United States over the age of 65. That number is expected to exceed 70 million over the next two decades.[9] Comfort Keepers' services may provide some seniors the option of staying in their homes as opposed to entering more costly assisted living centers. In August 1999, the company began franchising and by 2008 had over 600 franchise outlets throughout the United States, Canada, Ireland, Australia, New Zeeland, and Singapore.

The Comfort Keepers business idea lends itself to franchising because the company has a good trademark and a good business method. Moreover, because the nature of the business keeps the cost of starting a Comfort Keepers franchise relatively low, there is a substantial pool of people available to purchase the franchise. For Comfort Keepers and its franchisees, franchising is a win-win proposition. Comfort Keepers wins because it is able to use its franchisees' money to quickly grow its business and strengthen its brand. The franchisees win because they are able to start a business in a growing industry relatively inexpensively and benefit by adopting the Comfort Keepers trademark and method of doing business.

How Does Franchising Work?

There is nothing magical about franchising. It is a form of growth that allows a business to get its products or services to market through the efforts of business partners or "franchisees." As described previously, a franchise is an agreement between a franchisor (the parent company, such as College Nannies & Tutors or Comfort Keepers) and a franchisee (an individual or firm that is willing to pay the franchisor a fee for the right to sell its product, service, and/or business method).[10] Planet Smoothie, for example, is a very successful franchise system. The franchisor (Planet Smoothie, Inc.) provides the rights to individual businesspersons (the local franchisees) to use the Planet Smoothie trademark and business methods. In turn, the franchisees pay Planet Smoothie a franchise fee and an ongoing royalty for these privileges and agree to operate their Planet Smoothie restaurants according to Planet Smoothie Inc.'s standards.

Learning Objective

2. Describe the differences between a product and trademark franchise and a business format franchise.

There are two distinctly different types of franchise systems: the product and trademark franchise and the business format franchise. A **product and trademark franchise** is an arrangement under which the franchisor grants to the franchisee the right to buy its products and use its trade name. This approach typically connects a single manufacturer with a network of dealers or distributors. For example, General Motors has established a network of dealers that sell GM cars and use the GM trademark in their advertising and promotions. Similarly, British Petroleum (BP) has established a network of franchisee-owned gasoline stations to distribute BP gasoline. Product and trademark franchisees are typically permitted to operate in a fairly autonomous manner. The parent company, such as GM or BP, is generally concerned more with maintaining the integrity of its products than with monitoring the day-to-day activities of its dealers or station owners. Other examples of product and trademark franchise systems include agricultural machinery dealers, soft-drink bottlers, and beer distributorships. Rather than obtaining a royalty or franchise fee, the product and trademark franchisor obtains the majority of its income from selling its products to its dealers or distributors at a markup.

The second type of franchise, the **business format franchise**, is by far the more popular approach to franchising and is more commonly used by entrepreneurs and entrepreneurial ventures. In a business format franchise, the franchisor provides a formula for doing business to the franchisee along with training, advertising, and other forms of assistance. Fast-food restaurants, convenience stores, fitness centers, and tax preparation services are well-known examples of business format franchisees. While a business format franchise provides a franchisee a formula for conducting business, it can also be very rigid and demanding. For example, fast-food restaurants such as McDonald's and Burger King teach their franchisees every detail of how to run their restaurants, from how many seconds to cook french fries to the exact words their employees should use when they greet customers (such as "Will this

1-800-GOT-JUNK? is an example of a business format franchise. The company (called the "franchisor") provides its franchisees a formula for doing business, training, advertising, and other forms of support. In return, each franchisee pays an initial franchise fee of approximately $24,000 and an 8 percent royalty on gross sales. 1-800-GOT-JUNK? currently has over 300 franchises in four countries.

be dining in or carry out?"). Business format franchisors obtain the majority of their revenues from their franchisees in the form of royalties and franchise fees.

For both product and trademark franchises and business format franchises, the franchisor–franchisee relationship takes one of three forms of a franchise agreement (see Figure 15.1). The most common type of franchise arrangement is an individual franchise agreement. An **individual franchise agreement** involves the sale of a single franchise for a specific location. For example, an individual may purchase a CD Warehouse franchise to be constructed and operated at 901 Pearl Street in Boulder, Colorado. An **area franchise agreement** allows a franchisee to own and operate a specific number of outlets in a particular geographic area. For example, a franchisee may purchase the rights to open five CD Warehouse franchises within the city limits of Sioux Falls, South Dakota. This is a very popular franchise arrangement, because in most cases it gives the franchisee exclusive rights for a given area. Finally, a **master franchise agreement** is similar to an area franchise agreement, with one major difference. A master franchisee, in addition to having the right to open and operate a specific number of locations in a particular area, also has the right to offer and sell the franchise to other people in its area. For example, Barnie's Coffee & Tea is a coffee restaurant franchise. The company sells master franchise agreements that provide a master franchisee the right to open a certain number of Barnie's Coffee & Tea outlets in a defined geographic area. After its own outlets have been opened, the master franchisee can then sell the rights to open additional Barnie's Coffee & Tea locations in the same area to other individuals. The people who buy franchises from master franchisees are typically called **subfranchisees**.

An individual who owns and operates more than one outlet of the same franchisor, whether through an area or a master franchise agreement, is called a **multiple-unit franchisee**. Multiple-unit franchisees are common in both small and large franchise chains, and this source of growth far outpaces the units added by new franchisees in most franchise organizations.[11] (For example, over 70 percent of new Subway franchises are purchased by established franchisees.) For the franchisee, there are advantages and disadvantages to multiple-unit franchising. By owning more than one unit, a multiple-unit franchisee can capture economies of scale and reduce its administrative overhead per unit of sale. The disadvantages of multiple-unit franchising are that the franchisor takes more risk and makes a deeper commitment to a single franchisor. In general, franchisors encourage multiple-unit franchising. By selling an additional franchise to an

Learning Objective

3. Explain the differences among an individual franchise agreement, an area franchise agreement, and a master franchise agreement.

FIGURE 15.1

Different Types of
Franchise Systems

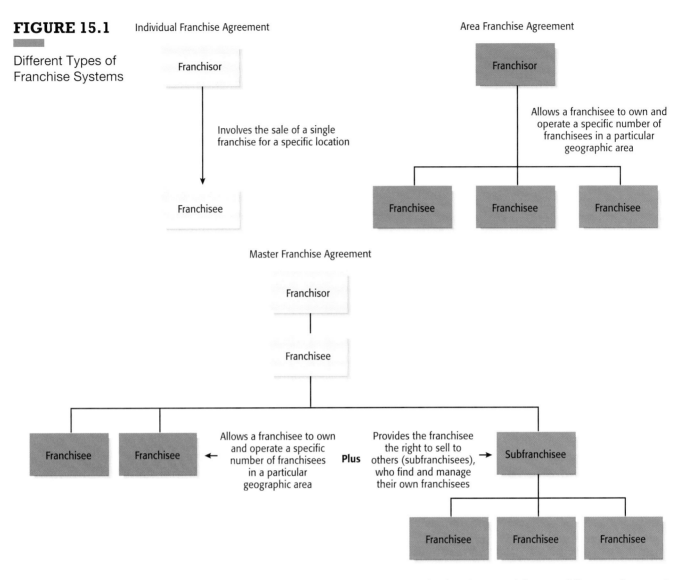

existing franchisee, a franchisor can grow its business without adding to the total number of franchisees with whom it must maintain a relationship to conduct its business.

An increasingly common practice among franchise organizations is to partner with one another through co-branding arrangements to increase systemwide sales and decrease costs. This practice is discussed in this chapter's "Partnering for Success" feature.

ESTABLISHING A FRANCHISE SYSTEM

Establishing a franchise system should be approached carefully and deliberately. While the process is a familiar one to a company such as McDonald's, which as of 2008 had 24,470 franchised units worldwide, franchising is quite an unfamiliar process to new businesses, such as College Nannies & Tutors and Comfort Keepers. Franchising is a complicated business endeavor, which means that an entrepreneur must look closely at all of its aspects before deciding to franchise. Indeed, franchising often involves the managerially demanding tasks of training, supporting, supervising, and nurturing franchisees.

An entrepreneur should also be aware that over the years a number of fraudulent franchise organizations have come and gone and left financially

Partnering for SUCCESS
Boosting Sales and Reducing Expenses Through Co-branding

Have you ever stopped at a gas station and caught a quick lunch at an Arby's or a Blimpie sub sandwich inside? Or have you ever noticed that Baskin-Robbins and Dunkin' Donuts often share the same building? If either of these two scenarios applies to you, then you have witnessed co-branding firsthand.

Co-branding takes place when two or more businesses are grouped together. Co-branding is becoming increasingly common among franchise organizations that are looking for new ways to increase sales and reduce expenses. As we describe next, there are two primary types of co-branding arrangements that apply to franchise organizations.

Two Franchises Operating Side by Side

The first type of co-branding arrangement involves two or more franchises operating side by side in the same building or leased space. This type of arrangement typically involves a franchise like a donut shop that is busiest in the morning and a taco restaurant that is busiest at lunch and dinner. By locating side by side, these businesses can increase their sales by picking up some business from the traffic generated by their co-branding partner and can cut costs by sharing rent and other expenses.

Side-by-side co-branding arrangements are not restricted to restaurants. Sometimes the benefit arises from the complementary nature of the products involved, rather than time of day. For example, a franchise that sells exercise equipment could operate side by side with a business that sells vitamins. By locating side by side, these two businesses could realize the same types of benefits as the donut shop and the taco restaurant.

Two Franchises Occupying the Exact Same Space

The second type of co-branding arrangement involves two franchises occupying essentially the same space. For example, it is increasingly common to see sub shops inside gasoline stations and other retail outlets. The relationship is meant to benefit both parties. The sub shop benefits by opening another location without incurring the cost of constructing a freestanding building or leasing expensive shopping mall space.

The gasoline station benefits by having a quality branded food partner to help it attract road traffic and by collecting lease income. Having a sub shop inside its store also helps a gasoline station become a "destination stop" for regular customers rather than simply another gas station serving passing cars.

Important Considerations

Although co-branding can be an excellent way for franchise organizations to partner for success, a firm should consider three questions before entering into a co-branding relationship:

- Will the co-branding arrangement maintain or strengthen my brand image?
- Do I have adequate control over how my partner will display or use my brand?
- Are there tangible benefits associated with attaching my brand to my partner's brand? For example, will my partner's brand have a positive effect on my brand and actually increase my sales?

If the answer to each of these questions is yes, than a co-branding arrangement may be a very effective way for a franchise organization to boosts sales and reduce expenses.

Questions for Critical Thinking

1. Do you think that co-branding will continue to gain momentum, or do you think it is a fad that will wane in terms of its popularity? Explain your answer.
2. What are the potential downsides of co-branding? What might make a franchise hesitant to enter into a co-branding relationship with another franchise organization?
3. Consider the College Nannies & Tutor's Opening Profile. Suggest some co-branding relationships that College Nannies & Tutors might consider forming.
4. Make a list of the types of businesses that might work well together in a co-branding relationship. Several initial examples include (1) a quick oil change and a tire store, (2) a bakery and a coffeehouse, and (3) a florist and a candy store.

ruined franchisees in their wake. Because of this, franchising is a fairly heavily regulated form of business expansion. Even with this regulation, though, caution is in order for those pursuing franchising as a business opportunity.

Despite the challenges, franchising is a popular form of growth. It is particularly attractive to new firms in retailing and services because it helps firms grow

Learning Objective

4. Describe the advantages of establishing a franchise system as a means of firm growth.

quickly and alleviates the challenge of raising substantial amounts of money. There is some anecdotal evidence, however, that many companies are hasty in putting together their franchise programs and as a result do a poorer job than they might have were they to take their time.[12] Although franchising is often touted as an easy way to rapidly expand a business, an effective franchise system needs to be as consciously initiated, managed, and supported as any other form of business expansion.[13] An example of a franchise organization that has gotten off to a good start via prudent management is Which Wich, a franchise with a new sandwich concept. Which Wich's unique twist is that customers "build their own sandwich" by checking off the ingredients they want on a paper bag with a Sharpie as they enter the restaurant. The company opened its first 12 restaurants in 2004 but didn't sell a franchise until 15 months later, preferring to wait until all the kinks were worked out of its approach. Which Wich now has about 40 franchise outlets and is growing.[14]

Now let's look more closely at the issues to consider when an entrepreneur is trying to decide if franchising is an appropriate approach to growing a business.

When to Franchise

Learning Objective

5. Identify the rules of thumb for determining when franchising is an appropriate form of growth for a particular business.

Retail firms grow when two things happen: first, when the attractiveness of a firm's products or services become well known, whether it is a new restaurant or a fitness center, and, second, when a firm has the financial capability to build the outlets needed to satisfy the demand for its products or services.

There are at least two options firms have as a means to grow. Building company-owned outlets is one of these options. However, this choice presents a company with the challenge of raising the money to fund its expansion. As discussed in Chapter 10, this option is typically pursued through debt, investment capital, or earnings, none of which is easy to achieve for a start-up venture.

Franchising is a second growth alternative available to firms. Franchising is perhaps especially attractive to young firms in that the majority of the money needed for expansion comes from the franchisees. Franchising is appropriate when a firm has a strong or potentially strong trademark, a well-designed business model, and a desire to grow. A franchise system will ultimately fail if the franchisee's brand doesn't create value for customers and its business model is flawed or poorly developed.

In some instances, franchising is simply not appropriate. For example, franchising works for Burger King but would not work for Wal-Mart. While Burger King has a large number of franchise outlets, each individual outlet is relatively small and has a limited menu, and policies and procedures can be written to cover almost any contingency. In contrast, although Wal-Mart is similar to Burger King in that it, too, has a strong trademark and thousands of outlets, Wal-Mart stores are much larger, more expensive to build, and more complex to run than Burger King restaurants. It would be nearly impossible for Wal-Mart to find an adequate number of qualified people who would have the financial capital and expertise to open and successfully operate a Wal-Mart store.

Steps to Franchising a Business

Let's assume that as an entrepreneur you have decided to use franchising as a means of growing your venture. What steps should you take to develop a franchise system? As illustrated in Figure 15.2, you, as an entrepreneur, should take nine steps in order to successfully set up a franchise system.

Step 1 **Develop a franchise business plan:** The franchise business plan should follow the format of a conventional business plan that we

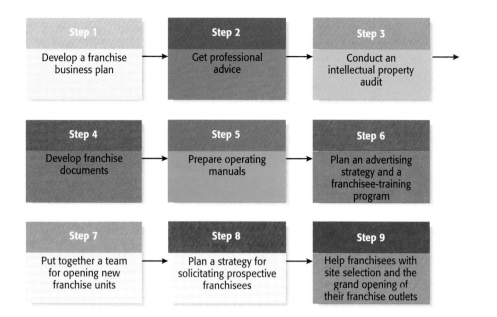

FIGURE 15.2

Nine Steps in Setting
Up a Franchise System

discussed in Chapter 4 and should fully describe the rationale for franchising the business and act as a blueprint for rolling out the franchise operation. Particular attention should be paid to the location of the proposed franchise outlet. For example, a Cold Stone Creamery restaurant that is successful in the food court of a mall in an upscale area doesn't mean that it will be successful in a less heavily trafficked strip mall in an average-income neighborhood.

Step 2   Get professional advice: Before going too far, a potential franchisor should seek advice from a qualified franchise attorney, consultant, or certified public accountant. If the business cannot be realistically turned into a franchise, then a qualified professional can save a potential franchisor a lot of time, money, and frustration by urging that the process be stopped. If the business can be turned into a franchise, then it is advisable to get professional advice to help direct the entire process.

Step 3   Conduct an intellectual property audit: As we discussed in Chapter 12, this step is necessary to determine the intellectual property a company owns and to ensure that the property is properly registered and protected. All original written, audio, and visual material, including operating manuals, training videos, advertising brochures, audiotapes, and similar matter, should be afforded copyright protection. If a firm has a unique business model that includes a unique business method, it should consider obtaining a patent for its business method. These protective measures are vital because once a company begins franchising, its trademarks and business model and any unique business methods are disseminated, making them more visible to customers and competitors. In addition, a franchisor should make sure that its trademark is not infringing on the trademark of any other firm.

Step 4   Develop franchise documents: Later in the chapter, we discuss the documents that are required to franchise a business. Here, we can note that at the beginning of the franchise evaluation process, a prospective franchisor should prepare the Franchise Disclosure Document (formally called the Uniform Franchise Offering Circular) and the franchise agreement. A franchise attorney can provide specific information regarding the content and format of these documents.

Step 5 **Prepare operating manuals:** Businesses that are suitable for franchising typically have a polished business system that can be fairly easily taught to qualified franchisees. The franchisor should prepare manuals that document all aspects of its business model.

Step 6 **Plan an advertising strategy and a franchisee-training program:** Prospective franchisees will want to see an advertising strategy and a franchisee-training program in place. The scope of each program should match the speed at which the franchisor wants to grow its business.

Step 7 **Put together a team for opening new franchise units:** A team should be developed and prepared to help new franchisees open their franchise units. The team should be well trained and equipped to provide the franchisee a broad range of training and guidance.

Step 8 **Plan a strategy for soliciting prospective franchisees:** There are many channels available to franchisors to solicit and attract potential franchisees. Franchise trade fairs, newspaper ads, franchise publications, and Internet advertising are examples of these channels.

Step 9 **Help franchisees with site selection and the grand opening of their franchise outlets:** Location is very important to most retail businesses, so a franchisor should be heavily involved in the site selection of its franchisees' outlets. The franchisor should also help the franchisee with the grand opening of the franchise outlet.

Along with the specific steps shown in Figure 15.2, it is important for a franchisor to remember that the quality of the relationships it maintains with its franchisees often defines the ultimate success of the franchise system. It is to the franchisor's advantage to follow through on all promises and to establish an exemplary reputation. This is an ongoing commitment that a franchisor should make to its franchisees.

Selecting and Developing Effective Franchisees

The franchisor's ability to select and develop effective franchisees strongly influences the degree to which a franchise system is successful. For most systems, the ideal franchisee is someone who has solid ideas and suggestions but is willing to work within the franchise system's rules. Bold, aggressive entrepreneurs typically do not make good franchisees. Franchisees must be team players to properly fit within the context of a successful franchise system.

Once franchisees are selected, it is important that franchisors work to develop their franchisees' potential. Table 15.1 contains a list of the qualities that franchisors look for in prospective franchisees and the steps that franchisors can take to develop their franchisees' potential.

Advantages and Disadvantages of Establishing a Franchise System

There are two primary advantages to franchising. First, early in the life of an organization, capital is typically scarce, and rapid growth is needed to achieve brand recognition and economies of scale. Franchising helps a venture grow quickly because franchisees provide the majority of the capital.[15] For example, if Comfort Keepers were growing via company-owned outlets rather than franchising, it

Table 15.1 SELECTING AND DEVELOPING EFFECTIVE FRANCHISEES

Qualities to Look For in Prospective Franchisees

- Good work ethic
- Ability to follow instructions
- Ability to operate with minimal supervision
- Team oriented
- Experience in the industry in which the franchise competes
- Adequate financial resources and a good credit history
- Ability to make suggestions without becoming confrontational or upset if the suggestions are not adopted
- Represents the franchisor in a positive manner

Ways Franchisors Can Develop the Potential of Their Franchisees

- Provide mentoring that supersedes routine training
- Keep operating manuals up-to-date
- Keep product, services, and business systems up-to-date
- Solicit input from franchisees to reinforce their importance in the larger system
- Encourage franchisees to develop a franchise association
- Maintain the franchise system's integrity

would probably have only a handful of outlets rather than the more than 600 it has today. Many franchisors even admit that they would have rather grown through company-owned stores but that the capital requirements needed to grow their firms dictated franchising. This sentiment is affirmed by an executive at Hardee's, who wrote the following about the growth of this fast-food chain:

> Hardee's would have preferred not to have franchised a single location. We prefer company-owned locations. But due to the heavy capital investment required, we could only expand company-owned locations to a certain degree—from there we had to stop. Each operation represents an investment in excess of $100,000; therefore, we entered the franchise business.[16]

Learning Objective

6. Discuss the factors to consider in determining if owning a franchise is a good fit for a particular person.

Second, a management concept called **agency theory**, argues that for organizations with multiple units (such as restaurant chains), it is more effective for the units to be run by franchisees than by managers who run company-owned stores. The theory is that managers, because they are usually paid a salary, may not be as committed to the success of their individual units as franchisees, who are in effect the owners of the units they manage.[17]

The primary disadvantage of franchising is that an organization allows others to profit from its trademark and business model. For example, each time Comfort Keepers sells a franchise it gets a $32,500 franchise fee and an ongoing royalty, which is 3 to 5 percent of gross sales. However, if Comfort Keepers had provided its service itself in the same location, it would be getting 100 percent of the gross sales and net profits from the location. This is the main reason some organizations that are perfectly suitable for franchising grow through company-owned stores rather than franchising. An example is Darden Restaurants Inc., the parent company of Red Lobster, Olive Garden, Bahama Breeze, Longhorn, The Capital Grill, and Seasons 52. With over 1,700 locations, this firm is the world's largest publicly held casual dining restaurant chain.[18] All of Darden's units are company owned. Starbucks is another company that is suitable for franchising but has only a small number of franchise outlets. We provide a more complete list of the advantages and disadvantages of franchising as a means of business expansion in Table 15.2.

Table 15.2 ADVANTAGES AND DISADVANTAGES OF FRANCHISING AS A METHOD OF BUSINESS EXPANSION

Advantages	Disadvantages
Rapid, low-cost market expansion. Because franchisees provide most of the cost of expansion, the franchisor can expand the size of its business fairly rapidly.	**Profit sharing.** By selling franchises instead of operating company-owned stores, franchisors share the profits derived from their proprietary products or services with their franchisees. For example, before being acquired by FedEx, Kinko's did not sell franchises, allowing it to retain all its profits.
Income from franchise fees and royalties. By collecting franchise fees, the franchisor gets a fairly quick return on the proprietary nature of its products/services and business model. The franchisor also receives ongoing royalties from its franchisees without incurring substantial risk.	**Loss of control.** It is typically more difficult for a franchisor to control its franchisees than it is for a company to control its employees. Franchisees, despite the rules governing the franchise system, still often view themselves as independent businesspeople.
Franchisee motivation. Because franchisees put their personal capital at risk, they are highly motivated to make their franchise outlets successful. In contrast, the managers of company-owned outlets typically do not have their own capital at risk. As a result, these managers may not be prone to work as hard as franchisees or be as attentive to cost savings.	**Friction with franchisees.** A common complaint of franchisors is dealing with the friction that often develops between franchisors and franchisees. Friction can develop over issues such as the payment of fees, hours of operation, caveats in the franchise agreement, and surprise inspections.
Access to ideas and suggestions. Franchisees represent a source of intellectual capital and often make suggestions to their franchisors. By incorporating these ideas into their business model, franchisors can in effect leverage the ideas and suggestions of their individual franchisees.	**Managing growth.** Franchisors that are in growing industries and have a strong trademark often grow quickly. Although this might seem like an advantage, rapid growth can be difficult to manage. A franchisor provides each of its franchisees a number of services, such as site selection and employee training. If a franchise system is growing rapidly, the franchisor will have to continually add personnel to its own staff to properly support its growing number of franchisees.
Cost savings. Franchisees share many of the franchisors' expenses, such as the cost of regional and national advertising.	**Differences in required business skills.** The business skills that made a franchisor successful in the original business are typically not the same skills needed to manage a franchise system. For example, Sam Jones may be a very effective owner/manager of a seafood restaurant. That does not necessarily mean, however, that he will be an effective manager of a franchise system if he decided to franchise his seafood restaurant concept.
Increased buying power. Franchisees provide franchisors increased buying power by enlarging the size of their business, allowing them to purchase larger quantities of products and services when buying those items.	**Legal expenses.** Many governments have specific laws pertaining to franchising. As a result, if a franchisor sells franchises in multiple areas, legal expenses can be high to properly interpret and comply with each government's laws. Unfortunately, from the franchisor's point of view, some of the toughest laws in the United States, for example, are in the most populated states.

When a company decides to investigate franchising as a means of growth, it should ensure that it and its product or service meet several criteria. Businesses that fail to satisfy these criteria are less likely to make effective franchise systems. Before deciding to franchise, a firm should consider the following:

■ **The uniqueness of its product or service:** The business's product or service should be unique along some dimension that customers value. Businesses with a unique product or service typically have the best potential to expand.

■ **The consistent profitability of the firm:** The business should be consistently profitable, and the future profitability of the business should be fairly easy to predict. When developing a franchise system, a company should have several prototype outlets up and running to test and ensure the viability of the business idea. Remember, a franchisee is supposed to be buying a way of doing business (in the form of a business model) that is "proven"—at least to a certain extent. Franchisors that learn how to run their businesses through the trial and error of their franchisees have typically franchised their businesses prematurely (especially from the franchisees' point of view).

■ **The firm's year-round profitability:** The business should be profitable year-round, not only during specific seasons. For example, a lawn and garden care franchise in Northern Europe should be set up to provide the franchisee supplemental products and services to sell during off-peak seasons. Otherwise, owning the franchise may not be an attractive form of business ownership. This issue is particularly problematic for some ice cream and smoothie franchises in northern locales, which experience a significant decline in sales during winter months.

■ **The degree of refinement of the firm's business systems:** The systems and procedures for operating the business should be polished and the procedures documented in written form. The systems and procedures should also be fairly easy to teach to qualified candidates.

■ **The clarity of the business proposition:** The business proposition should be crystal clear so that prospective franchisees fully understand the business proposition to which they are committing. The relationship between the franchisor and the franchisee should be completely open, and communication between them should be candid.

After determining that the firm satisfies these criteria, the entrepreneur should step back and review all the alternatives for business expansion. No single form of business expansion is the best under all circumstances. For any entrepreneurial venture, the best form of expansion is the one that increases the likelihood that the venture will reach its objectives.

One interesting development in franchising is the emergence of franchise systems that operate strictly online. This method of business growth via franchising is discussed in this chapter's "Savvy Entrepreneurial Firm" feature.

BUYING A FRANCHISE

Now let's look at franchising from the franchisee's perspective. Purchasing a franchise is an important business decision involving a substantial financial commitment. Potential franchise owners should strive to be as well informed as possible before purchasing a franchise and should be well aware that it is often legally and financially difficult to exit a franchise relationship. Indeed, an individual franchise opportunity should be meticulously scrutinized. Close scrutiny of a potential franchise opportunity includes activities such as meeting with the franchisor and reading the Franchise Disclosure Document, soliciting legal and financial advice, and talking to former franchisees who have dropped out of the system one is considering. In particularly heavily franchised industries, such as fast food and automobile repair, a prospective franchisee may have 20 or more franchisors from which to make a selection. It is well worth franchisees' time to carefully select the franchisor that best meets their individual needs.[19]

Some franchise organizations are designed to provide their franchisees a part-time rather than a full-time income, which is attractive to some people. An example is Stroller Strides, a company that gathers new mothers together to do

Savvy Entrepreneurial FIRM
Franchise Systems That Operate Strictly Online

TheGroceryStore: www.thegrocerystore.com
TruePresence: www.truepresence.com

Most people think of fast-food restaurants, fitness centers, tax preparation services, and tire stores when they think of franchise organizations. The idea is to create systems of nearly identical stores or businesses that consumers can rely on.

Franchise systems are now sprouting up that operate strictly online. They are called "virtual franchises" and do not have brick-and-mortar storefronts. An example is TheGroceryStore.com, a franchise organization that operates strictly online. The company tracks the best deals at grocery stores, drug stores, and retail stores, and charges its customers membership fees, which usually start at $10 for eight weeks of research for a specific store (like a local Wal-Mart store), and then a smaller amount for every eight-week period for each additional store. Launched in 1999, the company has franchisees and company-owned Web sites in all 50 U.S. states. A new franchisee gets a turnkey system that includes a training manual and access to TheGroceryStore's proprietary software and databases. When members log on to the company's main Web site, they are routed by postal code to their local franchisee's Web page, which lists the best deals at the stores they are signed up to follow.

Another example of an online franchise system is TruePresence, a company that sells Internet design and search engine marketing services. TruePresence's franchisees act as sales agents, signing up new clients and referring the work back to the main office for staff designers and programmers to complete. After paying an initial franchise fee, TruePresence's franchisees receive training, marketing materials, and other forms of support. Inquiries made through the corporate Web site are referred to the appropriate TruePresence franchisee,

and franchisees are trained on how to drum up business on their own. Franchisees basically sell the company's services at a retail price, and then pay TruePresence a wholesale price to complete the work. Because the company's franchisees spend most of their time in the field selling the company's services or taking care of existing clients, they don't need a physical storefront, and the virtual model is sufficient.

The biggest advantage of virtual franchising is that it eliminates the cost of obtaining commercial space, which is often frustrating and expensive for franchisees.

Questions for Critical Thinking

1. Do you think online or virtual franchising is an idea that will continue to gain momentum, or do you think the idea will wane over time?
2. Spend some time looking at the Web site of TheGroceryStore.com. Do you think this franchise system will continue to gain momentum? What are the upsides and the downsides of franchising for this company?
3. Think of a Web-based company, other than one of the companies mentioned in the feature, which might be suitable for franchising. Explain the rationale for franchising for this company.
4. What percentage of Web-based companies do you think are suitable to grow via franchising? Is it practical or impractical for the majority of Web-based companies to adopt the franchising growth model?

Source: C. DeBaise, "Virtual Copies," *Wall Street Journal,* October 1, 2007, R8.

45-minute power walks with their babies in strollers. The initial franchise fee ranges between $3,300 and $6,100. Owning a Stroller Strides franchise is ideal for a woman who wants to work two to three hours a day rather than eight and is passionate about fitness.

Franchising may be a particularly good choice for someone who wants to start a business but has no prior business experience. Along with offering a refined business system, well-run franchise organizations provide their franchisees training, technical expertise, and other forms of ongoing support. For example, if you buy a Curves franchise, your initial investment gets you a week-long training program at Club Camp—which is Curves' training center in Waco, Texas. Additional training is provided at regional events and at the company's annual meeting, and any franchisee needing a refresher can return to Club Camp for free. This type of support is what attracts people of all backgrounds to the franchise concept, regardless of prior work experience. Reflecting on this aspect of franchising, Cassie Findley, director of continuing education and research at Curves, said:

> We get people from all walks of life. We get homemakers who want to become entrepreneurs and run their own businesses. We get retirees who want to help women change their lives, and we get a small percentage of investors. They're not physical fitness professionals when they come to us.[20]

Is Franchising Right for You?

Entrepreneurs should weigh the possibility of purchasing a franchise against the alternatives of buying an existing business or launching their own venture from scratch. Answering the following questions will help determine whether franchising is a good fit for people thinking about starting their own entrepreneurial venture:

- Are you willing to take orders? Franchisors are typically very particular about how their outlets operate. For example, McDonald's and other successful fast-food chains are very strict in terms of their restaurants' appearance and how the unit's food is prepared. Franchising is typically not a good fit for people who like to experiment with their own ideas or are independent minded.

- Are you willing to be part of a franchise "system" rather than an independent businessperson? For example, as a franchisee you may be required to pay into an advertising fund that covers the costs of advertising aimed at regional or national markets rather than the market for your individual outlet. Will it bother you to have someone use your money to develop ads that benefit the "system" rather than only your outlet or store? Are you willing to lose creative control over how your business is promoted?

- How will you react if you make a suggestion to your franchisor and your suggestion is rejected? How will you feel if you are told that your suggestion might work for you but can be put in place only if it works in all parts of the system?

- What are you looking for in a business? How hard do you want to work?

- How willing are you to put your money at risk? How will you feel if your business is operating at a net loss but you still have to pay royalties on your gross income?

None of these questions is meant to suggest that franchising is not an attractive method of business ownership for entrepreneurs. It is important, however, that a potential franchisee be fully aware of the subtleties involved with franchising before purchasing a franchise outlet.

The Cost of a Franchise

The initial cost of a business format franchise varies, depending on the franchise fee, the capital needed to start the business, and the strength of the franchisor. For example, some franchisors, like McDonald's, own the land and buildings that their franchisees use, and lease the property to the franchisees. In contrast, other organizations require their franchisees to purchase the land, buildings, and equipment needed to run their franchise outlets. Table 15.3 shows the total costs of buying into several franchise organizations. As you can see, the total initial cost varies from a low of $59,600 for a Comfort Keepers franchise to more than $961,500 for a Gold's Gym franchise.

Learning Objective

7. Identify the costs associated with buying a franchise.

Table 15.3 INITIAL COSTS TO THE FRANCHISEE OF A SAMPLE OF FRANCHISE ORGANIZATIONS

Franchise Organization	Year Started Franchising	Company-Owned Units	Franchised Units	Franchise Fee	Ongoing Royalty Fee	Total Initial Investment
Comfort Keepers	1999	0	605	$32,500	3%–5%	$59,600–$90,000
Domino's Pizza	1967	565	7,945	$25,000	5.5%	$118,500–$460,300
GNC Nutrition Centers	1988	2,693	1,984	$35,000	6%	$132,700–$182,000
Gold's Gym	1980	53	583	$22,250	3%	$961,500–$3.6 million
McDonald's	1955	6,906	24,471	$45,000	12.5%+	$950,000–$1.8 million
Play It Again Sports	1988	0	375	$20,000	5%	$211,000–$402,400
Smoothie King	1988	1	505	$25,000	6%	$148,000–$299,000
Subway	1974	0	28,799	$12,500	8%	$80,000–$310,000

Source: Entrepreneur.com, www.entrepreneur.com (accessed October 28, 2008).

Also shown in Table 15.3 is a breakdown of the number of company-owned units and the number of franchise units maintained by different organizations. Company-owned units are managed and operated by company personnel, and there is no franchisee involved. Franchise organizations vary in their philosophies regarding company-owned versus franchised units. As we noted earlier in this chapter, some companies (e.g., Subway) are strictly franchisors and have no company-owned units. Other companies, such as General Nutrition Centers, maintain large numbers of both company-owned and franchised units. In addition, some U.S.-based franchise systems have nearly as many foreign as domestic franchises. For example, of the 7,945 franchises in Domino's Pizza's system, 4,571 are in the United States and 3,374 are in foreign countries.

When evaluating the cost of a franchise, prospective franchisees should consider all the costs involved. Franchisors are required by law to disclose all their costs in a document called the Franchise Disclosure Document and send it to the franchisee. (We'll talk about this document in more detail later in this chapter.) To avoid making a hasty judgment, a franchisee may not purchase a franchise for 14 days from the time the circular is received. The following costs are typically associated with buying a business format franchise:[21]

- **Initial franchise fee:** The initial franchise fee varies, depending on the franchisor, as shown in Table 15.3.
- **Capital requirements:** These costs vary, depending on the franchisor, but may include the cost of buying real estate, the cost of constructing a building, the purchase of initial inventory, and the cost of obtaining a business license. Some franchisors also require a new franchisee to pay a "grand opening" fee for its assistance in opening the business.
- **Continuing royalty payment:** In the majority of cases, a franchisee pays a royalty based on a percentage of weekly or monthly gross income. Note that because the fee is typically assessed on gross income rather than net income, a franchisee may have to pay a monthly royalty even if the business is losing money. Royalty fees are usually around 5 percent of gross income.[22]
- **Advertising fees:** Franchisees are often required to pay into a national or regional advertising fund, even if the advertisements are directed at goals other than promoting the franchisor's product or service. (For example,

advertising could focus on the franchisor's attempt at attracting new franchisees.) Advertising fees are typically less than 3 percent of gross income.

■ **Other fees:** Other fees may be charged for various activities, including training additional staff, providing management expertise when needed, providing computer assistance, or providing a host of other items or support services.

Although not technically a fee, many franchise organizations sell their franchisee products that they use in their businesses, such as restaurant supplies for a restaurant franchise. The products are often sold at a markup and may be more expensive than those the franchisee could obtain on the open market.

There are some franchise organizations that use a more hybrid fee structure than the pricing formula shown here. An example is Candy Bouquet, which charges an initial franchise fee starting at $3,900 but has no ongoing royalty fee. Instead, the company charges its franchisees a monthly association fee of $35 to $200, which is not tied to store volume.[23]

The most important question a prospective franchisee should consider is whether the fees and royalties charged by a franchisor are consistent with the franchise's value or worth. If they are, then the pricing structure may be fair and equitable. If they are not, then the terms should be renegotiated or the prospective franchisee should look elsewhere.

Finding a Franchise

There are thousands of franchise opportunities available to prospective franchisees. The most critical step in the early stages of investigating franchise opportunities is for the entrepreneur to determine the type of franchise that is the best fit. For example, it is typically unrealistic for someone who is not a mechanic to consider buying a muffler repair franchise. A franchisor teaches a franchisee how to use the contents of a business model, not a trade. Before buying a franchise, a potential franchisee should imagine operating the prospective franchise or, better yet, should spend a period of time working in one of the franchisor's outlets. After working in a print shop for a week, for example, someone who thought she might enjoy running a print shop might find out that she hates it. This type of experience could help avoid making a mistake that is costly both to the franchisee and to the franchisor.

There are many periodicals, Web sites, and associations that provide information about franchise opportunities. Every Thursday, for example, ads for franchise opportunities appear in special sections of the *Wall Street Journal* and *USA Today*. Periodicals featuring franchise opportunities include *Inc.* and *Entrepreneur* (especially the January issues) and franchise-specific magazines such as *Franchise Handbook*, *Franchise Opportunities Guide*, and *Franchise Times*. Prospective franchisees should also consider attending franchise opportunity shows that are held periodically in major U.S. cities and the International Franchise Exposition, which is held annually in Washington, D.C. The U.S. Small Business Administration is another good source of franchise information.

Because of the risks involved in franchising, the selection of a franchisor should be a careful, deliberate process. One of the smartest moves a potential franchise owner can make is to talk to current franchisees and inquire if they are making money and if they are satisfied with their franchisor. Reflecting on how this approach helped ease her inhibitions about buying a franchise, Carleen Peaper, the owner of a Cruise Planner franchise, said:

> I was really apprehensive about making an investment of my time and money into a franchise, so I e-mailed 50 Cruise Planner agents with a set of questions, asking for honest feedback. Everyone responded. That was a big thing and helped me determine that I wanted to join them.[24]

Table 15.4 QUESTIONS TO ASK BEFORE BUYING A FRANCHISE

Questions to Ask a Franchisor

- What is the background of the company and its performance record?
- What is the company's current financial status?
- What are the names, addresses, and phone numbers of existing franchisees in my trade area?
- Describe how you train and mentor your franchisees.
- If at some point I decide to exit the franchise relationship, how does the exit process work?
- In what ways do you work with a franchisee who is struggling?

Questions to Ask Current Franchisees

- How much does your franchise gross per year? How much does it net? Are the procedures followed to make royalty payments to the franchisee burdensome?
- Are the financial projections of revenues, expenses, and profits that the franchisor provided me accurate in your judgment?
- Does the franchisor give you enough assistance in operating your business?
- How many hours, on average, do you work a week?
- How often do you get a vacation?
- Have you been caught off-guard by any unexpected costs or expectations?
- Does your franchisor provide you ongoing training and support?
- If you had to do it all over again, would you purchase a franchise in this system? Why or why not?

Table 15.4 contains a list of sample questions to ask a franchisor and some of its current franchisees before investing. Potential entrepreneurs can expect to learn a great deal by studying the answers they receive in response to these questions.

Advantages and Disadvantages of Buying a Franchise

Learning Objective

8. Discuss the advantages and disadvantages of buying a franchise.

There are two primary advantages to buying a franchise over other forms of business ownership. First, franchising provides an entrepreneur the opportunity to own a business using a tested and refined business model. This attribute lessens the probability of business failure. In addition, the trademark that comes with the franchise often provides instant legitimacy for a business.[25] For example, an entrepreneur opening a new Curves fitness center would likely attract more customers than an entrepreneur opening a new, independently owned fitness center because many women who are a part of the target market of Curves have already heard of the firm and have a positive impression of it. Second, when an individual purchases a franchise, the franchisor typically provides training, technical expertise, and other forms of support. For example, many franchise organizations provide their franchisees periodic training both at their headquarters location and in their individual franchise outlets.

The main disadvantage of buying and operating a franchise is the cost involved. As mentioned earlier, the franchisee must pay an initial franchise fee. The franchisee must also pay the franchisor an ongoing royalty as well as pay into a variety of funds, depending on the franchise organization. Thus, franchisees have both immediate (i.e., the initial franchise fee) and long-term (i.e., continuing royalty payments) costs. By opening an independent business, an entrepreneur can keep 100 percent of the profits if it is successful.

Table 15.5 contains a list of the advantages and disadvantages of buying a franchise.

Table 15.5 ADVANTAGES AND DISADVANTAGES OF BUYING A FRANCHISE

Advantages	Disadvantages
A proven product or service within an established market. The most compelling advantage to buying a franchise is that the franchise offers a proven product or service within an established market.	**Cost of the franchise.** The initial cost of purchasing and setting up a franchise operation can be quite high, as illustrated in Table 15.3.
An established trademark or business system. The purchase of a franchise with an established trademark provides franchisees with considerable market power. For example, the purchaser of a McDonald's franchise has a trademark with proven market power.	**Restrictions on creativity.** Many franchise systems are very rigid and leave little opportunity for individual franchisees to exercise their creativity. This is an often-cited frustration of franchisees.
Franchisor's training, technical expertise, and managerial experience. Another important attribute of franchising is the training, technical expertise, and managerial experience that the franchisor provides the franchisee.	**Duration and nature of the commitment.** For a variety of reasons, many franchise agreements are difficult to exit. In addition, virtually every franchise agreement contains a noncompete clause. These clauses vary in terms of severity, but a typical clause prevents a former franchisee from competing with the franchisor for a period of two years or more.
An established marketing network. Franchisees who buy into a powerful franchise system are part of a system that has tremendous buying power and substantial advertising power and marketing prowess.	**Risk of fraud, misunderstandings, or lack of franchisor commitment.** Along with the many encouraging stories of franchise success, there are also many stories of individuals who purchase a franchise only to be disappointed by the franchisor's broken promises.
Franchisor ongoing support. One of the most attractive advantages of purchasing a franchise rather than owning a store outright is the notion that the franchisor provides the franchisee ongoing support in terms of training, product updates, management assistance, and advertising. A popular slogan in franchising is that people buy franchises to "be in business for themselves but not by themselves."	**Problems of termination or transfer.** Some franchise agreements are very difficult and expensive to terminate or transfer. Often, a franchisee cannot terminate a franchise agreement without paying the franchisor substantial monetary damages.
Availability of financing. Some franchisors offer financing to their franchisees, although these cases are the exception rather than the rule. This information is available in section 10 of the Franchise Disclosure Document.	**Poor performance on the part of other franchisees.** If some of the franchisees in a franchise system start performing poorly and make an ineffective impression on the public, that poor performance can affect the reputation and eventually the sales of a well-run franchise in the same system.
Potential for business growth. If a franchisee is successful in the original location, the franchisee is often provided the opportunity to buy additional franchises from the same franchisor. For many franchisees, this prospect offers a powerful incentive to work hard to be as successful as possible.	**Potential for failure.** Some franchise systems simply fail to reach their objectives. When this happens, franchisees' wealth can be negatively affected. Indeed, when a franchise system fails, it commonly brings its franchisees down with it.

Steps in Purchasing a Franchise

Purchasing a franchise system is a seven-step process, as illustrated in Figure 15.3. The first rule of buying a franchise is to avoid making a hasty decision. Again, owning a franchise is typically costly and labor-intensive, and the purchase of a franchise should be a careful, deliberate decision. Once the decision to purchase a franchise has been nearly made, however, the following steps should be taken. If at any time prior to signing the franchise agreement the prospective franchisee has second thoughts, the process should be stopped until the prospective franchisee's concerns are adequately addressed.

FIGURE 15.3

Seven Steps in
Purchasing a Franchise

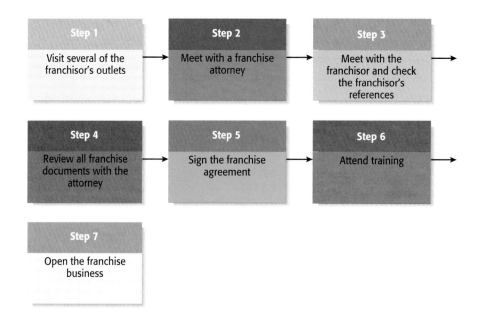

Step 1 **Visit several of the franchisor's outlets:** Prior to meeting with the franchisor, the prospective franchisee should visit several of the franchisor's outlets and talk with their owners and employees. During the visits, the prospective franchisee should continually ask, "Is this the type of business I would enjoy owning and operating or managing?"

Step 2 **Retain a franchise attorney:** Prospective franchisees should have an attorney who represents their interests, not the franchisor's. The attorney should prepare the prospective franchisee for meeting with the franchisor and should review all franchise documents before they are signed. If the franchisor tries to discourage the prospective franchisee from retaining an attorney, this is a red flag.

Step 3 **Meet with the franchisor and check the franchisor's references:** The prospective franchisee should meet with the franchisor, preferably at the franchisor's headquarters. During the meeting, the prospective franchisee should compare what was observed first-hand in the franchised outlets with what the franchisor is saying. Additional references should also be checked. The Franchise Disclosure Document is a good source for references. In section 20 of this document, there is a list of all the franchisees that have dropped out of the system in the past three years along with their contact information. Several of these should be called. Although it may seem to be overkill, the mantra for prospective franchisees is to check, double-check, and triple-check a franchisor's references.

Step 4 **Review all franchise documents with the attorney:** The franchise attorney should review all the franchise documents, including the Franchise Disclosure Document and the franchise agreement.

Step 5 **Sign the franchise agreement:** If everything is a go at this point, the franchise agreement can be signed. The franchise agreement is the document in which the provisions of the franchisor–franchisee relationship are outlined. We discuss this agreement in greater detail later in this chapter.

Step 6   **Attend training:** Almost all franchise organizations provide their franchisees training. For example, Comfort Keepers requires each of its new franchisees to attend an intensive five-day training program at its corporate headquarters, and ongoing opportunities for training are made available.

Step 7   **Open the franchise business:** For many franchises, particularly restaurants, the first two to three weeks after the business is opened may be its busiest period, as prospective customers "try it out." This is why many franchise organizations send experienced personnel to help the franchisee open the business as smoothly as possible. One goal of a franchisee is generating positive word of mouth about the business right from the start.

Watch Out! Common Misconceptions About Franchising

Despite the abundance of advice available to them, many franchisees make false assumptions about franchising. Part of the explanation for this is that franchising has an attractive lure. It is easy to become enthralled with the promise of franchising and not spend an adequate amount of time examining the potential pitfalls. The following is a list of misconceptions franchisees often have about franchising:

Learning Objective

9. Identify the common mistakes franchise buyers make.

■ **Franchising is a safe investment:** Franchising, in and of itself, is no safer an investment than any other form of business ownership.

■ **A strong industry ensures franchise success:** Although it is generally important to operate in a growing industry, the strength of an industry does not make up for a poor product, a poor business model, poor management, or inappropriate advertising. There are many firms that fail in growing industries just as there are firms that succeed in unattractive ones.

■ **A franchise is a "proven" business system:** A franchisor sells a franchisee the right to use a particular business model. Whether the model is proven or not is subject to the test of time. Obviously, companies such as Subway, Curves, and McDonald's are using models that are polished and that have worked well over time. Most prospective franchisees, however, cannot afford a McDonald's or a Subway unit and will be considering a lesser-known franchise. All too frequently, companies start selling franchises before their systems are anywhere close to being proven—a fact that should cause entrepreneurs to be wary.

■ **There is no need to hire a franchise attorney or an accountant:** Professional advice is almost always needed to guide a prospective franchisee through the franchise purchase process. A prospective franchisee should never give in to the temptation to save money by relying solely on the franchisor's advice.

■ **The best systems grow rapidly, and it is best to be a part of a rapid-growth system:** While some franchise systems grow rapidly because they have a good trademark and a polished business model, other franchise systems grow quickly because their major emphasis is on selling franchises. It is to a franchisee's benefit to be part of a system that has a solid trademark and business system—as that trademark and system will attract more customers—but some franchise systems grow so quickly that they outrun their ability to provide their franchisees adequate support.

■ **I can operate my franchise outlet for less than the franchisor predicts:** The operation of a franchise outlet usually costs just as much as the franchisor predicts.

■ **The franchisor is a nice person—he'll help me out if I need it:** Although it may be human nature to rely on the goodwill of others, don't expect anything from your franchisor that isn't spelled out in the franchise agreement.

Because these misconceptions are often hard to detect, some prospective franchisees attend seminars or franchise "boot camps" that teach them the ins and outs of franchising, including the things to watch out for when they talk to prospective franchisors. These types of seminars and boot camps are regularly offered by organizations such as Women in Franchising, the United States Hispanic Chamber of Commerce, and the International Franchising Organization.

LEGAL U.S. ASPECTS OF THE FRANCHISE RELATIONSHIP

According to the U.S. Federal Trade Commission (FTC), a franchise exists any time that the sale of a business involves (1) the sale of goods or services that bear a trademark, (2) the retention of significant control or assistance by the holder of the trademark on the operation of the business, and (3) royalty payments by the purchaser of the business to the owner of the trademark for the right to use the trademark in the business.

The legal and regulatory environment surrounding franchising is based on the premise that the public interest is served if prospective franchisees are as informed as possible regarding the characteristics of a particular franchisor. The offer and sale of a franchise is regulated at both the national and local levels. The legal aspects of the franchise relationship are unique enough that some attorneys specialize in franchise law.

U.S. Rules and Regulations

Except for the automobile and petroleum industries, U.S. laws do not directly address the franchisor–franchisee relationship. Instead, franchise disputes are matters of contract law and are litigated at the state level. During the 1990s, the United States considered several proposals for federal legislation to govern franchise relationships, but none became law.

Learning Objective

10. Describe the purpose of the Franchise Disclosure Document.

However, the offer and sale of a franchise is regulated at the national level. According to FTC Rule 436, franchisors must furnish potential franchisees with written disclosures that provide information about the franchisor, the franchised business, and the franchise relationship. The disclosures must be supplied at least 14 business days before a franchise agreement can be signed or the franchisee pays the franchisor any money.[26] In most cases, the disclosures are made through a lengthy document referred to as the Franchise Disclosure Document, which is accepted in all 50 states and parts of Canada. The **Franchise Disclosure Document (FDD)** contains 23 categories of information that give a prospective franchisee a broad base of information about the background and financial health of the franchisor. A summary of the information contained in the FDD is provided in Table 15.6. A prospective franchisee should fully understand all the information contained in the FDD before a franchise agreement is signed.

The FDD requires the franchisor to attach a copy of the franchise agreement and any other related contractual documents to the circular. The **franchise agreement**, or contract, is the document that consummates the sale of a franchise. Franchise agreements vary, but each agreement typically contains two sections: the purchase agreement and the franchise or license agreement. The purchase agreement typically spells out the price, the services to be provided by the franchisor to the franchisee, and the "franchise package," which refers to all the items the franchisee has been told to expect. The franchise or license agreement typically stipulates the rights granted to the franchisee (including the right to use the franchisor's trademark), the obligations and duties of the franchisor, the obligations and duties of the franchisee, trade restrictions, rights and limitations regarding the transfer or termination of the franchise agreement, and who is responsible for attorney fees if disputes arise. Most states have enacted a statute of frauds that requires franchise agreements to be in writing.

The federal government does not require franchisors to register with the FTC. The offer of a franchise for sale does not imply that the FTC has examined the franchisor and has determined that the information contained in the franchisor's FDD is accurate. The franchisor is responsible for voluntarily complying with the law, and it is the responsibility of prospective franchisees to exercise due diligence in investigating franchise opportunities. Although most franchisor–franchisee relationships are conducted in an entirely ethical manner, it is a mistake to assume that a franchisor has a fiduciary obligation to its franchisees. What this means is that if a franchisor had a **fiduciary obligation** to its franchisees, it would always act in their best interest, or be on the franchisees' "side." Commenting on this issue, Robert Purvin, an experienced franchise attorney, wrote:

> While the conventional wisdom talks about the proactive relationship of the franchisor to its franchisees, virtually every court case decided in the U.S. has ruled that a franchisor has no fiduciary obligation to its franchisees. Instead, U.S. courts have agreed with franchisors that franchise agreements are "arms length" business transactions.[27]

Purvin's statement suggests that a potential franchisee should not rely solely on the goodwill of a franchisor when negotiating a franchise agreement. A potential franchisee should have a lawyer who is fully acquainted with franchise law and should closely scrutinize all franchise-related legal documents.

State Rules and Regulations

In addition to the FTC disclosure requirements, 15 states have franchise investment laws that provide additional protection to potential franchisees. The states are California, Hawaii, Illinois, Indiana, Maryland, Michigan, Minnesota, New York, North Dakota, Oregon, Rhode Island, South Dakota, Virginia, Washington, and Wisconsin. The franchise investment laws require franchisors to provide presale disclosures, known as "offering circulars," to potential franchisees. Thirteen of the states have laws that treat the sale of a franchise like the sale of a security. These states require that a franchisor's FDD be filed with a designated state agency and be placed into public record.

Table 15.6 INFORMATION CONTAINED IN THE FRANCHISE DISCLOSURE DOCUMENT (FDD)
ALONG WITH EXPLANATIONS OF THEIR MEANINGS

Section and Item	Explanation
1. The franchisor, its predecessors, and affiliates 2. Business experience of the franchisor 3. Litigation experience of the franchisor 4. Bankruptcy on the part of the franchisor	These items provide information about the franchisor's operating history, business affiliations, and past litigation and bankruptcy experience, if any. It is not uncommon for a large company to have experienced some litigation. It would be a red flag, however, if a disproportionate percentage of the litigation involved suits with current or former franchisees.
5. Initial franchise fee 6. Other fees 7. Initial investment	These items specify the fees that the franchisee is subject to along with the franchisees' initial investment, which can be quite substantial. The "other fees" section should be carefully studied to avoid any surprises.
8. Restrictions on sources of products and services 9. Franchisee's obligations	These items stipulate the franchisee's obligations, along with restrictions pertaining to where the franchisee is permitted to purchase supplies and services. Some franchise agreements require the franchisee to purchase supplies from the franchisor.
10. Financing available 11. Franchisor's obligations	These items spell out the franchisor's obligations, along with a description of the financing (if any) that the franchisor offers to the franchisee. The franchisor's obligations typically include providing assistance in opening the franchise's unit, ongoing training, and advertising.
12. Territory 13. Trademarks 14. Patents, copyrights, and proprietary information	These items describe the territorial rights granted the franchisee (if any) and the franchisor's right to grant other franchises and open company-owned outlets. In addition, items 13 and 14 specify the principal trademarks, patents, and copyrights and other proprietary information owned by the franchisor and the extent to which these items can be used by the franchisee.
15. Obligation to participate in the actual operation of the franchise business	This section addresses the franchisee's obligation to participate personally in the operation of the franchise. Franchisors typically do not want absentee franchisees.
16. Restrictions on what the franchisee may sell 17. Renewal, termination, transfer, and dispute resolution	These sections deal with what the franchisee may sell and how the franchisor resolves disputes with its franchisees. Item 17 also contains important information about the manner in which franchisees can renew, terminate, and/or transfer their franchise.
18. Public figures	This section lists public figures affiliated with the franchise through advertising and other means.
19. Earnings claim	If a franchisor makes an earnings claim in connection with an offer of a franchise, then certain past and projected earnings information must be provided.
20. List of outlets	This section is quite exhaustive and contains (1) the number of franchises sold by the franchisor, (2) the number of company-owned outlets, (3) the names of all franchisees and the addresses and telephone numbers of all their outlets (within certain limitations), (4) an estimate of the number of franchises to be sold in the next year, and (5) a list of all franchisees (covering the past three years) who have dropped out of the system, including their last-known home addresses and telephone numbers.
21. Financial statements	This section contains the franchisor's previous two years of independently audited financial statements.
22. Contracts	These last two sections contain copies of the documents that franchisees have to sign.
23. Receipt **Attachments:** Franchise Agreement (or contract) Equipment Lease Lease for Premises Loan Agreement	These are the common exhibits attached to the FDD.

These state laws give franchise purchasers important legal rights, including the right to bring private lawsuits against franchisors for violation of state disclosure requirements.

By requiring franchisors to file their FDDs with a state agency, these states provide franchise purchasers important legal protection, including the right to sue a franchisor for violation of state disclosure requirements (if the franchise purchaser feels that full disclosure in the offering circular was not made). For example, if someone purchased a franchise in one of the states fitting the profile described previously and six months later discovered that the franchisor did not disclose an issue required by the FDD (and, as a result, felt that he or she had been damaged), that person could seek relief by suing the franchisor in state court. All 17 states providing additional measures of protection for franchisees also regulate some aspect of the termination process.[28] Although the provisions vary by state, they typically restrict a franchisor from terminating the franchise before the expiration of the franchise agreement, unless the franchisor has "good cause" for its action.

MORE ABOUT FRANCHISING

There are a number of additional issues pertaining to the franchisor–franchisee relationship. Three important topics, for both franchisors and franchisees, are franchise ethics, international franchising, and the future of franchising as a method of business ownership and growth.

Franchise Ethics

The majority of franchisors and franchisees are highly ethical individuals who are interested only in making a fair return on their investment. In fact, according to a recent FTC report, instances of problems between franchisors and their franchisees tend to be isolated occurrences rather than prevalent practices.[29] There are certain features of franchising, however, that make it subject to ethical abuse. An understanding of these features can help franchisors and franchisees guard against making ethical mistakes. These features are the following:

■ **The get-rich-quick mentality:** Some franchisors see franchising as a get-rich-quick scheme and become more interested in selling franchises than in using franchising as a legitimate means of distributing their product or service. These franchisors have a tendency to either oversell the potential of their franchise or overpromise the support they will offer to their franchisees.

■ **The false assumption that buying a franchise is a guarantee of business success:** Buying a franchise, as is the case with all other business investments, involves risk. Any statement to the contrary is typically misleading or unethical. A franchisor must steer clear of claims that it has the "key" to business success, and a franchisee needs to be wary of all such claims.

■ **Conflicts of interest between franchisors and their franchisees:** The structure of the franchise relationship can create conflicts of interest between franchisors and their franchisees. For example, franchisees benefit from the profits of a unit, while franchisors benefit from increased revenues (recall that a franchisor's royalty is typically paid on a percentage of gross profits rather than net profits). This anomaly in the franchise arrangement can motivate franchisors to take steps that boost revenues for the entire system but hurt profits for individual franchisees. For example, a franchisor might insist that a franchisee sell a product that has high revenue but low margins (or net income). Similarly, a franchisor might sell several franchises in a given geographic area to maximize the revenue potential of the area regardless of the effect on each individual franchisee's net income. These actions can at times be ethically questionable and can often lead to contentious conflicts of interest in franchise systems.

Despite the protection of law and the advocacy of franchise associations, individual franchisors and franchisees must practice due diligence in their relationships. "Buyer beware" is a good motto for franchisors selecting franchisees and prospective franchisees selecting franchisors. Entering into a franchise relationship is a major step for both parties and should be treated accordingly. The metaphor used frequently to describe the franchisor–franchisee relationship is marriage. Similar to marriage, the franchisor–franchisee relationship is typically close, long-term, and painful to terminate. Each side of the franchise partnership should scrutinize the past ethical behavior of the other before a franchise agreement is executed.

International Franchising

International opportunities for franchising are becoming more prevalent as the markets for certain franchised products in the United States have become saturated.[30] Indeed, heavily franchised companies, such as McDonald's, Kentucky Fried Chicken, and Century 21 Real Estate, are experiencing much of their growth in international markets. For example, Century 21 currently has more than 6,600 independently owned and operated franchised broker offices in over 30 countries and territories worldwide. The trend toward globalization in many industries is also hastening the trend toward international franchising, and the growing middle classes in many countries are creating large populations of consumers eager for American-style goods. In fact, to illustrate how global many familiar franchise systems have become, there is a Papa John's pizzeria in Karachi, Pakistan, a Denny's in Christchurch, New Zealand, and a Chili's Grill and Bar on a riverboat on the Egyptian Nile.[31]

A U.S. citizen who is thinking about buying a franchise abroad may be confronted with the choice of buying from an American company or a foreign company regardless of the location in the world. For U.S. citizens, these are some of the steps to take before buying a franchise in a foreign country:

- **Consider the value of the franchisor's name in the foreign country:** There are very few franchise systems whose names are known worldwide. Beyond a select few—McDonald's, Coca-Cola, and Budweiser come to mind—the majority of trademarks well known to Americans may be known to only a small percentage of the population of a foreign country. When considering the purchase of a U.S.-based franchise in a foreign country, carefully evaluate the value of the trademark in that country.

- **Work with a knowledgeable lawyer:** Many of the legal protections afforded to prospective franchisees in the United States are unavailable in foreign countries, highlighting the need for the purchaser of a franchise in a foreign country to obtain excellent legal advice. All the hazards involved

The restaurant industry remains one of the most rapidly growing areas of franchising because it caters to all ages and demographics. In 2008, *Entrepreneur* magazine ranked Papa John's the 10th fastest growing franchise with 2,122 franchises in the United States, 19 in Canada, and 474 in other foreign countries. Papa John's also has 674 company-owned stores.

with purchasing a domestic franchise are magnified when purchasing a franchise in a foreign country.

■ **Determine whether the product or service is salable in a foreign country:** Just because a product or service is desirable to Americans is no guarantee of success in a foreign culture. Before buying a franchise in a foreign country, determine if sufficient marketing research has been conducted to ensure that the product or service will have a sufficient market in the foreign country.

■ **Uncover whether the franchisor has experience in international markets:** It is typically not a good idea to be a franchisor's "test case" to see if the franchisor wants to operate in foreign markets. Be leery of franchisors with aggressive expansion plans but little international experience.

■ **Find out how much training and support you will receive from the franchisor:** If your franchise unit will be in a foreign country and the franchisor remains headquartered in the United States, make sure you fully understand the amount of training and support you can expect. Will the franchisor have an area representative in your country? If not, do you have to make an international phone call each time you want to talk to your franchisor? Will your franchisor be willing to travel to the foreign country to offer you training and support? Who pays for the international travel of the franchisor's training staff? Who is responsible for advertising in the foreign country, the franchisor or the franchisee?

■ **Evaluate currency restrictions:** Evaluate any restrictions that the foreign country places on the convertibility of its currency into U.S. dollars.

To avoid some of the potential problems alluded to here, U.S. franchisors typically structure their expansion into a foreign country through the following:

■ **Direct franchising arrangement:** Under a direct franchise arrangement, the U.S. franchisor grants the rights to an individual or a company (the developer) to develop multiple franchised businesses within a country or territory. For example, if Midas Muffler decided to sell franchises for the first time in Spain, Midas may grant the rights to a Spanish company to develop multiple Midas franchises there.

■ **Master franchise agreement:** Under a master franchise arrangement, the U.S. firm grants the right to an individual or company (the master franchisee) to develop one or more franchise businesses and to license others to develop one or more franchise businesses within the country or territory.

■ **Other agreements:** Combinations of other arrangements are also employed by franchisors expanding to foreign markets. Examples include joint-venture arrangements, direct-sales arrangements, or straight franchising agreements.

Even when a company adheres to these safeguards, there is plenty that can go wrong when opening franchise outlets overseas. This topic is addressed in this chapter's "What Went Wrong?" feature.

What Went WRONG?
Watch Out: Plenty Can Go Wrong in Opening Franchise Outlets Overseas

Although the Internet, satellite television, and Hollywood movies have increased the demand for American products and services abroad, franchisors should take care not to rush into opening franchise outlets overseas. Because many of the easiest countries into which U.S. firms can export their products and services, such as Canada and England, are already saturated with U.S. franchised outlets, this leaves only more difficult foreign markets. Differences in language and the customs associated with a nation's culture are examples of factors making franchising very challenging in these more difficult foreign markets. Indeed, plenty can go wrong because of the complexities of operating overseas.

Sometimes, franchisors run into unique challenges in foreign markets, sometimes they simply make mistakes, and sometimes they insist on trying to impose American tastes on overseas markets, which doesn't always work. All of these complications result from a lack of familiarity with the foreign markets the companies are trying to enter. Here are some examples of mistakes U.S. franchisors have made when trying to enter foreign markets:

- Burger King didn't register its trademark in Australia before another restaurant group did. If you walk through the Sydney airport, you'll pass hamburger stands called Burger King and Hungry Jack's. Burger King is a local company—U.S. Burger King sandwiches are sold at Hungry Jack's.
- A donut concept failed in Brazil because people felt the hole meant they were being shortchanged.

- In Malaysia, a company put up a hotel, but no one would go inside because the door was on the wrong side of the building, violating the residents' religious norms.
- The Coca-Cola Company bought one of India's most successful soft-drink companies, which distributed the popular brand Thums Up, to get access to its distribution channels. Although this acquisition gave Coca-Cola immediate access to distribution channels, Thums Up remained more popular than Coke for many years. Most Indians thought that Coke wasn't fizzy enough.
- TCBY, the yogurt maker, found that it couldn't use its slogan "None of the guilt, all of the pleasure" in Japan because the Japanese culture does not have the same interpretation of the word *guilt* as American culture does.

Fortunately, many U.S. franchisors are gaining experience and are making fewer mistakes in foreign countries. Flexibility is increasing too. For example, Domino's, which has almost 3,000 franchises overseas, is now encouraging its owner-operators to tweak menus according to local tastes. As a result, the company's overseas franchisees now offer pizzas topped with squid and peas in Taiwan, lamb and pickled ginger in India, and tuna in Iceland. Amazingly, Iceland is now home to three of Domino's four highest-grossing outlets. Similarly, in China, KFC outlets offer the chain's U.S. menu, plus "Duck Soup" and the "Old Beijing Twister," which is a wrap modeled on the way Peking duck is served, but with fried chicken inside.

Questions for Critical Thinking

1. In this feature, we considered a number of things that can go wrong when trying to pursue what appear to be franchising opportunities in some foreign markets. Using insights you've drawn from this chapter as well as your study of this book's first 14 chapters, prepare a list of reasons firms or entrepreneurs might be willing to accept the risks of establishing a franchise unit in a challenging foreign market. In slightly different words, what are the potential advantages of franchising in challenging international markets?

2. The examples of franchising mistakes made by Burger King and Coca-Cola, as described in this feature, may surprise you. Why is it that large organizations such as Burger King and Coca-Cola sometimes error when pursuing apparent franchising opportunities in difficult or challenging foreign markets? Prepare a list of factors you believe could cause large, long-lived organizations to make these types of mistakes.

3. Unlike Domino's Pizza, some restaurant chains sell the exact same food overseas as they sell in the United States. What are the pluses and the minuses of doing this?

4. Do some Internet research and identify a foreign-owned franchise organization that sells franchises in the United States. Do the company's U.S. franchises sell the same exact product as the company sells in its home country? If not, what types of changes or modification have been made to satisfy American consumers?

Sources: "Giving New Meaning to the Term 'Gross Revenue,'" *Business 2.0*, October 2005, 144; M. Haig *Brand Failures* (London: Kogan Page 2003); J. Bennett, "Some Franchises Don't Translate Well Overseas," *Wall Street Journal*, www.startupjournal.com (accessed October 28, 2003); J. Bennett, "Why U.S. Franchises Face Problems Abroad," *Wall Street Journal*, www.startupjournal. com (accessed October 28, 2003).

The Future of Franchising

The future of franchising appears bright. Franchise organizations represent a large and growing segment of the retail and service sectors of U.S. businesses and are in some cases replacing more traditional forms of small business ownership.[32] According to the International Franchise Association (IFA), franchising represents about $880 billion in annual retail sales in the United States and involves 900,000 franchised outlets in 75 industries. In addition, the IFA estimates that franchise organizations provide jobs for more than 11 million Americans. Including the additional economic activity that occurs outside of franchised businesses because of franchising activities, the overall economic activity of franchised businesses is around $2.3 trillion a year.[33] More and more college graduates are choosing careers in industries that are heavily dominated by franchising. The availability of digital business tools, which increase the effectiveness of franchise organizations in a variety of ways, is also making franchising more desirable. As franchising continues to become a more pervasive form of business, regulators and franchise associations are likely to intervene in ways that strengthen the viability of the franchise concept.[34]

Chapter Summary

1. A franchise is an agreement between a franchisor (the parent company, such as McDonald's) and a franchisee (an individual or firm that is willing to pay the franchisor a fee for the right to sell its product or service).

2. There are two distinctly different types of franchise systems: the product trademark franchise and the business format franchise. A product trademark franchise is an arrangement under which the franchisor grants to the franchisee the right to buy its products and use its trade name. Automobile dealerships and soft-drink distributorships are examples of

product trademark franchises. In a business format franchise, the franchisor provides a formula for doing business to the franchisee along with training, advertising, and other forms of assistance. Curves, Comfort Keepers, and College Nannies & Tutors are examples of this type of franchise system.

3. An individual franchise agreement involves the sale of a single franchise for a specific location. An area franchise agreement allows a franchisee to own and operate a specific number of outlets in a particular geographic area. A master franchise agreement is similar to an area franchise agreement with one major exception. In addition to having the right to operate a specific number of locations in a particular area, the franchisee also has the right to offer and sell the franchise to other people in the area.

4. The advantages of setting up a franchise system include rapid, low-cost market expansion; income from franchise fees and royalties; franchisee motivation; access to ideas and suggestions; cost savings; and increased buying power. The disadvantages of setting up a franchise system include sharing profits with franchisees, loss of control, friction with franchisees, managing growth, differences in required business skills, and legal expenses.

5. The rules of thumb for determining whether franchising is a good choice for growing a business are as follows: The product or service the business sells should be unique; the business should be consistently profitable; the business should be profitable year-round, not only during a specific season; the business system and procedures should be polished; and the business proposition should be clear so that prospective franchisees fully understand the relationship to which they are committing.

6. Preparing answers to the following questions helps the entrepreneur determine if franchising is a good fit as a way to launch a venture: Are you willing to take orders? Are you willing to be part of a franchise system? How will you react if you make a suggestion to your franchisor and your suggestion is rejected? What are you looking for in a business? How willing are you to put your money at risk?

7. The following costs are typically associated with buying a business format franchise: initial franchise fee, capital requirements (such as land, buildings, and equipment), continuing royalty payment, advertising fee, and other fees (depending on the franchise system).

8. The advantages of buying a franchise include a proven product or service within an established market; an established trademark or business system; the franchisor's training, technical expertise, and managerial experience; an established marketing network; ongoing franchisor support; availability of financing; and potential for business growth. The disadvantages of buying a franchise include cost of the franchise; restrictions on creativity; duration and nature of commitment; risk of fraud, misunderstanding, or lack of franchisor commitment; problems of termination or transfer; and the possibility of poor performance on the part of other franchisees.

9. The common mistakes made by franchise buyers include believing that franchising is a completely safe investment, believing that a great industry ensures franchise success, putting too much faith in the idea that a franchise is a "proven" business system, believing that there is no need to hire a franchise attorney or accountant, being overly optimistic about how fast the franchise outlet will grow, believing that "I can operate my franchise outlet for less than the franchisor predicts," and believing that just because the franchisor is a nice person, he or she will always be there to help out when needed.

10. The Franchise Disclosure Document (FDD) is a document with 23 categories of information. This document provides a prospective franchisee a broad base of information about a franchisor's background and financial health. The FDD must be provided by the franchisor to a prospective franchisee at least 10 business days before a franchise contract can be signed or the franchisee pays the franchisor any money.

Key Terms

agency theory, **521**
area franchise agreement, **515**
business format franchise, **514**
fiduciary obligation, **533**
franchise agreement, **533**
Franchise Disclosure
   Document (FDD), **532**

franchisees, **513**
franchising, **513**
franchisor, **513**
individual franchise
   agreement, **515**
master franchise
   agreement, **515**

multiple-unit
   franchisee, **515**
product and trademark
   franchise, **514**
subfranchisees, **515**

Review Questions

1. What is franchising? How does it differ from other forms of business ownership?
2. Describe the differences between a product and trademark franchise and a business format franchise. Provide at least two examples of both types of franchise arrangements.
3. What is the difference among an individual franchise agreement, an area franchise agreement, and a master franchise agreement? If you wanted to open a large number of ZENhome franchises (see "You Be the VC 15.2") in Northern California, which type of franchise arrangement would be best for you and why?
4. Why is it important for a franchisor to develop detailed and thorough operating manuals?
5. What are the advantages and disadvantages of establishing a franchise system?
6. What are the rules of thumb for determining whether franchising is a good choice for a particular business? Provide an example of a business that wouldn't be suitable for franchising.
7. What are some of the issues an entrepreneur should consider when answering the question "Is franchising a good choice for me?" Briefly describe the profile of someone who isn't suitable for franchising.
8. What are the costs involved in purchasing a business format franchise? Are these costs similar across franchise systems, or do they vary widely? Which costs are one-time costs and which costs continue indefinitely?
9. If an individual Planet Smoothie franchise is losing money, does it still have to pay a monthly royalty? Explain how this is possible.
10. Describe some of the resources available to prospective franchisees to identify franchise opportunities.
11. What are the principal advantages and disadvantages of buying a franchise?
12. Why is it important for a prospective franchisee to retain his or her own franchise attorney?
13. "Franchising is a safe investment." What would you think if you saw this statement in a book or magazine?

14. What is the purpose of the Franchise Disclosure Document (FDD)? Are there any regulations regarding when the FDD must be provided to a prospective franchisee? If so, what are they?

15. What is the purpose of a franchise agreement? Identify the two sections of the franchise agreement and describe the purpose of each one.

16. To date, every court case that has been adjudicated in the United States indicates that franchisors do not have a fiduciary responsibility to their franchisees. What do these rulings suggest to entrepreneurs considering the possibility of buying into a franchise system? Why?

17. What are some of the aspects of franchising that make it subject to ethical abuses? What steps can a prospective franchisee take to ensure that a specific franchisor is reliable and ethical?

18. For U.S. citizens, what are the main issues that should be considered before buying a franchise in a foreign country?

19. What are the main reasons that many U.S. franchise systems are expanding into global markets? Do you think this expansion will continue to gain momentum or will decline over time? Provide an example of a franchise organization, other than one referred to in the chapter, that is expanding rapidly oversees.

20. Does franchising have a bright or a dim future in the United States? Make your answer as substantive and thoughtful as possible.

Application Questions

1. Reread the Opening Profile, which focuses on Joseph Keeley and the franchise organization that he founded—College Nannies & Tutors. Think of an activity, other than nanny and tutoring services, that you think college students might be particularly good at, has a defined need, and can be turned into a franchise. Describe how that activity could be turned into a franchise organization.

2. Several executives from Intuit (the maker of Quicken and QuickBooks) have decided to leave their jobs to launch a chain of small offices that will provide financial advice to small businesses and keep their books. They want to grow quickly. Under what conditions would franchising be a good choice for them?

3. Pick a franchise organization that you admire. Spend some time looking at the company's Web site. Describe how the company is set up. Is it a product and trademark franchise or a business format franchise? Does it sell individual franchise agreements, area franchise agreements, master franchise agreements, or some combination of the three? How many company-owned stores and how many franchise outlets are in the system? Report any particularly interesting or unusual things you learned about the system.

4. Identify a franchise location near where you live and ask to talk to the owner. Show the owner one of the two "You Be the VC" features at the end of the chapter and ask the person whether he or she thinks the company will be successful. Write a brief summary of the owner's response.

5. Select a franchise organization that is located on your campus or near your campus that isn't involved in any co-branding arrangements. Suggest several co-branding relationships that would make sense for this company.

6. Bill Watts has decided to buy a sub shop franchise called Deluxe Subs. He lives in Cedar Falls, Iowa, and will be the first Deluxe Subs franchisee in the state. Along with buying a Deluxe Subs franchise, Bill would also like to purchase the rights to offer and sell Deluxe Subs franchises to other people in the Cedar Falls area. What type of franchise agreement should Bill negotiate with Deluxe Subs? For Bill, what are the advantages and disadvantages of this type of arrangement?

7. A friend of yours is thinking about opening a Planet Smoothie franchise. She has visited Planet Smoothie's headquarters in Atlanta, has been qualified as an eligible franchisee, and has enough money to pay the franchisee fee and get started. She asks you if there is anything else she should do before she signs the franchise agreement. What would you tell her?

8. A growing number of franchise organizations, including Wings Over, Great Harvest Bread Company, and Beef O' Brady's, are allowing their franchisees to tweak their menus and change the appearances of their facilities to better compete with local businesses. Do you think this is a good idea? What are the upsides and downsides of this approach?

9. Krispy Kreme is an example of a franchise organization that has suffered a number of setbacks over the past few years. Spend some time investigating Krispy Kreme, and write a short assessment of what went wrong at Krispy Kreme.

10. A friend of yours owns a construction company, which is a full-time job. To increase his income, he's thinking about buying a FASTSIGNS franchise, which is a franchise that prints and puts up signs. His thinking is that he already has all the equipment he needs to put up signs and has an experienced crew. Is your friend a good candidate for a FASTSIGNS franchise? If not, what type of franchise could he buy that would be a good fit with his current business?

11. Suppose you ran into an old friend who is just about to buy into a hand-held computer accessories retail franchise. He tells you that he is excited about the opportunity because the system he is about to buy into (1) is in an industry that virtually guarantees its success, (2) has a "proven" business model, and (3) is operated by people who are so honest that he can skip the expense of hiring a franchise attorney to review the documents he has to sign. If your friend asked you, "Be honest with me now—am I being naïve, or does this sound like a great opportunity?" what would you tell your friend? Why?

12. Suppose you became interested in opening a Clean Air Lawn Care franchise. You fly to Fort Collins, Colorado, and visit the company's headquarters. After learning more about the opportunity, you tell the Clean Air Lawn Care representatives that you're really interested and would like to move forward. If Clean Air Lawn Care follows the procedures it's suppose to in negotiating with you as a prospective franchisee, what should you expect from this point forward?

13. Recently, a good friend of yours gave a talk to a community group about franchising. Two of the people in the audience approached your friend after the talk to ask if their businesses are suitable for franchising. One owns a dance studio and the other owns a veterinary practice. Your friend has turned to you for advice. What would you say?

14. Do you think Starbucks could have benefited from placing a greater reliance on franchising over the years?

15. Suppose you are an American citizen living in England. You just lost your job with a telecommunications firm that merged with a French company. You would like to stay in England and are thinking about buying a franchise in an American cell phone retail company that is expanding to Europe. What are some of the issues you should evaluate before buying an outlet in an American franchise system that is selling franchises in England?

You Be the VC 15.1

Company: Clean Air Lawn Care

www.cleanairlawncare.com

Business Idea: Launch a lawn care franchise system that provides environmentally sound alternatives to traditional lawn care practices.

Pitch: Traditional lawn care practices have more downsides than one might imagine. According to the Environmental Protection Agency (EPA), gas powered mowers and other yard equipment account for 5 percent of fossil fuel emissions in the United States. In fact, one gas powered mower running for an hour emits the same amount of pollution as eight new cars driving 55 mph for the same amount of time. Gas powered mowers and lawn equipment are also noisy and smoky, which is irritating to many home owners and their neighbors.

Clean Air Lawn Care is launching a franchise system to address these problems. The company offers lawn care services for home owners and businesses, but does so in an environmentally friendly and a neighborhood friendly manner. The company uses electric mowers, trimmers, and blowers, and some biodiesel-powered equipment. It also uses organic fertilizers and pesticides. The company recharges its equipment at night in a conventional manner, but all of its trucks sport solar panels that can recharge the equipment between jobs. The company even purchases wind energy credits to offset the electricity that it does use in the evenings, to make its operations 100 percent carbon neutral.

Clean Air Lawn Care's service, which is price competitive, has several benefits for consumers. The most tangible benefit is environmental stewardship, which appeals to a certain clientele. Other positives include reduced noise (electric mowers are near silent) and the avoidance of gas and oil spills on grass, driveways, and sidewalks. According to the EPA, 17 million gallons of fuel are spilled each year while refueling lawn mowers. That amount is more than the oil leaked by the *Exxon Valdez* off the cost of Alaska in 1989. Spills have negative environmental consequences and can kill grass and stain driveways and sidewalks.

Clean Air Lawn Care sees itself as a triple win. It provides a necessary service, it's profitable, and it's good for the environment. The company is located in Fort Collins, Colorado, where it has rolled out its service. It plans to start franchising in 2008.

Q&A: Based on the material covered in this chapter, what questions would you ask the firm's founders before making your funding decision? What answers would satisfy you?

Decision: If you had to make your decision on just the information provided in the pitch and on the company's Web site, would you fund this company? Why or why not?

You Be the VC 15.2

Company: ZENhome

www.zenhomecleaning.com

Business Idea: Provide a menu of unique home services including green cleaning, professional organizing, eco-painting, and consulting on how to live an earth-friendly life.

Pitch: Many people pay professionals to help them clean and organize their homes, but they don't approach these tasks in an environmentally friendly or holistic manner. ZENhome offers a suite of green home services that deal with both the physical acts of cleaning and organizing and the emotional and spiritual well-being of the client. Its staple service is home cleaning. Many people hire housekeepers to clean their homes. A potential downside to this approach is that most housekeepers use traditional

cleaning supplies to do their work. This situation poses a problem for people who prefer to use nontoxic, ecofriendly products in their homes. ZENhome offers a solution to this problem by changing humdrum cleaning into something special. The company uses only nontoxic, environmentally friendly cleaning products, which appeals to both ecologically aware customers and people with allergies. In addition, ZENhome cleaners burn essential oils like jasmine while cleaning, spray linens with lavender mist, turn down beds, place organic chocolate bars on pillows, and leave small bowls of potpourri in their clients' homes. The entire effort is meant to help customers feel good about choosing an environmentally friendly cleaning service and feel good about themselves. Not only does ZENhome want its customers to come home to a clean house, they want them to come home to a peaceful, therapeutic setting as well.

ZENhome's other services are designed to have a similar impact. The company offers a professional organizing service, a green living consulting service, and an eco-painting service. The green living consulting service, for example, provides clients with access to experts in green living. From housepainting to energy use, ZENhome consultants help clients integrate green living into their lifestyle in a manner that complements their current daily lives.

ZENhome is currently operating in New York City and has a waiting list for its services. The company is thinking about using franchising to expand outside of the city.

Q&A: Based on the material covered in this chapter, what questions would you ask the firm's founders before making your funding decision? What answers would satisfy you?

Decision: If you had to make your decision on just the information provided in the pitch and on the company's Web site, would you fund this firm? Why or why not?

CASE 15.1

Snap Fitness: Fast, Convenient, and Intriguing Options for Growth
www.snapfitness.com

Bruce R. Barringer
Oklahoma State University
R. Duane Ireland
Texas A & M University

Imagine you're a police officer who works the evening shift. You go to work at 3:30 P.M. and are off at midnight. You've always enjoyed working out late in the day but don't have room for a home gym in your apartment. You've checked out the Gold's Gym and the Bally's Fitness Center near where you live. They both close at 11:00 P.M. so going to a fitness center isn't an option—until now! Snap Fitness is a rapidly growing franchise organization that features gyms that are open 24 hours a day, seven days a week. The state-of-the-art fitness concept began franchising in 2004 and already has over 1,500 franchise locations in the United States, Canada, and India.

Beginnings

Snap Fitness was founded by Pete Taunton. For most of his career, Taunton ran big-box fitness centers that offered all the amenities. By the time he opened his fifth center, he was burned out. He recalls seeing his kids twice a day—when they woke up in the morning and when they went to bed at night. He left the fitness industry, but a year later a group of former employees approached him about opening a new business. He was tired of 75-hour workweeks and didn't want to make a large investment. So he took a piece of paper and a pen and listed all the amenities that his former gyms had on the left-hand side of the paper and a smaller

number of "must haves" on the right side. Taunton had learned long ago that rock-climbing walls, racquetball courts, and swimming pools were nice to have but most people never used them. The "must haves" list became the blueprint for Snap Fitness.

Business Concept

Snap Fitness's centers are small gyms that are located near residential areas. They offer weights, treadmills, and exercise machines. The centers are staffed during the day and are available to members at night by swiping a key card at the main door. The equipment is state-of-the art, the centers are very clean, and they are secure. At night, security cameras monitor activities and members wear electronic devices around their necks that when pushed summon paramedics or police.

The centers offer their members a fast, convenient, and affordable way to stay fit. A membership costs around $35 a month, which is well below big-box fitness center rates. Because the centers are small—the average Snap Fitness center is 2,500 to 3,500 square feet compared to more than 20,000 square feet for a Gold's Gym or a Bally's Fitness Center—they can be located near where people live. In fact, the company claims that the majority of its members don't have more than a two-mile drive to the Snap Fitness center to which

(continued)

they belong. As a result, the members quickly learn each other's names and have things in common, such as kids that go to the same schools or they live in the same neighborhoods.

Snap Fitness recently launched www.mysnapfitness.com on which members can build their own Web pages. The Web pages allow members to construct their own wellness plan, tailor their meals to fit their weight loss goals, talk confidentially to health and wellness coaches by phone (for an extra fee), and build customized workout plans that can be tracked and are supported with video tutorials using 3-D animation. Members can also sign up for a vitamin and nutritional supplement plan that costs $69.95 per month. Eventually, members will be able to scan their membership cards on each piece of equipment they use and their personal Web page will record the duration and intensity of their workouts. Each facility will include a kiosk on which members can access their Web pages. Snap Fitness says that approximately 110,000 of its 200,000 members have set up personal Web pages.

Snap Fitness Centers are limited in the amenities they offer so they don't appeal to everyone. There are no locker rooms, child care, juice bars, aerobic classes, racquetball courts, or swimming pools. A Snap Fitness membership is a strict trade-off between cost and convenience versus a larger array of amenities. In addition, despite Curves' success, the small gym franchise concept is unproven. A number of small aerobics studios opened a number of years ago, and the vast majority of them failed.

Franchise Operations

Snap Fitness is actively selling franchises. To qualify, a prospective franchisee needs a minimum net worth of $250,000, a credit score of at least 700, and more than $60,000 in liquid assets. The initial franchise fee is $15,000, the royalty is a flat $399 per month (rather than a percentage of gross income), and there is a $75 per month advertising fee. It costs between $150,000 to $200,000 to get a Snap Fitness Center up and running. The buildings are leased so there is no real estate purchase involved.

The leanness of the company's business model makes it attractive to many franchisees. The franchisor handles all billing and collecting. Because the centers are not manned at night, a person can own and operate a Snap Fitness franchise and keep normal hours. Most franchisees own more than one location and have only one to two employees per location. A total of 70 percent of Snap Fitness locations are owned by absentee owners. Many of the owners are semiretirees or have other jobs.

Growth Alternatives

Moving forward, Snap Fitness has the following opportunities for growth.

1. Expand its domestic franchise network. Snap Fitness started franchising in 2004 and has grown to 1,500 centers. Curves International, a fitness center for women that has many similarities to Snap Fitness, started franchising in 1995 and has over 9,300 centers.
2. Expand internationally. The company has a small number of franchises in Canada and India. A challenge with international expansion is the availability of real estate in the most desirable markets and curfews that don't allow businesses to be open all night. For example Bangalore, one of the largest and most attractive cities in India, has an 11:30 P.M. curfew.
3. Set up "in-house" gyms for corporations. A growing number of corporations, especially those that operate 24/7 (such as oil refineries and large retail stores), are interested in opening on-site fitness centers for employees. Snap Fitness offers a turnkey solution that requires low overhead and minimal supervision.
4. Offer group discounts to local corporations. Snap Fitness can tie into the corporate wellness movement by offering group rates to local corporations to provide employees memberships to existing Snap Fitness locations.
5. Expand product and service offerings. Snap Fitness offers one-on-one personal training in its centers, wellness and weight loss consultations over the phone, and vitamin and nutrition supplements sales via www.mysnapfitness.com. These programs are offered on a fee basis and could be expanded.

While choice 1 seems obvious, the company must be careful to not overshoot its ability to properly manage its growth. Choices 2 through 5 all have pluses and minuses and are currently being weighed by the company's management team. Snap Fitness is still very young (founded in 2003). The choices it makes regarding these alternatives will shape the type of franchise organization it becomes.

Discussion Questions

1. Snap Fitness has positioned itself as a "neighborhood" chain of fitness centers and claims that the majority of its members are within a two-mile

drive of the center to which they belong. How big of a competitive advantage do you think this positioning strategy provides Snap Fitness?

2. Look at Figure 15-1 in the chapter. What type of franchise system makes the most sense for Snap Fitness?

3. Discuss the pluses and minuses of each of Snap Fitness's growth alternatives. Rank the alternatives on a scale from 1 to 5 (5 is the highest) in terms of desirability. Explain your rankings.

4. What do you think lies ahead for Snap Fitness? What are some of the things that can go right and what are some of the things that can go wrong as this firm continues to sell franchises and grows?

Application Questions

1. What similarities do you see between Snap Fitness and Curves International? Are the similarities strong enough that Snap Fitness will be able to match Curves International in terms of growth?

2. Analyze MySnapFitness.com, the online component of Snap Fitness's offering. How important of a component of Snap Fitness's business model do you think MySnapFitness.com will become? If the service is successful, do you think Snap Fitness's competitors will have a hard time or an easy time imitating it?

Sources: Snap Fitness homepage, www.snapfitness.com (accessed October 15, 2008); P. Taunton, "Trimming the Fat." *Fortune Small Business*, February, 2008, 61; J. Gustafson, "Small Gyms Proliferate Here," *Journal of Business* (September 11, 2008): A1.

CASE15.2

Pizza Fusion: Will Its Organic and Environmentally Friendly Concept Work Nationwide?

www.pizzafusion.com

Bruce R. Barringer
Oklahoma State University
R. Duane Ireland
Texas A & M University

Introduction

Pizza Fusion started as do many businesses. Two buddies, neither of whom was passionate about their current jobs, were venting over a couple of beers. Vaughan Lazar, who was running a design firm, and Michael Gordon, who was managing a real estate outfit, both liked pizza, and Lazar was eating organic at the time. So, they thought, "wouldn't it be great to open an organic pizza restaurant?" The idea stuck and began to gain momentum over the following days. What if the organic pizza was delivered in a hybrid car? It didn't seem right to serve organic and pollute the environment at the same time.

To flesh out their idea, Lazar and Gordon attended a Pizza Expo the next week in Orlando, three hours north of Deerfield Beach, Florida, their home town. They ran into a man named "Big Dave" Ostrander, also known as "The Pizza Doctor," and hired him as a consultant. Over the next five months, Lazar and Gordon, with the Pizza Doctor's help, fleshed out Pizza Fusion's business model, settled on a menu, and adopted the motto "Saving the Earth One Pizza at a Time." It wasn't a frivolous effort. Lazar and Gordon were sincere in their intentions and put together an impressive concept, using Newman's Own, Starbucks, and Patagonia's business practices as role models. On July 7, 2006, they opened the states' first organic pizza restaurant in Deerfield Beach, offering in-house dining and delivery. The pizzas were organic and tasty, the delivery vehicles were hybrids, and South Florida loved the concept.

(continued)

By sheer luck, one of the Pizza Fusion's first customers was Randy Romano, an individual with 20 years of franchise experience. He liked the food; the concept of an organic, environmentally friendly pizza restaurant; and the passion he saw in the restaurant's founders. Long story short, he introduced himself to Lazar and Gordon, talked up the idea of franchising the Pizza Fusion concept, and joined the firm as the VP of franchise development.

Pizza Fusion

Pizza Fusion serves gourmet pizzas, salads, sandwiches and wraps, appetizers, organic beers and wines, and other drinks. The menu is more than 75 percent organic, and it offers selections for vegans and products that are gluten free. The pizzas are untainted by preservatives, growth hormones, pesticides, nitrates, and trans fats. Most of the ingredients are locally grown. For customers with selective diets or food allergies, there are variations such as the Very Vegan Pizza, which is a $16 to $20 offering that includes Pizza Fusion's signature organic-flour or multigrain crust, organic sauce, 100 percent nondairy soy mozzarella cheese, and veggie topping. The pizzas are oblong rather than round (like a skateboard). The following table lists some of their menu items.

Pizza Fusion also champions environmental stewardship. It features furniture made from reclaimed wood, its countertops are made from recycled detergent bottles, its insulation is made out of blue jean scraps, and its restroom sinks are made from bamboo. One hundred percent of the electricity used to cook its products is offset through the purchase of renewable wind energy certificates. Its silverware and plastic-like containers are made from materials that will decompose within 50 days in a landfill.

To prove the legitimacy of its intentions and actions, Pizza Fusion's buildings are either Leadership in Energy and Design (LEED) certified or seeking certification. LEED is an independent organization that certifies buildings that meet certain environmental standards set by the U.S. Green Building Council. Similarly, the interiors of each of its restaurants is either certified or is seeking certification by Quality Assurance International (QAI), a third-party certifier that inspects restaurants that claim to sell organic products. One facet of their business that Lazar and Gordon, Pizza Fusion's founders, have been sensitive to from the beginning is that a restaurant that markets itself to the green consumer must have total integrity in its offerings. Green (or environmentally sensitive) consumers tend to be very savvy and will quickly expose a business that advertises itself as green but is really an imposter.

Franchising

Pizza Fusion has been careful to sell franchises at a moderate pace. In fall 2008, it had six locations open, 75 sold and in various stages of development, and plans to grow to 500 locations within five years. Each new location, at least to this point, has received the personal attention of the company's founders in terms of site selection, building construction, and training of the initial

---

Samples from Pizza Fusion's Menu

Appetizers and Bread

SIGNATURE BREADSTICKS
A mix of multigrain and organic white breadsticks warmed to perfection. Served with our award-winning crushed tomato marinara.

Salads

FUSION SIDE SALAD
Organic spring mix, cucumbers, tomatoes, and red onions.

PEAR AND GORGONZOLA
Organic spring mix, spinach, pear, Gorgonzola cheese, and walnuts.

Specialty Pies (Pizzas)

BBQ CHICKEN
Naturally raised chicken smothered in BBQ sauce, onion, garlic, mozzarella, parmesan, and fresh basil.

THREE CHEESE AND ORGANIC ROASTED GARLIC
Mozzarella, Gorgonzola, aged parmesan, roasted garlic, and light pesto sauce.

VEGGIE MEDLEY
Our signature organic tomato sauce with a variety of seasonal organic veggies.

---

staff. In preparation for ramping-up its pace of expansion, in October 2008, the company hired Mark Begelman as CEO. Begelman served as president and chief operating officer of Office Depot from 1991 to 1995, growing the company from 127 stores and $900 million in revenue to 460 stores and $4.5 billion in sales. He has been named Ernst & Young's "Entrepreneur of the Year" twice and was named *Financial News'* "CEO of the Year" once. Commenting on his appointment as Pizza Fusion's CEO, Begelman said:

> What attracted me most to Pizza Fusion was their menu . . . it's the best tasting pizza I have ever eaten. Pizza Fusion offers delicious food with a purpose. To have great food and be socially conscious is great for customers and franchisees alike. Pizza Fusion offers a healthy alternative to what has historically been referred to as "junk food." Pizza Fusion is everything I want my family to embrace. Healthy, delicious, and organic food served by a restaurant that's doing its part to contribute to the preservation of the planet.

Prior to joining Pizza Fusion, Begelman was managing director of Woodbridge Holdings, a diversified holding company. Woodbridge made an investment in Pizza Fusion at the time Begelman was hired.

It costs between $300,000 and $450,000 to build a Pizza Fusion restaurant. Franchisees also pay an initial franchise fee of $30,000 and royalties of 5 percent of gross sales.

Will It Work, Nationwide?

The question confronting Pizza Fusion is whether its concept will scale on a nationwide basis. Its core clientele are vegans, vegetarians, environmentalists, people who like organic food, people with food allergies, and people who will pay a premium to eat healthier and support the environment. Pizza Fusion is careful to locate its restaurants in areas that have a demographic mix that favors those tendencies. The four specific questions that Pizza Fusion's successful expansion hinges on are:

1. Is there a large enough critical mass of people in its core clientele to support 500 franchise restaurants? So far the company has had the advantage of locating in areas that perfectly fit its clientele. It will be harder to continually find "ideal" areas as the company grows.
2. Will Pizza Fusion be able to expand beyond its core clientele? In other words, in places where there aren't a large number of vegans, vegetarians, environmentalists, and other people who would naturally support a Pizza Fusion franchise, will enough "ordinary" people frequent the restaurants to make them successful?
3. Will Pizza Fusion attract direct competitors and how successful will the direct competitors (or imitators) be?
4. Is Pizza Fusion's management team capable of building out and managing a 500 franchise operation?

Discussion Questions

1. Pizza Fusion clearly is not competing on price. Instead, it is competing on the quality of its products and its organic/environmentally friendly themes. In your judgment is this a niche strategy or do you think Pizza Fusion can compete for the same customers that buy pizza from Domino's, Papa John's, and Pizza Hut?
2. Pizza Fusion's founders used Newman's Own, Starbucks, and Patagonia's business practices as role models when they designed Pizza Fusion's business concept. In general, what do you think Pizza Fusion's founders learned from those companies that you see reflected in Pizza Fusion's business practices and product offerings?
3. According to the case, Pizza Fusion's founders have been personally involved in the rollout of each of its franchise locations. Do you think the founders will be able to maintain this practice? If not, how can they ensure that each new Pizza Fusion franchise will be opened in a desirable manner if they're not physically present themselves?
4. In what ways was Mark Begelman a good choice or a poor choice to become Pizza Fusion's CEO? If you were the CEO of Domino's or Papa John's, what would the choice of Mark Begelman signal to you about Pizza Fusion's plans for the future?
5. Address each of the rhetorical questions posed at the end of the case.

Application Questions

1. If you had the choice to open a Pizza Fusion franchise or a Chili's Grill & Bar franchise, which would you choose? Why?
2. Pizza Fusion may be a strong draw for vegans, people who consume gluten-free products, and people with severe food allergies. What percent of the population falls into these categories? How can Pizza Fusion create buzz among these groups to attract them to Pizza Fusion restaurants?

Sources: Pizza Fusion homepage, www.pizzafusion.com (accessed October 15, 2008); "Pizza Fusion Appoints Mark Begelman as CEO," www.franchising.com (accessed August 15, 2008, posted on October 15, 2008); B. Ebenkamp, "Any Way You Slice It, Pizza Fusion Is Unique." *Brandweek*, May 12, 2008, 9.

Endnotes

1. L. Wolf, "Learning Curve," *Upsizemag.com*, www.upsizemag.com (accessed June 1, 2006).
2. Wolf, "Learning Curve."
3. Personal interview with Joseph Keeley, November 15, 2008.
4. V. K. Jolly, *Commercializing New Technologies* (Cambridge, MA: Harvard Business School Press, 1997).
5. International Franchise Organization, www.franchise.org (accessed October 30, 2008).
6. Franchising.com, www.franchising.com (accessed October 25, 2008).
7. T. Bates, "Analysis of Survival Rates Among Franchise and Independent Small Business Startups," *Journal of Small Business Management* 33, no. 2 (1995): 26–36.
8. Wikipedia, www.wikpedia.com (accessed June 3, 2006).
9. "Breaking the Silver Ceiling," *U.S. Congress Report from the Committee on Aging*, 2005; Start Your Own Business, "It Pays to Care," *Small Business Opportunities*, Spring 2002.
10. P. H. Rubin, "The Theory of the Firm and the Structure of the Franchise Contract," *Journal of Law and Economics* 21 (1978): 223–33.
11. J. G. Combs, D. J. Ketchen, and R. D. Ireland, "Effectively Managing Service Chain Organizations," *Organizational Dynamics* 35, no. 6 (2006): 357–71.
12. D. H. B. Welsh, I. Alon, and C. M. Falbe, "An Examination of Retail Franchising in Emerging Markets," *Journal of Small Business Management* 44, no. 1 (2006): 130–49.
13. B. Merrilees and L. Frazer, "Entrepreneurial Franchises Have Hidden Superior Marketing Systems," *Qualitative Market Research* 9, no. 1 (2006): 73–85.
14. R. Sloan, J. Sloan, and J. Sinelli, StartupNation Podcast, March 27, 2006.
15. G. J. Castrogiovanni, J. G. Combs, and R. T. Justis, "Shifting Imperatives: An Integrating View of Resource Scarcity and Agency Reasons for Franchising," *Entrepreneurship Theory and Practice* 39, no. 1 (2006): 23–40.
16. R. Bennett, "To Franchise or Not: How to Decide," in *Franchising Today: 1966–1967*, ed. C. L. Vaughn and D. B. Slater (New York: Matthew Bender and Company, 1967), 20.
17. J. Brickley and F. Dark, "The Choice of Organizational Form: The Case of Franchising," *Journal of Financial Economics* 18 (1987): 401–20.
18. "Darden Restaurants, Inc.," *Standard & Poor's Stock Report*, www.standardandpoors.com (accessed June 4, 2006).
19. J. E. Clarkin and S. M. Swavely, "The Importance of Personal Characteristics in Franchisee Selection," *Journal of Retailing and Consumer Services* 13, no. 2 (2006): 133–42.
20. "Learning Curves," *Franchise Times*, www.franchisetimes.com/content/story.php?article=00303 (accessed April 10, 2008).
21. Federal Trade Commission, *Consumers Guide to Buying a Franchise* (Washington, DC: U.S. Government Printing Office, 2002).
22. M. Grunhagen and M. Mittlestaedt, "Entrepreneurs or Investors: Do Multi-Unit Franchisees Have Different Philosophical Orientations?" *Journal of Small Business Management* 43, no. 3 (2005): 207–25.
23. Candy Bouquet homepage, www.candybouquet.com (accessed June 1, 2006).
24. J. Bennett, "Cruise Franchisee Says It's Been Smooth Sailing," *StartupJournal.com*, www.startupjournal.com (accessed May 30, 2006).
25. L. Altinay, "Selecting Partners in an International Franchise Organisation," *International Journal of Hospitality Management* 25, no. 1 (2006): 108–28.
26. Federal Trade Commission, "Guide to the FTC Franchise Rule," www.ftc.gov/bcp/franchise/netrule.html (accessed June 1, 2006).
27. R. L. Purvin, *The Franchise Fraud* (New York: John Wiley & Sons, 1994), 7.
28. American Bar Association, *Legal Guide for Small Business* (New York: Random House, 2000).
29. Federal Trade Commission, "Guide to the FTC Franchise Rule."
30. I. Alon and K. Bian, "Real Estate Franchising: The Case of Coldwell Banker Expansion into China," *Business Horizons* 48, no. 3 (2005): 223–31.
31. R. Gibson, "U.S. Restaurants Push Abroad," *Wall Street Journal*, June 18, 2008.

32. Federal Trade Commission, "Guide to the FTC Franchise Rule."
33. International Franchise Association, *Economic Impact of Franchised Businesses,*
    vol. 2, www.franchise.org/franchiseesecondary.aspx?id=37842 (accessed October 25,
    2008, published 2005).
34. E. Pfister, B. Deffians, M. Doriant-Duban, and S. Saussier, "Institutions and
    Contracts: Franchising," *European Journal of Law and Economics* 21, no. 1 (2006):
    53–78.

CASEAPPENDIX

Richard Ivey School of Business
The University of Western Ontario

IVEY

Case 1 San Francisco Coffee House: An American-Style Franchise in Croatia

Ilan Alon, Mirela Alpeza, and Aleksandar Erceg wrote this case solely to provide material for class discussion. The authors do not intend to illustrate either effective or ineffective handling of a managerial situation. The authors may have disguised certain names and other identifying information to protect confidentiality.

Copyright © Ivey Publishing.

All Rights Reserved. No part of the publication may be reproduced or transmitted in any form or by any means, or stored in a database or retrieval system without the written consent of Ivey Publishing. With respect to Ivey cases, Ivey Management Services prohibits any form of reproduction, storage or transmittal without its written permission. This material is not covered under authorization from any reproduction rights organization. To order copies or request permission to reproduce material, contact Ivey Publishing, Ivey Management Services, c/o Richard Ivey School of Business, The University of Western Ontario, London, Ontario, Canada, N6A 3K7; phone (519)661-3208, fax (519) 661-3882, email cases@ivey.uwo.ca

Version: (A) 2008-07-24

On the return to their homeland of Croatia following a six-year visit to the United States, Denis Tensek and Jasmina Pacek decided to open an American-style coffee house reminiscent of San Francisco's atmosphere. While Croatia had many coffee houses, few had the combination of service, quality, products, and atmosphere that they remembered from their time living in the United States.

Tensek and Pacek started with a single coffee house. From the beginning they felt that it had the potential to grow into a franchise. Instead of purchasing a franchise from someone else, they considered creating one that had all the elements of the modern franchise chains that were available on the international market plus the adjustments needed to the local market. They decided to use all of their U.S. lifestyle and professional experiences as well as understanding of habits and behaviors of the local market to create this new local concept in Croatia.

The initial coffee house became a success. The business steadily grew and operating profits had reached a satisfactory level. Motivated with the success of the first coffee shop in one of Croatia's poorest regions, the couple realized that the potential for this concept was national, if not regional. But, how would they grow? Should they develop their own outlets or open more company-owned outlets?

Growing organically by opening self-owned stores was costly, slow, and hard to control. They had neither the means nor the staff. They knew they did not want to put more capital at risk, and did not have the time to travel to various locations around the country. Furthermore, their concept had started to garner local publicity and inquiries from would-be franchisees began to arise. But, how could they franchise in Croatia?

Croatia had a small economy, changing legal system, and little experience in franchising. Growing through franchising was appealing, but they only had one store, the business was young, and franchising was unfamiliar to the emerging market of Croatia. The conditions for franchising were not ideal.

Aside from whether to franchise or not, how could they protect their intellectual property and business format know-how? How could they fight off imitators? What would happen if Starbucks or other major coffee chains entered the market? What should be the next steps? How could they become the biggest and most successful coffee house nationally or regionally?

The Entrepreneurs: Tensek and Pacek

Tensek and Pacek's creation of the San Francisco Coffee House (SFCH) in the winter of 2003 was an example of entrepreneurship where two people not only used their experiences in other countries, where a particular product or service was available, but also used their specific professional experiences to contribute to the creation of a unique visual identity and business opportunity. The managerial experience Tensek gained by working in large U.S. companies and the educational experience gained from a master's of business administration degree from California State University gave him an advantage in creating a business in Croatia that was world-class, towering above local offerings in service, quality, and satisfying customer expectations (see Exhibit 1).

On the other hand, Pacek's international design experience, experience working as art director in U.S. corporations, and masters of fine arts and design

553

EXHIBIT 1

Pictures of the San
Francisco Coffee
House (SFCH) Interior
and Exterior

degree from the University of California gave SFCH a recognizable visual identity and an interior in which visitors could feel the San Francisco–style coffee shop atmosphere. Thanks to the couple's successful careers and profitable real estate investments in the United States, they felt comfortable and confident to return to Croatia with enough capital to help them in their new venture, and help their country's development at the same time.

Tensek and Pacek recalled their days in the United States, and the economic success stories of all the major coffee franchise chains such as Starbucks. They even considered taking a master franchise license for Croatia, but the process was long, complicated, and extremely expensive in comparison to the expected return. The fact was that Starbucks had very low local brand recognition in

Croatia. The other problem with imported brands was that they often did not allow the adjustments needed to succeed in local markets, the major one being to the pricing of their product when it was simply too high for the local purchasing power of a developing country such as Croatia.

The Environment for Franchising in Croatia

The environment for franchising in Croatia was not ideal because of insufficient regulation, little market know-how about franchising, and low economic development. On the other hand, the emerging market and the new openness to European integration had created opportunities to start bringing in new businesses from the outside.

Annual Data	2007	Historical Averages (percent)	2003–07
Population (m)	4.0	Population growth	0.0
GDP (US$ bn; market exchange rate)	51,452	Real GDP growth	4.9
GDP (US$ bn; purchasing power parity)	69,211	Real domestic demand growth	5.0
GDP per head (US$; market exchange rate)	12,863	Inflation	2.6
GDP per head (US$; purchasing power parity)	17,303	Current-account balance (per cent of GDP)	−7.1
Exchange rate (av) HRK:US$	5.35(b)	FDI inflows (per cent of GDP)	6.4

EXHIBIT 2

Basic Socio-Economic Data on Croatia

Source: The Economist, 2008, http://www.economist.com/countries/Croatia/profile.cfm?folder=Profile-FactSheet, accessed June 11, 2008.

The Economic Environment

In 1991, after The Republic of Croatia gained its independence, the Croatian market increasingly opened to a great variety of international products and services. Due to the economic growth which began in the late 1990s, salaries had grown appreciably, especially in the larger cities and in certain other parts of Croatia.[1] Basic statistics on the economy are shown in Exhibit 2.

Salary growth resulted in increased consumer demand for higher-quality world brand names, which were not widely available in Croatia at the time. After independence, the Croatian market became flooded with imported goods of variable quality. The habits of younger Croatian consumers had changed as a result of this increased supply: international brands became the acquisition target of younger consumers, while older people tended to continue to seek out domestic brands. Inevitably, perhaps, purchasing habits also varied geographically.[2]

Financial institutions in Croatia were mostly owned by foreign banks—around 90 percent according to one source[3]—and many of these acquisitions had occurred in recent years. Although there was a predictable variety of capitalization options for would-be entrepreneurs, a main characteristic of the Croatian domestic market was the bankruptcy of small entrepreneurs as they struggled to collect their own debts. Although bartering was a common fixture of the domestic market (i.e., between local companies), the international ownership of local banks made such traditional arrangements problematic.

Political Environment

Creating a vibrant business environment in accordance with the standards of the European Union (EU) and with countries embedded in the local market economy was one of the major goals of the Croatian government's policies. The government's dedication to the reform of the national economy could be seen in its desire to attract foreign investment for the development of Croatia's domestic and international markets.

Foreign investments in Croatia were regulated by the Company Act and other legal norms. A foreign investor in Croatia had a number of organizational options available according to this act: a foreign investor would invest alone or as a joint-venture partner with a Croatian company or private citizen; there were no constraints as to the percentage of foreign ownership that was possible. In addition, in keeping with the government's desire for foreign investment, investors gained access to a number of newly opened markets; entrants could take advantage of a number of incentives, tax benefits, and customs privileges that were only available to foreign investors.

The Institutions of Franchising

In recent years, the Republic of Croatia had approved a number of laws which resulted in Croatia's acceptance into the World Trade Organization and CEFTA (Central European Free Trade Agreement); these legal changes also allowed Croatia to begin negotiations for acceptance into the EU. Nevertheless, there was no specific legal basis for franchising in Croatia. Franchising was mentioned in Croatian trade law (Narodne Novine, 2003), where the generalities of potential franchising agreements were stated, but mention was made in only one article and that mention was very condensed. Therefore, there was no legal standard for the development of franchising and no legal parameters (yet) for franchising

[1] *Državni zavod za statistiku, "Statistical information 2006," 2006, http://www.dzs.hr/Hrv_Eng/StatInfo/pdf/StatInfo2006.pdf, accessed on October 26, 2006.*
[2] *GfK, "Građani o markama," Survey conducted by GfK, March 2005, http://www.gfk.hr/press/marke.htm, http://www.gfk.hr/press/marke2.htm, accessed on January 3, 2007.*
[3] *Hrvatska narodna banka, "Standardni prezentacijski format," 2006, http://www.hnb.hr/publikac/prezent/hbanking-sector.pdf, accessed on October 20, 2006.*

agreements: business practices on the ground determined the appropriateness of such agreements.

Since the concept of franchising was relatively new to Croatia and to its inhabitants, little knowledge existed about franchising. There were two Centers for Franchising, one in Osijek and one in Zagreb, Croatia's most vibrant city. Each of these centers had worked with the Croatian Franchising Association to stimulate franchising development in several ways:

- **Educating about franchising**—The Franchise Center in Osijek, for example, had organized seminars, "Franchise A to Z," in order to educate entrepreneurs about franchising and its benefits;

- **Franchising promotion**—both centers and the association were trying to promote franchising as a way of doing business through local media—interviews, articles in the newspapers and magazines, etc.;

- **Creating Web sites with information about franchising on the Internet**—Information on the portal with current news about franchising in Croatia, information about new franchisors, and newly opened franchised locations;

- **Connecting franchisors with potential franchisees**—one section of the franchise portal contained offers from franchisors interested in the Croatian market; there were several inquiries each week from potential franchisees;

- **Helping domestic companies to become franchisors**—The Franchise Center in Osijek, with the help of Poduzetna Hrvatska, organized training for potential franchise consultants who could help domestic companies if they decided to use franchising as a growth strategy; and

- **Establishing franchise fairs and round tables.**

Foreign franchises tended to choose one of two potential pathways into the Croatian market: distribution-product franchising and/or business-format franchising. Larger, better-known franchisors like McDonald's opened their offices in Croatia and offered franchises to interested entrepreneurs in order to ensure quality control, while smaller and less well-known franchisors sold master franchises to local entrepreneurs in order to ensure the benefits of local knowledge and cost savings.

Barriers to Franchising Development

During September 2006, The Franchise Center of the Center for Entrepreneurship in Osijek conducted a survey of 50 people, asking what examinees (representatives of banks, entrepreneurs, and lawyers) thought about the barriers facing franchising in Croatia. Their responses included:

- **Laws**—there was no legal regulation of franchising in Croatia. The word "franchising" was only mentioned in trade law; the absence of clear legal precedent made it difficult for Croatian lawyers to help their clients, especially during the contracting phase—whether franchisor or franchisee, whether foreign or domestic investor;

- **Franchise professionals**—there was a dearth of professionals related to franchising; there were too few educational efforts, and too few franchise consultants who could help potential franchisors in developing their own networks or advise franchisees about selecting one;

- **Problems with banks (not familiar with franchising)**—banks did not recognize franchising as a relatively safe way of entering into a new business and did not have any specialized loans for the franchising industry; according to a survey conducted by The Franchise Center (2006), some banks' representatives said that they would ask a guarantee for a loan from the franchisor also; banks were not willing to educate their employees in order to learn about this way of doing business; banks seemed unable to distinguish between start-up entrepreneurs creating footholds in new franchise sectors and franchisees who were entering preexisting, proven franchise systems;

- **Small market**—because there were only about four million inhabitants in Croatia, examinees were doubtful that the largest franchisors would come to Croatia due to logistical problems: the perception was that it was much easier to open a location in London than in Croatia; large and famous franchisors were looking for bigger areas to capture the population, and they often resisted adapting to local standards and prices; smaller franchisors that would have liked to enter Croatia were not as well known to Croatian entrepreneurs and were, therefore, seldom selected; and

- **Franchising was not a well-known way of doing business**—people seldom recognized franchising; many thought it was connected with insurance; this was the biggest barrier according to the survey because people were not willing to enter into something with which they were unfamiliar; further seminars and round tables needed to be organized in order to educate entrepreneurs about franchising and its costs/benefits.

Franchisor	Industry	Number of Outlets
McDonald's	Fast food	16 restaurants
Subway	Fast food	6 restaurants
Fornetti	Bakeries	Over 150 locations
Dama service	Refilling toner cartridges	3 locations
Berlitz	Foreign language school	1 location
Firurella	Weight loss center for women	2 locations
Berghoff	Kitchen equipment	3 locations

EXHIBIT 3

Foreign Franchisors in Croatia

Source: "Round table—Franchising in Croatia," address given at EFF/IFA International Symposium, Brussels, October 24–25, 2006.

According to the above-mentioned survey, there were some identifiable reasons for the relatively slow development of franchising in the Republic of Croatia: entrepreneurial thinking, lack of franchising education, and a weak national franchising association. First, many entrepreneurs would rather own their own companies and have complete "business freedom" than submit to the restrictions they saw as related to becoming part of a system—from production and distribution to sales and to the "forced" cleaning of the premises. Second, Croatian entrepreneurs were not completely familiar with the benefits that would be gained by being a member of a successful franchising system.

Despite such a pessimistic tone, industry experts also reported that there was an excellent chance for franchising in Croatia, that there was the possibility of high growth in this sector (up to 30 percent), and that Croatia's membership in the EU would provide the necessary boost to franchising development. The survey showed that although franchising was not a familiar way of doing business, experts saw a bright future for franchising in Croatia.

Competition

Franchises had become more well-known in Croatia starting in the early 1990s, after the first McDonald's was opened in Zagreb. "McDonald's expansion into the Croatian market has tended to use two franchising methods: direct franchising and business-facility lease arrangements . . . Such lease arrangements allow for franchisees to become entry-level franchisees using less capital at the outset."[4]

Other franchisors followed McDonald's lead. For example, one of the relatively new restaurant franchising concepts in the Croatian market was the Hungarian company Fornetti, which managed to spread quickly its mini-bakeries business throughout

Croatia. They were founded in 1997, and by 2007 had more than 3,000 locations in Central and Eastern Europe.[5] Other international franchises represented in Croatia included Benetton, Subway, Dama Service, and Remax.

According to the Croatian Franchise Association, there were approximately 125 (25 of them domestic) franchise systems present in the Croatian market. These systems operated approximately 900 locations and employed almost 16,000 people.[6] Companies in more than 20 industries had chosen franchising as a growth option, with the sales industry and fast-food sectors accounting for more than 20 percent of the market. Other segments with important shares included the tourist industry, rent-a-car companies, courier services, and the fashion industry.

Exhibits 3 and 4 show the most well-known foreign and domestic franchisors in Croatia by industry and number of outlets as of 2007.

While a few restaurant franchisors had already entered the Croatian market, no well-known international coffee houses had done so. Competition for coffee houses was mostly local, dating back to Croatia's early days. Local competitors offered a roughly homogeneous product—coffee—and, most did not bother to create a visual identity, a brand, or a new concept. Price, location, and ambiance distinguished one coffee bar from another. Competitive rivalry from abroad, however, was imminent. The question was not if international coffee houses would come, but when?

Coffee consumption in Croatia was quite high; many Croatians spent time between meals, in the morning, or at night at coffee bars, which often also served beer and other alcoholic products. While regular bars and other restaurants competed

---

[4]*L. Viducic and G. Brcic in I. Alon and D. Welsh,* International Franchising in Emerging Markets: China, India and Other Asian Countries, *CCH Inc., Chicago, 2001, p. 217.*

[5]*K. Mandel, "Franchise in Hungary," address given at The Franchise Center Osijek seminar "Franšiza od A do ž," Osijek, November 2004.*

[6]*L. Kukec., "Round table—Franchising in Croatia," address given at EFF/IFA International Symposium, Brussels, October 24–25, 2006.*

EXHIBIT 4

Domestic Franchisors in Croatia

Source: "Round table—Franchising in Croatia," address given at EFF/IFA International Symposium, Brussels, October 24–25, 2006.

Franchisor	Industry	Number of Outlets
Elektromaterijal	Household appliances' distribution	Over 50 stores
X-nation	Fashion clothes	40 stores/corners
Rubelj Grill	Grill	17 restaurants
Skandal	Fashion clothes	15 stores
Body Creator	Weight loss center for women	4 centers
Bio & Bio	Health food	3 shops
Bike Express	Courier service	1 location
The San Francisco Coffee House	Coffee bar	1 location

with coffee shops for customers, coffee shops were relatively cheaper, providing a comfortable environment for socializing. Suppliers of coffee were many and included both international and local brands. Coffee, itself, was basically a commodity.

The Opening of "San Francisco Coffee House"

Osijek was a town with many coffee shops and bars, and visiting them was part of the lifestyle of the local population. But there was one competitive problem from which they all suffered: They all offered roughly the same limited product line without any differentiating concept. Tensek and Pacek noticed that what was missing in the market was an American-style coffee bar in which most of the offerings would consist of different types of coffee and that would include the novel (in Croatia) possibility of getting "coffee to go." They decided to adapt this ubiquitous American concept to the local Croatian market. They were under the impression that the "Made in USA" brand would be positively received in their "new" market, so they named the coffee bar "The San Francisco Coffee House." During the development of the business plan, Tensek traveled several times to the United States researching ideas, studying the technology of coffee making, and personally bringing back with him some of the supplies and crucial ingredients.

Tensek had chosen the location for The San Francisco Coffee House carefully: He was looking for a location with a minimum of 80 square meters near an area with heavy foot traffic, since his and Pacek's main target market was to be business people. He found an excellent location in the town's center—across from the green market, near three university departments and several lawyers' and public notaries' offices—for which he signed a five-year lease with provisions for extending the lease and a right to pre-emptive purchase in case the owner wanted to sell the premise. After the first few months, they found that their major client markets were students and business professionals of all ages.

Since SFCH was the first American coffee house in Croatia, this unique place where one could enjoy the authentic ambiance of the American city received excellent reviews and unusually large media attention in the first six months of existence. Elle Décor ranked it among six best decorated service industry interiors in the country, complimenting the brave mixture of styles and materials Pacek used to create the urban, bright, and sophisticated environment. The result was even more amazing taking into account that the entrepreneurs worked within a limited budget of € 40,000 as start-up capital.

The San Francisco Coffee House assortment was also unique for this market. It offered its customers coffee in 17 different latte (with milk) and mocha variants and American-style muffins in several varieties. Coffee could be taken in the relaxing but urban atmosphere of the bar or it could be taken out in "to-go" packaging. In order for Tensek and Pacek to adapt to their target market, guests were provided Croatian and international newspapers and magazines and free wireless access to the Internet (which was extremely rare in Croatia). The ambiance was also enhanced by smooth jazz and billboard music from the 1970s, 1980s, and 1990s.

SFCH had eight employees and was managed by Tanja Ivelj. The employees were all young people, some of them without any previous working experience and most of whom had worked in SFCH from its inception. When searching for employees, Tensek looked for trustworthy, loyal, and honest people. For each workstation, employees had a detailed job description and detailed checklists for each shift and for weekly and monthly routine duties.

After employment, all employees underwent training for working in a coffee shop/bar. Their salaries were almost 20 percent higher than those of comparable employees at other local coffee shops. Every six months all employees had scheduled performance reviews. If a review was satisfactory, there was a further five percent salary increase. Human resource management was one of the areas where Tensek had brought his American corporate experience into Croatia. In Croatia, employee rights, salaries, and general terms of employment were, in most cases, ambiguous. Also contrary to the common practice in Croatia, SFCH provided full paid vacation and benefits for its employees. As a result, in an industry where the turnover rate was extremely high, The San Francisco Coffee House was able to achieve less than 20 percent turnover over the first three years of operation. As Tensek mentioned, "Satisfied and motivated employees offer a high standard of service to the end customers."

SFCH made an extra effort to maintain excellent relationships with its suppliers, making timely payments in a market that was known for its irregularities. Wise and responsible financial management was the company's priority. For its good decisions, the market also rewarded SFCH. The summary of the financial performance of the company's operations is shown in Exhibit 5.

What Should Be Done Next?

Tensek and Pacek looked at the facts: Franchising was one of several possible models for business growth and was widely used in economically developed countries throughout the world. Some of the reasons why companies preferred to develop franchise networks rather than grow organically included lower financial investment, lower risk, faster growth, local market knowledge by franchisee, and the franchisee's motivation to succeed. They wanted these benefits too.

The barriers which the San Francisco Coffee House faced in franchising in the local market were challenging:

■ There was just not enough information about franchising; as a result, entrepreneurial and

institutional awareness of franchising was quite low;

■ There were no well-established support organizations for the development of franchise networks in Croatia; there were only two Entrepreneurship Centers in Croatia which offered services regarding franchise network development; and

■ There was no significant support from financial institutions; banks failed to recognize the relatively lower risk of investment in start-up entrepreneurs/franchisees than in independent start-up entrepreneurs.

Moreover, the company was still young and unproven in other locations. The couple could simply enjoy their local success. They could open additional stores by themselves. Or they could try to sell franchises of their concept. All three options had significant upsides and downsides. Their intuition told them they should use franchising, but serious limitations existed.

Could the couple develop franchising in a market where local conditions were less than conducive? Could they gain national prominence? The couple had never run a franchising business and did not have the necessary experience and knowledge. How could they overcome the weaknesses they possessed and the environmental threats? How could they seize the opportunities in the marketplace using their unique experiences, capabilities, and strengths?

This case was supported by The Franchise Center, part of the Center for Entrepreneurship Osijek, and Poduzetna Hrvatska, a USAID project in Croatia.

EXHIBIT 5

SFCH Financial Performance

	2006 (in EUR)	2007 (in EUR)
Income Data		
Net Revenues	13,333	166,666
Total Expenses	86,666	93,333
Direct Costs	50,666	54,000
Depreciation	2,666	7,333
Gross profit	80,000	105,333
Operating expenses	36,000	39,333
Earnings before I&T	44,000	66,000
Taxes	9,680	14,520
Earnings after I&T	34,320	51,480

Case 2   E+Co: A Tipping Point for Clean Energy Entrepreneurship (A)

Richard Ivey School of Business
The University of Western Ontario

IVEY

Kevin McKague and Oana Branzei wrote this case solely to provide material for class discussion. The authors do not intend to illustrate either effective or ineffective handling of a managerial situation. The authors may have disguised certain names and other identifying information to protect confidentiality.

Copyright © Ivey Publishing.

All Rights Reserved. No part of the publication may be reproduced or transmitted in any form or by any means, or stored in a database or retrieval system without the written consent of Ivey Publishing. With respect to Ivey cases, Ivey Management Services prohibits any form of reproduction, storage or transmittal without its written permission. This material is not covered under authorization from any reproduction rights organization. To order copies or request permission to reproduce material, contact Ivey Publishing, Ivey Management Services, c/o Richard Ivey School of Business, The University of Western Ontario, London, Ontario, Canada, N6A 3K7; phone (519)661-3208, fax (519) 661-3882, email cases@ivey.uwo.ca.

Version: (A) 2007-08-16

"How do we get from 10 million to 100 million people served by 2020?" asked Maria Gotbaum, an investment officer in E+Co's[1] Latin American office, as the organization's annual retreat wrapped up on September 8, 2006.

The question was directed to Phil LaRocco, E+Co's co-founder and executive director. LaRocco's contribution to spreading cleaner, affordable energy solutions to developing countries had just been recognized by the World Renewable Energy Congress (WREC) with its prestigious 2006 Honorary Award for outstanding achievement and vision in the global renewable energy sector. LaRocco and his team of 38 employees from nine regional offices in Africa, Latin America, Asia, Europe, and North America were extremely proud of the important work that E+Co had been doing: they had funded and supported 138 clean energy enterprises in 25 developing countries. E+Co's seed investments of $29 million[2] had helped leverage $114 million more from third parties to jointly fund local clean energy entrepreneurs. E+Co's portfolio included a wide range of investee enterprises, ranging from cookstove manufacturers and basic energy-efficiency companies to businesses that generated electricity from wind, geothermal, biogas, hydro, and solar technologies. (Exhibit 1 details E+Co's enterprise investments by geography and technology.)

These clean energy companies were replacing the burning of firewood, kerosene, charcoal, and oil and liquid petroleum gas with cleaner, more efficient energy technologies suited to local needs and demand. Together, these companies provided more than 3.6 million of the world's poorest people with access to modern energy services and generated 2,965 jobs, while simultaneously offsetting more than 2.2 million tons of carbon dioxide (CO_2) annually. (Exhibit 2 shows a summary of E+Co's triple bottom line performance.) As LaRocco had noted in his WREC award acceptance speech, he and his E+Co team fullheartedly believed that nurturing local clean energy enterprises in developing countries offered "enormous potential for eradicating energy poverty."

Gotbaum concluded:

> We now know how to do E+Co's daily work quite well. We know how to combine investment capital and business support services to bring clean energy entrepreneurs in developing countries to a place where they can have viable, sustainable enterprises. We've got that part down. And we know how to take E+Co from the 3 million people currently served to 10 million people served by 2010. What E+Co needs now, and what we need you to focus on is—how do we take this to scale?

Gotbaum's challenge was a welcome reminder that E+Co's key strategic objective was to build on its vision, learning, and successes thus far to bring the provision of clean energy to the poor in developing countries to a tipping point.

Energy Poverty + Energy Waste: Origins of the Business Model

Since its launch in 1994, E+Co's mission had been to empower local small and medium-sized enterprises to supply clean and affordable energy to households, businesses, and communities in developing countries through a combination of capital investment and business development support. (Exhibit 3 summarizes the company's "energy through enterprise" approach to greener energy.)

[1] *E+Co, pronounced "E and Co," http://www.eandco.net, accessed on July 11, 2007.*
[2] *This figure reflects combined investment by E+Co and local entrepreneurs.*

EXHIBIT 1

E+Co's Investment Profile (at December 31, 2006)

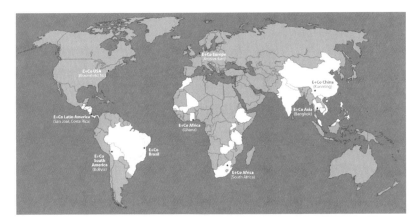

25 E+Co Countries of Operation

Bolivia, Brazil, Costa Rica, El Salvador, Guatemala, Honduras, Nicaragua, Ethiopía, Gambia, Ghana, Mali, Morocco, Senegal, South Africa, Tanzania, Uganda, Zambia, Cambodia, China, India, Malaysia, Nepal, Philippines, Thailand, Vietnam.

9 E+Co Regional Offices

Bolivia (La Paz), Brazil (Bahia), China (Kunming), Costa Rica (San José), Netherlands, Ghana (Accra), South Africa (Pretoria), Thailand (Bangkok), USA (Bloomfield, New Jersey)

Active Investments by Region

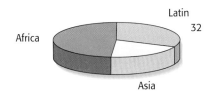

Active Investments by Technology (2006)

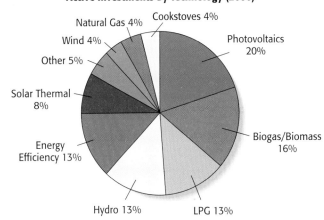

The brainchild of co-founders Phil LaRocco and Christine Eibs-Singer, E+Co's model was inspired by the idea that small and medium-sized energy enterprises held tremendous potential to simultaneously address the twin global issues of energy poverty and energy waste. The concept had begun forming four years earlier. Soon after LaRocco had stepped down as director of World Trade and Economic Development at the Port Authority of New York and New Jersey[3] (citing an entrepreneurial itch), he was approached by the Rockefeller Foundation to answer the question: "How could scarce resources be used in an effective way to do well for the global environment?"

Eibs-Singer had joined LaRocco on the consulting project. They went back to the Rockefeller Foundation with a simple, but challenging, proposal. They argued that if the Foundation cared about the global environment, it would have to care about energy. And if it cared about energy, it would have to focus on the developing world. And if it cared about energy in the developing world, it would have to learn the language of business and how to work with clean energy entrepreneurs in developing countries.

LaRocco and Eibs-Singer further argued that energy poverty and energy waste were two sides of the same coin; and unless tackled jointly, they would continue to thwart economic growth, threaten quality of life, and aggravate environmental problems. The same situation continues today: 2.5 billion people rely on biomass such as fuelwood, charcoal, agricultural waste, and animal dung to meet their energy needs for cooking.[4] In many countries, these resources

---

[3] *The Port Authority was a public purpose investment company—an arm's length organization from government—with the ability to make investments in companies for the development of the port and for the benefit of the public good. Phil LaRocco had been with the Port Authority for 20 years, and had worked his way up from parking auditor to head a staff of 550 and a budget of $750 million. Christine Eibs-Singer had worked for LaRocco at the Port Authority since 1982.*

---

[4] *International Energy Agency, "Energy for Cooking in Developing Countries," in* World Energy Outlook, *International Energy Agency, Paris, 2006 (pp. 419–445). Available at http://www.iea.org//textbase/weo/cooking.pdf, accessed on July 11, 2007.*

EXHIBIT 2

E+Co's Triple Bottom Line Performance*

Financial	Social and Economic		Environmental	
Investment Funds Disbursed	People with Access to Modern Energy Services	Households Served	CO_2 Offset by Enterprises Annually	CO_2 Offset (for life of project)
$14,721,633	3,607,559	721,253	2,201,780 tons	13,121,389 tons
Entrepreneur's Investment	Cumulative Clean Energy Generated	Energy Saved from Efficiency Initiatives	Value of CO_2 Offset (for life of project)	Reforested Land
$29,067,832	59,539,558 MWH	118,400 MWH	$65,606,946	228 hectares + ~220,000 trees
Leveraged from Third Parties	Jobs Supported	Improved Income	Clean Water Provided	Households with Access to Clean Water
$113,754,964	2,965	$7,394,073	140,157,750 liters	29,825
Potential Growth or Follow-On Capital	Clean Energy Enterprises	Women Ownership/ Shareholding	Charcoal Displaced	Firewood Displaced
$102,838,700	138	90	257,506 tons	207,984 tons
E+Co's Portfolio Return after Write-offs	Clean Energy Employees & Customers Trained	Customers Installing Energy-Efficient Equipment	Liquid Petroleum Gas Displaced	Kerosene Displaced
8.3%	73,960	29,545	2,379,000 kg	6,045,546 L
E+Co Repayments	Entrepreneurs Identified	Entrepreneurs Receiving Services	Barrels of Oil Displaced	Dollar Value of Oil Displaced
$4,178,748	1,574	854	259,743	$14,532,621

*Cumulative results through December 31, 2006. E+Co collects this information from its investee enterprises and reports it twice annually on its Web site at http://www.eandco.net.

account for more than 90 percent of household energy consumption. According to the International Energy Agency's 2006 World Energy Outlook:[5]

> The inefficient and unsustainable use of biomass has severe consequences for health, the environment and economic development. Shockingly, about 1.3 million people—mostly women and children—die prematurely every year because of exposure to indoor air pollution from biomass. There is evidence that, in countries where local prices have adjusted to recent high international energy prices, the shift to cleaner, more efficient ways of cooking has actually slowed and even reversed. In the Reference Scenario, the number of people using biomass increases to 2.6 billion by 2015 and to 2.7 billion by 2030 as population rises. That is, one-third of the world's population will still be relying on these fuels, a share barely smaller than today.

LaRocco and Eibs-Singer knew that, in the absence of new policies, energy waste and energy poverty were likely to persist. According to the World Energy Outlook[6] some 1.6 billion people—one-quarter of the world's population—had no access to electricity. Without radical interventions, 1.4 billion people

[5]World Development Report 1999/2000: Entering the 21st Century, World Bank, Washington, DC, 1999. Available at http://www.worldbank.org/wdr/2000, accessed July 11, 2007.

[6]International Energy Agency, 30 Key Energy Trends in the IEA and Worldwide, International Energy Agency, Paris, 2005. Available at http://www.iea.org//textbase/nppdf/free/2005/energy_trends.pdf, accessed on July 11, 2007; this data is based on the World Energy Outlook 2002 statistics.

EXHIBIT 3

E+Co Business Model

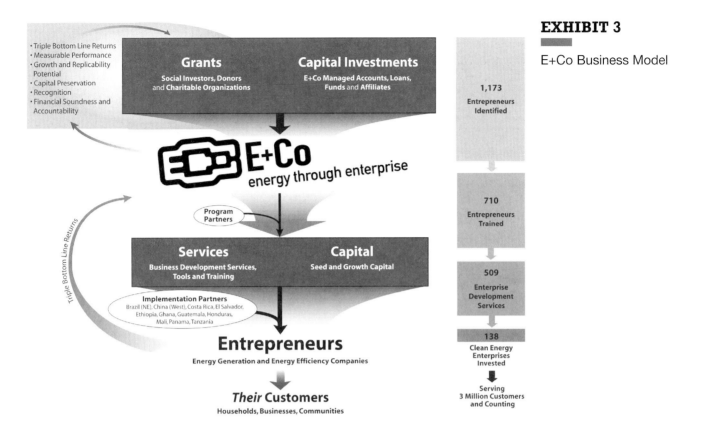

might still have no access to electricity in 2030. Four out of five people lacking access to electricity lived in rural areas of the developing world. About 80 percent of these people are located in sub-Saharan Africa and India.

LaRocco and Eibs-Singer knew that ability to pay wasn't the greatest barrier to accessing clean energy services. The poor often paid higher prices for traditional fuel sources (i.e., the so-called poverty premium) because modern energy technologies, such as wind and steam turbines, solar power or biofuels, which could offer cheaper and better energy sources, were often not available. Low-income households around the world spend about US$20 billion per year on expensive and environmentally damaging energy sources, such as kerosene, battery charging, charcoal, firewood, and disposable batteries.[7]

LaRocco and Eibs-Singer were also not concerned about a lack of either investor interest or investment. The 2004 World Energy Outlook of the International Energy Association (IEA) estimated that world energy use would grow 60 percent by 2030. Two-thirds of this growth was expected to be in developing countries. To finance this growth, US$7 trillion would be spent in the developing world

(with another US$9 trillion in the developed countries). The latest outlook adjusted this estimate upward by about US$3 trillion and called for a cumulative investment of just over $20 trillion (in year-2005 dollars) over 2005 to 2030. More than half of all the energy investment needed worldwide would be in developing countries.

Helping the poor in developing countries access cleaner energy remained, however, an important concern. LaRocco and Eibs-Singer had seen firsthand the limitations of the existing approaches for providing cleaner energy to the rural poor. From the middle of the 20th century onwards, the Breton Woods institutions (i.e., the World Bank and the International Monetary Fund) had approached energy provision in developing countries by undertaking high-visibility, major power plant projects. Contracts often focused on serving the capital city or major commercial centers, and were typically issued to reputable (often international) providers, who brought in their expertise on a project-by-project basis. But energy for the rural poor in developing countries often fell outside the scope of these large-scale, grid-focused interventions. Many non-governmental groups and civil society organizations had attempted to fill in the gap, but the effectiveness of their interventions was often limited to short-lived donor-funded projects. Many lacked a market-based approach, which meant that they offered technical solutions the poor could not afford, or failed to implement a financially sustainable

---

[7]World Development Report 1999/2000: Entering the 21st Century, *World Bank, Washington, DC, 1999. Available at http://www.worldbank.org/wdr/2000, accessed July 11, 2007.*

model for the provision of clean energy that could outlast donor funding—or sometimes both.

E+Co's Enterprise-Centered Alternative

While tackling the challenging question posed by the Rockefeller Foundation, LaRocco and Eibs-Singer had grown increasingly convinced that the best (perhaps the only) way to alleviate energy poverty and reduce energy waste was to encourage local solutions that fit the needs, and the means, of each community. LaRocco argued that grassroots entrepreneurs were the missing link needed to bridge the gaping disconnect between local needs and global investment:

> The critical element is not the local regulatory environment, or a country's macroeconomic circumstances, or the policy environment, or a big company ready to step in. It's the entrepreneur—the man or woman who decides to make his or her living selling clean energy to his or her neighbors.

By design, E+Co's intent was to nurture and tap into a pool of local entrepreneurial talent who would be in the best position to find the optimal balance between local needs and local means and would thus deliver desirable, feasible, and sustainable clean energy solutions where they were needed the most. E+Co's model had the local entrepreneurs—the drivers and champions of designing and implementing a viable clean energy enterprise—at its core. E+Co first identified and trained local entrepreneurs interested in starting clean energy businesses in developing countries. Then it offered seed capital along with a range of enterprise development services. E+Co's investments ranged in size from $29,000 to $800,000. Loans were typically given against the entrepreneur's commitment and a sound business plan, with less emphasis placed on collateral (especially for the smaller start-up loans). Growth capital was available for follow-on investments. Both financing and support services were tailored to fit local demand and then co-evolved with the needs of the entrepreneurs. Since 1998, E+Co had boasted an eight percent average internal rate of return (IRR) after write-offs and a 10 percent weighted average IRR for repaid loans.[8] (Exhibits 4 and 5 provide an overview of E+Co's financial performance.)

Up the Modern Energy Ladder

E+Co's enterprise-centered model was "technology neutral" (i.e., it was not driven by one particular renewable energy technology). Christine Eibs-Singer explained how the model enabled communities to climb the modern energy ladder at their own pace:

> If a household is using firewood or charcoal, sure it would be great to have them use a renewable source of electricity in their hut— but the first order of business is to get them to either use that firewood or charcoal more efficiently, to substitute that firewood or charcoal for an agricultural residue briquette or to use a more efficient stove for the burning of that firewood or charcoal. If the household and community could afford it, you want to get them off the firewood or charcoal to use LPG— liquid petroleum gas—as a substitute. And later, if economically viable, their energy needs could be met by a solar home system or a village mini-grid powered by run-of-river hydro. And so you basically want to move this population along the energy ladder, from the dirtiest to cleaner steps.[9]

The Tipping Point?

In the last 12 years, E+Co had grown dramatically in size and in its vision of what was possible. So had global concern and call to action for bringing the poor up the energy ladder. The 2006 World Energy Outlook[10] noted that:

> *Action to encourage more efficient and sustainable use of traditional biomass and help people switch to modern cooking fuels and technologies is needed urgently.* The appropriate policy approach depends on local circumstances such as per-capita incomes and the availability of a sustainable biomass supply. Alternative fuels and technologies are already available at reasonable cost. Halving the number of households using biomass for cooking by 2015—a recommendation of the UN Millennium Project—would involve 1.3 billion people switching to liquefied petroleum gas and other commercial fuels. This would not have a significant impact on world oil demand and the equipment would cost, at most, $1.5 billion per year. But vigorous and concerted government action—with support from

---

[8]*These calculations did not include E+Co's operating and enterprise development costs, which E+Co covered through contract revenues and grants.*

[9]*Interview with Christine Eibs-Singer, March 4, 2006.*
[10]*International Energy Agency,* World Energy Outlook Summary and Conclusions, *International Energy Agency, Paris, 2006, p. 11. Available at http://www.worldenergyoutlook.org/summaries 2006/English.pdf, accessed on July 11, 2007; emphasis in original.*

	December 04	December 05	December 06
Assets			
Cash	$ 4,034,625	$ 4,293,972	$ 6,444,793
Program Loans Receivable	$ 3,742,958	$ 3,942,019	$ 5,958,279
Program Equity Investments	$ 1,505,665	$ 1,170,665	$ 1,175,665
Promises to Give	$ 7,327,778	$ 5,856,322	$ 490,532
Other Assets	$ 445,055	$ 403,429	$ 47,623
Total	**$17,056,081**	**$15,666,407**	**$19,599,243**
Liabilities			
Program Loans Payable	$ 4,257,130	$ 3,871,811	$ 5,599,124
Other Liabilities	$ 184,324	$ 327,346	$ 336,188
Total	**$ 4,441,454**	**$ 4,199,157**	**$ 5,935,312**
Minority Interest in Subsidiary			$ (24,283)
Net Assets	$12,614,627	$11,467,250	$13,688,214
Total Liabilities & Net Assets	**$17,056,081**	**$15,666,407**	**$19,599,243**

Statement of Activity

	December 04	December 05	December 06
Revenue & Support			
Contributions	$5,593,014	$ 2,129,019	$4,566,994
Program Revenue	$ 242,924	$ 124,576	$ 762,758
Interest Income	$ 392,781	$ 652,095	$ 769,105
Other Income	$ 203,125	$ 7,530	$ 533,395
Total	**$6,431,844**	**$ 2,913,220**	**$6,542,252**
Expenses			
Program Services	$2,574,039	$ 2,332,266	$3,199,961
Management and General	$ 513,011	$ 743,671	$ 746,994
Grant Procurement	$ 259,240	$ 285,544	$ 398,616
Other	$ 40,000	$ 685,104	$ (10,271)
Total	**$3,386,290**	**$ 4,046,585**	**$4,335,300**
Increase In Net Assets	**$3,045,554**	**$(1,133,365)**	**$2,206,952**

EXHIBIT 4

E+Co Financial Statements Summary

the industrialised countries—is needed to achieve this target, together with increased funding from both public and private sources. Policies would need to address barriers to access, affordability and supply, and to form a central component of broader development strategies.

Maria Gotbaum's question was a suitable close to E+Co's annual retreat. In retrospect, Phil LaRocco, Christine Eibs-Singer, and their global team knew that E+Co had demonstrated the model's financial, environmental, and social impact; replicated it across technology sectors in 25 countries; and gradually

institutionalized successful practices in their global operations. These three steps kept them right on track for sustaining, and perhaps even organically tripling, E+Co's reach and impact—but would these steps be sufficient to scale up operations by a factor of 10? Could E+Co go it alone in its quest to implement its enterprise-centered clean energy paradigm in the developing world? Who else might adopt or perhaps help leverage E+Co's enterprise model to assist energy entrepreneurs in the developing world?

LaRocco did not yet have a good answer for Gotbaum's question. He and Eibs-Singer had long hoped that E+Co's enterprise-driven model to fighting poverty through energy would become infectious

EXHIBIT 5

E+Co Portfolio Performance Summary (January 1998 through December 31, 2006)

Total Debt Investments made	12,953,633
Total Equity Investments made	1,768,000
Total Portfolio	**14,721,633**
Number of Equity Investments	**15**
Number of Debt Investments	**129**
Total Investments	**144**
Write offs (26 Enterprises)	1,540,548
% of Total Investments made	10.5%
Debt Portfolio After Write Offs—(107 Investments)	**11,883,085**
Equity Portfolio After Write Offs—(11 Investments)	**1,298,000**
Total Portfolio After Write Offs	**13,181,085**
Projected Weighted Average IRR of Equity Portfolio	6.3%
Projected Weighted Average IRR of Debt Portfolio	8.5%
Projected Weighted Average IRR of Total Portfolio After Write Offs	**8.3%**
Total Equity 100% Exited (2 Investments)	**350,000**
Weighted Average IRR for Equity Buy-Outs	**9.0%**
Total Loans 100% Repaid (27 Investments)	**2,836,177**
Weighted Average IRR for Repaid Loans	**10.5%**

for many other organizations. They expected that the success of the enterprise-centered model for energy provision would focus the attention of energy policy-makers on local small and medium-sized energy enterprises. They wondered whether E+Co's success could even gradually change the "DNA" of large global organizations, such as the World Bank and the UN. The 2006 World Energy Outlook seemed to be in full support of what they had been doing for years. Could it be a sign of the tipping point to come?

Demonstrate

Phil LaRocco felt that E+Co's triple bottom line success had helped raise the profile of energy as a means to achieving global social and environmental targets, such as the Millennium Development Goals.[11] By 2006, E+Co's portfolio of investee enterprises had jointly displaced more than 450 million kilograms of firewood and charcoal, reforested more than 200 hectares of land, provided more than 140 million liters of clean water, and offset 13 million tons of CO_2. E+Co had helped raise local incomes by a total of $7.4 million. It had provided training or services to 854 entrepreneurs and actively encouraged women's entrepreneurship: women were owners or co-owners of 65 percent of E+Co's investee enterprises.

LaRocco recalled three of the many success stories that demonstrated the effectiveness of E+Co's enterprise-centered model: Thailand-based Clean Energy Development Ltd., Honduras-based hydroelectric project La Esperanza, and Ghana-based liquid petroleum gas provider Anasset.

Clean Energy Development Ltd. of Thailand (CleanThai) In Thailand, industrial-scale cassava processing was associated with huge lagoons of organic wastes often left to decompose in the open.[12] The methane given off by the cassava effluent was so toxic that flying birds rarely made it across the ponds, succumbing to the fumes in mid-air.

---

[11] *The Millennium Development Goals were adopted by the UN General Assembly in 2000, see www.un.org/millenniumgoals.*

[12] *Oana Branzei and Kevin McKague, "Green Thinking: Four Emerging Innovations from around the World Showcase a New Generation of Forward-looking Business Models,"* Corporate Knights, *Vol. 6, No. 1, http://www.corporateknights. ca/content/page.asp?name=green_thinking, accessed July 11, 2007.*

CleanThai saw a great waste-to-energy opportunity in these smelly lagoons. E+Co provided CleanThai with an early stage equity investment of $150,000, which supported the construction of E+Co's first commercial project with the largest cassava processing plant in the country. CleanThai used anaerobic digestion technologies to recover and convert these organic waste materials into methane. The captured biogas was used as replacement fuel for the plant's production boilers and generated almost all the electricity needed to operate the plant. One year later, E+Co provided CleanThai with a $35,000 investment to further develop its customer base.

E+Co's seed capital and enterprise development assistance was paying off. By 2003, CleanThai had successfully completed the construction of its first biogas system, which allowed it to develop prospects for 15 new cassava-based projects across Thailand. That same year, CleanThai built an in-ground covered lagoon biogas system for a large pig farm in Central Thailand. In June 2004, CleanThai entered into a shareholders' agreement with the Thai Biogas Energy Company for the construction and operation of a series of biogas power plants. CleanThai also signed a turnkey agreement to build a bioreactor for an ethanol distillery being installed by the Lanna Group in Thailand. In December 2005, CleanThai completed a buy back of E+Co shares, producing a profitable exit for E+Co's investment.

La Esperanza, Honduras La Esperanza developed a hydroelectric project using an abandoned dam and powerhouse foundation. In 2001, E+Co supported the developers with business plan preparation assistance and a $250,000 loan for the construction of the first two powerhouses with a combined installed capacity of 1.4 megawatts (MW). In March 2004, E+Co made a $200,000 preferred share investment that allowed La Esperanza to secure financing for the second powerhouse from the Central American Bank for Economic Integration and FinnFund.

Both powerhouses started operations in June 2004. In September 2006, E+Co approved a US$800,000 loan to further increase the size of the reservoir and improve flow.

As of early 2007, La Esperanza was generating approximately 24 MW per year, and had grown to a staff of 4 managers, 23 technicians, and 108 employees. The energy, distributed by the Empresa Nacional de Energía Eléctrica (ENEE) in Honduras, reached about 194 households (or an estimated 40.1 percent of the energy produced by La Esperanza).

Aside from its economic success, La Esperanza showcased the success of renewable energy projects on the environmental and social front. The hydro energy replaced an estimated total annual expenditure of $50,807 by 90 households in San Fernando and 70 households in Santa Anita previously spent on firewood, candles, and kerosene. La Esperanza's cleaner energy helped offset 19,063 tons of CO_2 annually. Thirty thousand trees were planted in 2006 through its reforestation program (3,572 in the project itself for slope stabilization, the remaining in surrounding communities). La Esperanza engaged in broad consultation with the communities, the local government, and different water administration councils to jointly decide on the reforestation priorities. La Esperanza also repaired an old greenhouse, using recycled materials, to establish a tree nursery. Three thousand seeds, all collected within the land of the project, were already planted. They also started the production of fruit trees.

In August 2005, La Esperanza became one of the first small-scale projects registered under the Clean Development Mechanism of the Kyoto Protocol. With support from the Citigroup Foundation, E+Co assisted La Esperanza in assessing and quantifying its 35,000 tons per year of carbon emissions reductions, which were then sold to the World Bank's Community Development Carbon Fund. During 2006, an agreement was signed between E+Co and La Esperanza to pilot E+Co's Erase Your Footprint Voluntary Carbon Offset program. Under the "Generando O2" (Generating O2), E+Co would purchase 350 tons of CO_2 offsets generated by La Esperanza's Tree Planting Program, at $4 per ton.

Anasset, Ghana In Ghana, where many low-income households still cooked with firewood or charcoal (which was expensive, time-consuming to collect, unhealthy when used indoors, and contributed to deforestation), E+Co's seed capital and enterprise development services helped Anasset profitably offer an alternative fuel source—liquid petroleum gas (LPG). Households accounted for 70 percent of Anasset's customers and 65 percent of its revenues; the remaining customers were commercial and institutional consumers, such as restaurants, hospitals, and schools, and those who purchased fuel for vehicles running on LPG.

Prior to working with E+Co, Anasset operated from rented premises, strategically located within the precincts of the middle-class Awudome Estates, one of the most densely populated areas of Ghana's capital city, Accra. In 2002, Anasset's owner, Seth Nanemeh, received a four-year, 7.5 percent loan of US$38,000 from E+Co and its partner African Rural Energy Enterprise Development (AREED).[13] E+Co's assistance with growth planning helped increase Anasset's sales by 57 percent by 2004, and almost doubled its monthly distribution of LPG, from 145,000 kilograms in 2004 to 220,000 kilograms in 2005. The seed loan also enabled Anasset to obtain an additional working capital loan from Unibank for opening a second plant at Afloa in south-eastern Ghana.

In 2006, Anasset sold 2.3 million kilograms of LPG, for annual sales of US$1.7 million. By the end of 2006, Anasset had provided 26,958 households with modern energy services and replaced the consumption of 16,174.8 tons of charcoal, or the equivalent of 114,841 tons of wood, every six months. Anasset employed 23 people and a planned third plant will add 13 more jobs.

Replicate

E+Co replicated these investments and business support services to companies such as CleanThai, La Esperanza, and Anasset across markets and cultures (see Exhibits 6, 7, and 8 for additional E+Co-financed ventures in Africa, Asia, and Latin America). As its portfolio of investee enterprises grew, E+Co learned to leverage its experience and impact through width and depth investing, pursuing opportunities for serial investing and broadening its partner base.

Investing for Width and Depth When E+Co started its quest to invest in energy entrepreneurs in emerging economies, exhaustive market research and feasibility studies were not just challenging to complete but often premature—many of E+Co's investee enterprises needed to blaze entirely new paths by creating a market for clean energy where none had existed before. Investing for width proved to be a suitable substitute for exhaustive upfront market research. Small initial investments in a wide variety of sectors helped E+Co test the waters by enabling local entrepreneurs to identify and signal which energy sectors, technologies, and business models were likely to be most viable in each regional market. Some of the venture ideas were brilliant. Others did not work out. Sampling a variety of enterprises in several different sectors provided a broad platform for creating small wins and for learning from early failures.

After local enterprises had identified the most promising sectors and technologies in each region (e.g., run-of-river hydro in Central America, solar hot water heating in South Africa, LPG in West Africa, or photovoltaics in parts of East Africa), E+Co channeled greater investment towards those sectors by organizing specialized managed accounts, funds, and affiliates that actively promoted specific types of clean energy enterprises in that region. In sum:

> E+Co's growth and sustainability plans are built on striking a balance between making investments in first-of-a-kind enterprises across a variety of clean energy sub-sectors ("investing for width") and making a number of subsequent investments in those sub-sectors that show the most promise for impact ("investing for depth").[14]

Serial Investing E+Co's model of Services+Capital (see Exhibit 3) had high start-up costs yet accrued rapidly increasing economies of scope. The average cost of business development services (e.g., business plan development, feasibility studies, market assessments, risk identification and mitigation, financial modeling, and ownership structuring) averaged about 40 cents on the dollar value of the loan. However, after 10 percent to 20 percent of E+Co's portfolio had grown to the point where the company could seek loans of more than half a million dollars, E+Co's return on these rapid-growth companies was enough to offset the high cost of business support services for a new set of initial investments. Each success story unleashed a small burst of growth: it helped provide seed investments and enterprise development services to a few more new start-ups.

[13]*African Rural Energy Enterprise Development Web site http:// www.areed.org, accessed on July 11, 2007.*

[14]*E+Co Progress Report, June 2006.*

EXHIBIT 6

Examples of E+Co
Ventures in Africa

Vent L'Eau pour la Vie, Senegal

In Senegal, where many local villages relied on wind-powered pumps for drinking water and subsistence agriculture, an E+Co seed loan of US$17,123 (five years, 12 percent interest) provided working capital for a local entrepreneur, Michel Tine, to found Vent L'Eau pour la Vie or VEV (French for Wind Water for Life).

VEV pumps now delivered 44,550,000 liters of clean water per year to 8,250 households in 166 villages.[1] VEV was launched in 1992, at the end of a decade-long project funded by an Italian aid agency, LVIA. Since 1981, LVIA had installed 110 wind-powered pumps in the Thies, Diourbel, Saint-Louis, and Casamance regions of Senegal. However, without continued repair and regular maintenance, these pumps would have had the same fate as most others in Senegal, where overall fewer than 10 percent of the pumps installed in the 1980s were still working.

Michel Tine, along with three other former LVIA employees, founded VEV to provide continued services to LVIA's former clients. The team had since grown to 13 employees and VEV had expanded its service offerings to include making and installing new pumps and windmills. VEV was also designing water supply projects for rural communities and had completed 12 such projects in 2005.

New Energies, South Africa

In South Africa, where 73 percent of energy generation came from fossil fuels and 25 percent of all electricity was used for water heating, the appeal of greener water-heating technologies was rising quickly. Although the country is bathed in sunshine, fewer than one percent of all households had solar thermal water heaters.[2] Yoram Gur Arie saw an opportunity to provide solar water-heating systems to large commercial institutions, such as schools, universities, hospitals, restaurants, and hotels, and founded New

Energies. The biggest entry barrier was the up-front investment cost in equipment. E+Co's helped New Energies develop a sound growth plan for the company. Starting in November 2004, E+Co disbursed a total investment of $253,179, in five sequential waves. New Energies is now one of South Africa's leading suppliers of industrial solar water-heating equipment.

[1]Kelvin Mason, "Pumping It up: Senegal, Equator Initiative," Series 5, 2005. Available at http://www.tve.org/ho/doc.cfm?aid=1500&lang=English, accessed on July 14, 2007.
[2]Gail Jennings, "Energy–South Africa: Putting Sunshine in Your Taps," 2007. Available at http://ipsnews.net/news.asp?idnews=38424, accessed on July 14, 2007.

Partnerships E+Co had also been successful in forging broad partnerships with like-minded organizations, including, among many others, Greenpeace International, the Bill & Melinda Gates Foundation, the International Finance Corporation, the Multilateral Investment Fund—Inter-American Development Bank, the Rockefeller Foundation, the Citigroup Foundation, the United Nations Environment Programme, the United Nations Foundation, the U.S. Agency for International Development, the U.S. Department of Energy, the Wallace Global Fund, and The Body Shop.

Institutionalize

E+Co also took steps to practice what it preached: it engaged in a formal business and growth planning exercise to help the team reach the "10 million

EXHIBIT 7

Examples of E+Co's
Ventures in Asia

Lotus Energy, Nepal*

In Nepal, E+Co helped Jeevan Goff grow his solar photovoltaic manufacturing and distribution company, Lotus Energy. A working capital loan of $150,000 from E+Co in 1997 helped serve 18,634 households with clean energy (replacing their regular kerosene consumption of about four liters per household each month). Before working with E+Co, Lotus Energy had installed a total of 350 solar home systems. Eight years later, Lotus had installed approximately 10,000 solar home systems (SHS), and one large water pump system for a 1,000-person village. Lotus Energy now employs 70 people, including three managers and 31 technicians, and generates 2.92 MW of green energy each day.

The environment benefited from the CO_2 savings. Socially, the cleaner energy brought education benefits, for adults and children, who could now study at night and receive news from the world. SHSs also have direct and indirect health care benefits: they prevent exposure to choking kerosene smoke and support the delivery of health care by local clinics now powered by sunshine. The systems even provide light for reading the Buddhist Mantras during the early morning and late evening prayers. In 1998, Lotus Energy had implemented two solar lighting systems for Buddhist monasteries in the remote Helambu district of Nepal.** Lotus Energy also promoted women's empowerment in Nepal: 37 percent of Lotus Energy's preference shares and 17 percent of its ordinary shares are owned by women.

Beijing Bergey Windpower Co., China

In China, Beijing Bergey Windpower Co. (BBWC) was established in 2001, with the help of an E+Co equity investment and working capital loan totaling $80,000. BBWC was responding to a growing awareness of the importance of wind systems in China's non-electrified areas. BBWC had produced more than 1,200 high-quality, low-cost 1 kW and 10 kW mini wind turbines for the Chinese market. The total installed capacity of Bergey systems had reached more than 1 MW. Now BBWC works with telecom companies, ocean traffic services, health clinics, and microbusinesses to provide custom electricity services. In most cases, the wind turbines displaced the use of diesel and kerosene for electricity generation and lighting.

*Photo: Hospital Solar Electrification Project, Ghami, upper Mustang: a 1.2 KW PV array with a TRSW3024W solar power converter provides AC power for the hospital equipment, including a Sun Works Ultra Violet water purifier and lights, http://www.lotusenergy.com/project.htm#Himalayan%20Lighting%20Gompa%20Project, accessed on July 14, 2007.
**Funds for 90 percent of the hard goods were made available by the Japanese consortium member of the Virtual Foundation and the rest of the funds and installation were supplied by the local Nepali villagers.

customers served" target. The planning task itself had been challenging:

> We needed a way forward that would allow us to grow and maintain our mission-driven focus at the same time. There were many examples of organizations drifting from their innovative development work because of the clearer precedent to create and manage highly specialized and commercial funds for investors. That might be a way forward. That might be a path to grow. But that would also be a path to potentially diluting the essence of E+Co: to create small and medium sized enterprises that rarely met the tests of conventional investor-driven funds.[15]

The exercise proved highly worthwhile. It helped make the E+Co case public in a clear, efficient manner. It also allowed E+Co to say "no" when no was appropriate.

The plan also charted E+Co's growth strategy. This strategy, summarized with two headlines—

---

[15]*Ibid.*

Geoteca, Guatemala*

Geoteca was the first private enterprise investment in a heat- and electricity-generating geothermal project in Central America. Although Guatemala had 32 volcanoes and geothermal reserves estimated at 1,800 MW (135 percent of the country's current installed capacity of 1325 MW), only 33 percent of the population had access to energy. A local enterprise, Bloteca, asked E+Co to support the completion of a 5-MW geothermal project. E+Co provided a $250,000 technical assistance loan (9 percent interest), which enabled the drilling of three new production wells, testing the productivity of the wells, making a reservoir assessment, and preparing a final pre-investment report. Geoteca, a fully owned subsidiary of Bloteca, provided the balance. The total cost of the project was $650,000. E+Co's investment was fully recovered by the fourth quarter of 2001. E+Co was instrumental in securing second-round financing by Banco Reformador and Citibank among others. The success of the geothermal project signaled the potential benefits of replication in Guatemala and Central America.

ASCIMA, Brazil

In Brazil, E+Co supported the greening of a community enterprise engaged in organic agriculture with a $50,000 loan in 2004. Fifteen families of small-holder farmers in a rural settlement in Maceio de Itapipoca, Ceará, partnered with two NGOs, NEPA and IDER,** to produce and distribute weekly assorted, seasonal baskets of goods for urban families in Fortaleza. The loan helped finance two photovoltaic water pumps; purchase equipment for the preparation of the land; and fund other initial inputs, such as a pickup truck to transport the produce and an amount to cover negative cash flow during the first seven months until sales began. The two NGO project implementers, IDER and NEPA, signed as co-borrowers; upon full repayment, the equipment would be transferred to the families.

*Photo: Cyclone Separador. Source: Luis Merida (1999). Eco-Fruit and Bloteca Guatemala, http://geoheat.oit.edu/bulletin/bull20-4/art4.pdf, accessed on July 14, 2007.
**IDER was an NGO partner of Brazil Rural Energy Enterprise Development (B-REED, also partner with E+CO and the Rockefeller Foundation); NEPA was a local NGO specialized in organic agriculture and distribution. Additional details on the partnership set-up and activities are available at http://www.b-reed.org/projects/doc/breed.prof.ascima.pdf, accessed July 14, 2007.

EXHIBIT 8

Examples of E+Co Ventures in Latin America

"Tradition of Experimentation Will Continue" and "Funds and Affiliates Approach Adopted to Tap Growth Potential"—involved a combination of width+depth investing, serial investing, and partnerships:

1. Entering markets through its traditional mode of making smaller, seed capital investments across a variety of technologies and niches. This approach allowed E+Co to learn the market dynamics, peculiarities, and players, and to realize which niches had most potential.

2. Creating a locally grounded fund where these smaller seed efforts could identify opportunities to concentrate on specific niches. This approach offered investors the focus they desired by creating an E+Co affiliated company. It also had the added benefit of being able to engage financial institutions in something familiar to them: a fund.

3. Using the accumulated experience in the market—and the established human and technical infrastructure—to lower the risk and the cost of each new development step.

E+Co Capital-Latin America was a good example for E+Co's increasing focus on funds and affiliates. Launched in 2005, it was E+Co's first such venture. E+Co Capital-Latin America served as fund manager for the Central American Renewable Energy and Cleaner Production Facility (CAREC).[16] The $15 million fund invested in renewable energy, energy efficiency, and cleaner production projects in Central America. Its focus was on small and medium-sized enterprises, with annual revenues of up to US$5 million and fewer than 100 employees. CAREC was structured to utilize mezzanine-financing mechanisms, such as subordinated debt, convertible debt, preferred shares, and other quasi-equity instruments. However, since its portfolio had excellent potential to reduce carbon emissions, CAREC would also undertake the packaging and selling of carbon emission reduction credits. Phil LaRocco hoped that this additional revenue stream would add to the financial viability of E+Co's growing portfolio of clean energy investee enterprises.

The formalization of a business plan and growth strategy followed several years of attention to standardizing key elements of E+Co's operations. Phil LaRocco and his team were particularly proud of three achievements: a web-based Global Management System, specialized loan servicing software, and a Web site boasting a multilingual media room.

Global Management System (GMS) Unveiled in November 2002, updated frequently, and accessible 24-7-365 with the latest information, the Global Management System (GMS) was E+Co's first line of management information and tools. GMS provided access to information on E+Co's investee enterprises, funders, and all facets of operations on five continents. Standardized documents could be readily downloaded and processed. The GMS also included the most recent reports, promotional information, progress photos, periodic presentations, and technology information.

Specialized Loan Servicing Software (LSS) Because most off-the-shelf accounting and loan servicing packages did not meet E+Co's needs, Phil LaRocco had asked a specialist software developer to design a system able to manage multiple currencies, varying loan periods, differing interest rates, and to automatically process and distribute invoices. The loan servicing software (LSS), launched in October 2005, was being integrated with the GMS to provide comprehensive, real-time information on each individual investment. In combination, the GMS and the LSS helped E+Co streamline many aspects of its initially boutique operations. Its investment due diligence, asset management, monitoring and evaluation templates, and accounting processes had all been standardized and simplified, which ensured more efficient operations and continued quality results.

Web Site In 2005, E+Co had upgraded and expanded its English-Spanish Web page to include a media room where site visitors could download many of E+Co's tools and publications. In 2006, E+Co launched sites in Chinese, French, and Portuguese.

Scaling Up

Phil LaRocco knew that scaling up E+Co's enterprise-centered model tenfold would require at least a hundred-fold increase in the initial number of interested entrepreneurs. For example, to reach three million customers, E+Co had identified 1,173 entrepreneurs. Of these, E+Co trained 710, offered enterprise development services to 509, and invested in 138 enterprises. To reach 100 million, E+Co would need to identify 40,000 potential entrepreneurs and work closely with about half of them.

LaRocco wondered how his team of 38 would develop the capacity to provide training and enterprise development services to so many. Could E+Co's experience and internal processes handle the increased responsibilities? What demands will such a scale of operation place on the working style of E+Co's tightly-knit team? What changes would need to be made in E+Co's organizational structure? See Exhibit 9 for E+Co's current organizational chart. What combination of top-down and bottom-up approaches could best propel E+Co to the 100 million customers served target?

However, the most important decision Phil LaRocco faced concerned E+Co's future strategy. Would scaling up operations by a factor of 10 require a radical departure from E+Co's current strategic path? Could E+Co continue to experiment with seed capital and width investing, or should it increasingly focus on depth and serial investments to leverage the experience accumulated thus far? Direct investment had proved to be an increasingly meaningful and lucrative opportunity but LaRocco knew that tapping into E+Co's growth potential would require a broader partner engagement and greater involvement of additional funds and affiliates. Would investments by funds and affiliates be sufficient to reach 100 million people served by 2020?

---

[16]*CAREC was initiated with core financial and institutional support from the Multilateral Investment Fund (MIF) of the Inter-American Development Bank.*

EXHIBIT 9

E+Co's Organizational Structure[1]

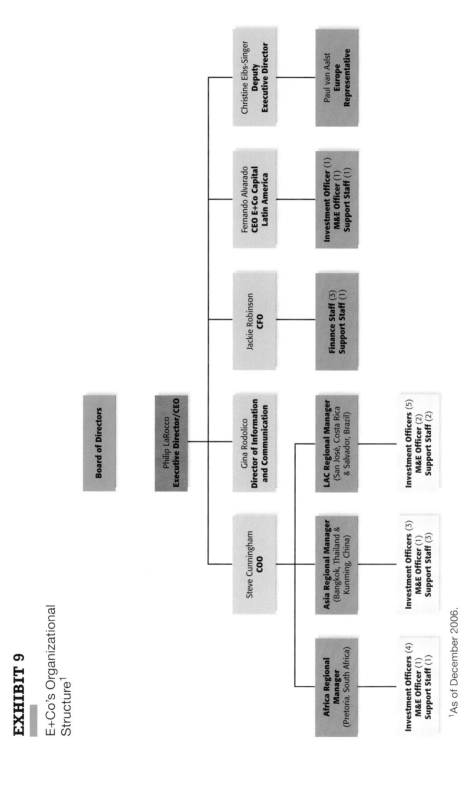

Board of Directors

Philip LaRocco
Executive Director/CEO

Steve Cunningham
COO

Gina Rodolico
Director of Information and Communication

Jackie Robinson
CFO

Fernando Alvarado
CEO E+Co Capital Latin America

Christine Eibs-Singer
Deputy Executive Director

Africa Regional Manager
(Pretoria, South Africa)

Asia Regional Manager
(Bangkok, Thailand & Kunming, China)

LAC Regional Manager
(San José, Costa Rica & Salvador, Brazil)

Finance Staff (3)
Support Staff (1)

Investment Officer (1)
M&E Officer (1)
Support Staff (1)

Paul van Aalst
Europe Representative

Investment Officers (4)
M&E Officer (1)
Support Staff (1)

Investment Officers (3)
M&E Officer (1)
Support Staff (3)

Investment Officers (5)
M&E Officer (2)
Support Staff (2)

[1]As of December 2006.

Case 3 Cineplex Entertainment: The Loyalty Program

Richard Ivey School of Business
The University of Western Ontario
IVEY

Renée Zatzman wrote this case under the supervision of Professor Kenneth G. Hardy solely to provide material for class discussion. The authors do not intend to illustrate either effective or ineffective handling of a managerial situation. The authors may have disguised certain names and other identifying information to protect confidentiality.

Copyright © Ivey Publishing.

All Rights Reserved. No part of the publication may be reproduced or transmitted in any form or by any means, or stored in a database or retrieval system without the written consent of Ivey Publishing. With respect to Ivey cases, Ivey Management Services prohibits any form of reproduction, storage or transmittal without its written permission. This material is not covered under authorization from any reproduction rights organization. To order copies or request permission to reproduce material, contact Ivey Publishing, Ivey Management Services, c/o Richard Ivey School of Business, The University of Western Ontario, London, Ontario, Canada, N6A 3K7; phone (519) 661-3208, fax (519) 661-3882, email cases@ivey.uwo.ca.

Version: (A) 2009-05-15

Introduction

Sarah Lewthwaite, marketing director for Cineplex Entertainment, was approached by chief executive officer (CEO) Ellis Jacob in August 2006 to resume the development of a loyalty program. The movie industry yielded inconsistent revenues each year, and Jacob wanted to increase and stabilize Cineplex's revenues. As chair of the Loyalty Steering Committee (the committee), Lewthwaite was scheduled to present her recommendations to the committee the following week. She would need to make a persuasive argument that included recommendations on program development, the reward structure, and the type of promotional campaign that would be most effective under the existing budget constraints. Finally, she needed to suggest whether the program should launch regionally or nationally. Her recommendations would be reviewed by senior Cineplex executives to ensure that the recommendations aligned with their criteria.

Cineplex Entertainment

Cineplex Entertainment (Cineplex) was founded in 1979 as a small chain of movie theaters under the Cineplex Odeon name. In 2003, under the direction of Onex Corporation, a Canadian private equity firm that held a major ownership claim in the company, Cineplex merged with Galaxy Entertainment Inc. (Galaxy). The CEO of Galaxy, Ellis Jacob, took over the newly merged company. In late 2005, Cineplex Galaxy acquired its largest competitor, Famous Players, and became Cineplex Entertainment—Canada's largest film exhibitor. With a box-office market share of 64 percent the chain enjoyed approximately 40 million visits per year under the Cineplex Odeon, Galaxy, Famous Players, and Cinema City brands.[1]

Cineplex's corporate mission focused on offering movie-goers "an exceptional entertainment experience." In addition to seeing a movie, customers could eat at various branded concession counters or play in the arcade. In 2005, Cineplex expanded its strategy to focus on developing new markets, using the theaters' large screens to showcase live events, such as major hockey games, wrestling matches, and the Metropolitan Opera. These events contributed greatly to Cineplex's success, which was measured primarily on customer traffic and revenue per guest (RPG), which was in turn composed of box-office and concession revenues.

In 2005, weak box-office attendance throughout the movie theater industry had affected Cineplex's operating performance (see Exhibit 1 for Cineplex's income statements for 2003, 2004, and 2005). Following the acquisition of Famous Players in 2005, Cineplex executives adjusted the pricing and products in the food and beverage concessions in 2006. With these moves, Cineplex was able to increase its average box-office RPG to $7.73 and its average concession RPG to $3.44 (see Exhibit 2).

A Growth Opportunity

Like the entire industry, Cineplex faced variable attendance levels depending on the crop of new movies. Additionally, RPG fluctuated based on the film genre. Cineplex executives knew that audiences for action-themed and children's movies purchased a high volume of concession items, which typically

---

[1] *Cineplex Galaxy Income Fund 2005 Annual Report, http://dplus.cineplexgalaxy.com/content/objects/ Annual%20Report%202005.pdf, accessed January 3, 2008.*

	2005	2004	2003
Total revenue	490,299	315,786	295,540
Cost of operations	421,529	248,818	242,636
Gross income	68,770	66,968	52,904
Amortization	42,948	22,530	18,404
Loss on debt	4,156	–	–
Impairment on assets	4,296	–	–
Loss (gain) on disposal of assets	122	(111)	(92)
Interest on long-term debt	18,401	8,280	4,020
Interest on loan	14,000	14,000	1,381
Interest income	(378)	(473)	(922)
Foreign exchange gain	–	–	(3,696)
Income taxes	(1,463)	(1,149)	366
Income from discontinued operations	28,116	6,357	6,184
Non-controlling interest	1,828	–	304
Net Income	**12,976**	**30,248**	**39,323**

EXHIBIT 1

Cineplex Entertainment Income Statements 2003–2005 (Cdn$ in Thousands)

Source: Cineplex Galaxy Income Fund 2005 Annual Report, http://dplus. cineplexgalaxy.com/content/ objects/annual%20report%20 2005.pdf, accessed January 3, 2008.

	2006E	2005	2004	2003
Attendance	61,000,000	39,945,000	28,096,000	27,073,000
Box-office RPG	–	$7.73	$7.45	$7.28
Concession RPG	–	$3.44	$3.04	$2.91
Film cost as a percent of box-office revenue	–	51.7%	51.6%	52.1%

EXHIBIT 2

Cineplex Entertainment Attendance and Revenue per Guest Data

Source: Cineplex Galaxy Income Fund 2005 Annual Report, http://dplus.cineplexgalaxy.com/content/ objects/annual%20report%202005.pdf, accessed January 3, 2008.

resulted in a higher RPG than dramas. From these viewing patterns, Cineplex executives were able to distinguish the groups of customers that were particularly valuable. However, with no actual link to individual customers, they faced challenges targeting customers for specific movies and special events. Although market research was helpful on an aggregate level, Cineplex executives wanted to link box-office and concession purchases to a particular customer. Senior executives were supportive of Lewthwaite and the committee collecting this information through a customer relationship management program.

Film Exhibition

The first Canadian film screening took place in 1896, in Montreal, Quebec, and the earliest cinema opened

in 1906.[2] Attending the cinemas, also known as theaters, became a popular social activity; by the 1930s, a variety of independent and studio-owned theaters competed for customer attention. In 1979, Canada's first 18-theater multiplex opened in Toronto, Ontario, with several other multiplexes following in subsequent years. After a series of consolidations, by 2005, only three major theater companies existed in the Canadian movie and event exhibition market.

To showcase films, theaters required licensing from distributors who purchased rights from the production studios. The licensing agreement stipulated the "box-office split," also known as the percentage of

---

[2]Marcus Robinson, *"A History of Film Exhibition in Canada,"* Playback: Canada's Broadcast and Production Journal *(2005), accessed December 30, 2007.*

Table 1   Observations on the Motivations and Frequency of Movie Attendance by Age

Frequency, reasons for attendance*	Age Segment Labels					
	13–15 "Teenagers"	16–19 "Young Adults"	20–24 "Young Working"	25–35 "Young Families"	36–54 "Older Families"	55+ "Retirees"
Low (Special Events)				X	X	
Medium (Special Movies)						X
High (Routine)	X	X	X			

*These observations were drawn from an independent focus group study conducted in 2003.

"Teenagers" — Teenagers use the movie theatre and arcade for social gatherings because locations are accessible and movie-viewing is considered by parents to be an appropriate social activity. They are among the highest frequency of visitors.

"Young Adults" — This segment has access to a variety of other social venues because they can drive. Some in this segment are still in high school and others are post-secondary students; this segment visits theatres with high frequency.

"Young Working" — This segment has disposable income and they combine movies with socializing at other venues such as bars and restaurants. This segment has a high frequency of movie visits.

"Young Families" — This segment struggles to balance family and work-related obligations; they take their children to special movies occasionally.

"Older Families" — With a busy work and family life and varying interests within the household, older families attend theatres only for special events, and seldom attend as a family unit.

"Retirees" — This segment has significant free time to attend movies. They attend movies at a medium frequency.

proceeds that the theater received from a given film over a specified duration. Although both parties were mutually dependent, distributors held the balance of power and theaters relied heavily on concession revenues, of which they retained 100 per cent of the receipts. The margins on customers' purchases of concession treats and beverages were 65 per cent on average. Table 1 (below) shows one way of characterizing the motivations and frequency of movie-going behavior according to various age segment.[3]

Customer Relationship Management (CRM)

Customer relationship management (CRM) is a marketing approach in which a company collects individual purchasing information to improve its ability to understand and respond to customer desires and buying patterns. The information is typically stored in a central database from which the company managers can analyze trends and the purchasing behavior of particular market segments. A better understanding of customers enables organizations to develop targeted campaigns to increase marketing effectiveness,

such as restructuring its products and services. For Cineplex, a CRM program could also be used to share valuable information with concession suppliers and movie distributors. Through the sharing of this information, partners would be better able to develop products for Cineplex's customer base.

Although several mechanisms were available to collect customer information, the most frequently used systems were point-of-sale systems, which scanned barcodes on wallet-sized cards or key chains. A recent trend for CRM programs was to offer incentives such as discounts or points that could be collected and redeemed for merchandise in return for the customer's permission for the company to collect data on the customer's buying habits. Among the Canadian companies following this trend were Shoppers Drug Mart with the Optimum card program, Air Canada with the Aeroplan rewards program, and Office Depot and Boston Pizza which both participated in the Flight Miles card campaign.

Creating Loyalty

Even with 65 percent market share in Canada, Cineplex had to aggressively compete for customer attention. Ongoing film piracy, rental movies, concerts, and sporting events, combined with inconsistent

---

[3] *Janet Wasko*, How Hollywood Works, *Sage Publications, London, 2003.*

Survey Period: May–June 17, 2005 Respondents: 4,261

- 95 percent of respondents were interested in joining a Cineplex Entertainment movie rewards program

- 87 percent of respondents currently belonged to the Flight Miles program, and 39 percent identified Flight Miles as their "favorite rewards program"

- 31 percent of respondents were interested in the opportunity to collect Aeroplan points

- 56 percent of respondents indicated that they would be interested in receiving a 10 percent discount at concessions

- The majority of respondents suggested that they would be more inclined to join if there were no additional card to carry

EXHIBIT 3

Highlights from Cineplex E-mail Survey of Current Customers

box-office revenues, encouraged Cineplex managers to explore ways to increase customer spending and frequency, particularly within the lucrative 16- to 24-year-old segment. Before merging with Cineplex Odeon, Galaxy Entertainment had established the Galaxy Elite card, which offered customers the opportunity to accumulate points toward free movie viewing. Although the program had no CRM capabilities, it had been successful in driving customer traffic. During the merger with Cineplex, the program had been disbanded and Galaxy's customer traffic had promptly waned. In a survey of Cineplex customers in May and June 2005, 95 percent of respondents stated they were interested in joining a movie rewards program (see Exhibit 3).

In 2004, a steering committee composed of different department representatives was established to investigate CRM opportunities for Cineplex. After being put on hold during the acquisition of Famous Players, the committee was anxious to move forward in investigating a joint loyalty/CRM program. Senior managers had several concerns, primarily regarding data control and ownership, which would be relevant if the program were disbanded. Another criterion concerned resource requirements; a program this size would be a costly investment and would likely require new employees to manage it. Lewthwaite would need to prove that it was a worthy financial investment. Finally, the committee needed to consider the length of time required to establish a new database because most committee members believed that conclusive information on customer behavior could be drawn only from a minimum of 500,000 members. Further, although they thought that an investment in such a program could be largely beneficial for Cineplex, if implemented poorly, the organization's image and its ability to deliver customer value could suffer widespread harm. Lewthwaite knew that although the following partner options might not meet all the committee's criteria, she had to evaluate the most important considerations.

Loyalty Partner Options

Internal Development

Under this option, Cineplex managers would develop and operate the program; they would then know their brand best and would have complete control over the direction of the program and the data ownership. However, the organization would incur the entire cost estimated at $5.5 million in the first year with diminishing costs in subsequent years. The company would also be fully exposed to the financial risk of unredeemed points and could face difficulty in divesting the program if it proved unsuccessful; a new department would need to be created to manage the exit of the program. This option would also require a new database, which, depending on promotional effectiveness, could take several years to create. However, because of the unlimited data access and control, this option appealed to several members of the committee.

Flight Miles Partnership

With 72 percent of Canadian households as active members, Flight Miles was the top Canadian loyalty program.[4] This program gave cardholders the opportunity to earn leisure and travel rewards by purchasing products at various retailers across the country. Flight Miles executives viewed Cineplex as an opportunity to increase its youth membership, and their executives approached Cineplex executives to propose a special joint program. In this program, traditional Flight Miles cards would be used to collect points. Supplementary key tags would be issued for movie customers who opted to receive additional member benefits and rewards. Although the key tags might confuse other existing Flight Miles

---

[4] *"Air Miles Rewards Program,"* http://www.loyalty.com/what/airmiles/index.html, accessed November 2, 2007.

members, the proposal seemed to offer numerous benefits to Cineplex, including immediate entrance into a database of seven million people. Cineplex would also have the opportunity to access data from other Flight Miles partners, which would be beneficial in targeting specific retail buyers for niche films.

Lewthwaite estimated that access to the Flight Miles program would cost Cineplex yearly fees of approximately $5 million. Cineplex would also be required to pay $0.09 for each point issued. Lewthwaite thought users of the program would expect each movie transaction to be worth a minimum of 10 Flight Miles points. Cineplex would also be required to pay each time it accessed the data, which Flight Miles would own. A commitment of three years would be required, and if Cineplex decided to leave the program, it would lose all access to accumulated data. Lewthwaite recognized that Cineplex would be required to adhere to the partnership's decisions; no easy out was available if she did not like some aspect of the program after they signed the deal. To make the proposal more attractive, Flight Miles executives offered to contribute $250,000 to launch a Cineplex-designed and -initiated marketing campaign.

Scotiabank Proposal

Just as Lewthwaite and her committee sat down to examine the two options in further detail, Scotiabank executives approached Cineplex as a potential loyalty partner. The bank had a relationship with Cineplex derived from earlier corporate sponsorships. As one of the Big Five banks in Canada, Scotiabank offered a diverse range of financial services, including domestic banking, wholesale banking, and wealth management. Through 950 branches, Scotiabank served approximately 6.8 million Canadians in 2005.[5] Because banks competed in an intensely competitive marketplace, many banks aligned their brands with sporting events, venues, and other companies through corporate sponsorship.

Scotiabank executives were interested in acquiring new youth accounts and increasing overall transactions, so they viewed a partnership with Cineplex as a means to achieve their objectives while sharing financial risk. Scotiabank, which had prior experience with data management companies through its gold credit card program, proposed 50-50 cost-sharing. In return for partnering on the program, Scotiabank

expected naming rights on three major theaters and an exclusivity agreement for Scotiabank bank machines in all Cineplex theaters.

Scotiabank proposed a three-card rewards strategy. The basic reward card would be Cineplex-branded and used at theaters; the Scotiabank debit and credit cards would act as reward accelerators that accumulated additional points based on customers' purchasing habits. Any Scotiabank debit- or credit-card user enrolled in this program would be issued the Cineplex card, and holders of basic Cineplex theater cards would not be required to open an account at Scotiabank.

Lewthwaite considered that the multiple card system might discourage some customers who disliked carrying additional cards. Secondly, because it would be a 50-50 partnership, Cineplex's decision-making power would be constrained, and the direction of the program would be subject to mutual agreement. Also, owing to privacy laws, Cineplex executives would not be able to access individual-level banking information on the Scotiabank program users, data that might be helpful in targeting specific retail consumers. However, this program could be promoted in theaters and bank branches across the country. The costs to develop and maintain Cineplex's portion of the partnership were estimated to be $3 million, $1.7 million, and $1.9 million in years 1, 2, and 3 respectively.

Lewthwaite had to fully consider the potential benefits and drawbacks of each proposal and weigh them against Cineplex's criteria before recommending which partner to select. She also acknowledged other options were available beyond those that were presented. She knew that this decision could not be made without analyzing the potential reward structure of the program because the committee would expect a detailed net benefit analysis to support her recommendation.

Structuring the Reward Program

Lewthwaite believed it was essential to create a program that would appeal to customers. However, creating a program with valuable and easy-to-gain rewards might be too costly to carry out for an extended period of time. If Cineplex went forward with the Flight Miles partnership, an offer of 10 Flight Miles points per transaction would be required to align with cardholder expectations and could be supplemented with Cineplex discounts. If Cineplex went forward with other loyalty partnerships, it would have full design control over the reward structure of the program. Points could be earned based on box-office transactions, concession transactions, or both. The

[5] *Scotiabank,* 2005 Annual Report, *http://cgi. scotiabank.com/annrep2005/en/rbl_ov.html, accessed February 10, 2008.*

- Membership fee possibilities, a one-time fee of $2 to $5

- Increase in concession RPG of from 5 percent to 15 percent

- Net increase in attendance (actual incremental attendance times 1-the estimated cannibalization rate)

- Cannibalization rate assumptions
  Worst: 50 percent
  Most Likely: 25 percent
  Best: 12.5 percent

EXHIBIT 4

Summary of Revenues and Cannibalization Rates

points could then be used towards movies and concession items. Determining the number and value of points to be given per transaction and the required price per transaction were aspects that Lewthwaite needed to determine. She also needed to decide on the number of points required for particular rewards and whether different reward levels should be created.

Among the other options, Cineplex could reward cardholders with a permanent discount on theater tickets or concession items (or both) or possibly provide first access to special events. If Lewthwaite went forward with free or discounted movies and concession items, she would need to estimate the extent to which she would be rewarding customers who would have attended without being offered any rewards,[6] the so-called cannibalization rate (see Exhibit 4). To determine the other potential revenues, Lewthwaite needed to perform a sensitivity analysis around any increases in the concession RPG, which she hoped might increase by 5 to 15 percent for loyalty program members. She also had the option of charging a nominal one-time or annual membership fee of $2 to $5. Finally, as with any loyalty point program, Lewthwaite knew that only 40 percent of earned points would be unredeemed annually. She drafted a preliminary list of four unique reward structures she thought could be effective, but was unsure which, if any, would maximize customer appeal through retail value while minimizing costs (see Exhibit 5).

Selecting the Database Vendor

If a recommendation were made to move forward with program development, the committee would need to select a database vendor to manage customer data and the e-communication site. This vendor would need strong Web site design capabilities and a technology platform that could collect a variety of data on Cineplex's customers. Because Canada had only a few such vendors, Cineplex released a request for proposal (RFP) to three major companies: Alpha, Kappa, and Gamma. Each company responded with a unique proposal for the project (see Exhibit 6).

The Marketing Communications Campaign

Cineplex executives wanted to enroll 500,000 customers per year for the first three years in any loyalty program. After the first year, Lewthwaite believed the data bank would be large enough to derive meaningful customer information, and the organization could then focus on customer retention. To meet these targets, Cineplex would need to build substantial awareness of the program, particularly in markets where the Galaxy Elite card had previously existed. Launching the loyalty card would also require a marketing campaign to fit a variety of geographic markets, including Quebec, a province whose official language was French. Lewthwaite had a budget of $300,000, and she needed to make some creative decisions, including the name of the program, the marketing message to customers, and the media to be used to deliver the message.

In-Theater Advertising

In 2005, Cineplex served 5.3 million unique visitors annually with an average of 7.5 visits per guest. No costs were associated with in-theater advertising, and Lewthwaite knew it was an excellent way to reach the market but she was unsure which media would be most effective without overwhelming movie-goers. The program could be promoted on concession products, point-of-purchase displays, backlit posters, or on the Web site. The program could also be advertised to a captive audience via the digital pre-show or during the presentation of upcoming attractions.

---

[6]*Cannibalization refers to the number of free visits redeemed that would have been paid visits in the absence of a loyalty program.*

EXHIBIT 5

Preliminary Reward
Structure Options

	Option 1	Option 2	Option 3	Option 4
Membership fee	No	One-time $2	Annually $5	No
Permanent concessions discount	–	10%	15%	10%
Points?	Yes	Yes	No	Yes
Sign-up points	500	100	–	250
Points per adult movie transaction	100	100	–	100
Points per concession combo transaction	–	75	–	–

Reward Items and Maximum Retail Value

Points Required								
500	Free child admission	$ 8.50	–		–		–	
750	Free concession combo	$12.37	–		–		–	
1,000	Free adult admission	$10.95	Free adult admission	$10.95	–	Free adult admission	$10.95	
1,500	Free event admission*	$19.95	Free event admission	$19.95	–	Free adult admission/ concession combo	($23.32)	
2,000	–		–		–	Free adult/2 children admission	$27.95	
2,500	–		Night out package**	$37.47	–	–		

*Includes admission to the following viewings: the Metropolitan Opera, NHL series, or WWE series.

**A Night out package includes two adult movie admissions, two large sodas, and one large popcorn.

Newspaper Advertising

Lewthwaite wondered whether the target market would respond to regional newspaper advertisements. She knew that the committee was opposed to advertising in a national newspaper, such as the *Globe and Mail*, because it did not have strong reach in every market in which Cineplex operated. However, Cineplex was accustomed to promoting events through half-page ads in regional papers. Although this option would be more costly than advertising solely in a national paper, several more movie-going markets could be reached. The average weekly cost per half-page ad in the small to medium markets was $1,200, and $3,600 for larger markets, with a development cost of $850 for each advertisement. If this option were selected, Lewthwaite would need to determine in which papers to advertise, and the message and frequency of the insertions (see Exhibit 7).

Radio Advertising

Local radio advertisements could achieve significant coverage in key markets across Canada. The average weekly cost per 30-second commercial was $160 in small- and medium-sized markets and $225 in larger markets. Development of local radio ads would cost approximately $1,100 per city. Because Cineplex had used this medium for other events, particularly in rural theater markets, Lewthwaite was confident Cineplex could also negotiate free advertisement space on many radio station's Web sites.

Online Advertising

In addition to advertising on the Cineplex Web site the program could be promoted through various Web sites such as Google, Muchmusic.ca, MTV.ca, and canoe.qc.ca, a French-language news site. Costs

EXHIBIT 6

Summary of Cineplex's Request for Proposal

Program Overview
Cineplex Entertainment is looking into the possibility of creating a new entertainment-focused loyalty program. Members will earn points that can be redeemed for free movies or other entertainment-related rewards. An ongoing marketing program requiring a member database and Web site is required.

Vendors to Provide
• A proposed approach and high-level design concept for the Web site that is creative and functional • Pricing for the database and Web site build

Web Site Goals
• Acquire new customers and deepen relationships with existing customers by enticing them to sign up, then encouraging them to remain active in the loyalty program • Provide an easy way to sign up, check status of points earned, get information on rewards that can be earned, redeem points, and interact with other members • The site will be a major marketing channel to reach members. It will be used for viral and targeted online promotions • Provide an online community for members

Database Use
• For program administration, analysis, and reporting • For analysis and reporting on moviegoer's behavior and preferences • For marketing to customers

The Target Market
• Is very comfortable with the online environment, text messaging, downloading, and browsing • Wants and expects discounts and free offers in an attainable timeframe • Wants simplicity and convenience

Web Site Requires
• A public section accessible to all, a member's section accessible with member ID and password, and an administrative site to be used for customer support • Site must connect to program database to collect, maintain, retrieve, and report member data including demographic information and points data • Integration with Cineplex's POS equipment and mobile channels for marketing • Site will link to and from the sites of main partners and vendors • Site must be available in English and French

Vendors' Responses to the Cineplex Request for Proposal
Alpha
Alpha was a leading marketing firm specializing in loyalty programs and performance improvement. As a global company, Alpha's clients include American Express, Coca-Cola, Hewlett-Packard, and Microsoft. Alpha has served the Canadian marketplace since 1980, and its focus is helping organizations identify, retain, and build customer relationships in order to maximize profit and drive long-term success. With a history of designing and implementing loyalty programs, Alpha's technology platforms focused on customer behavior tracking and loyalty rewards fulfillment. In preparing its response, Alpha held focus groups to help determine what type of Web site appealed to Cineplex's target market. These groups indicated the importance of security, easy navigation, and keeping site content up-to-date; they also spoke out against pop-up advertisements. All respondents were familiar with e-newsletters, and noted that loyalty members should have the option to opt in, because they do not want to be overwhelmed with promotional messages. Alpha used this information in conjunction with Cineplex's specifications to present how the Web site would be designed. The approximate investment cost for the program design was $500,000 with $40,000 per month required for Web site upkeep.

Kappa
Known for managing data for the Royal Bank of Canada, Kappa was one of the largest global marketing agencies. With a strong focus on customer loyalty programs, Kappa offered a high standard in data privacy and security and was the undisputed industry leader in mobile marketing, which linked strongly to Cineplex's target market. The Kappa proposal focused on creating a youth-driven brand identity that engaged viewers to join the program through program incentives and links to third-party social networking sites, such as MySpace. With a significant portfolio of integrated loyalty program solutions, Kappa also had entertainment industry experience, having previously worked on technology platforms with Famous Players, the Toronto International Film Festival, and IMAX. Kappa's main differentiating factor was its proposal to have two distinct sites, one for members and one for non-members. Although similar in nature, one site would focus on member acquisition and program information while the other would focus on member retention through contest promotions and access to personal account activity. Approximate costs would be $1 million.

Gamma
Gamma, a competitor in the Canadian marketplace for four years, had vast experience in information technology strategy and a track record of developing CRM programs for leading organizations, such as Kaplan University and Citi Financial. Gamma's response to the RFP included a proposal to plan, design, and manage Cineplex's marketing and technology programs on its specialized marketing platform that supported all aspects of e-mail management and e-communication campaigns. This platform would also enable Cineplex to track members on an ongoing basis through different promotional mediums, such as Web advertisements and search functions, and to respond instantly to member behavior through messaging for those leaving the site. Gamma's offer was appealing because it included a fixed-price, fixed-time model. Gamma was unable to provide costs for data management because it was unsure of Cineplex's technical capabilities, but preliminary planning and design costs were estimated at around $200,000.

EXHIBIT 7

Large Media Markets

Market	Newspaper	Radio
Calgary	Calgary Herald	VIBE 98.5
Edmonton	Edmonton Journal	Sonic 102.9
Montreal	Montreal Gazette	Q92
Ottawa	Ottawa Citizen	BOB FM
Toronto	Toronto Star	Mix 99.9
Vancouver	Vancouver Sun	Z95 FM

Small- and Medium-Sized Media Markets

Market	Newspaper	Radio
Barrie	Barrie Examiner	Rock 95 FM
Cornwall	Standard Freeholder	Rock 101.9
Guelph	Guelph Mercury	Magic FM
Kitchener	Kitchener Record	KOOL FM
London	London Free Press	Fresh FM
North Bay	North Bay Nugget	EZ Rock
Owen Sound	Owen Sound Sun Times	Mix 106
Quebec City	Quebec City Journale	Le 93.3
Regina	Regina Leader Post	Z-99
Saskatoon	The Star Phoenix	C95
Sault Ste. Marie	Sault Ste. Marie Star	EZ Rock 100.5
St. Thomas	St. Thomas Times-Journal	Fresh FM
Sudbury	Sudbury Star	Big Daddy 103.9 FM
Thunderbay	Chronicle Journal	Rock 94
Windsor	Windsor Star	89X
Winnipeg	Winnipeg Free Press	Q94

EXHIBIT 8

Cost per Thousand
Impressions (in Cdn$)

Web Site	Big Box Advertisement	Banner Advertisement
google.ca	20	12
mtv.ca	27	35
muchmusic.ca	29	32
yahoo.ca	19	13
imdb.com	17	9
canoe.qc.ca	26	–

varied according to advertisement format and site (see Exhibit 8).

Grass Roots Initiatives

Lewthwaite had also considered smaller initiatives with the goal of spreading word-of-mouth publicity. Event teams could promote on college and university campuses or at highly visited attractions, thereby raising awareness for the program. Cineplex could also engage in corporate sponsorships. She was unsure what costs would be associated with these options.

Launch

Launching the program was the final recommendation to be made. Cineplex's head office was located in Toronto, Ontario, and the company operated in six provincial markets—Quebec, Ontario, Manitoba, Saskatchewan, Alberta, and British Columbia—but none of the four Atlantic provinces.

Lewthwaite would have to decide whether the program should be launched regionally or across all six provinces. In early 2006, Cineplex had completed the installation of a new point-of-sale platform, which had the technological capability to support a national loyalty rollout. A national launch was appealing to Lewthwaite because it would be cost-efficient and would accrue revenues faster than a regional rollout. However, it was also riskier than a regional rollout: any problem would affect all markets. A regional launch would give Cineplex the opportunity to resolve problems before full implementation. The regional rollout would be more expensive at completion, but it would allow Cineplex to stretch funds over a longer time period. If Lewthwaite recommended the regional option, she would need to decide how the regional launch would be phased in.

Lewthwaite knew several complex decisions needed to be made, and she had little time before the steering committee's meeting the following week. Having a more comprehensive understanding of customer behavior and demographics was important in improving Cineplex's success, but could a loyalty program be implemented in such a way to fit senior management's criteria? If she recommended going ahead with the program, which loyalty partner should she use? How should the rewards be structured and promoted? What would the promotional campaign entail, and how should the launch take place? As she leaned back in her chair, she knew it was going to be a very long week.

Case 4   Williams Coffee Pub: The Franchising Opportunity[1]

Richard Ivey School of Business
The University of Western Ontario

IVEY

Hui Zhang wrote this case under the supervision of Professor Greg Zaric solely to provide material for class discussion. The authors do not intend to illustrate either effective or ineffective handling of a managerial situation. The authors may have disguised certain names and other identifying information to protect confidentiality.

Copyright © Ivey Publishing.

All Rights Reserved. No part of the publication may be reproduced or transmitted in any form or by any means, or stored in a database or retrieval system without the written consent of Ivey Publishing. With respect to Ivey cases, Ivey Management Services prohibits any form of reproduction, storage or transmittal without its written permission. This material is not covered under authorization from any reproduction rights organization. To order copies or request permission to reproduce material, contact Ivey Publishing, Ivey Management Services, c/o Richard Ivey School of Business, The University of Western Ontario, London, Ontario, Canada, N6A 3K7; phone (519)661-3208, fax (519) 661-3882, email cases@ivey.uwo.ca

Version: (A) 2008-01-04

The Williams Coffee Pub Franchising Opportunity

Shuying Chen had been looking for business opportunities since she immigrated to London, Ontario. Her research led her to consider becoming a franchisee for Williams Coffee Pub (WCP). The WCP promotional materials indicated that, for a typical restaurant, annual sales could be up to $1.7 million with a profit margin of 17.5 percent. The possibility of $300,000 profit per year was very attractive to Chen, so she decided to do some more in-depth investigation. In addition to visiting the WCP Web site, she contacted a real estate broker and a successful WCP franchisee.

WCP required a one-time franchise fee of $35,000 plus tax that was valid for 10 years. The royalty fee was 6 percent of gross sales. WCP helped franchisees with site selection, store design, training, store-opening assistance, and marketing support. WCP also provided a complete product line of coffee, specialty coffee, and food products. To start the business, the franchisee had to purchase furniture and decorate the store and would also incur various professional fees at start-up. WCP required a 1.5 percent advertising fund contribution and, in addition, recommended that each store should invest a minimum of 1 percent of gross sales into local marketing initiatives.

Variable costs included food, beverage, and labor costs. Labor costs covered management, staff, payroll taxes, and the benefits. Other operating expenses incurred by the franchisee included utilities, supplies, cleaning, staff uniforms, bank charges, and credit card commissions. Average expenses in each category were reported on the WCP Web site (see Exhibit 1). Actual costs could vary depending on location, sales volumes, and the franchisee's management skills.

Annual sales can range from $600,000 to $1.7 million depending on location, seating capacity, quality of the management team, and other factors. Store sizes typically ranged from 1,500 square feet to 4,300 square feet. Chen contacted a real estate broker and found that annual rent in the rapidly growing Fanshawe/Hyde Park area of London would be approximately $25–$30/square feet, plus $6 per square foot of additional rent to cover property maintenance and her share of property taxes. Utility bills would be separate. If she opted to include a drive-through window, then the store could generate an additional $2,000 to $7,000 of sales per week.

Sales growth varied from store to store. Chen felt that she could reach 65 to 85 percent of full capacity by the end of the first month of operation and that she would reach full capacity in one to three years. Chen realized that she would need a loan to finance the start-up costs of this venture. She estimated the interest rate to be 7 percent per annum. If she achieved a positive balance, she would save it in a risk-free investment that earned annual interest of 3 percent.

---

[1] *This case has been written on the basis of published sources only. Consequently, the interpretation and perspectives presented in this case are not necessarily those of Williams Coffee Pub or any of its employees.*

EXHIBIT 1

The Average Expenses of Operating a Williams Coffee Pub Restaurant

Source: Williams Coffee Pub, current opportunities, www.williamscoffeepub.com.

Items	Average
Food/beverage/paper	33.00%
Total labor	31.50%
Other operating	9.50%
Local store marketing	1.00%
Royalties	6.00%
Ad fund	1.50%
Profit before occupancy costs	17.50%

Richard Ivey School of Business
The University of Western Ontario

IVEY

Bin Zhao wrote this case under the supervision of Professor Fernando Olivera solely to provide material for class discussion. The authors do not intend to illustrate either effective or ineffective handling of a managerial situation. The authors may have disguised certain names and other identifying information to protect confidentiality.

Copyright © Ivey Publishing.

All Rights Reserved. No part of the publication may be reproduced or transmitted in any form or by any means, or stored in a database or retrieval system without the written consent of Ivey Publishing. With respect to Ivey cases, Ivey Management Services prohibits any form of reproduction, storage or transmittal without its written permission. This material is not covered under authorization from any reproduction rights organization. To order copies or request permission to reproduce material, contact Ivey Publishing, Ivey Management Services, c/o Richard Ivey School of Business, The University of Western Ontario, London, Ontario, Canada, N6A 3K7; phone (519) 661-3208, fax (519) 661-3882, email cases@ivey.uwo.ca

Version: (A) 2007-03-07

On April 29, 2004, Linlin Chen—a sales manager of Allnation Import and Export Co. Ltd., a Chinese company located in Beicheng, Jiangsu province—was in her office studying the revenue report of all the export transactions she had completed in the previous three months. The numbers were telling a very good story. If the numbers continued to increase at the same rate as they had in the past 11 months, Chen knew that, for her, a promotion and a shareholder certificate would surely be on their way. While she was pleased with her success, Chen also felt compelled to face a decision that was looming large: Should she leave this successful career path to open her own business?

Overview of Allnation Import and Export Co. Ltd.

Founded in 1999, Allnation was one of the fastest growing private corporations in the foreign trade industry in Beicheng, Jiangsu. The company specialized in the export of textile fabrics, clothing, and electrical and mechanical products. Allnation's sales value had increased by about 50 percent annually since its opening. By the end of 2003, the company had approximately 42 employees and reported more than RMB5 million in net income,

putting Allnation among the top five foreign trading companies in Beicheng.

Allnation's rapid growth could be attributed to the following three factors: location, state policies regulating the formation of import-export companies, and the company's growth strategy. First, for a company like Allnation, Beicheng was an ideal Chinese city in which to start and develop its business. Beicheng, located in Yangzi Delta, was a well-known assembling base for the textile industry in China. Up until the end of 2002, more than 5,200 textile manufacturing enterprises with assets of more than RMB16 billion operated in the city. These enterprises produced more than 300 million garments, 30,000 tons of cotton yarns, 36 million meters of cotton cloth, nearly 60,000 tons of chemical fibers, and 4.65 million sets of bedclothes each year. Textile fabrics and garments accounted for 40 percent of Beicheng's total export value.

Second, state policies regarding importing and exporting made it possible for Allnation to develop business promptly by offering agency services to companies and manufacturing plants that did not have an import-export license. Before 1997, only state-owned companies were allowed to perform importing and exporting in China. Due to economic reform and the adoption of the marketing economy, this policy was finally changed in 1997. The government started to sell state-owned import-export companies to private investors. Meanwhile, the government permitted entrepreneurs to establish their own import-export companies but expected them to comply with some very strict requirements. For example, a new company must have at least two owners with no less than RMB5 million of registered capital in order to get approval from the State Industrial and Commercial Bureau (SICB). Moreover, not every new company that was approved by the SICB could acquire an import-export licence from the Chinese Ministry of Foreign Trade and Economic Cooperation, which subjected all new companies to another round of rigorous examination. Therefore, when Allnation started its business in 1999, only a limited number of import-export companies existed in Beicheng. Many companies desired to carry on import and export business but did not have the license. The two founders and chief executive officers (CEOs) of Allnation, Min Gao and Bing Feng, grabbed this opportunity to provide agency services at a competitive price to those companies.

Third, Allnation grew quickly through extensive recruitment and flexible management of salespeople.

In order to ensure stable and swift business development, Allnation increased recruitment of salespeople yearly. One of the comments made most often by Gao to his managers was, "The more salespeople you have, the more sales you get." Moreover, Allnation adopted a very open management policy towards its sales force. Newly hired salespeople could export any product of their choosing and could make decisions thereafter fully at their own discretion. Allnation management made it crystal clear that they would not interfere in any salesperson's business as long as a salesperson was bringing product orders and profit into the company. For example, Chen's supervisor did not even know what specific textile product she was selling. Her supervisor was primarily concerned with whether a salesperson was making or losing money for the company. In addition, Allnation provided its salespeople with excellent and timely funding support for their business operations. Allnation had been very successful in getting big loans from banks, and none of its salespeople's business transactions had been delayed or foiled because of lack of money.

Linlin Chen Before Joining Allnation

Linlin Chen graduated in July 1993 with a college diploma in English. In August 1993, she found her first job with the MaxSilver Company in Beicheng. MaxSilver was a large firm with over 250 employees and an annual profit of RMB8 million. The company carried out business in highly diversified areas: real estate, auto repair, paint production, and, more importantly, the production of yarns and fabrics. Chen joined MaxSilver as a clerical staff member in the general manager's office. About two years later, because of her outstanding performance in international business operations, she was promoted to the position of chief management assistant to the general manager, Chao Jiang. Chen became a top manager in the company's international business activities, as well as acting as a translator and interpreter. She was also responsible for providing assistance and information support for Jiang's daily administrative work and decision making.

Chen developed a strong interest in entrepreneurship when she worked for MaxSilver. Her boss, Chao Jiang, was one of the most successful entrepreneurs in Beicheng. Most clients with whom Chen interacted were also entrepreneurs or business people with high entrepreneurial spirits. She heard many stories from them about the challenges involved in starting and developing one's own business. During the last five years at MaxSilver, Chen also actively participated in establishing three new subsidiary companies within the textile industry, and she had witnessed the successes and failures of these three subsidiaries since their inception. She had learned so much from this experience that she began to think about the possibility of one day becoming an entrepreneur herself.

In 2000, Chen joined the EMBA program at East China Industrial and Technical University. The training that she acquired in her EMBA made her aware of the management problems that existed at MaxSilver. At a strategic level, one of MaxSilver's greatest problems was that, despite its involvement in a broad array of industries, it had not established its own competitive advantage in any of them. There were also management problems. Decision making was done primarily by Jiang (as owner of MaxSilver), despite the fact that he lacked critical knowledge of the wide range of industries in which his company operated. Jiang used meetings to announce his decisions and to assign certain people to certain jobs, rather than first inviting the managers to provide input. MaxSilver's managers, including Chen, were not truly "managing" at all: they were simply executing Jiang's decisions. Employees like Chen could spot many mistakes made with respect to important decisions but could do nothing to stop them. When Chen decided to quit her job in the fall of 2002, it was not because of the steady decline in MaxSilver's business. The reason was simple: she could no longer stand working in an organization where she was expected to carry out other people's poor business decisions and where no one was interested in her input. Chen longed for the sense of achievement that she would get from doing a challenging job.

Linlin Chen at Allnation

Chen joined Allnation as a sales manager right after she left MaxSilver in the fall of 2002. A sales manager in Allnation was an independent salesperson, not a manager in charge of a sales department. Chen had two main responsibilities: training technical staff who knew little about foreign trade or building their own sales record. As with any new salesperson at Allnation, she was allowed to specialize in the exporting of any product of her choice, and she decided to start with yarns because of two considerations. First, no one in the company was exporting yarns even though Beicheng was a city famous for producing quality yarns. Second, when she had worked for MaxSilver, Chen had accumulated some knowledge about yarns and about the equipment and techniques used to produce them. This gave her a built-in advantage in that she was not starting from scratch with respect to product knowledge. However, two big questions still remained: Where should she start, given the large variety of yarns available? And where could she find clients? After some deliberation, Chen formulated a rough plan: she could start looking for clients on the Internet and then provide them with the yarns they wanted. This was a very bold idea because searching for clients on the Internet was not a popular business practice in China at that time. Almost all of Chen's colleagues at Allnation believed that it was too risky to try to find business opportunities through the Internet. Even so, Chen preferred this plan because it involved low costs. More importantly, she believed that e-business would be widely accepted sooner or later, considering the increasingly high success rate of e-business in developed countries, and she wanted to give it a try.

Soon after Chen started her client search on the Internet in December 2002, she noticed two large markets for yarns: India and Pakistan. The yarns demanded by these two markets could be readily found in almost every yarn factory in Beicheng. Clients in India and Pakistan contacted Chen immediately after she sent them some product samples. In March 2003, money had already come in from the first transaction. Once orders had become relatively stable in the Indian and Pakistani markets, North America and Europe were the next on the list. In June 2003, Chen received her first order from a client in the United States, and she received several large orders from Europe and North America after that.

Chen found that the European and North American market was quite a contrast to the Indian and Pakistani market. Indian and Pakistani clients had a well-established market in their own countries and in Europe for their products, which were usually medium-grade or mediocre clothing produced in bulk orders. Indian and Pakistani clients came to the Chinese market to purchase very specific and commonly used yarn products at cheaper prices, as there was very little difference in product quality compared to the yarns manufactured in their home countries. Consequently, competition for the Indian and Pakistani market was extremely intense because these clients could easily switch from one supplier to another. A Chinese supplier who could sell the same product at the cheapest price and/or who could be the quickest to deliver the order would win the deal.

Compared with the Indian and Pakistani market, the competition for North America and Europe was less fierce and the profit much higher. This was because European and North American clients demanded highly customized yarns for their usually high-end products. European and North American clients rarely came to the Chinese market with any specific yarn product in mind. These clients came

with the designs of their end products and the concepts and notions embodied in the designs, and asked suppliers to provide them with the type of yarns that could bring their designs into reality. In order to make a deal, a Chinese supplier had to be able to understand the clients' notions and designs and had to help them find the right yarn product in China. In most—if not all—cases, there was no ready yarn product in the market. Chinese suppliers had to design the required yarn (including choice of color and pattern as well as selection of raw materials used to produce the yarn) based on their own understanding of a specific client's desired end product. Therefore, two challenges existed in the European and North American market for Chinese yarn suppliers. First, to be a yarn designer, a supplier should not only be able to grasp clients' novel notions and designs but also had to be thoroughly familiar with yarn production (including production techniques and equipment and options of raw materials). Second, a successful supplier was expected to have strong, co-operative relationships with qualified yarn producers. After all, not every yarn factory had the facilities to produce a highly customized yarn product, and even if they did, they might not be willing to take part in the experimentation process. A small quantity of specially designed yarn samples was very troublesome to produce and yielded little profit, and the supplier had no certainty of making a deal in the end. A deal would be gained only if the client liked the sample.

Chen was all that North American and European clients could ask for in an excellent supplier. She was so successful in the North American and European market that, in February 2004, she decided to concentrate solely on these two markets.

The Big Decision

When Chen left MaxSilver, she had wanted to challenge herself and put herself, and especially her judgment and decision-making capabilities, to the test; success in the North American and European market confirmed her belief in herself: She knew she had what it takes to be successful in the export trade of textile products. When she was still working for MaxSilver, Chen had allowed herself to dream about owning her own company. Although these thoughts had continued to grow after she had developed a stable and successful business in the North American and European market, she did not take them seriously until she attended a high school reunion in January 2004. At the reunion, Chen found that some of her friends had already opened their own companies and were excited to share their success stories.

Still other friends, having shared the same ambitions and plans as the successful group back at the time when they were just college graduates, were complaining about their bosses or companies and were unhappy about their career development. This sharp contrast was a shock to Chen, because in her eyes, the only difference between these two groups of friends was the determination of one group to put their ideas into action while the other chose to let dreams be dreams. She explained, "It is just like a drama, like two movies with very similar beginnings but unfolding in totally different plots and ending with totally different sequels. I was already in my early 30s. I had begun to feel time pressures, and I couldn't help wondering what ending I wanted for my own career."

Since the reunion, Chen had been thinking a lot about establishing her own company, but she could not make up her mind. The advantages of staying at Allnation were obvious and multiple. She did not need to worry about funding for business operations or finding co-operative yarn producers. Allnation was already a well-established company in Beicheng, and banks and yarn producers were eager to work with it. In addition, compared to running one's own business, working for Allnation involved much less risk.

However, Chen also felt compelled to think seriously about starting her career as an entrepreneur. Although she enjoyed the discretion and autonomy that working at Allnation gave her, she was not so sure about Allnation's future, given the company's growth strategy. Allnation's owners/chief executive officers, Gao and Feng, simply relied on expanding their sales force for business growth in export trade. In February 2004, when Gao and Feng announced their decision to invest in real estate, Chen was not sure whether this was the correct direction for Allnation to pursue. None of the top management knew the real estate market well enough to make this rather large decision, and no detailed market analysis had been done before or after the decision was made public. It seemed to her that the company was just blindly following the investment trends.

Given the fame of Beicheng's advanced textile industry and quality textile products, Chen wanted to focus exclusively on the export of textile products for her own career development. She did not think that her sales strategy and performance was duly recognized by top management in Allnation, and she believed that this lack of acknowledgement would continue if she chose to stay. Allnation evaluated every salesperson's performance in terms of the value of profit that each individual brought to the company. The company did not care what product one was selling or how much innovation and creativity one put into promoting it. Money-wise, Chen believed that her salary was not proportional to the value she created for Allnation.

Personally, Chen believed that she was ready to start her own business. Her expertise and skills in the area of yarn product design had gained her success in the North American and European market and would remain as the source of competitive advantage for her own company. There was no doubt that the clients would remain with her. Not only her extraordinary performance but also her excellent design ability made her rare as a supplier.

Chen was also confident in her own ability to run a firm independently because her EMBA training had equipped her with the required knowledge about strategic planning, finance, and management. Moreover, she preferred to work for herself because she did not like the sense of dependence or of being subordinate to others for promotions and salary. She valued autonomy and independence, and she liked the idea of driving her own career progress.

Furthermore, Chen noticed that the social environment in China had become very encouraging for entrepreneurship because of changes in government policies. In August 1999, upon the increasing failure rate of state-owned companies in the market economy since the economic reform, the government published its new policy about private enterprises. The new policy eliminated many rigorous limitations in establishing private enterprises (e.g., there was no longer an upper limit on the number of people employed within a private company). It also simplified the application approval procedures. Given this favorable new policy, the growth in the number of private enterprises was about 36 percent annually in China. In Beicheng, hundreds of entrepreneurs were starting their own businesses each year, and the number kept increasing after China entered the World Trade Organization in 2001. About 38 Beicheng companies were exporting textile products by the end of 2003. Chen worried that if she did not start her own business quickly enough, the market would become too competitive for her to enter.

Nonetheless, opening her own company was not an easy choice to make. Chen must bear all the risks involved in each transaction. She had to "sell" her own company to banks and yarn producers, and it would take some time to establish the credibility of a new company. More importantly, although it was easier to acquire the import-export license in 2004 than in previous years, she could not get approval from the State Industrial and Commercial Bureau if she did not have two things: RMB5 million as registered capital and a business partner for her company. Chen's savings were far below the required amount of registered capital. The money problem might be solved if she could find the right partner (which was easier said than done), but she did not like the idea at all. Over the years, she had heard and witnessed enough of the kinds of problems that could be caused by a partner. Besides, she preferred to have her own company; a company where she could continue doing what she had been doing, but now as her own boss and with her own decision-making process. However, given the relevant policies and rules, Chen did not see a way that she could open a new company without enough money and without a partner.

The Deadline

To reward and keep top salespeople, Gao and Feng would invite these salespeople to buy the company's shares at a discount price and offer them a promotion and salary raise. After looking at the most recent revenue report for her sales in the previous three months, Chen knew for sure that she would be on that list. This explained why she got a sudden call from the CEO's office and was told that she was going to have a meeting with both Gao and Feng on May 8, 2004. She had been wondering what the meeting was for because she was expected to report to only one of the CEOs for routine work and performance reviews. Chen could clearly see that she had to make up her mind about her career direction as soon as possible. Allnation had not gone public and had no plans to do so in the near future. According to the current rules of Allnation, only an invited group of employees could become shareholders. Shareholders could sell their shares to the company only three years after they purchased them. That is, if Chen used her savings to buy shares, her money would be locked into the company for at least three years. If she was determined to open her own company, she would have no choice but to reject buying any shares of the company. Allnation was doing well, and an employee who intended to stay would not reject the idea of becoming a shareholder. The dividends were excellent, and becoming a shareholder would certainly bring in a lot more money. If Chen chose to say no to the owners on May 8, they would wonder why.

It was already April 29. There were only nine days left for Linlin Chen to reach her final decision.

GLOSSARY

7(A) loan guaranty program. The main Small Business Administration (SBA) program available to small businesses operating through private-sector lenders providing loans that are guaranteed by the SBA; loan guarantees reserved for small businesses that are unable to secure financing through normal lending channels. (355)

10-K. A report that is similar to the annual report, except that it contains more detailed information about the company's business. (278)

accounts receivable. The money owed to a firm by its customers. (276)

acquirer. The surviving firm in an acquisition. (491)

acquisition. The outright purchase of one firm by another. (491)

adverse selection. The challenge a firm must face as it grows such that as the number of employees a firm needs increases, it becomes more difficult to find the right employees, place them in appropriate positions, and provide adequate supervision. (463)

advertising. Making people aware of a product or service in hopes of persuading them to buy it. (391)

advisory board. A panel of experts who are asked by a firm's managers to provide counsel and advice on an ongoing basis; unlike a board of directors, an advisory board possesses no legal responsibilities for the firm and gives nonbinding advice. (321)

agency theory. A management concept that argues that managers, because they are paid a salary, may not be as commited to the success of the businesses they manage as the owners, who capture the business's profits. This theory supports the notion of franchising, because franchisees are in effect the owners of the units they manage. (521)

area franchise agreement. Agreement that allows a franchisee to own and operate a specific number of outlets in a particular geographic area. (515)

articles of incorporation. Documents forming a legal corporation that are filed with the secretary of state's office in the state of incorporation. (255)

assignment of invention agreement. A document signed by an employee as part of the employment agreement that assigns the employer the right to apply for the patent of an invention made by the employee during the course of his or her employment. (420)

assumptions sheet. An explanation in a new firm's business plan of the sources of the numbers for its financial forecast and the assumptions used to generate them. (152, 287)

balance sheet. A snapshot of a company's assets, liabilities, and owner's equity at a specific point in time. (281)

barriers to entry. Conditions that create disincentives for a new firm to enter an industry. (175)

board of advisors. A panel of experts asked by a firm's management to provide counsel and advice on an ongoing basis. (150)

board of directors. A panel of individuals who are elected by a corporation's shareholders to oversee the management of the firm. (150, 318)

bootstrapping. Using creativity, ingenuity, or any means possible to obtain resources other than borrowing money or raising capital from traditional sources. (344)

brainstorming. A technique used to quickly generate a large number of ideas and solutions to problems; conducted to generate ideas that might represent product or business opportunities. (82)

brand. The set of attributes—positive or negative—that people associate with a company. (384)

brand equity. The set of assets and liabilities that is linked to a brand and enables it to raise a firm's valuation. (386)

brand management. A program that protects the image and value of an organization's brand in consumers' minds. (384)

break-even point. The point where total revenue received equals total costs associated with the output. (289)

budgets. Itemized forecasts of a company's income, expenses, and capital needs that are also important tools for financial planning and control. (276)

burn rate. The rate at which a company is spending its capital until it reaches profitability. (341)

business angels. Individuals who invest their personal capital directly in new ventures. (349)

business concept blind spot. An overly narrow focus that prevents a firm from seeing an opportunity that might fit its business model. (213)

business format franchise. By far the most popular approach to franchising in which the franchisor provides a formula for doing business to the franchisee along with training, advertising, and other forms of assistance. (514)

business license. A legal authorization to operate a business in a city, county, or state. (249)

business method patent. A patent that protects an invention that is or facilitates a method of doing business. (418)

business model. A company's plan for how it competes, uses its resources, structures its relationships, interfaces with customers, and creates value to sustain itself on the basis of the profits it generates. (49, 202)

business model innovation. Initiative that revolutionizes how products are sold in an industry. (203)

business plan. A written document describing all the aspects of a business venture, which is usually necessary to raise money and attract high-quality business partners. (49, 136)

buyback clause. A clause found in most founders' agreements that legally obligates the departing founder to sell to the remaining founders his or her interest in the firm if the remaining founders are interested. (244)

buying intentions survey. An instrument that is used to gauge customers' interest in a product or service. (108)

buzz. An awareness and sense of anticipation about a company and its offerings. (385)

C corporation. A legal entity that in the eyes of the law is separate from its owners. (255)

carry. The percentage of profits that the venture capitalist gets from a specific venture capital fund. (351)

certification marks. Marks, words, names, symbols, or devices used by a person other than its owner to certify a particular quality about a product or service. (424)

channel conflict. A problem that occurs when two or more separate marketing channels (e.g., online sales and retail sales) are in conflict over their roles in selling a firm's products or services. (398)

closely held corporation. A corporation in which the voting stock is held by a small number of individuals and is very thinly or infrequently traded. (255)

code of conduct. A formal statement of an organization's values on certain ethical and social issues. (238)

collective marks. Trademarks or service marks used by the members of a cooperative, association, or other collective group, including marks indicating membership in a union or similar organization. (424)

common stock. Stock that is issued more broadly than preferred stock and that gives the stockholders voting rights to elect the board of directors of the firm. (255)

competitive analysis grid. A tool for organizing the information a firm collects about its competitors to see how it stacks up against its competitors, provide ideas for markets to pursue, and identify its primary sources of competitive advantage. (188)

competitive intelligence. The information that is gathered by a firm to learn about its competitors. (188)

competitor analysis. A detailed evaluation of a firm's direct, indirect, and future competitors. (149, 170)

Computer Software Copyright Act. In 1980, Congress passed this act which amended previous copyright acts; now, all forms of computer programs are protected. (428)

concept statement. A preliminary description of a business that includes descriptions of the product or service being offered, the intended target market, the benefits of the product or service, the product's position in the market, and how the product or service will be sold and distributed. (106)

concept test. A representation of the product or service to prospective users to gauge customer interest, desirability, and purchase intent. (106)

constant ratio method of forecasting. A forecasting approach using the percent of sales method in which expense items on a firm's income statement are expected to grow at the same rate as sales. (289)

consultant. An individual who gives professional or expert advice. Consultants fall into two categories: paid consultants and consultants who are made available for free or at a reduced rate through a nonprofit or governmental agency. (325)

copyright. A form of intellectual property protection that grants to the owner of a work of authorship the legal right to determine how the work is used and to obtain the economic benefits of the work. (428)

copyright bug. The letter c inside a circle with the first year of publication and the author copyright owner (e.g., © 2007 Dell Inc). (429)

copyright infringement. Violation of another's copyright that occurs when one work derives from another work or is an exact copy or shows substantial similarity to the original copyrighted work. (430)

core competency. A unique skill or capability that transcends products or markets, makes a significant contribution to the customer's perceived benefit, is difficult to imitate, and serves as a source of a firm's competitive advantage over its rivals. (215)

core strategy. The overall manner in which a firm competes relative to its rivals. (213)

corporate entrepreneurship. Behavior orientation exhibited by established firms with an entrepreneurial emphasis that is proactive, innovative, and risk taking. (31)

corporate venture capital. A type of capital similar to traditional venture capital, except that the money comes from corporations that invest in new ventures related to their areas of interest. (353)

corporation. A separate legal entity organized under the authority of a state. (254)

corridor principle. States that once an entrepreneur starts a firm and becomes immersed in an industry, "corridors" leading to new venture opportunities become more apparent to the entrepreneur than to someone looking in from the outside. (78)

cost-based pricing. A pricing method in which the list price is determined by adding a markup percentage to the product's cost. (390)

cost leadership strategy. Generic strategy in which firms strive to have the lowest costs in the industry relative to competitors' costs and typically attract customers on the basis of price. (214)

cost of sales. All of the direct costs associated with producing or delivering a product or service, including the material costs and direct labor costs (also cost of goods sold). (280)

cost reduction strategy. A marketing strategy which is accomplished through achieving lower costs than industry incumbents through process improvements. (185)

creative destruction. The process by which new products and technologies developed by entrepreneurs over time make current products and technologies obsolete; stimulus of economic activity. (45)

creativity. The process of generating a novel or useful idea. (79)

current assets. Cash plus items that are readily convertible to cash, such as accounts receivable, inventories, and marketable securities. (281)

current liabilities. Obligations that are payable within a year, including accounts payable, accrued expenses, and the current portion of long-term debt. (281)

current ratio. A ratio that equals the firm's current assets divided by its current liabilities. (283)

customer advisory boards. Panel of individuals set up by some companies to meet regularly to discuss needs, wants, and problems that may lead to new product, service, or customer service ideas. (85)

customer interface. The way in which a firm interacts with its customers. (219)

day-in-the-life research. A form of anthropological research used by companies to make sure customers are satisfied and to probe for new product ideas by sending researchers to the customers' homes or business. (85)

debt financing. Getting a loan; most common sources of debt financing are commercial banks and the Small Business Administration (SBA) guaranteed loan program. (346)

debt-to-equity ratio. A ratio calculated by dividing the firm's long-term debt by its shareholders' equity. (276)

declining industry. An industry that is experiencing a reduction in demand. (184)

derivative works. Works that are new renditions of something that is already copyrighted, which are also copyrightable. (428)

design patents. The second most common type of patent covering the invention of new, original, and ornamental designs for manufactured products. (419)

differentiation strategy. A strategy that firms use to provide unique or different products to customers. Firms using this strategy typically compete on the basis of quality, service, timeliness, or some other dimension that creates unique value for customers. (214)

disintermediation. The process of eliminating layers of intermediaries, such as distributors and retailers, to sell directly to customers. (398)

distribution channel. The route a product takes from the place it is made to the customer who is the end user. (396)

double taxation. Form of taxation in which a corporation is taxed on its net income. When the same income is distributed to shareholders in the form of dividends, it is taxed again on shareholders' personal income tax returns. (255)

due diligence. The process of investigating the merits of a potential venture and verifying the key claims made in the business plan. (352)

Economic Espionage Act. Passed in 1996, an act that makes the theft of trade secrets a crime. (433)

economies of scale. A phenomenon that occurs when mass-producing a product results in lower average costs. (176, 456)

efficiency. How productively a firm utilizes its assets relative to its rate of return. (276)

elevator speech (or pitch). A brief, carefully constructed statement that outlines the merits of a business opportunity. (346)

emerging industry. A new industry in which standard operating procedures have yet to be developed. (183)

employer identification number (EIN) A tax identification number; is used in filing various tax returns. (250)

entrepreneurial alertness. The ability to notice things without engaging in deliberate search. (78)

entrepreneurial firms. Companies that bring new products and services to market by creating and seizing opportunities. (42)

entrepreneurial intensity. The position of a firm on a conceptual continuum that ranges from highly conservative to highly entrepreneurial. (31)

entrepreneurial services. Those services that generate new market, product, and service ideas. (463)

entrepreneurship. The process by which individuals pursue opportunities without regard to resources they currently control. (30)

equity financing. A means of raising money by exchanging partial ownership in a firm, usually in the form of stock, for funding. (346)

ethical dilemma. A situation that involves doing something that is beneficial to oneself or the organization, but may be unethical. (240)

ethics training programs. Programs designed to teach employees how to respond to the types of ethical dilemmas that might arise on their jobs. (240)

exclusive distribution arrangements. An agreement that gives a retailer or other intermediary the exclusive rights to sell a company's products in a specific area for a specific period of time. (399)

execution intelligence. The ability to fashion a solid business idea into a viable business is a key characteristic of successful entrepreneurs. (37)

executive summary. A quick overview of the entire business plan that provides a busy reader everything that he or she needs to know about the distinctive nature of the new venture. (144)

external growth strategies. Growth strategies that rely on establishing relationships with third parties, such as mergers, acquisitions, strategic alliances, joint ventures, licensing, and franchising. (489)

fair use. The limited use of copyright material for purposes such as criticism, comment, news reporting, teaching, or scholarship. (430)

fast-track program. A provision in the SBIR Program in which some applicants can simultaneously submit Phase I and Phase II grant applications. (359)

feasibility analysis. A preliminary evaluation of a business idea to determine if it is worth pursuing. (102)

fictitious business name permit. A permit that's required for businesses that plan to use a fictitious name, which is any name other than the business owner's name (also called dba or doing business as). (250)

fiduciary obligation. The obligation to always act in another's best interest; it is a mistake to assume that a franchisor has a fiduciary obligation to its franchisees. (533)

final prospectus. Documents issued by the investment bank after the Securities and Exchange Commission (SEC) has approved the offering that sets a date and issuing price for the offering. (354)

financial feasibility analysis. A preliminary financial assessment of a new venture that considers the total start-up cash needed, financial performance of similar businesses, and the overall financial attractiveness of the proposed venture. (115)

financial management. The process of raising money and managing a company's finances in a way that achieves the highest rate of return. (274)

financial ratios. Ratios showing the relationships between items on a firm's financial statements that are used to discern whether a firm is meeting its financial objectives and how it stacks up against industry peers. (277)

financial statements. Written reports that quantitatively describe a firm's financial health. (276)

financing activities. Activities that raise cash during a certain period by borrowing money or selling stock, and/or use cash during a certain period by paying dividends, buying back outstanding stock, or buying back outstanding bonds. (285)

first-mover advantage. A sometimes significant advantage, created by the opportunity to establish brand recognition and/or market power, gained by the first company to produce a product or service or the first company to move into a market. (183)

first-to-invent rule. States that first person to invent an item or process is given preference over another person who is first to file a patent application. (420)

fixed assets. Assets used over a longer time frame, such as real estate, buildings, equipment, and furniture. (281)

fixed costs. The costs that a company incurs in operating a business whether it sells something or not (e.g., overhead). (456)

focus group. A gathering of five to ten people who have been selected based on their common characteristics relative to the issue being discussed; conducted to generate ideas that might represent product or business opportunities. (83)

follow-me-home testing. A product testing methodology in which a company sends teams of testers to the homes or businesses of users to see how its products are working. (128)

follow-on funding. Additional funding for a firm following the initial investment made by investors. (352)

forecasts. Estimates of a firm's future income and expenses, based on its past performance, its current circumstances, and its future plans. (276)

founders' agreement. A written document that deals with issues such as the relative split of the equity among the founders of a firm, how individual founders will be compensated for the cash or the "sweat equity" they put into the firm, and how long the founders will have to remain with the firm for their shares to fully vest (also shareholders' agreement). (244)

founding team. A team of individuals chosen to start a new venture; has an advantage over firms started by an individual because a team brings more talent, resources, ideas, and professional contacts to a new venture than does a sole entrepreneur. (313)

fragmented industry. An industry characterized by a large number of firms approximately equal in size. (183)

franchise agreement. The document that consummates the sale of a franchise, which typically contains two sections: (1) the purchase agreement and (2) the franchise or license agreement. (533)

Franchise Disclosure Document (FDD). Accepted in all 50 states and part of Canada, a lengthy document that contains 23 categories of information that give a prospective franchisee a broad base of information about the background and financial health of the franchisor. (532)

franchisee. An individual or firm that enters into a franchise agreement and pays an initial fee and an ongoing royalty to an franchisor in exchange for using the franchisor's trademark and method of doing business. (513)

franchising. A form of business organization in which a firm that already has a successful product or service (franchisor) licenses its trademark and method of doing businesses to other businesses (franchisees) in exchange for an initial franchise fee and an ongoing royalty. (513)

franchisor. A firm with a successful product or service that enters into a franchising agreement to license its trademark and method of doing business to other businesses in exchange for fee and royalty payments. (513)

fulfillment and support. The way a firm's product or service "goes to market" or how it reaches its customers; also, the channels a company uses and the level of customer support it provides. (220)

full business plan. A document that spells out a company's operations and plans in much more detail than a summary business plan; the format that is usually used to prepare a business plan for an investor. (142)

general partnership. A form of business organization in which two or more people pool their skills, abilities, and resources to run a business. (253)

geographic expansion. An internal growth strategy in which an entrepreneurial business grows by simply expanding from its original location to additional geographical sites. (486)

geographic roll-up strategy. When one firm starts acquiring similar firms that are located in different geographic areas. (183)

global industry. An industry that is experiencing significant international sales. (185)

global strategy. An international expansion strategy in which firms compete for market share by using the same basic approach in all foreign markets. (185)

guerilla marketing. A low-budget approach to marketing that relies on ingenuity, cleverness, and surprise rather than traditional techniques. (396)

heterogeneous team. A team whose individual members are diverse in terms of their abilities and experiences. (313)

historical financial statements. Reflects past performance and are usually prepared on a quarterly and annual basis. (278)

homogenous team. A team whose individual members' experiences and areas of expertise are very similar to one another. (313)

idea. A thought, impression, or notion. (67)

idea bank. A physical or digital repository for storing ideas. (85)

idea–expression dichotomy. The legal principle describing the concept that although an idea is not able to be copyrighted, the specific expression of an idea is. (429)

illiquid. Describes stock in both closely held and private corporations, meaning that it typically isn't easy to find a buyer for the stock. (256)

improving an existing product or service. Enhancing a product or service's quality by making it larger or smaller, making it easier to use, or making it more up-to-date, thereby increasing its value and price potential. (483)

income statement. A financial statement that reflects the results of the operations of a firm over a specified period of time: prepared on a monthly, quarterly, or annual basis. (279)

individual franchise agreement. The most common type of franchise agreement, which involves the sale of a single franchise for a specific location. (515)

industry. A group of firms producing a similar product or service, such as airlines, fitness drinks, or electronic games. (110, 170)

industry analysis. Business research that focuses on the potential of an industry. (170)

industry/market feasibility analysis. An assessment of the overall appeal of the industry and target market for the product or service being proposed. (113)

infomercial. A television commercial that runs as long as a television show and usually includes a pitch selling an item directly to the public. (394)

initial public offering (IPO). The first sale of a company's stock to the public and an important milestone for a firm for four reasons: it is a way to raise equity capital; it raises a firm's public profile; it is a liquidity event; and it creates another form of currency (company stock) that can be used to grow the company. (353)

innovation. The process of creating something new, which is central to the entrepreneurial process. (45)

inside director. A person on a firm's board of directors who is also an officer of the firm. (318)

insourcing. An approach that takes place when a service provider comes inside a partner's facilities and helps the partner design and manage its supply chain. (218)

intellectual property. Any product of human intellect, imagination, creativity, or inventiveness that is intangible but has value in the marketplace and can be protected through tools such as patents, trademarks, copyrights, and trade secrets. (86, 413)

intellectual property audit. A firm's assessment of the intellectual property it owns. (435)

intent-to-use trademark application. An application based on the applicant's intention to register and use a trademark. (427)

interference. An administrative proceeding overseen by a judge, which takes place when there is a dispute regarding who was the first person to invent a product. (421)

internal growth strategies. Growth strategies that rely on efforts generated within the firm itself, such as new product development, other product-related strategies, or international expansion. (480)

international new ventures. Businesses that, from inception, seek to derive significant competitive advantage by using their resources to sell products or services in multiple countries. (487)

intranet. A privately maintained Internet site that can be accessed only by authorized users. (85)

invention logbook. Documentation of the dates and activities related to the development of a particular invention. (420)

inventory. A company's merchandise, raw materials, and products waiting to be sold. (276)

investing activities. Activities that include the purchase, sale, or investment in fixed assets, such as real estate and buildings. (285)

investment bank. A financial institution that acts as an underwriter or agent for a firm issuing securities. (353)

joint venture. An entity created when two or more firms pool a portion of their resources to create a separate, jointly owned organization. (498)

Lanham Act. An act of Congress, passed in 1946, that spells out what is protected under trademark law. (425)

leadership strategy. A competitive strategy in which the firm tries to become the dominant player in the industry. (184)

lease. A written agreement in which the owner of a piece of property allows an individual or business to use the property for a specified period of time in exchange for regular payments. (358)

liability of newness. Situation that often causes new firms to falter because the people who start the firms can't adjust quickly enough to their new roles, and because the firm lacks a "track record" with customers and suppliers. (310)

licensee. A company that purchases the right to use another company's intellectual property. (495)

licensing. The granting of permission by one company to another company to use a specific form of its intellectual property under clearly defined conditions. (493)

licensing agreement. The formal contract between a licensor and licensee. (495)

licensor. The company that owns the intellectual property in a licensing agreement. (495)

lifestyle firms. Businesses that provide their owners the opportunity to pursue a particular lifestyle and earn a living while doing so (e.g., ski instructors, golf pros, and tour guides). (42)

limited liability company (LLC). A form of business organization that combines the limited liability advantage of the corporation with the tax advantages of the partnership. (257)

limited partnership. A modified form of a general partnership that includes two classes of owners: general partners and limited partners. The general partners are liable for the debts and obligations of the partnership, but the limited partners are liable only up to the amount of their investment. The limited partners may not exercise any significant control over the organization without jeopardizing their limited liability status. (254)

limited partnership agreement. Sets forth the rights and duties of the general and limited partners, along with the details of how the partnership will be managed and eventually dissolved. (254)

line of credit. A borrowing "cap" is established and borrowers can use the credit at their discretion; requires periodic interest payments. (354)

link joint venture. A joint venture in which the position of the parties is not symmetrical and the objectives of the partners may diverge. (499)

liquid market. A market in which stock can be bought and sold fairly easily through an organized exchange. (255)

liquidity. The ability to sell a business or other asset quickly at a price that is close to its market value; also, a company's ability to meet its short-term financial obligations. (251, 275)

liquidity event. An occurrence such as a new venture going public, finding a buyer, or being acquired by another company that converts some or all of a company's stock into cash. (346)

long-term liabilities. Notes or loans that are repayable beyond one year, including liabilities associated with purchasing real estate, buildings, and equipment. (281)

managerial capacity problem. The problem that arises when the growth of a firm is limited by the managerial capacity (i.e., personnel, expertise, and intellectual resources) that a firm has available to investigate and implement new business ideas. (463)

managerial services. The routine functions of the firm that facilitate the profitable execution of new opportunities. (463)

market analysis. An analysis that breaks the industry into segments and zeros in on the specific segment (or target market) to which the firm will try to appeal. (148)

market leadership. The position of a firm when it is the number-one or the number-two firm in an industry or niche market in terms of sales volume. (457)

market penetration strategy. A strategy designed to increase the sales of a product or service through greater marketing efforts or through increased production capacity and efficiency. (483)

market segmentation. The process of studying the industry in which a firm intends to compete to determine the different potential target markets in that industry. (149, 379)

marketing alliances. Typically matches a company with a distribution system with a company with a product to sell in order to increase sales of a product or service. (496)

marketing mix. The set of controllable, tactical marketing tools that a firm uses to produce the response it wants in the target market; typically organized around the four Ps—product, price, promotion, and place (or distribution). (386)

marketing strategy. A firm's overall approach for marketing its products and services. (149)

master franchise agreement. Similar to an area franchise agreement, but in addition to having the right to operate a specific number of locations in a particular area, the franchisee also has the right to offer and sell the franchise to other people in the area. (515)

mature industry. An industry that is experiencing slow or no increase in demand, has numerous (rather than new) customers, and has limited product innovation. (184)

mediation. A process in which an impartial third party (usually a professional mediator) helps those involved in a dispute reach an agreement. (247)

merchandise and character licensing. The licensing of a recognized trademark or brand, which the licensor typically controls through a registered trademark or copyright. (493)

merger. The pooling of interests to combine two or more firms into one. (491)

milestone. In a business plan context, a noteworthy event in the past or future development of a business. (146)

mission statement. A statement that describes why a firm exists and what its business model is supposed to accomplish. (146, 213)

moderate risk takers. Entrepreneurs who are often characterized as willing to assume a moderate amount of risk in business, being neither overly conservative nor likely to gamble. (40)

moral hazard. A problem a firm faces as it grows and adds personnel; the assumption is that new hires will not have the same ownership incentives or be as motivated to work as hard as the original founders. (463)

multidomestic strategy. An international expansion strategy in which firms compete for market share on a country-by-country basis and vary their product or services offerings to meet the demands of the local market. (185)

multiple-unit franchisee. An individual who owns and operates more than one outlet of the same franchisor, whether through an area or a master franchise agreement. (515)

net sales. Total sales minus allowances for returned goods and discounts. (280)

network entrepreneurs. Entrepreneurs who identified their idea through social contacts. (79)

networking. Building and maintaining relationships with people whose interests are similar or whose relationship could bring advantages to a firm. (316)

new product development. The creation and sale of new products (or services) as a means of increasing a firm's revenues. (481)

new-venture team. The group of founders, key employees, and advisors that move a new venture from an idea to a fully functioning firm. (114, 310)

niche market. A place within a large market segment that represents a narrow group of customers with similar interests. (380)

niche strategy. A marketing strategy that focuses on a narrow segment of the industry. (184)

noncompete agreement. An agreement that prevents an individual from competing against a former employer for a specific period of time. (247)

nondisclosure agreement. A promise made by an employee or another party (such as a supplier) to not disclose a company's trade secrets. (247)

one year after first use deadline. Requirement that a patent must be filed within one year of when a product or process was first offered for sale, put into public use, or was described in any printed publication. It this requirement is violated, the right to apply for a patent is forfeited. (418)

operating activities. Activities that affect net income (or loss), depreciation, and changes in current assets and current liabilities other than cash and short-term debt. (284)

operating expenses. Marketing, administrative costs, and other expenses not directly related to producing a product or service. (280)

operational business plan. A blueprint for a company's operations; primarily meant for an internal audience. (142)

opportunity. A favorable set of circumstances that creates a need for a new product, service, or business. (66)

opportunity gap. An entrepreneur recognizes a problem and creates a business to fill it. (66)

opportunity recognition. The process of perceiving the possibility of a profitable new business or a new product or service. (77)

organic growth. Internally generated growth within a firm that does not rely on outside intervention. (480)

organizational chart. A graphic representation of how authority and responsibility are distributed within a company. (151)

organizational feasibility analysis. A study conducted to determine whether a proposed business has sufficient management expertise, organizational competence, and resources to be successful. (113)

other assets. Miscellaneous assets including accumulated goodwill. (281)

outside director. Someone on a firm's board of directors who is not employed by the firm. (318)

outsourcing. Work that is done for a company by people other than the company's full-time employees. (485)

owner's equity. The equity invested in the business by its owner(s) plus the accumulated earnings retained by the business after paying dividends. (281)

pace of growth. The rate at which a firm is growing on an annual basis. (456)

partnership agreement. A document that details the responsibility and the ownership shares of the partners involved with an organization. (253)

passion for their business. An entrepreneur's belief that his or her business will positively influence people's lives; one of the characteristics of successful entrepreneurs. (33)

patent. A grant from the federal government conferring the rights to exclude others from making, selling, or using an invention for the term of the patent. (417)

patent infringement. This is when one party engages in the unauthorized use of another's patent. (422)

percent of sales method. A method for expressing each expense item as a percent of sales. (288)

piercing the corporate veil. The chain of effects that occurs if the owners of a corporation don't file their yearly payments, neglect to pay their annual fees, or commit fraud, which may result in the court ignoring the fact that a corporation has been established, and the owners could be held personally liable for actions for the corporation. (255)

place. The marketing mix category that encompasses all of the activities that move a firm's product from its place of origin to the consumer (also distribution). (396)

plant patents. Patents that protect new varieties of plants that can be reproduced asexually by grafting or cross-breeding rather than by planting seeds. (419)

position. How the entire company is situated relative to its competitors. (146, 170)

preferred stock. Stock that is typically issued to conservative investors, who have preferential rights over common stockholders in regard to dividends and to the assets of the corporation in the event of liquidation. (255)

preliminary prospectus. A document issued by an investment bank that describes the potential offering to the general public while the SEC is conducting an investigation of the offering (also red herring). (354)

press kit. A folder typically distributed to journalists and made available online that contains background information about a company and includes a list of the company's most recent accomplishments. (395)

price. The amount of money consumers pay to buy a product; one of the four Ps in a company's marketing mix. (389)

price/earnings (P/E) ratio. A simple ratio that measures the price of a company's stock against its earnings. (281)

price-quality attribution. The assumption consumers naturally make that the higher-priced product is also the better-quality product (390).

primary research. Research that is original and is collected firsthand by the entrepreneur by, for example, talking to potential customers and key industry participants. (103)

prior entrepreneurial experience. Prior start-up experience; this experience has been found to be one of the most consistent predictors of future entrepreneurial performance. (314)

private corporation. A corporation in which all of the shares are held by a few shareholders, such as management or family members, and the stock is not publicly traded. (255)

private placement. A variation of the IPO in which there is a direct sale of an issue of securities to a large institutional investor. (354)

product. The element of the marketing mix that is the good or service a company offers to its target market; often thought of as something having physical form. (388)

product and trademark franchise. An arrangement under which the franchisor grants to the franchisee the right to buy its product and use its trade name. (514)

product attribute map. a map which illustrates a firm's positioning strategy relative to it's major rivals. (381)

product/customer focus. A defining characteristic of successful entrepreneurs that emphasizes producing good products with the capability to satisfy customers. (36)

product line extension strategy. A strategy that involves making additional versions of a product so they will appeal to different clientele. (485)

product/market scope. A range that defines the products and markets on which a firm will concentrate. (213)

product/service feasibility analysis. An assessment of the overall appeal of the product or service being proposed. (105)

productive opportunity set. The set of opportunities the firm feels it is capable of pursuing. (463)

pro forma balance sheet. Financial statements that show a projected snapshot of a company's assets, liabilities, and owner's equity at a specific point in time. (294)

pro forma financial statements. Projections for future periods, based on a firm's forecasts, and typically completed for two to three years in the future. (153, 279)

pro forma income statement. A financial statement that shows the projected results of the operations of a firm over a specific period. (293)

pro forma statement of cash flows. A financial statement that shows the projected flow of cash into and out of a company for a specific period. (295)

profit margin. A measure of a firm's return on sales that is computed by dividing net income by average net sales. (281)

profitability. The ability to earn a profit. (275)

promotion. The marketing mix category that includes the activities planned by a company to communicate the merits of its product to its target market with the goal of persuading people to buy the product. (391)

prototype. The first physical depiction of a new product. (152)

provisional patent application. A part of patent law that grants "provisional rights" to an inventor for up to one year, pending the filing of a complete and final application. (421)

public corporation. A corporation that is listed on a major stock exchange, such as the New York Stock Exchange or the NASDAQ, in which owners can sell their shares at almost a moment's notice. (255)

public relations. The efforts a company makes to establish and maintain a certain image with the public through networking with journalists and others to try to interest them in saying or writing good things about the company and its products. (394)

ratio analysis. Ratios showing the relationships between items on a firm's financial statements that are used to discern whether a firm is meeting its financial objectives and how it stacks up against industry peers. (154)

reference account. An early user of a firm's product who is willing to give a testimonial regarding his or her experience with the product. (389)

regression analysis. A statistical technique used to find relationships between variables for the purpose of predicting future values. (288)

relevant industry experience. Experience in the same industry as an entrepreneur's current venture that includes a network of industry contacts and an understanding of the subtleties of the industry. (314)

resource leverage. The process of adapting a company's core competencies to exploit new opportunities. (215)

road show. A whirlwind tour taken by the top management team of a firm wanting to go public; consists of meetings in key cities where the firm presents its business plan to groups of investors. (354)

rounds. Stages of subsequent investments made in a firm by investors. (352)

salary-substitute firms. Small firms that yield a level of income for their owner or owners that is similar to what they would earn when working for an employer (e.g., dry cleaners, convenience stores, restaurants, accounting firms, retail stores, and hairstyling salons). (41)

sales forecast. A projection of a firm's sales for a specified period (such as a year); though most firms forecast their sales for two to five years into the future. (287)

Sarbanes-Oxley Act. A federal law that was passed in response to corporate accounting scandals involving prominent corporations, like Enron and WorldCom. (353)

SBA Guaranteed Loan Program. An important source of funding for small businesses in general in which approximately 50 percent of the 9,000 banks in the United States participate. (355)

SBIR Program. Small Business Innovation Research (SBIR) competitive grant program that provides over $1 billion per year to small businesses for early stage and development projects. (359)

scale joint venture. A joint venture in which the partners collaborate at a single point in the value chain to gain economies of scale in production or distribution. (499)

secondary market offering. Any later public issuance of shares after the initial public offering. (353)

secondary meaning. This arises when, over time, consumers start to identify a trademark with a specific product. For example, the name CHAP STICK for lip balm was originally considered to be descriptive, and thus not afforded trademark protection. (427)

secondary research. Data collected previously by someone else for a different purpose. (103)

service. An activity or benefit that is intangible and does not take on a physical form, such as an airplane trip or advice from an attorney. (388)

service marks. Similar to ordinary trademarks but used to identify the services or intangible activities of a business rather than a business's physical product. (424)

shareholders. Owners of a corporation who are shielded from personal liability for the debts and obligations of the corporation. (255)

signaling. The act of a high-quality individual agreeing to serve on a company's board of directors, which indicates that the individual believes that the company has the potential to be successful. (319)

single-purpose loan. One common type of loan in which a specific amount of money is borrowed that must be repaid in a fixed amount of time with interest. (354)

skills profile. A chart that depicts the most important skills that are needed and where skills gaps exist. (316)

sole entrepreneurs. Entrepreneurs who identified their business idea on their own. (79)

sole proprietorship. The simplest form of business organization involving one person, in which the owner maintains complete control over the business and business losses can be deducted against the owner's personal tax return. (251)

sources and uses of funds statement. A document, usually included in the financial section of a business plan, that lays out specifically how much money a firm needs, where the money will come from, and what the money will be used for. (152)

spin-in. A transaction that takes place when a large firm that has a small equity stake in a small firm, decided to acquire a 100% interest in the firm. (499)

spin-out. The opposite of a spin-in that occurs when a larger company divests itself of one of its smaller divisions. (499)

stability. The strength and vigor of the firm's overall financial posture. (276)

statement of cash flows. A financial statement summarizing the changes in a firm's cash position for a specified period of time and detailing why the changes occurred. Similar to a month-end bank statement, it reveals how much cash is on hand at the end of the month as well as how the cash was acquired and spent during the month. (283)

stock options. Special form of incentive compensation providing employees the option or right to buy a certain number of shares of their company's stock at a stated price over a certain period of time. (256)

strategic alliance. A partnership between two or more firms that is developed to achieve a specific goal. (496)

strategic assets. Anything rare and valuable that a firm owns, including plant and equipment, location, brands, patents, customer data, a highly qualified staff, and distinctive partnerships. (215)

strong-tie relationships. Relationships characterized by frequent interaction that form between like-minded individuals such as coworkers, friends, and spouses; these relationships tend to reinforce insights and ideas the individuals already have and, therefore, are not likely to introduce new ideas. (79)

STTR Program. A government grant program, similar to the SBIR program, which requires the participation of a research organization, such as a research university or a federal laboratory? (360)

subchapter S corporation. A form of business organization that combines the advantages of a partnership and C corporation; similar to a partnership, in that the profits and losses of the business are not subject to double taxation, and similar to a corporation, in that the owners are not subject to personal liability for the behavior of the business. (256)

subfranchisees. The people who buy franchises from master franchisees. (515)

summary business plan. A business plan 10 to 15 pages long that works best for companies very early in their development that are not prepared to write a full plan. (141)

supplier. A company or vendor that provides parts or services to another company. (216)

supply chain. A network of all the companies that participate in the production of a product, from the acquisition of raw materials to the final sale. (216)

supply chain management. The coordination of the flow of all information, money, and material that moves through a product's supply chain. (216)

sustainable competitive advantage. A competitive advantage that is sustainable normally as the result of the unique combination of core competencies and strategic assets that a firm possesses. (215)

sustained growth. Growth in both revenues and profits over an extended period of time. (450)

sweat equity. The value of the time and effort that a founder puts into a new firm. (343)

tagline. A phrase that is used consistently in a company's literature, advertisements, promotions, stationery, and even invoices to develop and to reinforce the position the company has staked out in its market. (382)

target. In an acquisition, the firm that is acquired. (491)

target market. The limited group of individuals or businesses that a firm goes after or tries to appeal to at a certain point in time. (219, 279)

technological alliances. Business alliances that cooperate in R&D, engineering, and manufacturing. (496)

technology licensing. The licensing of proprietary technology, which the licensor typically controls by virtue of a utility patent. (495)

trademark. Any work, name, symbol, or device used to identify the sources or origin of products or services and to distinguish those products and services from others. (423)

trade secret. Any formula, pattern, physical device, idea, process, or other information that provides the owner of the information with a competitive advantage in the marketplace. (433)

trade show. An event at which the goods or services in a specific industry are exhibited and demonstrated. (395)

triggering event. The event that prompts an individual to become an entrepreneur (e.g., losing a job, inheriting money, accommodating a certain lifestyle). (48)

Uniform Trade Secrets Act. Drafted in 1979 by a special commission in an attempt to set nationwide standards for trade secret legislation; although the majority of states have adopted the act, most revised it, resulting in a wide disparity among states in regard to trade secret legislation and enforcement. (433)

utility patents. The most common type of patent covering what we generally think of as new inventions that must be useful, must be novel in relation to prior arts in the field, and must not be obvious to a person of ordinary skill in the field. (418)

value. Relative worth, importance, or utility. (42)

value-based pricing. A pricing method in which the list price is determined by estimating what consumers are willing to pay for a product and then backing off a bit to provide a cushion. (390)

value chain. The string of activities that moves a product from the raw material stage, through manufacturing and distribution, and ultimately to the end user. (208)

variable costs. The costs that are not fixed that a company incurs as it generates sales. (456)

venture capital. The money that is invested by venture capital firms in start-ups and small businesses with exceptional growth potential. (351)

venture-leasing firms. Firms that act as brokers, bringing the parties involved in a lease together (e.g., firms acquainted with the producers of specialized equipment match these producers with new ventures that are in need of the equipment). (358)

viral marketing. A new marketing technique that facilitates and encourages people to pass along a marketing message about a particular product or service. (396)

virtual prototype. A computer-generated 3-D image of an idea. (152)

weak-tie relationships. Relationships characterized by infrequent interaction that form between casual acquaintances who do not have a lot in common and, therefore, may be the source of completely new ideas. (79)

window of opportunity. The time period in which a firm or an entrepreneur can realistically enter a new market. (67)

working capital. A firm's current assets minus its current liabilities. (283)

NAME INDEX

SUBJECT INDEX

A

Accounts receivable, 276
Acquirer, 491
Acquisitions. *See* Mergers and acquisitions
Adverse selection, 463
Advertising, 391–394
Advisory boards, 243
Agency theory, 521
Agents of change, 45
Alliances, strategic, 496, 497, 498
Allnation Import and Export Co. Ltd., 586–590
Appendix of business plan, 154
Aquaculture, 194
Area franchise agreement, 515
Articles of incorporation, 255
Assets, 281
Assignment of invention agreement, 420
Assumption sheet, 152–153, 287
Attorneys, 241–243, 530

B

Backward integration, threat of, 180
Balance sheet, 281, 283, 284
Bargaining power, 178–180
Barrier to entry, 175–176
Board of advisors, 150, 321–323
Board of directors, 150, 318, 320
Bootstrapping, 344–345
Brainstorming, 82–83
Brand equity, 386
Brand management, 384
Brands, 384–387
Break-even point, 289, 291
Budgets, 276
Bug report, 83
Burn rate, 341
Business angels, 349–351
Business concept blind spot, 213
Business format franchise, 514–515
Business growth
  case examples of, 504–508
  challenges of, 462–466
  core strategy commitment, 453, 454–455
  managing, 458, 459
  pace of, 451–452, 453, 456
  planning for, 455–456
  reasons for, 456–457
  scale of success, 452–453, 454
  sustained, 450
  as two-edged sword, 452
  See also External growth strategies; Internal growth strategies; Organizational life cycle
Business licenses, obtaining, 249–250
Business method patents, 418–419
Business model, 49, 202
  clearly articulated, importance of
  components of, 211–221
  described, 203
  development of, 204
  diversity of, 207

emergence of, 208–209, 210
fatal flaws in, potential, 210–211
importance of, 206–207
innovation, 203, 205
of online companies, 208
value chain, 208–209, 210
Business model innovation, 203, 205
Business ownership, choosing, 250–251
  comparison of, 252
  corporations, 254–257
  limited liability company, 257–258
  partnerships, 253–254
  sole proprietorship, 251, 253
Business partnerships. *See* Partnerships in business
Business permits, 250
Business plans, 49, 136
  appendix, 154
  company description, 146
  cover page, 144
  executive summary, 144, 145–146
  financial projections, 152, 153, 154
  for firm's employees, 139
  franchise, 518–519
  full business plan, 142
  industry analysis, 148
  for investors and external stakeholders, 139–140
  management team and company structure, 150–151
  market analysis, 148–149
  marketing plan, 149–150
  operational business plan, 142
  operations plan, 151
  oral presentation, 155
  outline of, 144–154
  partnerships common in, 147
  PowerPoint slides to include, 156
  presenting to investors, 154–155
  product design and development plan, 152
  purpose of, 137
  putting it all together, 154
  questions and feedback to expect, 155, 156
  questions answered by, 154
  reasons for writing, 137–139
  red flags in, 140
  structure of the business plan, 140–141
  style or format of the business plan, 141
  summary business plan, 141
  table of contents, 154
  types of, 141–142
  writing, guidelines for, 140–144
Business trends, 173
Buyback clause, 244
Buyer group concentration, 179
Buyers, 179–180
Buying group, 277
Buying intentions survey, 108–109
Buzz, 385

C

Capital constraints in business growth, 466
Capital investments, 341
Capital requirements, 176
Carry, 351
Cash flow
  challenges, 341
  management in business growth, 464
  statements, 283, 284–285, 286
CEFTA (Central European Free Trade Agreement), 555
Centers for Franchising, 555–556
Certification marks, 424
Channel conflict, 398
Character licensing, 495–496
Cineplex Entertainment (Cineplex), 574–583
Closely held corporation, 255
Co-branding, 517
Code of conduct, establishing, 238–240
Collective marks, 424
College students as entrepreneurs, 44
Commercial banks, 355
Common stock, 255
Company description in business plan, 146
Company structure, business plan and, 150–151
Comparison data, 285, 286
Competitor analysis, 149, 170, 185–187
Competitors, 186–188
Concept statement, 106–108
Concept test, 106
Constant ratio method of forecasting, 289
Consultants, 325–326
Context-dependent memory, 102
Continuous growth stage of organizational life cycle, 461–462
Copyright bug, 429
Copyrights, 428–432
Core competency, 215
Core strategy, 213-214
Corporate entrepreneurship, 31
Corporate venture capital, 353
Corporations, 254–257
Corridor principle, 78
Cost advantages independent of size, 176
Cost-based pricing, 390
Cost leadership strategy, 214
Cost reduction strategy, 185
Costs
  buyer's, 179
  of buying franchise, 525–527
  fixed, 178
  of sales and other items, forecasting, 287–289
  of sales on income statement, 280
  switching, 179
  variable, 456
Counterfeit goods, 417–418
Cover page of business plan, 144
Creative destruction, 45
Creativity, 79–81, 85–86
Croatia. *See* San Francisco Coffee House in Croatia

Croatian Franchising Association, 556, 557
Current assets, 281
Current liabilities, 281
Current ratio, 283
Customer advisory boards, 85, 322
Customer interest, gauging, 108
Customer interface, 219–221
Customer relationship management (CRM), 576

D

Day-in-the-life research, 85
Dba (doing business as), 250
Debt financing, 346
  advantages of, 354
  commercial banks, 355
  disadvantages of, 354–355
  line of credit, 354
  other sources of, 356–357
  SBA guaranteed loans, 355–356
  single-purpose loan, 354
Debt-to-equity ratio, 276
Deceptive matter, 426
Decline stage of organizational life cycle, 462
Declining industry, 184–185
Descriptive marks, 426
Design patents, 419
Development plan in business plan, 152
Differentiation, 176–178, 214
Direct competitors, 186
Direct franchise arrangement, 537-538
Direct-sales arrangements in international franchising, 538
Direct selling, 398
Disclosure Document, 87
Disintermediation, 398
Distribution (or place), 396, 398–399
Distribution channels, 177, 396
Doing business as (dba), 250
Double taxation, 255
Drop shipping, 147
Due diligence, 352–353

E

E+Co, 560–573
Early growth stage of organizational life cycle, 460–461
Economic Espionage Act, 433
Economic forces, 69–70
Economics, pursuing unsound, 211
Economies of scale, 176, 456
Economies of scope, 456–457
Education in entrepreneurship, 44
Efficiency, 276
Elaboration, 81
Elevator speech (pitch), 346–348
Emerging industry, 183
Employees
  attracting and retaining for business growth, 458
  recruiting, 316–318, 331–336
Employer identification number (EIN), 250
Entrepreneur, defined, 30
Entrepreneurial alertness, 78

L

Lack of experience,
  overcoming, 315
Lanham Act, 425
Leadership strategy, 184
Leading by example, 237–238
Leasing, 358
Legal disputes, avoiding,
  244–249
Legal issues for new firms
  attorneys, choosing for a firm,
    241–243
  business licenses, obtaining,
    249–250
  business permits, 250
  founders' agreement, drafting,
    243–244
  legal disputes, avoiding,
    244–249
  in naming your business,
    269–271
  start-up, case example of,
    264–266
Lenders and investors, 323
Liabilities, 281
Liability of newness, 310–311
Library research, 84–85,
  109–110
Licensee, 495
Licensing, 493–496
Licensor, 495
Lifestyle firms, 42
Limited liability company (LLC),
  257–258
Limited partnership
  agreement, 254
Limited partnerships, 254
Line of credit, 354
Link joint venture, 499
Liquidity, 251, 275–276
Liquidity event, 346
Liquid market, 255
Local call buffering, 126
Logbooks, 420, 435
Logos, 415, 425
Long-term liabilities, 281

M

Management prowess, 114
Management team, 150–151,
  313–314, 316
Managerial capacity problem,
  462–463, 464
Managerial services, 463
Market analysis, 148–149
Marketing
  establishing a brand,
    384–386
  guerrilla, 396, 397
  selling benefits rather than
    features, 383
  viral, 396
  See also 4Ps of marketing
Marketing alliances, 496
Marketing mix, 386, 390
Marketing plan, 149–150
Marketing strategy, 149–150
Market leadership, 457
Market segmentation,
  149, 379–380
Master franchise
  agreement, 515
Master franchise
  arrangement, 540
Mature industry, 184
Maturity stage of organizational
  life cycle, 461
Mediation, 247, 249
Mentors, 349

Merchandise licensing, 495–496
Mergers and acquisitions,
  492–496
Milestone, 146
Minority entrepreneurs, 43
Misconduct, most common
  types of, 238
Mission statements, 146, 213
Moderate risk takers, 40
Moral hazard, 463
Multidomestic strategy, 185
Multiple-unit franchisee,
  515–516

N

Naming your business,
  269–271
National Business Ethics
  Survey, 237, 240
Net sales, 280
Network entrepreneurs, 79
Networking, 316
New entrants, threat of,
  175–177
New product development, 481
  feasibility analysis in, 483
  geographic expansion, 486
  improving existing products
    or service, 483
  internal growth strategies,
    481–483
  market penetration strategy,
    483, 484–485
  pricing in, 483
  product lines, extending,
    485–486
  target markets in, 483
  See also Internal growth
    strategies; International
    new ventures
New-venture team, elements of
  board of advisors, 321–323
  board of directors, 318, 320
  founder/founders of, 313–316
  key employees, recruiting,
    316–318, 331–336
  lenders and investors, 323
  management team,
    313–314, 316
  other professionals, 325–326
Niche market, 380
Niche strategy, 184–185
No Child Left Behind Act of
  2002, 71
Noncompete agreement, 247
Nondisclosure agreement, 247
Nonlawyer professionals, 243

O

Office Action report, 421
One year after first use
  deadline, 416, 418
Online companies, 208
Operating activities, 284
Operating expenses, 280
Operational business plan, 142
Operations plan in business
  plan, 151
Opportunities, identifying
  gaps in the marketplace,
    76–78
  vs. ideas, 67
  problems, recognizing and
    solving, 73–76
  qualities of, 67
  recognition process, 82
  window of opportunity,
    importance of, 67
  See also Environmental trends

Opportunity, defined, 66
Opportunity gap, 66
Opportunity recognition, 77
Oral presentations, 155
Organic growth, 480
  See also Internal growth
    strategies
Organizational chart, 151
Organizational feasibility
  analysis, 113–115
Organizational life cycle,
  459–462
Outside director, 318
Outsourcing, 485
Overseas selling, 487
Owners' equity, 281

P

Pace of growth, 451–452,
  453, 456
Partnership agreement,
  253–254
Partnership network,
  215–219
Partnerships in business,
  253–254
Passion for their business,
  33–35
Password protection, 435
Patents, 417
  applying for, 419
  assignment of invention
    agreement, 420
  business method patents,
    418–419
  design patents, 419
  eligibility, case example of,
    442–444
  first-to-invent rule, 420–421
  growth in patent applications
    in U.S., 417–418
  history of, 417
  infringement, 422–423
  interference, 421
  invention logbook, 420
  obtaining, 420–421
  one year after first use
    deadline, 416, 418
  partnering for, 422
  plant patents, 419
  provisional patent
    application, 421
  requirements for, 418
  USPTO regulation, 417–418
  utility patents, 418
P/E, 281
Percent-of-sales method,
  288–289, 288–291
Piercing the corporate veil, 255
Pitch (elevator speech),
  346–348
Place (or distribution),
  396–399
Plant patents, 419
Political changes, 71–72
Position, 146
Positioning strategy, 379
PowerPoint slides, 156
Preferred stock, 255
Preliminary prospectus, 354
Preparation, 81
Price/pricing, 389–391
Price-quality attribution,
  390–391
Price stability in business
  growth, 465
Primary research, 103
Prior entrepreneurial
  experience, 314

Private corporation, 255–256
Private placement, 354
Product and trademark
  franchise, 514
Product attribute map,
  381–382
Product/customer focus, 36
Productive opportunity
  set, 463
Product line extension strategy,
  485–486
Product/market scope,
  213–214
Products, 388–389, 397
  co-branding, 517
  core *vs.* actual, 388–389
  design in business
    plan, 152
  development (*See* New
    product development)
  development cycles,
    lengthy, 341
  differentiation, 176
    degree of, 177, 178
  initial rollout, 389
  reference account, 389
  standardization of, degree of,
    179–180
Product/service demand,
  108–110
Product/service feasibility
  analysis
  case example of, 124–126
  product/service demand,
    108–110
  product/service desirability,
    106–108
  purpose of, 105
Professional employer
  organizations (PEOs), 167
Profitability, 174, 275
Profit-and-loss statement,
  279–281
Profit margin, 281
Pro forma balance sheet,
  294–295
Pro forma financial statements,
  291–297
Pro forma income statement,
  293–294
Pro forma statement of cash
  flows, 295–297
Promotion, 391–396
Prototype, 152
Provisional patent
  application, 421
Public corporations, 255
Public relations, 394–395

Q

Quality control in business
  growth, 465–466

R

Ratio analysis, 154, 285,
  287, 297
Ratio analysis financial
  statements, 297
Red herring, 354
Reference account, 389
Regression analysis, 288
Regulatory changes, 71–72
Relevant industry
  experience, 314
Resource sufficiency, 114
Rivalry among existing firms,
  177, 178
Road show, 354
Rounds, 352

COMPANY INDEX